TEACHING READING IN TODAY'S ELEMENTARY SCHOOLS

Third Edition

TEACHING READING IN TODAY'S ELEMENTARY SCHOOLS

Paul C. Burns

late of University of Tennessee at Knoxville

Betty D. Roe

Tennessee Technological University

Elinor P. Ross

Tennessee Technological University

HOUGHTON MIFFLIN COMPANY   BOSTON
Dallas   Geneva, Illinois   Hopewell, New Jersey   Palo Alto

Dedicated to Michael H. Roe
and James R. Ross

Cover photograph by James Scherer.

Chapter opener photo credits:
Chapter 1: © Leif Skoogfors/Woodfin Camp • Chapter 2: © Sepp Seitz/ Woodfin Camp • Chapter 3: © Teri Leigh Stratford/Monkmeyer • Chapter 4: © Elizabeth Crews • Chapter 5: © Elizabeth Crews/Stock, Boston • Chapter 6: © Ed Lettau/Photo Researchers • Chapter 7: © Peter Vandermark/Stock, Boston • Chapter 8: © Hugh Rogers/Monkmeyer • Chapter 9: © David R. Frazier/Photo Researchers • Chapter 10: © Sybil Shelton/ Peter Arnold • Chapter 11: © David S. Strickler/Monkmeyer • Line drawing on page 37 rerendered from an original by Michelle R. Banks, Tennessee Technological University.

Printed in the U.S.A.
Library of Congress Catalog Number: 83-082564
ISBN: 0-395-34234-1

Contents

Preface

Audience and Purpose

This book has been written primarily for the preservice elementary school classroom teacher. It is intended for a first course in reading methods. Inservice classroom teachers and teachers preparing to become reading specialists may also use the book as part of an introductory reading education course. Although primarily oriented to teachers, the book will also be suitable for administrators, for there is much information in the text that would be helpful in the administration and direction of a school's reading program.

This book is designed to familiarize teachers with all the important aspects of elementary reading instruction. It presents much practical information about the process of teaching reading. Theoretical background and the research base behind suggestions have also been included to give the teacher or prospective teacher a balanced perspective.

The primary aim of the book is to prepare teachers for developing reading readiness, all fundamental reading and study skills, and enjoyment of reading in their students. The large amount of the school day spent on reading instruction in the primary grades makes this content especially important to the primary grade teacher. In the intermediate grades students must handle reading assignments in the content areas as well as in reading periods. Our book—in particular the chapters on content area reading and study skills—also contains much information that can help teachers teach the skills appropriate for content area reading tasks.

Revisions in this Edition

This book has been extensively revised. Four chapters—those on reading readiness, major approaches to reading instruction, literature and recreational reading, and readers with special needs—have been substantially reorganized and rewritten. Among the significant changes in these chapters are the inclusion of a comprehensive discussion of Piaget; the expansion of the section on computer-assisted and computer-managed instruction; the addition of discussions, by exceptionality, of the implications of PL 94-142 for classroom reading instruction; and the addition of a section on corrective and remedial readers.

In addition, recent topics of concern have been added throughout the entire book. For instance, discussions of schema theory, subskill theories, semantic webbing, story grammars, alternatives to the use of the directed reading activity, and several new procedures for reading in the content areas are now treated in considerable detail. Also, throughout every chapter important sections have been expanded and updated from the second edition. For example, the discussions of vocabulary development, questioning, critical reading, creative reading, basal readers, study guides, criterion-referenced tests, and grouping for reading instruction have all been significantly revised.

Another important aspect of the revision is the addition of many new activities and worksheets. For instance, the chapter on readiness now has an extensive appendix consisting of dozens of activity suggestions. All activities have been grouped, labeled, and identified in a more accessible manner. Example facsimiles of elementary school reading materials continue to be plentiful, and have been updated throughout.

Coverage and Features

The first chapter discusses the components of the reading act, theories related to reading, and principles of teaching reading. Chapter 2 presents information on reading readiness and a multitude of activities useful in developing readiness. The next two chapters are devoted to techniques of teaching word recognition and comprehension skills, major approaches to reading instruction are described in Chapter 5. Chapter 6 discusses methods of teaching reading/study skills, and Chapter 7 tells how to present the reading skills necessary for reading in individual content areas. Chapter 8 deals with literary appreciation and recreational reading. Assessment of pupil progress is discussed in Chapter 9, and classroom management and organization are treated in Chapter 10. Chapter 11 covers the teaching of reading to exceptional students. The Appendixes contain answers to Test Yourself quizzes.

This text provides an abundance of practical activities and strategies for improving students' reading performance. Illustrative lesson plans, learning-center ideas, worksheets, independent task or activity cards, and instructional games are all presented in this text. Thus, it should continue to be a valuable reference for inservice teachers.

In order to make this text easy to study, we have included the following features:

Introductions to each chapter help readers develop a mental set for reading the chapter and give them a framework into which they can fit the ideas they will read about.

Setting Objectives, part of the opening material in each chapter, provides objectives to be met as the chapter is read.

Self-Checks are keyed to the objectives and are located at strategic points *throughout* each chapter to help readers check whether they have grasped the ideas presented.

Test Yourself, a section at the end of each chapter, includes questions that check retention of the material in the chapter as a whole; these questions may also serve as a basis for discussion.

Vocabulary, a list of important terms with which readers should be familiar, is included for students to review their knowledge of key chapter concepts.

Self-Improvement Opportunities suggests activities in which the readers can participate in order to further their understanding of the ideas and methods presented in the chapter.

Acknowledgments

We are indebted to many people for their assistance in the preparation of this text. In particular, we would like to recognize the contribution that Paul C. Burns made to the first and second editions of this book. Many of his ideas and much of his organization have been incorporated in this text. His death in the summer of 1983 was a loss to us as his colleagues and friends and a loss to the field of reading as well. As a prolific writer and an outstanding teacher, his contributions to reading education were exceptional.

Although we would like to acknowledge the many teachers and students whose inspiration was instrumental in the development of this book, we cannot name all of them. We offer grateful recognition to the following reviewers, whose constructive advice and criticism helped greatly in the writing and revision of the manuscript: John Christoffersen, Western Illinois University; Susan Daniels, University of Akron; Helen Dermer, Bowling Green State University; J. Eldredge, Brigham Young University; Juanita Garfield, Eastern Michigan University; Cal Greatsinger, Central Washington University; Maribeth Henney, Iowa State University; Bob Jerrolds, University of Georgia; Paula Laurence, Texas Tech University; Dorothy McGinnis, Western Michigan University; Walter A. Nelson, California State University (Northridge); Florence N. Odle, Northern Arizona University; Charles Rice, Slippery Rock College; Davida Schuman, Kean College; Gary Shaffer, James Madison University; Lawrence Smith, University of Southern Mississippi; Shela Snyder, Central Missouri State; Virginia Stanley, Clemson University; and Janet W. Lerner, Northeastern Illinois University. In addition, appreciation is expressed to those who have granted permission to use sample materials or citations from their respective works. Credit for these contributions has been given in the footnotes.

Betty D. Roe
Elinor P. Ross

CHAPTER 1

The Reading Act

Introduction

Attempts to define reading have been numerous, and a great variety of definitions has been developed. This is partly because of the complexity of the reading act, which includes two major components—a process and a product—each of which is complicated. Teachers need to be aware of these components and of their different aspects in order to respond effectively to reading needs. In addition, they will find that familiarity with some theories related to the reading process and with important principles of teaching reading can be helpful in planning reading activities.

This chapter analyzes the components of the reading act and discusses the reading product and process. It describes two divergent theories about the reading process and presents some sound principles for reading instruction, with explanatory comments.

Setting Objectives

When you finish reading this chapter, you should be able to

1. Discuss the reading product.
2. Describe the reading process.
3. Explain two divergent theories of the reading process: subskill and psycholinguistic.
4. Name some principles upon which effective reading instruction is based.

COMPONENTS OF THE READING ACT

The reading act is composed of two parts: the reading process and the reading product. By *process* we mean a method, a movement toward an end that is accomplished by going through all the necessary steps. Eight aspects of the reading process combine to produce the reading product. When they blend and interact harmoniously, good communication between the writer and reader results. But the sequences involved in the reading process are not always exactly the same, and they are not always performed in the same way by different readers. Example 1.1 is a diagram of the reading act, listing the various aspects of the process that lead to the product.

A *product* is the consequence of utilizing certain aspects of a process in an appropriate sequence. The product of reading is the communication of thoughts and emotions by the writer to the reader. Because your main goal as a teacher of reading is to help students achieve the reading product, we will discuss the reading product first.

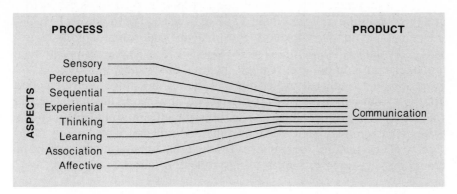

The Reading Product

As we have pointed out, the product of the reading act is communication, the reader's understanding of ideas that have been put in print by the writer. A wealth of knowledge is available to people living today because we are able to read material that others wrote in the past. Americans can read of events and accomplishments that occur in other parts of the globe. Knowledge of great discoveries does not have to be laboriously passed from person to person by word of mouth; such knowledge is available to all who can read.

As well as being a means of communicating generally, reading is a means of communicating specifically with friends and acquaintances who are nearby. A note may tell a child that Mother has gone to town or it can inform a babysitter about where to call in case of an emergency. A memo from a person's employer can specify which work must be done.

Reading can be a way of sharing another person's insights, joys, sorrows, or creative endeavors. Being able to read can make it possible for a person to find places he or she has never visited before (through maps, directional signs), to take advantage of bargains (through advertisements), or to avert disaster (through warning signs). What would life be like without this vital means of communication?

Communication is dependent upon comprehension, which is affected by all aspects of the reading process. Word recognition skills, the associational aspect of the reading process, are essential, but comprehension involves much more than decoding symbols into sounds; the reader must derive meaning from the printed page. Some people have mistakenly considered reading to be a single skill, exemplified by pronouncing words, rather than a combination of many skills that lead to deriving meaning. Thinking of reading in this way may have fostered the unfortunate educational practice of using a reading period for extended drill on word calling, in which the teacher asks each child to "read" aloud while classmates follow in their books. When a child cannot pronounce a word, the teacher may supply the pronunciation or ask another child to do so. When a child miscalls, or mispronounces, a word, the teacher usually corrects the mistake. Some pupils may be good pronouncers in such a situation, but are they readers? They may be able to pronounce words beautifully and still not understand anything they have read. Although pronunciation is important, reading involves much more.

Teachers who realize that all aspects of the reading process have an effect on comprehension of written material will be better able to diagnose children's reading difficulties and as a result offer a sound instructional program based on children's needs. Faulty performance related to any of the aspects of the reading process may result in an inferior product or in no product at all. Three examples of this condition follow.

1. If a child does not clearly see the graphic symbols on a page, he or she may be unable to recognize them.
2. If a child has developed an incorrect association between a grapheme (written symbol) and a phoneme (sound), incorrect word recognition will result and will hamper comprehension.
3. If a child does not have much experience in the area written about, he or she will comprehend the passage less completely than one who has a rich background. For example, a child who has lived on or visited a farm will understand a passage concerning farm life with greater ease and more complete comprehension than a child who has never been outside an urban area.

✔ **Self-Check: Objective 1**
Discuss the product of the reading process.
(See Self-Improvement Opportunities 1 and 2.)

The Reading Process

The process of reading is extremely complex. In reading, children must be able to

1. perceive the symbols set before them (sensory aspect);
2. interpret what they see as symbols or words (perceptual aspect);
3. follow the linear, logical, and grammatical patterns of the written words (sequential aspect);
4. recognize the connections between symbols and sounds, between words and what they represent (associational aspect);
5. relate words back to direct experiences to give the words meaning (experiential aspect);

6. remember what they learned in the past and incorporate new ideas and facts (learning aspect);
7. make inferences from and evaluate the material (thinking aspect);
8. deal with personal interests and attitudes that affect the task of reading (affective aspect).

Reading seems to fit into the category of behavior called a skill, which has been defined by Frederick McDonald as an act that "demands complex sets of responses—some of them cognitive, some attitudinal, and some manipulative" (Downing, 1982, p. 535). Understanding, rather than simple motor behavior, is essential. The key element in skill development is *integration* of the processes involved, which "is learned through practice. Practice in integration is only supplied by performing the whole skill or as much as is a part of the learner's 'preliminary fix.' . . . one learns to read by reading" (Downing, 1982, p. 537). This idea is supported by a great deal of current opinion. A child can learn all of the subskills (such as word recognition) of reading and still not be able to read until a teacher shows him or her how to put the subskills together (May, 1982, p. 15).

Not only is the reading process complex, but each aspect of the process is complex as well. The whole process, as shown in Example 1.2, could be likened to a series of books, with each aspect represented by a hefty volume.

▶ **EXAMPLE 1.2:** Aspects of the Reading Process

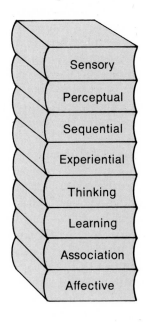

Sensory

Perceptual

Sequential

Experiential

Thinking

Learning

Association

Affective

Sensory Aspects of Reading

The reading process begins with a sensory impression, either visual or tactile. A normal reader perceives the printed symbol visually; a blind reader uses the tactile sense. (Discussion of the blind reader is beyond the scope of this text, although the visually handicapped reader is discussed in Chapter 11, "Readers with Special Needs.") The auditory sense is also very important, since a beginning stage in reading is the association of printed symbols with spoken language. A person with poor auditory discrimination may find some reading skills, especially those involved with phonics, difficult to master.

Vision Many visual demands are imposed upon children by the reading act. They must be able to focus their eyes on a page of print that is generally fourteen to twenty inches away from them, as well as on various signs and visual displays that may be twenty feet or more away. In addition to having visual acuity (or sharpness of vision), children must learn to discriminate visually among the graphic symbols (letters or words) that are used to represent spoken language. Reading is impossible for a person who cannot differentiate between two unlike graphic symbols. Because of these demands, teachers should be aware of how a child's sight develops and of the physical problems that can handicap reading.

Babies are farsighted at birth and gradually become less farsighted as they mature. By the time they are five or six years old, most children have attained 20/20 vision; however, some do not reach this point until later. Several authorities feel that the eyes of many children are not ready for the demands of reading until the children are eight years old. To complicate matters, visual deterioration begins almost as soon as 20/20 vision is attained. Some research indicates that approximately 30 percent of people who once had 20/20 vision no longer have it in both eyes by age seventeen (Leverett, 1957).

Farsighted first graders may learn reading skills more easily through work on charts and chalkboards than through workbooks and textbooks. Near-sighted children may do well when working with books, but are often unable to see well enough to respond to directions or exercises written on charts or chalkboards.

Some children may have an eye disorder call astigmatism, which results in blurred vision. This problem, as well as the problems of nearsightedness and farsightedness, can generally be corrected by glasses.

If a child's eyes do not work well together, he or she may see two images instead of one. Sometimes when this occurs the child manages to suppress the image from one eye. If suppression continues over a period of time, he or she may lose sight in that eye entirely. If suppression occurs for only short periods, the child may be likely when reading to lose the appropriate place on the page and become confused and frustrated.

Eye movement during reading appears to the casual observer as a smooth sweep across a line of print. Actually, a person makes numerous stops, or

fixations, when reading in order to take in the words and phrases and react to
them. A high proportion of total reading time is spent on fixations; therefore,
fixation time is closely related to speed of reading. Both the time and the
frequency of fixations will vary according to the difficulty of the material.
Easy material involves fewer and briefer fixations.

Eye movements back to a previously read word or phrase in order to reread
are called *regressions.* Although they can become an undesirable habit,
regressions are useful if the reader performs them to correct false first
impressions.

It takes time for children to learn to move their eyes across a page in a left-
to-right progression and to execute a return sweep from the end of one line to
the beginning of the next line. This is a difficult maneuver. Those who have
not yet mastered the process will find themselves rereading and skipping
lines. Both of these activities hamper comprehension. Although teachers
often attempt to correct faulty eye movements, such movements are more
often *symptoms* of other problems (for example, poor muscle coordination or
poor vocabulary) than *causes* of problems. When the other problems are
removed, these symptoms usually disappear.

Hearing If a child cannot discriminate among the different sounds
(phonemes) represented by graphic symbols, he or she will be unable to make
the sound-symbol assocations necessary for decoding unfamiliar words. Of
course, before a child can discriminate among sounds, he or she must be able
to hear them; that is, auditory acuity must be adequate. Deaf and hearing
impaired children are deprived of some methods of word identification
because of their disabilities. (See Chapter 11 for more information.)

Perceptual Aspects of Reading

Perception involves interpretation of the sensory impressions that reach the
brain. Each person processes and reorganizes the sensory data according to
his or her background and experiences. When a person is reading, the brain
receives a visual sensation of words and phrases from the printed page. It
recognizes and gives meaning to these words and phrases as it associates them
with the reader's previous experience with the objects, ideas, or emotions
represented.

Visual sensations reach the brain through the optic nerve. The brain
compares each pattern of nerve impulses that reaches it with memory traces
of similar patterns: its visual form, its verbal label, and the meanings that the
person has accumulated for it. A child can recognize a printed word when he
or she associates its sensory trace with the other two types of traces in
memory. Thereafter, when the child encounters that word in print, the
pattern of nerve impulses elicited by that word matches its memory trace in
the brain, which arouses the traces of the verbal label and the cluster of
meanings (Harris and Sipay, 1979, p. 19).

Reading is not a single skill but a combination of many skills leading to deriving meaning from print and to the enjoyment of sharing another person's insights.   (©Leif Skoogfors/Woodfin Camp)

For example, the printed words *apple pie* have no meaning for a person until that person associates them with the object they represent. Perception of the term *apple pie* can result not only in a visual image of a pie but also in a recollection of its smell and taste. Of course, prior experience with the thing named by the word(s) is necessary for the person to make these associations.

Since different people have had different experiences with apple pies, and apple pies can smell, taste, and look many ways, people will attach different meanings to the words *apple pie*. Therefore, individuals will have slightly different perceptions when they encounter these or any other words. The clusters of information that people develop about things (such as apple pies), places (such as restaurants or airports), or ideas (such as justice or democracy) are sometimes referred to as *schemata*. Every person has many of these schemata. Recent theories describe reading comprehension as the act of relating textual information to existing schemata (Pearson et al., 1979). More information about this relationship is located in Chapter 4.

Visual Perception   Visual perception involves identification and interpretation of size, shape, and relative position of letters and words. *Visual discrimination,* the ability to see likenesses and differences in visual forms, is an important part of visual perception because many letters and words are very similar in form but very different in pronunciation and meaning.

Accurate identification and interpretation of words results from detecting the small variations in form. A child might have good visual acuity and not be able to discriminate well visually. Teachers can help children develop this skill through carefully planned activities (discussed in Chapter 2).

Auditory Perception   Auditory perception involves *auditory discrimination,* detecting the likenesses and differences in speech sounds. Children must be able consciously to separate a phoneme (sound) from one spoken word and compare it with another phoneme separated from another word. Since many children have not developed the ability to do this well by the age of five or six years, a phonics-oriented beginning reading program can be very demanding (Pearson et al., 1979). As is true of visual discrimination, a child can have good auditory acuity and not be able to discriminate well auditorily. The skill can be taught, however. (Instructional activities for auditory discrimination are also discussed in Chapter 2.)

Sequential Aspects of Reading

Printed material that is written in English generally appears on a page in a left-to-right, top-to-bottom sequence. A person's eyes must follow this sequence in order to read. We pointed out earlier that readers occasionally regress, or look back to earlier words and phrases, as they read. While these regressions momentarily interrupt the reading process as the reader checks the accuracy of initial impressions, the reader eventually returns to the left-to-right, top-to-bottom sequence. This sequence is discussed in more detail in Chapter 2, as a part of prereading activities.

Reading is also a sequential process because oral language is strung together in a sequential pattern of grammar and logic. Since written language is a way of representing speech, it is expressed in the same manner. The reader must be able to follow the grammatical and logical patterns of spoken language in order to understand written language.

Experiential Background and Reading

As indicated in the section on perceptual aspects, meaning derived from reading is based upon the reader's experiential background. Children with rich background experiences have had more chances to develop understanding of the vocabulary and concepts they encounter in reading than have children with meager experiences. For example, a child who has actually been in an airport is more likely to be able to attach appropriate meaning to the word *airport* when he or she encounters it in a reading selection than a child who has not been to an airport. Direct experience with places, things, and processes described in reading materials makes understanding of the materials much more likely.

Vicarious (indirect) experiences are also helpful in conceptual development, although they are probably less effective than concrete experiences. Hearing other people tell of or read about a subject; seeing photos or a movie of a place, event, or activity; and reading about a topic are examples of vicarious experiences that can build concept development. Since vicarious experiences do not involve as many of the senses as do direct, concrete experiences, the concepts gained from them may be developed less fully.

Some parents converse freely with their children, read to them, tell them stories, show them pictures, and take them to movies and on trips. These parents are providing rich experiences. Other parents, for a variety of reasons, do not offer these experiences to their children. A child's experiential background may be affected by parental rejection, indifference, or overprotection, by frequent illness, by the use of a nonstandard dialect in the home, or by any number of other reasons. Consider an example of how overprotection can limit a child's experiences: a first-grade boy enters school unable to use scissors, to color, or to play games effectively. At home he has been denied the use of scissors so he will not hurt himself, the use of crayons so the house will not be marred, and permission to play outside or on the floor so he will not get dirty. This child's teacher will need to give him a great deal of help in order to build up his experiential background.

Teachers can help to broaden children's concrete experiences through field trips, displays of objects, and class demonstrations. They can also help by providing rich vicarious experiences, such as photographs, filmstrips, movies, records and tape recordings, many classroom discussions, and storytelling and story-reading sessions.

If reading materials contain vocabulary, concepts, and sentence structures that are unfamiliar to children, their teacher must help them develop the background necessary to understand the materials. Because the children's experiential backgrounds will differ, some will need more preparation for a particular selection than others will.

Teachers can help children learn the standard English found in most books by telling and reading stories, encouraging show-and-tell activities, leading or encouraging class discussions, utilizing language experience stories (accounts developed cooperatively by teacher and class members about interesting happenings), and encouraging dramatic play (enactment of roles or imitations of people or things). The new words encountered during field trips and demonstrations will also help.

The Relationship Between Reading and Thinking

Reading is a thinking process. The act of recognizing words requires interpretation of graphic symbols. In order to comprehend a reading selection thoroughly, a person must be able to use the information to make inferences and read critically and creatively—to understand the figurative language, determine the author's purpose, evaluate the ideas presented, and apply the ideas to actual situations. All of these skills involve thinking processes.

Chambers and Lowry point out that

reading is more than merely recognizing the words for which certain combinations of letters bring about a correct recall. It includes the whole gamut of thinking responses: feeling and defining some need, identifying a solution for meeting the need, selecting from alternative means, experimenting with choices, rejecting or retaining the chosen route, and devising some means of evaluating the results. (1975, p. 114)

Teachers can guide students' thinking by asking appropriate questions. Students will be more likely to evaluate the material they are reading if they have been directed to do so. "How" and "why" questions are particularly good. However, questions can also limit thinking: if children are asked only to locate isolated facts, they will probably not be very concerned about main ideas in a passage or the purpose of the author. Test questions also affect the way students read assignments: if the usual test questions ask for evaluation or application of ideas, children will be apt to read the material more thoughtfully than if they are asked to recall isolated facts.

The Relationship of Reading to Learning

Reading is a complex act that must be learned. It is also a means by which further learning takes place. In other words, a person learns to read and reads to learn.

Learning to read depends upon motivation, practice, and reinforcement. Teachers must show children that being able to read is rewarding in many ways—that it increases success in school, helps in coping with everyday situations outside of school, bestows status, and provides recreation. Children are motivated by the expectation that they will receive these rewards, which then provide reinforcement to continue reading. Reinforcement encourages them to continue to make associations between printed words and the things to which they refer and to practice the skills they need for reading.

After children have developed some facility in reading, it becomes a means through which they learn other things. They read to learn about science, mathematics, social studies, literature, and all other subjects—a topic treated in depth in Chapter 7.

Reading as an Associational Process

Learning to read depends upon a number of types of association. First, children learn to associate objects and ideas with spoken words. Next they are asked to build up associations between spoken words and written words. In some cases—for instance, when a child is presented with an unfamiliar written word paired with a picture of a familiar object—the child makes a direct association between the object or event and the written word, without an intermediate connection with the spoken word. In teaching phonics, teachers set up associations between graphic symbols (graphemes) and sounds (phonemes).

This type of learning is called *paired-associate learning.* In order to learn through association, a child must be presented with the written stimulus (for example, a printed letter or word) along with the response that the teacher expects it to elicit (the spoken sound or word). The child must pay attention during this process to both the stimulus and the expected response. Mediation takes place at this point.

Gagné defines mediation in this way: "Most investigators agree that the efficient learning of a two-element verbal association requires the use of an *intervening link,* having the function of *mediation* or coding. . . . Such links are usually implicit ones, that is, they occur inside the learner and do not appear as overt behavior" (1965, p. 99). The more such links a person has available, the faster he or she will be likely to learn.

The child should practice the association, even to the extent of "overlearning," and he or she should respond actively. Immediate reinforcement of correct answers and correction of wrong ones can help to establish the association. The sooner the teacher provides the reinforcement after the child makes the response, the more effective the reinforcement is likely to be. For example, the teacher might show a child the word *time* and tell him or her that this printed word is "time." Then the teacher would show the word again and ask the child to respond with the word "time." The teacher may drill the child in a variety of situations, requiring the child to respond with "time" each time that word is presented.

Practice in and of itself, however, is not always enough to set up lasting associations. The more meaningful an association is to a child, the more rapidly he or she will learn it. Children can learn words after only a single exposure if the words have vital meaning for them (Ashton-Warner, 1963).

Affective Aspects of the Reading Process

Interests, attitudes, and self-concepts are three affective aspects of the reading process. These aspects influence how hard children will work at the reading task. For example, children who are interested in the materials presented to them will put forth much more effort in the reading process than will children who have no interest in the available reading materials.

In the same manner, children with positive attitudes toward reading will expend more effort on the reading process than children with negative attitudes will. Positive attitudes are nurtured in homes where the parents read for themselves and to their children and where reading materials are provided for children's use. In the classroom, teachers who enjoy reading, who seize every opportunity to provide pleasurable reading experiences for the children in their classes, and who allow time for recreational reading during school

hours are encouraging positive attitudes. Reading aloud to the children
regularly can also help accomplish this objective. Also, if a child's peers view
reading as a positive activity, that child is likely to view reading in the same
way.

Negative attitudes toward reading may be developed in a home environment where parents, for a variety of reasons, do not read. Children from such
homes may be told that "reading is for sissies." They may bring such ideas to
the classroom and spread them among children who have not previously
been exposed to such attitudes. The "reading is for sissies" attitude affects
everyone in the classroom negatively, regardless of gender.

Attitudes, or the affective domain, can be classified in five main levels
(Krathwohl, Bloom, and Masia, 1964). The first three, presented here with
descriptions of how to recognize them in reading behavior, are most
appropriate for the elementary school years.

1. Receiving (attending): Students are at least willing to hear or study the
   information, as indicated by
   a. perceiving the reading concepts.
   b. reading on occasion, particularly on a topic of interest.
   c. identifying what they do not understand in reading.
2. Responding: Students will respond to the material being studied through
   a. completing reading assignments.
   b. making an effort to figure out words and to understand what they read.
   c. seeking out reading opportunities.
3. Valuing: Students have a commitment to what they are learning and
   believe it has worth, as suggested by
   a. voluntarily working to improve their skills through wide reading.
   b. choosing reading when other activities are available.
   c. reading in their spare time.

Children with poor opinions of themselves may be afraid to attempt a
reading task because they are sure that they will fail. They find it easier to
avoid the task altogether and to develop "don't care" attitudes than to risk
looking "dumb." Children with good self-concepts, on the other hand, are
generally not afraid to attack a reading task, since they feel that they are going
to be successful.

There are several ways to help children build positive self-concepts. First, in
every possible way, help the children feel accepted. A definite relationship
exists between a teacher's attitude toward a child, as perceived by the child,
and the child's self-concept. One of the best ways to make children feel
accepted is to share their interests, utilizing those interests in planning for
reading instruction. Accept children's contributions to reading activities even
if they are not clearly stated.

Second, help children feel successful by providing activities that are simple enough to guarantee satisfactory completion. For poorer readers, we recommend the language experience approach (see Chapter 5), as well as appropriate materials such as high-interest, low-vocabulary books.

Third, avoid comparing a child with other pupils. Instead, compare children's reading progress with their own previous work. Private records of books read, skills mastered, or words learned are much better than public records in which one child consistently compares unfavorably with others.

Fourth, minimize the differences between reading groups to avoid giving children the idea that unless they are members of the top group they are not worthy people. Avoid comparisons and competition among groups, and vary the bases on which groups are formed.

✔ Self-Check: Objective 2

List the eight aspects of the reading process presented in this section and explain each one briefly. Reread the section to check your explanations.
(See Self-Improvement Opportunity 1.)

The Reading Process: Selected Theories

A theory is a set of assumptions or principles designed to explain phenomena. Research findings have resulted in many theories related to the reading process, but as Richard Smith and others have pointed out, no current theory adequately explains "all of the mysteries of reading" (1978, p. 19). Theories that are based on good research and practical observations can be helpful when you are planning reading instruction, but do not lose sight of the fact that current theories do not account for all aspects of this complex process. In addition, theories are hypotheses—educated guesses. New information may be discovered that proves part or all of a theory invalid.

It would not be practical to try to present all of the theories related to reading in the introductory chapter of a survey textbook. Therefore, we have chosen to discuss two relatively divergent theoretical approaches, subskill and psycholinguistic theories, to give you a feeling for the complexities inherent in choosing a theoretical stance.

Subskill Theories

Some educators see reading as a set of subskills that children must master and integrate. They believe that although good readers have learned and integrated these subskills so well that they use them automatically, beginning readers have not learned them all and may not integrate well those that they have learned. This situation results in slow, choppy reading for beginners and perhaps also in reduced comprehension, because the separate skills of word recognition take so much concentration. Teaching these skills until they become automatic and smoothly integrated is thus the approach that these educators take to reading instruction (Weaver, 1978).

Richard J. Smith and others (1978) point out that teachers need to teach specific skills in order to focus instruction. Otherwise, instruction in reading would be reduced to assisted practice—a long, laborious trial-and-error approach. Phyllis Weaver suggests that

although some research suggests that *skilled* reading is a single, holistic process, there is no research to suggest that children can learn to read and develop reading skill if they are taught using a method that treats reading as if it were a single process. Therefore, for instructional purposes, it is probably best to think of reading as a set of interrelated subskills. (1978, p. 7)

Proponents of the subskill theory are not, however, in agreement as to what subskills are involved. Most would present one list for decoding subskills (for example, knowledge of letter–sound correspondences and recognition of prefixes and suffixes) and another list for comprehension subskills (for example, identifying details and making inferences), but their sets of lists are rarely identical. In this textbook, we have identified the word recognition (Chapter 3) and comprehension (Chapter 4) subskills that we feel are most important.

A body of research supports the subskill theory. For example, John Guthrie (1973) found that reading subskills correlated highly with each other for students who were good readers. These students seemed to have integrated the skills to produce a good reading product. The correlations among reading subskills for poor readers were low. These students seemed to be operating at a level of separate rather than integrated skills. Guthrie's findings led to the conclusion that "lack of subskill mastery and lack of integration of these skills into higher order units" was a source of disability among poor readers (Samuels, 1980, pp. 209–10).

David LaBerge and S. Jay Samuels's hierarchical model of perceptual learning suggests that

the sequence of learning is from distinctive features, to letters, to letter clusters, and to words. In the process of learning to recognize a letter, the student must first identify the features that comprise it. For the lower case letters *b, d, p,* and *q,* the features are a vertical line and a circle in a particular relationship to each other; that is, the circle may be high or low and to the left or right side of the vertical line. Having identified the parts and after an extended series of exposure to the letters, the learner sees it as a unit; that is, the parts are perceptually unitized. (1980, p. 211)

This model illustrates the process by which students master smaller units before larger ones and integrate them into larger units after mastery. Many lists of decoding subskills include the ones mentioned here.

S. Jay Samuels (1980) reports a supportive study in which Donald Shankweiler and Isabelle Liberman tried to determine how well a child's fluency in oral reading of paragraph material could be predicted from his or her ability to read selected words in tests. They found that "roughly 50 percent of the variability in oral reading of connected words is associated with how well one can read these words in isolation" (p. 212). In other words, a child's oral reading of connected discourse tended to be only as good as his or her oral reading of individual words. Recognition of words in isolation (sight words) is one decoding subskill. Since some research on perception and reading indicates that people do master smaller units before larger ones, teaching subskills (smaller units) rather than expecting students to learn to read without such instruction is supported.

Harry Silberman found that an experimental skill-based program for teaching beginning reading was not at first successful with all of the children in the program; although the brighter children acquired the reading skill, less bright children could not apply their knowledge to words that had not specifically been taught. Evaluators found that an important subskill had been omitted, and after the subskill was added to the program, all the children managed to master the transfer to words not specifically taught (Samuels, 1980).

Those who teach a set of subskills as a means of instructing children in reading generally do recognize the importance of practicing the subskills in the context of actual reading in order to ensure integration. But some teachers overlook this vital phase and erroneously focus only upon the subskills, overlooking the fact that they are the means to an end and not an end in themselves.

Psycholinguistic Theories

Psycholinguistic theories, as the name implies, are based on the disciplines of psychology and linguistics. Kenneth Goodman, a noted psycholinguist, describes reading as a psycholinguistic guessing game in which readers "select the fewest, most productive cues necessary to produce guesses which are right the first time." He points out the importance of the reader's ability to anticipate the material that he or she has not yet seen (Goodman, 1973, p. 31). He also points out that readers bring to their reading all of their accumulated experience, language development, and thought in order to anticipate meanings in the printed material (p. 34).

The contrast between subskill and psycholinguistic theories is apparent in this statement, which describes a psycholinguistic view:

Learning to read does not require memorization of letter names, or phonic rules, or large lists of words, all of which are in fact taken care of in the course of learning to read, and little of which will make sense to a child without some experience of reading. Nor is learning to read a matter of application to all manner of exercises and drills, which can only distract and perhaps even discourage a child from the business of learning to read. And finally learning to read is not a matter of a child relying upon instruction, because the essential skills of reading—namely the uses of nonvisual information—cannot be taught. (Frank Smith, 1978, p. 179)

Smith, like other psycholinguists, believes that children learn to read as they learn to speak, by generating and testing hypotheses about the reading material and getting appropriate feedback. In addition, he believes that although reading cannot be taught, children can be given opportunities to learn. First they need to have people read to them, and then they need the chance to read for themselves, with help. The contrast between this position and the subskills approach is striking. Teaching a sequential set of subskills to be integrated into the reading process is vastly different from merely establishing conditions that will allow students to learn to read.

Psycholinguists point out that although the ability to combine letters to form words is related to learning to read, it has little to do with the process of fluent reading. When a person reads for meaning, he or she does not always need to identify individual words. A person can comprehend a passage without having identified all of the words in it. The more experience a reader has had with language and the concepts presented, the fewer clues from visual configurations he or she will need to determine the meaning of the material. Fluent readers make frequent use of semantic (meaning) and syntactic (word-order) clues within the material as well. They engage in the following activities as they process print:

1. The reader discovers the distinctive features in letters, words, and meaning.
2. The reader takes chances—risks errors—in order to learn about printed text and to predict meaning.
3. The reader reads to identify meaning rather than to identify letters or words.
4. The reader guesses from context at unfamiliar words, or else just skips them.
5. The reader takes an active role, bringing to bear his or her knowledge of the world and of the particular topic in the text.
6. The reader reads as though he or she expects the text to make sense.
7. The reader makes use of redundancies—orthographic, syntactic, and semantic—to reduce uncertainty about meaning.
8. The reader maintains enough speed to overcome the limitations of the visual processing and memory systems.
9. The reader shifts approaches for special materials.
10. The reader shifts approaches depending on the purpose. (Cooper and Petrosky, 1976, pp. 191–95)

The reading process is described in the following way by psycholinguistic theorists:

the brain directs the eye to pick up visual information from the configurations on the page; once the information starts coming into the brain, the brain processes it for meaning using its prior knowledge of language (syntactical rules that lend themselves to prediction) and content. The initial incoming information, if we conceive of this model working in slow motion, resides in the visual configurations on the page. The bridge between the visual configurations (surface structure) and meaning (deep structure) is syntax, and the frame of reference for this entire process is the knowledge and experience already stored in the brain in memory. The final outcome of the process is the identification of meaning. Psycholinguistics, then, combines cognitive psychology and linguistics in order to analyze and understand the language and thinking process, including reading, as it occurs in humans. (Cooper and Petrosky, 1976, p. 185)

Psycholinguists point out the importance of syntax (word order in sentences) in decoding written material. In the English language certain syntactic or word-order clues are predictable. These clues are listed below.

1. adjective/noun sequence (happy children, tall buildings, intelligent woman)
2. verb/adverb sequence (walked slowly, talks rapidly, works quietly)
3. adverb/verb sequence (cheerfully gave, truthfully spoke, lovingly cared)
4. article/noun sequence (the toy, a top, an egg)
5. article/adjective/noun sequence (the friendly cow, the clever girl, the beautiful mountains)
6. verb/complement sequence (weighed ten pounds, served six years, had many friends)
7. preposition/article/noun sequence (into the woods, over the hill, inside the tent)
8. qualifier/adjective or adverb sequence (very tall, rather well, quite late)
9. possessive noun/noun sequence (dog's tail, Seward's folly, child's toy)

Some sentence patterns that occur often are

1. noun/verb (The boy ran.).
2. noun/verb/noun, noun/verb/adverb, or noun/verb/adjective (Mary drove the tractor. Mary walked rapidly. Mary seems happy.).
3. noun/verb/noun/noun (Bill gave Bev a watch.).
4. noun/linking verb/noun or -/adjective or -/adverb (My boss is a tyrant. The apples were sweet. Ms. Jones was out.).

These basic sentence structures are commonly transformed in the following ways:

Negative: Terry is here. → Terry is not here.
Question: She is singing. → Is she singing?
Use of *there:* A pencil is in the desk. → There is a pencil in the desk.
Request: You rake the leaves. → Rake the leaves.
Passive: A baseball broke the window. → The window was broken by a baseball.
Possessive: Pat owns that dog. → That is Pat's dog.

The four common sentence patterns and six transformations cited above are a part of the speaking repertoire of most children; therefore, most children are prepared for encountering them in reading instructional materials. Other language structures that are not a part of children's speaking repertoires may appear in their reading materials. In the following cases, the teacher needs to be alert for possible difficulties in understanding:

Appositives: Mary, my aunt, came in.
Infinitives as sentence subjects: To exercise is healthy.
Conjunctive adverbs: Since it's raining, take your umbrella.
Paired conjunctions: Either he leaves or I do.
Clauses as sentence subjects: What you do is your business.
Absolute constructions: The meeting over, she left.

Children usually enjoy putting sets of words together to make sentences. In the beginning years of school teachers can teach sentence patterns by showing examples rather than by attempting linguistic descriptions. Later they can ask children to identify sets of sentences or to build fragments into sentences according to some particular patterns. They can develop exercises in which sentences of varying patterns are compared; ask students to examine articles and stories for evidence of sentence patterns; and use excerpts from a child's own writing to provide examples of sentence patterns. For ideas on how to emphasize semantic cues, see the section on context clues in Chapter 4.

Robert Canady (1980) has described some good classroom practices based upon a psycholinguistic view of the reading process.

1. Allow children to read an entire meaningful story without providing assistance. Encourage logical guesses, regressions to self-correct, and skipping words if necessary. After reading, have students tell what they remember.
2. Use the language experience approach.

3. Help children become aware that they are reading when they read labels, signs, or advertisements.
4. Let children learn reading skills as they read meaningful materials. Focus on reading as comprehension.

Constance Weaver (1980) also recommends the language experience approach (see Chapter 5). In addition, she suggests using sustained silent reading and sharing and experiencing reading (both discussed in Chapter 8), as well as reading for a specific purpose (stressed throughout this book).

✔ Self-Check: Objective 3
Compare and contrast the subskill and psycholinguistic theories of the reading process.
(See Self-Improvement Opportunity 1.)

TWELVE PRINCIPLES OF TEACHING READING

Principles of teaching reading are generalizations about reading instruction based on research in the field of reading and observation of reading practices. The principles listed here are not all-inclusive; many other useful generalizations about teaching reading have been made in the past and will continue to be made in the future. However, the principles listed here are ones that we believe are most useful in guiding teachers in planning reading instruction.

Principle 1   Reading is a complex act with many factors that must be considered.

The discussion earlier in this chapter of the eight aspects of the reading process makes this principle clear. The teacher must understand all parts of the reading process if he or she is to plan reading instruction wisely.

Principle 2   Reading is the interpretation of the meaning of printed symbols.

If a person does not derive meaning from a passage, he or she has not been reading, even if the person has pronounced every word correctly.

Principle 3   There is no one correct way to teach reading.

Some methods of teaching reading work better for some children than for others. Each child is an individual who learns in his or her own way. Some are visual learners; some are auditory learners; some are kinesthetic learners. Some need to be instructed through a combination of modalities, or avenues of perception, in order to learn. The teacher should differentiate instruction to fit the diverse needs of children in the class. Of course, some methods also work better for some teachers than they do for others. Teachers need to be acquainted with a variety of methods so they can help all of their pupils.

Principle 4   Learning to read is a continuing process.

Children learn to read over a long period of time, acquiring more advanced reading skills after they master prerequisite skills. Even after they have been introduced to all reading skills, refinement continues. No matter how old people are, or how long they have been out of school, they can continue to refine their reading skills.

Principle 5   Students should be taught word recognition skills that will allow them to unlock the pronunciations and meanings of unfamiliar words independently.

Children cannot memorize all the words they will meet in print. Therefore, they need to learn techniques of figuring out unfamiliar words so that they can read when the assistance of a teacher, parent, or friend is not available.

Principle 6   The teacher should diagnose each student's reading ability and use the diagnosis as a basis for planning instruction.

Teaching all children the same reading lessons and hoping to deal at one time or another with all of the different pupils' difficulties is a shotgun approach and should be avoided. Such an approach wastes the time of those children who have attained the skills that are currently being emphasized and may not ever meet some of the desperate needs of other children. Avoid this approach by using standardized and teacher-made tests to pinpoint the strengths and weaknesses of each individual in the classroom. Then divide the children into needs groups and teach them what will really be of help to them, or give each of them an individual course of instruction.

Principle 7   Reading and the other language arts are closely interrelated.

Reading—the interaction between a reader and written language, through which the reader tries to reconstruct the writer's message—is closely related to all other major language arts (listening, speaking, and writing). For example, children can learn much about their language while being taught reading skills. For children five years old and younger, experiences with listening and speaking are part of the growth process toward learning to read (see Chapter 2).

A special relationship exists between listening and reading, which are *receptive* phases of language, as opposed to the *expressive* phases of speaking and writing. Mastering listening skills is important in learning to read, for direct association of sound, meaning, and word form must be established from the start. The ability to identify sounds heard at the beginning, middle, or end of a word and the ability to discriminate among sounds are essential to the successful phonetic analysis of words. Listening skills also contribute to interpretation of reading material.

Students' listening comprehension is generally superior to their reading comprehension in the elementary school years, particularly with easy materials. Listening and reading become more equal in both word recognition rate and in word-per-minute rate later on. Not until the latter part of the sixth or the seventh grade does reading proficiency reach the stage where students prefer reading to listening in many learning situations. This implies that it is profitable to present instruction orally in the elementary school. Generally, more advanced children prefer to learn by reading; slower ones prefer to learn by listening, particularly when the concepts and vocabulary are especially difficult. While reading and listening are not identical and each has its own advantages, there are many ways in which they are alike. Teachers must be aware of these similarities so they can provide efficient instruction.

People learn to speak before they learn to read and write. Through experience with their environments, they begin to associate oral symbols or words with certain people, places, things, and ideas. Children's reading vocabularies are generally composed largely of words in their speaking vocabularies. These are words for which they have previously developed concepts and words that they can comprehend.

One means of relating early writing experiences with reading experiences, or the language experience approach, is described in Chapter 5. The need to develop and expand concepts and vocabulary, essential to reading, is reflected in the entire language arts curriculum. Skills are also interrelated. For example, whereas reading involves decoding skills, spelling, which is also related to writing experiences, involves encoding skills.

Principle 8   Reading is an integral part of all content area instruction within the educational program.

Teachers must consider the relationship of reading to other subjects within the curriculum of the elementary school. Other curricular areas frequently provide outlets for the skills taught in the reading period. For instance, the need to write a report in social studies can involve many reading and study skills: locating information (using the alphabet and the dictionary, note-taking); organizing information (outlining, preparing bibliographies); using the library (using the card catalog, call numbers, classification systems, and references such as the encyclopedia and atlas). The teacher who gives reading instruction only within a reading period and who treats reading as separate from the rest of the curriculum will probably achieve teacher frustration rather than pupil change and growth. While a definitely scheduled period

specifically for reading instruction may be recommended, this does not mean that teachers should ignore reading when teaching content subjects. The ideal situation at any level is not "reading" for an hour's period, followed by "study" of social science or science for the next period. Instead, although the emphasis will shift, both reading and studying should be integrated during all periods at all levels.

Elaboration of these points may be found in Chapter 6, "Reading/Study Skills," and in Chapter 7, "Reading in the Content Areas," but we should clarify one further idea at this time. Teachers sometimes assume the existence of a dichotomy—that children learn to read in the primary grades and read to learn in the intermediate and upper grades. While it may be true that teachers devote less attention to the actual process of learning to read at the intermediate level, there is still need for attention to the primary reading skills as well as to higher-level skills.

Principle 9   The student needs to see why reading is important.

Children who cannot see any advantage in learning to read will not be motivated to learn this skill. Learning to read takes effort, and children who see the value of reading in their personal activities will be more likely to work hard than those who fail to see the benefits. Teachers should have little trouble demonstrating to youngsters that reading is important: it helps people to travel from place to place, to make needed purchases, to keep informed about current conditions, and so on. In addition to emphasizing the children's future needs for reading, teachers should attempt to show the children immediate, personal values of reading in the classroom each day.

Principle 10   Enjoyment of reading should be considered of prime importance.

It is possible for our schools to produce capable readers who do not read; in fact, today it is a common occurrence. Reading can be entertaining as well as informative. Teachers can help children to realize this by reading interesting material to them and by making available good books of appropriate difficulty for them to read on their own.

Principle 11   Readiness for reading should be considered at all levels of instruction.

Not only when reading instruction begins, but whenever instruction in any reading skill takes place, at all grade levels, teachers should consider the readiness of the child for instructional activity. A teacher should ask, "Does the child have the prerequisite skills necessary for learning this new skill?" If the answer is no, then the prerequisite skills should be thoroughly developed before the teacher presents the planned activity.

One of the most important principles of reading instruction is that reading should be taught in a way that allows each child to experience success.   (© Michal Heron/Woodfin Camp)

Principle 12   Reading should be taught in a way that allows each child to experience success.

Asking children to try to learn to read from materials that are too difficult for them is insuring failure for a large number. Teachers should give children instruction at their own levels of achievement, regardless of grade placement. Success generates success. If children are given a reading task at which they can succeed, they gain the confidence to attack in a positive way other reading tasks that are presented to them. This makes the likelihood of their success at these later tasks much greater. In addition, some recent studies have shown that if a teacher *expects* his or her students to be successful readers, they will in fact *be* successful.

No matter what teaching approaches are used in a school or what patterns of organization predominate, these principles of teaching reading should apply. Each teacher should consider carefully his or her compliance or lack of compliance with such principles.

We have discussed twelve principles related to teaching reading.
Explain how knowledge of each principle should affect your
teaching of reading.
(See Self-Improvement Opportunity 3.)

Test Yourself

True or False

_____ 1. Over a period of time a single, clear-cut definition of reading has emerged.
_____ 2. Reading is a complex of many skills.
_____ 3. Youngsters entering first grade are often farsighted.
_____ 4. When children read, their eyes move smoothly over the page from left to right.
_____ 5. Faulty eye movements usually cause serious reading problems.
_____ 6. Regressions are always undesirable.
_____ 7. Perception involves interpretation of sensation.
_____ 8. Questions can affect the way students think while reading.
_____ 9. The more meaningful learning is to a child, the more rapidly associative learning takes place.
_____ 10. Word calling and reading are synonymous.
_____ 11. Teachers go to school so that they can learn the one way to teach reading.
_____ 12. People can continue to refine their reading skills as long as they live.
_____ 13. Diagnosis of reading problems for every child in a class is a waste of a teacher's valuable time.
_____ 14. Diagnosis can help a teacher plan appropriate instruction for all of his or her pupils.
_____ 15. Reading and the other language arts are closely interrelated.
_____ 16. Content area instruction should not have to be interrupted for teaching of reading skills; reading instruction should remain strictly within a special reading period.
_____ 17. Understanding the importance of reading is unimportant to the reading progress of a child.
_____ 18. Teachers should stress reading for enjoyment as well as for information.
_____ 19. Readiness for reading is a concept that applies only to beginning reading instruction.
_____ 20. One of the early sentence transformations used by many children is the passive transformation.
_____ 21. Reading seems to fit in the "skill" category of behavior.

_____ 22. Current theories about reading account for all aspects of the reading process.

_____ 23. No research supports the view that reading is a set of subskills that must be mastered and integrated.

_____ 24. LaBerge and Samuels' model of perceptual learning indicates that the sequence of learning is from distinctive features, to letters, to letter clusters, to words.

_____ 25. Psycholinguistic theory, as explained by Frank Smith, indicates that the essential skills of reading cannot be taught.

Vocabulary

Check your knowledge of these terms. Reread parts of the chapter if necessary.

affective	paired-associate	schemata
auditory discrimination	learning	self-concept
auditory sense	perception	semantic cues
fixations	phoneme	subskill approach
grapheme	psycholinguistic	syntax
kinesthetic	theories	tactile
modality	regressions	vicarious experience
motivation	reinforcement	visual acuity
		visual discrimination

Self-Improvement Opportunities

1. Study the following definitions of reading, which have been suggested by well-known authorities. Decide which aspect or combination of aspects of the reading process has been emphasized most in each definition.

   a. "Reading may be defined as the attaining of meaning as a result of the interplay between perceptions of graphic symbols that represent language, and the memory traces of the reader's past verbal and nonverbal experiences." (Albert J. Harris and Edward R. Sipay, _How to Teach Reading: A Competency-Based Program._ New York: Longman, 1979, p. 27.)

   b. "Reading is both a communication process and a decoding process. A mature reader perceives reading as communication. A beginning reader may perceive it primarily as decoding." (Frank B. May, _Reading As Communication._ Columbus, Ohio: Charles E. Merrill, 1982, p. 11.)

   c. "Reading means getting meaning from certain combinations of letters. Teach the child what each letter stands for and he can read." (Rudolph Flesch, _Why Johnny Can't Read and What You Can Do About It._ New York: Harper & Row, 1955, pp. 2–3.)

d. "Reading is a process of looking at written language symbols, converting them into overt or covert speech symbols, and then manipulating them so that both the direct (overt) and implied (covert) ideas intended by the author may be understood." (Lawrence E. Hafner and Hayden B. Jolly, *Teaching Reading to Children*. 2nd ed. New York: Macmillan, 1982, p. 4.)

e. "Reading is thinking . . . reconstructing the ideas of others." (Robert Karlin, *Teaching Elementary Reading*. 3rd ed. New York: Harcourt Brace Jovanovich, 1980, p. 7.)

f. "Reading involves the identification and recognition of printed or written symbols which serve as stimuli for the recall of meanings built up through past experience, and further the construction of new meanings through the reader's manipulation of relevant concepts already in his possession. The resulting meanings are organized into thought processes according to the purposes that are operating in the reader." (Miles A. Tinker and Constance M. McCullough, *Teaching Elementary Reading*. 4th ed. Englewood Cliffs, N.J.: Prentice-Hall, 1975, p. 9.)

g. "Reading involves nothing more than the correlation of a sound image with its corresponding visual image, that is, the spelling." (Leonard Bloomfield and Clarence L. Barnhart, *Let's Read: A Linguistic Approach*. Detroit: Wayne State University Press, 1961, dustjacket.)

h. "Reading typically is the bringing of meaning *to* rather than the gaining of meaning *from* the printed page." (Henry P. Smith and Emerald V. Dechant, *Psychology in Teaching Reading*. Englewood Cliffs, N.J.: Prentice-Hall, 1961, p. 22.)

2. Note the points of agreement in the various definitions given above.

3. After studying the principles of reading instruction given in this chapter, see if you can formulate other principles based upon your reading in other sources.

4. Study a story presented in a basal reader for a grade level of your choice. Giving illustrative sentences, list the kinds of sentence patterns and transformed sentences presented in the story.

5. To help in your further study of elementary school reading, participate in the activities of organizations such as the International Reading Association. The meetings, publications (particularly *The Reading Teacher*), and projects sponsored by the organization provide some of the best ways to keep informed about new ideas on teaching reading. Other periodicals dealing with timely ideas on reading instruction include:

Elementary School Journal—University of Chicago Press, 5835 Kimbark Avenue, Chicago, IL 60637

Exceptional Children—Council for Exceptional Children, 1141 South Jefferson Davis Highway, Jefferson Plaza, Suite 900, Arlington, VA 22202

Horn Book Magazine—Horn Book, Inc., 585 Boylston Street, Boston, MA 02116

Journal of Reading Behavior—National Reading Conference, Inc., Clemson
University, Clemson, SC 29150

Instructor—Instructor Publications, Inc., P.O. Box 6099, Duluth, MN 55806

Language Arts (Elementary English)—National Council of Teachers of English,
1111 Kenyon Road, Urbana, IL 61801

National Elementary Principal—Department of Elementary School Principals,
NEA, 1201 Sixteenth Street, N.W., Washington, D.C. 20036

Perceptual and Motor Skills—Perceptual and Motor Skills, Box 9229, Missoula,
MT 59807

Reading Newsreport—Multi-Media Education, Inc., 11 West 42nd St., New
York, NY 10036

Reading Research Quarterly—International Reading Association, Inc., 800
Barksdale Road, Newark, DE 19711

Reading World—College Reading Association, Box 462, Shippensburg State
College, Shippensburg, PA 17257

6. Compare critically the suggestions made in this and the following chapters
with those in other professional references, to achieve a more intensive
study of the subject. The suggested readings listed at the end of this chapter
provide a beginning place for such study.

Bibliography

Ashton-Warner, Sylvia. *Teacher.* New York: Simon and Schuster, 1963.

Canady, Robert J. "Psycholinguistics in a Real-Life Classroom." *The
Reading Teacher* 34 (November 1980): 156–59.

Chambers, Dewey, and Heath Lowry. *The Language Arts: A Pragmatic
Approach.* Dubuque, Iowa: William C. Brown, 1975.

Cooper, Charles R., and Anthony R. Petrosky. "A Psycholinguistic
View of the Fluent Reading Process." *Journal of Reading* 20 (December
1976): 184–207.

Downing, John. "Reading—Skill or Skills?" *The Reading Teacher* 35
(February 1982): 534–37.

Gagné, Robert M. *The Conditions of Learning.* New York: Holt, Rinehart
and Winston, 1965, pp. 98–107.

Goodman, Kenneth S. "Reading: A Psycholinguistic Guessing Game." In
Perspectives on Elementary Reading, Robert Karlin, ed. New York: Harcourt
Brace Jovanovich, 1973, pp. 30–41.

Guthrie, John T. "Models of Reading and Reading Disability." *Journal of
Educational Psychology* 65 (1973): 9–18.

Harris, Albert J., and Edward R. Sipay. *How to Teach Reading.* New
York: Longman, 1979.

Johnson, Peter H. *Reading Comprehension Assessment: A Cognitive Basis.*
Newark, Del.: International Reading Association, 1983.

Krathwohl, David, B. Bloom, and B. Masia. *Taxonomy of Educational Objectives: The Classification of Educational Goals, Handbook 2: The Affective Domain.* New York: McKay, 1964, Appendix A, pp. 176–85.

Leverett, Hollis M. "Vision Test Performance of School Children." *American Journal of Ophthalmology* 44 (October 1957): 508–19.

May, Frank B. *Reading As Communication.* Columbus, Ohio: Charles E. Merrill, 1982, Chapter 1.

Pearson, P. David, et al. *The Effect of Background Knowledge on Young Children's Comprehension of Explicit and Implicit Information.* Urbana: University of Illinois, Center for the Study of Reading, 1979.

Samuels, S. Jay. "The Age-Old Controversy between Holistic and Sub-skill Approaches to Beginning Reading Instruction Revisited." In *Inchworm, Inchworm: Persistent Problems in Reading Education,* Constance McCullough, ed. Newark, Del.: International Reading Association, 1980, pp. 202–21.

Smith, Frank. *Understanding Reading.* 2nd ed. New York: Holt, Rinehart and Winston, 1978.

Smith, Richard J., et al. *The School Reading Program.* Boston: Houghton Mifflin, 1978.

Weaver, Constance. *Psycholinguistics and Reading: From Process to Practice.* Cambridge, Mass.: Winthrop, 1980, pp. 251–91.

Weaver, Phyllis, and Fredi Shonkoff. *Research Within Reach: A Research-Guided Response to Concerns of Reading Educators.* St. Louis, Mo: CEMREL, 1978.

Suggested Readings

Beery, Althea, et al. *Elementary Reading Instruction: Selected Materials.* 2nd ed. Boston: Allyn and Bacon, 1974.

Bush, Clifford L., and Mildred H. Huebner. *Strategies for Reading in the Elementary School.* 2nd ed. New York: Macmillan, 1979, Chapter 1.

Dallman, Martha, et al. *The Teaching of Reading.* 6th ed. New York: Holt, Rinehart and Winston, 1982, Chapters 2 and 3.

Fry, Edward. *Elementary Reading Instruction.* New York: McGraw-Hill, 1977, Chapter 1.

Guszak, Frank J. *Diagnostic Reading Instruction in the Elementary School.* 2nd ed. New York: Harper & Row, 1978, Chapter 1.

Hafner, Lawrence E., and Hayden B. Jolly. *Teaching Reading to Children.* 2nd ed. New York: Macmillan, 1982, Chapter 1.

Harris, Larry H., and Carl B. Smith. *Reading Instruction: Diagnostic Teaching in the Classroom.* 3rd ed. New York: Holt, Rinehart and Winston, 1980, Chapter 2.

Heilman, Arthur W., et al. *Principles and Practices of Teaching Reading.* 5th ed. Columbus, Ohio: Charles E. Merrill, 1981, Chapter 1.

Hittleman, Daniel R. *Developmental Reading: A Psycholinguistic Perspective.* 2nd ed. Boston: Houghton Mifflin, 1983, Chapter 3.

Karlin, Robert. *Teaching Elementary Reading: Principles and Strategies.* 3rd ed. New York: Harcourt Brace Jovanovich, 1980, Chapter 1.

Kennedy, Eddie C. *Methods in Teaching Developmental Reading.* 2nd ed. Itasca, Illinois: F. E. Peacock Publishers, Inc., 1981, Chapter 1.

Lamb, Pose, and Richard D. Arnold. *Reading: Foundations and Instructional Strategies.* Belmont, California: Wadsworth, 1976, Chapters 1 and 2.

Malmstrom, Jean. "Psycholinguistics and Reading" in *Reading: Process and Product,* Harold Newman, ed. Forest Hills, N.Y.: Prestige Education, 1976, pp. 51–56.

Miller, Wilma H. *The First R: Elementary Reading Today.* 2nd ed. New York: Holt, Rinehart and Winston, 1977, Chapter 1.

Olson, Joanne P., and Martha H. Dillner. *Learning to Teach Reading in the Elementary School: Utilizing a Competency-Based Instructional System.* 2nd ed. New York: Macmillan, 1982, Chapter 1.

Quandt, Ivan J. *Teaching Reading: A Human Process.* Boston: Houghton Mifflin, 1977, Chapter 1.

Ransom, Grayce A. *Preparing to Teach Reading.* Boston: Little, Brown, 1978, Chapters 1 and 2.

Rubin, Dorothy. *A Practical Approach to Teaching Reading.* New York: Holt, Rinehart and Winston, 1982, Chapter 1.

Ruddell, Robert B., et al., eds. *Resources in Reading-Language Instruction.* Englewood Cliffs, N.J.: Prentice-Hall, 1974, Chapter 2.

Smith, Richard J., and Dale D. Johnson. *Teaching Children to Read.* 2nd ed. Reading, Mass.: Addison-Wesley, 1980, Chapter 1.

Wardhaugh, Ronald. "Linguistics-Reading Dialogue." In *Linguistics for Teachers: Selected Readings,* John F. Savage, ed. Chicago: Science Research Associates, 1973, pp. 281–91.

CHAPTER 2

Prereading Experiences for Children

Introduction

This chapter begins with a discussion of the important concept of reading readiness and the six major factors to be considered in a readiness program: experiential background, language facility, interest in reading, social and emotional development, physical development, and cognitive development. In developing a prereading program teachers must base decisions about their approach on the needs of their students; the program may be activity-based, structured, discovery-oriented, or organized around published workbooks. It is important to remember that the readiness period does not end when reading begins but continues as the child moves on into reading. Teachers must develop readiness for each new reading task a child attempts.

Setting Objectives

When you finish reading this chapter you should be able to

1. Identify some strategies for helping young children develop concepts and vocabulary.
2. Discuss the prereading value of group and individually dictated story experiences.
3. Explain reasons for the importance of storytelling and story reading and describe how to present a story to a class.
4. Discuss how visual and auditory skills can be developed.
5. Understand some implications of Piaget's theory of cognitive development for teaching children during the reading readiness period.
6. List some strategies for helping young children to recognize letters and words.
7. Discuss whether formal reading instruction should begin in kindergarten.

THE READINESS CONCEPT

The prereading period extends from birth to the time when a child is taught to recognize and read words. During this period, the child learns to understand and speak words, to follow directions, to follow the cumulative development of a story, to study and interpret pictures, to acquire skill in perceiving small sight and sound differences, to handle crayons, chalk, and scissors, and to feel an interest in printed words. These and many other interests and abilities grow gradually until the child reaches a stage of "readiness" for beginning reading instruction.

The modern concept holds that readiness is made up of various factors. It is neither physical nor intellectual maturation alone, although both are involved (since they affect the physical structure of the eye, degree of interest, and level of knowledge). Nor do modern educators believe that readiness is something to wait for passively; they believe that it is a stage into which the child may be guided.

While this chapter focuses upon beginning reading readiness, readiness is important at all reading levels. Even if readers are ready for one level of reading instruction, they will not necessarily be adequately prepared at a higher level. Developing readiness for any reading experience at any level is an important task for teachers.

The concept of readiness has significant implications for designing formal or systematic reading experiences. When a child is not prepared to succeed at a reading task, his or her frustration can produce negative and detrimental effects. If repeated over a period of time, the frustration can become more intense.

Three conditions that a teacher cannot change are likely to affect a child's readiness for reading: gender, home environment, and participation in preschool programs. Teachers should be aware of these in order to understand the possible reasons for certain behaviors or lack of progress; however, they must also guard against developing preconceived ideas about children based on these conditions.

Research studies in North America have revealed that girls surpass boys in reading performance, especially in the lower grades, possibly because of cultural factors (Lehr, 1982). Home environment, including socioeconomic level, family size, type of neighborhood, educational level of the parents, and verbal interaction among family members, also affects children's success in reading. Coleman (1972) reported a positive relationship between socioeconomic level and reading achievement, and Loban (1976) found that children from homes of a higher socioeconomic level had superior verbal ability. Teachers have observed that children who have participated in some sort of preschool program usually make an easier transition into the reading program than other children do. Most likely, such children have already developed many of the social, communication, and other skills that are basic to beginning reading. Both black and white children who attended preschool educational programs scored higher than non-preschool attenders in achievement and readiness to learn (Knox and Glover, 1978).

Children who enter first grade also vary widely in other ways, such as rate of growth and attitude toward learning. In the following section we present six major factors in which children exhibit differing degrees of readiness and suggest some activities for developing each factor. Additional activities are listed in Appendix A of this chapter.

At times it may be appropriate to view these activities in isolation, but most of the time they become more meaningful when coordinated around units of related experiences. For example, a unit or project may evolve around a central theme, such as "different kinds of weather." Activities for a unit on weather could include listening to stories or poems about weather, interpreting weather pictures, and planning a trip to a weather station, then dictating a class story about the trip, drawing pictures about the trip, and telling the class about it. Such a coordinated experience provides a wealth of opportunities for oral expression, writing practice, artistic expression, and practice of social manners. Some unit themes with many possibilities are

Our School and School Helpers
What Makes a Home a Home
People Who Help Us
Seasons
Celebrations
Everything Grows Together
How We Go Places
Places We Buy Things in the Community
Five Senses

Teachers should clearly delineate goals, activities, helpful materials, and methods of evaluation in planning units of work.

IMPORTANT READINESS FACTORS

Six important readiness factors—experiential background, language facility, interest in reading, social and emotional development, physical development, and cognitive development—are discussed in this section.

Experiential Background

Providing an adequate background of experience is an integral part of the reading readiness program. The school can supply some of this background; the rest must come from the home. Because the child who is intellectually curious reaps the most from his or her experiences, those who are associated with children should try to stimulate their curiosity about new or unknown things.

A broad experiential background is essential for success in reading because children must be familiar with the concepts and vocabulary they will see in written form in order to gain meaning from them. Experiences are the foundation for building concepts, and concepts are the foundation for building vocabulary. Through their experiences children gain an understanding of ideas and concepts, and they learn words, or labels, for them. Later they will understand more of what they read because they can relate their experiences to the symbols on the printed page. As children encounter a variety of experiences, they modify and refine their perceptions until they get a clear picture of each concept they have acquired. A child may need many experiences to attain a well-rounded impression of a single idea. *School,* for example, is a concept that children will not completely understand until they have experienced it in different ways.

Teachers may build a broad background of experiences in a variety of ways. The important things to keep in mind are the needs of the children and the available resources. As teachers observe and talk with their students, they can perceive gaps in experience and find ways to fill them. They can provide many experiences within the classroom by inviting guests or by taking the children on a field trip (if the expense and distance are not too great and transportation and supervisory personnel are available). Children learn basic concepts through activities such as constructing mobiles and collages, cooking, playing with puzzles, following directions in playing finger games, and so on. Particularly useful are activities that involve the senses; those like the following ones provide opportunities for using words to describe sensations.

1. taking *sight* walks
2. making *sound* mobiles (from pieces of wood, bells, buttons, tin cans, aluminum foil)
3. using a *feel* box or bag for guessing objects by touch
4. holding a *tasting* party (tasting salt, sugar, vinegar)
5. playing a *smelling* game (identifying aromatic objects tied in small, thin cloth bags, as a piece of banana, fresh orange peel, onion, apple)

Having a news period can be useful. From the reported news, the teacher can make a chart, including items like "We had a fire drill today. We talked about the farm." Students can help compile the week's news, decide on a headline, and make illustrations for some items.

Since young children enjoy games, playing them is a good way to stimulate vocabulary development. Try a game using prepositions. For example, put an object *in* (*on, under*) a box and ask children to identify the various positions. Play a game with adverbs, for example, *walking quickly, slowly, sadly, quietly, noisily, happily,* or one with adjectives, pretending you are *big, little, brave,* or *happy.*

Teachers should make every effort to use whatever experience is available for developing concepts and language. Use correct terminology—*printing press, homogenized, card catalog*—in class discussions. Elicit descriptive words from the children or introduce such words to them as they recall their sensory impressions of an experience. Both before and after the experience, the teacher should involve the children in related language activities. In this way children increase their verbal ability; that is, their vocabularies and stock of concepts expand as they learn words for colors, shapes, textures, and numbers.

Experiences may be either direct or vicarious. Children generally remember direct experiences with actual physical involvement best, but it may not always be feasible to provide direct experiences. Good vicarious experiences, such as listening to stories and watching films, provide opportunities to expand concepts and vocabulary indirectly. Some appropriate experiences of both types are

field trips	films, filmstrips, slides, tapes
resource people	selected television programs
story reading	photographs, pictures, posters
demonstrations	neighborhood walks
exhibits	class holiday celebrations

A class project like the one described below can promote growth in vocabulary and concept development.

● **MODEL ACTIVITY:** *Direct Experience*

Start by saying to the children: "Tomorrow we will make some vegetable soup. Try to remember to bring a vegetable to put in the soup. Now we will write a chart story about the ingredients we will need for our soup." The next morning say: "Tell us about your vegetable. What is it called? What color is it? How does it feel? How does it smell?" Give each child a chance to handle and talk about the vegetables. Then ask: "What do we need to do first to make the soup? What must we do to the vegetables before we put them in the pot? What else should we add?" (Answers include getting and heating the water, washing and cutting up the vegetables, and adding spices and alphabet noodles.)

When the soup is ready to eat, give each child a cupful. As the children eat, ask: "How does your soup taste? Are the colors of the vegetables the same as when we put them into the soup? How have the alphabet noodles changed? Can you name some of the letters that are in your soup?" After they have finished eating, let the children dictate another chart story about the sequence of making the soup and/or their reactions to eating it.

Some of the concepts you can help children acquire from this experience and related discussions are (1) soup is made from firm, fresh, brightly colored vegetables; (2) after they are cooked, the vegetables change in texture and appearance; (3) the noodles get larger from absorbing the water; (4) it takes time to heat water and cook soup; (5) the water absorbs flavor and color from the vegetables and spices; (6) cold water becomes hot when it is placed on a heated surface; (7) certain foods are classified as vegetables. As a result of the experience, children's vocabularies might now include the words *boil, simmer, dissolve, melt, ingredients, squash, celery, turnips, slice, chop, shred, dice, liquid,* and *flavor.* A bonus comes from letting the children manipulate the alphabet letters—identifying them, matching them, and finding the first letters of their names. ●

Looking at pictures is one type of vicarious experience. Pictures are extremely fruitful sources of new ideas and experiences and are useful in developing vocabulary and concepts. Good pictures to use for building experiences are those that tell a story. In order to help children interpret pictures fully, teachers should ask them questions like those in Model Activity: Vicarious Experience.

● **MODEL ACTIVITY:** *Vicarious Experience*

1. Where is the little boy? How do you know?
2. What kinds of things usually happen at the veterinarian's office?
3. Why do you think he took his cat there?
4. Why are the other people there?
5. Who is at the door? How do you know?
6. Why is the boy there without his father or mother?
7. What is the boy doing?
8. What do you think will happen soon? ●

Story writing is a logical extension of either direct or vicarious experiences. It may occur as an introduction to or as an outcome of an experience. If a class writes a story following a field trip, the students should first discuss the trip. By asking carefully selected questions, the teacher can encourage them to form valid concepts and use appropriate vocabulary words. The students then dictate sentences for the teacher to write on a chart like that in Example 2.1.

38 ▶ **EXAMPLE 2.1:** Experience Chart Story

Teaching
Reading in
Today's
Elementary
Schools

Our Trip to the Zoo

We rode in the school bus.
Mr. Spring was the bus driver.
The bus took us to the zoo.
We saw many animals.
We ate popcorn and peanuts.
We thanked Mr. Spring.
Our trip was fun.

Dictated story experiences provide an excellent opportunity to introduce the coordinated language experience approach discussed in Chapter 5.

Stories about an experience may be dictated by a whole class, a group, or an individual. When individual children tell stories, parents, aides, older children, classroom volunteers, or the teacher can act as scribes. These stories should be about things that are important to the children, such as their families, their pets, or their favorite activities. The children may illustrate them and combine them into booklets which are then shared around the library table and eventually taken home by the authors. Some appropriate experiences for story writing are listed below.

taking a field trip	observing an animal
watching an experiment	popping corn
visiting a science or book fair	experimenting with paints
tasting unusual foods	planting seeds or bulbs
	building a pretend space ship

An older sibling's or a parent's reading to a young child is one important way of building readiness for reading. (© Judith D. Sedwick/Woodfin Camp)

✔ Self-Check: Objective 1

Several ways in which experience can help build concepts and vocabulary have been presented. Name as many as you can. Can you think of some others?
(See Self-Improvement Opportunity 3.)

Perhaps the most important reason for story writing is that children begin to realize that writing is recorded speech. This awareness occurs as the teacher reads the story back to the children in the words they have just dictated. After repeated readings by the teacher, the children may also be able to "read" the story. The teacher may make copies of the story for all of the children to take home and share with their families. As a result of involvement with the story, children may learn to recognize some high-interest words and words that are used more than once (such as *we* and *bus* in the experience chart story).

Many reading readiness skills are learned through story writing. Children watch as the teacher forms letters that make up words; they notice that language consists of separate words which are combined into sentences. They see the teacher begin at the left side and move to the right and go from top to bottom; they become aware that dictated stories have titles in which the first letter of each important word is capitalized; they realize that sentences begin with capital letters and end with a punctuation mark. In addition to becoming familiar with mechanical writing skills, children develop their thinking skills. The teacher's questions are useful in helping them develop skill in organizing and summarizing. As the children retell events in the order of their occurrence, they begin to understand sequence. As they recall the *important* ideas, they begin to form a concept of a main idea.

✔ Self-Check: Objective 2
State why it is important to include group and individually dictated stories in the prereading program.
(See Self-Improvement Opportunity 6.)

Language Facility

Good listening and speaking skills are essential for effective communication. Because the concepts and vocabulary derived from listening and speaking are the basis for effective reading and writing, and because language is part of the curriculum at all levels, a good foundation in speaking and listening skills is necessary for academic progress. Children should be encouraged to see the relationships among these language components.

Young children are naturally eager to engage in activities involving the senses, where sight, sound, smell, taste, and touch are ways of perceiving surroundings. Through these experiences they can be encouraged to enlarge their speaking and listening vocabularies. Conversations with parents, teachers, and peers provide opportunities to observe and practice oral skills— to learn to express ideas and to think about the ideas of others. Planning trips, discussing how to care for a pet, and talking over daily experiences are valuable opportunities for stimulating conversation with young children. Language facility is enhanced when teachers and parents give their complete attention to children while they read to them, look at pictures with them, or listen to them tell stories about pictures or activities in which they have engaged. Even shy children can usually be encouraged to say a few words about something they have made, an enjoyable experience, or a prized toy.

Such uses of language develop the ability to communicate orally with reasonable fluency—to articulate common sounds clearly, to choose words, to use sentence structures. In all of their communication with children, teachers should model good speech. They should encourage the children's efforts to use new words and speak in correctly formed sentences.

The ability to listen is a language skill that is highly important in learning to read as well as in other schoolwork. In training children to listen, teachers should choose subjects that interest the children, that are related to their own experiences, and that make use of words and concepts they understand. In order to be good listeners, children need to learn to concentrate and to develop their attention spans. Being good listeners as members of an audience should be stressed. There are several ways of facilitating various types of listening and speaking skills.

Storytelling and Story Reading

Reading aloud to children should be a daily occurrence. This story-sharing time creates far-reaching benefits for the listener. Some reasons for reading aloud are given below.

Books extend experiences by telling about other cultures and lifestyles.
Classics introduce children to fine literature.
Children can develop good comprehension and thinking skills as they listen to stories.
Story time creates a warm feeling and a sense of rapport.
Some stories help children solve their problems and be more tolerant of others.
Stories acquaint children with new words and concepts.
Well-chosen stories can be the basis for creative expression, such as drama, music, and art.
Hearing stories read aloud brings about an interest in reading and a desire to learn to read.
Good readers encourage children to become attentive listeners.
Story time is a time to relax, enjoy, and share a laugh or a tear.

You may find that some situations lend themselves better to storytelling, some to story reading. To decide which stories to tell rather than read ask yourself: Is the story interesting and entertaining to you? Does the story fit your personality, style, and talents? Will it appeal to the interests of the children for whom it is intended? Is the story appropriate to the age and ability level of the children? Is there ample dialogue and action in the story? Are there few lengthy descriptive passages, and can they be easily condensed? Will the story be relatively easy to prepare? Will it add variety and contrast to the storyteller's repertoire of stories? Is it a story that would be better told than read aloud (Coody, 1979, pp 25–37)?

There are several guidelines for a teacher who is preparing a story to tell. Read the story carefully. Reread it to get the incidents clearly in mind and to get a clear picture of the details. Tape yourself as you practice telling the story. Use cue cards—of opening lines, main points, climaxes, and closing lines—if they will help you. Memorize essential parts that provide atmosphere or imagery (for example, "'Who's that tripping over my bridge?' roared the troll," or "In the high and far-off times, O best beloved"). Retape your story, concentrating upon improving pitch, range, and voice quality. Make sure you are enunciating clearly and that you are making good use of pauses. Continue to practice telling the story. Use gestures sparingly; do not be overly dramatic. Young children enjoy listening to a story if it stimulates their imaginations and depicts experiences that are understandable, and if they are listening to a good storyteller or reader.

● *MODEL ACTIVITY: Storytelling*

Say to the children: "This morning I'm going to tell you a story that you may already know. It is called 'The Three Little Pigs.' How many of you know it? This story is about three little pigs and a mean old wolf who tries to blow down their houses. I want you to help me tell the story. When the wolf says, 'I'll huff and I'll puff and I'll blow your house in,' I want you to say it along with me. Let's try it now, all together." The children practice saying this line with you. Then tell the story and signal to the children when it is the right time for them to say the line. The same ideas may be used with other stories that have repeated lines, such as "The Three Billy Goats Gruff" and "The Gingerbread Man." ●

Real vs. Imaginary Stories   As stories are read and told to them, children learn to differentiate between the real and the imaginary ones. This learning experience can be helped through asking a series of questions such as

1. Could this story really happen? Why do you say so?
2. What is there in the story that shows that it could not happen in real life?
3. How is the character _____ like someone you have known?
4. How could anything like _____ (event) ever happen to you?
5. What in the story is like something in modern life?
6. Where have you ever been or what have you heard about that is like the place described in the story?

Very young children can learn to detect the difference between fantasy and events that might have happened. Children enjoy changing a factual presentation to a fantasy by incorporating talking animals, magical events, or other imaginary elements. The purpose of differentiating between real and imaginary stories is neither to discount fantasy nor to dismiss a story as unworthy because it is untrue; the distinction is part of the foundation necessary for later reading of fiction, particularly of tall tales and humorous stories. Learning to make the distinction may be one of the first critical reading skills developed by young children.

Story Sequence   Understanding the concept of story sequence is difficult for many youngsters. The teacher should begin with just two or three ideas for the children to arrange in order and gradually increase the number of ideas as children show mastery of this skill.

Find three identical copies of books from a discarded basal reader series. Then cut three or four pictures from a story out of two of the books, mount the pictures, and cover them with clear plastic. Say to the children: "This morning I am going to read you a story about a big black bear. As I read, I am going to show you pictures of the story. I want you to listen and look carefully to see what happens first in the story, then what happens next, and finally what happens at the end of the story. When I am finished reading, I will ask you to put these pictures in the same order that you saw them as I read the story." After the story, let the children take turns arranging the cutout pictures in the correct sequence. ●

Creative Responses   The ability to make predictions is an important reading skill that children can begin to develop during the readiness period. One purpose of reading stories to children is to encourage them to begin to make predictions about what will happen next.

As children learn to anticipate story endings, they should be urged to be creative and to develop their own endings. You can use the following books in a situation where you ask the pupil to complete an unfinished story.

Katy and the Big Snow by Virginia L. Burton. Boston: Houghton Mifflin, 1943. Read up to the point where it says "Slowly and steadily Katy started to plow out the city." Ask, "What do you think Katy did?"

Harry by the Sea by Gene Zion. New York: Harper & Row, 1965. Read up to the point where Harry was jumping with joy at the hot dog stand. Stop after "He jumped so much that suddenly. . . ." Ask, "What happened when he jumped? What did Harry do then?"

Story of the Three Bears by Eleanor Mure. New York: H. Z. Walck, 1967. Read up to the point where the bears reenter the house. Say, "What happened then?"

The Three Little Pigs by Paul Galdone. New York: Seabury Press, 1970. Read up to the point where the wolf visits the first little pig's house. Ask, "What happened next?"

Listening for Information

In using factual books, the teacher should relate the child's experience in the classroom to the experience provided by the book. For example, *Your First Pet and How to Care for It* (Carla Stevens. New York: Macmillan, 1978) is a good book to use when there is a pet in the classroom. Relevant books should be read and made available to children before and after visiting various places on field trips. In other words, books should be an integral part of many classroom activities and experiences. Some general guidelines for use of factual books are

1. Do not read aloud only the part of the book that answers a specified question. Lead students to decide for themselves when an answer has been supplied.
2. Read more than one book on the topic being taught, and ask students to specify what new information was in the second or third book. Also ask them to find the "conflicts" in the sources.
3. Reread parts of a book to emphasize and to provide fuller information, and read from several books that provide the same information.
4. Teach locational skills. "In what part of the book did we find that information?"

The following activity shows the possible use of books in a lesson on plants in a kindergarten room.

● **MODEL ACTIVITY:** *Listening for Information*

Set up a science center with books and displays about plants. Say to the children: "Today we are going to talk about plants. First, I am going to read you a book about plants. Listen to see if you can find out how plants grow. Then we will plant something for our room." Read the book and ask questions such as those listed below.

Questions
Where do seeds come from?
What do plants need to make them grow?
How are seeds planted?
How do we take care of plants?
If we want to plant something, what will we need?

Sources for Center
Eat the Fruit, Plant the Seed by Millicent Selsam and Jerome Wexler. New York: Morrow, 1980.
Science Experiences for Young Children: Seeds by Rosemary Althouse and Cecil Main. New York: Teachers College Press, 1975.
Plant Fun: Ten Easy Plants to Grow Indoors by Anita Holmes. New York: Four Winds, 1974.
Projects with Plants by Seymour Simon. New York: Watts, 1973.
How Plants Travel by Joan E. Rahn. New York: Atheneum, 1973.
Vegetables from Stems and Leaves by Millicent Selsam. New York: William Morrow, 1972. ●

What are some reasons for storytelling and story reading? How would you present a story to a group of children? (See Self-Improvement Opportunities 2 and 5.)

Following Directions

Children must listen attentively to follow directions and must be familiar with many directional terms, such as *row, top of the page,* and *under.* A teacher may find many ways during the day to help children develop the ability to follow directions well. The next activity develops skill in listening and following directions; it also allows the teacher to check a child's understanding of colors and shapes.

● *MODEL ACTIVITY: Following Directions*

See that each child has a large piece of unlined paper and a box of crayons. Give this series of directions: "Make a big red *X* in the middle of your paper. Draw a blue circle around the outside of the *X*. Put a yellow line across the middle of the *X*. Put green dots inside the circle." ●

Oral Expression

Children learn to use language through informal conversations with other children and with the teacher. These conversations may be carried on while the children work quietly together at centers or on projects. The schoolroom environment provides many subjects and opportunities for descriptive talk. Children can compare different building blocks and note their relationships— size, weight, color; they can observe several kinds of animals and consider differences in their feet, skin covering, and size; they can compare a variety of fabrics for texture, weight, and purpose.

One means of helping children with description is for the teacher to describe a prominent object in the room. The children listen to the description and take turns identifying what they think the teacher has described. Later, children should describe objects while other children guess what has been described.

On certain occasions children may speak to a group or to the entire class, explaining their artwork or telling how to do something. One popular sharing activity is often referred to as show-and-tell. Children share something interesting with the class by telling about it and sometimes by showing it. Show-and-tell can be an effective way of developing oral language, but it can also be a waste of time if it is mishandled.

● *MODEL ACTIVITY:* *Oral Expression (Show-and-Tell)*

Say to the children: "This morning we are going to have show-and-tell. Let's review the rules before we start. I will call on one of you to begin and that one will be the leader for today. After the first time, the leader will call on the other children. Remember that you are to share something important. Don't just tell about a television show or what you had for dinner last night. Think about what you want to say before you raise your hand. The rest of you will be the audience. You should be good listeners. Who would like to start?" ●

Opportunities for oral expression occur frequently during the day. Teachers should encourage children to use these opportunities to develop their skills in oral communication. Some good ideas for class activities that develop oral expression are

making the daily schedule
choosing a current event to record on the chalkboard
planning projects, activities, or experiences
discussing a new bulletin-board display
interpreting pictures
discussing what to include in an experience story
brainstorming ideas from "What if . . ." situations (Example: "What if we had four arms instead of two arms?")
acting out stories
carrying on pretend telephone conversations with play telephones
reviewing the day's events
engaging in dramatic play.

Interest in Reading

Since readiness for an activity requires an interest in that activity, one of the first and most important tasks of a reading readiness program is building an interest in reading. Children's attitudes may range from disinclination to indifference to anticipation, exhibited in such behavior as showing interest in signs, enjoying listening to stories, being able to tell stories and recite poems or rhymes, enjoying looking at pictures in books, being able to attend to a sequential picture book, making up stories about a picture, and asking to take books home. In order to develop interest in learning to read, children need to be exposed to language and literature. They need to experience the delight that comes from listening and responding to stories, to handle books and examine pictures, and to see reasons for reading in their daily activities.

Wordless Picture Books

Picture books without words serve three major purposes in the reading readiness program. They develop positive attitudes toward reading because most children enjoy "reading" them. Any reasonable interpretation is acceptable, so children are unlikely to fail in their storytelling. Children also develop oral language skills as they tell their impressions of what is happening, using correct sentence structure and appropriate vocabulary. Finally, they begin working with comprehension skills that they will use later in reading: identifying details, becoming aware of sequence, making inferences, predicting what will happen next, seeing cause-and-effect relationships, and drawing conclusions.

When using wordless picture books, a teacher can help students gain the greatest benefit from the experience by observing a few guidelines. He or she should select books with illustrations that are clear and easy to understand and with story lines that are readily discernible. The teacher should instruct children to look all the way through a book to get an overall perspective before trying to tell the story. (Otherwise, they may interpret each page individually.) He or she should ask questions to develop comprehension (for example, "What is this called?" for vocabulary; "Why does Jack look angry?" for inference).

There are different types of wordless picture books.[1] Most tell stories (Raymond Briggs' *The Snowman*); some develop concepts (Tana Hoban's *Is It Red? Is It Yellow? Is It Blue?*); and others give information (Iela and Enzo Mari's *The Apple and the Moth*). Mercer Mayer's humorous books about a boy and his frog are well liked *(Frog, Where Are You?, Frog Goes to Dinner)*. John Goodall has written several wordless picture books that use half-page inserts to change the illustrations *(Ballooning Adventures of Paddy Pork)*. A good wordless picture storybook is *Changes, Changes* by Pat Hutchins. This book captivates children with its fast-moving sequence of events; two brightly colored wooden dolls rearrange wooden building blocks to create whatever is needed. Children can see cause and effect, perceive logical sequence, and predict what will happen next.

Poetry

Nothing better acquaints children with the melody, rhythm and flow of language than poetry. By repeating favorite verses, children can develop an

---

[1]Richard F. Abrahamson, "An Update on Wordless Picture Books with an Annotated Bibliography," *The Reading Teacher* 34 (January 1981): 417–21; Charlotte S. Huck, *Children's Literature*, 3rd ed. updated (New York: Holt, Rinehart and Winston, 1979), pp. 106–108; Donna Read and Henrietta M. Smith, "Teaching Visual Literacy through Wordless Picture Books," *The Reading Teacher* 35 (May 1982): 928–33; Zena Sutherland et al., *Children and Books*, 6th ed. (Glenview, Ill.: Scott, Foresman, 1981), pp. 100–102, 117–18.

appreciation and love of language and experiment with sounds and rhythmic phrases. They may like poetry for its humor, its vivid and sometimes ridiculous images, its quick action, and its delightfully expressive words. The alliteration and rhyming words are not only fun to use, they help in developing phonics skills.

Having the right poem on hand for the occasion, such as Lillian Moore's "Wind Song" on a windy day, is a good way to introduce children to the rich possibilities of poetry. An anthology for young children or a personal card file of children's favorite poems, classified so that you can quickly find what you want, is a useful resource. Some possible classifications for a poetry file are holidays, seasons, animals, humorous verse, and fantasy. Occasionally, teachers may wish to use records, tapes, or filmstrips with sound effects during poetry time. One possible card for a poetry file is shown in Example 2.2.

Hearing poetry read by a teacher should be a pleasant experience for children. When reading to the class, the teacher should select poems that have variety and include such qualities as worthwhile ideas, honesty, uniqueness, imagery, musical quality, and mood and emotional appeal. Poems should stimulate the children's imaginations and foster their enjoyment. A few excellent poems to read aloud at the prereading level are

"Galoshes" by Rhoda W. Bacmeister   (rhythm and sound)
"The Monkeys and the Crocodile" by Laura E. Richards   (story, humor)
"Eletelephony" by Laura E. Richards   (humor)
"Snow" by Dorothy Aldis   (imagery)

▶ **EXAMPLE 2.2:** A Poem for a Poetry Card File

Poetry Card
"Once I Caught a Fish"
Ages 4 – 6
    1st Half Class: 1, 2, 3, 4, 5
    2nd Half Class: Once I caught a fish alive,
    1st Half Class: 6, 7, 8, 9, 10,
    2nd Half Class: I let it go again.
    1st Half Class: Why did you let it go?
    2nd Half Class: Because it bit my fingers so.
    1st Half Class: Which finger did it bite?
    2nd Half Class: The little finger on the right.

                                                    Anon.

Suitability: Choral reading (antiphonal)
Type: Humorous

"Hiding" by Dorothy Aldis   (story, humor)

"Who Has Seen the Wind?" by Christina Rossetti   (mood)

"Mice" by Rose Fyleman   (humor)

"The Owl and the Pussy-Cat" by Edward Lear   (story, humor)

"Every Time I Climb a Tree" by David McCord   (mood)

"The Swing" by Robert Louis Stevenson   (action, mood)

"Indian" by Rosemary and Stephen Vincent Benét   (action)

"Stocking Fairy" by Winifred Welles   (fantasy)

"Hello and Goodbye" by Mary A. Haberman   (mood)

"The King's Breakfast" by A. A. Milne   (story)

"Doorbells" by Rachel Field   (characterization)

"The Coin" by Sara Teasdale   (wisdom)

Other poets whose work is appropriate for this age group include Harry Behn, Myra C. Livingston, and Walter de la Mare. Mother Goose is still popular with children because of its language patterns, story quality, characterization, and possibilities for active involvement.

● **MODEL ACTIVITY:** *Poetry*

Say to the children: "Boys and girls, we have been reading Mother Goose rhymes and you can say many of them by yourselves now. Let's say some of our favorites together." The children recite rhymes that you suggest. Then say to them: "I have written some of these rhymes on paper. I would like you to make pictures for them. Then we will put these papers together and make pages for a book. I will give each one of you a different rhyme. When you get your rhyme, I will tell you which one you have. Then think about what kind of picture to draw to go with the rhyme. When you are finished, we will have a new book for our library table."   ●

Children enjoy participation poems and finger plays in which they can move their bodies or their fingers along with the poem. When listening to "Jump or Jiggle" by Evelyn Beyer, different children can be "lions stalking," "snakes sliding," or "sea gulls gliding." An example of a finger play is "Little Brown Rabbit," (shown in Model Activity: Finger Play), for which children can use their fingers to act as rabbits.

Informal Drama

Informal dramatic activities create interest in language and stories. Informal drama is spontaneous and unrehearsed, as opposed to formal drama, in which people memorize lines and wear costumes, and settings may be elaborate. Children assume the roles of characters, either from real life or from stories they have heard. They think, feel, move, react, and speak in accordance with their interpretation of the characters.

● *MODEL ACTIVITY: Finger Play*

Gather the children around you and say, "I am going to tell you a poem about a little brown rabbit. Listen carefully and watch my fingers. Then I'm going to let you say the poem with me. Are you ready?" When you have everyone's attention, recite the poem and move your fingers accordingly. Then say: "Now I will say the poem again, and this time you say it with me. Hold up your hands, but keep your fingers tucked in until it's time for them to pop out."

Little Brown Rabbit

A little brown rabbit popped out of the ground.
(right index finger pops up)

Wriggled his whiskers and looked around.
(right index finger wriggles)

Another wee rabbit who lived in the grass
(left index finger pops up)

Popped his head out and watched him pass.
(right hand hops over left, wrists crossed)

Hoppity, hoppity, hoppity, hop
(both index fingers hop forward)

Till they came to a wall and had to stop.
(both fingers stop suddenly)

Then both the wee rabbits turned themselves round.
(hands uncross)

And scuttled off home to their holes in the ground.
(hands hop back and finish in pockets)[2]

[2]Elizabeth Matterson, *Games for the Very Young. A Treasury of Nursery Songs and Finger Plays* (New York: American Heritage Press, 1969), p. 151; and *This Little Puffin* (Harmondsworth, England: Penguin Books, 1969), p. 151. Reprinted with permission of McGraw-Hill Book Co. and Penguin Books Ltd.

Informal drama may take one of many forms. It may begin with simple
rhythmic movements or actions in response to poems or songs. Later,
children may pantomime stories or actions as the teacher reads. Dramatic
play occurs when children simulate real experiences, such as cooking dinner
or being a cashier.

In an activity such as the one presented below, children are able to practice
language skills as they play the roles of customer, cashier, food preparer, and
order taker. They learn to follow directions, fill out forms, and recognize the
words for menu items. They also develop mathematical skills as they use play
money to pay for their orders and make change.

● *MODEL ACTIVITY:* Dramatic Play

After the children have been discussing their experiences at various fast-food
restaurants, say to them: "How could we make a pretend fast-food restaurant in our
own classroom? Where could we put it? What are some things we would need? How
could we get these things?" Have the children come up with answers and develop a
plan. Ask some children to bring in cups, napkins, bags, and plastic containers from
a fast-food restaurant and have others paint a sign. One child can bring in a toy cash
register. Make an illustrated price list to place above an improvised counter and
copies of order forms for the children to use. Help the children learn to read the food
words and the prices by asking: "What is the first item on the list? How much does it
cost? Can you find it on the order form?" Keep the list simple at first and add new
items later. When the fast-food center is ready, different children can assume the
roles of customers and workers.[3] ●

Acting out stories spontaneously, or creative dramatics, builds interest in
reading because children love to hear stories and then act them out. As the
teacher reads a story, the children need to pay close attention to the sequence
of events, the personalities of the characters, the dialogue, and the mood.
Before acting out the story, the class reviews what happened and identifies
the characters. As they act, the children must use appropriate vocabulary,
enunciate distinctly, speak audibly, and express themselves clearly. Children
will want to dramatize some stories several times, with different youngsters
playing the characters each time. The rest of the class forms the audience and
must listen carefully.

Use simple stories or selected parts of longer stories with young children
who are engaging in creative dramatics. Some good stories are the following:

One Fine Day by Nonny Hogrogian. New York: Macmillan, 1971.
Ask Mr. Bear by Marjorie Flack. New York: Macmillan, 1932.
Caps for Sale by Esphyr Slobodkina. New York: William R. Scott, 1947.
The Three Billy Goats Gruff by Peter Asbjornsen and Jorgan Moe. New York:
   Harcourt Brace Jovanovich, 1957.

[3]For a detailed account of setting up a McDonald's center, see Gaye McNutt and Nancy Bukofzer,
"Teaching Early Reading at McDonald's," *The Reading Teacher* 35 (April 1982): 841–42.

The Ox-Cart Man by Barbara Cooney. New York: Viking, 1979.

Where the Wild Things Are by Maurice Sendak. New York: Harper & Row, 1963.

Puppets are also useful in creative dramatics. Some shy children who are unwilling to speak as themselves are willing to talk through puppets. Children develop good language skills as they plan puppet shows and spontaneously speak their lines (see Model Activity: Puppets).

● *MODEL ACTIVITY: Puppets*

Provide a simple puppet theater and a box of puppets that may be used to represent different characters. The puppet theater can be an old appliance carton with the back cut off and a hole cut near the top of the front.

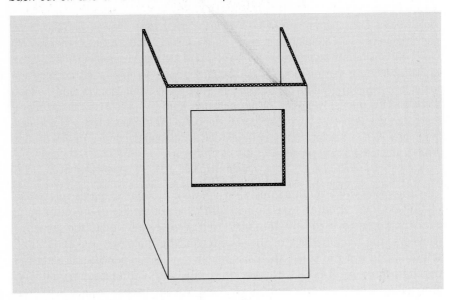

Here are some of the kinds of puppets that the children may use, along with directions for making them:

1. *Finger puppets.* Use fabric or construction paper to make a snug tube that fits over a finger. Decorate it to make it resemble a character.
2. *Paper-bag puppets.* Use paper lunch bags and apply facial features with scraps of fabric or construction paper. The mouth opening should fall on the fold of the bag.
3. *Sock puppets.* Using a child's sock that can fit over a hand, apply buttons, yarn, and bits of felt to make a character's head.
4. *Stick puppets.* Cut out characters that have been colored from coloring books. Mount them on the end of a ruler or a stick. ●

If teachers want to encourage children to participate in dramatic play, they should have the following kinds of supplies on hand:

costume box
strips of old tickets
order forms and pencils
cash register
old cardboard boxes
old clock with movable hands
calendars, pamphlets, and
  postcards
oak tag strips with felt-tip pens
empty food containers

beauty shop equipment and
  supplies
housekeeping materials
catalogues and seed packets
fast-food paper products
shopping bags
play money
building blocks
tools and kitchen utensils
library cards

Dramatic play has many benefits. Because children need to carry on conversations, they must use good language skills. By interacting with others, they are developing social and emotional readiness. Frequently children use printed words in their play, which later become sight words. These words may be found on package labels, order forms, street signs, or ticket booths. Children discover the need to read when they must recognize words in order to play the situation. Seeing this need stimulates interest in learning to read.

Social and Emotional Development

Individual and group communication and participation are important factors in social and emotional development. Many children have had little or no experience with a group as large as that found in an ordinary classroom. Each child must learn to work independently and to follow certain patterns in order not to disrupt the learning situation for others. However, many group activities in the classroom call for cooperation and sharing among students and help children develop from self-centered individuals into social beings. Language is the most important basis of cooperation. Both the social patterns within the class and the authority of the teacher are established through language. Communication experiences should be structured so that children feel adequate and secure and can develop desirable attitudes toward themselves and others. Every effort must be made in the classroom to avoid threatening a child's security and disrupting the learning experience of the others in the group. Emotionally, every child has a need for love, attention, and acceptance. If these needs are denied, a child will react with behavior that hinders achievement of her or his goals or those of the school. Aggressive, hostile, and withdrawn children pose problems that are potentially detrimental to the learning process.

A child's social and emotional development can affect his or her success in learning to read. Certain activities can help a child reach maturity. Here we present the characteristics of socially and emotionally mature children, along with ideas for promoting the development of each characteristic.

Carrying on sensible conversations; interacting well with other children. Give children opportunities to participate in small group discussions and work on projects with other children. Form groups for various purposes. Encourage children to generate ideas, reach decisions, take turns talking, and complete tasks cooperatively.

Controlling temper; accepting disappointments. Praise children who control their tempers and who accept disappointments gracefully. Ignore inappropriate behavior whenever possible.

Following directions. Encourage children to follow directions, by using exercises such as those described under Listening Activities. Establish routines so that children will know what to expect.

Sharing and taking turns. Show children how to share and take turns by role-playing proper behavior. Stress the need to be patient, to consider the feelings of others, and to take care of property.

Being self-reliant; completing tasks. Give children simple tasks that they can complete independently. Gradually increase the complexity of the tasks. Praise children who are self-reliant.

Having good attention spans. Plan short, high-interest activities. Work with children on an individual basis if necessary. Reward children who maintain their attention with privileges.

Having a positive attitude toward school; seeming eager to learn. Make school an interesting and happy place to be. Allow each child to be successful at something every day. Create a cheerful environment.

Handling school materials competently. Demonstrate the use of scissors, crayons, paste, and paint. Allow children the privilege of using them when they can handle them correctly and put them away as instructed.

Knowing what to do in different situations. Role-play what to do if the teacher must leave the room, if a guest comes, if a child gets sick, if something is lost, and so on. Explain fire drills and routine procedures. Show children what choices they have when they have completed their work.

Working independently at centers. In small groups, show children how to work at centers. Stress how important it is for each child to do his or her own work without interfering with other children. Allow children to work in centers only when they observe the rules.

Putting away and cleaning up. Give children a five-minute warning when free time is nearly over. Have a place for everything, with labels to indicate where things belong. Be sure that paper towels and other supplies required for cleaning up are readily available.

Finding resources independently. Familiarize children with the resources in the classroom. Keep things in their proper places. Allow children to be responsible for using and returning materials.

An activity such as that shown in Model Activity: Duty Chart can help children foster mature social and emotional attitudes.

● *MODEL ACTIVITY: Duty Chart*

Say to the children: "In our classroom we need many helpers. What kinds of helpers do we need?" The children suggest answers. Then say: "We will need different boys and girls to help us each week. I have made a duty chart to help us remember whose turn it is to help. Each week we will change the names beside the jobs. Let's read the chart together. We will see who has a job this week."

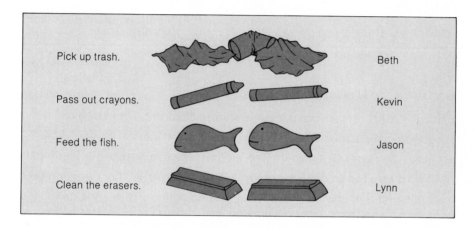

Physical Development

Other than general good health, good vision and hearing are most essential for learning to read. Good visual acuity, at near and far distances, and eye coordination are important for adequate visual functioning in reading. The child's need to make fine visual discriminations (to see likenesses and differences) is obvious, and suggests the usefulness of early activities that involve forms and shapes (such as picture puzzles) and later activities that involve letter recognition (words beginning or ending alike, and so on). Auditory acuity is also important in learning to read. Phonics is based on the ability to hear sounds and discriminate among them. Activities that emphasize beginning sounds and rhyming words are especially useful in developing auditory skills.

Children must also develop skill in motor coordination to be successful with reading. One reason for permitting and encouraging them to use blocks, brushes, clay, crayons, paints, scissors, paper, pencils, and other equipment is that these things help to develop motor (muscle) coordination.

A teacher can use many types of physical activities to prepare children for working with letters and words. The activities that follow are divided into three major categories: visual skills, auditory skills, and motor skills. Some of the activities involve the use of letters and words, but others do not.

Visual Skills

Visual perception, memory, and discrimination are necessary for reading, in addition to good visual acuity. Perception refers to the brain's processing and understanding of visual stimuli; memory, to a child's ability to recall what he or she has seen; and discrimination, to the ability to distinguish between likenesses and differences. In order to achieve this last skill, the child must first understand the concepts of *like* and *different*.

The visual perception, visual memory, and visual discrimination activities in this section should be helpful in developing each of these skills. Appendix A to this chapter presents additional visual activities.

● *MODEL ACTIVITY: Visual Perception*

Say to the children: "I am going to put a word on the board. The word is *car*. Now I am going to draw a box around it. Karen, come up and trace over the box." ▢car "I will put another word on the board. The word has some tall letters in it. The word is *call*. I will draw a box around it, too. Andy, will you trace over this box?" ▢call "Let's try another word. In this word one letter goes up and one letter goes down. The word is *dog*. Look at the box I am drawing around *dog*. Trace over this box for us, Skip." ▢dog Repeat this process with several other short words with different shapes (ride, said, go, hide). Then give each child a sheet of paper with some large printed words on it. Say to them: "Look at the words on your paper. I want you to look at each word carefully. Then I want you to make a box around it with your crayon." ●

● *MODEL ACTIVITY: Visual Memory*

Write a series of letters on the board, such as *f, o, t, s, m,* and *k*. Say to the children: "I have written some letters on the board. Let's say the names of these letters together." The children say the letter names with you. Then say: "Think carefully about the letters that are on the board. I am going to ask you to close your eyes while I erase one of them. When you open your eyes, see if you can tell me which letter I erased." ●

● *MODEL ACTIVITY: Visual Discrimination*

Write on the board some letters that are similar in appearance (*b, d, g, p,* and *d*) and also some similarly shaped or identical words (*hot, pat, top, pat, ton*). Say to the children: "Let's look at these letters. Are any of them alike? Which ones are the same? How are the first two letters different? What is different about the other letters?" Ask the same questions about the words. Some children may draw boxes around the letters and words or trace them. Then say to them: "Now I am going to give you a piece of paper with some letters and words on it. Look at the first group of letters. Do you see the letter above the blocks of letters? Can you find a block with a letter in it that is exactly like the letter on top of the blocks? If you can, I want you to color that block red." Repeat the activity with a sample set of words. Then say: "Does everyone understand what to do? Go ahead and color the blocks that have the same letters or words as the ones on top."

b	
g	d
p	b

bad	
dad	bat
bad	bed

Auditory Skills

As is true of visual skills, auditory skills necessary for reading involve acuity, perception, memory, and discrimination. Auditory perception is the way the brain comprehends information it receives by sound. Many auditory perception activities can help children develop an awareness of their environment as well as help them with reading.

● **MODEL ACTIVITY:** *Auditory Perception*

Most of the children in this class can recognize the letters of the alphabet. Say to them: "We are going to play a game. I want you to close your eyes and listen while I write a letter on the board. Then I want you to tell me what letter I wrote without looking. First I will write an *s* or a *t* on the board. Think how you make these letters. Then close your eyes and listen while I make either an *s* or a *t*." Make a *t*. Then say: "Which letter did I make?" Most of the children answer "*t*." Say: "Open your eyes and see if you are right. How did you know it was *t* and not *s*? That's right. You heard me crossing the *t*." Other pairs of letters to use are *i* and *l*, *j* and *n*, *x* and *o*, and *f* and *c*. ●

Auditory memory refers to a child's ability to recall information or stimuli that he or she has heard. Several activities will promote the development of auditory memory; although there is some overlap, they fall into three major categories: echo activities, remembering connected speech, and following directions. Here is one possible echo activity.

● **MODEL ACTIVITY:** *Auditory Memory*

Play the following game with a small group of children. Say to them: "We are going to pretend to go to the store and buy some food. Each one of us will remember what everyone else has bought. Then we will buy one more thing. Let's try it. I will begin. 'I went to the store and bought some bread.' Now Mark must say, 'I went to the store and bought some bread and something else.'" If Mark says, "I went to the store and bought some bread and butter," tell him, "That's the right idea. Now, Sandra, it's your turn." Sandra says: "I went to the store and bought some bread and butter and popsicles." The children continue around the circle, each adding a new item. ●

Skill in auditory discrimination enables a child to hear the likenesses and differences in sounds. Before working with the sounds of letters and words, a teacher should talk about things in the room that sound alike or different. For instance, moving a table and moving a desk sound nearly alike. Opening a window and opening a door make different sounds.

Introducing children to simple rhymes is a good way to sensitize them to likenesses and differences in verbal sounds. Ask children to pick out the words that rhyme and to supply words to rhyme with a given word. This ability is fundamental to the construction of "word families." Children should also be able to hear similarities and differences in word endings and in middle vowels; for example, they should be able to tell whether *rub* and *rob*, or *hill* and *pit*, have the same middle sound. Finally, they should be able to listen to the pronunciation of a word sound by sound and mentally fuse or blend the sounds to recognize the intended word. The two activities presented below should help develop such auditory discrimination abilities.

● **MODEL ACTIVITY:** *Auditory Discrimination (Beginning Sounds)*

Name several puppets with double names to stress initial consonant sounds (Molly Mouse, Freddie Frog, Dolly Duck, and Bennie Bear). While holding a puppet, say: "I'd like you to meet Molly Mouse. Molly Mouse only likes things that begin the same way that her name begins. Molly Mouse likes milk, but she doesn't like water. I am going to name some things that Molly Mouse likes or doesn't like. You must listen closely to the way the word begins. Raise your hand if I say something that Molly Mouse likes. Keep your hand down if I say something that Molly Mouse doesn't like. Let's begin. Molly Mouse likes meat." The children should raise their hands. If they don't seem to understand why she likes meat, talk about the beginning sound and give additional examples. Then say: "Molly Mouse likes cheese." The children should keep their hands down. ●

● *MODEL ACTIVITY: Auditory Discrimination (Whole Word)*

Give each child in the group or class two cards that are identical except that one has S written on it and one has D written on it. Say to the children: "Each of you has two cards. Hold up the one that has S on it." Demonstrate which card has the S by holding it up. Then follow the same procedure with the D card. Continue by saying: "I am going to say two words. If the two words sound exactly the same, hold up the card with S on it. If the two words do not sound exactly the same, hold up the card with D on it. The S card means *same*. The D card means *different*. The first two words are *boy* and *horse*. All of you should be holding up the D card because these two words sound different. The next two words are *funny* and *funny*. Now everyone should be holding up the S card because these two words sound the same." Continue with other examples. ●

Additional activities to develop each of these skills are presented in Appendix A in this chapter.

Motor Coordination

The ability to control and coordinate physical movement seems to have a positive effect on learning to read. Young children begin with gross motor activities (throwing, pushing) and move toward fine motor coordination (using a paintbrush). Their ability to coordinate hand-eye activities is important for learning to read and write. Visual-motor coordination is necessary for following a line of print from left to right and returning to the next line, and for focusing attention on words and symbols in order to decode them. Children also require a high level of visual-motor coordination in order to form letters correctly when writing. The activities described below relate to children's motor-skill development, kinesthetic-tactile skills, and sense of directionality, but nearly all movement activities, from swinging on the jungle gym to cutting, pasting, and drawing, contribute to development of motor skills.

● *MODEL ACTIVITY: Motor Coordination*

Say to the children: "We are going to make a book about the girls and boys in our class. I have put some magazines and catalogues on the table in the back of the room. I have also put some scissors and paste on the table. I want each one of you to make a page for our book. When you are ready to make your page, come to me and I will give you a piece of paper with your name on it. Then go to the table and look through the magazines and catalogues. Find some pictures that will tell us something about you. Maybe you will find something that you like to play with or something that you like to eat. Cut out some pictures very carefully. Decide how you want to arrange the pictures on your page. Then paste the pictures on the page." ●

Children can develop readiness skills such as eye-hand coordination and recognition of similar shapes and sizes as they cut, paste, and draw.   (©Sepp Seitz/Woodfin Camp)

Most children learn to read readily through an auditory-visual approach, but kinesthetic-tactile activities are also useful for teaching letter and word shapes. These activities utilize the sense of touch and whole body movements for learning letter forms. Some educators believe that children who use body movements to work with letters pay closer attention to the shapes. The kinesthetic-tactile approach is good reinforcement for the average learner and an alternate way to teach the special learner.

● *MODEL ACTIVITY: Kinesthetic-Tactile Learning*

Give each child in the group a card with the word *down* printed on it. Say to the children: "Today we are going to learn to read and write a new word. This word is *down*. Look at your card and say the word with me. Listen to a sentence that has the word *down* in it. 'Put this book down.' Will you do this for me, Jenny? Now I want all of you to start with the tall letter *d* and move your finger under the word as we say it together. Let's do that three times. This time I want you to trace each letter with your finger as we say the word again. Remember to start with the tall letter *d*. Now look at your card and use your finger to write the word *down* in giant letters in the air. See if you can do it this time without looking at your card. Look at your card again and see if you did it right. Turn your card over and try writing the word *down* with your finger on the back of the card. Check to see if you did it right." ●

Children need to establish directionality in reading and writing; that is, they must learn to read from left to right and from top to bottom. Some children can write their names as easily from right to left as from left to right. Such directional errors are common for beginners; they will usually disappear as a child moves along in reading.

● **MODEL ACTIVITY:** *Directionality*

The children are sitting facing you. Say to them: "How many hands do you have? That's right. You have two hands. One hand is your left hand. The other hand is your right hand." Show the children which hand is left and which is right. Then say: "Raise your left hand up high. Your other hand is your right hand. Now raise your right hand up high." Repeat this process with arms, legs, and feet. Then say: "I want you to listen carefully and do exactly what I say. Hold up your right hand. Stamp your right foot. Put your left hand on your left leg." Give directions slowly and pause long enough to make sure everyone is following directions. ●

Appendix A in this chapter includes additional motor coordination activities.

🖊 **Self-Check: Objective 4**
List some activities that you would like to try for developing visual, auditory, and motor skills. (Refer to Appendix A for additional ideas.)
(See Self-Improvement Opportunity 4.)

Cognitive Development

A child's intelligence is vital in learning to read. At one time a mental age of six and one-half years was considered to be the factor that determined when a child could learn to read. In recent years, however, educators have realized that many other factors also affect readiness for reading, including, as we have pointed out, the child's experiential background and degree of language development.

A more significant criterion than mental age is a child's level of cognitive development, or way of acquiring knowledge. Jean Piaget, a Swiss psychologist highly respected for his theory of cognitive development, asserted that thought comes before language and that language is a way of representing thought. His theory, which relates to the associational, sequential, and learning aspects of the reading process that we described in Chapter 1, as well as to the thinking aspect, divides cognitive development into four stages: sensorimotor, preoperational, concrete-operational, and formal-operational.

The *sensorimotor period* extends approximately from birth to two years of age. During this period children learn about objects and form ideas about the world around them through physical manipulation. These ideas are quite simple, of course, and nonverbal. According to Piaget, manipulation of a wide variety of objects seems to be most important for the child's intellectual development at this point.

The *preoperational period* extends approximately from age two to age seven. During this period children engage in symbolic thought by representing ideas and events with words and sentences, drawings, and dramatic play. They are rapidly developing concepts, but are as yet unable to think logically. Children in this phase are also hampered in their reading development because they have not yet achieved an understanding of "conservation of substance"—the understanding that something remains the same regardless of changes in shape or division. In other words, a change may occur in a system without changing the fundamental characteristics of that system.

The *concrete-operational period* extends approximately from age seven to eleven. In this period children become capable of performing various logical operations, but only with concrete objects. They usually understand the operations of identity (permitting them to remember the original condition of an element) and reversibility. They can observe a system, change it, and then return it to its original state; thus, they are capable of manipulating the elements of language. During this period children are usually able to reason well about things they read only if what they read is closely related to their direct experiences.

The *formal-operational period* appears sometime between the ages of eleven and fifteen. In this period children are able to reason about ideas that do not relate to direct experiences. These youngsters can manipulate symbols without referring to the actual objects represented.

Children of the same chronological age are not necessarily at the same level of cognitive development, but they do go through each stage in the sequence outlined by Piaget. There is little, if any, value in trying to accelerate a child's rate of progress. Rather, Piaget believed, parents and educators should attempt to broaden and enrich a child's experiences at each level in order to develop a solid foundation for future stages of development.

Most children who enter first grade are nearing the end of the preoperational period; therefore, we will describe this stage more fully than the others because of its relevance to reading readiness. During the early part of the preoperational period (ages two to four), children do not separate language from experiences and objects. The name of an object seems to be inherently related to it; the name and the object seem to be inseparable. At this stage children need to continue to have a wide variety of experiences while they rapidly attach verbal labels to objects and physical operations. Because of their limited concept formation and language development, these children are not yet ready for formal reading instruction. An activity like the following could help develop children's familiarity with concrete objects.

● *MODEL ACTIVITY:* *Concrete Experience*

Say to a child: "Some things float when you play with them in the bathtub, and some things sink. See if you can tell me which things will float on top of the water and which things will sink to the bottom. Take this golf ball and feel it. Do you think it will float on top or sink to the bottom? Why? Let's try it and see." Follow the same procedure with other objects, such as a tennis ball, a crayon, a penny, a sponge, and a nail. ●

The second phase of the preoperational period (ages five to seven) is characterized by rapid development in symbolic thought. Children are able to see simple relationships and classify objects according to certain features. For example, they realize that pennies, nickels, and dimes are all money. They are generally unable to talk about their reasons for grouping things together, however. Piaget therefore referred to this period as *intuitive,* the phase when children's thinking is based on their perceptions rather than on their knowledge of specific criteria for classification (Evans, 1975, pp. 198–99).

Preoperational children possess several characteristics that limit their thinking. They are egocentric; that is, they consider things from only their own point of view. They cannot understand that other people may have different viewpoints and that their own point of view may actually be incorrect. They cannot disassociate themselves from objects and events in order to understand how a situation might be perceived differently by someone else. For instance, a child who snatches a toy from another child is motivated to act by a desire to play with the toy and fails to realize how the other child feels when the toy is taken away. This characteristic prevents children from thinking clearly about the events in a story, except from their own limited perspective.

Preoperational children also lack all but the most elementary skills of classification. They are unable to understand that something can be a member of two classes at the same time. They do not see that a banana can belong to a classification of fruit and also to a classification of things that are yellow. Similarly, if a teacher shows children ten wooden blocks—eight red ones and two blue ones—and asks if there are more red blocks or more wooden blocks, most children will say there are more red blocks. The relationships between sounds and symbols in the English language are inconsistent and hard to classify; thus, a beginning reading program based on phonics generalizations is questionably useful for children in this stage. However, an activity such as the following can help children to practice classification skills.

● *MODEL ACTIVITY:* *Classification*

Cut out pictures of objects that might be found in a large discount store (furniture, shoes, appliances, toys, and so on). Put the collection of pictures on a table along with several small, empty boxes. Say to a child: "Let's pretend that we are in a large store. Each box is a different part of the store. Can you put all the things together that belong in each part?" The child places the items. Then, in order to understand the child's reasoning, ask questions such as "Why did you put the bicycle with the television set? Why is the toy box with the furniture? Why did you put the tennis shoes with the toys?" ●

Since preoperational children do not understand conservation of substance, they have difficulty handling even slightly altered situations, which they tend to treat as entirely new ones. Yet in reading, children are expected to recognize letters produced in varied scripts, cases, and typefaces as being the same.

Two abilities that result from comprehending conservation of substance are *reversibility* and *decentration*. Reversibility is the ability to reverse an operation to produce what was there initially—in other words, to return an object to its original shape after its form has been changed. In reading, children must convert printed symbols (graphemes) into spoken sounds (phonemes), then check the results by reversing the process. Decentration refers to the ability to consider more than one aspect of a situation at a time. For instance, a child who is working on a jigsaw puzzle may focus only on how one edge of the puzzle piece seems to fit into the puzzle, without considering the other edges. Reading requires children to deal with words both as linear patterns to be remembered and as representations of meaning to be understood, a process requiring decentration. Since they do not usually understand conservation of substance, preoperational children often lack reversibility and decentration skills. The following activity may be helpful in developing their concept of conservation of substance.

● **MODEL ACTIVITY:** *Conservation of Mass*

Have in hand one ball of clay (or dough) and enough material to make another ball of the same size. Say to the child: "Take this clay and make another ball exactly the same size as this ball." After the child is satisfied that the second ball is the same size as the first, change the ball by flattening it into a pancake, rolling it into a sausage, or cutting it into small pieces. Then ask: "Do these two pieces have the same amount of clay?" or "Does this pile have the same amount as this ball?" After the child answers, ask: "How do you know?" ●

Additional activities to help children gain experience with each of the concepts mentioned are presented in Appendix A in this chapter.

Implications for Instruction

Several studies show a relationship between reading and Piaget's theory. A rather high correlation between beginning reading achievement and the ability to conserve concrete substances was reported by Almy (1966). Cox (1976) also found that a group of second graders reading at grade level could conserve, but youngsters reading below grade level were unable to conserve. In a summary of the relationship between reading achievement and the attainment of concrete-operational thought, however, Waller (1977) found only low to moderate relationships.

Schools have not yet applied Piaget's theory to the curriculum in any precise ways, but many schools are incorporating his general ideas into activity-based curricula that focus on three basic tenets. First, teachers should use Piaget's cognitive development sequence as a guide for determining program content at various levels. They should not expect children to work successfully at a task for which they have not yet acquired the necessary thinking skills. Second, children need social interaction with their peers to facilitate cognitive, social, emotional, and moral development. Their egocentricity is reduced as they contemplate the viewpoints of others. Third, instructional programs should emphasize self-directed discovery and learning. According to Piaget, the goal of education is to create possibilities for children to discover and invent (Evans, 1975, p. 245).

The broad meaning of Piaget's theory for education is that thought processes differ at various periods of life and children should not be expected to think like adults. The theory points out that children learn better by moving and manipulating than by sitting and listening; they understand by experimenting and exploring, not by memorizing rules. Piaget's theory supports those who provide more opportunities for thinking before introducing reading to the young child (Furth, 1970). Thinking, rather than reading and writing, should be stressed when the child first comes to school. According to Furth, teachers should encourage but never impose reading, and a delay in learning to read will have no negative effect on a child's eventual level of reading achievement. Certainly Piaget's theory does not support the teaching of reading at the preschool level.

Therefore, encouraging logical thought should be one goal of the reading readiness program. Even though prereaders do not as yet possess abstract thinking skills, they can engage in activities that will prepare them for logical thinking and problem-solving skills (Nevius, 1977). Because children may need time to discover relationships between objects and ideas and between causes and outcomes, reading readiness and beginning reading programs should move gradually from concrete examples to more abstract material, from literal reading skills to higher-level reading skills. It is important to remember that when children begin to read, they will need to use higher-level cognitive abilities than those that are typical of the intuitive phase of the preoperational period. Among these abilities are dealing with logical rules and classifications, perceiving the outstanding features of letters and words, understanding concepts found in books, and relating sounds to symbols (Kirkland, 1978). A broad base of experiences with Piagetian types of tasks will help to develop the kinds of thinking skills that are necessary for success in beginning reading. More extensive information about Piaget's theories may be found in numerous sources.[4]

✔ Self-Check: Objective 5

Briefly describe Piaget's four stages of cognitive development. (See Self-Improvement Opportunity 7.)

MOVING INTO READING

According to research, knowledge of letter names is a good predictor of success in reading (Hillerich, 1966). This finding, however, does not mean that knowing letter names makes a good reader. It is probable that children who know the names of letters when they enter school are also intelligent, curious, aware, and from a good home environment. Any of these factors could influence their progress in beginning reading.

Most children are eager to learn to read and write, but many find reading more difficult than they anticipated. One problem that frequently occurs is that children are confused by terminology and cannot understand words related to learning to read (Roberts, 1981; Downing, 1976). For instance, when a teacher says, "Point to the second word in the last sentence," a child might not understand the words *second, word, last,* or *sentence;* he or she may not have developed concepts for these words. Teachers must observe children carefully to see what concepts they do not know and then find ways of teaching these concepts in natural language situations.

Teaching Letters and Words

Teachers need to keep several points in mind while teaching letters and words to beginning readers. Letter names should be taught early so that the teacher

---

[4]See Ronald J. Raven and Richard J. Salzer, "Piaget and Reading Instruction," in *Perspectives on Elementary Reading: Principles and Strategies of Teaching,* Robert Karlin, ed. (New York: Harcourt Brace Jovanovich, 1973), pp. 21–30; Alfred L. Baldwin, *Theories of Child Development* (New York: Wiley, 1967); John H. Flavell, *The Developmental Psychology of Jean Piaget* (Princeton, N.J.: D. Van Nostrand, 1963); Millie Almy, "Young Children's Thinking and the Teaching of Reading," in *Issues and Innovations in the Teaching of Reading,* Joe L. Frost, ed. (Glenview, Ill.: Scott, Foresman, 1967), pp. 89–93; Millie Almy, E. Chittenden, and Paula Miller, *Young Children's Thinking: Studies of Some Aspects of Piaget's Theory* (New York: Teachers College Press, 1966), pp. 139–40; Kenneth Lovell, "The Philosophy of Jean Piaget," *New Society* 11 (August 1966), 222–26.

and the class have a common referent—for example, understanding when the teacher talks about the letter *f* or the letter *n* (Farr and Roser, 1979, p. 105). Knowledge of letter *names* is important for talking about similarities and differences in printed words, but knowledge of letter *sounds* is more useful in decoding words (Hafner and Jolly, 1982, p. 26). It is more difficult to discriminate between some letters (such as *d* and *b* or *p* and *q*), than others, and the teacher should not teach similar letters or letters that are reversals of each other at the same time. Beginning readers have no reason to memorize the letters of the alphabet in order. An activity such as the following can be used in early teaching of letters. Additional activities are presented in Chapter Appendix A.

● *MODEL ACTIVITY: Letter Recognition*

Print the letters *E* and *e* on the chalkboard. Point to each letter and ask: "What letter is this?" The children should identify the letters as the capital and lower-case *e*. Then say: "I am going to give each of you a page from the newspaper. Some of these letters will be in the newspaper. Each time you find one, cut it out. Then paste your letters on a piece of paper. Some of the letters may be very big and some may be small." ●

Children are naturally fascinated by their names, and should be provided with numerous opportunities to see their names and other familiar words in print. Activities for teaching letter and word recognition that focus on names include

1. comparing lengths of names—longest and shortest.
2. counting letters in names.
3. identifying individual coat hooks from name cards.
4. writing names, using name cards for models.
5. examining names for double letters.
6. identifying duplicate first names in the class.
7. repeating letters of names after teacher.
8. identifying daily tasks by reading names and interpreting adjacent pictures.

At this stage in their development children are rapidly acquiring sight words, especially names, color words, and number words. They are also learning words from experience stories and television commercials. A more extensive discussion of sight words is found in Chapter 3. One activity to build sight word knowledge is presented in Model Activity: Sight Word Recognition.

● *MODEL ACTIVITY:* Sight Word Recognition

Make a color chart like the one pictured below. On one side of the chart print a list of color words in their corresponding colors. On the other side make some color splotches that match the words, but arrange them in a different sequence from the words. Attach colored yarn tipped with tape or glue to the appropriate color words. Punch a hole beside each splotch of color on the right side of the chart. While working with a small group of children, say: "Here are some colors that you know. Let's name the colors together." Say the colors with the children. "Now let's read these color words together." Read the color words with the children. "Frank, I would like you to read us one of the color words. Then put the piece of yarn from that word through the hole that is beside the same color as the word." Continue in the same way with the other children.

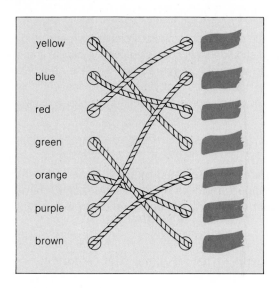

✔ **Self-Check: Objective 6**

What are some good ways to teach letter and word recognition? (See Self-Improvement Opportunities 8 and 11.)

Beginning Reading and Writing

Predictable books—those that use repetition, rhythmic language patterns, and familiar concepts—are excellent resources for introducing children to the pleasure and ease of reading. Even during a first reading by the teacher, children join in on the repetitive lines or familiar chants. Stories such as Bill Martin's *Brown Bear, Brown Bear* (New York: Holt, Rinehart and Winston, 1970) and the folk tale "The Old Woman and Her Pig" (Paul Galdone; New York: McGraw-Hill, 1960) contain familiar sequences. Children are soon reading these books for themselves if the teacher has reread them and pointed out the corresponding words (Rhodes, 1981).

As children learn to read, they also learn to write. They copy their names onto their papers, and they copy other words that they want to use. If they have had a wide variety of fine motor coordination activities, they should possess the skill needed for forming letters. They will see the value of learning to write if they are given some purposes for writing, such as writing invitations, thank-you notes, captions for artwork, and words in story booklets.

A child is often ready to write when he or she

1. spontaneously shows an interest in learning to print his or her own name.
2. has developed facility in the use of scissors, crayons, paintbrushes, and pencils in a variety of informal activities.
3. can copy simple geometric or letter-shaped figures.
4. has established handedness (whether right- or left-handed).
5. has participated in composing and sending written messages.
6. feels a personal need to learn to write.

These criteria provide clues to the types of activities that promote handwriting readiness. (Incidentally, children should be permitted to use their preferred hand. If a child is ambidextrous, help him or her to make a choice and develop a preference by determining which hand is most frequently used and has the better control.)

Most prereading programs for teaching beginning reading and writing skills use reading readiness workbooks that serve as the first level of a basal reading series (Paradis and Peterson, 1975). These workbooks introduce the children gradually and sequentially to such skills as visual discrimination, letter sounds, and left-to-right directionality. The accompanying teacher's manual gives detailed directions for using the workbook and suggests a wealth of ideas for supplementary enrichment activities. A sample lesson from a teacher's guide, including the student workbook page and explanation for the teacher, is shown in Example 2.3.

Workbooks and skill sheets should never be considered a total reading program, however, nor should they become drudgery for children. Some preschoolers quickly become frustrated and discouraged by too much drill. Though workbooks are useful for building certain skills, a complete prereading program must also include many other types of experiences. Teachers should ask themselves the following questions regarding their use of workbooks:

1. What is (are) the specific objective(s) of this material?
2. Does this material meet this child's specific prereading skill need?
3. Does the child need to review a previously developed skill to be successful?

4. Does the child understand terms needed for doing the work (*underline* the *matching letter*)?
5. Is the skill being developed actually necessary for learning to read?
6. What concrete manipulative activities—involvement with real objects—can I provide to build background and motivation for the material?
7. How can I use the material to help the child develop oral language?
8. After completing the material, does the child still need further practice with its objective(s)?
9. What kind of records should I keep to indicate the child's progress through the use of the material?
10. What follow-up activities (non-workbook) can I provide to reinforce the objective(s)? What creative ways will extend the learning?

Assessment of Readiness

Assessment of each child's level of reading readiness is a critical element in the total readiness program. Teachers must not assign children reading-related tasks that are too difficult for them, nor place them in structured reading programs until they have the necessary coping skills. The danger that children will develop lasting negative or indifferent attitudes toward reading is great when they are frustrated. If a teacher is in doubt about a child's readiness for formal reading instruction, he or she should wait and be sure, rather than take a chance on starting the child too soon.

On an informal basis, the teacher makes assessments daily as he or she observes how a child reacts to situations, participates in activities, and communicates with others. Rate of learning is not steady, and the teacher will need to be sensitive to variations in growth rates. When a child's curiosity surges ahead, the teacher must find new ways to challenge him or her. If, on the other hand, a child indicates that he or she doesn't really understand a skill or concept, the teacher may need to backtrack and repeat a lesson. A teacher chooses strategies by assessing the needs, interests, and abilities of the students. See Chapter 9 for a more complete discussion of assessment at the readiness level.

Pre–First-Grade Reading Instruction: Pros and Cons

A trend currently exists toward pre–first-grade formal instruction in reading and writing skills. Articles in popular magazines are urging parents to begin teaching reading at home and to seek out preschools that teach reading skills. Many schools are responding to pressure from parents by initiating direct reading instruction in kindergarten (O'Donnell, 1979). Most research supports the idea that formal reading instruction is effective for young children; moreover, these young readers maintain their lead over comparable children who are taught at later ages (Wilson, 1976). According to one study, a highly structured program of language and cognitive development produced better

Matching Beginning Sounds with Letters   f g

To have children correctly associate the sounds for *f* and *g* with the letters *f* and *g* at the beginning of words.

MATERIALS FOR THE LESSON

Getting Ready to Read: page 67
Getting Ready to Read, Big Book: page 67
Pencils or Crayons

PREPARING FOR THE LESSON

Model activities are provided in the Reference Handbook for your use with those children who, in your judgment, still need preparatory exercises. See Reference Handbook, page 408.

TEACHING THE LESSON

Distribute copies of *Getting Ready to Read*.
Help children find page 67.

ROW 1 Say: Find Row 1. **Point to number 1.** Put your finger under number 1. . . . **Point to *f*.** What letter is at the beginning of this row? . . . *(f)* This is the letter *f*. **Point to the pictures.** Now look at these pictures. Who will name these pictures? . . . *(five, bus, fence, feather)* Point to the pictures in left-to-right order and have them named.

Some of these picture names begin with the sound for *f*. **Point to *five*.** Does *five* begin with the sound for *f*? . . . *(yes)* Five begins with the sound for *f*. **Point to *bus*.** Does *bus* begin with the sound for *f*? . . . *(no)* Bus does not begin with the sound for *f*. **Point to *fence*.** Does *fence* begin with the sound for *f*? . . . *(yes)* Fence begins with the sound for *f*. **Point to *feather*.** Does *feather* begin with the sound for *f*? . . . *(yes)* Feather begins with the sound for *f*.
Ask: Which picture names in this row begin with the sound for *f*? . . . *(five, fence, feather)* Five, fence, feather begin with the sound for *f*. Which picture name does not begin with the sound for *f*? . . . *(bus)* Bus does not begin like *five, fence, feather*.

Continue using the same procedure for the remaining three rows:

ROW 2 LETTER: *g*
         PICTURES: *garden, goat, girl, hook*

ROW 3 LETTER: *f*
         PICTURES: *key, fox, four, fish*

ROW 4 LETTER: *g*
         PICTURES: *game, guitar, lion, ghost*

PRACTICE

Distribute pencils or crayons.

ROW 1 Point to number 1. Say: Find Row 1 and put your finger under number 1 again. . . . **Point to *f*.** Put a line under the letter *f*. . . . Some of the picture names in this row begin with the sound for *f*. Say the name of each picture to yourself. Put a line under each picture whose name begins with the sound for *f*. Do not put a line under a picture if the picture name does not begin with the sound for *f*.
   When children have finished marking the pictures, ask: Which picture names begin with the sound for *f*? . . . *(five, fence, feather)* Five, fence, feather begin with the sound for *f*. You should have a line under *five, fence, feather*.

Continue using the above procedure with the remaining three rows:

ROW 2 LETTER: *g*
         PICTURES: *garden, goat, girl, hook*

ROW 3 LETTER: *f*
         PICTURES: *key, fox, four, fish*

ROW 4 LETTER: *g*
         PICTURES: *game, guitar, lion, ghost*

OPTIONAL RESOURCE MATERIALS

Practice Book: page 67
Reference Handbook: Activities 59–65 (pages 408–411)
Reading Bonus: Lesson 67

Source: William K. Durr, et al. *Getting Ready to Read, Teacher's Guide,* pp. 243–45. Copyright © 1981 by Houghton Mifflin Company. Used by permission. ◀

readiness for reading in four-year-olds than an incidental approach did (Karnes and others, 1968). Children from different economic and social backgrounds also showed significant gains from early instruction in reading skills (Di Lorenzo and Salter, 1968).

Research confirming the effectiveness of early reading instruction does not tell the whole story, however. Lesiak (1978) pointed out that this research is still unclear in several respects. For example, it gives no guidelines for selecting the best methods and materials, since different studies used different strategies. The length of the reading readiness instructional period varied, as did ways of measuring achievement. The research is inconclusive on the emotional effects of early reading instruction. Those studies that checked the progress of early readers in upper grades found that even though these children did maintain their lead in the primary grades, their lead disappeared or decreased in the intermediate grades.

Those who oppose direct reading instruction for preschoolers point out some potential dangers. Young children who are exposed to a highly structured, paper-and-pencil readiness program may become bored or frustrated. Feeling the pressure to finish their work, they may begin to dislike reading. What learning takes place may be superficial and rote rather than broadly based on language and concept development (Davis, 1980). Highly structured, published programs are unlikely to meet the needs of individual learners or of a teacher who observes and works with children on a day-to-day basis.

We wish to stress that children who come to kindergarten or first grade knowing how to read should be encouraged to continue reading; their instruction, of course, should be in keeping with their level of achievement. These children are usually high achievers throughout school. Keep in mind that other children may not be ready for reading until the end of first grade or even later. As this chapter has pointed out, readiness for reading is a matter of individual development.

Finally, we urge you to read carefully the following joint statements of concerns and recommendations about practices in pre–first-grade reading instruction, prepared by a number of professional organizations concerned with the education of children.[5]

A Perspective on Pre-First Graders and the Teaching of Reading
Pre-First Graders need:
> Opportunities to express orally, graphically, and dramatically their feelings and responses to experiences.

AND

> Opportunities to interpret the language of others whether it is written, spoken, or nonverbal.

[5]"Reading and Pre-First Grade: A Joint Statement of Concerns About Present Practices in Pre-First Grade Reading Instruction," *Language Arts* 54 (April 1977), pp. 460–461. Copyright © by the National Council of Teachers of English. Reprinted by permission of the publisher and the author.

Teachers of Pre-First Graders need:

Preparation that emphasizes developmentally appropriate language experiences for all pre-first graders, including those ready to read or already reading.

AND

The combined efforts of professional organizations, colleges, and universities to help them successfully meet the concerns outlined in this document.

Concerns:

1. A growing number of children are enrolled in pre-kindergarten and kindergarten classes in which highly structured prereading and reading programs are being used.
2. Decisions related to schooling, including the teaching of reading, are increasingly being made on economic and political bases instead of on our knowledge of young children and of how they best learn.
3. In a time of diminishing financial resources, schools often try to make "a good showing" on measures of achievement that may or may not be appropriate for the children involved. Such measures all too often dictate the content and goals of the programs.
4. In attempting to respond to pressures for high scores on widely used measures of achievement, teachers of young children sometimes feel compelled to use materials, methods, and activities designed for older children. In so doing, they may impede the development of intellectual functions such as curiosity, critical think-ing, and creative expression, and, at the same time, promote negative attitudes toward reading.
5. A need exists to provide alternative ways to teach and evaluate progress in pre-reading and reading skills.
6. Teachers of pre-first graders who are carrying out highly individualized programs without depending upon commercial readers and workbooks need help in articulating for themselves and the public *what* they are doing and *why*.

Recommendations:

1. Provide reading experiences as an integrated part of the broader communication process that includes listening, speaking, and writing. A language experience approach is an example of such integration.
2. Provide for a broad range of activities both in scope and in content. Include direct experiences that offer opportunities to communicate to different persons.
3. Foster children's affective and cognitive development by providing materials, experiences, and opportunities to communicate what they know and how they feel.
4. Continually appraise how various aspects of each child's total development affects his or her reading development.
5. Use evaluative procedures that are developmentally appropriate for the children being assessed and that reflect the goals and objectives of the instructional program.
6. Insure feelings of success for all children in order to help them see themselves as persons who can enjoy exploring language and learning to read.
7. Plan flexibly in order to accommodate a variety of learning styles and ways of thinking.

8. Respect the language the child brings to school, and use it as a base for language activities.

9. Plan activities that will cause children to become active participants in the learning process rather than passive recipients of knowledge.

10. Provide opportunities for children to experiment with language and to simply have fun with it.

11. Require that pre-service and in-service teachers of young children be prepared in the teaching of reading in a way that emphasizes reading as an integral part of the language arts as well as the total curriculum.

12. Encourage developmentally appropriate language learning opportunities in the home.

✔ Self-Check: Objective 7
From what you have read and from your own experiences, list the advantages and disadvantages of formal reading instruction before first grade.
(See Self-Improvement Opportunity 11.)

Test Yourself

True or False

_____ 1. Reading readiness is an important consideration only at the initial reading instruction stage.

_____ 2. Boys are usually better readers than girls, especially in the lower grades.

_____ 3. Speaking and listening skills are closely related to learning to read.

_____ 4. Children in first grade are too young to understand informational books.

_____ 5. Wordless picture books are useful for building reading readiness skills.

_____ 6. Being ready for an activity requires having an interest in it, and learning to read is no exception.

_____ 7. One way to develop social and emotional readiness is to help children learn how to share and take turns.

_____ 8. Two very important physical factors in reading readiness are visual and auditory acuity.

_____ 9. Following directions is one way for children to develop auditory memory.

_____ 10. Teachers should read aloud to children about once a week.

_____ 11. Picture reading is an example of a *direct* experience through which a child can learn concepts and vocabulary.

_____ 12. Jean Piaget developed a kinesthetic-tactile approach to reading.

_____ 13. Piaget's theory supports formal reading instruction at the pre-school level.

_____ 14. According to Piaget, language comes before thought.

_____ 15. The concrete-operational period of cognitive development generally occurs between the ages of two and seven.

_____ 16. If a child is egocentric, he or she sees things only from a personal point of view.

_____ 17. Most children at the readiness level are able to "conserve."

_____ 18. One reason that some children have trouble with worksheets is that they don't understand the meanings of such words and phrases as _first, draw a circle around,_ and _word._

_____ 19. Beginning readers need to know the letters of the alphabet in order.

_____ 20. Most prereading programs use reading readiness workbooks.

_____ 21. If you are not sure whether a child is ready for formal reading instruction, you should go ahead and start anyway.

_____ 22. Knowledge of letter names is a good predictor of success in beginning reading.

_____ 23. Prereading experiences are more meaningful when incorporated into units of related experiences.

_____ 24. Drawing, painting, rhythmic exercises, and play are related to important reading skills.

_____ 25. Formal instruction in reading is the most important function of the kindergarten.

_____ 26. There is a trend toward pre–first-grade reading instruction.

Vocabulary

auditory discrimination
auditory perception
cognitive development
conservation of substance
creative dramatics
decentration
dramatic play
egocentric
experience chart story
experiential background

kinesthetic-tactile
language facility
motor coordination
preoperational period
reading readiness
reversibility
vicarious experience
visual discrimination
visual perception
wordless picture book

Self-Improvement Opportunities

1. Interview two kindergarten children. Write a report on their readiness for initial reading instruction in terms of the major readiness factors.
2. Start a file of read-aloud books and stories for kindergarten and/or first-grade children.
3. Ask a child to interpret a picture. Report your findings and start your own picture file.

4. Start a collection of rhymes, riddles, and poems that you can use to promote auditory discrimination skills.
5. Use a trade book to help develop the concepts and vocabularies of a small group of children. Report your results.
6. Elicit an individual story from a young child. Write or type it and share it with your peers.
7. Try a conservation activity with a child of five or six. What can you say about the child's level of cognitive development?
8. To focus on names with a group of young children, use an activity like one of those described for recognizing names, words, and letters of the alphabet.
9. Study a set of commercially available reading readiness materials. Discuss their strengths and weaknesses.
10. Prepare mini-lessons for one to three children or peers on such topics as visual discrimination, auditory discrimination, or names of colors or numbers.
11. Visit a preschool. How much direct or indirect reading instruction is part of the program?

Bibliography

Almy, Millie, E. Chittenden, and Paula Miller. *Young Children's Thinking: Studies of Some Aspects of Piaget's Theory.* New York: Teachers College Press, 1966.

Coleman, John S. "The Evaluation of Equality of Educational Opportunity." In *On Equality of Educational Opportunity,* F. Mosteller and D. P. Moynihan, eds. New York: Random House, 1972.

Coody, Betty. *Using Literature with Young Children.* 2nd ed. Dubuque, Iowa: William C. Brown, 1979, pp. 25–37.

Cox, Mary B. "The Effect of Conservation Ability on Reading Competency." *The Reading Teacher* 30 (December 1976): 251–58.

Davis, Hazel Grubbs. "Reading Pressures in the Kindergarten." *Childhood Education* (November/December 1980): 76–79.

Di Lorenzo, L. S., and R. Salter. "An Evaluative Study of Prekindergarten Programs for Educationally Disadvantaged Children: Follow-up and Replication." *Exceptional Children* 35 (October 1968): 111–19.

Downing, John. "Reading Instruction Register." *Language Arts* 53 (October 1976): 762–66.

Evans, Ellis D. *Contemporary Influences in Early Childhood Education.* 2nd ed. New York: Holt, Rinehart and Winston, 1975, p. 245.

Farr, Roger, and Nancy Roser. *Teaching a Child to Read.* New York: Harcourt Brace Jovanovich, 1979, p. 105.

Furth, Hans G. *Piaget for Teachers.* Englewood Cliffs, N.J.: Prentice-Hall, 1970, Letter 13.

Hafner, Lawrence E., and Hayden B. Jolly. *Teaching Reading to Children.* 2nd ed. New York: Macmillan, 1982, p. 26.

Hillerich, Robert L. "An Interpretation of Research in Reading Readiness." *Elementary English* 43 (April 1966): 359–64, 372.

Karnes, M. B., et al. "Evaluation of Two Preschool Programs for Disadvantaged Children: A Traditional and a Highly Structured Experimental Preschool." *Exceptional Children* 34 (May 1968): 667–76.

Kirkland, Eleanor R. "A Piagetian Interpretation of Beginning Reading Instruction." *The Reading Teacher* 31 (February 1978): pp. 497–503.

Knox, Bobbie J., and John A. Glover. "A Note on Preschool Experience Effects on Achievement, Readiness, and Creativity." *The Journal of Genetic Psychology* 132 (March, 1978): 151–52.

Lehr, Fran. "Cultural Influences and Sex Differences in Reading." *The Reading Teacher* 35 (March 1982): 744–46.

Lesiak, Judi. "Reading in Kindergarten: What the Research Doesn't Tell Us." *The Reading Teacher* 32 (November 1978): 135–38.

Loban, Walter D. *Language Development: Kindergarten Through Grade Twelve.* Research Report No. 18. Urbana, Ill.: National Council of Teachers of English, 1976.

McNutt, Gaye, and Nancy Bukofzer. "Teaching Early Reading at McDonald's." *The Reading Teacher* 35 (April 1982): 841–42.

Nevius, John R., Jr. "Teaching for Logical Thinking Is a Prereading Activity." *The Reading Teacher* 30 (March 1977): 641–43.

O'Donnell, Holly. "What Do We Know about Preschool Reading?" *The Reading Teacher* 33 (November 1979): 248–52.

Paradis, Edward, and Joseph Peterson. "Readiness Training Implications from Research." *The Reading Teacher* 30 (February 1975): 445–48.

Rhodes, Lynn K. "I Can Read! Predictable Books as Resources for Reading and Writing Instruction." *The Reading Teacher* 34 (February 1981): 511–18.

Roberts, Leslie. "First Graders' Understanding of Reading and Reading Instructional Terminology." Unpublished doctoral dissertation, University of Tennessee, 1981.

Waller, Gary. *Think First, Read Later! Piagetian Prerequisites for Reading.* Newark, Del.: International Reading Association, 1977.

Wilson, Susan I. *A Content Analysis of Kindergarten Reading Curricula in Thirteen Large American Cities.* New Brunswick, N.J.: Rutgers University, 1976. [ED 128 760]

Aukerman, Robert C., and Louise R. Aukerman. *How Do I Teach Reading?* New York: John Wiley and Sons, 1981, Chapters 2 and 3.

Dallman, Martha, et al. *The Teaching of Reading.* 6th ed. New York: Holt, Rinehart, and Winston, 1982, Chapters 5A and 5B.

Day, Mary Carol, and Ronald K. Parker. *The Preschool in Action.* 2nd ed. Boston: Allyn and Bacon, 1977, Chapters 14 and 15.

Downing, John, et al. "Conceptual and Perceptual Factors in Learning to Read." *Educational Research* 21 (November 1978): 11–17.

Durkin, Dolores. *Teaching Them to Read.* 3rd ed. Boston: Allyn and Bacon, 1978, Chapters 6 and 7.

Forman, George E., and David S. Kuschner. *The Child's Construction of Knowledge: Piaget for Teaching Children.* Monterey, Calif.: Brooks/Cole, 1977.

Hall, MaryAnne, et al. *Reading and the Elementary School Child.* 2nd ed. New York: D. Van Nostrand, 1979, Chapter 4.

Harris, Larry H., and Carl B. Smith. *Reading Instruction Through Diagnostic Teaching.* 3rd ed. New York: Holt, Rinehart, 1980, Chapters 7–9.

Heilman, Arthur W., et al. *Principles and Practices of Teaching Reading.* 5th ed. Columbus, Ohio: Charles E. Merrill, 1981, Chapter 2.

Hillerich, Robert. *Reading Fundamentals for Preschool and Primary Children.* Columbus, Ohio: Charles E. Merrill, 1977.

Hittleman, Daniel R. *Developmental Reading: K–8, Teaching Reading from a Psycholinguistic Perspective.* 2nd ed. Boston: Houghton Mifflin, 1983, Chap. 6.

Kamii, Constance, and Rheta De Vries. *Physical Knowledge in Preschool Education: Implication of Piaget's Theory.* Englewood Cliffs, N.J.: Prentice-Hall, 1978.

Mangrum, Charles T., II, and Harry W. Forgan. *Developing Competencies in Teaching Reading.* Columbus, Ohio: Charles E. Merrill, 1979, Module 3.

Mason, George E. *A Primer on Teaching Reading.* Itasca, Ill.: F. E. Peacock, 1981, Chapter 2.

McCarthy, Melodie A., and John P. Houston. *Fundamentals of Early Childhood Education.* Cambridge, Mass.: Winthrop, 1980, Chapter 4.

Ollilia, Lawrence, ed. *The Kindergarten Child and Reading.* Newark, Del.: International Reading Association, 1977.

Otto, Wayne, et al. *How to Teach Reading.* Reading, Mass.: Addison-Wesley, 1979, Chapter 5.

Pulaski, Mary Ann Spencer. *Understanding Piaget: An Introduction to Children's Cognitive Development.* New York: Harper & Row, 1980.

Quandt, Ivan J. *Teaching Reading: A Human Process.* Chicago: Rand McNally, 1977, Chapter 4.

Raven, Ronald J., and Richard T. Salzer. "Piaget and Reading Instruction." *The Reading Teacher* 24 (April 1971): 630–39.

Read, Donna, and Henrietta M. Smith. "Teaching Visual Literacy

Through Wordless Picture Books." *The Reading Teacher* 35 (May 1982): 928–33.

Robinson, Helen F. *Exploring Teaching in Early Childhood Education.* Boston: Allyn and Bacon, 1977, Chapter 12.

Rubin, Dorothy. *A Practical Approach to Teaching Reading.* New York: Holt, Rinehart, and Winston, 1982, Chapter 4.

Singer, Dorothy G., and Tracey A. Revenson. *A Piaget Primer: How a Child Thinks.* New York: New American Library, 1978.

Smith, Richard J., and Dale D. Johnson. *Teaching Children to Read.* 2nd ed. Reading, Mass.: Addison-Wesley, 1980, Chapter 2.

Spache, George D., and Evelyn B. Spache. *Reading in the Elementary School.* 4th ed. Boston: Allyn and Bacon, 1977, Chapters 6 and 7.

Sund, Robert B. *Piaget for Educators.* Columbus, Ohio: Charles E. Merrill, 1976.

CHAPTER APPENDIX A: ACTIVITIES

I. LANGUAGE ACTIVITIES

A. *Storytelling*

1. Cut out scenes and/or characters from an inexpensive storybook of a familiar tale (*Little Red Riding Hood*). Fasten adhesive to the backs of the cutouts and use them for a flannel-board presentation. You may put the pictures up the first time or two, but then let the children place the pictures as you tell the story.

2. A puppet can help with a story presentation, either by actually telling the story or by being a character who says its part in a different voice.

3. Type the text of a picture storybook on one or two sheets of paper and mark the places where the pages are to be turned. Then tape these papers to the outside cover of the book. Hold the book so that the children can look at the pictures in the book while you read the story which is taped to the outside cover.

4. Before reading the story, tell the children that they will later dramatize it. After the reading, they either pantomime it as you reread or act out parts of the story independently.

5. Record some favorite stories on tapes. Make a sound (a bell or a clicking sound) when the pages are to be turned. Send children to a listening station to hear a tape and appoint one child to hold the book and turn the pages.

6. To enhance the story, use visual aids, such as having a pair of goggles for the children to try on after they listen to Ezra Jack Keats's *Goggles* (New York: Macmillan, 1969).

B. *Story Sequence*

1. Let children dramatize a story that you have read to them. Tell them before you read to listen carefully to what happens first, next, and last.
2. Place felt pictures from a familiar story randomly on a flannel board. Children arrange the pictures in the correct sequence, moving from left to right.
3. Give children a strip of paper about four inches wide and sixteen inches long, which they fold into fourths so that there are four squares. The children draw one picture in each square to retell the story in the proper order.
4. Have one child retell the major events of a story in the correct order. Let other children listen to see if they agree.

C. *Following Directions*

1. Have the children play Simon Says.
2. Give a three-step direction ("Clap your hands twice, stamp your foot, cross your arms") and then call on a child to carry it out. The class judges whether or not the child performs the actions correctly and in sequence. If the child is right, he or she gives the next series of directions and calls on a classmate.
3. Hand each child a piece of paper and give directions for making an airplane, a hat, a snowflake, or something else.
4. To check a child's understanding of directional terms, ask him or her to come to the front of the room and put the eraser *on* the table, hold it *beside* the table, or place it *under* the table. If the child does everything correctly, he or she may select the next child.
5. Have the children form a circle on the playground or in the gym. Give directions, such as "Turn to your right, march like soldiers, hop on your left foot, clap your hands above your head, swing your arms."
6. Explain a new game to the class; the children must follow the directions in order to play.

D. *Other Listening Comprehension Activities*

1. Have the children find the silly word in a sentence that you say. Example: "Bill had a *noffelhumper* for supper" (noffelhumper).
2. Name three or four items that are related and ask the children to name the category. Example: dogs, cats, sheep, cows (animals).
3. Name three things that are related and one that is not. The children must select the one that does not belong. Example: books, paper, ice cream, pencils (ice cream).
4. Make a tape of some familiar sounds and ask the children to identify what they hear. Examples: running water in the sink, splashing water, pouring water, a chiming clock, a barking dog, a ringing telephone.
5. The children close their eyes while you do several things that make noise. When you are finished, the children open their eyes and tell what

happened in sequence. Examples: write on chalkboard, drop chalk, open door, close window, pull out chair.

6. Ask the children to answer riddles. Example: "I am big. I have four wheels. Many people can ride on me. I take children to school. What am I?" (bus)

7. Show a picture to the class. Say several sentences that may or may not refer to the picture. If the sentence is about the picture, the children raise their hands. If the sentence has nothing to do with the picture, the children keep their hands down.

8. Slowly read sentences with selected vocabulary words. Have the children dramatize the meaning of the sentences. Example: "The king *slouched* on his *throne* and *frowned* at his *subjects*."

9. Tell the children that you are going to pretend to be different people; from what you say they must guess who you are. Use statements like the following: "There's Goldilocks and she's sleeping in my bed" (Baby Bear) or "I want to help boys and girls cross the street safely" (safety patrol or police officer).

II. INTEREST ACTIVITIES

A. Poetry

1. Choose poems for choral speaking. Have the class say some poems in unison so that children can imitate good phrasing and intonation. Do other poems "a line a child," with different children saying different lines. An example of this type is "One, two, buckle my shoe."

2. Select some poems for singing, such as "Twinkle, Twinkle, Little Star," "Over in the Meadow," and "London Bridge Is Falling Down." Poetry set to music brings out the phrasing and melodic patterns of language.

3. Read a poem that children can respond to with art. Choose media that are in keeping with the tone of the poem. Crayon resists are good for spooky poems ("Hallowe'en" by Harry Behn); finger painting works well for poems with motion ("The Swing" by Robert Louis Stevenson); and chalk is appropriate for soft, quiet poems ("Pussy Willows" by Aileen Fisher).

4. Choose poems with wonderfully descriptive words. Talk about the sounds of the words and how they make you feel. A good example is "Skins" by Aileen Fisher.

5. Act out nursery rhymes, such as "Jack Be Nimble" and "Little Miss Muffet." This is a good way to check children's understanding of the verses.

6. Have a collection of popular Mother Goose characters for your flannel board. Try using characters from "Jack Spratt Could Eat No Fat," "Mary Had a Little Lamb," "Simple Simon Met a Pie Man," and "The Old Woman Who Lived in a Shoe." Let the children put up the characters and say the corresponding rhymes.

7. Make a bulletin board for poetry. Select a poem that the children enjoy, copy it on a large poster, and let the children make illustrations and put their work on the bulletin board. Change poems as children lose interest.

A. *Visual Perception*
1. Get a set of beginning basal readers that use a lot of repetition. Show the children a word, such as *jump;* then ask them to see how many times that word appears on a certain page.
2. Print each child's name on an envelope. Then print the letters of the child's name on an index card, cut the card apart between the letters, and put these letters in the envelope. Let the child take the letters out and arrange them in the right order. (The same activity may be done with word cards.)
3. Let children supply missing letters. Example: Print the word *play* on each child's paper. Then print portions of the word (pl___y, p___ay, p___a___) on the paper for the child to complete.
4. Arrange straws or toothpicks in a pattern and have the children reproduce the pattern.

B. *Visual Memory*
1. Place several objects on a table and hide them (cover them with a box). Ask the children to name as many objects as they can remember.
2. Show the children a simple pattern or geometric design. Remove it and ask the children to draw from memory what they saw.
3. Three children stand in front of the class while the class notices their clothing. These children leave the room, and one child changes something about his or her appearance before returning. The classmates try to discover what has been changed.
4. Show a card with the word *dog* written on it, but only long enough for the children to study it (about five seconds). Then place it out of sight. From four cards on each child's desk (the *dog* card and cards with the words *man, boy,* and *bus*), ask the children to select the word they were shown.

C. *Visual Discrimination*
1. Point out likenesses and differences in the objects in the classroom. Example: How are desks and chairs alike and different?
2. Print similar letters on the board and help students discover how they are alike and how they are different. Example: *d b, p q, m n.*
3. From a series of pictures, letters, or words, have the children find the one that is different. Begin with pictures, then move to shapes, and end with letters and words. Example: *on on no on.*
4. Let the children fill in the missing letters. Example: *j p q g   j ___ q g   j ___ q ___   j ___ ___ ___   ___ ___ ___ ___*
5. Ask the children to circle the letter that is different in a series of letters. Example: *s s z   m n m   o c o   d b b*

D. *Auditory Perception*
1. Tap on a desk, a glass, a chalkboard, and other objects while the children are looking the other way. Ask them to identify the object you tapped.

2. Ask children to identify noises you make with objects, such as tearing a sheet of paper, closing a book, zipping a zipper, and writing on the chalkboard. They should close their eyes while you are making the sound.
3. Go on a "listening walk." Come back and discuss what the class heard.
4. Say polysyllabic words and have the children clap, tap, or hit a drum for each syllable.
5. Give a letter sound. Then give a word and ask the students if the letter occurs at the beginning, middle, or end of the word. Example: *m, summer, middle.*
6. Tell students a word that begins with a certain sound (*bell*). Then say a sentence that contains the sound several times. Ask the children to raise their hands when they hear the sound. Example: *Betty bounces the ball in the back yard.*

E. *Auditory Memory*
   1. Tap on a table or a desk. Ask the children to repeat the rhythm.
   2. Play a tape of sounds and let the children reproduce them.
   3. Have each child repeat two nonsense words after hearing them once. Example: *soo-sye, bloop-bleep.*
   4. Let the children pretend to be in a cave and echo the sounds or words made by the leader of their "expedition."
   5. Teach children jingles and rhymes such as nursery rhymes, which focus on rhyming sounds. Example: "Jack be nimble, Jack be quick, Jack jump over the candlestick."
   6. Give each child crayons. Name three colors and have the children make dots or lines on their papers in sequence. Example: red dot, blue line, green dot, red line, blue dot, green dot.

F. *Auditory Discrimination (beginning sounds)*
   1. Say a group of words and ask the children to indicate, by raising their hands, which one starts with a different sound. Begin with vastly different sounds and move to similar sounds. Example: *hat, head, mask, home.*
   2. Make a chart featuring a letter sound. Write the name of the letter at the top of the chart in both upper and lower case (*B, b*). Ask the children to find pictures of a ball, baby, book, etc., to glue on the chart.
   3. Play a guessing game. Ask if there is anyone in the room whose name starts with the same sound as the beginning of the word *top.* The child whose name starts with this sound may give the next clue.
   4. Find poems that repeat certain sounds. Examples: "Wee Willie Winkie," "Lucy Locket," "Bye-Baby Bunting," and "Deedle, Deedle Dumpling."

G. *Auditory Discrimination (medial and final sounds, whole word)*
   1. Use pictures and ask questions. Example: "Is this a *pat* or a *pet*?"
   2. Use riddles to relate sounds to words. For example, ask each child to

guess what word, illustrated by the following riddle, begins with the same sound as *pig*.

> I am good to eat.
> I rhyme with teach.
> I am a fruit.
> What am I?

3. Let the children supply the missing rhyming word in a familiar verse.
4. Give an example of rhyming word pairs; then ask the children to tell you which word pairs rhyme. Example: *boy, toy; toy, head.*
5. Ask the children to supply the second line of a rhyming couplet. Example: I saw Sam (eat a ham). I saw Mabel (set the table).

H. *Motor Coordination*
1. Give children activity sheets for connecting dots, first in a straight line and later in various shapes.
2. Provide different types of art media (paints, crayons, chalk, felt-tip pens) for children to use.
3. Make a large letter on a sheet of paper. Tell the children they can make rainbows by tracing over the letter with five or six different colors.
4. Let the children take sticks and make shapes, letters, or numbers in clay or damp sand. Then they can trace the forms with their fingers.
5. Play music for the children to respond to through dancing, skipping, and other rhythmic movements.
6. Give children all kinds of opportunities to work with their hands: cardboard carpentry, sewing, jigsaw puzzles, tracing, cutting out geometric shapes, lacing cards with punched-out shapes, and stringing beads.
7. Let children write on the chalkboard and magic slates (where the letters disappear when you raise the clear acetate cover).
8. Make a display of fastenings for the children to manipulate, including zippers, hooks, buttons, laces, and snaps.

I. *Kinesthetic-Tactile Learning*
1. Mount sandpaper, cardboard, or linoleum letters on a piece of smooth cardboard. Let the children trace the letters and feel their shapes. They may close their eyes and move their fingers lightly over the letters. Then have them reproduce each letter with their pencils.
2. Prepare different kinds of surfaces for writing with the finger in various textures. Use finger paint, shaving cream, or a thin layer of salt or sand on the bottom of a large baking pan.
3. Let children make shapes, numbers, and letters with their bodies, working with partners.
4. Have children walk out letter shapes that you have placed on the floor with tape, chalk, or string.
5. Let the children tear letter and number shapes out of old newspapers.

J. *Directionality*

   1. Stress moving from left to right in reading. Move your arm from left to right along a line of print in an experience story or on an overhead transparency.

   2. Play games that require a knowledge of left and right. Examples: Looby Loo, Hokey Pokey, Simon Says.

   3. Put an arrow pointing to the right across the top of a page or put an *X* at the top left corner of a child's paper to remind him or her where to start.

   4. Have children arrange sequential pictures from left to right.

   5. When children are trying to match word cards, stress the importance of looking at the left letter first and moving on through the word from left to right.

IV. COGNITIVE DEVELOPMENT ACTIVITIES

A. *Concrete Experiences*

   1. Let the children experiment with objects to see what happens. For example, let a child see how tall a tower of blocks he or she can build before it falls over.

   2. Let children guess what objects are in the "feel box." Place items (ruler, apple, sponge) in a box with a hole in the top big enough for a child's arm. Put a sock with the toe cut out over the hole so that the children cannot see inside; then let each child reach through the sock and into the box to identify objects by touch.

   3. Give children opportunities to experiment with placing objects of different sizes and weights on a balance scale.

   4. Ask children to move objects by blowing on them, pushing them, rolling them, throwing them, and swinging them. For example, let children blow feathers, push a desk, roll a ball down a slanted board, throw a bean bag, and swing an object on a rope suspended from the ceiling.

   5. Let children cut up pictures into three or four puzzle pieces and then reassemble them.

   6. Encourage children to create original designs by arranging pegs, parquetry blocks, and other materials.

B. *Classification*

   1. Let children group objects together by form, color, size, and function. For example, have children shelve blocks together according to size and shape, string a necklace of blue beads, and group together pictures that belong in the same category (vehicles, food, people).

   2. Have children match objects that belong together, such as shoe and sock or knife and fork.

   3. Ask the children to separate objects that are alike from those that are different. For example, let them put all the green crayons from the coloring box in one pile.

   4. Provide coins for the children to classify according to type: pennies, nickels, and dimes.

5. Ask each child to pick out the one item that doesn't belong from a group of items. For example, a child should remove the pencil from a collection of dollhouse furniture.
6. Give children small objects to sort, such as rice, dried beans, pebbles, macaroni, and popcorn.
7. Ask children to bring in leaves and sort them according to kind.

C. *Conservation*
1. Conservation of number: Place two identical rows of pennies in front of the child. Spread one row of pennies out and ask if each row now has the same number of pennies.
2. Conservation of volume: Put equal amounts of water in two tall, thin glasses. Pour the water from one glass into a short, wide glass. Ask if the two glasses contain the same amount of water.
3. Conservation of length: Lay two strings of the same length side by side on a table. Then shape one string into a curve and leave the other one straight. Ask if the strings are now the same length.

V. BEGINNING READING ACTIVITIES

A. *Letter Recognition*
1. Let children match cards that are coded on the back by color. For instance, when children find *r* to go with *R,* they can turn the cards over to see if they have a match.
2. Teach alphabet songs to the class. You may want to point to the letters on a chart as you sing them.
3. Show alphabet picture books and talk about the letters.
4. Provide movable cardboard or wooden letters for children to manipulate. Also let children place felt letters on a flannel board and magnetic letters on a metal surface. Encourage them to name the letters and copy words.
5. Play bingo with the children by saying letter names and having the children cover the corresponding letters on their cards. Beginning players should cover all of the letters in order to win. Later, when children understand the concepts for vertical, diagonal, and horizontal rows, they may win by completing one of these patterns.

k	s	r
b	o	t
a	l	p

6. Let children form letters by bending pipe cleaners, writing a letter with glue and covering it with glitter, or shaping it from clay or dough.

B. *Sight Word Recognition*
1. Tape children's names to their desks so that they may see them and copy them frequently.
2. Label objects in the room with oak-tag strips. Use words or short sentences. For example, one label might read *chalkboard,* and another might say *This is our piano.*
3. Put on the board daily schedules of things that you plan to do, and read them with the class.

CHAPTER APPENDIX B: RESOURCES

For Teachers

Adamson, Pamela. *The First Book of Number Rhymes.* New York: Franklin Watts, 1970.

Arbuthnot, May Hill, and Shelton L. Root, Jr., eds. *Time for Poetry.* 3rd ed. Glenview, Ill.: Scott, Foresman, 1968.

Association for Childhood Education, Literature Committee. *Sung Under the Silver Umbrella.* New York: Macmillan, 1962.

Brewton, Sara, and John Brewton. *Birthday Candles Burning Bright: A Treasury of Birthday Poetry.* New York: Macmillan, 1960.

Briggs, Nancy E., and Joseph A. Wagner. *Children's Literature Through Storytelling and Drama.* 2nd ed. Dubuque, Iowa: William C. Brown, 1979.

Coody, Betty. *Using Literature with Young Children.* 2nd ed. Dubuque, Iowa: William C. Brown, 1979.

De Forest, Charlotte B. *The Prancing Pony: Nursery Rhymes from Japan.* New York: Walker, 1968.

Hopkins, Lee Bennett. *I Think I Saw a Snail: Young Poems for City Seasons.* New York: Crown, 1969.

Hopkins, Lee Bennett. *Pass the Poetry, Please!* New York: Citation Press, 1972.

Huck, Charlotte S. *Children's Literature.* 3rd ed. updated. New York: Holt, Rinehart, and Winston, 1979.

Larrick, Nancy. *Green Is Like a Meadow of Grass.* Champaign, Ill.: Garrard, 1968.

Livingston, Myra Cohn, ed. *Listen, Children, Listen.* New York: Atheneum, 1972.

Matterson, Elizabeth. *Games for the Very Young.* New York: American Heritage, 1971.

Sechrist, Elizabeth. *One Thousand Poems for Children.* Philadelphia: Macrae, 1946.

Sutherland, Zena, et al. *Children & Books*. 6th ed. Glenview, Ill.: Scott, Foresman, 1981.

Wallace, Daisy, ed. *Fairy Poems*. New York: Holiday, 1980.

Children's Books

Alphabet Picture Books

Anno, Mitsumasa. *Anno's Alphabet: An Adventure in Imagination*. New York: Thomas Crowell, 1975.

Brown, Marcia. *All Butterflies: An ABC*. New York: Scribner's, 1974.

Burningham, John. *John Burningham's ABC*. Indianapolis: Bobbs-Merrill, 1967.

Eichenberg, Fritz. *Ape in a Cape*. New York: Harcourt, Brace, 1952.

Feelings, Muriel. *Jambo Means Hello: Swahili Alphabet Book*. New York: Dial, 1974.

Musgrove, Margaret. *Ashanti to Zulu*. New York: Dial, 1976.

Wildsmith, Brian. *Brian Wildsmith's ABC*. New York: Watts, 1963.

Informational/Concept/Vocabulary Books

Borten, Helen. *Do You Go Where I Go?* New York: Abelard-Schuman, 1972.

Brown, Marcia. *Walk With Your Eyes*. New York: Franklin Watts, 1979.

Cole, Joanna. *A Chick Hatches*. New York: William Morrow, 1976.

Hoban, Tana. *Push-Pull, Empty-Full*. New York: Macmillan, 1972.

Hoban, Tana. *Over, Under and Through*. New York: Macmillan, 1973.

Ruben, Patricia. *What Is New? What Is Missing? What Is Different?* New York: J.B. Lippincott, 1978.

Spier, Peter. *Gobble, Growl, Grunt*. New York: Doubleday, 1971.

Tresselt, Alvin. *It's Time Now!* New York: Lothrop, 1969.

Udry, Janice May. *A Tree Is Nice*. New York: Harper & Row, 1966.

White, Paul. *Janet at School*. New York: Thomas Crowell, 1979.

Predictable/Repetitive Books

Adams, Pam. *This Old Man*. New York: Grosset and Dunlap, 1974.

Aliki. *Go Tell Aunt Rhody*. New York: Macmillan, 1974.

Bonne, Rose, and Alan Mills. *I Know an Old Lady*. New York: Rand McNally, 1961.

Carle, Eric. *The Very Hungry Caterpillar*. Cleveland: Collins World, 1969.

Langstaff, John. *Oh, A-Hunting We Will Go*. New York: Atheneum, 1974.

Martin, Bill. *Brown Bear, Brown Bear*. New York: Holt, Rinehart and Winston, 1970.

Martin, Bill. *Fire! Fire! Said Mrs. McGuire*. New York: Holt, Rinehart and Winston, 1970.

Peppe, Rodney. *The House That Jack Built*. New York: Delacorte, 1970.

Shaw, Charles B. *It Looked Like Spilt Milk*. New York: Harper & Row, 1947.

Tolstoy, Alexei. *The Great Big Enormous Turnip*. New York: Franklin Watts, 1968.

Wager, Justin (illustrator). *The Bus Ride*. New York: Scott, Foresman, 1971.

Wordless Picture Books

Briggs, Raymond. *The Snowman*. New York: Random House, 1978.

De Paola, Tomie. *Pancakes for Breakfast*. New York: Harcourt Brace, 1978.

Goodall, John S. *The Ballooning Adventures of Paddy Park*. New York: Harcourt Brace, 1969.

Goodall, John S. *Creepy Castle*. New York: Atheneum, 1975.

Hoban, Tana. *Is It Red? Is It Yellow? Is It Blue?* New York: Greenwillow, 1978.

Hutchins, Pat. *Changes, Changes*. New York: Macmillan, 1971.

Krahn, Fernando. *Catch That Cat!* New York: Dutton, 1978.

Mari, Iela, and Enzo Mari. *The Apple and the Moth*. New York: Pantheon, 1970.

Mayer, Mercer. *Frog, Where Are You?* New York: Dial, 1969.

Mayer, Mercer. *Frog Goes to Dinner*. New York: Dial, 1974.

Turkle, Brinton. *Deep in the Forest*. New York: Dutton, 1976.

Films, Filmstrips, and Recordings

Caedmon Records, 1995 Broadway, New York, NY 10023.

CMS Records, Inc., 14 Warren Street, New York, NY 10007.

Connecticut Films, Inc., 6 Cobble Hill Road, Westport, CT 06880.

Encyclopedia Britannica Educational Corp., 425 N. Michigan Avenue, Chicago, IL 60611.

McGraw-Hill Films, 110 15 Street, Del Mar, CA 92014.

Miller-Brody Productions, 201 E. 50th Street, New York, NY 10022.

Pathways of Sound, Inc., 102 Mount Auburn Street; Cambridge, MA 02138.

Pyramid Films, Box 1048, Santa Monica, CA 90406.

Society for Visual Education, Inc., 1345 Diversey Parkway, Chicago, IL 60614.

Texture Films, Inc., 1600 Broadway, New York, NY 10019.

The Viking Press, 625 Madison Avenue, New York, NY 10022.

Weston Woods Studios, Inc., Weston, CT 06883.

CHAPTER 3

Word Recognition

Good readers differ from poor readers both in size of sight vocabularies and in the ability to decode words. Good readers tend to have larger sight vocabularies than poor readers, resulting in a decreased need to stop and analyze words. However, when they do have to analyze words, they often have a more flexible approach than do poor readers, since they generally have been taught several strategies and have been encouraged to try a new one if one fails (Jenkins, 1980). Poor readers frequently know only a single strategy for decoding words, and there is not one strategy that is appropriate for all words. Thus these children are at a disadvantage when they encounter words for which their strategy is not useful. Even if they have been taught several strategies, poor readers may not have learned a procedure to follow that will allow them to decode unfamiliar words as efficiently as possible.

This chapter presents a variety of methods of word recognition and stresses a flexible approach to unfamiliar words, encouraging application of those word recognition skills that are most helpful at the moment. It also explains how to use a number of word recognition skills in conjunction to help in decoding a word.

Setting Objectives

When you finish reading this chapter, you should be able to

1. Describe some ways to help a child develop a sight vocabulary.
2. Describe some activities for teaching use of context clues.
3. Discuss the place of phonics in the reading program.
4. Define each of the following terms: *consonant blend, consonant digraph, vowel digraph, diphthong.*
5. Describe how to teach a child to associate a particular sound with a particular letter or group of letters.
6. Discuss ways of teaching the various facets of structural analysis.
7. Name the skills that children need in order to use a dictionary as an aid in word recognition.

WORD RECOGNITION SKILLS

Word recognition skills help a reader recognize words while reading. They include developing a store of words that can be recognized immediately on sight and being able to use context clues, phonics, structural analysis, and dictionaries for word identification. The last four skills are sometimes referred to as word attack skills.

Children need to be able to perform all of the different word recognition skills, since some will be more useful in certain situations than others.

Teaching a single approach to word identification is not wise, because a child may be left without the proper tools for specific situations. Additionally, some word recognition skills are easier to learn than others, depending on the student's abilities. For example, a child who has a hearing loss may not become very skillful at using phonics but may learn sight words easily and profit greatly from the use of context clues.

Sight Words

Developing a store of sight words, or words that are recognized immediately without having to resort to analysis, is important to a young reader. The larger the store of sight words a person has, the more rapidly and fluently he or she can read a selection. Comprehension of a passage and reading speed suffer if a person has to pause too often to analyze unfamiliar words. The more mature and experienced a reader becomes, the larger his or her store of sight words becomes. For instance, most, if not all, of the words used in this textbook are a part of the sight vocabularies of college students. One goal of reading instruction is to turn all of the words that students continuously need to recognize in print into sight words.

A sight word approach (also referred to as a look-and-say or whole word approach) to teaching beginning reading makes sense for several reasons.

1. The English language contains a multitude of irregularly spelled words, that is, words that are not spelled the way they sound. Many of these are among the most frequently used words in our language. The spellings of the following common words are highly irregular as far as sound-symbol associations are concerned: *of, through, two, know, give, come,* and *once.* Rather than trying in vain to sound out these words, children need to learn to recognize them on sight as whole configurations.
2. Learning several sight words at the very beginning of reading instruction gives the child a chance to engage in a successful reading experience very early and consequently promotes a positive attitude toward reading.
3. Words have meaning for youngsters by the time they arrive at school, but single letters have no meaning for them. So presenting chldren with whole words at the beginning allows them to associate reading with meaning rather than with meaningless memorization.
4. After children have built up a small store of sight words, the teacher can begin phonics instruction with an analytic approach. More about this approach can be found later in this chapter.

A teacher must carefully choose which words to teach as sight words. Extremely common irregularly spelled words *(the, of, to, two)* and frequently used regularly spelled words *(at, it, and, am, go)* should be taught as sight words so children can read connected sentences early in the program. The first sight words should be useful and meaningful; a child's name should be one of them. Days of the week, months of year, and names of school subjects are other prime candidates. Words that stand for concepts that are unfamiliar to youngsters are poor choices. Before children learn *democracy* as a sight word, they need to have an understanding of what a democracy is. Therefore, this word is not a good one to teach in the primary grades.

Teaching some words with regular spelling patterns as sight words is consistent with the beliefs of linguists who have become involved with development of reading materials (see Chapter 5 for further details). Words with regular spelling patterns are also a good base for teaching "word families" in phonics—for example, the *an* family consists of *ban, can, Dan, fan, man, Nan, pan, ran, tan,* and *van*.

Sight Word Lists

Lists of basic sight words may give teachers an indication of what words are used most frequently in reading materials and therefore needed most frequently by students. Some of these lists are included or discussed in the following publications:

Dolch, Edward W. *A Manual for Remedial Reading.* 2nd ed. (Champaign, Ill.: Garrard, 1945).

Durr, William. "Computer Study of High Frequency Words in Popular Trade Juveniles." *The Reading Teacher* 27 (October 1973): 37–42.

Ekwall, Eldon E. *Diagnosis and Remediation of the Disabled Reader.* (Boston: Allyn and Bacon, 1976), p. 70.

Fry, Edward. *Elementary Reading Instruction.* (New York: McGraw-Hill, 1977), p. 73.

Harris, Albert J., and Milton Jacobson. *Basic Elementary Reading Vocabularies.* (New York: Macmillan, 1976).

Hillerich, Robert L. "Word Lists—Getting It All Together," *The Reading Teacher* 27 (January 1974): 353–60.

Mangieri, John N., and Michael S. Kahn. "Is the Dolch List of 220 Basic Sight Words Irrelevant?" *The Reading Teacher* 30 (March 1977): 649–51.

Moe, A. J. "Word Lists for Beginning Readers." *Reading Improvement* 10 (Fall 1973): 11–15.

Otto, Wayne, and R. Chester. "Sight Words for Beginning Readers." *Journal of Educational Research* 65 (July 1972): 435–43.

Walker, Charles Monroe. "High Frequency Word List for Grades 3 Through 9." *The Reading Teacher* 32 (April 1979): 803–12.

Garrard Press (Champaign, Illinois) publishes basic vocabulary flash cards, including the words on the Dolch list of 220 most common words found in reading materials (excluding nouns). Garrard also publishes picture word cards, which have ninety-five common nouns printed on the front and the identifying pictures printed on the back. Games for learning these basic sight words are also available through this publisher.

Another well-known list of basic sight words is Fry's list of "Instant Words" shown in Table 3.1. This list presents the words most frequently used in reading materials.

Richard Culyer (1982) recommends developing a locally relevant basic sight word list by charting the levels at which words are introduced in the basal series a school system uses. In other words, the words found in the different series used in a school system are combined into a single list, based on the point of introduction of each word in the pertinent series. Teachers can then use words of concern to the children in their area, rather than words determined on a nationwide basis, in their sight word instruction.

Teaching Sight Words

Before children begin to learn sight words, they must have developed visual discrimination skills. That is, they must be able to see likenesses and differences among printed words. It is also helpful, although not essential, for them to know the names of the letters of the alphabet, because discussion of likenesses and differences in words is easier. For example, a teacher could point out that whereas *take* has a *k* before the *e, tale* has an *l* in the same position.

A potential sight word must initially be identified for the learners. A teacher should show the children the printed word as he or she pronounces it, or pair the word with an identifying picture. Regardless of the method of presentation, one factor is of paramount importance: the children must *look* at the printed word when it is identified in order to associate the letter configuration with the spoken word or picture. If children fail to look at the word when it is pronounced, they have no chance of remembering it when they next encounter it.

Teachers should also encourage children to pay attention to the details of the word by asking them to notice ascending letters (such as *b, d, h*), descending letters (such as *p, g, q*), word length, and particular letter combinations (such as double letters). Careful scrutiny of words can greatly aid retention.

Children learn early to recognize some sight words by visual configurations, or shapes. This technique is not one teachers should stress too much, since many words have similar shapes. But since many children seem to use the technique in the early stages of reading, regardless of the teacher's methods, a teacher can use configuration judiciously to develop early sight words. One way to do this is to call attention to shape by having the children frame the words to be learned.

money   trip   make

That configuration soon loses its usefulness is demonstrated by the following words:

saw   car   was   see   ran

Teachers can call attention to word makeup through comparison and contrast, comparing a new word to a similar known word: *fan* may be compared to *can* if the children already have *can* in their sight vocabularies. The teacher can point out the fact that the initial letters of the words are different and the other letters are the same, or the students can discover this on their own. The latter method is preferable because the students are likely to remember their own discoveries longer than they will remember something they have been told by the teacher.

Few words will be learned by the students after a single presentation, although Sylvia Ashton-Warner (1963) claims that children will instantly learn words that are extremely important to them. Generally, a number of repetitions will be necessary before a word actually becomes a sight word.

The teacher should carefully plan practice with potential sight words. It should be varied and interesting, because children will more readily learn those things in which they have an interest. Games are useful if they emphasize the words being learned rather than the rules of the game.

Practice with potential sight words should involve using the words in context. Out of context, children cannot pronounce many words with certainty, for example, *read, desert,* and *record.* The following sentences indicate the importance of context.

I *read* that book yesterday.   I can't *read* without glasses.
We drove for miles through the   How can you *desert* him when he
desert.   needs you most?
Will you *record* these figures for   I bought a new *record* today.
me?

Another reason for using context when presenting sight words is that many commonly used words have little meaning when they stand alone. Prime examples are *the, a,* and *an.* Context for words may be a sentence (*The* girl ate *a* pear and *an* apple) or short phrases (*the* girl, *a* pear, *an* apple). Context is also useful in a situation where pronunciation is not as clear as it should be. A teacher may say *thing* and have it confused with *think* unless he or she has presented context for the word: "I haven't done a useful thing all day."

Joyce Hood (1972) suggests using phrase cards or, even better, story context for sight word practice. She correctly asserts that if readers can be

TABLE 3.1 Fry's List of "Instant Words"

First Hundred Words (approximately first grade)				Second Hundred Words (approximately second grade)				Third Hundred Words (approximately third grade)			
Group 1a	Group 1b	Group 1c	Group 1d	Group 2a	Group 2b	Group 2c	Group 2d	Group 3a	Group 3b	Group 3c	Group 3d
the	he	go	who	saw	big	may	fan	ask	hat	off	fire
a	I	see	an	home	where	let	five	small	car	sister	ten
is	they	then	their	soon	am	use	read	yellow	write	happy	order
you	one	us	she	stand	ball	these	over	show	try	once	part
to	good	no	new	box	morning	right	such	goes	myself	didn't	early
and	me	him	said	upon	live	present	way	clean	longer	set	fat
we	about	by	did	first	four	tell	too	buy	those	round	third
that	had	was	boy	came	last	next	shall	thank	hold	dress	same
in	if	come	three	girl	color	please	own	sleep	full	tell	love
not	some	get	down	house	away	leave	most	letter	carry	wash	hear
for	up	or	work	find	red	hand	sure	jump	eight	start	yesterday
at	her	two	put	because	friend	more	thing	help	sing	always	eyes
with	do	man	were	made	pretty	why	only	fly	warm	anything	door
it	when	little	before	could	eat	better	near	don't	sit	around	clothes
on	so	has	just	book	want	under	than	fast	dog	close	through
can	my	them	long	look	year	while	open	cold	ride	walk	o'clock
will	very	how	here	mother	white	should	kind	today	hot	money	second
are	all	like	other	run	got	never	must	does	grow	turn	water
of	would	our	old	school	play	each	high	face	cut	might	town
this	any	what	take	people	found	best	far	green	seven	hard	took
your	been	know	cat	night	left	another	both	every	woman	along	pair
as	out	make	again	into	men	seem	end	brown	funny	bed	now
but	there	which	give	say	bring	tree	also	coat	yes	fine	keep
be	from	much	after	think	wish	name	until	six	ate	sat	head
have	day	his	many	back	black	dear	call	gave	stop	hope	food

The Second 300 Words
(approximately fourth grade)

Group 4a	Group 4b	Group 4c	Group 4d	Group 4e	Group 4f	Group 4g	Group 4h	Group 4i	Group 4j	Group 4k	Group 4l
told	time	word	wear	hour	grade	egg	spell	become	herself	demand	aunt
Miss	yet	almost	Mr.	glad	brother	ground	beautiful	body	idea	however	system
father	true	thought	side	follow	remain	afternoon	sick	chance	drop	figure	line
children	above	send	poor	company	milk	feed	became	act	river	case	cause
land	still	receive	lost	believe	several	boat	cry	die	smile	increase	marry
interest	meet	pay	outside	begin	war	plan	finish	real	son	enjoy	possible
government	since	nothing	wind	mind	able	question	catch	speak	bat	rather	supply
feet	number	need	Mrs.	pass	charge	fish	floor	already	fact	sound	thousand
garden	state	mean	learn	reach	either	return	stick	doctor	sort	eleven	pen
done	matter	late	held	month	less	sir	great	step	king	music	condition
country	line	half	front	point	train	fell	guess	itself	dark	human	perhaps
different	remem-ber	fight	built	rest	cost	hill	bridge	nine	them-selves	court	produce
bad	large	enough	family	sent	evening	wood	church	baby	whose	force	twelve
across	few	feet	began	talk	note	add	lady	minute	study	plant	rode
yard	hit	during	air	went	past	ice	tomor-row	ring	fear	suppose	uncle
winter	cover	gone	young	bank	room	chair	snow	wrote	move	law	labor
table	window	hundred	ago	ship	flew	watch	whom	happen	stood	husband	public
story	even	week	world	business	office	alone	women	appear	himself	moment	consider
sometimes	city	between	airplane	whole	cow	low	among	heart	strong	person	thus
I'm	together	change	without	short	visit	arm	road	swim	knew	result	least
tried	sun	being	kill	certain	wait	dinner	farm	felt	often	continue	power
horse	life	care	ready	fair	teacher	hair	cousin	fourth	toward	price	mark
something	street	answer	stay	reason	spring	service	bread	I'll	wonder	serve	president
brought	party	course	won't	summer	picture	class	wrong	kept	twenty	national	voice
shoes	suit	against	paper	fill	bird	quite	age	well	impor-tant	wife	whether

Source: From *Elementary Reading Instruction* (p. 73) by Edward Fry. Copyright © 1977. Used with permission of McGraw-Hill Book Company.

Practice with potential sight words—such as these five common prepositions—should involve using the words in context.   (© Michael Goss)

encouraged to pay attention to context, they can learn to correct their own errors. She and her associates reward children verbally or with special privileges for paying attention to context and correcting their own mistakes.

The language experience approach, in which students' own language is written down and used as the basis for their reading material, is good for developing sight vocabulary. This approach (described in detail in Chapter 5) provides meaningful context for learning sight words, and it can be used productively with individuals or groups. The word-bank activities associated with it are particularly helpful.

Another context for presenting a word is a picture. Teachers may also present words in conjunction with the actual objects they name, such as chairs and tables, calling attention to the fact that the labels name the items. These names can be written on the board, so that youngsters can try to locate the items in the room by finding the matching labels.

Constructing picture dictionaries, in which children illustrate words and file the labeled pictures alphabetically in a notebook, is a good activity for helping younger children develop sight vocabulary. This procedure has been effective in helping children whose primary language is not English learn to read and understand English words.

Children can also learn to recognize their own names and the names of some of their classmates through a labeling process. On the first day of school, give each child a name tag and label each child's desk with her or his name. The area where the child is supposed to hang a coat or store supplies may also be labeled. Explain to each child that the letters written on the name tag, desk, and storage area spell her or his own name. Nobody else is supposed to use these areas. Encourage the child to look at the name carefully so she or he will remember it when locating belongings. At first, the child may use the name tag to match the labels on the desk and storage area, but by the time the name tag has been worn out or lost the child should be able to identify her or his own printed name.

The teacher can generally accelerate this process by teaching children how to write their names. Encourage children to trace the name label on desks with fingers and then to try to copy the label on a sheet of paper, using a primary-sized pencil or crayon. At first you should label all students' work and drawings with the students' names, but as soon as they are capable of writing their names they should label their own papers. From the very beginning, the children's names should be written in a mixture of capital and lower-case letters rather than all capitals, as this is the way a name most commonly appears in print.

To encourage learning the days of the week as sight words, write "Today is" on the chalkboard and fill in the name of the appropriate day each morning. At first you may read the sentence to the children at the beginning of each day, but soon you will be able to ask for volunteers to read the sentence and be assured of successful responses.

Function words—words that have only syntactic meaning rather than concrete content—are often particularly difficult for children to learn, because of their lack of concrete meaning and because many of them are similar in physical features. Hayden Jolly (1981) suggests the following ideas for teaching these troublesome words:

1. Teach only one word at a time of a pair that is likely to be confused (for example, *was* and *saw*).
2. First teach words that have large differences in features, then those that have finer differences. For example, teach *that* with words like *for* and *is* before presenting it with *this* and *the*.
3. Teach three or four dissimilar words in each session in a small group setting. Present them on individual cards to each student, in isolation and in context. The teacher identifies them and the students analyze them, learning to spell each word. They read the words in context orally after the teacher reads the phrases to them; then they are given some simple sentences in which they have multiple choices for target words and are asked to underline the correct word. Finally the students have a flash card drill.
4. Give parents suggestions for helping children practice these words in a game.
5. Use the cloze procedure (deleting target words and leaving blanks for the children to fill in) for a review method.

100

Teaching
Reading in
Today's
Elementary
Schools

Much teaching of sight word recognition takes place as a part of basal reader lessons. The teacher frequently introduces the new words, possibly in one of the ways discussed above, before reading, discussing meanings at the same time. Then students have a guided silent reading period during which they silently read material containing the new words in order to answer questions asked by the teacher. Purposeful oral rereading activities offer another chance to use the new words. Afterwards, teachers generally provide practice in workbooks or on the worksheets suggested in the teacher's manual of the basal reading series. Other follow-up activities include games, manipulative devices, and special audiovisual materials.

Writing new words is helpful to some learners, especially to kinesthetic learners, who learn through muscle movement. Recent basal readers have made use of writing by providing incomplete sentences with choices of words that the children can use to complete the sentences. The children choose the words that fit the sentences and write each word in the blank provided. Example:

Janet forgot _____ she put the doll.
                    (where, which)

This approach forces the children to pay attention to small details in the words presented as choices and is likely to increase their word retention because the writing activity reinforces the letter sequence.

Games such as word bingo are useful for practice with sight words. The teacher or a leader calls out a word, and the children who recognize that word on their cards cover it. (Cards may look something like the ones shown.) When a child covers an entire card, he or she says "cover," and the teacher or leader checks the card to see if all the covered words were actually called.

saw	can	on
have	FREE	again
never	said	will

have	was	no
want	FREE	many
even	so	here

can	want	on
was	FREE	see
to	will	many

Card games in which children accumulate "books" of matching cards can be developed into word recognition games. Use a commercial pack of Old Maid cards with sight words carefully lettered on them, or form an original deck. Use the regular rules of the game, except to claim a book a child must name the word on the matching cards.

Another technique is to list sight words on a circular piece of cardboard and to have children paper-clip pictures to appropriate words. The teacher can make this activity self-scoring by printing the matching words on the back of the pictures as shown below.

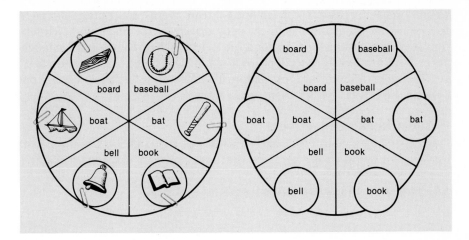

Some teachers use tachistoscopes to expose words rapidly for sight-word recognition practice. The advantage of this technique is that children become accustomed to the idea of recognizing the word immediately, not sounding it out. However, special equipment is not necessary; the teacher can slide a file card with a slot cut out of it down a list of words, exposing each word for a brief period of time and thereby controlling the presentation.

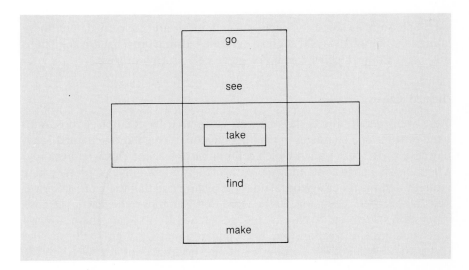

Maria Ceprano (1981) reviewed research on methods of teaching sight words and found that no one method alone was best for every student. She found evidence that teaching the distinctive features of words helped children

102

Teaching
Reading in
Today's
Elementary
Schools

learn. She also found evidence that use of picture clues along with specific instruction to focus attention on the words facilitated learning. However, she reported that some research indicates that teaching words in isolation or with pictures does not assure the ability to read words in context. In fact, indications are "that most learners need directed experience with written context while learning words in order to perceive that reading is a language process and a meaning-getting process" (p. 321). Therefore, when teachers are working with sight word instruction, it seems wise to include presentation of words in context rather than in isolation.

✔ Self-Check: Objective 1

Should sight words be presented alone or in context? Justify your answer. Describe two activities that can be used for teaching sight words.
(See Self-Improvement Opportunities 1 and 2.)

Context Clues

Context clues—the words, phrases, and sentences surrounding the words to be decoded—help readers determine what the unfamiliar words are. Here we will focus on the function of context clues as *word recognition* aids; Chapter 4 offers a consideration of the function of context clues as *comprehension* aids.

Since research has found that readers' identification of a word is influenced by syntactic and semantic context, it is important that word recognition skills be introduced and practiced in context (Jones, 1982). Much of the written material that primary-level readers are introduced to is well within their comprehension as far as vocabulary and ideas are concerned, but these youngsters cannot always recognize in printed form words that are familiar in oral form. Context clues can be of great help in this process.

Picture Clues

These are generally the earliest context clues used by children. Exposure to many pictures of a character in readiness materials, such as one named Sally, may develop the situation in which children recognize the character instantly. When shown a page containing a picture of Sally and a single word, they may naturally assume that the word names the picture and that the word is *Sally*. If they do not relate the picture to the word in this manner, the teacher can ask a question, such as "Who is in the picture?" to lead them toward understanding the relationship. If a child responds, "A girl," the teacher might ask, "What kind of letter is at the beginning of the word?" The response "A capital letter" would prompt the question, "What kinds of words have we talked about that begin with capital letters?" After eliciting the answer "Names," the teacher can then ask, "What is the name of the girl in the picture?" This question should produce the response "Sally." Finally, the teacher asks, "Now what do you think the word is?" At this point a correct response is extremely likely. The teacher should use a procedure that encourages the use of picture clues *along with,* rather than apart from, the clues available in the printed word.

Teachers should not overly emphasize picture clues. They may be useful in the initial stages of instruction, but they become less useful as the child advances to more difficult material, which has a decreasing number of pictures and an increasing proportion of print. Encouraging too much reliance on pictures may result in too little time spent on developing word analysis skills.

Semantic and Syntactic Clues

As soon as possible, teachers should encourage first-grade children to use written context as a clue to unknown words. The idea of using context clues can be introduced by oral activities like this one.

● *MODEL ACTIVITY: Use of Oral Context*

Read sentences such as the ones below to the children, leaving out words as indicated by the blanks. After reading each sentence, ask the children what word they could use to finish the sentence in a way that would make sense. The children will find that the sentences that have missing words at the end are easier. In some cases, the children may suggest several possibilities, all of which are appropriate. Accept all of these contributions.

Sample sentences:
1. Jane went out to walk her _____.
2. John was at home reading a _____.
3. They were fighting like cats and _____.
4. I want ham and _____ for breakfast.
5. Will you _____ football with me? ●

In the sample sentences above, children could use both semantic (meaning) and syntactic (grammar) clues in choosing words to fill in the blanks. Youngsters generally utilize these two types of clues in combination, but for the purpose of clarifying their differences, we will first consider them separately.

Semantic clues are clues derived from the meanings of the words, phrases, and sentences surrounding the unknown word. In the example just given, children can ask themselves the following questions to decide what words would make sense:

Sentence 1—What are things that can be walked?
Sentence 2—What are things that can be read?

104

Teaching
Reading in
Today's
Elementary
Schools

Sentence 3—What expression do I know about fighting that has "like cats and" in it?

Sentence 4—What food might be eaten with ham for breakfast?

Sentence 5—What things can you do with a football?

There are various kinds of semantic clues, including the following:

1. Definition clues. A word may be directly defined in the context. If the child knows the word in oral form, he or she can recognize it in print through the definition.

   > The *register* is the book in which the names of the people who come to the wedding are kept.
   >
   > The *dictionary* is a book in which the meanings of words can be found.

2. Appositive clues. An appositive may offer a synonym or description of the word, which will cue its recognition. Children need to be taught that an appositive is a word or phrase that restates or identifies the word or expression it follows, and that it is usually set off by commas, dashes, or parentheses.

   > They are going to *harvest,* or gather in, the season's crops.
   >
   > That model is *obsolete* (outdated).
   >
   > The *rodents*—rats and mice—in the experiment learned to run a maze.

3. Comparison clues. A comparison of the unfamiliar word with one the child knows may offer a clue. In the examples the familiar words *sleepy* and *clothes* provide the clues for *drowsy* and *habit.*

   > Like her sleepy brother, Mary felt *drowsy.*
   >
   > Like all of the clothes she wore, her riding *habit* was very fashionable.

4. Contrast clues. A contrast of the unknown word to a familiar one may offer a clue. In the examples the unfamiliar word *temporary* is contrasted with the familiar word *forever,* and the unfamiliar word *occasionally* is contrasted with the familiar word *regularly.*

   > It will not last forever; it is only *temporary.*
   >
   > She doesn't visit regularly; she just comes by *occasionally.*

5. Common-expression clues. Familiarity with the word order in many commonly heard expressions, particularly figurative expressions, can lead children to the identity of an unknown word. In the context activity discussed earlier, children needed to know the expression "fighting like

cats and dogs'' to complete the sentence. Children with varied language backgrounds are more likely to be able to use figurative expressions to aid word recognition than are children with less developed backgrounds.

> He was as quiet as a *mouse*.
>
> Daryl charged around like a bull in a *china* shop.

6. Example clues. Sometimes examples are given for words that may be unfamiliar in print, and these examples can provide the needed clues for identification.

> Mark was going to talk about *reptiles*, for example, snakes and lizards.
>
> Andrea wants to play a *percussion* instrument, such as the snare drum or the bells.

Syntactic clues are contained in the grammar or syntax of our language. Certain types of words appear in certain positions in spoken English sentences. Thus, word order can give readers clues to the identity of an unfamiliar word. Because most children in schools in the United States have been speaking English since they were preschoolers, they have a feeling for the grammar or syntax of the language. Syntactic clues help them discover that the missing words in sentences 1 through 4 in the oral-context activity on page 103 are nouns, or naming words, and that the missing word in sentence 5 is a verb, or action word.

Looking at each item, we see that in number 1 *her* is usually followed by a noun; *a* is usually followed by a singular noun, as in number 2. Items 3 and 4 both employ *and*, which usually connects words of the same type. In number 3 children are likely to insert a plural animal name because of the absence of an article (*a, an, the*). Similarly, in number 4 *and* will signal insertion of another food. Number 5 has the verb marker *will*, which is often found in the sequence "Will you (verb) . . .?''

As we pointed out earlier, semantic and syntactic clues should be used *together* to unlock unknown words.

Teaching Strategies

Early exercises with context clues may resemble the oral exercise explained above. Sometimes teachers supply multiple-choice answers and ask the children to circle or underline the correct choice in a writing exercise. An example follows.

> Sandy ate the _____. (cookie, store, shirt)

The child might need to apply some knowledge of phonics as well as context clues to complete the following sentence.

> Pat wore a new _____. (hate, hat, heat)

106

Teaching
Reading in
Today's
Elementary
Schools

It is good practice for a teacher to introduce a new word in context and let the children try to identify it, rather than simply to tell them what the word is. Then children can use any phonics and structural analysis knowledge that they have, along with context clues, to help identify the word. The teacher should use a context in which the only unfamiliar word is the new word; for example, use the sentence "My *umbrella* keeps me from getting wet when it rains" to present the word *umbrella*. The children will thus have graphic examples of the value of context clues in identifying unfamiliar words.

When a child encounters an unfamiliar word in oral reading to the teacher, instead of supplying the word, the teacher can encourage the child to read on to the end of the sentence (or even to the next sentence) to see what word would make sense. The teacher can encourage use of the sound of the initial letter or cluster of letters, sounds of other letters in the word, or known structural components, along with context. In a sentence where *hurled* appears as an unknown word, in the phrase *hurled the ball,* a child might guess *held* from the context. The teacher could encourage this child to notice the letters *ur* and try a word that contains that sound and makes sense in the context. Of course, this approach will be effective only if the child knows the meaning of the word *hurled.* Encouraging the child to read subsequent sentences could also be helpful, since these sentences might disclose situations in which *held* would be inappropriate but *hurled* would fit.

Use of context clues can help children make educated guesses about the identity of unfamiliar words. Context clues are best used with phonics and structural analysis skills since they help identify words more quickly than use of phonics or structural analysis clues alone would do. But without the confirmation of phonics and structural analysis, context clues provide only guesses. As we mentioned earlier, when a blank is substituted for a word in a sentence, students can often use several possibilities to complete the sentence and still make sense. When a child encounters an unknown word, he or she should make an educated guess based on the context and verify that guess by using other word analysis skills.

If a child encountered the sentence below, containing a blank instead of a word at the end, she might fill in the blank with either *bat* or *glove.*

> Frank said, "If I am going to play Little League baseball this year, I need a new ball and _____."

If the sentence gave the initial sound of the missing word, the child would know that *bat* was the appropriate word, instead of *glove.*

> Frank said, "If I am going to play Little League baseball this year, I need a new ball and *b_____."

Structural analysis clues can be used in the same way. In the sentence below, a child might insert such words as *stop* or *keep* in the blank.

> I wouldn't want to _____ you from going on the trip.

The child would choose neither if he had the help of a familiar prefix to guide his choice. The word *prevent* would obviously be the proper choice.

> I wouldn't want to *pre*_____ you from going on the trip.

Suffixes and ending sounds are also very useful in conjunction with the context to help in word identification. Teachers can utilize exercises similar to the one below to encourage children to use phonics and structural analysis clues along with context clues.

● **WORSHEET:** *Word Identification*

Directions: From the clues given, identify the incomplete words in the following sentences. Fill in the missing letters.
1. This package is too *h___ __ __y* for me. Let someone else carry it.
2. I want to join the Navy and ride in a *s u b __ __ __ __ __ __*.
3. If you keep up that arguing, you will *s p __ __ __* the party for everyone.
4. If you want to be strong, eat your *v __ __ __ __ __ __ __ __ s*.
5. John rides a *m __ __ __ __ __ c l e* to school.
6. You can't hurt it. It's *i n __ __ s t r __ __ __ i b l e*.
7. She lives in a *p e n t __ __ __ __ __* apartment.
8. My grandmother has a home *r __ __ __ d y* for any disease. ●

Some words are difficult to pronounce unless they are in context, for example, homographs—words that look alike but have different meanings and pronunciations, such as *row, wind, bow, read, content, rebel, minute, lead, record,* and *live.* Here are examples of how context can clarify pronunciations of these words.

1. I'll let you *row* the boat when I get tired.
   If I had known it would cause a *row,* I would never have angered you by mentioning the subject.
2. The *wind* is blowing through the trees.
   Did you *wind* the clock last night?
3. She put a *bow* on the gift.
   You should *bow* to the audience when you finish your act.
4. Can you *read* the directions to me?
   I *read Tom Sawyer* to my class last year.
5. I am *content* living in the mountains.
   The book has a nice cover, but I didn't enjoy the *content.*
6. Would you *rebel* against that law?
   I have always thought you were a *rebel.*
7. I'll be there in a *minute.*
   You must pay attention to *minute* details.
8. Nikki wants to *lead* the parade.
   Some gasoline has *lead* in it.

108

Teaching
Reading in
Today's
Elementary
Schools

9. Did your father *record* his gas mileage?

Suzanne broke Jill's *record* for the highest score in one game.

10. I *live* on Main Street.

We saw a *live* octopus.

Although most of the examples in this section show only a single sentence as the context, children should be encouraged to look for clues in surrounding sentences as well as the sentence in which the word occurs. Sometimes an entire paragraph will be useful in defining a term.

A cloze passage, in which words have been systematically deleted and replaced with blanks of uniform length, can be a good way to work on context-clue use. For this purpose, the teacher can delete certain types of words (nouns, verbs, adjectives, etc.) if he or she wishes, rather than have random deletion. The class should discuss reasons for the words chosen to be inserted in the blanks, and the teacher should accept synonyms and sometimes nonsynonyms for which the students have a good rationale. The point of the exercise is to have the students think logically about what would make sense in the context.

✔ Self-Check: Objective 2

Describe a procedure to help children learn to use context clues. (See Self-Improvement Opportunities 6 and 7.)

Phonics

Before you read this section, go to "Test Yourself" at the end of the chapter and take the multiple-choice phonics test. It will give you an idea of your present knowledge of phonics. After you study the text, go back and take the test again to see just what you've learned.

Phonics is the association of speech sounds (phonemes) with printed symbols (graphemes). In some languages this sound-symbol association is fairly regular, but not in English. A single letter or combination of letters in our alphabet may stand for many different sounds. For example, the letter *a* in each of the following words has a different sound: *cape, cat, car, father, soda*. On the other hand, a single sound may be represented by more than one letter or combination of letters. The long *e* sound is spelled differently in each of the following words: *me, mien, meal, seed,* and *seize*. To complicate matters further, the English language abounds with letters that stand for no sound, as in island, knight, write, lamb, gnome, psalm, and rhyme.

The existence of spelling inconsistencies does not imply that phonics is not useful in helping children decode written language. We discuss inconsistencies to counteract the feeling of some teachers that phonics is an infallible guide to pronouncing words in written materials. Teaching phonics does not constitute a complete reading program; rather, phonics is a valuable aid to word recognition when used in conjunction with other skills, but it is only *one* useful skill among many. Mastering this skill, with the resulting ability to pronounce most unfamiliar words, should not be considered the product of the reading program. Children can pronounce words without understanding them, and getting *meaning* from the printed page should be the objective of all reading instruction.

Using twenty-four phonetically regular consonant-vowel-consonant words, Douglas Carnine (1977) studied the transfer effects of phonics and whole word approaches to reading instruction and found superior transfer to new words for the students who were taught phonics. The phonics group even had greater transfer to irregular words, although it was not extensive. Carnine pointed out that Gibson and Levin have interpreted research with adults as indicating that teachers should present *several* sound-symbol correspondences for each grapheme rather than one-to-one correspondences, thereby providing their students with a set for diversity. If such a procedure had been used in this study, it might have produced more transfer to irregular words; further examination of this possibility is needed.

✔ Self-Check: Objective 3

Can you justify teaching phonics as the only approach to word recognition? Why or why not?
(See Self-Improvement Opportunity 3.)

Terminology

To understand written material about phonics, teachers need to be familiar with the terms discussed below.

Vowels   The letters *a, e, i, o,* and *u* represent vowel sounds, and the letters *w* and *y* take on the characteristics of vowels when they appear in the final position in a word or syllable. The letter *y* also has the characteristics of a vowel in the medial (middle) position in a word or syllable.

Consonants   Letters other than *a, e, i, o,* and *u* generally represent consonant sounds. *W* and *y* have the characteristics of consonants when they appear in the initial position in a word or syllable.

Consonant Clusters (or Blends)   Two or more adjacent consonant sounds blended together—with each individual sound retaining its identity—constitute a consonant cluster. For example, although the first three sounds in the word *strike* are blended smoothly, listeners can detect the separate sounds of *s, t,* and *r* being produced in rapid succession. Many teaching materials refer to these letter combinations as consonant blends rather than consonant clusters.

110

Teaching
Reading in
Today's
Elementary
Schools

Consonant Digraphs   Two adjacent consonant letters that represent a single speech sound constitute a consonant digraph. For example, *sh* is a consonant digraph in the word *shore*, since it represents one sound and not a blend of the sounds of *s* and *h*.

Vowel Digraphs   Two adjacent vowel letters that represent a single speech sound constitute a vowel digraph. In the word *foot*, *oo* is a vowel digraph.

Diphthongs   Vowel sounds that are so closely blended that they can be treated as single vowel units for the purposes of word identification are called diphthongs. These sounds are actually vowel blends, since the vocal mechanism produces two sounds instead of one, as is the case with vowel digraphs. An example of a diphthong is the *ou* in *out*.

Some authorities object to the use of the terms *long* and *short* vowel sounds, since some readers may think that these terms refer to the duration of the sound. For this reason the terms *glided* (for long) and *unglided* (for short) have been used in some publications. A majority of readers are more familiar with *long* and *short*, however, so we have used them in this text.

Of course, teachers may choose to use neither set of terms. Instead of saying, "The vowel sound is usually long," a teacher may say, "The vowel has the sound of its alphabet name." For short vowel sounds, the teacher can say that the sound is the same as the one heard in a key word like *pet, cat, mitt, cot,* or *cup*.

✔ Self-Check: Objective 4

Define and give an example of a consonant blend, a consonant digraph, a vowel digraph, and a diphthong.

Sequence for Presenting Phonics Skills

Teachers do not usually determine the sequence for presenting phonics materials, which is usually dictated by materials chosen for use in the school, but they might find it helpful to understand the reasoning behind a particular order. Teachers who understand a reasonable sequence for presenting phonics elements are better equipped to choose new materials when given the opportunity to do so.

There seems to be agreement over the fact that good auditory and visual discrimination are prerequisites for learning sound-symbol relationships. We know that a child must be able to distinguish one letter from another and one sound from another before he or she can associate a particular letter with a particular sound. However, some controversy exists over the relative merits of teaching vowel sounds or consonant sounds first. Those who favor teaching vowel sounds first point out that every syllable of every word has a vowel sound and that vowels can be pronounced in isolation without undue distortion, whereas many consonants must be accompanied by vowels in order to be pronounced properly. These educators do not agree among themselves about *which* vowels should be presented first. Some prefer to teach the long vowels first because their sounds correspond to their letter names, while others believe that the short vowels should be presented first because they occur in more words in the beginning reading materials. Still others advocate teaching both types at the same time in order to take advantage of contrasts available in the children's vocabularies (*tap—tape, cot—coat*). They do seem to agree that the *r*- and *l*-controlled vowels, the schwa (ə) sound, and diphthongs should be presented after the long and short vowel sounds.

A majority of the authorities on reading instruction favor the presentation of consonant sounds before the introduction of vowel sounds, citing the following reasons:

1. Consonant letters are more consistent in the sounds they represent than vowel letters are. Many consonants represent a single sound (although they are not always sounded in a word), whereas all vowels represent numerous sounds. *B, f, h, k, l, m, p, r,* and *t* are among the most consistent consonant sounds.
2. Consonants usually make up the more identifiable features of a word. As an example, decide which of these representations of the word *tractor* is easiest to decipher: *t r __ c t __ r* or __ __ *a* __ __ *o* __.
3. More words start with consonants than with vowels, and words are generally attacked in a left-to-right sequence.

These reasons seem more practical than the reasons for presenting vowels first. We can overcome the problem that many consonants cannot be pronounced in isolation through an analytic approach to phonics, which is explained later in this chapter.

Words with consonants in the initial position are usually presented first, then consonants in the final position. Consonants that represent fairly consistent sounds are usually presented before those that represent several sounds (*c, g, s, x* and so on). Consonant digraphs (voiced *th,* voiceless *th, sh, wh, ch, ck, ng, ph,* and so on) and consonant blends (*br, bl, st, str, gl,* and so on) are usually not presented until students have been taught the single consonant sounds in the initial positions. Consonant letters that appear in words but are not sounded ("silent" letters) must also receive attention, for they occur quite often (lam*b, p*neumonia, *g*nat).

Some authorities suggest teaching vowel and consonant sounds simultaneously, thus making possible the complete sounding of entire short words early in the program. For example, a teacher can present the short *a* sound along with several consonants (perhaps *m, t, f, c*) to make the building of several words possible (*mat, fat, cat*).

112

Teaching
Reading in
Today's
Elementary
Schools

A sequence for presenting letter-sound correspondences is reproduced below. The first part of the sequence was suggested by Dale Johnson.

Single Consonants
  Set 1: *d, n, l, m, b*
  Set 2: *p, f, v, r, h, k, y, s, c, t*
  Set 3: *j, w, z, x, q (u), g*
Consonant Clusters
  Digraphs: *sh, th, ch, ng, ph*
Double Consonants
  ss, ll, rr, tt, mm, nn, ff, pp, cc, dd, gg, bb, zz
Single Vowels
  i, a, o, u, e
Vowel Clusters
  Set 1: *io, ea, ou, ee, ai, au*
  Set 2: *oo, ow, oi, ay*
  Set 3: *ia, oa, ie, ue, iou, ua, ui*[1]
Consonant Blends
  consonant plus *l,* consonant plus *r, s* plus consonant
Patterned irregularities
  knee, knife, knew, bomb, comb, lamb
Syllabication
  VCV [Vowel-Consonant-Vowel] *ba/by*
  VCCV [Vowel-Consonant-Consonant-Vowel] *nap/kin*
  VCle [Vowel-Consonant-le] *a/ble*

Phonics Generalizations

Many teachers believe that good phonics instruction is merely the presentation of a series of principles that children are expected to internalize and utilize in the process of word identification. Difficulties may arise from this conception.

First, pupils tend to internalize a phonics generalization more rapidly and effectively when they can arrive at it inductively. That is, by analyzing words to which a generalization applies and by deriving the generalization themselves from this analysis, children will understand it better and remember it longer.

Second, the irregularity of our spelling system results in numerous exceptions to phonics generalizations. Children must be helped to see that generalizations help them to derive *probable* pronunciations rather than infallible results. When applying a generalization does not produce a word that makes sense in the context of the material, readers should try other

[1]Dale D. Johnson, "Suggested Sequences for Presenting Four Categories of Letter-Sound Correspondence," *Elementary English* 50 (September 1973): 888–96. Copyright © 1973 by the National Council of Teachers of English. Reprinted with permission of the publisher and the author.

reasonable sound possibilities. For example, in cases where a long vowel
sound is likely according to a generalization but results in a nonsense word, the child should be taught to try other sounds, such as the short vowel sound, in the search for the correct pronunciation. Some words are so totally irregular in spelling that even extreme flexibility in phonic analysis will not produce a close approximation of the correct pronunciation. In a situation such as this, the child should be taught to turn to the dictionary for help in word recognition. Further discussion of this approach to word recognition can be found later in this chapter.

Third, students can be so deluged with rules that they cannot memorize them all. This procedure may result in failure to learn any generalization well.

Teachers can enhance a phonics program by presenting judiciously chosen phonics generalizations to youngsters. Authorities vary on which ones to present (Bailey, 1967; Clymer, 1963; Emans, 1967; Burmeister, 1978), but they agree on some of them. Considering the findings of phonics studies and past teaching experience, we feel that the following generalizations are useful under most circumstances:

1. When the letters *c* and *g* are followed by *e, i,* or *y,* they generally have soft sounds: the *s* sound for the letter *c* and the *j* sound for the letter *g.* (Examples: *cent, city, cycle, gem, ginger, gypsy.*) When *c* and *g* are followed by *o, a,* or *u,* they generally have hard sounds: *g* has its own special sound, and *c* has the sound of *k.* (Examples: *cat, cake, cut, go, game, gum.*)
2. When two like consonants are next to each other, only one is sounded. (Examples: *hall, glass.*)
3. *Ch* usually has the sound heard in *church,* although it sometimes sounds like *sh* or *k.* (Examples of usual sound: *child, chill, china.* Examples of *sh* sound: *chef, chevron.* Examples of *k* sound: *chemistry, chord.*)
4. When the letters *ght* are side by side in a word, the *gh* is not sounded. (Examples: *taught, light.*)
5. When *kn* are the first two letters in a word, the *k* is not sounded. (Examples: *know, knight.*)
6. When *wr* are the first two letters in a word, the *w* is not sounded. (Examples: *write, wrong.*)
7. When *ck* are the last two letters in a word, the sound of *k* is given. (Examples: *check, brick.*)
8. The sound of a vowel preceding *r* is neither long nor short. (Examples: *car, fir, her.*)
9. In the vowel combinations *oa, ee,* and *ay,* the first vowel is generally long and the second one is not sounded. This may also apply to other double vowel combinations. (Examples: *boat, feet, play.*)
10. The double vowels *oi, oy,* and *ou* usually form diphthongs. While the *ow* combination frequently stands for the long *o* sound, it may also form a diphthong. (Examples: *boil, boy, out, now.*)
11. In a word that has only one vowel which is at the end of the word, the vowel usually represents its long sound. (Examples: *me, go.*)

114

Teaching
Reading in
Today's
Elementary
Schools

12. In a word that has only one vowel which is *not* at the end of the word, the vowel usually represents its short sound. (Examples: *set, man, cut, hop, list.*)

13. If there are two vowels in a word and one is a final *e*, the first vowel is usually long and the final *e* is not sounded. (Examples: *cape, cute, cove, kite.*)

14. The letter combination *qu* often stands for the sound of *kw*, although it sometimes stands for the sound of *k*. (Examples of *kw* sound: *quick, queen*. Example of *k* sound: *quay*.)

15. The letter *x* most often stands for the sound of *ks*, although at times it stands for the sound of *gz* or *z*. (Examples of *ks* sound: *box, next*. Example of *gz* sound: *exact*. Example of *z* sound: *xylophone*.)

Barbara Rosso and Robert Emans (1981) tried to determine whether knowledge of phonic generalizations helps children decode unrecognized words and whether children have to be able to state the generalizations to use them. They found statistically significant relationships between knowledge of phonic generalizations and reading achievement, but pointed out that this does not necessarily indicate a cause-and-effect relationship. They also discovered that "inability to state a phonics rule did not seem to hinder these children's effort to analyze unfamiliar words . . . this study supports Piaget's theory that children in the concrete operations stage of development may encounter difficulty in describing verbally those actions they perform physically" (p. 657). Teachers may need to investigate techniques for teaching phonics generalizations that do not require children to verbalize a generalization.

It is wise to teach only one generalization at a time, presenting a second only after students have thoroughly learned the first. The existence of exceptions to generalizations should be freely acknowledged, and children should be encouraged to treat the generalizations as possible rather than infallible clues to pronunciation.

Consonants Although consonant letters are more consistent in the sounds they represent than vowel letters are, they are not perfectly consistent. The list below shows some examples of variations with which a child must contend.

Consonant	Variations	Consonant	Variations
b	board, lamb	n	never, drink
c	cable, city, scene	p	punt, psalm
d	dog, jumped	q(u)	antique, quit
f	fox, of	s	see, sure, his, pleasure, island
g	go, gem, gnat		
h	hit, hour	t	town, listen
j	just, hallelujah	w	work, wrist
k	kitten, knee	x	fox, anxiety, exit
l	lamp, calf	z	zoo, azure, quartz

Consider the cases in which *y* and *w* take on vowel characteristics. Both of these letters represent consonant sounds when they are in the initial position in a word or syllable, but they represent vowel sounds when they are in a final or medial position. For example, *y* represents a consonant sound in the word *yard,* but a vowel sound in the words *dye, myth,* and *baby.* Notice that actually three different vowel sounds are represented by *y* in these words.

Consonant Digraphs   Several consonant digraphs represent sounds not associated with either of the component parts. These are shown in the list below.

Consonant digraph	*Example*
th	then, thick
ng	sing
sh	shout
ph	telephone
gh	rough
ch	chief, chef, chaos

Other consonant digraphs generally represent the usual sound of one of the component parts, as in *wr*ite, *pn*eumonia, and *gn*at. Some sources consider one of the letters in each of these combinations as a "silent" letter and do not refer to these combinations as digraphs.

Vowels   The variability of the sounds represented by vowels has been emphasized before. Some examples of this variability are given in the list below.

Vowel letter	*Variations*
a	ate, cat, want, ball, father, sofa
e	me, red, pretty, kitten, her, sergeant
i	ice, hit, fir, opportunity
o	go, hot, today, women, button, son, work, born
u	use, cut, put, circus, turn

In the examples here, the first variation listed for each vowel is a word in which the long vowel sound, the same as its letter name, is heard. In the second variation the short sound of the vowel is heard. These are generally the first two sounds taught for each vowel.

Another extremely common sound that children need to learn is the schwa sound, a very soft "uh" or grunt usually found in unaccented syllables. It is heard in the following words: sof*a,* kitt*e*n, opportun*i*ty, butt*o*n, circ*u*s. The schwa sound is, as you can see, represented by each of the vowel letters.

116

Teaching
Reading in
Today's
Elementary
Schools

Three types of markings represent the three types of vowel sounds we have discussed:

Marking	Name of mark	Designation
ā, ē, ī, ō, ū	macron	long vowel sound
ă, ě, ĭ, ŏ, ŭ	breve	short vowel sound
ə	schwa	soft "uh" sound

Some dictionaries place no mark at all over a vowel letter that represents the short sound of the vowel.

Vowel Digraphs   Some vowel digraphs represent sounds not associated with either of the letters involved. These digraphs are illustrated below:

Vowel Digraph	Example
au	taught
aw	saw
oo	food, look

Other vowel digraphs generally represent the usual sound of one of the component parts, as in br*ea*k, br*ea*d, b*oa*t, s*ee*d, and *ai*m. Some sources treat one of the letters in these combinations as "silent" and do not refer to them as digraphs.

Diphthongs   There are four common diphthongs, or vowel blends.

Diphthong	Example in context
oi	foil
oy	toy
ou	bound
ow	cow

Notice that the first two diphthongs listed (*oi* and *oy*) stand for identical sounds, as do the last two (*ou* and *ow*). Remember that the letter combinations *ow* and *ou* are *not always diphthongs*. In the words *snow* and *blow*, *ow* is a vowel digraph representing the long *o* sound. In the word *routine*, *ou* represents an $\overline{oo}$ sound.

Teaching Strategies

There are two major approaches to phonics instruction, the synthetic approach and the analytic approach.

In a synthetic method the teacher first instructs children in the speech sounds that are associated with individual letters. Since letters and sounds

Games and game-like activities, in addition to worksheets and chalkboard exercises, can offer students practice in letter-sound associations. (© Teri Leigh Stratford/Monkmeyer)

have no inherent relationships, this task is generally accomplished by repeated drill on sound-symbol associations. The teacher may hold up a card on which the letter *b* appears, and the children are expected to respond with the sound ordinarily associated with that letter. The next step is blending the sounds together to form words. The teacher encourages the children to pronounce the sounds associated with the letters in rapid succession so that they produce a word or an approximate pronunciation of a word, which they can then recognize and pronounce accurately. This blending process generally begins with two- and three-letter words and proceeds to much longer ones. Sometimes the children are asked to pronounce nonsense syllables because these syllables will appear later in their written materials as word parts. Reading words in context does not generally occur until these steps have been

118

Teaching
Reading in
Today's
Elementary
Schools

repeatedly carried out and the children have developed a moderate stock of words.

The analytic approach involves teaching some sight words and then the sounds of the letters within those words. It is preferred by many and is used in many basal reader series, partly because it avoids the distortion that occurs when consonants are pronounced in isolation. For example, trying to pronounce a *t* in isolation is likely to result in the sounds *tə*. Pronouncing a schwa sound following the consonant can adversely affect the child's blending, since the word *tag* must be sounded as *tə-a-gə*. No matter how fast the child makes those sounds, he or she is unlikely to come very close to *tag*. The same process may be used to introduce other consonants, consonant blends, consonant digraphs, vowels, diphthongs, and vowel digraphs in initial, medial, and final positions.

The analytic method is illustrated in the three sample lesson plans presented below. The first two lesson plans are *inductive*. The children look at a number of specific examples related to a generalization and then derive the generalization. A *deductive* plan consists of the teacher's first stating a generalization and then having the children apply the generalization in decoding unfamiliar words. The third lesson plan illustrates this approach.

● **MODEL ACTIVITY:** *Analytic-Inductive Lesson Plan for Initial Consonant* D

Write on the chalkboard the following words, all of which the children have learned previously as sight words:

dog	did
daddy	donkey
do	Dan

Ask the children to listen carefully as you pronounce the words. Then ask: "Did any parts of these words sound the same?" If you receive an affirmative reply, ask, "What part sounded the same?" This should elicit the answer that the first sound in each word is the same or that the words sound alike at the beginning.

Next ask the children to look carefully at the words written on the board. Ask: "Do you see anything that is the same in all these words?" This should elicit the answer that all of the words have the same first letter or all of the words start with *d*.

Then ask what the children can conclude about words that begin with the letter *d*. The expected answer is that words that begin with the letter *d* sound the same at the beginning as the word *dog* (or any other word on their list).

Next invite the children to name other words that have the same beginning sound as *dog*. Write each word on the board. Ask the children to observe the words and draw another conclusion. They may say, "Words that sound the same at the beginning as the word *dog* begin with the letter *d*."

Ask the children to watch for words in their reading that begin with the letter *d* in order to check the accuracy of their conclusions. ●

Write the following list of words on the board, all of which are part of the children's sight vocabularies:

sit	in
at	man
hot	Don
met	wet
cut	bun

Ask the children how many vowels they see in each of the words in the list. When you receive the answer "one," write on the board "One vowel letter."

Then ask: "Where is the vowel letter found in these words?" The children will probably say, "At the beginning in some and in the middle in others." Write on the board, "At the beginning or in the middle."

Then ask: "Which of its sounds does the vowel have in the word *sit*? In the word *at*? and so on until the students have discovered that the short sound is present in each word. Then write "Short sound" on the board.

Next ask the children to draw a conclusion about the vowel sounds in the words they have analyzed. The generalization may be stated, "In words that contain only one vowel letter, located at the beginning or in the middle of the word, the vowel usually has its short sound." The children will be likely to insert the word "usually" if they have been warned about the tentative nature of phonics generalizations.

Finally, ask the children if they should have included in their generalization words having only one vowel letter located at the end of the word. The children can check sight words such as *he, no,* and *be* in order to conclude that these words do not have a short vowel sound and therefore should not be included in the generalization. ●

● **MODEL ACTIVITY:** *Analytic-Deductive Lesson Plan for Soft Sound of* c

Tell the children: "When the letter *c* is followed by *e, i,* or *y,* it generally has its soft sound, which is the sound you have learned for the letter *s*." Write the following examples on the chalkboard: *city, cycle,* and *cent.* Point out that in *cycle* only the *c* that is followed by *y* has the soft sound. Follow this presentation with an activity designed to check the children's understanding of the generalization. The activity might involve a worksheet with items like this:

Directions: Place a checkmark beside the words that contain a soft *c* sound.

_____ cite	_____ cider	_____ cape
_____ cord	_____ cede	_____ cymbal
_____ cut	_____ cod	_____ cell

The soft *c* sound is the sound we have learned for the letter _____. ●

120

Teaching
Reading in
Today's
Elementary
Schools

Teachers should keep in mind a caution concerning the teaching of phonics generalizations, involving the use of such terms as *sound* and *word.* Studies by Reid and Downing indicate that young children (five-year-olds) have trouble understanding terms used to talk about language, such as *word, letter,* and *sound* (Downing, 1973), and Meltzer and Herse (1969) found that first-grade children do not always know where printed words begin and end. In addition, Tovey (1980) found that the group of second through sixth graders that he studied had difficulty in dealing with abstract phonics terms such as *consonant, consonant blend, consonant digraph, vowel digraph, diphthong, possessive, inflectional ending,* and others. His study also showed that the children had learned sound-symbol associations without being able to define the phonics terms involved. Lessons such as those described are worthless if the students do not have these basic concepts. Before teaching a lesson using linguistic terms, the teacher should check to be sure that students grasp such concepts. Technical terminology should be deemphasized when working with students who have not mastered the terms.

Anna Cordts (1965) suggests using key words to help children learn the sounds associated with vowels, consonants, vowel digraphs, consonant digraphs, diphthongs, and consonant blends. These words in all cases should already be part of the children's sight vocabularies. Cordts suggests that a key word for a vowel sound be one that contains that vowel sound and can be pictured, while a key word for a consonant sound should be one that can be pictured and has that consonant sound at the end. She feels that consonant sounds can be more clearly heard at the ends than at the beginnings of words.

From the suggestions given by Cordts, we have constructed the list of key words shown in Table 3.2.

Other authorities also encourage the use of key words, but most suggest using words with the consonant sounds at the beginning. The sounds may be harder to distinguish, but usable key words are much easier to find when initial sounds are used.

Key words are valuable in helping children remember sound-symbol associations which are not inherently meaningful. People remember new things through associations with things that they already know. The more associations that a person has for an abstract relationship, such as the letter *d* and the sound of *d,* the more quickly that person will learn to link the sound and symbol. The person's retention of this connection will also be more accurate. Schell (1978) refers to a third-grade boy who chose as key words for the consonant blends *dr, fr,* and *sp* the character names *Dracula, Frankenstein,* and *Spiderman.* These associations were both concrete and personal for him. The characters were drawn on key-word cards to aid his memory of the associations.

Consonant substitution activities are useful for helping students see how their knowledge of some words helps them to decode other words. To teach consonant substitution, the teacher writes a known word, such as *pat,* on the board and asks the students to pronounce the word. Then he or she writes on the board a letter for which the sound has been taught (for example, *m*). If

TABLE 3.2 Sample Key Words

121

Word
Recognition

Sample Key Words for Vowel Sounds

Short Vowels	Long Vowels	Diphthongs	Special Vowel Digraphs
cat	snake	coin	saw
bed	key	boy	auto
ship	dime	house	moon
top	cone	cow	foot
bug	fuse		

Sample Key Words for Consonant Sounds

Single Consonants	Single Consonants (cont'd)	Special Consonant Digraphs	Only Heard at the Beginning of Words
b—tub	p—hoop or pipe	ch—match	h—hat
d—head	s—glass	th—cloth	w—wing
f—chief	t—coat	sh—dish	j—jail
g—rug	v—sleeve or	ng—ring	wh—whale
k—chalk	dove		y—yard
l—rail	x—box		
m—arm	z—prize		
n—pen			
r—rope (The *r* sound is more consistent at the beginning than at the end of words.)			

the letter sound can be pronounced in isolation without distortion, the teacher asks the students to do so; if not, he or she asks for a word beginning with this sound. Then the students are asked to leave the *p* sound off when they pronounce the word on the board. They will respond with "at." Next they are asked to put the *m* sound in front of the "at," and they produce "mat." The same process is followed with other sounds, such as *s, r,* and *b.*

This procedure is also useful with sounds at the ends of words or in medial positions. Vowel substitution activities, in which the teacher may start with a known word and have the students omit the vowel sound and substitute a different one (for example: m*a*t, m*e*t, m*i*tt; p*a*t, p*e*t, p*i*t, p*o*t), can also be helpful.

Drill on letter-sound associations does not have to be dull. Teachers can use many game activities, and activities that are more businesslike in nature will not become boring if they are not overused. Always remember when planning games that, although competitive situations are motivational for some youngsters, others are adversely affected by being placed in win/lose situations, especially if they have little hope of being a winner at least part of the time. Continuously being forced into losing situations can negatively affect a child's self-concept and can promote negative attitudes toward the activity involved in the game (in this instance, reading). This effect is less likely if children with similar abilities compete with each other; however,

122

Teaching
Reading in
Today's
Elementary
Schools

even then competitive games should be used with caution. Game situations in which children cooperate or in which they compete with their *own previous records* rather than with one another are often more acceptable. Here are some practical examples.

ACTIVITIES

1. Construct cards resembling bingo cards, like the ones below. Pronounce a word beginning with the sound of one of the listed consonants or consonant digraphs. Instruct the children to check their cards for the letter or letter combination that represents the word's initial sound. Tell those who have the correct grapheme on the card to cover it with a token. Continue to pronounce words until one child has covered his or her entire card. The first child to do this can be declared the winner, or the game may continue until all cards are covered.

b	d	f	g
h	j	k	l
m	n	p	r
s	t	v	w

y	z	th	sh
h	ch	b	p
r	m	t	k
n	s	g	n

d	y	g	th
h	ch	k	p
m	r	s	v
sh	n	l	j

2. Give each child a sheet of paper that is blank except for a letter at the top. Have the children draw pictures of as many items as they can think of that have names beginning with the sound of the letter at the top of the page. Declare the child with the most correct responses the winner.
3. Make five decorated boxes, and label each with a short vowel. Have the children locate pictures of objects whose names contain the short vowel sounds and file them in the appropriate boxes. Each day take out the pictures, ask the children to pronounce the names, and check to see if the appropriate sounds are present. Do the same thing with long vowel sounds, consonant sounds, consonant blends, digraphs, diphthongs, and rhyming words.
4. Use worksheets such as those that follow. In each case, read the directions for the worksheet to the children before they begin.

● **WORKSHEET:** *Medial Vowels*

Directions: Listen to the word that the teacher says for each line. Circle the word that you hear.

1. cat   cut   cot
2. sit   set   sat
3. hit   hat   hut
4. fan   fun   fin

5. cop	cap	cup
6. pup	pip	pop
7. mad	mod	mud

● WORKSHEET: *Rhyming Words*

Directions: Draw a line connecting the words in Column 1 with the words in Column 2 that rhyme.

Column 1	Column 2
lake	coat
pig	big
size	cake
mat	mail
boat	prize
sail	sat

● WORKSHEET: *Long o Sound*

Directions: Underline the words that contain the long o sound.

1. cot	7. soul
2. coat	8. hog
3. snow	9. won
4. cow	10. moose
5. cone	11. cold
6. pole	12. tone

5. Place a familiar word ending on a cardboard disc like the one pictured here. Pull a strip of cardboard with initial consonants on it through an opening cut in the disc. Show the children how to pull the strip through the disc, pronouncing each word that is formed.

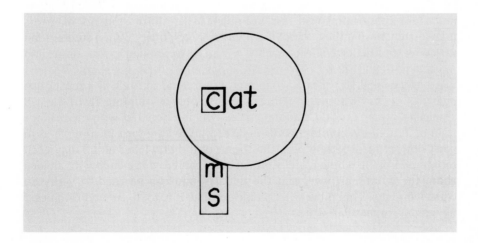

124

Teaching
Reading in
Today's
Elementary
Schools

6. Divide the children in the room into two groups. Give half of them initial consonant, consonant blend, or consonant digraph cards. Give the other half word-ending cards. Instruct the children to pair up with other children holding word parts that combine with their parts to form real words. Have the children hold up their cards and pronounce the word they have made when they have located a combination.

7. Use riddles. For example, "I have in mind a word that rhymes with *far*. We ride in it. It's called a _____."

8. Give students silly sentences to read orally. Construct these sentences so that they require the application of phonics skills taught previously. Examples: She said it was her fate to be fat. Her mate sat on the mat. He charged a high rate to kill the rat.

9. Let the children find a hidden picture by shading in all of the spaces that contain words with long vowel sounds.

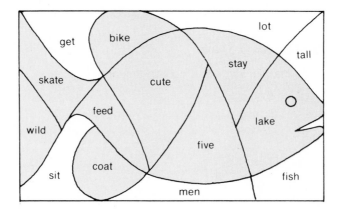

Practice exercises should always be preceded by instruction and followed by feedback on results if they are to be effective. The absence of prior instruction may cause practice of the wrong response. Feedback, which should come either directly from the teacher or through a self-correcting procedure (posted answers, for example), will inform students of errors immediately so that they do not learn incorrect responses. When students fail to see reasons for errors, the teacher will need to provide explanations and reteaching of the skill.

A phonics skill is a means to an end, not an end in itself. If a reader can recognize a word without resorting to letter-by-letter sounding, he or she will recognize it more quickly, and the process will interfere less with the reader's train of thought. When the words to be recognized are seen in context, as in most normal reading activities, the sound of the first letter alone may elicit recognition of the whole word. Context clues can provide a child with an idea about the word's identity, and the initial sound can be used to verify an educated guess. This procedure is efficient and is a good method of quickly identifying unfamiliar words.

Phonics skills receive extensive attention in the primary grades (1–3), and teachers of these grades are generally aware that they need to be well-informed in this area. Review and reteaching of phonics skills should, however, take place at successively higher grade levels. Not all children internalize phonics principles during the first three grades, and these children should have help until they have attained proficiency. Therefore, intermediate and upper-grade teachers should also be well versed in teaching these skills.

✔ Self-Check: Objective 5

Describe a procedure for teaching one of the phonics generalizations listed in this section.
(See Self-Improvement Opportunity 4.)

Structural Analysis

Structural analysis skills are closely related to phonics skills and have several significant facets:

1. inflectional endings
2. prefixes, suffixes
3. contractions
4. compound words
5. syllabication and accents

Structural analysis skills enable children to decode unfamiliar words by using units larger than single graphemes; this procedure generally expedites the decoding process. Structural analysis can also be helpful in understanding word meanings, a function discussed in Chapter 4.

Inflectional Endings

Inflectional endings are added to nouns to change number, case, or gender; added to verbs to change tense or person; and added to adjectives to change degree. They may also change the part of speech of a word. Since inflectional endings are letters or groups of letters added to the endings of root words, some people call them inflectional suffixes. The words that result are called variants, and some examples are found in the list below.

Root Word	Variant	Change
boy	boys	Singular noun changed to plural noun
host	hostess	Gender of noun changed from masculine to feminine
Karen	Karen's	Proper noun altered to show possession (change of case)

Root Word	Variant	Change
look	looked	Verb changed from present tense to past tense
make	makes	Verb changed from first or second person singular to third person singular
mean	meaner	Simple form of adjective changed to the comparative form
happy	happily	Adjective changed to adverb

Generally, the first inflectional ending that children are exposed to is *s*. This ending often appears in preprimers and primers and should be learned early in the first grade. Other inflectional endings that children are likely to encounter in these early materials are *ing* and *ed*.

A child can be shown the effect of the addition of an *s* to a singular noun by illustrations of single and multiple objects. An activity such as that shown in Worksheet: Recognizing Inflectional Ending *s* can be used to practice this skill. Another sample worksheet for various inflectional endings and a commercial workbook activity (Example 3.1) demonstrate further practice with different inflectional endings.

● **WORKSHEET:** *Recognizing Inflectional Ending* s

Directions: Circle the word that describes two things.

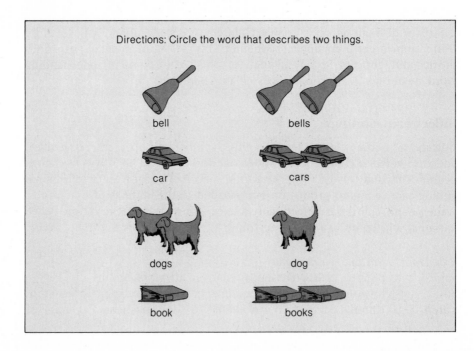

Directions: Circle the word that describes two things.

bell   bells

car   cars

dogs   dog

book   books

Directions: In each sentence below, circle the endings you have studied.

1. He walk(ed) around the block with the boy(s).
2. She found Jane('s) grape(s) in her lunchbox.
3. Bob is going with Jack('s) group.
4. Ray('s) motorcycle need(ed) to be fix(ed).
5. Kristy has many toy truck(s).
6. Toby pick(ed) up my glass(es). ●

▶ **EXAMPLE 3.1:** Practice Sheet for Word Endings

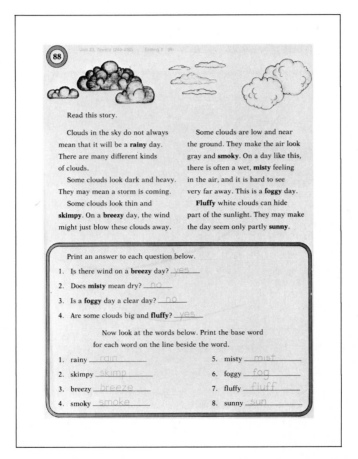

Source: William K. Durr et al.: *Practice Book: Towers, Teacher's Annotated Edition* (Houghton Mifflin Reading Program), p. 88. Copyright © 1981 by Houghton Mifflin Company. Used by permission. ◀

128

Teaching
Reading in
Today's
Elementary
Schools

Children should not be given the impression that the inflectional ending *s* always sounds like the *s* in *see;* this pronunciation occurs only after an unvoiced *th, t, p, k,* and *f.* After other consonant sounds and after long vowel sounds, the ending *s* has the sound associated with the letter *z.*

The teacher should also emphasize variations in pronouncing the inflectional ending *ed.* When the *ed* follows *d* and *t,* the *e* is sounded, but after other letters the *e* is silent. When the *e* is sounded, a separate syllable is formed, but when it is not sounded, the inflectional ending does not form a separate syllable. (Examples: dusted—dust' ed; begged—begd.) In addition, the *d* in *ed* is given the sound ordinarily associated with *t* in many words, especially those ending with *s, ch, sh, f, k,* and *p.* (Examples: asked—askt; helped—helpt; wished—wisht.)

An activity that can help children recognize the varied sounds of the *d* in the ending *ed* follows.

● **MODEL ACTIVITY:** *Sounds of* d *in* ed *Ending*

Distribute worksheets containing the following words to the children:

1. dropped ———
2. canned ———
3. worked ———
4. passed ———
5. stopped ———

Then say: "Listen carefully as I pronounce each of the words on your paper. If the *d* in the ending *ed* sounds like *d,* write a *d* after the word. If the *d* sounds like *t,* write a *t* after the word." Give the children time to fill in their worksheets, and then say: "Now check your answers. Do you have *t* for 1, 3, 4, and 5 and *d* for 2? If so, you have a perfect paper. If you missed some, please come to the skills corner, and I will help you." ●

Children in the primary grades are frequently exposed to the possessive case formed by *'s.* An activity designed for work with this inflectional ending follows.

● **MODEL ACTIVITY:** *The* 's *Ending*

Tell the children: "When I say, 'This is the book of my brother,' I mean that the book belongs to my brother. Another, shorter way of saying the same thing is 'This is my brother's book.' The apostrophe *s* on the end of the word *brother* shows that the noun following *brother* (book) belongs to brother. Reword these phrases without changing their meaning by using the apostrophe *s* ending." Pass out the following phrases on a handout or write them on the chalkboard or a transparency.

Example: the coat of my aunt   *my aunt's coat*

1. the cat that belongs to my friend _____
2. the hat of my father _____
3. the sister of my mother _____
4. the brother of Bill _____
5. the ball that belongs to Merryl _____
6. the house of my grandmother _____
7. the ranch of my uncle _____   ●

This activity could also become a matching exercise. For example:

the cat that belongs to my friend ———————— my father's hat
the hat of my father ———————— my friend's cat
the sister of my mother ———————— my mother's sister

✔ Self-Check: Objective 6
Describe a procedure for teaching the inflectional ending *s*.

Prefixes and Suffixes

Prefixes and suffixes are affixes or sequences of letters that are added to root words to change their meanings and/or parts of speech. A prefix is placed before a root word, and a suffix is placed after a root word.

Children can learn the pronunciations and meanings of some common prefixes and suffixes. Good readers learn to recognize common prefixes and suffixes instantly; this helps them recognize words more rapidly than they could if they had to resort to sounding each word letter by letter. Knowledge of prefixes and suffixes can help readers decipher the meanings as well as the pronunciations of unfamiliar words. Common, useful prefixes and suffixes are shown in the list below.

Prefix	*Meaning*	*Example*
un-	not	unable
in-	in or not	inset, inactive
bi-	two, twice	bicycle, biweekly
dis-	apart from, reversal of	displace, dismount
multi-	many	multicolored
non-	not	nonliving
pre-	before	preview
re-	again	reread
pro-	in favor of	prolabor
post-	after	postscript
semi-	partly	semicircle

130

Teaching
Reading in
Today's
Elementary
Schools

Prefix	Meaning	Example
sub-	under	subway
super-	over	superhuman
trans-	across	transatlantic
tri-	three	tricycle

Suffix		
-ful	full of	careful
-less	without	painless
-ment*	state of being	contentment
-ship*	state of being	friendship
-ous	full of	joyous
-ward	in the direction of	westward
-tion*	state of being	action
-sion*	state of being	tension
-able	capable of being	likable
-ness*	state of being	happiness

NOTE: The starred (*) suffixes are best taught simply as visual units because their meanings are abstract.

Some very common prefixes, such as *ad-, com-,* and *con-,* are not included in the list above because they generally occur with word parts that do not stand alone and are not recognizable meaning units to children. Examples are *admit, advice, combine, commerce, commit, conceal,* and *condemn.*

The suffixes *-ment, -ous, -tion,* and *-sion* have especially consistent pronunciations. Thus, they are particularly useful to know. The suffixes *-ment* and *-ous* generally have the pronunciations heard in the words *treatment* and *joyous.* The suffixes *-tion* and *-sion* have the sound of *shun,* as heard in the words *education* and *mission.*

When prefixes and suffixes are added to root words, the resulting words are called derivatives. Whereas prefixes simply modify the meanings of the root words, suffixes may change the parts of speech in addition to modifying the meaning. Some of the modifications that can result are listed below.

Root Word	Affix	Derivative	New Meaning or Change
happy	un-	unhappy	not happy
amuse	-ment	amusement	verb is changed to noun
worth	-less	worthless	meaning is opposite of original meaning

Use worksheets like the two shown below following instruction in prefixes and suffixes.

● **WORKSHEET:** *Recognition of Prefixes and Suffixes*

Directions: Circle the prefixes and suffixes you see in the words below.

1. disagree	8. premeditate
2. reuse	9. transport
3. inhuman	10. reload
4. honorable	11. likely
5. contentment	12. treatment
6. joyful	13. dangerous
7. unusable	14. westward ●

● **WORKSHEET:** *Adding Prefixes and Suffixes*

Directions: Make as many new words as you can by adding prefixes and suffixes to the following root words.

1. *agree* 2. *move* 3. *construct*

_____ _____ _____

_____ _____ _____

_____ _____ _____

_____ _____ _____ ●

Contractions

The apostrophe used in contractions indicates that one or more letters have been left out when two words were combined into one word. Children need to be able to recognize the original words from which the contractions were formed. The following are common contractions, with their meanings, that teachers should present to children:

can't/cannot	I'll/I will
couldn't/could not	I'm/I am
didn't/did not	I've/I have
don't/do not	isn't/is not
hadn't/had not	let's/let us
hasn't/has not	she'd/she would or she had
he'll/he will	she'll/she will
he's/he is	she's/she is
I'd/I had or I would	shouldn't/should not

132

Teaching
Reading in
Today's
Elementary
Schools

they'd/they had or they would
they'll/they will
they're/they are
they've/they have
wasn't/was not
we're/we are
weren't/were not

we've/we have
won't/will not
wouldn't/would not
you'll/you will
you're/you are
you've/you have

Use a worksheet such as the following for practice with contractions.

● **WORKSHEET:** *Contractions*

Directions: Match the contractions in Column 1 with their proper meanings in Column 2 by drawing a line from each contraction to its meaning.

Column 1	Column 2
don't	cannot
can't	do not
he's	we are
we're	I am
you'll	he is
I'm	will not
won't	you will ●

Compound Words

Compound words consist of two (or occasionally three) words that have been joined together to form a new word. The original pronunciations of the component words are usually maintained, and their meanings are connected to form the meaning of the new word. For example, *dishpan* is a pan in which dishes are washed. Children can be asked to underline or circle component parts of compound words or to put together familiar compound words. Examples of exercises illustrating these activities follow.

● **WORKSHEET:** *Recognizing Parts of Compound Words*

Directions: Circle the two words that make up each of the following compound words.

1. dishwasher	5. workbook
2. newspaper	6. weekend
3. beehive	7. footprint
4. earthquake	8. daylight ●

Directions: Find a word in Column 2 that, when combined with a word in Column 1, will form a compound word. Write the words you form in Column 3. One example word has been filled in for you.

Column 1	*Column 2*	*Column 3*
pocket	burn	pocketbook
letter	hive	_____
sun	book	_____
grass	carrier	_____
bee	hopper	_____ ●

Syllabication/Accent

Since many phonics generalizations apply not only to one-syllable words but also to syllables within longer words, many people feel that breaking words into syllables can be helpful in determining pronunciation. Gerald Glass (1967), however, says that syllabication is usually done after the reader has recognized the sound of the word. Most of the participants in his study used the sounds to determine syllabication rather than syllabication to determine the sounds. If this procedure is the one normally used by children in attacking words, syllabication would seem to be of little use in a word analysis program. On the other hand, many authorities firmly believe that syllabication is helpful in decoding words. For this reason, a textbook on reading methods would be incomplete without discussions of syllabication and a related topic, stress or accent.

A syllable is a letter or group of letters that forms a pronunciation unit. Every syllable contains a vowel sound. In fact, a vowel sound may form a syllable by itself (a mong'). Only in a syllable that contains a diphthong is there more than one vowel sound. Diphthongs are treated as single units, although they are actually vowel blends. While each syllable has only one vowel sound or diphthong, there may be more than one vowel letter in a syllable. Letters and sounds should not be confused. For example, the word *peeve* has three vowel letters, but the only vowel sound is the long *e* sound. Therefore, *peeve* contains only one syllable.

There are two types of syllables: open syllables and closed syllables. Open syllables end in vowel sounds; closed syllables end in consonant sounds. Syllables may in turn be classified as accented (given greater stress) or unaccented (given little stress). Accent has much to do with the vowel sound that we hear in a syllable. Multisyllabic words may have primary (strongest), secondary (second strongest), and even tertiary (third strongest) accents. The vowel sound of an open accented syllable is usually long (*mī' nus, bā' sin*); the second syllable of each of these example words is unaccented, and the vowel sound represented is the schwa, often found in unaccented syllables. A

134

Teaching
Reading in
Today's
Elementary
Schools

single vowel in a closed accented syllable generally has its short sound, unless it is influenced by another sound in that syllable (*căp' sule, cär' go*).

Several useful rules concerning syllabication and accent are given below.

1. Words contain as many syllables as they have vowel sounds (counting diphthongs as a unit). Examples: *se/vere*—final *e* has no sound; *break*—*e* is not sounded; *so/lo*—both vowels are sounded; *oil*—diphthong is treated as a unit.

2. A word with more than one sounded vowel, when the first vowel is followed by two consonants, is generally divided between the two consonants. Examples: *mar/ry, tim/ber*. If the two consonants are identical, the second is not sounded.

3. Consonant blends and consonant digraphs are treated as units and are not divided. Examples: *ma/chine, a/bridge*.

4. A word with more than one sounded vowel, when the first vowel is followed by only one consonant or consonant digraph, is generally divided after the vowel. Examples: *ma/jor, ri/val* (generally long initial vowel sounds). There is, however, an abundance of exceptions to this rule, which makes it less useful. Examples: *rob/in, hab/it* (generally short initial vowel sounds).

5. When a word ends in *le* preceded by a consonant, the preceding consonant plus *le* constitutes the final syllable of the word. This syllable is never accented, and the vowel sound heard in it is the schwa. Examples: *can/dle, ta/ble*.

6. Prefixes and suffixes generally form separate syllables. Examples: *dis/taste/ful, pre/dic/tion*.

7. Some syllable divisions come between two vowels. Examples: *cru/el, qui/et*.

8. A compound word is divided between the two words that form the compound, as well as between syllables within the component words. Examples: *snow/man, thun/der/storm*.

9. Prefixes and suffixes are usually not accented. (*dis/grace' ful*)

10. Words that can be used as both verbs and nouns are accented on the second syllable when they are used as verbs and on the first syllable when they are used as nouns. (*pre/sent'*—verb; *pres' ent*—noun)

11. In two-syllable root words, the first syllable is usually accented, unless the second syllable has two vowel letters. (*rock' et, pa/rade'*)

12. Words containing three or more syllables are likely to have secondary (and perhaps tertiary) accents, as well as primary accents. (*reg' i/men/ta' tion*)

Readiness for learning syllabication includes the ability to hear syllables as pronunciation units. Teachers can have youngsters listen to words and clap for every syllable heard as early as first grade. An early written exercise on syllabication follows.

Directions: On the line following each word, write the number of syllables that the word contains. If you need to do so, say the words aloud and listen for the syllables. Pay attention to the sounds in the words. Don't let the letters fool you!

1. ruin _____
2. break _____
3. table _____
4. meaningful _____
5. middle _____
6. excitement _____
7. disagreement _____
8. human _____
9. cheese _____
10. happen _____

11. right _____
12. person _____
13. fingertip _____
14. hotel _____
15. grandmother _____
16. elephant _____
17. name _____
18. schoolhouse _____
19. scream _____
20. prepare _____ ●

Generalizations about syllabication can be taught by the same process, described earlier in this chapter, as phonic generalizations can. Present many examples of a particular generalization, and lead the children to state the generalization.

Waugh and Howell (1975) point out that in dictionaries it is the syllable divisions in the phonetic respellings, rather than the ones indicated in the boldface entry words, that are of use to students in pronouncing unfamiliar words. The divisions of the boldface entry words are a guide for hyphenations in writing, not for word pronunciation.

Accentuation is generally not taught until children have a good background in word attack skills and is often presented in conjunction with the study of the dictionary as a tool for word attack. More will be said about that in the next section of this chapter.

Dictionary Study

Dictionaries are valuable tools to use in many different kinds of reading tasks. They can help students determine pronunciations, meanings, derivations, and parts of speech for words they encounter in reading activities. They can also help with spellings of words, if children have some idea of how the word is spelled and need only to confirm the order of letters within the word. Picture dictionaries are primarily used for sight word recognition and spelling assistance. This section deals mainly with the part the dictionary plays in helping children with word recognition; discussion of the dictionary as an aid to comprehension can be found in Chapter 6.

Although the dictionary is undeniably useful in determining the pronunciation of unfamiliar words, students should turn to it only as a last resort for

136

Teaching
Reading in
Today's
Elementary
Schools

this purpose. They should consult it only after they have applied phonics and structural analysis clues along with knowledge of context clues. There are two major reasons for this. First, applying the appropriate word recognition skills immediately, without having to take the time to look up the word in the dictionary, is less of an interruption of the reader's train of thought and therefore less of a hindrance to comprehension. Second, a person does not always have a dictionary readily available; however, if he or she practices other word recognition skills, they will always be there when they are needed.

When using other word attack skills has produced no useful or clear result, a child should turn to the dictionary for help. Obviously, before a child can use the dictionary for pronunciation, he or she must be able to locate a word in it. This skill is discussed in Chapter 6.

After the child has located the word, he or she needs the following two skills to pronounce the word correctly.

Interpreting Phonetic Respellings and Accent Marks

The pronunciation key and knowledge of sounds ordinarily associated with single consonants help in interpreting phonetic respellings in dictionaries. There will be a pronunciation key somewhere on every page spread of a good dictionary. Pupils do not need to memorize the diacritical (pronunciation) markings used in a particular dictionary. Different dictionaries use different markings, and learning the markings for one could cause confusion when students are using another. The sounds ordinarily associated with relatively unvarying consonants may or may not be included in the pronunciation key. Because they are not always included, it is important for children to master a knowledge of phonics.

Here are four activities for interpretation of phonetic spellings.

ACTIVITIES

1. Have the pupils locate a particular word in their dictionaries. [Example: *cheat* (*chēt*)] Call attention to the phonetic respelling beside the entry word. Point out the location of the pronunciation key and explain its function. Have the children locate each successive sound-symbol in the key—*ch*, *ē*, *t*. (If necessary, explain why the *t* is not included in the key.) Have the children check the key word for each symbol to be sure of its sound value. Then have them blend the three sounds together to form a word. Repeat with other words. (Start with short words and gradually work up to longer ones.)

2. Code an entire paragraph or joke using phonetic respellings. Provide a pronunciation key. Let the children compete to see who can write the selection in the traditional way first. Let each child who believes he or she has done so come to your desk. Check his or her work. If it is correct, keep it and give it a number indicating the order in which it was finished. If it is incorrect, send the student

back to work on it some more. Set a time limit for the activity. This activity may be
carried out on a competitive or a noncompetitive basis.

3. Give the children a pronunciation key and let them encode messages to friends.
   Check the accuracy of each one before it is passed on to the friends to be
   decoded.
4. Use a worksheet such as the following.

● **WORSHEET:** *Pronunciation Key*

Directions: Pretend that the following list of words is part of the pronunciation key for
a dictionary. Choose the key word or words that would help you pronounce each of
the words listed below. Place the numbers of the chosen key words in the blank
beside the appropriate word.

Pronunciation Key: (1) cat, (2) āge, (3) fär, (4) sōfə, (5) sit

1. cape (cāp) _____
2. car (cär) _____
3. ago (ə/gō′) _____
4. aim (ām) _____
5. fad (fad) _____
6. race (rās) _____
7. rack (rak) _____
8. affix (ə/fiks′) _____ ●

Some words will have only one accent mark, whereas others will have
marks to show different degrees of accent within a single word. Children need
to be able to translate the accent marks into proper stress when they speak the
words. Following are two ideas for use in teaching accent marks.

● **WORKSHEET:** *Accent Marks*

Directions: Pronounce the following words and decide where the accent is placed in
each one. Indicate its placement by putting an accent mark (′) after the syllable
where you feel the accent belongs. Look up the words in the dictionary and check
your placement. Make the correction on the line to the right of the word if you were
wrong.

1. truth ful _____
2. lo co mo tion _____
3. fric tion _____
4. at ten tion _____
5. ad ven ture _____
6. peo ple _____
7. gig gle _____
8. emp ty _____
9. en e my _____
10. ge og ra phy _____ ●

● *MODEL ACTIVITY: Syllabication and Accent*

Distribute sheets of paper with a list of words such as the following ones.

(1) des' ti na' tion
(2) con' sti tu' tion
(3) hob' gob' lin
(4) mys' ti fy'
(5) pen' nant
(6) thun' der storm

Ask volunteers to read the words, applying the accents properly. When they have done so, give them a list of unfamiliar words with both accent marks and diacritical (pronunciation) marks inserted. (Lists will vary according to the ability of the children.) Once again, ask the children to read the words, applying their dictionary skills. ●

✔ Self-Check: Objective 7

Name two skills needed to enable a child to pronounce words correctly.
(See Self-Improvement Opportunity 8.)

Introducing the Dictionary

Children can be introduced to picture dictionaries as early as the first grade. They can learn how dictionaries are put together and how they function by making their own picture dictionaries. Intermediate grade pupils can develop dictionaries of special terms like *My Science Dictionary* or *My Health Dictionary.* From these they can advance to junior dictionaries. See Example 3.2 for a sample page of a junior dictionary.

Some thesauruses are also available for youngsters. Two examples are

In Other Words: A Beginning Thesaurus, by W. Cabell Greet et al. New York: Lothrop, 1969.
In Other Words: A Junior Thesaurus, by W. Cabell Greet et al. Chicago: Scott, Foresman, 1977.

WORD RECOGNITION PROCEDURE

It is helpful if children know a procedure for decoding unfamiliar words. A child may discover the word at any point in the following procedure; he or

she should then stop the procedure and continue reading. Sometimes it is necessary to try all of the steps.

Step 1. Apply context clues.
Step 2. Try sound of initial consonant, vowel, or blend along with context clues.
Step 3. Check for structure clues (prefixes, suffixes, inflectional endings, compound words, or familiar syllables).
Step 4. Begin sounding out the word using known phonics generalizations. (Go only as far as necessary to determine the word.)
Step 5. Consult the dictionary.

140

Teaching
Reading in
Today's
Elementary
Schools

A teacher may explain this five-step procedure in the following way:

1. First try to decide what word might reasonably fit in the context where you found the unfamiliar word. Ask yourself: "Will this word be a naming word? A word that describes? A word that shows action? A word that connects two ideas?" Also ask yourself: "What word will make sense in this place?" Do you have the answer? Are you sure of it? If so, continue to read. If not, go to Step 2.
2. Try the initial sound(s) along with the context clues. Does this help you decide? If you are sure that you have the word now, continue reading. If not, go to Step 3.
3. Check to see if there are familiar word parts that will help you. Does it have a prefix or suffix that you know? If this helps you decide upon the word, continue reading. If not, go to Step 4.
4. Begin sounding out the word, using all your phonics skills. If you discover the word, stop sounding and go back to your reading. If you have sounded out the whole word and it does not sound like a word you know, go to Step 5.
5. Look up the word in the dictionary. Use the pronunciation key to help you with the pronunciation of the word. If the word is one you have not heard before, check the meaning. Be sure to choose the meaning that fits the context.

A crucial point for teachers to remember is that children should not consider use of word recognition skills important *only* during reading classes. They should apply these skills whenever they encounter an unfamiliar word, whether it happens during reading class, science class, during a free reading period, or in out-of-school situations. Teachers should emphasize to their students that the procedure explained above is applicable to *any* situation in which an unfamiliar word occurs.

Test Yourself

True or False

_____ 1. It is wise to teach a single approach to word attack.
_____ 2. All word recognition skills are learned with equal ease by all children.
_____ 3. Sight words are words that readers recognize immediately without needing to resort to analysis.
_____ 4. The English language is noted for the regularity of sound-symbol associations in its written words.

_____ 5. Teaching a small store of sight words can be the first step in inaugurating an analytic approach to phonics instruction.

_____ 6. Early choices for sight words to be taught should be words that are extremely useful and meaningful.

_____ 7. Games with complex rules are good ones to use for practice with sight words.

_____ 8. Most practice with sight words should involve the words in context.

_____ 9. If teachers teach phonics well, they do not need to bother with other word recognition skills.

_____ 10. Consonant letters are more consistent in the sounds they represent than vowel letters are.

_____ 11. Phonics generalizations often have numerous exceptions.

_____ 12. It is impossible to teach too many phonics rules, since these rules are extremely valuable in decoding unfamiliar words.

_____ 13. In a word that has only one vowel letter at the end of the word, the vowel letter usually represents its long sound.

_____ 14. It is wise to teach only one phonics generalization at a time.

_____ 15. Structural analysis skills include the ability to recognize prefixes and suffixes.

_____ 16. The addition of a prefix to a root word can change the meaning.

_____ 17. Inflectional endings can change the tense of a verb.

_____ 18. The apostrophe in a contraction indicates possession or ownership.

_____ 19. Every syllable contains a vowel sound.

_____ 20. There is only one vowel letter in each syllable.

_____ 21. Open syllables end in consonant sounds.

_____ 22. The vowel sound in an open accented syllable is usually long.

_____ 23. The schwa sound is often found in unaccented syllables.

_____ 24. When dividing words into syllables, we treat consonant blends and consonant digraphs as units and do not divide them.

_____ 25. Prefixes and suffixes generally form separate syllables.

_____ 26. Prefixes and suffixes are usually accented.

_____ 27. Picture clues are the most useful word recognition clues for sixth-grade pupils.

_____ 28. A comparison or contrast found in printed material may offer a clue to the identity of an unfamiliar word.

_____ 29. Context clues used in isolation provide only educated guesses about the identities of unfamiliar words.

_____ 30. Children should be expected to memorize the diacritical markings used in their dictionaries.

_____ 31. Accent marks indicate which syllables are stressed.

_____ 32. Some words have more than one accented syllable.

_____ 33. Another term meaning short vowel sound is "unglided" vowel sound.

142

Teaching
Reading in
Today's
Elementary
Schools

_____ 34. Writing new words is helpful to some learners in building sight vocabulary.

_____ 35. The language experience approach is good for developing sight vocabulary.

_____ 36. One method of teaching sight words is best for all students.

Multiple Choice

_____ 1. In the word *myth* the *y*
   a. has the characteristics of a vowel.
   b. is silent.
   c. has the characteristics of a consonant.

_____ 2. When it occurs in the initial position in a syllable, the letter *w*
   a. stands for a vowel sound.
   b. is silent.
   c. stands for a consonant sound.

_____ 3. In the word *strong*, the letters *str*
   a. represent a consonant blend.
   b. are silent.
   c. represent a single sound.

_____ 4. Consonant digraphs
   a. represent two blended speech sounds.
   b. represent a single speech sound.
   c. are always silent.

_____ 5. The word *sheep* is made up of
   a. five sounds.
   b. four sounds.
   c. three sounds.

_____ 6. In the word *boat,* the *oa* is
   a. a vowel digraph.
   b. a diphthong.
   c. a blend.

_____ 7. In the word *boy,* the *oy* is
   a. a vowel digraph.
   b. a consonant digraph.
   c. a diphthong.

_____ 8. The word *diphthong* contains
   a. three consonant blends.
   b. three consonant digraphs.
   c. a consonant digraph and two consonant blends.

_____ 9. In the word *know,* the *ow* is
   a. a diphthong.
   b. a vowel digraph.
   c. a consonant blend.

_____ 10. In the word *his,* the letter *s* has the sound usually associated with the letter
    a. *s.*
    b. *z.*
    c. *sh.*

_____ 11. When the inflectional ending *ed* follows the letter *d* or the letter *t,* the *e* is
    a. sounded.
    b. silent.
    c. long.

_____ 12. In the word *helped,* the *d*
    a. is silent.
    b. has the sound of *d.*
    c. has the sound of *t.*

_____ 13. In the word *canned,* the *d*
    a. is silent.
    b. has the sound of *d.*
    c. has the sound of *t.*

_____ 14. Which type of accent mark indicates the heaviest emphasis?
    a. primary
    b. secondary
    c. tertiary

Vocabulary

Check your knowledge of these terms. Reread parts of the chapter if necessary.

analytic approach to phonics instruction	irregularly spelled words	syntactic clues
derivatives	phonics	synthetic approach to phonics instruction
homographs	semantic clues	variants
inflectional endings	sight words	word configuration
	structural analysis	

Also check your knowledge of words in the section entitled "Terminology," which is part of the discussion on phonics.

Self-Improvement Opportunities

1. Compare the Dolch List of 220 Service Words and the Dolch List of 95 Picture Words with the words found in the preprimers and primers of a

144

Teaching
Reading in
Today's
Elementary
Schools

contemporary basal reading series. Are the words on the Dolch lists still high-usage words, even though the lists were compiled many years ago?

2. Plan exercises for presenting the words on a basic sight word list in context; many of these are function words and have meanings that are hard for the child to conceptualize. For example, *for* and *which* produce no easy images, but a child would understand the following sentences:

> I bought this *for* you.
>
> *Which* one is mine?

Try your exercises in a classroom if you have the opportunity.

3. React to the following statement: "Going back to teaching basic phonics skills will cure all of our country's reading ills."

4. Make arrangements to observe a phonics lesson in which the teacher uses the synthetic approach and another lesson in which the teacher uses the analytic approach. Evaluate the two approaches. Be sure you evaluate the methods rather than the instructors.

5. Look up references related to the controversy concerning the value of teaching syllabication as part of a word recognition program. Prepare a paper on this topic.

6. React to the following statement: "I do not believe in teaching children to use context clues. It just produces a group of guessers."

7. Compile a list of words whose pronunciation depends upon the context. Plan a lesson for presenting some of these words to a group of youngsters in the grade level of your choice.

8. Compare the dictionary pronunciations of the following words in old and new dictionaries and in dictionaries published by different companies. Analyze the differences among diacritical markings. Use the words *gypsy, ready, lecture, away, ask, believe, baker,* and *care.*

9. Gather the necessary material and construct a skill-development game for some aspect of word recognition.

Bibliography

Ashton-Warner, Sylvia.   *Teacher.* New York: Simon and Schuster, 1963.

Bailey, Mildred Hart.   "The Utility of Phonic Generalizations in Grades One Through Six." *The Reading Teacher* 20 (February 1967): 413–18.

Burmeister, Lou E.   "Usefulness of Phonic Generalizations." *The Reading Teacher* 21 (January 1968): 349–56, 360.

Carnine, Douglas W.   "Phonics Versus Look-Say: Transfer to New Words." *The Reading Teacher* 30 (March 1977): 636–40.

Ceprano, Maria A.   "A Review of Selected Research on Methods of Teaching Sight Words." *The Reading Teacher* 35 (December 1981): 314–22.

Clymer, Theodore.   "The Utility of Phonics Generalizations in the Primary Grades." *The Reading Teacher* 16 (January 1963): 252–58.

Cordts, Anna D.   *Phonics for the Reading Teacher.* New York: Holt, Rinehart and Winston, 1965.

Culyer, Richard.   "How to Develop a Locally-Relevant Basic Sight Word List." *The Reading Teacher* 35 (February 1982): 596–97.

Downing, John.   "How Children Think About Reading." In *Psychological Factors in the Teaching of Reading,* Eldon E. Ekwall, comp. Columbus, Ohio: Charles E. Merrill, 1973, pp. 43–58.

Ekwall, Eldon E., comp.   *Psychological Factors in the Teaching of Reading.* Columbus, Ohio: Charles E. Merrill, 1973.

Emans, Robert.   "The Usefulness of Phonic Generalizations Above the Primary Grades." *The Reading Teacher* 20 (February 1967): 419–25.

Fry, Edward.   *Elementary Reading Instruction.* New York: McGraw-Hill, 1977.

Glass, Gerald G.   "The Strange World of Syllabication." *The Elementary School Journal* 67 (May 1967): 403–405.

Hood, Joyce.   "Why We Burned Our Basic Sight Vocabulary Cards." *The Reading Teacher* 27 (March 1972): 579–82.

Jenkins, Barbara L., et al.   "Children's Use of Hypothesis Testing When Decoding Words." *The Reading Teacher* 33 (March 1980): 664.

Johnson, Dale D.   "Suggested Sequences for Presenting Four Categories of Letter-Sound Correspondence." *Elementary English* 50 (September 1973): 888–96.

Jolly, Hayden B., Jr.   "Teaching Basic Function Words." *The Reading Teacher* 35 (November 1981): 136–40.

Jones, Linda L.   "An Interactive View of Reading: Implications for the Classroom." *The Reading Teacher* 35 (April 1982): 775.

Meltzer, Nancy S., and Robert Herse.   "The Boundaries of Written Words as Seen by First Graders." *Journal of Reading Behavior* I (Summer 1969): 3–14.

Rosso, Barbara Rak, and Robert Emans.   "Children's Use of Phonic Generalizations." *The Reading Teacher* 34 (March 1981): 653–57.

Schell, Leo M.   "Teaching Decoding to Remedial Readers." *Journal of Reading* 31 (May 1978): 878.

Tovey, Duane R.   "Children's Grasp of Phonics Terms vs. Sound-Symbol Relationships." *The Reading Teacher* 33 (January 1980): 431–37.

Waugh, R. P., and K. W. Howell.   "Teaching Modern Syllabication." *The Reading Teacher* 29 (October 1975): 20–25.

Suggested Readings

Crutchfield, Marjorie.   *Individualized Reading: A Guide for Teaching Word Analysis Skills.* Los Angeles: Gramercy Press, 1975.

Cunningham, Patricia M.   "A Compare/Contrast Theory of Mediated Word Identification," *The Reading Teacher* 32 (April 1979): 774–78.

146
Teaching
Reading in
Today's
Elementary
Schools

Cunningham, Patricia M. "Decoding Polysyllabic Words: An Alternative Strategy." *The Reading Teacher* 21 (April 1978): 608–14.

Dahl, Patricia R., and S. Jay Samuels. "Teaching Children to Read Using Hypothesis/Test Strategies." *The Reading Teacher* 30 (March 1977): 603–606.

Dallman, Martha, et al. *The Teaching of Reading.* 6th ed. New York: Holt, Rinehart and Winston, 1982, Chapters 6A and 6B.

Durkin, Dolores. *Phonics, Linguistics, and Reading.* New York: Teachers College Press, Columbia University, 1972.

Durkin, Dolores. *Teaching Them to Read.* 3rd ed. Boston: Allyn and Bacon, 1978, Chapters 8, 9, 11, and 12.

Freshour, Frank W. *Word Recognition Skills for Teachers of Reading.* 2nd ed. Minneapolis: Burgess, 1977.

Fry, Edward. *Elementary Reading Instruction.* New York: McGraw-Hill, 1977, Chapters 2, 3, and 4.

Harris, Larry, and Carl B. Smith. *Reading Instruction Through Diagnostic Teaching in the Classroom.* 3rd ed. New York: Holt, Rinehart and Winston, 1980, Chapters 8, 9, and 10.

Heilman, Arthur W. *Phonics in Proper Perspective.* 4th ed. Columbus, Ohio: Charles E. Merrill, 1981.

Heilman, Arthur W., et al. *Principles and Practices of Teaching Reading.* 5th ed. Columbus, Ohio: Charles E. Merrill, 1981, Chapters 6 and 7.

Hull, Marion A. *Phonics for the Teacher of Reading.* 3rd ed. Columbus, Ohio: Charles E. Merrill, 1981.

Ives, Josephine P., et al. *Word Identification Techniques.* Boston: Houghton Mifflin, 1979.

Karlin, Robert. *Teaching Elementary Reading: Principles and Strategies.* 3rd ed. New York: Harcourt Brace Jovanovich, 1980, Chapter 6.

Kennedy, Eddie C. *Methods in Teaching Developmental Reading.* 2nd ed. Itasca, Ill.: Peacock, 1981, Chapters 7 and 8.

Lamb, Pose M., and Richard D. Arnold. *Reading: Foundations and Instructional Strategies.* Belmont, Calif.: Wadsworth, 1976, Chapter 10.

Lapp, Diane, and James Flood. *Teaching Reading to Every Child.* New York: Macmillan, 1978, Chapters 7 and 8.

Miller, Wilma H. *The First R: Elementary Reading Today.* 2nd ed. New York: Holt, Rinehart and Winston, 1977.

Olson, Joanne P., and Martha H. Dillner. *Learning to Teach Reading in the Elementary School: Utilizing a Competency Based Instructional System.* 2nd ed. New York: Macmillan, 1982, Chapters 2 and 15.

Ransom, Grayce A. *Preparing to Teach Reading.* Boston: Little, Brown, 1978, Chapters 8 and 9.

Schell, Leo M. *Fundamentals of Decoding for Teachers.* 2nd ed. Boston: Houghton Mifflin Company, 1980.

Spache, George D., and Evelyn B. Spache. *Reading in the Elementary School.* 4th ed. Boston: Allyn and Bacon, 1977, Chapters 11 and 12.

CHAPTER 4

Comprehension

Introduction

The objective of all readers is, or should be, comprehension of what they read. This chapter discusses how to achieve that comprehension through background information and important comprehension skills, suggests methods of developing those skills, and points out techniques for ascertaining how well children have comprehended. It explores comprehension from two angles: the written units that a child must understand and the different levels of comprehension that he or she should achieve. As David Pearson and Dale Johnson have pointed out, "reading comprehension is at once a unitary process and a set of discrete processes" (1978, p. 227). We discuss the individual processes separately, yet teachers must not lose sight of the fact that there are many overlaps and many interrelationships among the processes. There are even close relationships between comprehension and decoding. Research has shown, as Maryann Eads (1981) has pointed out, that good comprehenders are able to decode quickly and accurately. Thus, developing decoding skills to the automatic stage seems to be important. However, teachers should always keep in mind that decoding skills are merely a means of understanding the written material.

The content of this chapter is particularly important in view of some recent research findings. Dolores Durkin (1978–79) and her associates observed fourth-grade classrooms chosen by principals as exemplary to determine how much time teachers spend on instruction in reading comprehension. They found that less than one percent of instructional time was taken up by such instruction, while children spent a great deal of time on noninstructional activities such as answering questions in writing and completing workbook pages. In general, teachers spent more time on testing comprehension than on teaching. They often just mentioned a skill, saying just enough about it to justify making a related assignment. In another study Durkin (1981) discovered that teacher's manuals for basal reading series did not always make adequate suggestions for teaching comprehension; instead, they emphasized practice and assessment activities and often only briefly described instructional procedures. This finding underscores the need for teachers to know a great deal about comprehension instruction, for they cannot depend completely on guidance from teacher's manuals.

Setting Objectives

When you finish this chapter, you should be able to

1. Explain what schema theory has to say about reading comprehension.
2. Describe how context clues can aid in determining meanings of unfamiliar words.

3. Explain how you can help a child use the dictionary to find the particular meaning of a word that fits the context.
4. Name some problems that homophones and homographs can cause, and tell how you can help children understand synonyms and antonyms.
5. Explain how to help pupils understand the meanings of sentences.
6. Suggest some ways to teach children to recognize main ideas of varied types of paragraphs.
7. Describe some ways in which selections are organized.
8. Describe ways to promote reading for literal meanings.
9. Discuss some of the things a critical reader must know.
10. Explain what "creative reading" means.
11. Explain how to construct questions that will check depth of comprehension.

BACKGROUND INFORMATION

Educators have long believed that if a reader has not been exposed to the language patterns that a writer uses or the objects and concepts to which a writer refers, his or her comprehension will at best be incomplete. This belief is supported by recent theories that hold that reading comprehension involves relating textual information to pre-existing knowledge structures, or schemata (Pearson et al., 1979). "These schemata represent generic knowledge, that is, what is believed to be generally true, based on experience, of a class of objects, actions, or situations" (Hacker, 1980, p. 867). Each of our schemata is incomplete, as though it contained empty slots that could be filled with information collected from new experiences. Reading of informational material is aided by the existing schemata and also fills in some of the empty slots in them (Durkin, 1981).

Some research studies have supported this theory. For instance, Anderson, Reynolds, Schallert, and Goetz "found that recall and comprehension of passages which invited two schematic interpretations (wrestling versus a prison break or card-playing versus a music rehearsal) were highly related to the background knowledge of the readers and/or environment in which the testing occurred" (Pearson et al., 1979, p. 3). Bransford and Johnson discovered that college students' recall of obscure passages was increased if a statement of the topic for the passage or a picture related to it was provided.

A study by Pearson and others (1979) focused on younger students (second graders), who were tested on their background knowledge of spiders, given a selection about spiders to read, and then given a posttest including questions to elicit both implicit (implied) and explicit (directly stated) information. The researchers found that background knowledge had more effect on understanding of implied than on explicit information. Such studies suggest that the prior development of background information is likely to enhance reading

150

Teaching
Reading in
Today's
Elementary
Schools

comprehension, especially inferential comprehension. Kathleen Stevens (1982) found similar results among ninth graders reading about topics of which they had high and low levels of prior knowledge. She then provided tenth graders with background information about a topic before reading and discovered that their reading on that topic was improved.

Although these studies did not all involve elementary school children, they indicate that teachers should plan experiences that will help children to understand written material that they are expected to read. Such background material will assist them in choosing appropriate schemata to apply to the reading. The prediction strategies in a directed reading–thinking activity (described in Chapter 7) may help set up such schemata, as may the preview step of the SQ3R study method (described in Chapter 6) (Hacker, 1980) and the purpose questions of the directed reading activity (described in Chapter 5).

Teachers need to find out whether a child lacks the necessary schemata or possesses them but cannot use them effectively when reading (Jones, 1982). If the child lacks the schemata, the teacher should plan direct and vicarious experiences to build them, such as examining and discussing pictures that reveal information about the subject, introducing new terminology related to the subject, and taking field trips or watching demonstrations. If children already know about the subject, letting them share their knowledge, preview the material to be read, and predict what might happen can be helpful (Jones, 1982).

Marcia Sheridan has pointed out that research on schemata provides evidence of the holistic nature of comprehension. Although she acknowledges that educators will still need to teach reading skills, Sheridan believes that schema theory has made the overlapping nature of those skills more apparent. Along with many others in the field of reading education, she hopes that the teaching of skills in isolation will cease through the application of schema research (Lange, 1981). Teachers should always approach comprehension skills by emphasizing their application in actual reading of connected discourse. One way to accomplish this is to relate the skills to whole selections in which students can apply the skills immediately after learning about and practicing them with less complex material. Another way is to stress the relationships of the various skills (for example, point out that details are the building blocks used to recognize main ideas and that following directions necessitates integrating the skills of recognizing details and detecting sequence).

Rand Spiro (1979) and his colleagues have conducted studies that indicate that readers vary in the relative degrees to which they emphasize two processes of comprehension. Text-based processes are those in which the reader is primarily trying to extract information from the text. Knowledge-based processes are those in which the reader primarily brings prior knowledge and experiences to bear on the interpretation of the material. For example, consider this text: "The children were gathered around a table upon which sat a beautiful cake with *Happy Birthday* written on it. Mrs. Jones said, 'Now Maria, make a wish and blow out the candles.'" Readers must use a text-based process to answer the question "What did the cake have written on it?" because the information is directly stated in the material. They must use a knowledge-based process to answer the question "Whose birthday was it?" Prior experience will provide them with the answer, "Maria," because they have consistently seen candles blown out by the child who has the birthday at parties they have attended. Of course, before they use the knowledge-based process they have to use a text-based process to discover that Maria was told to blow out the candles.

151
Comprehension

Skilled readers may employ one type of process more than the other when the situation allows them to do this without affecting their comprehension. Less able readers may tend to rely too much on one type of processing, with the result of poorer comprehension. Unfortunately, some students have the idea that knowledge-based processing is not an appropriate reading activity, so that they fail to use knowledge they have.

Richard Rystrom presents a good argument that reading cannot be exclusively knowledge-based, or "top down": if it were, two people reading the same material would rarely arrive at the same conclusions, and the probability that a person could learn anything from written material would be slight. He has an equally convincing argument that reading is not exclusively text-based, or "bottom up": if it were, then all people who read a written selection would agree about its meaning. It is far more likely that reading is interactive, involving both information supplied by the text and information brought to the text by the reader, which combine to produce a person's understanding of the material (Strange, 1980).

✔ Self-Check: Objective 1
What aspects of schema theory have direct application to the teaching of reading?

UNITS OF COMPREHENSION

The basic comprehension units in reading are words, sentences, paragraphs, and whole selections. These units combine to form all written material children encounter.

Words

In Chapter 3 we referred to the importance of decoding words and developing a sight vocabulary, but these abilities have little value if students do not understand the words. Children's sight vocabularies should be built from words they already comprehend, words that are a part of their meaning vocabularies. This section is concerned with the development of extensive

152

Teaching
Reading in
Today's
Elementary
Schools

meaning vocabularies and the difficulties that certain types of words may present to youngsters.

The growth of vocabulary is essentially the development of labels for the child's schemata. Because students must call upon their existing schemata to comprehend, vocabulary development is an important component of comprehension skill (Jones, 1982).

It is difficult to pinpoint the age at which children learn the precise meanings of words. They first learn to differentiate between antonyms (opposites), making more discriminating responses as they grow older. Sometimes they overgeneralize about word meanings: for example, once a very young child learns the word *car,* he or she may apply it to any motor vehicle, making no discrimination between cars and trucks or other kinds of vehicles. Carol Chomsky's research has shown that some children as old as nine years have trouble distinguishing between the meanings of *ask* and *tell,* as well as between other words—a finding in congruence with Piaget's discovery that some children as old as ten years had not yet differentiated between the words *brother* and *boy* and the words *sister* and *girl* (McConaughy, 1978). As children mature they learn more about choosing specific words.

Eve Clark has indicated that words can be broken down into semantic features, or smaller components of meaning, which a child learns in order to develop understanding of words. When a child first uses a word, he or she may be aware of only one or two of its semantic features and therefore may use it incorrectly—for example, calling all birds *ducks.* As the child develops the meaning of the word more fully, he or she narrows down application of the word to the correct category—for example, adding the feature of webbed feet to eliminate robins from the *duck* category.

Clark has predicted that in order to recognize the overlapping meanings of synonyms, a child has to learn the semantic features of each word separately. Clark represents the features with positive (+) and negative (−) indicators. For example, children first find the word *before* to be related to time (+ time) and later to be related to sequence of time (− simultaneous). Finally, they add the feature that distinguishes *before* from *after* (+ prior). The semantic-features theory even explains figurative usage, such as metaphor. In this case, the child chooses only specific semantic features in the particular context; a "blanket of snow" would utilize the covering feature of a blanket and a snowfall.

Emotional reactions to words can also be expressed as semantic features. All readers do not develop the same emotional features for the same word, because of their varied backgrounds (McConaughy, 1978).

Children increase their vocabularies at a rapid rate during the elementary school years. It has been estimated that the typical child increases his or her vocabulary at a rate of about 1,000 words a year in the primary grades and 2,000 words a year in the intermediate grades, and some suggest that the rate

is even higher. While estimates vary, they do reflect the general trend of a
growing vocabulary with increasing age.

153
Comprehension

Vocabulary building is a complex process involving many kinds of words: *double function* words (psychological characteristics of persons and physical characteristics of objects such as *sweet*); abstract definitions; *homophones* (She will take the *plane* to Lexington. He has on *plain* trousers.); *homographs* (I will *read* the newspaper. I have *read* the magazine.); *synonyms* (Marty was *sad* about leaving. Marty was *unhappy* about leaving.); and *antonyms* (Bill is a *slow* runner. Mary is a *fast* runner.). Children must also acquire meanings for a number of relational terms, such as *same, more, less, different, taller/shorter, older/younger, higher/lower,* and so on.

Teachers can approach vocabulary instruction in a variety of ways. A researcher found that a context method (requiring students to read a new word in meaningful contexts and apply the word based on their own experiences) was more effective for teaching vocabulary than an association method (pairing an unknown word with a familiar synonym), a category method (requiring students to add to a list of words in a category), or a dictionary method (looking up the word, writing a definition, and using it in a sentence) (Gipe, 1980). The most important aspect of the context method may be that after the students derive the meaning of the word from a variety of contexts, including a definition context, they then *apply* the word to their own personal experiences in a written response.

Although this method may often have advantages, other ways of improving vocabulary have also produced good results, and teachers should be familiar with several different approaches. Four of the most common methods for teachers to help children discover the meanings of unfamiliar words are discussed below.

Context Clues

We discussed use of context clues to help recognize words that are familiar in speech but not in print in Chapter 3. Context clues can also key the meaning of an unfamiliar word by directly defining the word, providing an appositive, or comparing or contrasting the word with a known word. For example:

A *democracy* is a government run by the people being governed. (definition)

He made an effort to *alleviate,* or relieve, the child's pain until the doctor arrived. (appositive)

Rather than encountering hostile Indians, as they had expected, many settlers found the Indians to be *amicable.* (contrast)

Context can also offer clues in different sentences from that in which the new word is found, so children should be encouraged to read surrounding

154

Teaching
Reading in
Today's
Elementary
Schools

sentences for clues to meaning. Sometimes an entire paragraph embodies the explanation of a term, as in the following example:

> I've told you before that measles are *contagious*! When Johnny had the measles, Beatrice played with him one afternoon, and soon Beatrice broke out with them. Joey caught them from her, and now you tell me you have been to Joey's house. I imagine you'll be sorry when you break out with the measles and have to miss the party on Saturday.

When introducing new words in context, teachers should use sentences that students can relate to their own experiences and that have only one unfamiliar word. It is best not to use the new word at the very beginning of the sentence, since the children will not have had any of the facilitating context before they encounter it (Duffelmeyer, 1982).

Teachers can have students apply context clues fruitfully in conjunction with other kinds of clues, which are discussed below.

✔ Self-Check: Objective 2

Discuss different ways in which context clues can help key the meanings of unfamiliar words.

(See Self-Improvement Opportunity 2.)

Structure Clues

Structural analysis, discussed in Chapter 3 as a word recognition skill, can also be used as an aid in discovering meanings of unknown words. Knowing meanings of common affixes and combining them with meanings of familiar root words can help pupils determine the meanings of many new words. For example, if a child knows the meaning of *joy* and knows that the suffix *-ous* means *full of,* he or she can conclude that the word *joyous* means *full of joy.* Students can often determine meanings of compound words by relating the meanings of the component parts to each other (*watchman* means a *man* who *watches*).

Children begin to learn about word structure very early. First they deal with words in their simplest, most basic forms, as morphemes, the smallest units of *meaning* in a language. The word *cat* is one morpheme. If an *s* is added to form the plural, *cats,* the final *s* is also a morpheme, since it changes the word's meaning. There are two classes of morphemes, distinguished by function: *free* morphemes, which have independent meaning and can be used by themselves (*cat, man, son*), and *bound* morphemes, which must be combined with another morpheme in order to have meaning. Affixes and inflectional endings are bound morphemes; the *er* in *singer* is an example.

Worksheets can help children see how prefixes and suffixes change meanings of words. An example is shown.

● **WORKSHEET:** *Prefix* un-

Directions: The word *unhappy* is made up of the prefix *un-* and the root word *happy*. The prefix *un-* means *not*, so the word *unhappy* means *not happy*. Write the meanings for each of the following words on the lines beside the words.

1. unable _____
2. unbelievable _____
3. undeserving _____
4. undesirable _____

5. untrue _____
6. unused _____
7. unavailable _____
8. unappreciated _____ ●

Worksheets such as the one that follows can offer practice in determining meanings of compound words.

● **WORKSHEET:** *Compound Words*

Directions: Using the meanings of the two words that make up each of the compound words below, write a definition for each word on the line beside it.

1. snowfall _____
2. coverall _____
3. doorstop _____
4. driveway _____
5. bookcase _____
6. bedroom _____ ●

Analogies and Word Lines

Analogies compare two similar relationships and thereby bolster word knowledge. Educators may teach analogies by displaying examples of categories, relationships, and analogies; asking guiding questions about the examples; allowing students to discuss the questions; and applying the ideas that emerge (Bellows, 1980).

Students may need help in grouping items into categories and understanding relationships among items. For example, the teacher might write *nickel, dime,* and *quarter* on the board and ask, "How are these things related? What name could you give the entire group of items?" (Answer: *money.*) Teachers can use pictures instead of words in the primary grades; in either case, they might ask students to apply the skill by naming other things that would fit the

156

Teaching
Reading in
Today's
Elementary
Schools

category (*penny* and *dollar*). Or the teacher could write *painter* and *brush* and ask, "What is the relationship between the two items?" (Answer: *A painter uses a brush to work.*) Teachers should remember to simplify their language for discussions with young children, and to have students give other examples of the relationship (*butcher* and *knife*). After working through many examples such as these, the students should be ready for examples of simple analogies, such as "Light is to dark as day is to night," "Glove is to hand as sock is to foot," "Round is to ball as square is to block." Students can discuss how analogies work—"How are the first two things related? How are the second two things related? How are these relationships alike?" They can then complete incomplete analogies, such as "Teacher is to classroom as pilot is to _____." Younger children should do this orally; older ones can understand the standard shorthand form of *come : go : : live : die* if they are taught to read ":" as *is to* and ": :" as *as* (Bellows, 1980). Once children are familiar with analogies, they can use worksheets such as the following in class.

● **WORKSHEET:** *Analogies*

Directions: Fill in the blanks with words that complete the same relationship in the second word pair that was indicated in the first word pair.

1. hot is to cold as black is to _____.
2. milk is to drink as steak is to _____.
3. toe is to foot as finger is to _____
4. blue is to blew as red is to _____
5. coat is to coats as mouse is to _____
6. up is to down as top is to _____ ●

Teachers may use word lines to show the relationships among words, just as they use number lines for numbers. Arrange related words on a graduated line that emphasizes their relationships—for young children, use pictures and words to match or ask them to locate or produce appropriate pictures. Ask upper-grade students to arrange a specified list of words on a word line themselves. Word lines can concretely show antonym, synonym, and degree analogies, as in this example:

| enormous | large | medium | small | tiny |

Analogies that students could develop include "enormous is to large as small is to tiny" (synonym); "enormous is to tiny as large is to small" (antonym);

Vocabulary instruction should be interesting and varied, focusing on such factors as context clues, structural analysis, and study of etymology. (© Sybil Shelton/Peter Arnold)

and "large is to medium as medium is to small" (degree). Challenge children to make their own word lines and analogies (Macey, 1981).

Dictionary Use

We know that the dictionary is an excellent source to use in discovering meanings of unfamiliar words, particularly for determining the appropriate meanings of words that have multiple definitions or specific, technical definitions. In some instances children may be familiar with several common meanings of a word, but not with a specialized meaning found in a content area textbook. For example, a child may understand a reference to a *base* in a baseball game but not a discussion of a military *base* (social studies material), a *base* that turns litmus paper blue (science material), or *base* motives of a character (literature). Words that have the greatest number of different meanings are frequently very common, such as *run* or *bank.*

Teachers should instruct children to consider the context surrounding a word, to read the different dictionary definitions, and to choose the definition that makes most sense in the context. Students will have to practice this

158

Teaching
Reading in
Today's
Elementary
Schools

activity because they will have a strong tendency to read only the first dictionary definition and try to force it into the context.

Give children help in developing this skill through activities such as the ones below.

● **WORKSHEET:** *Appropriate Dictionary Definitions*

Directions: Find the dictionary definition of *sharp* that fits each of the sentences below. Write the appropriate definition on the line following each sentence.

1. Katherine's knife was very sharp. _____

_____

2. There is a sharp curve in the road up ahead. _____

_____

3. Sam is a sharp businessman. That's why he has been so successful. _____

_____

4. I hope that when I am seventy my mind is as sharp as my grandmother's is.

_____

5. We are leaving at two o'clock sharp. _____

_____ ●

● **WORKSHEET:** *Multiple Meanings of Words*

Directions: Some words mean different things in textbooks from what they mean in everyday conversation. In each of the following sentences, find the special meanings for the words and write these meanings on the lines provided.

1. Frederick Smith has decided to *run* for mayor. _____

_____

2. The park was near the *mouth* of the Little Bear River. _____

_____

3. The management of the company was unable to avert a *strike*. _____

_____

4. That song is hard to sing because of the high *pitch* of several notes. _____

_____

5. That numeral is written in *base* two. _____

_____ ●

When using activities that involve worksheets or workbooks, teachers should go over the pages with the children after they have completed their work and discuss reasons for right and wrong responses.

Students can also use dictionaries to study etymology, the origin and history of words. The origin of a word is often given in brackets after the phonetic respelling (although not all dictionaries do this in the same way), and archaic or obsolete definitions are frequently given and labeled so that pupils can see how words have changed. Older students may be introduced to the *Oxford English Dictionary,* whereas younger children may appreciate such sources as *The First Book of Words,* by S. Epstein and B. Epstein (New York: Franklin Watts, 1954), or *They Gave Their Names,* by Richard A. Boning (Baldwin, N.Y.: Barnell Loft, 1971).

✔ Self-Check: Objective 3

What must children remember when using the dictionary to discover the meanings of unfamiliar words?
(See Self-Improvement Opportunity 1.)

Special Words

Special types of words, such as the ones mentioned below, need to be given careful attention.

Homophones   Homophones (also known as *homonyms*) can trouble young readers because they are spelled differently but pronounced the same way. Some common homophones are

I want to *be* a doctor.
That *bee* almost stung me.

She has *two* brothers.
Will you go *to* the show with me?
I have *too* much work to do.

I can *hear* the bird singing.
Maurice, you sit over *here.*

That is the only *course* they could take.
The jacket was made from *coarse* material.

Mark has a *red* scarf.
Have you *read* that book?

I *ate* all of my supper.
We have *eight* dollars to spend.

ACTIVITIES

1. Have children play a card game to work on meanings of homophones. Print homophones on cards and let the children take turns drawing from each other, as in the game of Old Maid. When a child has a pair of homophones, he or she can put them down if he or she can give a correct sentence using each word. The child who claims the most pairs wins.

160

Teaching
Reading in
Today's
Elementary
Schools

2. Have the children play a game called Homophone Hunt, in which they are given a list of words for which they are to locate as many homophones as possible. Some words to use follow:

be	one
beat	pain
dear	pair
eight	peace
fair	red
hair	road
hall	sea
hour	sum
knew	sun
knight	tale
made	waste
mail	way

Homographs Homographs are words that have identical spellings but not the same meanings. Their pronunciations may or may not be the same. Readers must use context clues to identify the correct pronunciations, parts of speech, and meanings of homographs. Examples include:

I will *read* my newspaper. (pronounced *rēd*)
I have *read* my newspaper. (pronounced *rĕd*)

I have a *contract* signed by the president. (noun: pronounced *cŏn' trăkt;* means a document)
I didn't know it would *contract* as it cooled. (verb: pronounced *cən/trăkt';* means to reduce in size)

Synonyms Synonyms are words that have the same or very similar meanings. Work with synonyms can help expand children's vocabularies.

ACTIVITIES

1. Provide a stimulus word and have the pupils find as many synonyms as they can.
2. Use a worksheet like the following one:

● *WORKSHEET: Synonyms*

Directions: Rewrite each sentence, substituting a synonym for the word in italics.

1. Gretchen had a *big* dog.
2. We *hurried* to the scene of the fire.
3. Will you *ask* him about the job?
4. I have *almost* enough money to buy the bicycle.
5. Curtis made an *error* on his paper.

6. Suzanne is a *fast* runner.
7. It was a *frightening* experience.
8. Marty was *sad* about leaving. ●

Antonyms Antonyms are two words that have opposite meanings from each other. Working with antonyms will also expand students' vocabularies. Exercises similar to the ones mentioned for use with synonyms can be used with antonyms, as can the one below.

● **WORKSHEET:** *Antonyms*

Directions: Draw lines connecting the words in Column A with their antonyms in Column B.

Column A	*Column B*
slow	small
big	skinny
weak	young
fat	fast
ugly	pretty
old	strong ●

New Words New words are constantly being coined to meet the new needs of society and are possible sources of difficulty. Have students search for such words in their reading and television viewing and then compile a dictionary of words so new that they are not yet in standard dictionaries. The class may have to discuss these words to derive an accurate definition for each one, considering all the contexts in which the students have heard or seen it (Koeller and Khan, 1981).

Additional Vocabulary Development

This section focuses on clarifying meanings of words in print; however, teachers should use every opportunity to expand children's listening and speaking vocabularies. Understanding printed materials depends upon a knowledge of word meanings. The teacher's responsibility includes both a quantitative and a qualitative approach to vocabulary. Here are some more ways to develop vocabularies.

ACTIVITIES

1. Provide firsthand experiences (field trips, excursions, and other concrete experiences that permit children to associate words with real situations) and elicit oral and written accounts and descriptions of them as a follow-up.

162

Teaching
Reading in
Today's
Elementary
Schools

Vicarious experiences, including storytelling and oral reading, are a good substitute when concrete experiences are not possible.

2. Use audiovisual aids and printed materials to illustrate words that students have encountered in reading and to suggest other words. Filmstrips, records, television, thesauruses, children's dictionaries, and trade books about words (such as *Words from the Myths,* by Isaac Asimov, Boston: Houghton Mifflin, 1961) are useful sources.

3. To help students master the concepts in every subject area, carefully develop vocabulary to make sure that students understand the specialized or technical words they encounter. Vocabulary building of this type should take place throughout the school day, not just during reading class.

4. Encourage variety in word choice and exactness in expressing thoughts both verbally and in writing.

5. When you read aloud or give explanations to the class, discuss new words you use and encourage the children to use them too. Your oral language has a definite effect on the growth of students' vocabularies. If you use and explain appropriate words, even if they are unfamiliar to the children, you have provided a first step toward students' incorporating these terms into their vocabularies.

6. Help children understand the different ways in which words can be formed—for instance, portmanteau words, such as *smog* (from *smoke* and *fog*); acronyms, such as radar (from the phrase "*ra*dio *d*etecting *a*nd *r*anging"); abbreviated words, such as *phone* (shortened form of *telephone*); and words borrowed from other languages, such as *lasso* (from the Spanish *lazo*). When students encounter such words in reading materials, have them discuss the origins of the terms and encourage them to come up with other words that have been formed in a similar manner.

7. Play classification games with words. For example, divide the children into groups of three or four and make category sheets like the one below for each group. When you give a signal, the children should start writing as many words as they can think of that fit in each of the categories; when you signal that time is up, a person from each group should read the group's words to the class. Have the children compare their lists and discuss why they placed certain words in certain categories.

Cities	States	Countries

Other appropriate categories are meat, fruit, and vegetables; mammals, reptiles, and insects; or liquid, solid, and gas.

8. Children in the intermediate grades can learn about the kinds of changes that
have taken place in the English language by studying words and definitions that
appear in very old dictionaries and differences between American English and
British English. Some sources follow:

Epstein, Sam, and Beryl Epstein. *The First Book of Words*. New York: Franklin
Watts, 1954.
Funk, Wilfred. *Word Origins and Their Romantic Stories*. New York: Funk &
Wagnalls, 1950.
Nurnburg, Maxwell. *Fun with Words*. Englewood Cliffs, N.J.: Prentice-Hall, 1970.

9. Encourage children's use of word play.

a. Have them write words in ways that express their meanings—for example,
they may write *backward* as *drawkcab,* or *up* slanting upward and *down*
slanting downward.
b. Ask them silly questions containing new words. Example: "Would you have a
terrarium for dinner? Why or why not?"
c. Discuss what puns are and give some examples; then ask children to make
up or find puns to bring to class. Let them explain the play on words to
classmates who do not understand it. Example: "What is black and white and
read all over?" Answer: A newspaper (word play on homophones *red* and
read).
d. Use Hink Pinks, Hinky Pinkies, and Hinkety Pinketies, rhyming definitions for
terms with one, two, and three syllables, respectively. Give a definition, tell
whether it is a Hink Pink, Hinky Pinky, or Hinkety Pinkety, and let the children
guess the expression. Then let the children make up their own terms. Several
examples follow.

Hink Pink: Unhappy father—Sad dad
Hinky Pinky: Late group of celebrators—Tardy party
Hinkety Pinkety: Yearly handbook—Annual manual

10. Select a concept word related to something you are teaching and write it on the
board. Give the children a specified time limit in which to write down related
words. Then let them share their word lists (Kaplan and Tuchman, 1980). For
children who do not respond well under time pressure, simply have students call
out the related words, and write them on the board.
11. Using a selection the students are going to read, take an unfamiliar word, put it
into a title, and construct several sentences that offer clues to its meaning. Show
the title on the overhead projector; then show one sentence at a time, letting the
students guess the meaning of the word at each step (Kaplan and Tuchman,
1980).
12. Give the students a list of clues ("means the same as . . .", "is the opposite

164

Teaching
Reading in
Today's
Elementary
Schools

of . . .", and so forth) to words in a reading selection, along with page numbers, and tell them to go on a scavenger hunt for the words, writing them beside the appropriate clues (Criscuolo, 1980).

13. Dramatizing words, thereby clarifying their meanings by associating situations with them, is a vicarious experience that is more effective than mere verbal explanation of terms, and under some circumstances it has proved to be more effective than use of context clues, structural analysis, or dictionaries (Duffelmeyer and Duffelmeyer, 1979; Duffelmeyer, 1980).

14. To teach word origins, place on the bulletin board a "word tree" that has limbs labeled Greek, Latin, Anglo-Saxon, French, Native American, Dutch, and so on, with words on each limb (Gold, 1981).

15. Use students' names as a springboard for vocabulary development, devoting a day to each child's name. For example, discuss several meanings of the name ("Bill" is good for this one); find words that contain the name ("Tim" is in "Timbuktu"); study the etymology of one ("Patricia" means "high born" in Latin and is related to *patriotic* and *paternal*); or relate the name to colloquialisms or figurative language ("Johnny on the spot"). Or you may find examples of the name in literature in stories such as *Heidi* and *Kim,* biographies of real people such as Rachel Jackson or George Washington, mythology (Diana, Jason, and Helen), or authors' names (Carl Sandburg and Robert Frost). You may also relate a name to geography (Charleston, for example) or to the language of its origin ("Juan" is Spanish), or make limericks or write poems with names that have easy rhymes. There are many other possibilities (Crist, 1980); you might even want to spend a week on a name.

16. Familiar product names can be utilized to initiate vocabulary activities. Have students bring in empty product containers and place them in a box. Each student can reach into the box, draw out an item, and use its name in a sentence, giving it a common meaning. For example, the sentence for Joy dishwashing liquid could be "It is a joy to use this product" or "My new bicycle brought me much joy."

17. Use a technique called musical cloze. First select a song appropriate for the children and the unit of study. Make deletions in its text: certain parts of speech, words that fit into a particular category, words that show relationships, or something else. Using the original text, have the children practice until they learn the song; then sing it with the deletions and ask the children to suggest alternatives for the omitted words or phrases. Write these on the board and sing the song several times, using the children's suggestions in place of the original words. Afterward lead the students in a discussion of their replacement choices (Mateja, 1982).

18. Vocabulary notebooks, in which students list new words heard in conversations, found in general reading, or heard over radio or on television, are a good way for children to maintain a record of their increasing vocabularies.

19. Students might also enjoy crossword puzzles that highlight new words in their textbooks or other instructional materials.

Sentences

Children may find complicated sentences difficult to understand, so they need to know ways to attack them, or derive their meaning. Research has shown that systematic instruction in sentence comprehension increases reading comprehension. For example, Phyllis Weaver had students arrange cut-up sentences in the correct order by finding the action word first and then asking who, what, where, and why questions (Durkin, 1978–79). Another approach is to have children discover the essential parts of sentences by writing them in telegram form, as in this example:

> Original sentence: The angry dog chased me down the street.
> Telegram: Dog chased me.

Teachers should help children learn that some sentence parts can be moved around without changing the sentence's meaning. For instance, these two sentences say the same thing: (1) On a pole in front of the school, the flag was flying. (2) The flag was flying on a pole in front of the school.

Sentence Difficulty Factors

A number of types of sentences, including those with relative clauses, complex sentences, those in the passive voice, those containing pronouns, those with missing words, and those with implicit (implied) relationships, have been found to cause comprehension difficulty for children. Children understand material better when the syntax is like their oral language patterns, but the text in some primary-grade basal readers is syntactically more complex than the students' oral language.

For example, relative clauses (including restrictive and nonrestrictive clauses) are among the syntactic patterns that do not appear regularly in young children's speech. Both restrictive clauses, which restrict the information in the main clause by adding information, and nonrestrictive or appositive clauses, which add information, are troublesome. In the example "The man *who called my name* was my father," the restrictive clause indicates which particular man to designate as "my father." "My father, who is a doctor, visited me today" is an example of a sentence with a nonrestrictive clause. John Bormuth and associates found that 33 percent of the fourth graders they studied made errors in processing singly embedded restrictive clauses when reading paragraphs (Kachuck, 1981).

166

Teaching
Reading in
Today's
Elementary
Schools

Younger children also find it hard to understand sentences that delete linguistic units; for example, in "The man *calling my name* is my father," the words *who is* have been deleted and must be inferred (Kachuck, 1981). Yet Beatrice Kachuck found that in second-grade readers, relative clauses occurred from six to twenty times per one hundred sentences. When reduced relative clauses—constructions such as "calling my name"—were considered, the incidence rose to twenty-eight to sixty-eight times per one hundred sentences. In higher-grade materials, an increase in such clauses was usual. When researchers examined standardized reading tests, they found that the proportions of relative clauses rose dramatically in fourth-grade materials, which could account for the apparent decline in reading progress of many children in the fourth grade: the children's inability to deal with these syntactic patterns may affect their scores.

Teachers should ask questions that test understanding of particular syntactic patterns in the reading material, and when misunderstanding is evident they should point out the clues that help children discover the correct meaning. Students who need more work with relative clauses can be asked to turn two-clause sentences into two sentences. They could move from this activity into sentence combining. Finally, they should apply their understanding in reading whole passages (Kachuck, 1981).

To introduce breaking down complex sentences into main ideas in order to discover the information included, use a chalkboard activity such as the following:

Although they don't realize it, people *who eat too much* may be shortening the amount of time *that they will live.*

1. People may shorten their lifespan.
2. They may do this by overeating.
3. They may not realize this possible bad effect of overeating.

Teachers can reverse this activity to provide another learning situation by giving the children three short sentences and asking them to combine the information into a single sentence.

Children should explore other ways in which sentences may be altered and still say the same thing, for example: (1) Jackie kicked the ball. (2) The ball was kicked by Jackie. Here the sentence has been transformed from the active to the passive voice. Children can work on understanding this without using the technical labels. Give them a sentence, such as "Terry hit Chris," and tell them to write a sentence that says the same thing but begins with the word "Chris."

Since children frequently have trouble identifying the noun to which a pronoun refers, they need practice in deciding who, or what, the pronouns refer to in sentences such as these:

1. Joan put the license plate on *her* bicycle.
2. Since the book was old, *it* was hard to replace.

Problems also sometimes arise when sentences have words that are left out but are supposed to be "understood." In sentences such as the following, children need to practice determining what word or words are left out:

1. I have plenty of flower seeds. Do you need any more?
2. Tony knows he shouldn't drink so many soft drinks, but he claims he can't stop.

When short sentences such as those found in many primary readers are used to make reading "easier" but in the process leave out the connectives that signal relationships, students may find the material harder to read than longer sentences with explicit causal, conditional, and time-sequence relationships. When these are not explicitly stated, as below,

Because he was angry, he screamed at his brother.

they must be inferred by the reader, as in this example:

He was angry. He screamed at his brother.

Implicit relationships are harder for children to comprehend than explicit ones. Teachers must be aware of this problem and attempt to help children deal with it by focusing discussions and questions on implicit connective relationships and talking about the need to discover them (Irwin, 1980).

Punctuation

Punctuation can greatly affect the meaning conveyed by a sentence: it represents pauses and pitch changes that would occur if the passage were read aloud. While punctuation marks imperfectly represent the inflections in speech, they greatly aid in turning written language into oral language.

A period occurs at the end of a statement, a question mark at the end of an interrogative sentence, and an exclamation point at the end of an emphatic utterance. All of these punctuation marks signal a pause between sentences and also alter the meaning:

He's a crook. (Making a statement)
He's a crook? (Asking a question)
He's a crook! (Showing surprise or dismay at the discovery)

168

Teaching
Reading in
Today's
Elementary
Schools

Commas and dashes indicate pauses within sentences and are often used to set off explanatory material from the main body of the sentence. Commas are also used to separate items in a series or to separate main clauses joined by coordinate conjunctions.

To help students see how punctuation can affect the meaning of the material, use sentences such as the following:

Mother said, "Joe could do it."
Mother said, "Joe could do it?"
"Mother," said Joe, "could do it."

We had ice cream and cake.
We had ice, cream, and cake.
We had ice cream and cake?

Discuss the differences in meaning among each set of sentences, highlighting the function of each punctuation mark.

Underlining and italics, which are frequently used to indicate that a word or group of words is to be stressed, are also clues to underlying meaning. For example, here are several stress patterns for a single sentence:

Pat ate a snail.
Pat *ate* a snail.
Pat ate *a* snail.
Pat ate a *snail.*

In the first example, the stress immediately indicates that Pat, and not anyone else, ate the snail. In variation two, stressing the word *ate* shows that the act of eating the snail was of great importance. In variation three, the writer indicates that only one snail was eaten, whereas the last variation implies that eating a snail was unusual and that the word *snail* is more important than the other words in the sentence.

Teachers need to be sure that children are aware of the aids to comprehension found in punctuation and that they practice interpreting these marks.

✔ Self-Check: Objective 5

Explain how children can discover essential parts of sentences by writing them in telegram form and how to break down complex sentences in order to discover the information included in them. Discuss the effect of punctuation marks on the meaning of sentences.

Paragraphs

Paragraphs are groups of sentences that serve a particular function within a whole selection or passage. They may be organized around a main idea or topic. Understanding their functions, their general organization, and the

relationships between the sentences in a paragraph is important to reading
comprehension.

Different Functions

Different types of paragraphs perform different functions, and children can increase their ability to understand selections by learning to recognize these. All of the different types except the narrative paragraph occur primarily in informational materials in the elementary grades, and teachers should discuss them as students encounter them in these materials, if the children are to understand them fully. Some common types of paragraphs are

1. *Narrative paragraphs* are found primarily in story selections in basal readers or in literature, and simply present a narration of events to move the plot along.
2. *Introductory paragraphs* inform the reader of the topics that will be covered and stimulate interest in the material. They usually occur at the beginnings of whole selections or major subdivisions of lengthy readings.

    If children are searching for a discussion of a particular topic, they can check the introductory paragraph of a selection to determine whether they need to read the entire selection. The "Introduction" sections that accompany each chapter in this book are intended to be used in this manner. Introductory paragraphs can also help readers establish a proper mental set for the material to follow; they may offer a framework for categorizing the facts that readers will encounter in the selection.
3. *Transitional paragraphs* help readers to change gears by indicating a shift from one line of thought to another. They assist the reader in moving smoothly from idea to idea and in seeing the relationships among these ideas.
4. *Illustrative paragraphs* contain examples that help to clarify ideas presented in the text. They may present specific examples of the processes, materials, and functions described.
5. *Topical paragraphs* usually form the body of an expository selection. Most contain a topic sentence, which sets forth the central thought or idea of the paragraph, and the other sentences in the paragraph are closely related to the topic sentence, supplying supporting details. Sometimes, however, the main idea is not directly stated in a topic sentence but must be inferred from the related details.
6. *Summary paragraphs* occur at the ends of whole selections or major subdivisions and summarize what has gone on before, stating the main points of the selection in a concise manner and omitting explanatory material and supporting details. They offer a tool for rapid review of the material.

Teaching Main Ideas   To understand written selections fully and to summarize long selections, children must be able to determine the main ideas of

170

Teaching
Reading in
Today's
Elementary
Schools

paragraphs. Teachers should provide them with opportunities to practice recognizing main ideas and help them to realize the following facts:

1. A topic sentence often states the main idea of the paragraph.
2. The topic sentence is often, though not always, the first sentence in the paragraph; sometimes it appears at the end or in the middle.
3. Not all paragraphs have topic sentences.
4. The main idea is supported by all of the details in a well-written paragraph.
5. When the main idea is not directly stated, readers can determine it by discovering the topic to which all of the stated details are related.

Dan Donlan (1980) recommends a three-stage process for teaching the relationships in paragraphs and helping students locate main ideas. First he suggests exercises related to word relationships: equal relationships, such as *general* and *admiral;* opposite relationships, such as *war* and *peace;* superior/ subordinate relationships, such as *corporal* and *private;* and no relationship, such as *tank* and *porch.* Next the teacher should use exercises on sentence relationships, which fall into the same four types. Finally students should try exercises dealing with complete paragraphs, analyzing them by examining the relationships among their sentences. The superior/subordinate relationships found in the paragraphs represent the main idea and supporting details. Consider the following paragraph:

My brothers all joined the armed forces. Tom joined the Army. Robert joined the Navy. Bill became a Marine.

This paragraph could be diagramed as follows:

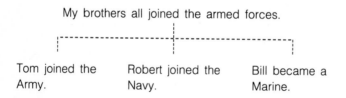

Exercises such as those below are helpful in giving pupils practice in locating main ideas in paragraphs. Also look at the examples of commercial materials in Example 4.1.

● **WORKSHEET:** *Topic Sentences*

Directions: In the following paragraph, underline the sentence that states the main idea.

Edward Fong is a solid citizen of this city and this state. He is well educated, and he keeps his knowledge of governmental processes up-to-date. He has served our

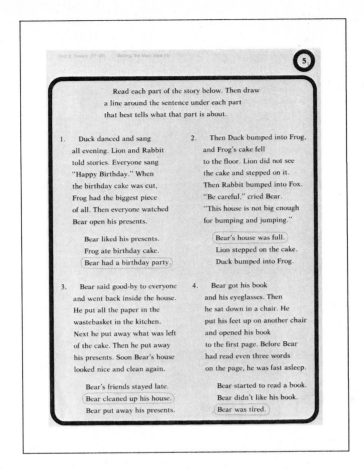

Source: William K. Durr et al. *Practice Book: Towers, Teacher's Annotated Edition*, p. 5 (Houghton Mifflin Reading Program). Copyright © 1981 by Houghton Mifflin Company. Used by permission. ◄

city well as a mayor for the past two years, exhibiting his outstanding skills as an administrator. Edward Fong has qualities that make him an excellent choice as our party's candidate for governor. ●

● **WORKSHEET:** *Unstated Main Ideas*

Directions: In the following paragraph, the main idea is implied rather than directly stated. On the line following the paragraph, write the main idea.

Scenic Lake is crowded each year with enthusiastic vacationers. The lake is extremely large and is an ideal place for water-skiing. It abounds with numerous varieties of fish and has an abundant supply of quiet inlets. The water is practically

172

Teaching
Reading in
Today's
Elementary
Schools

free of pollutants, making swimming a pleasant experience. Roped-off areas are available for swimmers, and lifeguards are provided by the state. The grounds near the swimming areas are supplied with picnic tables and grills.

Main idea: _____ ●

● **WORKSHEET:** *Provide a Title*

Directions: Read the following paragraph. Decide on a good title for it and place the title on the line provided.

_____ (Title)

Johnny's teddy bear was five years old. It had dirty brown fur that was torn in two places. The cotton stuffing was visible at the torn spots. At one time there had been two button eyes, but only one was left. In spite of the bear's bad appearance, Johnny refused to throw him away. ●

● **MODEL ACTIVITY:** *Main Idea—''Rim Rat's Dilemma''*

Gather old newspapers and cardboard for mounting. Tell the children that a rim rat is a newspaper worker who writes headlines and that they will pretend to be "rim rats" in this activity. Cut a number of articles from the newspaper that you feel will be of interest to the children and separate the text of each article from its headline. The child's task is to read each article and locate the most suitable headline for it. Mount article and title on cardboard. To make the task easier, match captions to pictures, use very short articles, or use articles that are completely different in subject matter.

For evaluation purposes, make the activity self-checking by coding articles and headlines. To follow up you might use these ideas: have children make pictures and captions to share in the skills center; write articles and prepare headlines separately and let children match them; have them try to match advertisements to pictures or captions to cartoons. ●

✔ **Self-Check: Objective 6**   **173**

Name six types of paragraphs and describe the functions of each.   Comprehension
How can teachers help children recognize main ideas of paragraphs?

Whole Selections

We know that entire selections consist of words, sentences, and paragraphs, and that understanding of whole selections depends upon understanding the smaller units.

Narrative selections are generally composed of a series of narrative paragraphs, which present the unfolding of a plot. Though they are usually arranged in chronological order, paragraphs may be flashbacks, or narrations of events from an earlier time, to provide the reader with background information he or she needs to understand the current situation.

Expository selections are composed of a variety of types of paragraphs, usually beginning with an introductory paragraph and primarily composed of a series of topical paragraphs, with transition paragraphs to indicate shifts from one line of thought to another and illustrative paragraphs to provide examples to clarify the ideas. These selections generally conclude with summary paragraphs, which present the main points of the selection in a concise manner. If a selection is extremely long, it may include summary paragraphs at the ends of the main subdivisions, as well as at the end of the entire work.

The topical paragraphs within an expository selection are logically arranged in order to carry the reader through the author's presentation of an idea or process. Since the writer's purpose will dictate the order in which he or she arranges the material, a number of different types of organization are possible.

1. *Chronological order.* In some selections, events are presented in the order in which they occur.
2. *Cause-and-effect organization.* Some selections emphasize causes and effects. For example, a history textbook might present the causes of the Civil War and lead the reader to see that the war was the effect of these causes.
3. *Comparison-and-contrast organization.* Some written materials make points through comparison and contrast. For example, social studies materials may compare and contrast life in another country with life in the United States, or life in the past with present-day life.
4. *Enumeration.* Some selections are primarily lists of points that support the main idea. Material designed to explain how consumers can save energy might contain phrases such as "One way to help," "A second way," "Still another possibility," and so on.
5. *Topical order.* Some written material is organized around specific topics. For example, this textbook has a topical arrangement.

174

Teaching
Reading in
Today's
Elementary
Schools

At times a writer may use more than one form of organization in a single selection, such as chronological order and cause-and-effect organization in history materials.

Teachers may use a number of strategies to help students understand whole selections, including the cloze procedure, semantic webbing, listening-reading transfer lessons, and story grammar activities.

Cloze Procedure

In using the cloze procedure, the teacher deletes some of the words in a passage and asks students to fill them in as they read, utilizing the clues within the language to do so. This procedure is helpful in improving comprehension (Grant, 1979).

Completing cloze passages requires use of both semantic and syntactic clues. Teachers should be careful to leave the initial and final sentences of the selection intact and delete no more than 10 percent of the words in a passage designed for teaching, rather than testing. They can choose a passage of any length and make deletions randomly or space them regularly (though neither random nor regularly spaced deletions will focus on a particular skill). If a teacher *does* wish to focus on a particular skill, he or she can delete only a particular part of speech, provide multiple-choice answers or phonic clues for the deleted words, or indicate word length by leaving a space for each letter in the word. Cloze lessons can focus on any specific comprehension skill, such as relating pronouns to their referents, but they should follow instruction about the skill by the teacher (Schoenfield, 1980).

Semantic Webbing

"Semantic webbing is a process for constructing visual displays of categories and their relationships" (Freedman and Reynolds, 1980, p. 877) that can help students organize and integrate concepts. Each web consists of a core question, strands, strand supports, and strand ties. The teacher chooses a core question, which becomes the center of the web, to which the entire web is related. The students' answers are web strands, facts and inferences taken from the story and students' experiences are the strand supports, and the relationships of the strands to each other are strand ties. Below is an example of a semantic web based on "How D. Y. B. worked for April," an excerpt from *Bright April*, by Marguerite de Angeli, included in the basal reader *Panorama* (Houghton Mifflin, 1974). In preparing to construct this web, children were given the task of reading a portion of the story to predict what would happen next. The core question focuses on this. Students answered the question, and their answers became web strands (for example, "cry") if the other children judged them reasonable. Support for strands was drawn from the story and from their experiences. The support was also accepted or excluded according to the class's evaluation. If strands were found to be unsupportable, they were rejected at this point, just before the strands were related through strand ties (shown in the example with broken lines). The web was then used as a basis for further activity, such as reading the end of the story to see what really happened (Freedman and Reynolds, 1980).

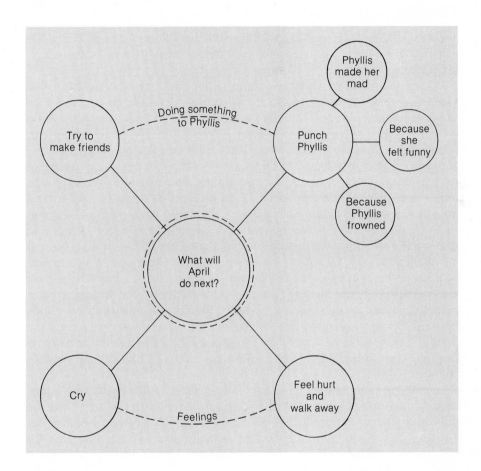

Reprinted with permission of Glenn Freedman and Elizabeth Reynolds and the International Reading Association.

Listening-Reading Transfer Lesson

A listening-reading transfer lesson can also be useful in improving comprehension skills. In such a lesson, the teacher asks students to listen to a selection and respond to a purpose (such as determining sequence of events) that he or she has set. As the class discusses the detected sequence, the teacher provides guidance, helps children explain how they made their decisions, and

176

Teaching
Reading in
Today's
Elementary
Schools

rereads the material if it is necessary to resolve controversies. Then the children read a different selection for the same purpose, and a similar follow-up discussion is conducted. Teachers can use this type of lesson with any comprehension skill (Cunningham, 1982).

Story Grammar Activities

A story schema is a person's mental representation of story structures and the way they are related. Knowledge of such structures appears to facilitate both comprehension and recall of stories.

A story grammar provides rules that define these story structures. Jean Mandler and Nancy Johnson developed a story grammar that includes six major structures: setting, beginning, reaction, attempt, outcome, and ending (Whaley, 1981). In a simplified version of Perry Thorndyke's story grammar, the structures are setting, characters, theme, plot, and resolution (McGee and Tompkins, 1981). Teachers may be able to help students develop a concept of story by using these or other story grammars. For instance, they may read stories and talk about the structure in terms that children understand (folktales and fairy tales have easily identifiable parts and make good choices), or they may have children retell stories. Reading or listening to stories and predicting what comes next is a good activity, as is discussion of the predicted parts. Teachers may give students stories in which whole sections are left out, indicated by blank lines in place of the material, and ask students to supply the missing material and then discuss the appropriateness of their answers. By dividing a story into different categories and scrambling the parts, teachers can provide students with the opportunity to rearrange the parts to form a good story. Or they can give all the sentences in the story on strips of paper to the children and ask them to put together the ones that fit (Whaley, 1981).

To provide independent practice for beginning readers and prereaders, teachers can videotape stories, giving an introduction to the story and the story structure to be studied. The children should receive directions for listening that focus attention on that structure, as well as directions for follow-up activities such as drawing pictures of characters, setting, or resolution, choosing pictures related to theme from several provided by the teacher, and arranging pictures that relate the plot in sequence. To make sure the procedures are clear, have the entire group do the activity under the teacher's direction the first time such tapes are used (McGee and Tompkins, 1981).

Even though there is much interest in the use of story grammars, questions remain about this technique. Mariam Dreher and Harry Singer (1980) studied the effects of teaching story grammar to fifth graders and discovered that such instruction did not increase how much story information the pupils recalled. Fifth graders may already have story structures in their mental repertoires, so that there is no need to offer them instruction in this area. More on story grammars can be found in the section on questioning techniques.

✔ Self-Check: Objective 7

Name five ways in which entire selections are often organized. (See Self-Improvement Opportunity 4.)

LEVELS OF COMPREHENSION

It is possible to understand materials on a number of different levels. To take in ideas that are directly stated is literal comprehension; to read between the lines is interpretive comprehension; to read for evaluation is critical reading; and to read beyond the lines is creative reading. Perhaps because literal comprehension is easiest to attain, teachers have given it a disproportionate amount of attention in the classroom; but children need to achieve higher levels of reading comprehension to become informed and effective citizens.

Literal Reading

Reading for literal comprehension, which involves acquiring information that is directly stated in a selection, is important in and of itself and is also a prerequisite for higher-level understanding. Examples of the skills involved are the ability to follow directions and the ability to restate the author's material in other words. For instance, if the author wrote, "The man's tattered coat was not effective against the cold," a child could show evidence of literal comprehension by saying, "The man's ragged coat didn't keep him warm."

Recognizing *stated* main ideas, details, causes and effects, and sequences is the basis of literal comprehension, and a thorough understanding of vocabulary, sentence meaning, and paragraph meaning is important. Exercises for developing literal comprehension include those described earlier under "Units of Comprehension" as well as those below.

Details

The specific, explicitly stated parts of a paragraph or passage that contain the basic information are the details upon which main ideas, cause-and-effect relationships, inferences, and so on are built. For example, in the sentence, "The man wore a red hat," the fact that a red hat was being worn is one detail that readers must note and remember. Some activities for developing the skill of locating details are presented below. (Recognizing details is also important in completing exercises under the topics "Sequence" and "Following Directions.")

178 *ACTIVITIES*

Teaching
Reading in
Today's
Elementary
Schools

1. After students have read a paragraph, ask them questions for which the answers are directly stated in the paragraph.

   Tom's favorite toy was his dump truck. Although Tom was usually a generous boy, he never offered to let anyone else play with the truck. He had had the truck for three years, and it was still as good as new. Tom was afraid that other children would be careless with his toy.

   a. What was Tom's favorite toy?
   b. Describe the condition of Tom's toy.
   c. How long had Tom had his favorite toy?

2. Give the children a set of directions, and have them number the important details (or steps), as in the following example. Go through one or more examples before you ask them to work alone.

   To make a good bowl of chili, first (1) sauté the onions for about ten minutes. Then (2) add the ground beef and brown it. (3) Stir the mixture frequently so that it will not burn. Finally, (4) add the tomatoes, tomato sauce, Mexican-style beans, salt, pepper, and chili powder. (5) Cook over low heat for forty-five minutes to one hour.

3. Make some copies of a menu. After showing pupils how to locate items and prices, ask them to read it and answer specific questions such as these:

   a. What is the price of a soft drink?
   b. Can you order a baked potato separately? If so, under what heading is it found?
   c. What else do you get when you order a rib steak?
   d. How many desserts are available?

4. Using a description like the one below and reading each step aloud, draw an object on the board. Then give the children a written description of another object and ask them to draw it.

   The flower has five oval petals. The petals are red. The center, at which the petals meet, is brown. The flower has a long green stem. At the bottom of the stem are overlapping blade-shaped leaves, which are half as tall as the stem.

5. Have the children read paragraphs like the one in the Worksheet below and answer the listed questions. Newspaper articles are good for practice of this sort, since lead paragraphs tend to include information about who, what, where, when, why, and how.

Directions. Read this newspaper article and answer the questions.

Jane and John Stone, who own the local grocery, had one hundred dollars stolen from them as they left the store last night at eleven o'clock. The robber stepped from behind a shrub outside the door of the grocery store and pulled a gun from his pocket, saying, "Hand over that cash sack!" Stone handed the robber the sack of money he had just removed from the cash register, and the man turned and fled, leaving both Mr. and Mrs. Stone unharmed.

a. Who was involved in this event?
b. What took place?
c. Where did it take place?
d. When did it take place?
e. How or why did it take place? ●

Main Ideas

As we discussed earlier, the main idea of a paragraph is the central thought around which a whole paragraph is organized. It is often, but not always, expressed in a topic sentence.

ACTIVITIES

1. Demonstrate the idea that the topic sentence is the main idea and that the other sentences in the paragraph relate to it by taking a paragraph, locating the topic sentence, and showing the relationship of each of the other sentences to the topic sentence. Then give the students paragraphs and ask them to underline the topic sentence and tell how each of the other sentences relates to it.
2. Have the students read a story that has a clearly stated main idea and point it out, explaining why you chose that idea. Then ask them to read another story, select the main idea from a list of options, and explain why they chose as they did.
3. Using copies of newspaper articles from which you have removed the titles, ask students to match a list of titles with the articles. Provide more titles than articles so that students cannot make their decisions by default.
4. Again working with newspaper articles without titles, have students construct titles using the information in the lead paragraph. Show them how to do this before you ask them to work on the task alone.
5. Discuss how main headings and subheadings in textbooks give information about the main ideas in sections.

Cause and Effect

Recognizing and understanding the cause-and-effect relationship in a written passage is an important reading skill. It is considered a literal skill when the relationship is explicitly stated ("Bill stayed out *because* he was ill"). Teachers can use the following activities when the cause and effect are directly stated in the passage; when they are implied, teachers can use procedures similar to the ones listed in the section on interpretive reading.

ACTIVITIES

1. Have the children read a paragraph that contains a cause-and-effect relationship. Then state the cause of the action and have them identify the effect. Carefully explain the process through a number of examples before asking them to work alone.

   > Bobby, Jill, Leon, and Peggy were playing softball in Bobby's yard. Peggy was up at bat and hit the ball squarely in the direction of Bobby's bedroom window. As the group watched in horror, the softball crashed right through the window, shattering the glass.
   >
   > Question: What happened when the softball hit the window?

2. Use the procedure described in the first activity, but describe the effect and have the children identify the cause. Using the same paragraph as an example, the question would be "What made the window break?"

Sequence

Sequence—the order in which events in a paragraph or passage occur—is signaled by time-order words such as *now, before, when, while, yet, after,* and so on. Children must learn to recognize straightforward chronological sequence as well as flashbacks and other devices that describe events "out of order."

ACTIVITIES

1. Have the children read a short selection. Then list the events in the selection out of sequence and show students how to reorder them. Using another selection—like that in the Worksheet below—ask the children to list the events in sequence. (Use shorter selections for younger children.)

Directions: Read this story and then place the list of events in order.

We were all excited on Friday morning because we were going to go to the circus. We had trouble concentrating on eating breakfast, but Mother wouldn't allow us to leave the table before we were finished.

Immediately after breakfast we piled into the station wagon. Everyone was talking at once and bouncing around on the seats as Dad started the car and backed out of the driveway. We were making so much noise and moving around so much that Dad didn't hear or see the truck turn the corner. The truck driver honked his horn, but it was too late. Dad backed right into the side of the truck.

The angry driver jumped out of his truck, but when he saw the crowd of us in the station wagon, he calmed down. He and Dad talked to each other for a while, staring at the damaged side of the truck occasionally. Then they went into the house to report the accident to the police.

Mother immediately recovered from the shock and told us to get out of the car. "We'll have a long wait before we will be able to leave," she said.

Story Events
The family got into the station wagon.
The truck driver honked his horn.
The family ate breakfast.
Dad backed out of the driveway.
Dad and the truck driver talked.
Mother told the children to get out of the car.
Dad backed into the side of the truck.
Dad and the truck driver went into the house.
The driver jumped out of his truck. ●

2. After they have read a selection, ask the children to answer questions about the order of events. For example, using an article entitled "Wars in Which United States Citizens Have Fought," ask the children questions such as "Which came first, the Civil War or the War of 1812?" "Was the Korean Conflict before or after World War II?"

3. Cut the separate frames of comic strips apart, back them with cardboard to make them durable, scramble them, and place them in envelopes; then ask the children to read the separate frames and arrange them in the correct order. If you wish to have students check this activity themselves, indicate the correct order by assigning a number to each frame on the back. To vary the difficulty of this task, use some strips that have little or no dialogue, some with a moderate amount, and some with a great deal of dialogue, or strips with different numbers of frames.

4. A similar activity is to cut a story apart so that each paragraph forms a separate section, back the sections with cardboard, scramble them, and give them to pupils to place in the proper sequence. You may put numbers on the backs of the sections to indicate the order if you want students to do a self-check.

Following Directions

The ability to read and follow directions is a prerequisite for virtually all successful schoolwork. This skill is considered a part of literal reading comprehension. It involves understanding details and sequence; therefore, some of the exercises under those headings are appropriate to use in teaching children to follow written directions. In addition, the activities below may prove useful.

ACTIVITIES

1. Alert children to the functions of such key words as *first, next, last,* and *finally* by giving them a paragraph containing these words and asking them to underline the words that help to show the order of events.
2. Prepare handouts with uncolored pictures. Have the children color the pictures according to directions such as "Color the girl's sweater red. Color her skirt gray. Color her hair brown."
3. Use a worksheet such as the one that follows for intermediate grades; primary-level worksheets would have much simpler directions, such as "Draw a dog."

● **WORKSHEET:** *Following Directions*

Directions: Follow the directions in the sentences below.

1. Circle the number that is largest: 10, 55, 6, 19.
2. Underline all of the even numbers in this list: 1, 5, 8, 11, 12, 14, 15, 19, 20.
3. Draw a line through the first and last words in this sentence.
4. Circle every word in this sentence that begins with the letter *t.*
5. Add 3 to 2. Take the result and subtract 1. Divide that result by 2. What is your answer? _____ . ●

4. Use a practice sheet similar to the one that follows:

● **WORKSHEET:** *Following Directions*

Directions: Read all of the items before you begin to carry out each instruction. Work as quickly as you can; you have five minutes to finish this activity.

1. Write your name at the top of the paper.
2. Turn the paper over and add 15 and 25. Write the answer you get on this line: _____ .
3. Stand up and clap your hands three times.
4. Count the number of times the word *the* is written on this page. Put the answer on this line: _____ .
5. Subtract 9 from 99. Put your answer on this line: _____ .
6. Go to the board and write your name.

7. Count the people in this room. Put the answer under your name at the top of the page.
8. Now that you have read all of the directions, take your paper to the teacher. It should have no marks on it. ●

5. Make it a practice to refer children to written directions instead of telling them how to do everything orally. Ask them to read the directions silently and then tell you in their own words what they should do.
6. Teach the children the meanings of words commonly encountered in written directions, such as *underline, circle, divide, color, example, left, right, below, over,* and *match.* Other words that might need attention are listed in an article by Helen Newcastle (1974).
7. Have children follow directions for making things in art class.
8. Write directions on slips of paper, place them in a box, and let each child in turn draw a slip of paper and follow the instructions. In the initial stages of learning to follow written directions, each slip should list one step; later, two or more steps may be included per slip. Individualize this activity by giving one-step directions to those who are just beginning to learn to follow directions and multistep directions to those who have acquired some facility.

> Close the door. (one step)
> Walk to the pencil sharpener. Turn around in a circle. (two steps)
> Hop three times on your left foot. Hop two times on your right foot. Bow to the class. (three steps)

9. Use activities such as the one shown in Example 4.2.

✔ Self-Check: Objective 8
Describe a procedure for developing literal comprehension of
1. the main idea.
2. details.
3. cause and effect.
4. sequence.
5. following directions.
(See Self-Improvement Opportunities 5 and 6.)

Interpretive Reading

Interpretive reading involves reading between the lines or making inferences. It is the process of deriving ideas that are implied rather than directly stated. Skills for interpretive reading include

1. inferring main ideas of passages in which the main ideas are not directly stated,
2. inferring cause-and-effect relationships when they are not directly stated,
3. inferring referents of pronouns,

184

Teaching
Reading in
Today's
Elementary
Schools

4. inferring referents of adverbs,
5. inferring omitted words,
6. detecting mood,
7. detecting the author's purpose in writing, and
8. drawing conclusions.

Bob Lange has pointed out that "readers make inferences consistent with their schemata" (1981, p. 443), yet it is important to realize that children have less prior knowledge than adults and do not always make inferences spontaneously, even when they possess the necessary background knowl-

▶ **EXAMPLE 4.2:** Following Directions Practice Worksheet

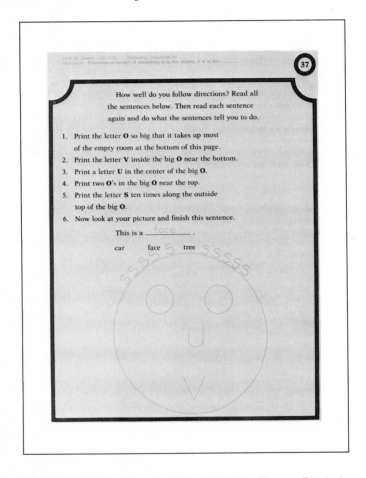

Source: William K. Durr et al. *Practice Book: Towers, Teacher's Annotated Edition*, p. 37 (Houghton Mifflin Reading Program). Copyright © 1981 Houghton Mifflin Company. Used by permission. ◀

edge. Using a group setting in which children heard about each other's experiences, listened to each other's predictions about a story, and then wrote down their own experiences and guesses, Jane Hansen (1981b) found that primary-grade children were able to increase their ability to make inferences about the story. Hansen (1981a) also tested two methods designed to convince children that they can and should make inferences about what they read, drawing from their prior knowledge. The Strategy method employed prereading activities to relate children's knowledge to the text; the Question method provided practice in answering inferential questions. Using a control group that was asked to answer primarily literal questions, Hansen found that the Strategy method increased the likelihood that the children would draw inferences spontaneously in the instructional setting, and the Question method also enhanced the children's ability to draw inferences spontaneously.

Main Ideas

For some selections readers must infer the main idea from related details. A good way to develop readiness to make such inferences is to ask children to locate the main ideas of pictures first. Then ask them to listen for main ideas as you read to them, and finally have them look for main ideas of passages they read.

The teacher should model the thought process students need to follow in deciding upon the main idea of a selection before asking them to try this independently. In the example below the teacher could compare each of the possible choices to the details in the selection, rejecting those that fail to encompass the details. As students practice and become more proficient at identifying implied main ideas, the teacher should delete the choices and ask them to state the main idea in their own words (Moore and Readence, 1980). In addition, teachers can increase passage length as the children gain proficiency, beginning with paragraphs that do not have directly stated topic sentences and moving gradually to entire selections. Because of the obvious morals, Aesop's fables are good for teaching implied main ideas; the teacher can give students a fable and ask them to state the moral, then compare the actual morals to the ones the children stated, discuss any variations, and examine reasoning processes.

● **WORKSHEET:** *Inferring Unstated Main Ideas*

Directions: In the selection below, the main idea is implied but not directly stated. Choose the correct main idea from the list of possible ones.

The mayor of this town has always conducted his political campaigns as name-calling battles. Never once has he approached the basic issues of a campaign. Nevertheless, he builds himself up as a great statesman, ignoring the irregularities that have been discovered during his terms of office. Do you want a man like this to be re-elected?

186

Teaching
Reading in
Today's
Elementary
Schools

The main idea of this selection is

1. The current mayor is not a good person to re-elect to office.
2. The mayor doesn't say nice things about his opponents.
3. The mayor is a crook.
4. The mayor should be re-elected. ●

Another activity on inferring unstated main ideas appears in the discussion on comprehending paragraphs.

Cause and Effect

Sometimes a reader needs to be able to infer a cause or effect that has been implied in the material, as in the following activity. Brainstorming about causes and effects out loud may help children develop more skill in this area. The teacher can ask: "What could be the effect when a person falls into the lake? What could be the cause of a crying baby?" Elicit the reasoning behind children's answers.

● **WORKSHEET:** *Inferring Cause-and-Effect Relationships*

Directions: Read the following paragraphs and answer the question.

Jody refused to go to bed when the babysitter told her it was time. "This is a special occasion," she said. "Mom and Dad said I could stay up two hours later tonight."

Reluctantly, the babysitter allowed Jody to sit through two more hour-long TV shows. Although her eyelids drooped, she stubbornly stayed up until the end of the second show.

This morning Jody found it hard to get out of bed. All day there was evidence that she was not very alert. "What is wrong with me?" she wondered.

Question: What caused Jody to feel the way she did today? ●

Pronoun Referents

Writing seldom, if ever, explicitly states the connection between a pronoun and its referent, so the task of determining the referent is an inferential one. Working with third graders, Margaret Richek found that, given a sentence paraphrase choice such as the one shown below, children understood the repeated subject most easily, the pronominalized form next, and the deleted form least easily (Barnitz, 1979).

Bill saw Jane, and Bill spoke to Jane.
Bill saw Jane, and he spoke to her.
Bill saw Jane and spoke to her.

John Barnitz (1979) found that students recalled structures in which the
referent was a noun or noun phrase more easily after reading than ones in which the referent was a clause or sentence.

> Mark wanted an ice-cream cone but did not have enough money for it. (noun phrase referent)
> Mike plays the guitar for fun, but he does not do it often. (sentence referent)

Similarly, children found it easier to remember structures in which the pronoun followed its referent than ones in which the pronoun came first (Barnitz, 1979).

> Because it was pretty, Marcia wanted the blouse.
> Marcia wanted the blouse because it was pretty.

Teachers should present these structures in the order of difficulty indicated by the studies just cited. They should explain the connections between the pronouns and referents in a number of examples before giving students exercises in which to make the relationship themselves.

After presenting all of the structures separately, teachers could use a worksheet such as the following to provide practice in integrating learning.

● **WORKSHEET:** *Pronoun Referents*

Direction: Circle the word or group of words to which each italicized word refers.

1. Don hit Jasper and then ran away from *him*.
2. Janice wanted a five-string banjo, but Janice's mother would not buy *it*.
3. Daniel works at the car wash, but he does not do *it* on school days.
4. Because *it* was the last one left, Terry did not take the piece of cake.
5. Sandra mopped the floor because she had gotten *it* dirty. ●

Adverb Referents

At times adverbs refer to other words or groups of words without an explicitly stated relationship. Teachers can explain these relationships, using examples such as the ones below, and then let children practice making the connections independently.

> I'll stay at home, and you come here after you finish. (In this sentence, the adverb *here* refers to *home*.)

> I enjoy the swimming pool, even if you do not like to go there. (In this sentence, the adverb *there* refers to *swimming pool*.)

Omitted Words

Sometimes in writing, words are omitted and said to be "understood," a structure known as ellipsis. Ellipsis can cause problems for some students, so again teachers should provide examples and explain the structure and then give children practice in interpreting sentences.

Are you going to the library? Yes, I am. (In the second sentence, the words *going to the library* are understood.)

Who is going with you? Bobby. (The words *is going with me* are understood.)

I have my books. Where are yours? (Here the second sentence is a shortened form of *Where are your books?*)

After this structure has been thoroughly discussed, students may practice by restating the sentences, filling in the deleted words.

Detecting Mood

Certain words and ways of using words tend to set a mood for a story, poem, or other literary work. Have children discuss how certain words trigger certain moods—for example, *ghostly, deserted, haunted, howling* (scary); *lilting, sparkling, shining, laughing,* (happy); *downcast, sobbing, dejected* (sad). Give them copies of selections in which you have underlined words setting the mood. Then give them a passage such as the one below and tell them to underline the words that set the mood.

● **WORKSHEET:** *Detecting Mood*

Directions: Underline the words that set the mood of the paragraph.

Jay turned dejectedly away from the busy scene made by the movers as they carried his family's furniture from the house. "We're going away forever," he thought sadly. "I'll never see my friends again." And a tear rolled slowly down Jay's cheek, further smudging his unhappy face. ●

Detecting the Author's Purpose

Writers always have a purpose for writing: to inform, to entertain, to persuade, or to accomplish something else. Teachers should encourage their students to ask, "Why was this written?" by presenting them with a series of stories and explaining the purpose of each one, then giving them other stories and asking them to identify the purposes. Discuss reasons for the answers.

● **WORKSHEET:** *Detecting Author's Purpose*

Directions: Read the following materials and decide for each one whether the author was trying to inform, entertain, or persuade.

Television Works Like This, by Jeanne and Robert Bendick. New York: McGraw-Hill, 1965.

The Story of Doctor Doolittle, by Hugh Lofting. Philadelphia: Lippincott, 1920.

"Put Safety First," a pamphlet. ●

Drawing Conclusions

In order to draw conclusions, a reader must put together information gathered from several different sources or places within the same source. Students may develop readiness for this skill by studying pictures and drawing conclusions from them. Answering such questions as the following may also help.

1. What is taking place here?
2. What happened just before this picture was taken?
3. What are the people in the picture preparing to do?

Cartoons may be used to good advantage in developing this comprehension skill. Show the students a cartoon such as the one below and ask a question that leads them to draw a conclusion, such as "What kind of news does Dennis have for his father?" Putting together the ideas that an event happened today and that Dennis's father needs to be relaxed to hear about it

DENNIS the MENACE

"LET ME KNOW WHEN YOU'RE RELAXED ENOUGH TO HEAR ABOUT SOMETHIN' THAT HAPPENED TODAY."

190

Teaching
Reading in
Today's
Elementary
Schools

enables students to conclude that Dennis was involved in some mischief or accident that is likely to upset his father. The teacher can model the necessary thinking process by pointing out each clue and describing how he or she related it to a personal knowledge about how parents react. Then students can practice on other cartoons.

In the early grades, riddles such as "I have a face and two hands. I go tick-tock. What am I?" are good practice in drawing conclusions. Commercial riddle books, which allow readers to answer riddles and explain the reasoning behind their answers, may also be used for developing this skill.

● **WORKSHEET:** *Drawing Conclusions*

Directions: Read each paragraph and answer the question that follows it.

1. Ray went through the line, piling his plate high with food. He then carried his plate over to a table, where a waitress was waiting to find out what he wanted to drink. Where was Ray?_____

2. Cindy awoke with pleasure, remembering where she was. She hurried to dress so that she could help feed the chickens and watch her uncle milk the cows. Then she would go down to the field, catch Ginger, and take a ride through the woods. Where was Cindy?_____ ●

Another way to help children draw conclusions is to ask questions about sentences that imply certain information. For example, the teacher may write on the chalkboard "The uniformed man got out of his truck and climbed the telephone pole with his tools." Then he or she may ask, "What do you think is this man's job? What are your reasons for your answers?" Even though the sentence does not directly state that the man is a telephone repair person, the details all imply this occupation. With help, children can become adept at detecting such clues to implied meanings.

Critical Reading

Critical reading is evaluating written material—comparing the ideas discovered in the material with known standards and drawing conclusions about their accuracy, appropriateness, and timeliness. The critical reader must be an active reader, questioning, searching for facts, and suspending judgment until he or she has considered all of the material. Critical reading depends upon literal comprehension and interpretive comprehension, and grasping implied ideas is especially important.

If people are to make intelligent decisions based upon the material that they read, such as which political candidate to support, which products to buy, which movies to attend, which television programs to watch, and so on, they must read critically. Since children are faced with many of these decisions early in life, they should receive instruction in critical reading early.

Teachers can begin promoting critical reading in the first grade, or even kindergarten, by encouraging critical thinking. When reading a story to the class, they can ask, "Do you think this story is real or make-believe? Why do you think so?" If the children have difficulty in answering, questions such as "Could the things in this story really have happened? Do you know of any children who can fly? Have you ever heard of any *real* children who can fly? Have you ever heard of anyone who stayed the same age all of the time? Do all people grow up after enough years have passed?" can be helpful. By asking "Can animals really talk? Have you ever heard an animal talk?" teachers can help children understand how to judge the reality or fantasy in a story.

Critical thinking can also be promoted at an early stage through critical reading of pictures. If children are shown pictures that contain inaccuracies (for example, a car with a square wheel), they can identify the mistakes. Children's magazines often contain activities of this type, and illustrators of books often inadvertently include incorrect content. After the children have read (or have been read) a story containing such a picture, ask them to identify what is wrong in the picture according to the story.

To foster critical reading skills in the classroom, teachers can encourage pupils to read with a questioning attitude. Lead them to ask questions such as the following when reading nonfiction:

1. Why did the author write this material?
2. Does the author know what he or she is writing about? Is he or she likely to be biased? Why?
3. Is the material up-to-date?
4. Is the author approaching the material logically or emotionally? What emotional words does he or she use?
5. Is the author employing any undesirable propaganda techniques? Which ones? How does he or she use them?

Fiction can be read critically also, but the questions that apply are a little different.

1. Could this story really have happened?
2. Are the characters believable within the setting furnished by the story? Are they consistent in their actions?
3. Is the dialogue realistic?
4. Did the plot hold your interest? What was it that kept your interest?
5. Was the ending reasonable or believable? Why, or why not?
6. Was the title well chosen? Why, or why not?

Newspaper editorials offer one good way, especially in the intermediate grades, for children to practice distinguishing fact from opinion. Students can underline each sentence in the editorial with colored pencils, one color for

192

Teaching
Reading in
Today's
Elementary
Schools

Reading newspaper articles and editorials is a good way for students to practice the critical reading skill of distinguishing fact from opinion. (© Elizabeth Crews)

facts and another for opinions. They can then be encouraged to discuss which opinions are best supported by facts. Worksheets similar to the following might also be used to help children differentiate fact from opinion.

● **WORKSHEET:** *Fact or Opinion?*

Directions: Read each sentence carefully. Decide whether it states a fact or an opinion. Write an *F* on the line after the sentence if the statement is a fact; write an *O* if it is an opinion.

1. Michael Jackson is a terrific singer._____
2. Austin is the capital of Texas._____
3. There are twelve inches in a foot._____
4. I believe that people were never intended to visit other planets._____
5. Mark thinks that there is other intelligent life in our solar system._____
6. The discovery of polio vaccine was probably the most important discovery of the century._____
7. Emily has brown eyes._____
8. Everyone who is worth knowing will be at the party._____
9. It appears that Martin is the most eager worker in the plant._____
10. There are two pints in a quart._____ ●

The mature critical reader must consider and evaluate the person who wrote the material, considering the four categories that follow.

Author's Purpose   The critical reader will try to determine whether the author wrote the material to inform, to entertain, to persuade, or for some other purpose. This is an interpretive reading skill.

Author's Point of View   The critical reader will want to know if the writer belonged to a group, lived in an area, or held a strong view that would tend to bias any opinions about a subject in one way or another. Two accounts of the Civil War might be very different if one author was from the North and the other from the South.

Author's Style and Tone   The author's style is the manner in which he or she uses vocabulary (vividness, precision, use of emotional words, use of figurative language) and sentence structure (the order within the language). Special attention should be given to use of *figurative language*, expressions that are not meant to be taken literally (discussed in Chapter 7), and use of emotional words, which do much to sway the reader toward or away from a point of view or attitude. Note the effects of the two sentences below.

> Author 1: Next we heard the *heartrending* cry of the wounded tiger.
> Author 2: When the tiger was shot, it let out a *vicious* roar.

Teachers should be aware of the undesirable aspects of the style or tone of some writers of material for youngsters. A condescending tone, for example, will be quickly sensed and resented.

Author's Competence   The reliability of written material is affected by the competence of the author to write about the subject in question. If background information shows that a star football player has written an article on the nation's foreign policy, intermediate-grade youngsters will have little trouble determining that the reliability of the statements in this article is likely to be lower than the reliability of a similar article written by an experienced diplomat.

To determine an author's competence, students should consider his or her education and experience, referring to books such as *Current Biography* (H. W. Wilson, 1980) and *Fourth Book of Junior Authors and Illustrators* (H. W. Wilson, 1978) or to book jacket flaps, to find such information. Give students a topic and ask them to name people who might write about it. Let them discuss which ones might be most qualified, or have them compare two authors of books on the same subject and decide which one is better qualified. Class members who are knowledgeable about a topic and others who are not

194

Teaching
Reading in
Today's
Elementary
Schools

can write reports on that topic, while remaining pupils predict which people are likely to have the most accurate reports. The students can follow up with a comparison for accuracy (Ross, 1981).

Material

In addition to comprehending the material literally, the critical reader needs to be able to determine and evaluate the following things about it.

Timeliness   The critical reader will wish to check the date that the material was published, because the timeliness of an article or book can make a crucial difference in a rapidly changing world. For example, an outdated social studies book may show incorrect boundaries for countries or fail to show some countries that now exist; similarly, an outdated science book may refer to a disease as incurable when a cure has recently been found. A science or history book with a 1950 copyright date would contain no information about astronauts or moon shots.

Accuracy and Adequacy   Nonfiction material should be approached with this question in mind: "Are the facts presented here true?" The importance of a good background of experience becomes evident here. A reader who has had previous experience with the material will have a basis of comparison not available to one lacking such experience. A person with only a little knowledge of a particular field can often spot such indications of inadequacy as exaggerated statements, one-sided presentations, and opinion offered as fact. Obviously, readers can check reference books to see if the statements in the material are supported elsewhere.

Appropriateness   Critical readers must be able to determine whether the material is suitable for their purposes. A book or article can be completely accurate and not be applicable to the problem or topic under consideration. For example, a child looking for information for a paper entitled "Cherokee Indian Ceremonies" needs to realize that an article on the invention of the Cherokee alphabet is irrelevant to the task at hand.

Differentiation of Fact from Opinion   This skill is vital for good critical readers. People often unquestioningly accept as fact anything they see in print, though printed material is often composed of statements of opinion. Some authors intermix facts and opinions, giving little indication that they are presenting anything but pure fact. Also, many readers are not alert to clues that signal opinions. By pointing out these clues and providing practice in the task of discrimination, teachers can promote the ability to discriminate between facts and opinions.

Some readers have trouble reading critically because they do not have a clear idea of what constitutes a fact. Facts are statements that can be verified through direct observation, consultation of official records of past events, or

scientific experimentation. The statement "General Lee surrendered to
General Grant at Appomattox" is a fact that can be verified by checking
historical records. For various reasons, opinions cannot be directly verified.
For example, the statement "She is the most beautiful girl in the world" is
unverifiable and is therefore an opinion. Even if every girl in the world could
be assembled for comparison, different people's standards of beauty are
different, and a scale of relative beauty would be impossible to construct.

Knowledge of key words that signal opinions, such as *believe, think, seems,
may, appears, probably, likely,* and *possibly,* can be extremely helpful to readers.
Teachers often find that pointing out such indicators to children and giving
the children practice in locating them is highly beneficial.

Children must also understand that not all opinions are of equal value,
since some have been based upon solid facts, whereas others are unsupported. Critical readers try to determine the relative merits of opinions as well
as to separate the opinions from facts.

Recognition of Propaganda Techniques Elementary school children, like
adults, are constantly deluged with writing that attempts to influence their
thinking and actions. Some of these materials may be used for good purposes
and some for bad ones. For example, most people would consider propaganda designed to influence people to protect their health "good," whereas
they would label propaganda designed to influence people to do things that
are harmful to their health "bad." Since propaganda techniques are often
utilized to sway people toward or away from a cause or point of view,
children should be made aware of them so that they can avoid being unduly
influenced by them.

The Institute for Propaganda Analysis has identified seven undesirable
propaganda techniques which good critical readers should know about:

1. name calling—using derogatory labels (*yellow, reactionary, troublemaker*) to
   create negative reactions toward a person without providing evidence to
   support such impressions
2. glittering generalities—using vague phrases to influence a point of view
   without providing necessary specifics
3. transfer technique—associating a respected organization or symbol with a
   particular person, project, product, or idea, thus transferring that respect to
   the person or thing being promoted
4. plain-folks talk—relating a person (for example, a politician) or a proposed program to the common people in order to gain their support
5. testimonial technique—using a highly popular or respected person to
   endorse a product or proposal
6. bandwagon technique—playing on the urge to do what others are doing
   by giving the impression that everyone else is participating in a particular
   activity
7. card stacking—telling only one side of a story by ignoring information
   favorable to the opposing point of view.

196

Teaching
Reading in
Today's
Elementary
Schools

Children can learn to detect propaganda techniques by analyzing newspaper and magazine advertisements, printed political campaign material, and requests for donations to various organizations. Activities like the first three in the list below are also helpful. The other eleven activities can be used to provide children with practice in other critical reading skills.

ACTIVITIES

1. Number several newspaper advertisements and attach them to the bulletin board. Have children number their papers and write beside the number of each advertisement a description of the propaganda technique or techniques it uses.
2. Have a propaganda hunt. Label boxes with the names of the seven propaganda techniques discussed above, and ask children to find examples of these techniques in a variety of sources and drop their examples into the boxes. As a class activity, evaluate each example for appropriateness to the category in which it was placed.
3. Make skill sheets similar to the one below to give the students practice with recognizing propaganda techniques.

● **WORKSHEET:** *Propaganda Techniques*

Directions: Read each statement carefully. On the line after the statement, put the letter of the propaganda technique it illustrates.

Techniques
A. Name calling
B. Glittering generalities
C. Transfer technique
D. Plain-folks talk
E. Testimonial technique
F. Bandwagon technique
G. Card stacking

Statements
1. Everybody is buying Cool Kola. You buy some too._____
2. Jennifer Johnson, tennis superstar, uses our new improved hair spray.
   _____
3. Elect Jane Brown, who represents all working people. She says, "Those of us who have worked hard for our living all our lives have to stick together against the professional politicians."_____
4. Join the gang! Don't be left out! Eat at the new Biggie Burger._____
5. Senator Mitts is a conniving troublemaker!_____

6. Mack Barker, the most outstanding football player in the country, says, "I wouldn't be without my Sparkling Mouthwash. It helps me keep the girls interested."_____

7. Olin Moore believes in our country; show that our country believes in Olin Moore._____

8. This car is the only car to buy because it has power steering, power brakes, AM-FM radio, stereo tape player, air conditioner, special oversized tires, and plenty of room for seven people to ride in comfort._____●

4. Ask students to compare two biographies of a well-known person by answering questions such as "How do they differ in their treatment of the subject? Is either of the authors likely to be biased for or against the subject? Are there contradictory statements in the two works? If so, which one seems most likely to be correct? Could the truth be different from both accounts?"

5. Have students compare editorials from two newspapers with different philosophies or from different areas. Have them decide why differences exist and which stand, if any, is more reasonable, based on facts.

6. Ask students to examine newspaper stories for typographical errors and to determine whether or not the typographical error changed the message of the article.

7. Have the class interpret political cartoons from various newspapers.

8. Ask students to examine the headlines of news stories and decide whether or not the headlines fit the stories.

9. Using a list of optional topics—school policies, parental restrictions, and so forth—ask students to write editorials, first presenting facts, then their opinions, and finally their reasons for the opinions (Rabin, 1981).

10. Locate old science or geography books containing statements that are no longer true and use them to show the importance of utilizing current sources. Let students compare old books with new ones to find the differences (new material included, "facts" that have changed, etc.), and discuss what types of material are most and least likely to be dependent on recent copyright dates for accuracy (Ross, 1981).

11. Have students become acquainted with the typical point of view of a particular writer or newspaper and then predict the position that writer or newspaper will take on an issue, later checking to discover the accuracy of their predictions (Ross, 1981).

12. Let children compare the results when they write about the same topic from different viewpoints (Ross, 1981).

13. Direct students to write material that will persuade their classmates to do something. Then examine the results for the techniques they used.

14. Discuss the nutritional aspects of sugar and chemical food additives and the foods that contain them. Then have students examine the ingredient lists from popular snacks. What food value do various snacks have, based upon their labels (Neville, 1982)?

198

Teaching
Reading in
Today's
Elementary
Schools

✓ **Self-Check: Objective 9**

**What does a critical reader need to know about the authors of the
selections he or she is reading?**
**React to this statement: "I know it is correct because it is here in this
book in black and white."**
**Name seven commonly used propaganda techniques. Give an exam-
ple of each.**
(See Self-Improvement Opportunity 7.)

Creative Reading

Creative reading involves going beyond the material presented by the author.
It requires readers to think as they read, just as critical reading does, and it
also requires them to use their imaginations. According to Helen Huus (1967)
"it is concerned with the production of new ideas, the development of new
insights, fresh approaches, and original constructs." Teachers must carefully
nurture creative reading, trying not to ask only questions that have absolute
answers, since these will tend not to encourage the diverse processes
characteristic of creative reading. Creative readers must be skilled in the areas
discussed below.

Cause and Effect

Creative readers must understand cause-and-effect relationships in a story so
well that they know why a character acts as he or she does at a particular
time. For example, by analyzing the reasons for the actions in the story
"Stone Soup," the creative reader will know why the townspeople finally
produced their food supplies to be used in the soup after being so careful to
hide them and deny their existence. Such readers will also be able to imagine
what might have happened in a story if a particular event had not occurred or
if something quite different had happened.

To help students acquire the skill of reading creatively, teachers should
model the thought process involved. After the students practice on various texts, ask them to explain their reasons for thinking as they did.
Some questions they might answer for *Heidi,* for example, are presented
below:

> What would have happened in the book if Peter had not pushed Klara's wheelchair
> down the side of the mountain?
> What would have happened if Herr Sessman had refused to send Heidi back to the
> Alm, even though the doctor advised it?

Some questions for *Wind in the Willows* include:

> Why was Mole so dissatisfied with life at the beginning of the story?
> Why did Ratty search for Mole in the Wild Woods? Why was Toad boastful?

By vividly visualizing the events depicted by the author's words, creative readers allow themselves to become a part of the story—they see the colors, hear the sounds, feel the textures, taste the flavors, and smell the odors described by the writer. They will find that they are living the story as they read. Exercises that encourage visualization are listed below.

ACTIVITIES

1. Give students copies of a paragraph that vividly describes a scene or situation and have them illustrate the scene or situation in a painting or a three-dimensional art project.
2. Using a paragraph or statement that contains almost no description, ask students questions about details they would need in order to picture the scene in their minds.

   Example: The dog ran toward Jane and Susan. Jane held out her hands toward him and smiled.
   Questions: What kind of dog was it? How big was it? Why was it running toward the girls? Were the girls afraid of the dog? What happened when the dog reached the girls? Where did this action take place? Was the dog on a leash, behind a fence, or running free?

3. Have the children dramatize a story they have read, such as the folktale "Caps for Sale."

THE FAMILY CIRCUS   **By Bil Keane**

3-4
Copyright 1983
The Register and Tribune
Syndicate, Inc.

"I like reading. It turns on pictures in your head."

The Family Circus reprinted courtesy of The Register and Tribune Syndicate, Inc.

Making Value Judgments

Creative readers need to be able to determine whether actions of characters are reasonable or unreasonable. In order to help them develop this ability, teachers may ask questions such as the following:

> Was the little red hen justified in eating all of the bread she had made, refusing to share with the other animals?
>
> Was it a good thing for Heidi to save bread from the Sessmans' table to take back to the grandmother?

Solving Problems

Creative readers relate the things they read to their own personal problems, sometimes applying the solution of a problem encountered in a story to a different situation. For instance, after reading the chapter in *Tom Sawyer* in which Tom tricks his friends into painting a fence for him, a child may use a similar ruse to persuade a sibling to take over her chores or even her homework.

To work on developing this problem-solving skill, teachers need to use books in which different types of problems are solved, choosing an appropriate one to read or to let the children read and then asking the children questions, such as the following:

1. What problem did the character(s) in the story face?
2. How was the problem handled?
3. Was the solution a good one?
4. What other possible solutions can you think of?
5. Would you prefer the solution in the book or one of the others?

Predicting Outcomes

In order to predict outcomes, readers must put together available information and note trends, then project the trends into the future, making decisions about what events might logically occur next. A creative reader is constantly predicting what will happen next in a story, reacting to the events he or she is reading about and drawing conclusions about their results. Russell Stauffer and Ronald Cramer (1968) describe in detail ways of promoting this approach to reading, and a condensed version of their approach is presented in Chapter 7 under the heading "DRTA."

An enjoyable way to work on this skill is to have students read one of the action comic strips in the newspaper for several weeks and then predict what will happen next, based upon their knowledge of what has occurred until that

time. Record these predictions on paper and file them; later, students can
compare the actual ending of the adventure with their predictions. Be sure that students can present reasons to justify what they predict. When judging their theories, be sure to point out that some predictions may seem as good a way to end the story as the one the comic-strip artist used. On the other hand, some may not make sense, based on the evidence, and reasons for this should be made clear.

Improving Story Presentation

Creative readers may be able to see how a story could be improved in order to make it more interesting—for example, excessive description may cause a story to move too slowly, and certain parts could be deleted or changed to be more concise. Or students may suggest that a story did not have enough description to allow them to picture the setting and characters well enough to really become involved. In this case, ask them to add descriptive passages that make visualization easier. Perhaps one child will feel that a story would be better with more dialogue and will write scenes for the characters, to replace third-person narration. Another child may feel that a story needs a more gripping opening paragraph. The possibilities for skill development are extensive, but remember that this skill is extremely advanced and may only be attained by the best readers in the elementary grades, although many others will attain it before their school years are finished.

Producing New Creations

Art, drama, and dance can be useful in elaborating on what students read. By creating a new ending for a story, adding a new character, changing some aspect of a character, or adding an additional adventure within the framework of the existing story, students approach reading creatively. Possible activities are listed below.

ACTIVITIES

1. Have students write plays or poems based on books of fiction they have read and enjoyed.
2. Ask students to illustrate a story they have read, using a series of pictures or of three-dimensional scenes.
3. Have the students write a prose narrative based upon a poem they have read.
4. After the children have read several stories of a certain type (such as *Just So Stories*), ask them to write an original story of the same type.
5. Transfer the story of *Heidi* to the Rocky Mountains or Appalachia.

202

Teaching
Reading in
Today's
Elementary
Schools

✔ Self-Check: Objective 10

Define creative reading and discuss some of the things that creative readers must be able to do.

QUESTIONING TECHNIQUES

All reading done by children should be purposeful, because (1) children who are reading with a purpose tend to *comprehend* what they read better than those who have no purpose, and (2) children who read with a purpose tend to *retain* what they read better than those who have no purpose. For these reasons teachers should set purposes for youngsters by giving them questions rather than merely telling them, "Read chapter seven for tomorrow." This approach avoids presenting children with the insurmountable task of remembering everything they read and allows them to know that they are reading to determine main ideas, locate details, understand vocabulary terms, or meet some other well-defined goal. As a result, they can apply themselves to a specific, manageable task. However, if the teacher always uses the same type of purpose question, children may not develop the ability to read for a variety of purposes.

Even when teachers do not provide purpose questions, children are often guided in the way they approach their reading assignments by the types of questions that teachers have used in the past, on tests. If a teacher tends to ask in test questions for factual recall of small details, children will concentrate on such details, perhaps overlooking the main ideas entirely. In class discussion, the teacher may be bewildered by the fact that the children know many things that happened in a story without knowing what the basic theme was.

Whether teachers prepare only test questions or both purpose and test questions, they all use both written and oral questions as a part of class activities. And it is significant that the bulk of research indicates that regardless of when they are used, questions foster increased comprehension, apparently because readers give more time to the material related to answering them (Durkin, 1981b). Since this situation exists, teachers need to understand thoroughly the process of preparing questions.

Preparing Questions

Teachers often ask questions they devise on the spur of the moment. This practice is no doubt due to the pressure of the many different tasks that a teacher must perform during the day, but it is a poor one for at least two reasons. First, questions developed hastily, without close attention to the material involved, tend to be detail questions ("What color was the car? Where were they going?"), since detail questions are much easier to construct than most other types. But detail questions fail to measure more than simple recall. Second, many hastily constructed questions tend to be poorly worded, vague in their intent, and misleading to students.

One of the bases for planning questioning strategies is to try to construct questions of particular types to tap different levels of comprehension and different comprehension skills. There are seven major types of questions that we have found to be useful in guiding reading.

1. Main idea—ask the children to identify the central theme of the selection
2. Detail—ask for bits of information conveyed by the material
3. Vocabulary—ask for the meanings of words used in the selection
4. Sequence—require knowledge of events in their order of occurrence
5. Inference—ask for information that is implied but not directly stated in the material
6. Evaluation—ask for judgments about the material
7. Creative response—ask the children to go beyond the material and create new ideas based on the ideas they have read.

Main Idea Questions   These may give children some direction toward the nature of the answer. The question "What caused Susie to act so excited?" could direct readers toward the main idea of a passage in which Susie was very excited because she had a secret. An example of a question that offers no clues to the main idea is "What would be a title for this selection that would explain what it is about?" Main idea questions help children to be aware of details and the relationships among them.

Detail Questions   These ask for such information, as in "Who was coming to play with Maria? What was Betty bringing with her? What happened to Betty on the way to Maria's house? When did Betty finally arrive? Where had Betty left her bicycle?" Whereas it is important for students to assimilate the information conveyed by these questions, very little depth of comprehension is necessary to answer them all correctly. Therefore, even though these questions are easy to construct, they should not constitute the bulk of the questions the teacher asks.

Vocabulary Questions   Such questions check children's understanding of word meaning. For discussion purposes, a teacher might ask children to produce as many meanings of a particular word as they can, but purpose questions and test questions should ask for the meaning of a word as it is used in the selection under consideration.

Sequence Questions   These check the child's knowledge of the order in which events occurred in the story. The question "What did Alex and Robbie do when their parents left the house?" is not a sequence question, since children are free to list the events in any order they choose. The question "What three things did Alex and Robbie do, in order, when their parents left the house?" requires children to display their grasp of the sequence of events.

204
Teaching
Reading in
Today's
Elementary
Schools

When students have a clearcut purpose for reading, they will be better able to understand and retain what they read. (© Elizabeth Crews)

Inference Questions These require some reading between the lines. The answer to an inference question is implied by statements in the selection, but it is not directly stated, as in the example below.

Passage:
Margie and Jan were sitting on the couch listening to Barry Manilow records. Their father walked in and announced, "I hear that Barry Manilow is giving a concert at the Municipal Auditorium next week." Both girls jumped up and ran toward their father. "Can we go? Can we go?" they begged.

Question:
Do you think Margie and Jan liked to hear Barry Manilow sing? Why or why not?

Evaluation Questions Such questions require children to make judgments. Although these judgments are inferences, they depend upon more than the information implied or stated by the story; the children must have enough experience related to the situations involved to establish standards for comparison. An example of an evaluation question is "Was the method Kim used to rescue Dana wise? Why or why not?" These questions are excellent for open-ended class discussion but hard to grade as test questions.

Creative Response Questions Questions requiring creative response are also good for class discussions. As a means of testing comprehension of a passage, however, they are not desirable, since almost any response could be considered correct. Examples of creative response questions include "If the story stopped after Jimmie lost his money, what ending would you write for it?" and "If Meg had not gone to school that day, what do you think might have happened?"

Other Question Types Doris Crowell and Kathryn Au (1981), who recommend use of different question types, have developed a scale of comprehension questions arranged in order from easiest to most difficult:

1. Association—designed to discover any detail from a story that a child can recall. Example: "What was this story about?"
2. Categorization—requires a simple categorization. Example: "Did you like Anna Marie? Why or why not?"
3. Seriation—asks for interrelationships among details, such as sequence of events or cause and effect. Example: "What happened first? What happened next? And then what?"
4. Integration—requires combining elements in the story into a coherent structure. Example: "What was the problem in this story?" followed by a question specific to the story, such as "What problem did Nino have?"
5. Extension—asks for application beyond the bounds of the immediate story structure. Example: "Tell me another way this story could have ended."

Other Bases for Questioning

Two other bases for questioning deserve attention: use of story grammar and use of a story map.

A story is a series of events related to each other in particular ways. As people hear and read many stories, they develop expectations, sometimes called story schemata, about the types of things they will encounter; these help them organize information. Related story schemata are described by a *story grammar*. As Marilyn Sadow (1982) suggests, questions based on story grammar may help children develop story schemata. The questions should be chosen to reflect the logical sequence of events.

206

Teaching
Reading in
Today's
Elementary
Schools

David Rumelhart proposed a simple story grammar that "describes a story as consisting of a setting and one or more episodes" (Sadow, 1982, p. 519). The setting includes the main characters and the time and location of the events, and each episode contains an initiating event, the main character's reaction to it, an action of the main character caused by this reaction, and a consequence of the action, which may act as an initiating event for a subsequent episode. (Sometimes some of the elements of an episode are not directly stated.) Sadow suggests the following five generic questions as appropriate types to ask about a story:

1. Where and when did the events in the story take place and who was involved in them? (Setting)
2. What started the chain of events in the story? (Initiating Event)
3. What was the main character's reaction to this event? (Reaction)
4. What did the main character do about it? (Action)
5. What happened as a result of what the main character did? (Consequence). (Sadow, 1982, p. 520)

Such questions can help students see the underlying order of ideas in a story, but of course teachers should reword them to fit the story and the particular children. For example, Question 1 can be broken into three questions (where, when, who), and the teacher can provide appropriate focus by using words or phrases from the story. After pupils address these story grammar questions, which establish the essential facts, they should answer questions that help them relate the story to their experiences and knowledge (Sadow, 1982).

Each of Sadow's generic questions could include detail or inference questions, as described in the suggested list of seven question types on page 203. For example, her setting question would fit under the detail category if the answer was directly stated in the material, as is true for Steven Vincent Benét's short story "A Tooth for Paul Revere," and under the inference category if the answer was implied, as in Benét's "By the Waters of Babylon." Similarly, Sadow's initiating-event question is a type of sequence question, whereas her reaction question could be a detail or an inference question, according to our chosen types, as could her action and consequence questions.

Isabel Beck and Margaret McKeown (1981) suggest use of a *story map*, "a unified representation of a story based on a logical organization of events and ideas of central importance to the story and interrelationships of these events and ideas. The map is derived from an integration of explicit and implicit ideas, since even the most basic understanding of a story requires the making of inferences as well as recall of explicit events" (Beck and McKeown, 1981, pp. 914–15). In order to develop a story map, the teacher first determines the premise or starting point of the story and then lists the major events and ideas that make up the plot, including implied ideas and relationships. Then he or she designs questions (both detail and inference types) that elicit the information in the map and follow the sequence of the story. Extension questions (evaluation or creative-response type) can be used to extend discussion to broader perspectives; such questions that elicit tangential information should not be placed in the story-map question sequence.

Guidelines for Preparation

Some guidelines for preparing questions may be of use to teachers who wish to improve their questioning techniques. The following suggestions may help teachers avoid the pitfalls that have been detected by other educators.

1. When trying to determine overall comprehension skills, ask a variety of questions designed to reflect different types of comprehension. *Avoid overloading the skill evaluation with a single type of question.*
2. Don't ask questions about obscure or insignificant portions of the selection. Such questions may make a test harder, but they don't convey realistic data about comprehension. *"Hard" tests and "good" tests are not necessarily synonymous.*
3. Avoid ambiguous or tricky questions. *If a question has two or more possible interpretations, more than one answer for it has to be acceptable.*
4. Questions that a person who has not read the material can answer correctly offer you no valuable information about comprehension. *Avoid useless questions.*
5. Don't ask questions in language that is more difficult than the language of the selection the question is about. *Sometimes you can word questions so as to prevent a child who knows the answer from responding appropriately.*
6. Make sure the answers to sequence questions require knowledge of the *order* of events. *Don't confuse questions that simply ask for lists with sequence questions.*
7. Don't ask for unsupported opinions when testing for comprehension. Have children give support for their opinions, by asking, "Why do you think that?" or "What in the story made you think that?" *If you ask for an unsupported opinion, any answer would be correct.*
8. Don't ask for opinions, if you want facts. *Ask for the type of information you want to receive.*
9. Avoid questions that give away information. Instead of saying, "What makes you believe the boy was angry?" say, "How do you think the boy felt? Why?" *Questions may lead students to the answers by supplying too much information.*
10. If a question can be answered with a *yes* or *no*, or if a choice of answers is offered, the child has a chance to answer the question correctly without having to read the selection at all. *Avoid questions that offer choices.*

Helping Children Question

The Reciprocal Questioning (ReQuest) procedure, developed by Anthony V. Manzo (1969), seems a promising way of improving reading comprehension as well as of helping children develop questioning techniques. ReQuest is a one-to-one teaching technique that encourages children to think critically and formulate questions. A condensed outline of the procedure is given below.

1. Both child and teacher have copies of the selection to read.
2. Both silently read the first sentence. The child may ask the teacher as many questions as he or she wishes about that sentence. The child is told to try to ask the kind of questions that the teacher might ask, in the way the teacher might ask them.
3. The teacher answers the questions but requires the child to rephrase those questions that he or she cannot answer because of their poor syntax or incorrect logic.
4. After the teacher has answered all the child's questions, both read the second sentence, and the teacher asks as many questions as he or she feels will profitably add to the child's understanding of the content.
5. The teacher periodically requires the child to verify his or her responses.
6. After reading the second sentence, the teacher requires the child to integrate the ideas from both sentences.

All through this interaction, the teacher constantly encourages the child to imitate the teacher's questioning behavior, reinforcing such behavior by saying, "that's a good question" or by giving the fullest possible reply.

This procedure continues until the child can read all the words in the first paragraph, can demonstrate literal understanding of what he or she has read, and can formulate a reasonable purpose, stated as a question, for completing the remainder of the selection.[1]

✔ Self-Check: Objective 11

Name seven types of questions that are useful in guiding reading and checking comprehension.

Name five of the ten guidelines for question preparation mentioned in this section.

(See Self-Improvement Opportunities 8 and 9.)

---

[1]For a specific illustration of helping children to ask questions by using a technique called DRTA, see Elaine Schwartz and Alice Sherf, "Student Involvement in Questioning for Comprehension," *The Reading Teacher* 29 (November 1975): 150–54. Also see Barbara Olmo, "Teaching Students to Ask Questions," *Language Arts* 52 (November/December 1975): 1116–19 for more ideas on questioning.

True or False

_____ 1. Context clues are of little help in determining the meanings of unfamiliar words, although they are useful for recognizing familiar ones.

_____ 2. Structural analysis can be an aid to determining meanings of new words containing familiar prefixes, suffixes, and root words.

_____ 3. When looking up a word in the dictionary to determine its meaning, a child needs to read only the first definition listed.

_____ 4. Homophones are words that have identical, or almost identical, meanings.

_____ 5. Antonyms are words that have opposite meanings.

_____ 6. Punctuation marks are clues to pauses and pitch changes.

_____ 7. The main idea of a paragraph is always stated in the form of a topic sentence.

_____ 8. Literal comprehension involves acquiring information that is directly stated in a selection.

_____ 9. Students must attend to details when they follow directions.

_____ 10. Comic strips can be used to develop an activity for recognizing sequence.

_____ 11. Critical reading is reading for evaluation.

_____ 12. Critical reading skills are easier to teach than literal reading skills.

_____ 13. Readers at the critical and interpretive levels are interested in determining the author's purpose.

_____ 14. Critical readers are not interested in copyright dates of material they read.

_____ 15. An inference is an idea that is implied in the material rather than directly stated.

_____ 16. Elementary school children are too young to be able to recognize propaganda techniques.

_____ 17. A bandwagon approach takes advantage of the desires of people to conform to the crowd.

_____ 18. Critical thinking skills should first be given attention in the intermediate grades.

_____ 19. Critical readers read with a questioning attitude.

_____ 20. Creative reading involves going beyond the material presented by the author.

_____ 21. Teachers should give little class time to creative reading because it is not practical.

_____ 22. All reading that children do should be purposeful.

_____ 23. When making out comprehension questions for testing purposes, teachers should use several different types of questions.

_____ 24. A good test is a hard test and vice versa.

_____ 25. Listing questions and sequence questions are the same thing.

210
Teaching
Reading in
Today's
Elementary
Schools

_____ 26. Word play is one good approach to building vocabulary.

_____ 27. Punctuation marks do not function as clues to sentence meaning.

_____ 28. Children sometimes make overgeneralizations in dealing with word meanings.

_____ 29. Research has shown that teachers spend the majority of their time on instruction in reading comprehension.

_____ 30. Reading comprehension involves relating textual information to pre-existing knowledge structures.

_____ 31. Comprehension skills should be taught in a way that emphasizes their application when students are actually reading connected discourse.

_____ 32. Less able readers may rely too much on either text-based or knowledge-based processing.

_____ 33. Richard Rystrom has presented an argument that reading is exclusively a top-down process.

_____ 34. The development of vocabulary is essentially a child's development of labels for his or her schemata.

_____ 35. Work with analogies bolsters word knowledge.

_____ 36. Restrictive clauses cause few comprehension problems for children.

_____ 37. Semantic webbing involves systematically deleting words from a printed passage.

_____ 38. Children make inferences that are consistent with their schemata.

_____ 39. Some children have difficulty determining referents of pronouns and adverbs.

Vocabulary

Check your knowledge of these terms. Reread parts of the chapter if necessary.

analogies
antonyms
appositive
cloze procedure
creative reading
critical reading
ellipsis
etymology
figurative
   language
homographs

homophones
idiom
interactive processing
interpretive reading
juncture
knowledge-based
   processing
literal comprehension
morpheme
nonrestrictive clauses

propaganda
   techniques
relative clauses
restrictive clauses
schema
semantic webbing
synonyms
text-based
   processing
topic sentence
visualization

Also look back to the section on propaganda techniques and check your knowledge of those terms.

1. Plan a dictionary exercise that requires children to locate the meaning of a word that fits the context surrounding that word.
2. In a chapter of a textbook for a content area such as science, social studies, math, language arts, or health, locate examples of difficult words whose meanings are made clear through context clues. Decide which kind of clue is involved in each example.
3. Construct a board game which requires the players to respond with synonyms and antonyms when they land on certain spaces or draw certain cards. Demonstrate the game with your classmates role-playing elementary students, or as an alternative, actually use the game with children in a regular classroom setting.
4. Construct a time line for a chapter in a social studies text that has a chronological order organizational pattern. Describe to your classmates how you could use the time line with children to teach this organizational pattern.
5. Use old newspapers to devise teaching materials for
   a. finding main ideas.
   b. locating propaganda techniques.
   c. distinguishing fact from opinion.
   d. recognizing sequence.
6. Make a "Following Directions" board game.
7. Make a file of examples of each of the propaganda techniques listed in the chapter. File ideas for teaching activities, games, bulletin boards, and so on, and show your files to your classmates, sharing with them the possible instructional uses of your file.
8. Make up questions of the seven types listed on the content found in this chapter or on the content of another chapter in this book. Bring the questions to class and ask classmates to respond.
9. Study the selection below and make up questions of the seven different types listed in this chapter. Check the ten guidelines to make sure your questions are well written. Then have pupils read the selection and answer your questions. Evaluate their comprehension skills.

Miguel had decided that everything that wasn't Mexican or Spanish must be better. He enjoyed going to Ramón's house, but he didn't enjoy it when Ramón came home with him.

Mr. Diaz frequently had homework to do, too. One afternoon, Mr. Diaz was at home when Miguel and Ramón came in. He was studying at the kitchen table, and he had a lot of paper in front of him.

"My friend and I have assignments to do, Father," Miguel said, "and we need this table for our papers." He hoped that his father would leave the room.

However, Mr. Diaz shifted some of his papers out of the way and explained, "Now there is room for all."

212

Teaching
Reading in
Today's
Elementary
Schools

"No, no," Miguel said. "You can't work here, Father. We talk while we do our work, and you couldn't get yours done."

"Oh, we can be quiet, Mike," Ramón said. "Your father can work here, too."

The two boys started their homework. Then Ramón saw that Mr. Diaz was looking strangely at what he was reading. "Can I help you with something?" Ramón asked. He walked over to Mr. Diaz.

"My father does not need your help," Miguel said. He didn't want Ramón to see what his father was doing.

"Thank you, Ramón," Mr. Diaz said. "I do need your help. I do not know what this word is."

Ramón looked at the book Mr. Diaz was holding. "That word is 'shivered.' It's a hard word to read." Then Ramón said, "Are you coming to our school tonight, Mr. Diaz?"

Mr. Diaz looked surprised. "Why should I go to your school tonight?" he asked.

"All the parents will be there tonight. Our school is having an open house so the parents can talk to the teachers. Didn't Mike tell you about tonight?"

Miguel didn't look at his father when he said, "I didn't tell him."

Mr. Diaz saw that Miguel didn't want him to visit the school. He also saw that Miguel didn't want the teachers to meet his parents.

Mr. Diaz said to Ramón, "Miguel's mother has been sick this week with a bad cold. But I will be happy to come to the school tonight." Mr. Diaz didn't say anything to Miguel.[2]

Bibliography

Barnitz, John G. "Developing Sentence Comprehension in Reading." *Language Arts* 56 (November/December 1979): 902–908, 958.

Beck, Isabel L., and Margaret G. McKeown. "Developing Questions That Promote Comprehension: The Story Map." *Language Arts* 58 (November/December 1981): 913–18.

Bellows, Barbara Plotkin. "Running Shoes Are to Jogging as Analogies Are to Creative/Critical Thinking." *Journal of Reading* 23 (March 1980): 507–11.

Criscuolo, Nicholas P. "Creative Vocabulary Building." *Journal of Reading* 24 (December 1980): 260–61.

Crist, Barbara. "Tim's Time: Vocabulary Activities from Names." *The Reading Teacher* 34 (December 1980): 309–12.

Crowell, Doris C., and Kathryn Hu-pei Au. "A Scale of Questions to Guide Comprehension Instruction." *The Reading Teacher* 34 (January 1981): 389–93.

[2]"My Name is Miguel" by Eth Clifford. From Leo Fay et al., *Telephones and Tangerines. Level 10* of the Rand McNally Reading Program (Chicago: Riverside Publishing Company, 1978), pp. 108–110. Reprinted by permission of the publisher.

Cunningham, Pat. "Improving Listening and Reading Comprehension." *The Reading Teacher* 35 (January 1982): 486–88.

Donlan, Dan. "Locating Main Ideas in History Textbooks." *Journal of Reading* 24 (November 1980): 135–40.

Dreher, Mariam Jean, and Harry Singer. "Story Grammar Instruction Unnecessary for Intermediate Grade Students." *The Reading Teacher* 34 (December 1980): 261–68.

Duffelmeyer, Frederick A. "The Influence of Experience-Based Vocabulary Instruction on Learning Word Meanings." *Journal of Reading* 24 (October 1980): 35–40.

Duffelmeyer, Frederick A. "Introducing Words in Context." *The Reading Teacher* 35 (March 1982): 724–25.

Duffelmeyer, Frederick A., and Barbara Blakely Duffelmeyer. "Developing Vocabulary Through Dramatization." *Journal of Reading* 23 (November 1979): 141–43.

Durkin, Dolores. "Reading Comprehension Instruction in Five Basal Reader Series." *Reading Research Quarterly* 16 (1981a): 515–44.

Durkin, Dolores. "What Classroom Observations Reveal about Reading Comprehension Instruction." *Reading Research Quarterly* 14 (1978–79): 481–533.

Durkin, Dolores. "What Is the Value of the New Interest in Reading Comprehension?" *Language Arts* 58 (January 1981b): 23–43.

Eads, Maryann. "What To Do When They Don't Understand What They Read—Research-Based Strategies for Teaching Reading Comprehension." *The Reading Teacher* 34 (February 1981): 565–71.

Freedman, Glenn, and Elizabeth G. Reynolds. "Enriching Basal Reader Lessons with Semantic Webbing." *The Reading Teacher* 33 (March 1980): 667–84.

Gipe, Joan P. "Use of a Relevant Context Helps Kids Learn New Word Meanings." *The Reading Teacher* 33 (January 1980): 398–402.

Gold, Yvonne. "Helping Students Discover the Origins of Words." *The Reading Teacher* 35 (December 1981): 350–51.

Grant, Patricia L. "The Cloze Procedure as an Instructional Device." *The Reading Teacher* 22 (May 1979): 699–705.

Hacker, Charles J. "From Schema Theory to Classroom Practice." *Language Arts* 57 (November/December 1980): 866–71.

Hansen, Jane. "The Effects of Inference Training and Practice on Young Children's Reading Comprehension." *Reading Research Quarterly* 16, no. 3 (1981a): 391–417.

Hansen, Jane. "An Inferential Comprehension Strategy for Use with Primary Grade Children." *The Reading Teacher* 34 (March 1981b): 665–69.

Huus, Helen. "Critical and Creative Reading." In *Critical Reading*, Martha L. King, Bernice Ellinger, and Willavene Wolf, eds. New York: J. B. Lippincott, 1967, pp. 84–89.

214

Teaching
Reading in
Today's
Elementary
Schools

Irwin, Judith Westphal. "Implicit Connectives and Comprehension." *The Reading Teacher* 33 (February 1980): 527–29.

Jones, Linda L. "An Interactive View of Reading: Implications for the Classroom." *The Reading Teacher* 35 (April 1982): 772–77.

Kachuck, Beatrice. "Relative Clauses May Cause Confusion for Young Readers." *The Reading Teacher* 34 (January 1981): 372–77.

Kaplan, Elaine M., and Anita Tuchman. "Vocabulary Strategies Belong in the Hands of Learners." *Journal of Reading* 24 (October 1980): 32–34.

Koeller, Shirley, and Samina Khan. "Going Beyond the Dictionary with the English Vocabulary Explosion." *Journal of Reading* 24 (April 1981): 628–29.

Lange, Bob. "Making Sense with Schemata." *Journal of Reading* 24 (February 1981): 442–45.

Macey, Joan Mary. "Word Lines: An Approach to Vocabulary Development." *The Reading Teacher* 35 (November 1981): 216–17.

Manzo, Anthony V. "The ReQuest Procedure." *Journal of Reading* 13 (November 1969): 123–26.

Mateja, John. "Musical Cloze: Background, Purpose, and Sample." *The Reading Teacher* 35 (January 1982): 444–48.

McConaughy, Stephanie H. "Word Recognition and Word Meaning in the Total Reading Process." *Language Arts* 55 (November/December 1978): 946–56, 1003.

McGee, Lea M., and Gail E. Tompkins. "The Videotape Answer to Independent Reading Comprehension Activities." *The Reading Teacher* 34 (January 1981): 427–33.

Moore, David W., and John E. Readence. "Processing Main Ideas Through Parallel Lesson Transfer." *Journal of Reading* 23 (April 1980): 589–93.

Neville, Rita. "Critical Thinkers Become Critical Readers." *The Reading Teacher* 35 (May 1982): 947–48.

Newcastle, Helen. "Children's Problems with Written Directions." *The Reading Teacher* 28 (December 1974): 292–94.

Olmo, Barbara. "Teaching Students to Ask Questions." *Language Arts* 52 (November/December 1975): 1116–19.

Pearson, P. David, and Dale D. Johnson. *Teaching Reading Comprehension.* New York: Holt, Rinehart and Winston, 1978.

Pearson, P. David, et al. *The Effect of Background Knowledge on Young Children's Comprehension of Explicit and Implicit Information.* Urbana: University of Illinois, Center for the Study of Reading, 1979.

Rabin, Annette T. "Critical Reading." *Journal of Reading* 24 (January 1981): 348.

Ross, Elinor Parry. "Checking the Source: An Essential Component of Critical Reading." *Journal of Reading* 24 (January 1981): 311–15.

Sadow, Marilyn W. "The Use of Story Grammar in the Design of Questions." *The Reading Teacher* 35 (February 1982): 518–22.

Schoenfeld, Florence G. "Instructional Uses of the Cloze Procedure." *The Reading Teacher* 34 (November 1980): 147–51.

Schwartz, Elaine, and Alice Sheff. "Student Involvement in Questioning for Comprehension." *The Reading Teacher* 29 (November 1975): 150–54.

Spiro, Rand J. *Etiology of Comprehension Style.* Urbana: University of Illinois, Center for the Study of Reading, 1979.

Stauffer, Russell G., and Ronald Cramer. *Teaching Reading at the Primary Level.* Newark, Del.: International Reading Association, 1968.

Stevens, Kathleen C. "Can We Improve Reading by Teaching Background Information?" *Journal of Reading* 25 (January 1982): 326–29.

Strange, Michael. "Instructional Implications of a Conceptual Theory of Reading Comprehension." *The Reading Teacher* 33 (January 1980): 391–97.

Whaley, Jill Fitzgerald. "Story Grammars and Reading Instruction." *The Reading Teacher* 34 (April 1981): 762–71.

Suggested Readings

Baker, Deborah Tresidder. "What Happened When? Activities for Teaching Sequence Skills." *The Reading Teacher* 36 (November 1982): 216–18.

Brown, Bonnie. "Enrich Your Reading Program with Personal Words." *The Reading Teacher* 35 (October 1981): 40–43.

Crafton, Linda K. "Comprehension Before, During, and After Reading." *The Reading Teacher* 36 (December 1982): 293–97.

Dallman, Martha, et al. *The Teaching of Reading.* 6th ed. New York: Holt, Rinehart and Winston, 1982, Chapters 7A and 7B.

Durkin, Dolores. *Teaching Them to Read.* 3rd ed. Boston: Allyn and Bacon, 1978, Chapters 14 and 15.

Fagan, William T. "Transformations and Comprehension." *The Reading Teacher* 25 (November 1971): 169–72.

Farrar, Mary Thomas. "Another Look at Oral Questions for Comprehension." *The Reading Teacher* 36 (January 1983): 370–74.

Fodor, J. A., and M. Garrett. "Some Syntactic Determinants of Sentential Complexity." *Perception and Psychophysics* 2 (July 1967).

Fowler, Gerald. "Developing Comprehension Skills in Primary Students Through the Use of Story Frames." *The Reading Teacher* 36 (November 1982): 176–79.

Goodman, Kenneth S., and Catherine Buck. "Dialect Barriers to Reading Comprehension Revisited." *The Reading Teacher* 27 (October 1973): 6–12.

Heilman, Arthur W., et al. *Principles and Practices of Teaching Reading.* 5th ed. Columbus, Ohio: Charles E. Merrill, 1981, Chapters 6 and 7.

216

Teaching
Reading in
Today's
Elementary
Schools

Hittleman, Daniel R. *Developmental Reading, K–8: Teaching From a Psycholinguistic Perspective.* 2nd ed. Boston: Houghton Mifflin, 1983, Chapter 8.

Hunkins, Frances P. *Questioning Strategies and Techniques.* Boston: Allyn and Bacon, 1972.

Johnson, Dale D., and P. David Pearson. *Teaching Reading Vocabulary.* New York: Holt, Rinehart and Winston, 1978.

Karlin, Robert. *Teaching Elementary Reading: Principles and Strategies.* 3rd ed. New York: Harcourt Brace Jovanovich, 1980, Chapter 7.

Kennedy, Eddie C. *Methods in Teaching Developmental Reading.* 2nd ed. Itasca, Ill.: Peacock, 1981, Chapters 9 and 10.

Lamb, George S., and John C. Towner. "The Portent of Reading." *The Reading Teacher* 28 (April 1975): 638–42.

Lapp, Dianne, James Flood, and Gary Gleckman. "Classroom Practices Can Make Use of What Researchers Learn." *The Reading Teacher* 35 (February 1982): 578–85.

McCabe, Patrick P. "Cohesive Ties in Text." *Language Arts* 58 (November/December 1981): 945–46.

Merlin, Shirley B., and Sue F. Rogers. "Direct Teaching Strategies." *The Reading Teacher* 35 (December 1981): 292–97.

Moberly, Peggy. "Anaphoric Relationships." Unpublished paper, Renton, Washington, 1982.

Monson, Dianne. "Effect of Type and Direction on Comprehension of Anaphoric Relationships." Paper presented at International Reading Association Word Research Conference, Seattle, Washington, 1982.

Olmo, Barbara. "Teaching Students to Ask Questions." *Language Arts* 52 (November–December 1975): 1116–19.

Pearson, P. David, and Dale D. Johnson. *Teaching Reading Comprehension.* New York: Holt, Rinehart and Winston, 1978.

Raphael, Taffy E. "Question-Answering Strategies for Children." *The Reading Teacher* 36 (November 1982): 186–90.

Schwartz, Elaine, and Alice Sheff. "Student Involvement in Questioning for Comprehension." *The Reading Teacher* 29 (November 1975): 150–54.

Smith, Richard J., and Dale D. Johnson. *Teaching Children to Read.* 2nd ed. Reading, Massachusetts: Addison-Wesley, 1980, Chapter 6.

Tyson, Eleanore S., and Lee Mountain. "A Riddle or Pun Makes Learning Words Fun." *The Reading Teacher* 36 (November 1982): 170–73.

Wilson, Carol Roller. "Teaching Reading Comprehension by Connecting the Known to the New." *The Reading Teacher* 36 (January 1983): 382–89.

Wood, Karen D., and Nora Robinson. "Vocabulary, Language, and Prediction: A Prereading Strategy." *The Reading Teacher* 36 (January 1983): 392–95.

Zintz, Miles V. *The Reading Process: The Teacher and the Learner.* 3rd ed. Dubuque, Iowa: William C. Brown, 1980, Chapters 10 and 12.

CHAPTER 5

Major Approaches to
Reading Instruction

Introduction

Over the years educators have developed many approaches to teaching reading, some of which have gained wide acceptance. These are discussed in this chapter. You will notice that these approaches are not mutually exclusive; in many instances teachers use more than one method simultaneously. In fact, educators who advocate an eclectic approach urge teachers to use the best techniques and materials from each approach in order to meet the varied needs of the individuals in any classroom.

Setting Objectives

When you finish reading this chapter, you should be able to

1. Name the types of materials that are a part of most basal reader series.
2. Describe a directed reading activity.
3. Explain the rationale behind the language experience approach.
4. Discuss the characteristics of the individualized reading approach.
5. Name some other ways of individualizing reading instruction.
6. Discuss the features of linguistic approaches.

BASAL READER APPROACH

Basal reader series are the most widely used materials for teaching reading in the elementary schools of America. They help children become ready for reading and they provide for development and practice of reading skills in each grade. For example, the following books are included in the Houghton Mifflin Reading Program:

Readiness—*Ready Steps*
Prereading—Level A, *Getting Ready to Read*
Preprimer—Level B, *Bears*
Preprimer—Level C, *Balloons*
Preprimer—Level D, *Boats*
Primer—Level E, *Sunshine*
1st Reader—Level F, *Moonbeams*
2^1 Reader—Level G, *Skylights*
2^2 Reader—Level H, *Towers*
3^1 Reader—Level I, *Spinners*
3^2 Reader—Level J, *Weavers*
4th Reader—Level K, *Gateways*
5th Reader—Level L, *Banners*

6th Reader—Level M, *Beacons*
7th Reader—Level N, *Emblems*
8th Reader—Level O, *Awards*

In addition, basal reader series include teacher's manuals, which have detailed lesson plans that help teachers use the readers to best advantage. Teachers who follow these plans use what is called a directed reading activity (DRA), described later in this chapter. Basal reader series also include workbooks that children can use to reinforce skills they have previously learned in class. Workbooks are not designed to teach the skills and should not be used for this purpose. Many publishing companies offer other supplementary materials to be used in conjunction with basal series such as ''big books'' (chart-sized replicas of readiness book pages and preprimer stories), read-aloud libraries for the teacher, duplicating masters, unit tests, and various other items.

The major strengths of basal reader programs are listed below.

1. The books are carefully graded in difficulty. The vocabularies of most series are carefully controlled so that children do not meet too many unfamiliar words in a single lesson, and repetition of words is planned so that the children have a chance to fix them in their memories.
2. The teacher's manuals have many valuable suggestions about teaching reading lessons, and thus can save much lesson preparation time.
3. Most basal reader series deal with all phases of the reading program, including word recognition, comprehension, oral reading, silent reading, reading for information, and reading for enjoyment. This comprehensive coverage helps a teacher avoid overemphasis or underemphasis of any aspect.
4. The series provide for systematic teaching of skills and systematic review.

Nevertheless, basal readers have frequently been the object of criticism in the past. The weaknesses that have been mentioned most often are:

1. Controlling vocabularies causes dull, repetitive stories with little literary merit.
2. The sentence structure found in most basal readers is not like that used by children who read them. It is too stiff and formal, devoid of the contractions and sentence fragments used in normal conversation.
3. Settings and characters tend to be familiar to middle-class suburban white children from intact families, but not to other racial and socioeconomic groups or groups from rural or urban backgrounds.
4. The characters tend to be presented in stereotyped male/female roles and situations.

220

Teaching
Reading in
Today's
Elementary
Schools

5. Basal series are often advertised as *total* reading programs. If teachers accept this assertion, they may fail to provide the variety of experiences that children need for a balanced program.

6. Teachers are often led to believe that if they do not carry out *all* the suggestions in the teacher's manuals, they will fail to provide adequate instruction. By trying to do everything suggested, they use up valuable time with inappropriate activities for some groups of children, leaving no time for appropriate ones. Basal readers should not be used from front to back in their entirety without considering the special needs of particular children in the class.

Recently two other complaints have surfaced. One is based on research by Dolores Durkin (1981), which uncovered the fact that teacher's manuals of basal reader series give much more attention to comprehension assessment and practice than to direct, explicit instruction. The teaching suggestions that are included tend to be very brief, and often ideas for instruction in comprehension are offered *after* a selection, when such instruction would have been helpful in understanding the selection itself. In addition, manuals only infrequently bring together related materials (such as different ways of showing possession) in review so that teachers can emphasize the relationships.

The second complaint is about the readability levels of the workbooks accompanying basal readers, as opposed to the readability levels of the readers themselves. Gisela Fitzgerald (1979) and Carol Stensen (1982) found that, in general, workbooks were too difficult for the grade levels at which they are placed, and those for grades four through six were especially difficult, being at seventh-grade level or above.

Authors of basal readers have been trying, with a good deal of success, to overcome the causes of these criticisms. In order to provide stories with high quality, limited vocabulary, and extensive repetition, they have included folk tales in some of the early readers. Other good literature is also included. Authors have tried to make the language more like normal conversation, and they have diversified the characters, introducing people of various races, roles, and backgrounds. Female children now sometimes wear jeans and play ball rather than being permanently relegated to the kitchen to bake cookies. Dad has ceased to dress perpetually in a business suit, and Mom appears without an apron. All of these modifications show sensitivity to the needs of textbook users and the changes in society.

Recently, interest in the characteristics and content of basal readers has surfaced, as reflected by several studies that have discovered pertinent information. Victoria Chou Hare (1982) studied the teacher's manuals of four series, two of which had an early meaning-getting emphasis and the other two of which had an early decoding emphasis, to determine whether comprehension questions reflected the philosophical stance of the series. She hypothesized that the meaning-emphasis series would have more questions requiring inferential thinking and use of prior knowledge, whereas the decoding-emphasis series would use more literal and text-based questions. This hypothesis was affirmed to some extent, but Hare found many similarities between the two types of readers. Both had larger numbers of literal questions in the first-grade text than at the higher levels, although the decoding-emphasis texts had slightly larger percentages of these questions than the meaning-emphasis texts did. When Hare also considered grades three and five, however, she found no significant differences in the number of strictly literal questions in the two types of series. In the fifth-grade texts, both types of series had more questions requiring children to integrate passage information with prior knowledge, although the meaning-emphasis series, considered together, had a higher percentage of these than the decoding-emphasis series, considered together, did. This study appears to indicate that a series' philosophy is only somewhat evident in the relative concentration of question types asked.

Robert Aaron and Martha Anderson (1981) analyzed three basal reader series to discover the values expressed in them, and learned that the series were alike in stressing work/success/failure, cooperation/helpfulness/togetherness, solicitude for others/kindness, good and bad moral rules, strength/activity/power, novelty/excitement, cleanliness/orderliness, responsibility, independence/toughness, trying hard/don't give up, courage, smartness/cleverness/thinking, generosity/doing more than required/noncommercialism, sense of emergency, fairness, and honesty. Each of these values appeared in at least three of the sixty-three stories analyzed. Many of them were found in basals of earlier periods. Unlike earlier readers, however, today's basals were found to have strong female models in nontraditional roles.

In another research effort in this field, Geraldine Snyder (1979) studied basal stories to see if they offered role models of people reading. The results were somewhat disappointing. Although the readers depicted people reading a wide variety of printed forms, the different forms (for example, blueprints, labels, addresses on letters) did not appear often. Characters were shown reading storybooks and signs most frequently, generally in the home, and males were shown reading more than females. Even animals were shown reading more than females.

Finally, Florence Pieronek (1980) studied the degree to which basal readers reflect the interests of intermediate students and found that, with minor exceptions, the books reflect the students' interests reasonably well. Only mystery and humor seem to be somewhat slighted.

It is worth noting that educators have expressed considerable concern about the misuse of workbooks that accompany basal readers—some teachers use them to keep children busy while they meet with other children or do paperwork. It is important to note that the fault here is with the

222

Teaching
Reading in
Today's
Elementary
Schools

Assignments in basal workbooks should always be purposeful; they should be used to help students practice skills already taught.   (© Walter S. Silver)

teachers' procedure and not with the workbooks. Workbook activities should always be purposeful, and a teacher should never assign a workbook page simply to occupy students. He or she should grade and return completed workbook assignments promptly, since children need to have correct responses reinforced immediately and to be informed about incorrect responses so that they will not continue to practice them.

Sumner Schachter (1981) has suggested ways in which teachers can increase the effectiveness of their use of workbooks. First, teachers should decide to use the pages to provide children with appropriate practice needed to master a skill previously taught and to provide successful experiences. To achieve these goals in a group setting, a teacher can use the every-pupil response technique, having all students respond to instructions ("underline," "circle," and so forth) at the same time. When a spoken response is required, the teacher asks the question and then gives the child's name, so that everyone attends to the question. Incorporation of trimodal responses, in which children respond to each task in visual, auditory, and kinesthetic or tactile modes, is also helpful. For example, they see the word, hear its pronunciation, and write it. At times the teacher may wish to do an exercise with the children to be sure they complete it successfully. And some children may need more practice than others, which they can get without extra pages if the teacher offers multiple practice for each item on one page.

For example, first the teacher might read himself or herself, then have the students underline, and then ask the students to read.

In this discussion we have generalized about basal readers; it is not our intention to imply that all basal reader series are alike. On the contrary, series differ in their basic philosophies, their order of presentation of skills, their degree and type of vocabulary control, and their types of selections. Most are eclectic in approach, but some emphasize one particular method, such as a linguistic or an intensive phonics approach. Some contain no pictures; some have line drawings or photographs; and some provide a mixture of drawings and photographs. Before a school system adopts a basal series, teachers should examine many series. The one that best fits the student population should be selected.

✔ Self-Check: Objective 1

List some types of materials that are a part of most basal reading series and explain the purpose of each.
(See Self-Improvement Opportunity 1.)

Directed Reading Activity (DRA)

The DRA is a teaching strategy used to extend and strengthen a child's reading abilities. It can be used with either a basal story or any other reading selection, including content area materials. The five steps that usually comprise the DRA are summarized below.

1. *Motivation and development of background.* During this part the teacher attempts to interest pupils in reading about the topic by helping them associate the subject matter with their own experiences or by using audiovisual aids to arouse interest in unfamiliar areas. It may not be necessary to work on motivation for all stories.

   At this point the teacher can determine whether the children have the background of experiences and language necessary for understanding the story, and if necessary, he or she can develop new concepts and vocabulary before the story is read.

2. *Directed story reading (silent and oral).* Before children read the story silently the teacher provides them with purpose questions (or a study guide) to direct their reading (on a section-by-section basis at lower grade levels). Following the silent reading, the teacher may ask the children to read aloud their answers to the purpose or study-guide questions or to read orally for a new purpose. This section of the lesson is designed to aid children's comprehension and retention of the material. Using questioning procedures in the directed reading of a DRA is frequently the teacher's primary approach to improving comprehension skills.

224

Teaching
Reading in
Today's
Elementary
Schools

3. *Skill-building activities.* Either before the silent reading or after it, the teacher provides direct instruction in one or more word recognition or comprehension skills.

4. *Follow-up practice.* During this portion of the lesson, children practice skills they have already been taught, frequently by doing workbook exercises.

5. *Enrichment activities.* These activities may connect the story with art, music, or creative writing, or may lead the children to read further material on the same topic or by the same author.

Although the steps may vary from series to series, most basal reading lessons have parts that correspond to the preceding list of components. Directed reading of a story generally involves the teacher asking questions and the children reading to find the answers.

To illustrate the directed reading activity used in a basal reading series, representative parts of a sample lesson for a first-grade level story are presented in Example 5.1. This lesson is taken from the teacher's edition of the series. The section entitled "Reading the Selection" incorporates parts that correspond both to the first step of the DRA, motivation and development of background, and to the second step, directed story reading. "Reading the Selection" includes purpose questions, directions for both silent and oral reading of the story, and comprehension questions to help develop students' understanding. The next major section, "Teaching Reading Skills," corresponds to steps three and four of the DRA and presents both basic reading skill activities and follow-up practice, the latter indicated by the Practice Book symbol and reference. Finally, the "Reteaching and Enrichment" section includes the enrichment activities that form the final step of the DRA. In the facsimile in Example 5.1 only representative parts of each section, including the basal story, are shown.

A second example of a directed reading activity is presented in Example 5.2 (page 231), showing a lesson plan from an intermediate-level basal reader.

▶ **EXAMPLE 5.1** DRA as Presented in a Basal Reading Series

The Big Turnip

Summary

In this old Russian folk tale, an industrious old man plants a little turnip which grows into a big problem. The turnip grows so large that the old man cannot pull it up, so he enlists the help of the old woman. This starts the cumulative tale as the old man and the old woman, then a girl, a dog, a cat, and a mouse are added to the chain of turnip pullers until at last the mammoth root comes out of the ground. The story helps prove that through group effort, even the tiniest of creatures can help to solve a big problem.

The Big Turnip

by ALEXEI TOLSTOY

One day an old man planted
a little turnip.

The little turnip grew and grew.

It grew into a very big turnip.

69

Then one day, the old man went
to pull up the turnip.

He pulled and pulled.

But he could not pull it up.

So he asked the old woman to help.

The old woman pulled the old man.

The old man pulled the turnip.

And they pulled and pulled.

But they could not pull it up.

70

71

1 Reading the Selection

Vocabulary and Concept Development

In today's story you will read about an old man who plants a turnip and then has a problem with it. Before you begin reading, let's look at two words that may be new to you.

See Pages 5–8 for model.

▶ could

Print: I did not need help.

I **could** open the box myself.

Say: In this word the letters *ould* stand for the sounds you hear at the end of *wood*.

Checking words: cold *(no sense)*

forced *(wrong sounds)*

▶ woman

Print: I can tell you who she is.

That **woman** is Susan's grandmother.

Checking words: woolen *(no sense)*

lady *(wrong sounds)*

If you prefer to introduce all the new words in advance of the reading, see guide page 235 or pages 111–112 for Unit 9 in the Instruction Charts.
Now we are ready to begin the story about the old man and the turnip that he planted. Does anyone know what a turnip is? . . . *(a vegetable)* **If necessary, explain that a turnip is a vegetable and that both the leaves and the rounded yellow or white root are eaten. If the children are unfamiliar with turnips, you may wish to show them one.** Now open your books to page 69.

Pages 69–71 Motivation and Silent Reading

Read the title of this story to yourself. . . . Who will read the title aloud? . . . The author of this story is Alexei Tolstoy.

Look at the picture on this page. The plant that the old man is looking at is a turnip. Which is larger, the old man or the turnip? . . . Do you think a turnip would ever really grow to be this big?

Now turn to page 70. . . . What is the old man doing? . . . *(pulling on the turnip)*

Look at the picture on the next page. Who is with the old man? . . . *(an old woman)* What is she doing? . . . *(pulling on the old man)* Turn back to page 69. Read pages 69, 70, and 71 to yourself and find out what the old man has trouble doing.

Checking and Developing Comprehension

What couldn't the old man do? . . . *(pull up the turnip)* Why couldn't he pull it up? . . . *(It was too big.)* Who will read aloud the sentence on page 69 that tells you the turnip was big?

Do you think the old man really tried hard to pull up the turnip? . . . *(yes)* Who will read aloud the words on page 70 that make you think that?

What did the old man do when he couldn't pull up the turnip by himself? . . . *(He asked the old woman to help him.)*

What did the old woman do? . . . *(pulled the old man)* What did the old man do while the old woman was pulling him? . . . *(pulled the turnip)* Who will find and read the sentences on page 71 that tell what the old man and the old woman did?

Comprehension Questions

Now that the children have finished the story, have them close their books. Then conduct a short discussion of the story, using some of the following questions as stimuli.

1. Who was the first one who asked to help pull up the turnip? *(the old woman)* Who did the old woman ask to help? *(the little girl)* Who was the last one to help? *(the mouse)* Literal: sequence of events
2. What do you think would have happened if the mouse hadn't helped? *(The turnip would have had to stay in the ground; the cat would have asked someone else to help.)* Interpretive: making inferences
3. Why do you think the turnip finally came up? *(The people and animals together were strong enough to pull it up.)* Interpretive: drawing conclusions
4. What are some other ways the story characters could have tried to get the turnip out of the ground? Evaluative: thinking creatively
5. Do you think the mouse could have pulled up the turnip alone? Why or why not? Evaluative: thinking creatively
6. Why was the mouse such a help? *(The mouse provided just that extra little bit of strength that was needed to get the turnip out of the ground.)* Interpretive: drawing conclusions
7. Why do you think the old man wanted to pull up the turnip? Evaluative: thinking critically

Oral Rereading of the Selection

"The Big Turnip" lends itself to dramatization as well as choral reading. Choose children to act out the roles of the old man, old woman, little girl, dog, cat, and mouse. As each new character is introduced, the child will act out his or her role. This will help to emphasize the sequential aspect of the story, as well as point out how enormous the turnip was. You may wish to have children construct a gigantic turnip as a prop. This could be done using papier mâché or cardboard.

You may wish to have the story reread in the following manner: Choose different children to read each page aloud. When the child who is reading comes to the lines "And they pulled and they pulled. But they could not pull it up" on pages 71–74, have the entire reading group read those lines. The entire

228

Teaching
Reading in
Today's
Elementary
Schools

reading group could also read the final two sentences on page 76. When they read the words "at last," have them use strong emphasis.

Encourage children to read with good expression.

2 Teaching Reading Skills

Basic Skill Instruction

Decoding: Contractions with 's, n't, 'll (D1•7f) LESSON 9

Children whose native language is Spanish may have difficulty with this skill. For teaching suggestions, see Guide page 249.

Print: I think that's for you.

Why can't James get down?

Say: Read these sentences to yourself. . . . Who will read the sentences aloud? . . . **Point to *that's.*** Who will say just this word? . . . You have learned that *that's* is a shorter way of saying *that is.* . . . **Point to *can't.*** You have learned that *can't* is a shorter way to say *can not.*

In your reading you will sometimes meet words like *that's* and *can't* that have been made by putting two words together with some of their letters left out. **Point to the apostrophe in *that's* and *can't.*** An apostrophe takes the place of the letter or letters that have been left out. A word made this way is called a *contraction.* Today you will learn about another contraction.

Print: I will tell you a story.

I'll tell you a story.

Say: You know all the words in these sentences. Read the sentences to yourself. . . . Who will read them aloud? . . . Do both these sentences mean the same thing? . . . **Point to the second sentence.** What is the contraction in this sentence? . . . **Draw a line under *I'll.*** From what two words is the contraction *I'll* made? . . . ***(I will)* Draw a line under *I will.* Point to the apostrophe.** What two letters does the apostrophe take the place of? . . . ***(An apostrophe was put in place of the w and i.)*** *I'll* is a shorter way of saying *I will.* When a contraction ends with *apostrophe -l-l,* the *apostrophe -l-l* usually stands for the word *will.*

Now let's see if you can read some sentences with contractions in them. **Print the following sentences, underlining the words that are in boldface type:**

1. **"We'll** have to go now," said Tony.
2. Susan **couldn't** see the duck.
3. **He'll** make the bread.
4. **Who's** coming for lunch?
5. She thinks **they'll** all come.

Have children read each sentence silently. Then call on individual children to read each sentence aloud, to name the contraction in each sentence, and to tell from what two words the contraction was made.

Remember, a contraction is a word made by putting two words together with some of their letters left out. An apostrophe takes the place of those letters.

━━ Practice Book: page 31

Decoding: Sound Associations for   oo   (D1•7m) LESSON 10

229

Major
Approaches to
Reading
Instruction

Children whose native language is Spanish may have difficulty with this skill. For teaching suggestions, see Guide page 249.

Print: school
Say: You know this word. What is it? . . . **Draw a line under the oo.** Say *school* softly to yourself and listen for the sound that *oo* stands for.
Print: look
Say: Here is another word you know. What is it? . . . **Draw a line under the oo.** Say *look* softly to yourself and listen for the sound for *oo.* . . . Is that the same sound you hear for *oo* in *school?*

   When two *o*'s come right together in a word, they usually stand for either the sound you hear for those letters in *school* or the sound you hear for those letters in *look.* Listen to the words as I say them. **Say school and look, emphasizing the oo sound in each word.**

   When in your reading you come to a word that has *oo* in it, you can tell which sound *oo* stands for by using the sounds for the other letters in the word and the sense of the other words in what you are reading.

   Let's see how well you can use what you know about the sounds *oo* can stand for to help you figure out some new words. **Print the following sentences, underlining the words that are in boldface type:**
1. You can put your hat on this **hook.**
2. Grandmother pulled my **tooth** out.
3. May we swim in your **pool?**
4. What did you **cook** for lunch?
   Have children read the sentences silently. Then call on individual children to read each sentence aloud and to identify the underlined word.

   Today you have learned about two sounds *oo* can stand for. When you come to a word with two *o*'s together, what sounds can *oo* stand for? . . . **(either the sound for oo in school or in look)** You can tell which sound *oo* stands for by using the sounds for the other letters in the word and by using the sense of the other words in what you are reading.

≡ Practice Book: page 32
≡ Assessment: Forms A, B   Sound Associations for oo

3 Reteaching and Enrichment

Reading and Language Enrichment

1. Have six children pantomime the story "The Big Turnip." Another child should read the words of the story, while the six children pantomime the actions described in the story. The turnip should be imaginary.
   Dramatizing the story
2. The sequence of the characters and their actions in "The Big Turnip" lends itself to illustrations. Individual children could draw a sequence strip retelling the story.

230

Teaching
Reading in
Today's
Elementary
Schools

The completed pictures can be displayed on a bulletin board or they can be developed as roller movies.
Story-related art activity: noting correct sequence

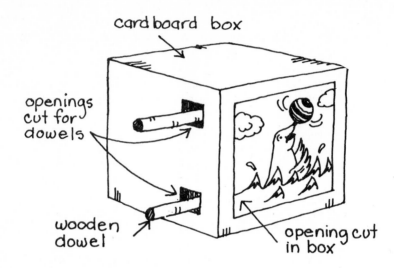

card board box

openings
cut for
dowels

wooden
dowel

opening cut
in box

3. Collect books about vegetables and flowers from your school library or public library and place them in the learning center for children to examine. After children have looked at these books, have them decide whether they would like to have a vegetable garden, a flower garden, or a combination of both. Have available old magazines, seed catalogs, and art materials so children can make a picture of the garden they would like to have. Provide a time for children to share and tell about their pictures.
Learning Center: concept development (gardens)

4. Individual children may be interested in growing their own plants in the classroom. Obtain seedlings such as marigolds, some potting soil, and some empty six-ounce juice cans to be used as pots.

   Have each child plant one seedling in a clean juice can, water it, and place it in the sun. Each child should then be responsible for watering his or her plant as needed. Children might wish to decorate their "pots" by wrapping foil around the cans.
   Story-related science activity

Source: William K. Durr, et al.: *Sunshine, Teacher's Annotated Edition*, pp. 91–100 (Houghton Mifflin Reading Program). Copyright © 1981 by Houghton Mifflin Company. Used by permission. ◄

In Example 5.2 the skill objectives are all designed for maintenance and expansion, meaning that pupils have already had skill instruction. Words that could cause difficulty are identified for the teacher, along with the number of the page on which they appear, so that he or she can ask children to try to get

▶ **EXAMPLE 5.2:** Sample Directed Reading Activity

231

Major
Approaches to
Reading
Instruction

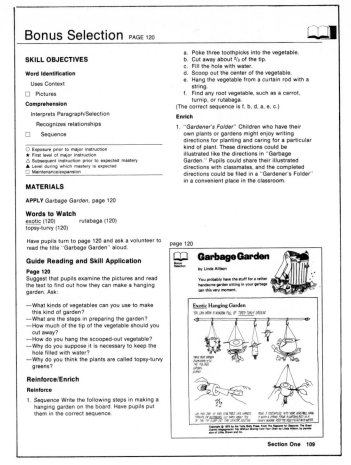

Source: From SCOTT, FORESMAN BASICS IN READING, TEACHER'S
EDITION, FINS AND TALES by Ira E. Aaron, Dauris Jackson, Carole
Riggs, et al. Copyright © 1978 by Scott, Foresman and Company.
Reprinted by permission. ◀

the meanings of these words from context. The Example selection states a
purpose; offers guiding questions to make the reading of the material
purposeful and to enhance comprehension; provides practice material for
reinforcing the skill of detecting sequence; and suggests an enrichment
activity to encourage application of skills.

✔ Self-Check: Objective 2

What are the parts of a directed reading activity?
(See Self-Improvement Opportunity 2.)

Alternatives to Use of DRA

The directed reading activity has for many years been the format for basal reader lessons, and it is a valuable procedure. However, teachers desire variety in lessons to add spice to reading instruction, so Dixie Lee Spiegel (1981) has suggested alternatives to the DRA, including ReQuest (described in Chapter 4), the directed reading-thinking activity (described in Chapter 7), the expectation outline, the prereading guided reading procedure, Word Wonder, and semantic webbing (described in Chapter 4).

An expectation outline is most appropriate for a factual story and can be used with content area materials as well as basal readers. The teacher asks children to tell what they think they will learn about the topic, writing questions that the children expect to have answered on the chalkboard, in related groups. Vocabulary words are emphasized during this procedure, and the teacher clarifies them as necessary, also filling in some needed background information. The children make up titles for each related group of questions, then read the story to find the answers. They read the proof of their answers orally.

For a selection such as "The Gift of Corn" by Aliki, found in *Weavers,* one of the third-grade readers of the Houghton Mifflin Reading Program, the children might indicate that they expect to find answers to the following questions:

1. Where did the corn in this country come from?
2. Who gave someone a gift of corn?
3. Who received a gift of corn?
4. How is corn grown?
5. Where does corn grow?
6. In what ways is corn used?
7. Are the corn kernels seeds?

Given this set of questions, the teacher might group Questions 2 and 3 and Questions 4, 5, and 7. The children might name the first group "Gift Questions" and the second group "Growing Corn." The only vocabulary word that is likely to need attention is *kernels.* If the class includes many children who have seen corn only in cans, the teacher may wish to bring in an ear or at least pictures of ears of corn to provide some background information before the children read the story.

The prereading guided reading procedure is also particularly useful with factual material. The teacher asks the children to tell everything they know about the topic while she or he writes their contributions on the board. Then the children analyze the contributions for inconsistencies, connecting the numbers of inconsistent statements with lines and noting information of questionable accuracy with a question mark. After categorizing the informa-

tion, the children read to discover whether or not it is correct.

Use of the prereading guided reading procedure with "The Gift of Corn" would begin with the teacher writing on the board such contributions from the children as

1. Corn is a vegetable.
2. Corn grows on stalks.
3. Corn has kernels.
4. The Indians showed the Pilgrims how to grow corn.
5. Corn is good to eat.
6. Corn can be boiled on the cob.
7. Corn can be fried.
? 8. Corn grows on trees.
? 9. Hair grows on corn.

The pupils might then divide the statements into categories, such as "Characteristics of Corn," "Early Users of Corn," and "Ways to Cook Corn."

With Word Wonder, children name the words they expect to encounter in a story they are about to read, and then they read to check their predictions. The teacher may also list words and let the children decide whether each one is likely to appear in the story, offering their reasons for choosing particular words. After reading, discussions of why certain words were not included may help clear up misconceptions. Students may read orally the parts in which they found specific vocabulary words.

A final instructional technique is horizontal reading (Cunningham, 1980), which can be used as an adjunct to the basal reader approach. Horizontal reading gives children additional experiences and practice at the level they have just completed instead of moving them on to the next level immediately. It allows students to review skills in their current level and practice them while reading different stories, thus developing automaticity at each level. *Encore Readers*, published by Scott, Foresman, are horizontal readers correlated with grades one to three of that publisher's *Basics in Reading* program; *Text Extenders*, published by Scholastic, include collections of books correlated with each level (grades one through six) of basals published by Houghton Mifflin, Ginn, Holt, Macmillan, Economy, Harcourt Brace Jovanovich, and Scott, Foresman.

LANGUAGE EXPERIENCE APPROACH (LEA)

The language experience approach interrelates the different language arts and uses the experiences of the children as the basis for reading materials. The

234

Teaching
Reading in
Today's
Elementary
Schools

rationale for this approach has been stated very concisely by one of its leading proponents, R. V. Allen.

What I can think about, I can talk about.
What I can say, I can write—or someone can write for me.
What I write, I can read.
I can read what I write, and what other people can write for me to read. (Karlin, ed., 1973, p. 158)

This approach to reading is not totally new; in fact, one of its major components, the experience chart, has been used since the 1920s. Originally, experience charts were group-composed stories that were transcribed by the teacher on the chalkboard or chart paper and then read by the children. Today, they may be either group or individual compositions: stories about field trips, school activities, or personal experiences outside of school, or charts that contain directions, special words, observations, job assignments, questions to be answered, imaginative stories or poems, or class rules.

Because the charts used in the language experience approach are developed by children, they are motivational; because they use the language of the children, the reading material on the charts is meaningful. (Frequently, basal reader stories are not meaningful to many children, especially those we often refer to as disadvantaged.) A child's background may be limited, but every child has experiences that can be converted into stories. In addition, the teacher can plan interesting first-hand experiences that can result in reading material that is meaningful for all pupils.

The language experience approach is consistent with schema theory. Because it uses the child's experiences as the basis for written language, the child necessarily has adequate schemata to comprehend the material and can thus develop a schema for reading that includes the idea that written words have meaning (Hacker, 1980). The language patterns found in stories composed by children are usually much more mature than those found in basal readers, since children use compound and complex sentences and a wide vocabulary. Nevertheless, children seem to find their own language patterns much easier to read than those in a basal reader, probably because clues in a familiar context are easier to use. In fact, pupils often pick up the long, unusual words in experience stories faster than many of the short service words, probably because the distinctive configurations of these words contribute to recognition.

With the language experience approach, reading grows out of natural, ongoing activities. Children can see the relationships between reading and their oral language. This approach helps them to visualize reading as "talk written down" and offers good opportunities for developing the concepts of *writing, word,* and *sentence.* During the language experience process children see the transformation from oral language to print take place, including directionality, the spacing between words, and punctuation and capitalization. Framing the individual language units with the hands is also helpful in illustrating their meanings (Blass et al., 1981).

Implementation in Kindergarten

In order to use the language experience approach in the kindergarten, the teacher should fill the classroom with stimulating things such as building blocks, a kitchen corner, a science corner, etc. He or she must also provide children with opportunities to engage in many concrete and vicarious experiences designed to enrich their backgrounds, including field trips, demonstrations, experiments, and movies.

At the kindergarten level, experience charts are usually individual ones, although group charts may be composed following a special activity. The child (or children) dictates the experience story to the teacher, who either writes the story in manuscript or types it. The teacher then reads the story back to the child. Although an especially adept pupil may begin to recognize some of the words on the chart, at this point the teacher should emphasize that writing is just talk written down rather than have the child read the chart. Watching the teacher write the chart also helps the child become accustomed to the left-to-right progression of print, which the teacher can emphasize by sweeping the hand across the page under each line when he or she reads the chart.

In addition to using experience charts, the teacher can label desks with the owners' names to show students that everything has not only an oral name but a written name. As time passes children will recognize many of these names by sight. Lists of class helpers, the date of each day, and other regularly used announcements (for example, "today's weather," "library day") also provide opportunities for learning words by sight, as does labeling children's drawings with a word or phrase.

Those children who are ready to read may move into a program similar to the one described below, which is appropriate for use in the first grade.

Implementation in First Grade

After the children have participated in a common experience and have talked it over thoroughly, the group is ready to compose an experience story. First the teacher may ask for suggestions for a title, allowing the students to select their favorite by voting. The teacher then records the title on the chalkboard or a transparency. Each child offers details to add to the story, which the teacher also records. She may write "Joan said" by Joan's contribution, or she may simply write the sentence, calling attention to capitalization and punctuation as she does so. After she writes each idea, the teacher reads it aloud. After all contributions have been recorded, she reads the entire story to the class, sweeping her hand under each line to emphasize the left-to-right progression. Then she asks the class to read the story with her as she moves her hand under the words. Under cover of the group, no child will stand out if he or she doesn't know a word.

If this is the group's first actual reading experience, the teacher will probably stop at this point. On the second day, the class can be divided into

236

Teaching
Reading in
Today's
Elementary
Schools

three or four groups, with which the teacher can work separately. To begin each group session, the teacher rereads the story to the children, using a master chart she made the day before. Then the group rereads it with her. Next she asks for a volunteer who reads the story with her, filling in the words he or she knows while the teacher supplies the rest. After each child in the group has had a chance to read, the teacher asks students to find certain words on the chart. She may also show the children sentence strips (also prepared the day before) and have the children match these with the lines on the chart, either letting volunteers reconstruct the entire chart from the sentence strips or using this as a learning-center activity to be completed individually while other groups are meeting. Group charts can be useful in developing many skills and are commonly utilized for lessons in word endings, compound words, long and short vowels, rhyming words, initial consonants, capitalization, punctuation, and other areas.

If the teacher makes a copy of the story for each student, she may underline on that copy the words that the student recognizes as he or she reads the story. The teacher may then make word cards of these words, which serve as the beginnings of the children's "word banks." (Word cards containing the words a child has used in stories can eventually be used to drill on sight vocabulary, to work on word recognition skills, and to develop comprehension skills.) As a group of students finishes meeting with the teacher, the students may be given the opportunity to illustrate their stories individually.

After this first attempt, students will write most experience stories in small groups, sometimes working on a story together and sometimes producing and sharing individual stories. At times, slower learners may dictate their stories to the faster learners or to helpers from higher grades. Some teachers use tape recorders for dictation.[1]

Sharing stories, whether orally or in written form, is very important, since group members will soon see that certain words occur over and over again and that they can read the stories written by their classmates. The experience stories written by the group as a whole may be gathered into a booklet under a general title chosen by the group, and individuals may also bind their stories into booklets. Recopying a story to be included in a booklet is excellent motivation for handwriting practice. Pupils will enjoy reading each other's booklets, and a collection of their own stories provides both a record of their activities and evidence of their growth in reading and writing.

In one school a multicultural group of first graders wrote language experience stories, illustrated them, made them into books, and set up a classroom library. The books were given library pockets and check-out cards and were catalogued and shelved as they might be in a regular library, and children assumed jobs as reference librarians, check-out librarians, check-in

---

[1]A plan for teaching paraprofessionals and volunteers to utilize the language-experience approach with children is described by Linda C. Askland in "Conducting Individual Language Experience Stories," *The Reading Teacher* 27 (November 1973): 167–70. The suggestions given could be easily followed by teachers who have these helpers in their classrooms.

librarians, and so forth. Both older and younger children in the school were

scheduled for visits to use the library, which was operated for six days, and the student librarians accomplished an extensive amount of learning during the progress of the project (Powers, 1981).

As time passes and the children learn to write and spell, they may wish to write experience stories by themselves, asking the teacher or turning to their word banks or dictionaries for help in spelling. Teachers should allow them to spell phonetically when they are writing, since they can go back and correct spelling and rewrite the story in a neater form later if the story is to be read by others.

Rereading and editing require children to make judgments about syntax, semantics, and the topic and whether the written account can be understood by others. They provide ways to emphasize comprehension when using language experience stories. At first this should be done with extensive teacher guidance; later children can work more independently (Sulzby, 1980).

Related Activities

When children have accumulated a sufficient number of word cards, they can use them to compose new stories or to play word-matching or visual and auditory discrimination games. To develop comprehension skills a teacher can use classification games, asking such questions as "How many of you have a color word? A word that shows action? A word that names a place?" When each student has as many as ten word cards, the children can begin to alphabetize them by the first letter, which gives them a practical reason to learn alphabetical order. They can also develop a picture dictionary representing the words on their cards. Or they can search for their words in newspapers and magazines. After they recognize that their words appear in books, they will realize that they can read the books. The uses for word banks seem to be limited only by the teachers' and pupils' imaginations.[2]

LEA: Pros and Cons

This approach offers something for children regardless of the modes through which they learn best, as it incorporates all modes. For instance, the learners use the auditory mode when stories are dictated or read aloud, the kinesthetic (motor) mode when they write stories, and the visual mode when they read stories.

Use of the language experience approach promotes a good self-concept. It shows children that what they have to say is important enough to write down and that others are interested. It also promotes close contact between teachers and pupils. Finally, this approach has been highly successful as a remedial technique in the upper grades, allowing remedial readers to read material that

[2]See Ivan Quandt, "Investing in Word Banks—A Practice for Any Approach," *The Reading Teacher* 27 (November 1973): 171–73, for tips on use of word banks.

238

Teaching
Reading in
Today's
Elementary
Schools

interests them rather than lower-level materials that they quickly recognize as being designed for younger children.

Of course, there are some potential disadvantages to the LEA. They are as follows:

1. The lack of sequential development of reading skills because of the unstructured nature of the approach is seen as a disadvantage by some. It must be remembered, however, that there is no one correct sequence for presenting reading skills. Children learn from a variety of programs which provide different skill sequences, and with careful planning a good teacher can provide some sequence when using this approach.
2. Some educators regard the lack of systematic repetition of new words and the lack of vocabulary control in general as drawbacks.
3. The charts may be lacking in literary quality.
4. Charts can be memorized, resulting in recitation rather than actual reading.
5. Repetition of the same reading material may become boring, causing students to "tune it out." An alert teacher, however, can avoid allowing repetition to continue to this point.
6. Making charts is very time-consuming.
7. If this approach is used to the exclusion of other methods of reading instruction, at some point the limitations of the children's backgrounds of experiences may keep them from developing in reading as they should; but this approach is rarely used in isolation.

Some teachers fail to use the children's own language in the language experience stories because it does not fit the teachers' ideas of basic words. These teachers are not likely to reap the full benefits of this approach.

✔ Self-Check: Objective 3
What is the rationale behind the language experience approach? What are some advantages of the LEA? Some disadvantages? (See Self-Improvement Opportunity 3.)

INDIVIDUALIZED APPROACHES

The traditional Individualized Reading Approach—as well as alternative individualized approaches—are discussed in this section.

Individualized Reading Approach

The individualized reading approach encourages children to move at their own pace through reading material that they have chosen instead of to move through teacher-prescribed material at the same pace as other children placed in the same group for reading instruction. With the individualized reading approach, which is designed to encourage independent reading, each child receives assistance in improving performance when need for such assistance becomes apparent.

A number of characteristics are nearly always attributed to the individualized reading approach, including the following:

1. Self-selection. Children are allowed to choose material that they are interested in reading. Each child in the class may choose a different book. The teacher may offer suggestions or give help if it is requested, but the decision ultimately rests with the child. Thus, the individualized reading approach has a built-in motivation—children want to read the material because they have chosen it.
2. Self-pacing. Each child reads the material at his or her own pace. Slower students are not rushed through in order to keep up with the faster ones, and faster children are not held back until others have caught up with them.
3. Skills instruction. The teacher helps students, either on an individual basis or in groups, develop their word recognition and comprehension skills as these skills are needed.
4. Record-keeping. The teacher keeps records of the progress of each child. He or she must know the levels of a child's reading performance in order to know which books the child can read independently, which are too difficult or frustrating, and which the child can read with the teacher's assistance. The teacher must also be aware of a student's reading strengths and weaknesses, and should keep a record of the skills help that has been planned and given to the child. Each child must keep records of books read, new words encountered, and new ways of attacking words experienced.
5. Student-teacher conferences. One or two times a week, the teacher schedules a conference with each child, varying from three to fifteen minutes depending on the purpose.
6. Sharing activities. The teacher plans some time each week for the children to share books with each other that they have read individually. The children may share with the entire class or with a small group.
7. Independent work. The children do a great deal of independent work at their seats, rather than spending the majority of the assigned reading period in a group with the teacher.

Since exposure to different types of literature can help children build schemata for these *types* and should thus increase their efficiency in processing the text, this approach is congruent with schema theory (Hacker, 1980). In addition, the variety of material pupils read provides vicarious experiences that help build other schemata and thus enhance future comprehension.

To set up an individualized reading program, a teacher must have available a large supply of books, magazines, newspapers, and other reading materials—at least three to five books per child, covering a variety of reading levels and many different interest areas. This collection will need to be supple-

240

**Teaching
Reading in
Today's
Elementary
Schools**

mented continuously after the program begins, for many children will quickly read all of the books that are appropriate for them. Sources of books are school, city, and county libraries; book clubs; parent-teacher associations; and class members' personal collections.

The teacher should have read a large number of the books available to the children, since doing so makes it much easier to check the comprehension of pupils. Starting a file of comprehension questions and answers for the books being used in the program is a good idea; these questions will be available year after year and help refresh the teacher's memory of the books.

The teacher will also find it convenient to have a file of skill-developing activities, covering the entire spectrum of word recognition and comprehension and a wide range of difficulty levels.

When starting an individualized program, the teacher should determine the reading levels and interests of the children through standardized or informal tests in order to choose books for the program. Informal reading inventories that provide information about a child's levels of performance (discussed at length in Chapter 9) yield a great deal of useful information, as does an interest inventory, such as the one shown in Example 5.3. Administer the inventory to primary-level children orally.

▶ **EXAMPLE 5.3:** Interest Inventory

1. The things I like to do after school are:
    a. _____
    b _____
    c. _____
2. The television programs I enjoy most are:
    a. _____
    b. _____
    c. _____
3. My hobbies are:
    a. _____
    b. _____
    c. _____
4. If I could take a trip, I would like to go to:
    a. _____
    b. _____
    c. _____
5. The sports I like best are:
    a. _____
    b. _____
    c. _____
6. The school subjects I like best are:
    a. _____
    b. _____
    c. _____

7. I like to hear these types of stories read to me:
   a. _____
   b. _____
   c. _____
8. I like to read these types of stories on my own:
   a. _____
   b. _____
   c. _____ ◀

Before initiating an individualized program, the teacher can plan routines to follow in the classroom, considering questions such as (1) How are books to be checked out? (2) How will conferences be set up? (3) What should a child who is working independently at his or her desk do when in need of assistance? The room arrangement can also be planned in advance to allow for good traffic flow. If books are located in a number of places instead of being bunched together in a single location, pupils will have less trouble finding them and the potential noise level in the room will be lower.

The teacher may find that having a file folder for each child will help in organizing and record-keeping. Each file folder could contain both a reading skills checklist (such as the one prepared by Walter Barbe[3]) on which to record skill strengths and weaknesses and a form noting conference dates and skill help given. Students can keep their own records in file folders that are accessible to both teacher and children. These records will take different forms, depending upon the maturity of the children. A primary-level record might look like the one below.

Name of Book	Author	Evaluation (Circle One)		
		Good	O.K.	Bad
		Good	O.K.	Bad
		Good	O.K.	Bad
		Good	O.K.	Bad

An intermediate-level record might look like this one.

Name of Book	Author	Comments

[3]Walter Barbe, *Educator's Guide to Personalized Reading Instruction* (Englewood Cliffs, N.J.: Prentice-Hall, 1961).

242

Teaching
Reading in
Today's
Elementary
Schools

A form that could be used by children at all levels might look like this one.

New Words from Reading		
Word	Pronunciation	Definition

Student-teacher conferences serve a variety of purposes, including:

1. To help with book choices. To overcome the fear that children will not be able to select books wisely, teachers should spend some time showing children how to choose appropriate books. Encourage them to read one or two pages of the books that they think might appeal to them and to consider the number of unfamiliar words they encounter. If there are more than five unfamiliar words per page, the book might be too difficult, whereas if there are no unfamiliar words, the child should consider the possibility that he or she could read more difficult material. If the teacher has given an interest inventory, he can suggest potentially interesting books to pupils who find it hard to make a choice.
2. To check comprehension. Conferences help determine how well the children are comprehending the books and other materials they are reading. Ask a variety of types of comprehension questions—main idea, detail, inference, cause and effect, sequence, and vocabulary.
3. To check word attack and oral reading skills. The teacher can ask a child to read orally, observing his or her methods of attacking unfamiliar words and of using oral reading skills such as appropriate phrasing and good oral expression.
4. To give skill assistance. If a child is the only one in the room who needs help with a particular reading skill, the teacher can help him or her on a one-to-one basis during a conference.
5. To plan for sharing. Some conferences help children prepare for sharing their reading experiences with others. If a child wishes to read a portion of a book to the other class members, the teacher might use a conference to listen to the child practice audience reading and to give help with the presentation.

There is nothing contradictory about using group instruction in an individualized reading program. A teacher can group together children with similar skill difficulties to give help. The important thing is to be sure that all children get the instruction they need when they need it and are not forced to sit through instruction they do not need.

The student-teacher conference, an important part of the individualized reading approach, may be used to check comprehension, word attack skills, and oral reading skills. (© Elizabeth Crews/Stock, Boston)

When an individualized reading program is in effect, each child is expected to be involved in independent silent reading a great deal of the time. This time should be uninterrupted by noisy surroundings, classmates' projects, or non-task-oriented activities such as daydreaming, wandering around the room, or talking to other students. The teacher should make the rules for the quiet reading time very clear, and acceptable activities should be well defined: taking part in student-teacher conferences, selecting a book, reading silently, giving or receiving specific reading assistance, taking part in a skills group, completing a skill-development practice activity, or keeping records concerned with reading activity. Strict adherence to the rules will make the program run more smoothly.

Individualizing a reading program is a huge undertaking, but such a program can be introduced gradually in two ways.

1. Use part of the time. Introduce the individualized program one day a week while using the basal program the other four days. Then increase time spent in the individualized program one day at a time over a period of weeks until all five days of the week are devoted to it.

244

Teaching
Reading in
Today's
Elementary
Schools

2. Use part of the class. Introduce the program to one reading group at a time while the remaining groups continue the basal program. If the children are grouped by ability, the top group will be a good first choice because they are likely to have more independent work habits and will probably learn the routines more quickly than the other children would. After one group has become familiar with the approach, other groups can be introduced to it, until the entire class is participating in the individualized reading program.

The main advantages of an individualized reading approach are that

1. there is built-in motivation in reading books that the child chooses himself or herself.
2. a child is not compared negatively with other children, since every child has a different book and the books are primarily trade books, which have no visible grade designation.
3. each child has an opportunity to learn to read at his or her own rate.
4. a great deal of personal contact is made possible by the pupil-teacher conferences.

Characteristics of this approach that are considered disadvantages by some are

1. the necessity of amassing a large quantity of reading material that must be continually replenished.
2. the time difficulties inherent in trying to schedule so many individual conferences and skill-group meetings.
3. the enormous amount of bookkeeping that is necessary.
4. the lack of a sequential approach to skill development.

An excellent source for teachers who would like to individualize their programs is *Reading in the Elementary School,* 2nd. ed., by Jeannette Veatch (New York: John Wiley, 1978), and many teachers have found *Individualized Reading Program Units* (New York: Scholastic Book Service, 1970) and *Random House Reading Program, Grades 2–9* (Westminister, Md.: Random House) helpful in implementing an individualized program.

✔ Self-Check: Objective 4
Name seven characteristics that are usually associated with an individualized reading approach.
What are some advantages and disadvantages of this approach?
(See Self-Improvement Opportunity 4.)

Other Means of Individualizing Instruction

245

Major
Approaches to
Reading
Instruction

Ways to individualize instruction other than the traditional individualized reading approach include the following methods.

Objective-Based Approach

An objective-based approach offers each child instruction based upon his or her needs, which are determined through criterion-referenced tests that check on the student's mastery of a list of skill objectives (see Chapter 9 for a description of these tests). Instruction is prescribed to help the child master skills in which he or she shows weakness and uses materials of various types and from various sources, including basal readers, filmstrips, mechanical devices (such as controlled readers), programmed materials, games, and so on. These materials may be placed in learning centers for individual use, or they may be used with teacher direction.

The Wisconsin Design, which uses commercial materials from a variety of publishers along with some specially developed techniques as a basis for prescriptions, serves as a good example of an objective-based program (also called "management systems" and "diagnostic/prescriptive"). It has the following characteristics:

1. It has a set of behavioral objectives for the various reading skills.
2. Special tests determine whether children have mastered the skills.
3. Materials are specially designed or listed to correspond to these skills, to be used with those who fail to attain a particular level of achievement on the tests.
4. It has a method of recording and reporting results.

The major operations called for in the Wisconsin Design's framework for organizing instruction are identification of essential content, statement of objectives, assessment, identification of appropriate teaching/learning activities, and evaluation. A management component, included in the framework because systematic student accounting is necessary, is comprised of mechanisms for keeping records of students' skill development—a card-sorting system in which the basic skill data for each pupil are kept on a profile card. An "Outline of Reading Skills" is essentially a scope and sequence statement of reading skills for kindergarten through grade six.

The remaining components of the Design—the assessment exercises, profile cards, and aids to instruction—are keyed to the specific skills listed in the outline. A "Statement of Skills and Objectives" states the objectives of the first three skill areas—word attack, comprehension, and study skills—as closed, behavioral objectives. The objectives of the last three areas—self-directed reading, interpretive reading, and creative reading—are stated as open, describing behaviors and activities. *The Wisconsin Tests of Reading Skill*

246

Teaching
Reading in
Today's
Elementary
Schools

Development test for most of the skills in word attack, comprehension, and study skills, either as written tests or in the form of directions for teacher observation. Skills in each of the six areas are clustered at levels that correspond generally to traditional grade levels, as shown in Table 5.1.

The Teacher's Resource Files key the skills in the outline to selected published materials and techniques in the teacher's resource file and include a variety of materials and procedures that can be used to develop a specific skill. "Guides to Individual Skill Assessment" are filed in the appropriate folders of the Teacher's Resource File for Word Attack and are intended to assist teachers in observing specific skill-related behaviors and to serve as models for the development of additional individual guides or exercises. A sample page of a Teacher's Resource File for Skill 3, Level C of Study Skills is provided in Example 5.4. The file also includes a list of ten concept development activities, along with materials and procedures for each activity.

Some basal reading series that have a self-contained objective-based approach have their own identified skill objectives, criterion-referenced tests, and materials designed for development of each objective. A detailed outline of the procedures for teaching with a basal series of this type is found in Example 5.5.

Some of the advantages of management systems in general are the following:

1. They work well with many approaches to reading, although they do not fit into some of the less rigid methods, such as the language experience approach.
2. The teacher has an overall picture of the child's strengths and weaknesses.
3. Children work only on the skills they need the most.
4. Success is likely because children work at their own levels; self-concepts are thus enhanced.
5. Learners may have as much time as they need for skill mastery.
6. Grouping can be flexible to include children's short-term common skills needs.
7. Teachers can report progress in specific skills to parents.

TABLE 5.1 *Wisconsin Design* Skills by Area and Level

				Grade			
Skill Area	*K*	*1*	*2*	*3*	*4*	*5*	*6*
Word Attack	A	B	C	D	—	—	—
Comprehension	A	B	C	D	E	F	G
Study Skills	A	B	C	D	E	F	G
Self-Directed Reading	A	B	C	D	←	E	→
Interpretive Reading	A	B	C	D	←	E	→
Creative Reading	A	B	C	D	←	E	→

Source: *The Wisconsin Design for Reading Skill Development: Overview* © 1972. The Board of Regents of the University of Wisconsin System for the Wisconsin Research and Development Center for Cognitive Learning.

► **EXAMPLE 5.4:** Sample Page of a Teacher's Resource File

247
Major
Approaches to
Reading
Instruction

---

the Wisconsin Design for Reading Skill Development
Teacher's Resource File: Study Skills

Study Skills—Level C
■■■■■ Skill 3: Number-Letter Grids ■■■■■
Objective

The child uses coordinates to locate points and to describe the locations of points on number-letter grids.

Printed Materials

Allyn and Bacon, *Study Skills for Information Retrieval*, Book 2, teacher's ed. (1970), p 58

American Education Publications, *Map Skills for Today*, Book C (1971), pp. 25, 26

American Education Publications, *Map Skills for Today*, Book D (1971), p 14

American Education Publications, *Map Skills for Today*, Book E (1971), p 17

Benefic, *How Charts and Drawings Help Us* (1965), p 76

Benefic, *How Maps and Globes Help Us* (1970), p 28

Educational Development Laboratories, *Reference EEE* (1961), EEE-10

Field Educational Publications, *Cyclo-Teacher Learning Aid School Kit* (1968), Finding Places

Follett, *Study Lessons in Map Reading* (1965), pp. 10†, 52, 60†

Rand McNally, *Where?* (1965), pp. 9, 16-17

Rand McNally, *Where?*, Pupil's Activity Book (1965), pp 8-9, 16-17

Scholastic Book Services, *Map Skills Project*, Book II (1964), pp. 18-19

Scott, Foresman, *Where Do We Live?* (1970)†

Franklin Watts, *The First Book of Maps and Globes* (1959), pp. 16-17

Audiovisual Materials

Coronet Films, *Maps Are Fun* (1963)

Creative Visuals, *Typical Road Map* (1969)

Encyclopaedia Britannica, *Locating Places on Maps* (1958)

Eye Gate, *Elements of a Map* (1959)

Eye Gate, *Reviewing the Elements of a Map* (1971)

Eye Gate, *Using Common Maps* (1959)

GAF, *Maps Location Grid* (1964)†

Hammond, *Map Skills*, Set II (1970), transparency no 72

Instructo, *Key & Index* (1967)

Library Filmstrip Center, *Introduction to the Use of Globe, Map, Atlas* (1971)†

Library Filmstrip Center, *Map, Atlas Survey* (1969)

McGraw-Hill, *Latitude and Longitude: Finding Places and Directions* (1962)

McGraw-Hill, *Special Maps* (1968)

Sterling Films, *Finding Locations and Distance on a Map* (1969)

Visualcraft, *Map and Globe Skills* (1969), Road Map, Location Skills

Source: The Wisconsin Design for Reading Skill Development © 1972, 1973—The Board of Regents of the University of Wisconsin System. ◄

248

**Teaching
Reading in
Today's
Elementary
Schools**

▶ **EXAMPLE 5.5:** *Reading 720* Cycle of Instruction

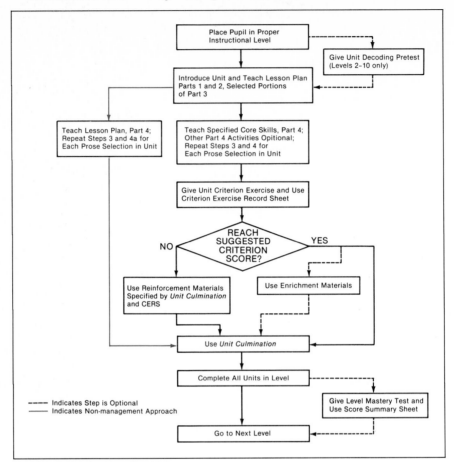

Source: From *Teacher's Edition, One to Grow On,* of the *Reading 720* series by Theodore Clymer and others © Copyright, 1976, by Ginn and Company (Xerox Corporation). Used with permission. ◀

Some of the disadvantages are:

1. It takes planning and time to organize a room to facilitate needed skill practice.
2. The wide variety of materials needed may be discouraging to some teachers.
3. Record-keeping is a vital element but is time-consuming.
4. Some important aspects of reading may be neglected; more attention is given to skills than reading interests.[4]

[4]For other evaluations of such systems, see Robert T. Rude, ''Objective-Based Reading Systems: An Evaluation,'' *The Reading Teacher* 28 (November 1974): 169–75. Also see Dale D. Johnson and P. David Pearson, ''Skills Management Systems: A Critique,'' *The Reading Teacher* 28 (May 1975) 757–64.

More diagnostic/prescriptive programs are becoming available for teacher selection, including:

Criterion Reading. Random House, 201 E. 50th St., New York, NY 10022

Fountain Valley Support System. Richard L. Zweig Associates, 20800 Beach Blvd., Huntington Beach, CA 92648

Harper & Row Classroom Management System. Harper & Row, 10 E. 53rd St., New York, NY 10022

Prescriptive Reading Inventory. CTB/McGraw-Hill, Del Monte Research Park, Monterey, CA 93940

Read On. Random House School Division, 201 E. 50th St., New York, NY 10022

Skills Monitoring System—Reading. Harcourt Brace Jovanovich 757 Third Ave., New York, NY 10017

SRA Diagnosis. Science Research Associates, 259 East Erie Street, Chicago, IL 60611

Programmed Instruction

Some attempts to individualize include programmed materials, which instruct in small, sequential steps, each of which is referred to as a frame. The pupil is required to respond in some way to each frame and is instantly informed of the correctness of his or her response (giving immediate reinforcement). Because the instruction is presented to an individual child, rather than to a group, each child moves through the material at his or her own pace, thereby benefiting from some individualization. An even greater degree of individualization is provided by branching programs, which offer review material to children who respond incorrectly to frames, thereby indicating that they have not mastered the skills being presented.

Programmed instruction can also provide follow-up reinforcement for instruction presented by the teacher, thereby freeing the teacher from many drill activities and allowing him or her more time to spend on complex teaching tasks. The programmed materials are designed to be self-instructional and do not require direct teacher supervision.

On the other hand, programmed instruction does not lend itself to teaching many complex comprehension skills, such as those involving analysis and interpretation, nor does it promote flexibility of reading rate. Word analysis and vocabulary-building skills are most prominently treated in programmed materials, so teachers may wish to use other materials (for example, basal texts) or techniques (semantic webbing) to present and provide practice for the complex comprehension skills.

Perhaps the best-known programmed material for reading instruction is Sullivan Associates' *Programmed Reading*, 3rd edition, published by McGraw-Hill in 1973. The program consists of two readiness kits and three programmed reading series, including teacher's guides and other available support materials such as duplicating masters, cassette tapes, alphabet strips, pupil alphabet cards, teacher alphabet cards, sound-symbol cards, activity

250

Teaching
Reading in
Today's
Elementary
Schools

books, achievement tests, filmstrips, teacher's guides to filmstrips, two Read and Think Series, duplicating masters for Read and Think Series, response books and vinyl overlays which make readers reusable, and placement tests. Criterion-referenced tests follow each unit in the programmed readers, and the teacher's guide contains suggestions for appropriate corrective exercises that do not repeat previously presented materials. Both word attack and comprehension receive attention in this program: Series I focuses on word attack but introduces comprehension skills in the sixth of seven books, and comprehension receives increasing emphasis in Series II and Series III.

Computer Approaches

There are two broad categories of computer use for individualizing instruction: computer-assisted instruction (CAI), in which a computer administers a programmed instructional sequence to a student, and computer-managed instruction (CMI), in which the computer takes care of such tasks as record-keeping, diagnosis, and prescription of individualized assignments. These two approaches are sometimes available in a single coordinated package.

Computer-Assisted Instruction   Of the two basic types of CAI that are currently used for reading instruction—drill-and-practice and tutorial (Blanchard, 1980)—the simplest and most common is the drill-and-practice program, which consists of practice lessons on skills that students have previously been taught. Students receive material in a programmed sequence (as described above, under Programmed Instruction) and immediate feedback on correctness of answers; sometimes they are given more than one opportunity to answer before they are told the correct answer.

Tutorial programs are really advanced forms of drill-and-practice programs in which the computer actually presents instruction, then follows it with practice activities. Depending upon the correct and incorrect responses a student gives as the program progresses, he or she may be branched to a remedial sequence of instruction, taken back through the initial instruction, directed through the typical sequence for the instruction, or skipped ahead in the program to avoid unnecessary practice. In some programs the student has no direct control over the sequence; in others, he or she may request review, remedial help, or additional practice as part of the program design.

Teachers who are unfamiliar with computer technology in general may find it difficult to picture the implementation of CAI in the school; therefore, it is helpful to know something about computer equipment (hardware). When computers are mentioned, many teachers think of early, huge main-frame computers, which were prohibitive in both size and cost for single-school use. These computers, usually located at a point remote from the school and connected by telephone lines to the terminals in the school, allowed several users access in a "time-sharing" arrangement. Terminals were varied: some were simply teletypewriters that communicated with the student by typing information on a sheet of paper; some had audio input to the student through headsets; some had video displays that resembled television screens; and a few allowed students to touch a "light pen" to the screen to enter a response. Irene Gersten and others (1981) have commented that most massive main-frame computer systems were generally viewed negatively because they were "plagued by high cost, low reliability, inadequate programming and, as the number of users grew, extremely slow response time" (p. 45).

Microcomputers, on the other hand, as many have pointed out, are cheaper, portable, and have rapid response capabilities. This has moved microcomputers into education's mainstream. Most microcomputers used in reading education vary from the size of a large electric typewriter to a little over twice that. They have a typewriter keyboard for student input, a video display for presenting instruction to students, and a built-in microprocessor and memory which allows them to operate as discrete units. A printer may be attached to provide printed output. A microcomputer system can be so inexpensive that an individual classroom might have one or more of its own.

Minicomputers are smaller than main-frame computers but larger than microcomputers and range in price between the two. Minicomputers generally serve an entire school rather than a single classroom.

The heart of a CAI system is the software, the programs that actually provide the instruction. These programs are developed by people and therefore vary in quality; the computer can only carry out the instructions the programmer has given it. Programs may be written on printed pages so that someone has to enter them into the computer's memory by using a typewriterlike keyboard, or they may be on prerecorded cassettes or disks. Teachers are wise to try out software before purchasing it (Spindle, 1981), because, as Art Botterell (1982) points out, "the lack of good software is the biggest barrier to the growth of educational computing. . . . There is a great deal of bad educational software on the market today" (p. 149). Botterell goes on to state that commercial publishers and materials developers have been slow to enter the field of educational computing. Fortunately, they do seem to be moving in this direction.

In the meantime teachers will need to be careful about programs they purchase, asking themselves such questions as the following:

1. Is the material instructionally sound?
2. Is the program easy for the learner to use?
3. Does use of the program accomplish something that is needed in this classroom?

To be instructionally sound, the program should present accurate information in a reasonable sequence with an appropriate amount of pupil interac-

252

Teaching
Reading in
Today's
Elementary
Schools

tion. It should not give responses to incorrect answers that reward the learner with clever messages or graphics, while not doing this for correct answers. Ease of use encompasses clear instructions on what to do to advance material on the screen, to respond to questions (Do students use a letter or an entire typed-out answer to respond to a multiple-choice question? Do they touch the screen on or beside the correct answer?), and to receive help when needed. Erroneous keystrokes should not "dump" a student out of the program but allow him or her to recover in a clear and easy way.

Even good programs are not useful if they do not accomplish something that needs to be done. Only the teacher can decide that. John Herriott has noted that the computer can:

1. Impart information on a one-to-one basis with a high success rate when well-written and thoroughly validated programs are used.
2. Provide imbedded remedial instruction of which the student may not necessarily be aware.
3. Provide enrichment material within the program.
4. Keep accurate track of progress throughout the program, and indeed, throughout a series of programs on varied material.
5. (Perhaps the most important.) Allow the student to progress at his own rate.
6. Provide video and audio support via peripheral devices linked directly to the computer.
7. Provide a massive information retrieval base—either by direct display of the material itself or by directing the student to the appropriate medium.[5]

Thorwald Esbensen (1981) points out that drill-and-practice routines can conserve a teacher's time while providing individualized instruction for students who need help learning facts and skills. The interactive nature of CAI can make this drill more interesting, and it helps keep the learner involved with the task.

Furthermore, computer-assisted instruction has been successfully used to teach initial reading skills. One system was developed at Stanford University primarily to teach decoding skills. It utilized a "Model 33" teletypewriter and an audio headset.[6] Children using this CAI program along with regular instruction scored better on tests given at the end of first grade than a control group, and the same group also scored better on tests given at the end of second grade, although no CAI was administered to either group during the second grade.

[5]REPRINTED FROM CREATIVE COMPUTING MAGAZINE, Copyright © 1982 AHL COMPUTING, INC.
[6]For more information, see Richard C. Atkinson and John D. Fletcher, "Teaching Children to Read with a Computer," *The Reading Teacher* 25 (January 1972): 319–27.

When Lois Avaunne Hed examined "the effects math, reading and language arts CAI had on regular classroom, special education, and disadvantaged elementary school students in fifteen different studies, she concluded that students advanced because the CAI approach compressed learning time, individualized instruction, and provided more hours of concentrated instruction for each learner" (Gersten et al., 1981, p. 45).

Of the many public schools that currently use CAI, the Chicago public school system has a particularly large program incorporating commercial drill-and-practice programs in reading instruction for grades two through six. Decoding, literal and figurative comprehension, and some study skills are covered (Blanchard, 1980).

Although comprehension materials are not yet as numerous as word recognition materials, attempts are being made to develop good programs in this area. The Center for the Study of Reading (University of Illinois at Urbana-Champaign) has designed two microcomputer-based reading activities based on how comprehension occurs and what makes up effective instructional software: "Story Maker" and "Textman."

In "Story Maker," which works on problem-solving, reasoning, inference, and evaluation skills, a child can work toward a goal the computer has generated, which describes something that will happen in a story. An inverted tree design allows the child to make choices that add to the story line at each branch; when he or she has made decisions from the top to the bottom of the tree, the child has a complete story. Early decisions affect the ending, and as the child moves through the story he or she has to assess new information, make predictions about consequences, and decide which choice will lead to the desired outcome. If the outcome does not match the child's goal, the computer responds that the result is not the one expected. A printer provides a copy of the completed story to the child, which has motivated some children to do creative things, such as making books.

In "Textman" students guess which sentences go together to form a paragraph in a specific selection. The child is informed about what kind of text is involved. He or she may be told about the purpose of the material and the author and given some paragraphs that come before and after the missing one. He or she tries to choose the sentence that comes next in the paragraph from a list of choices; incorrect answers result in parts being added to a hanging figure, as in the familiar game of Hangman. The computer also gives feedback on whether incorrectly chosen sentences are elsewhere in the text or do not occur in the text at all. Such programs obviously are educationally desirable. These two programs will be made available for minimal charge (Zacchei, 1982).[7]

---

[7]Write to Andee Rubin, Bolt Beranek and Newman, Inc., 10 Moulton St., Cambridge, Massachusetts 02238, for information.

254

Teaching
Reading in
Today's
Elementary
Schools

Some educational publishers who are currently producing CAI programs for reading are listed below. Sample selections from these companies are given here.

(*Reading Comprehension*)
Milliken Publishing Company
1100 Research Blvd.
St. Louis, MO 63132

(*Tutorial Phonics and Word Attack; Fundamental Comprehension; Homonyms in Context*)
Random House School Division
2970 Brandywine Road
Atlanta, GA 30341

(*Critical Reading; Word Structure*)
Borg-Warner Educational Systems
600 W. University Drive
Arlington Heights, IL 60004

(*Read and Solve Math Problems; How to Read in the Content Areas; Literal Comprehension Program; Reading with Understanding; Critical Reading Program: Reading with Critical Understanding*)
Educational Activities
P.O. Box 392
Freeport, NY 11520

(*The Cloze Technique for Developing Comprehension; Word Factory; Vocabulary Builders; Active Reading—World of Nature Series; Adventures Around the World; Strange Encounters: You Decide*)
Orange Cherry Media
7 Delano Drive
Bedford Hills, NY 10507

(*Reading Ads; Understanding Labels; How to Read a Map*)
Philip Roy, Inc.
P.O. Box 68
Indian Rocks Beach, FL 33535

(*Base Words and Affixes; Noting Details/Visualization; Comprehension—Sequence and Cause/Effect; Comprehension—Interpretive Thinking Skills; Vowel Sounds; Following Directions*)
Houghton Mifflin Company
One Beacon Street
Boston, MA 02108

Programs are also available from educational software houses. *Swift's 1983–84 Educational Software Directory* (Austin, Texas: Sterling Swift) is a good source of these materials and of non-commercial software.

Computer-Managed Instruction Computer-managed instruction can help teachers keep track of student performance and guide learning activities. For example, some systems provide tests on specific objectives that are computer-scored. The computer then matches the student's deficiencies to available instructional materials, suggests instructional sequences for the teacher to use, or assigns material directly to the student. The computer may also perform tasks such as averaging grades on a series of tests, thereby removing quite a bit of burdensome record-keeping from the teacher's shoulders (Hedges, 1981; Coburn et al., 1982).

Houghton Mifflin Company supplies a CMI program for reading that gives an on-the-computer survey test, made up of items from the Individual Pupil Monitoring System's criterion-referenced test, after the teacher has provided instruction. Evidence of mastery of a skill allows a student to move to the next skill, but if the student needs to practice, the computer can assign appropriate materials. A posttest then determines whether reteaching is needed; if a student fails, the computer can prescribe work in outside materials. The system provides the teacher with thirteen types of reports on pupils' learning, including a Work Report, which provides a skill-by-skill analysis of each student's progress; a Survey Statistics Report, which shows at a glance how the class has performed overall on the survey; a Survey Alert Report, which tells which students failed to show mastery of a particular skill; and an Assignment Status Report, which indicates skills assigned, mastered, and bypassed. This CMI system is implemented on a minicomputer. Some other companies, such as Milliken and Educational Development Corporation, have smaller systems that run on microcomputers.

The computer generation is here. Children are unintimidated by computers, and teachers need to keep in step. The use of computers holds much promise for education, but the technology is changing rapidly, so teachers need to stay up-to-date.

✔ Self-Check: Objective 5

What are some advantages of programmed instruction?
What kinds of questions should teachers ask about the computer software that they purchase for reading instruction?
(See Self-Improvement Opportunity 5.)

LINGUISTIC APPROACHES

Linguistics is the scientific study of human speech. Linguistic scientists (also referred to as linguists) have attempted to provide an accurate description of the structure of the English language by identifying the sound units, the meaning units, and the patterns that occur in the language, concentrating upon the oral aspects rather than the written aspects of the language.

There is no *one* linguistic approach to teaching reading; however, a number of approaches have been built around linguistic principles. The earliest such

256

Teaching
Reading in
Today's
Elementary
Schools

program for teaching reading was developed for parents by Leonard Bloomfield, who was not an educator but who had strong feelings about the impact of linguistic principles on reading instruction. (See Leonard Bloomfield and Clarence Barnhart, *Let's Read, A Linguistic Approach*, Detroit, Mich.: Wayne State University Press, 1961, for Bloomfield's approach.) Some other materials built upon linguistic principles are Charles C. Fries et al., *Merrill Linguistic Readers* (Columbus, Ohio: Merrill, 1975); *Linguistic Readers* (New York: Benzinger, 1965); and Ralph F. Robinett et al., *Miami Linguistic Readers* (Indianapolis: D.C. Heath, 1970).

Some ways in which linguistic studies have affected instructional materials are explained below.

1. Beginning readers are presented with material in which each letter has only a single phonetic value (sound); therefore, if the short *a* sound is being used in early material, the long *a* sound or other sounds associated with the letter *a* are not used. Naturally, after students have thoroughly learned one phonetic value of a letter, other values are presented.
2. Irregularly spelled words are avoided in beginning reading material, although some (for example, *a* and *the*) are used to construct sentences that have somewhat normal patterns.
3. Word-attack skills are taught by presenting minimally contrasting spelling patterns, words that vary by a single letter. For example, one lesson may contain the words *can, tan, man, ban, fan, ran*, and *pan*. This exposure to minimally contrasting patterns is believed to help the child understand the difference that a certain letter makes in the pronunciation of a word. However, sounds are not isolated from words, because when the sounds are pronounced outside the environment of a word they are distorted. This is particularly true of isolated consonant sounds; *buh, duh*, and *puh* are sounds incorrectly associated with the letters *b, d*, and *p*.
4. Reading orally in a normal speaking fashion is emphasized. Reading is looked upon as turning writing back into speech.

Among linguists' many disagreements about the proper ways of presenting reading material to children, two of the most prominent concern the context of words. First, some linguistic reading materials present children with lists of words (with minimally contrasting spelling patterns) to pronounce. Structural linguists object to this because it isolates words from context. They point out that sentences are basic meaning-bearing units and that many words that do not appear in context cannot be pronounced, defined, or categorized as to part of speech. Second, some linguistic reading materials (for example, *Merrill Linguistic Readers*) have no illustrations because the authors feel that a child, using extraneous picture clues, may fail to perceive and utilize the clues to word identification inherent in the language. Other linguistic readers (for example, Benzinger Press's *Linguistic Readers*) use pictures to provide a context that the limited vocabulary cannot provide.

Example 5.6 conveys a feeling for the type of material contained in linguistic readers.

▶ **EXAMPLE 5.6:** Sample of Linguistic Reading Material

● Direct pupils' attention to the title of the story. Have them place the markers below it. Have the title read aloud. Then say, "Let's read the story to see what we can find out about a cat."
● Guide the silent reading of each sentence by asking the suggested question above it. At this early stage, have oral reading follow the silent reading of each sentence. Demonstrate moving the marker down the page as each sentence is read.

A Cat

Who is Nat?
   Nat is a cat
What can you tell about how he looks?
   Nat is fat.
What does the last sentence say about Nat?
   Nat is a fat cat.

● After the story has been read, ask pupils what they have learned about the cat.
● Proceed with the oral rereading of the entire story. Have several pupils read each sentence until normal intonation is achieved.
● If a particular pattern word proves difficult, offer help in the following sequence. First, have the pupil spell the word. If this procedure does not activate recall, write other words of the pattern on the chalkboard. If neither plan is successful, supply the word and provide practice at a later time.
● If a circled word is not recognized, pronounce it for the pupil who is having difficulty.

Source: Mildred K. Rudolph et al. *I Can, Teacher's Guide, The Merrill Linguistic Reading Program* (Columbus, Ohio: Merrill, 1975), p. 6. ◀

✔ **Self-Check: Objective 6**
Describe some features of linguistic reading approaches.

ECLECTIC APPROACHES

Eclectic approaches combine the desirable aspects of a number of different methods rather than strictly adhering to a single one. Teachers often choose an eclectic approach to fit their unique situations. Following are some

258

Teaching
Reading in
Today's
Elementary
Schools

examples; they are only possibilities, and teachers should remember that the only limitations are school resources and their own imaginations.

1. A teacher may supplement a basal reader approach with language experience charts by having children write ''books about the book,'' that is, dictate stories about the basal selection using the new vocabulary. This approach has been found to enhance comprehension and vocabulary skills (Grabe, 1981). In a classroom in which there are two reading periods each day, the teacher may use the basal reader during the first period and the language experience approach during the second, relating the experience story to the basal story and thereby helping the children gain additional practice with much of the same vocabulary.
2. To encourage sequential skill development, use a basal reader approach two or three days a week; use an individualized reading approach for the remaining days to gain the motivational value of self-selected activities.
3. For children who are reading at grade level and below, a basal reader approach might be better because these children have a greater need for direct teacher interaction and structured materials. The children reading above grade level could be involved in an individualized reading approach, doing much more work independently at their seats and being given skill instruction only when specific needs become evident.
4. Programmed instruction can be utilized with any approach, as can computer-assisted instruction. The use of the word processing function of the computer as described by Glenn Kleiman and Mary Humphrey (1982) makes the computer a natural tool for implementation of the language experience approach. Children who tend to always produce short stories, due to difficulties in writing, are freed to write more extensively with the ease of editing offered by the computer.

Classroom Example

To see how a teacher who embraces an eclectic approach to reading instruction might operate, let us look in on a classroom during one reading period. The following activities are taking place:

1. The teacher is working with a grade-level basal reading group in a corner of the room.
2. Children from another reading group are illustrating a language experience story that they wrote on the previous day. As they finish their illustrations, pairs of children from this group are forming sentences with their word-bank words.
3. Several children who are reading far above grade level are busy reading self-selected library books at their seats.
4. Three other children, also reading above grade level, have returned to the room from the library and seated themselves together to discuss some research reading they have been doing on space travel.

5. A boy who is reading two years below grade level is working independently in a programmed reading textbook.
6. A girl is in another corner of the room, working on a microcomputer program on prefixes and suffixes.

All of the students are busy at reading tasks, but the tasks involve many different approaches to reading instruction.

Test Yourself

True or False
_____ 1. Teacher's manuals in basal reading series generally provide detailed lesson plans for teaching each story in a basal reader.
_____ 2. Basal reader workbooks are designed to teach reading skills and do not require teacher intervention.
_____ 3. Workbook activities are a good way to keep children busy while the teacher is engaged in other activities.
_____ 4. Authors of today's basal readers are trying to reflect today's world realistically.
_____ 5. The language experience approach (LEA) makes use of child-created material for reading instruction.
_____ 6. A word bank is a collection of words that the teacher believes the children should learn.
_____ 7. The language experience approach promotes a better self-concept in many children.
_____ 8. The individualized reading approach utilizes self-selection and self-pacing.
_____ 9. The individualized reading approach involves no direct skills instruction.
_____ 10. Student-teacher conferences are an integral part of the individualized reading approach.
_____ 11. A disadvantage of the individualized reading approach is the absence of sequential skill development.
_____ 12. Beginning linguistic reading materials make use of words that conform to regular spelling patterns.
_____ 13. Programmed instruction involves the presentation of instructional material in small, sequential steps.
_____ 14. Eclectic approaches combine the best features of a number of different approaches.
_____ 15. Sometimes computers are useful in diagnosing students' reading difficulties and prescribing corrective programs.
_____ 16. Basal readers should always be used from front to back in their entirety.
_____ 17. Behavioral objectives are provided for each of the elements in the Wisconsin Design.

260

Teaching
Reading in
Today's
Elementary
Schools

_____ 18. The language experience approach is not consistent with schema theory.

_____ 19. Drill-and-practice programs are among the rarest and most complex CAI programs.

_____ 20. Microcomputers are much less expensive than main frame computers, and therefore it is easier for schools to purchase them for CAI purposes.

_____ 21. No commercial educational publishers have as yet ventured into the new field of CAI.

Vocabulary

Check your knowledge of these terms. Reread parts of the chapter if necessary.

computer-assisted
  instruction
computer-managed
  instruction
directed reading
  approach
eclectic approaches

experience charts
individualized read-
  ing approach
interest inventory
language experience
  approach
linguistics

minimally contrasting
  spelling patterns
objective-based
  approach
programmed
  instruction
word bank

Self-Improvement Opportunities

1. Visit an elementary school classroom and discuss the instructional materials used in the reading program with the teacher(s).
2. Visit a school and watch an experienced teacher using a DRA plan.
3. Develop a language experience chart with a group of youngsters. Use it to teach one or more word-attack skills.
4. Plan an individualized reading approach for a specific group of youngsters. Explain what materials will be used (include reading levels and interest areas of the materials) and where they will be obtained. Outline the record-keeping procedures; explain how conferences will be scheduled and the uses to which they will be put; and describe the routines the children will follow for selecting books, checking out books, and receiving help while reading.
5. Look into the possibility of utilizing CAI programs in your area. Find out, as nearly as possible, what the cost would be and what equipment would be necessary. Evaluate the feasibility of using CAI in your area in the near future.

Bibliography

261

Major
Approaches to
Reading
Instruction

Aaron, Robert L., and Martha K. Anderson. "A Comparison of Values Expressed in Juvenile Magazines and Basal Reader Series." *The Reading Teacher* 35 (December 1981): 305–13.

Allen, R. V. "The Language-Experience Approach." In *Perspectives on Elementary Reading: Principles and Strategies of Teaching,* Robert Karlin, ed. New York: Harcourt Brace Jovanovich, 1973.

Atkinson, Richard C., and John D. Fletcher. "Teaching Children to Read with a Computer." *The Reading Teacher* 25 (January 1972): 319–27.

Barbe, Walter B., and Jerry Abbot. *Personalized Reading Instruction.* Englewood Cliffs, N.J.: Prentice-Hall, 1975.

Blanchard, Jay S. "Computer-assisted Instruction in Today's Reading Classrooms." *Journal of Reading* 23 (February 1980): 430–34.

Blass, Rosanne J., Nancy Allan Jurenka, and Eleanor G. Zirzow. "Showing Children the Communicative Nature of Reading." *The Reading Teacher* 34 (May 1981): 926–31.

Botterell, Art. "Why Johnny Can't Compute." *Microcomputing* 6 (April 1982): 146–50.

Coburn, Peter, et al. *Practical Guide to Computers in Education.* Reading, Mass.: Addison-Wesley, 1982, pp. 46–49.

Cunningham, Pat. "Horizontal Reading." *The Reading Teacher* 34 (November 1980): 222–24.

Durkin, Dolores. "Reading Comprehension Instruction in Five Basal Reader Series." *Reading Research Quarterly* 16, No. 4 (1981): 515–44.

Esbensen, Thorwald. "Personal Computers: The Golden Mean in Education." *Personal Computing* 5 (November 1981): 115–16, 120.

Fitzgerald, Gisela G. "Why Kids Can Read the Book But Not the Workbook." *The Reading Teacher* 32 (May 1979): 930–32.

Gersten, Irene Fandel, James A. Schuyler, and Lesley I. Czechowicz. "The Personal Computer Phenomenon in Education," *Sourceworld* 2 (November/December 1981): 44–47.

Grabe, Nancy White. "Language Experience and Basals." *The Reading Teacher* 34 (March 1981): 710–11.

Hacker, Charles J. "From Schema Theory to Classroom Practice." *Language Arts* 57 (November/December 1980): 866–71.

Hare, Victoria Chou. "Beginning Reading Theory and Comprehension Questions in Teacher's Manuals." *The Reading Teacher* 35 (May 1982): 918–23.

Hedges, William D. "Lightening the Load with Computer-Managed Instruction." *Classroom Computer News* 1 (July/August 1981): 34.

Herriott, John. "CAI: A Philosophy of Education and a System to Match." *Creative Computing* 8 (April 1982): 80–86.

Karlin, Robert, ed. *Perspectives on Elementary Reading: Principles and Strategies of Teaching.* New York: Harcourt Brace Jovanovich, 1973.

262

Teaching
Reading in
Today's
Elementary
Schools

Kleiman, Glenn, and Mary Humphrey. "Learning with Computers: Word Processing in the Classroom." *Compute* 4 (March 1982): 96, 98–99.

Pieronek, Florence T. "Do Basal Readers Reflect the Interests of Intermediate Students?" *The Reading Teacher* 33 (January 1980): 408–12.

Powers, Anne. "Sharing a Language Experience Library with the Whole School." *The Reading Teacher* 34 (May 1981): 892–95.

Quandt, Ivan J. "Investing in Word Banks—A Practice for Any Approach." *The Reading Teacher* 27 (November 1973): 171–73.

Schachter, Sumner W. "Using Workbook Pages More Effectively." *The Reading Teacher* 35 (October 1981): 34–37.

Snyder, Geraldine V. "Do Basal Characters Read in Their Daily Lives?" *The Reading Teacher* 33 (December 1979): 303–306.

Spiegel, Dixie Lee. "Six Alternatives to the Directed Reading Activity." *The Reading Teacher* 34 (May 1981): 914–20.

Spindle, Les. "Computer Corner: What Software Is, and What It Does." *Radio-Electronics* 52 (December 1981): 88, 90, 106.

Stenson, Carol M. "Yes, Workbooks Are Too Hard to Read." *The Reading Teacher* 35 (March 1982): 725–26.

Sulzby, Elizabeth. "Using Children's Dictated Stories to Aid Comprehension." *The Reading Teacher* 33 (April 1980): 772–78.

Zacchei, David. "The Adventures and Exploits of the Dynamic Storymaker and Textman." *Classroom Computer News* (May/June 1982): 28–30, 76–77.

Suggested Readings

Allen, Elizabeth G., and Lester L. Laminack. "Language Experience Reading—It's a Natural," *The Reading Teacher* 35 (March 1982): 708–14.

Allen, Roach Van, and Claryce Allen. *Language Experiences in Reading: Teachers Resource Book.* Chicago: Encyclopaedia Britannica Press, 1966.

Aukerman, Robert C. *Approaches to Beginning Reading.* New York: John Wiley & Sons, 1971.

Aukerman, Robert C. *The Basal Reader Approach to Reading.* New York: John Wiley & Sons, 1981.

Barbe, Walter B., and Jerry Abbot. *Personalized Reading Instruction.* Englewood Cliffs, N.J.: Prentice-Hall, 1975.

Durkin, Dolores. *Teaching Them to Read.* 3rd ed. Boston: Allyn & Bacon, 1978, Chapters 3, 4, and 10.

Hall, MaryAnne. *Teaching Reading as a Language Experience.* 3rd ed. Columbus, Ohio: Charles E. Merrill, 1981.

Hall, MaryAnne. *The Language Experience Approach for Teaching Reading: A Research Perspective.* 2nd ed. Newark, Del.: International Reading Association, 1978.

Hittleman, Daniel R. *Developmental Reading: A Psycholinguistic Perspective.*
2nd ed. Boston: Houghton Mifflin, 1983, Chapter 7.

Kennedy, Eddie C. *Methods in Teaching Developmental Reading.* 2nd ed.
Itasca, Ill.: Peacock, 1981, Chapters 4 and 5.

Lamb, Pose, and Richard Arnold. *Reading: Foundations and Instructional
Strategies.* Belmont, Calif.: Wadsworth, 1976, Chapters 7 and 8.

Lapp, Dianne, and James Flood. *Teaching Reading to Every Child.* New
York: Macmillan, 1978, Chapter 12.

Lee, Dorris M., and Roach V. Allen. *Learning to Read Through Experience.*
2nd ed. Englewood Cliffs, N.J.: Prentice-Hall, 1966.

Miller, Wilma H. *The First R: Elementary Reading Today.* 2nd ed. New York:
Holt, Rinehart and Winston, 1977.

Olson, Joanne P., and Martha H. Dillner. *Learning to Teach Reading in
the Elementary School: Utilizing a Competency Based Instructional System.* 2nd
ed. New York: Macmillan, 1982, Chapters 2 and 15.

Quandt, Ivan J. "Investing in Word Banks—A Practice for Any Approach." *The Reading Teacher* 27 (November 1973): 171–73.

Quandt, Ivan J. *Teaching Reading: A Human Process.* Chicago: Rand
McNally, 1977, Chapters 9, 10, 11, 12, and 13.

Ransom, Grayce A. *Preparing to Teach Reading.* Boston: Little, Brown,
1978, Chapters 8 and 9.

Sartain, Harry, comp. *Individualized Reading.* Rev. ed. Newark, Del.:
International Reading Association, 1970 (annotated bibliography, listing
periodicals, books, and research).

Smith, Richard J., and Dale D. Johnson. *Teaching Children to Read.* 2nd
ed. Reading, Mass.: Addison-Wesley, 1980, Chapters 3, 8, and 9.

Spache, George D., and Evelyn B. Spache. *Reading in the Elementary
School.* 4th ed. Boston: Allyn & Bacon, 1977, Chapters 11 and 12.

Stauffer, Russell G. *The Language Experience Approach to the Teaching of
Reading.* 2nd ed. New York: Harper & Row, 1980.

Veatch, Jeannette, et al. *Key Words to Reading.* 2nd ed. Columbus, Ohio:
Charles E. Merrill, 1979.

Veatch, Jeannette. *Reading in the Elementary School.* 2nd ed. New York:
John Wiley & Sons, 1978.

Vilscek, Elaine C., ed. *A Decade of Innovative Approaches to Beginning
Reading.* Newark, Del.: International Reading Association, 1968.

Walcutt, Charles C., et al. *Teaching Reading: A Phonic/Linguistic Approach
to Developmental Reading.* New York: Macmillan, 1974.

Zintz, Miles V. *The Reading Process: The Teacher and the Learner.* 3rd ed.
Dubuque, Iowa: William C. Brown, 1980, Chapters 10 and 12.

CHAPTER 6

Reading/Study Skills

Introduction

Reading/study skills are techniques that enhance comprehension and retention of information contained in printed material and thus help children cope successfully with reading assignments in content area classes. Students need to develop the ability to use a good study method that can help them in retaining material they read, flexibility of reading habits, and the ability to locate and organize information effectively. Knowledge of how to gain the greatest amount of information possible from graphic aids (maps, graphs, tables, and illustrations) in content area reading materials is also useful.

Teaching study skills is not only the job of the intermediate-grade teacher, although the need for it is more obvious at this level. Primary-grade teachers must lay the foundation by developing readiness for this instruction and making children aware of the need for study skills. They can do this with activities such as making free-form outlines related to stories the children have heard or read, occasionally writing group experience charts in outline form, letting the children see them using indexes and tables of contents of books to find needed information, encouraging the children to watch them use the card catalog to help locate a book, and reading aloud information related to content area study from a variety of reference books. Primary teachers can begin actual study skill instruction in use of some parts of books (tables of contents, glossaries), dictionary use (alphabetical order, use of picture dictionaries), library use (location of the easy-to-read books, check-in and check-out procedures), map reading (titles, directional indicators, legends), graph-reading (picture graphs, circle graphs, simple bar graphs), and picture-reading.

Since some children are ready for more advanced skills, such as note-taking, much more quickly than others, intermediate-grade teachers should determine the readiness of particular children for study skills instruction and offer instruction to fit the students' capabilities. Those children who are ready for more advanced skills should be helped to develop these skills as early as possible, because study skills help children succeed in all subjects.

Teachers may present study skills during a content class when the need arises or during a reading class, but they should be sure they are applied to content soon after a reading class. Children will retain skills longer if they apply them, and they will see them as useful tools, not as busywork exercises. The likelihood of their applying their new knowledge is increased if they practice skills in the context in which they are to be used, so a teacher may find it very effective to set aside time during a content class to teach a study skill that students will need immediately in that class.

Setting Objectives

When you finish reading this chapter, you should be able to

1. Discuss the features of the SQ3R study method.
2. Explain the importance of developing flexible reading habits.

266

Teaching
Reading in
Today's
Elementary
Schools

3. Name some skills that a child needs in order to locate information in a book or in a library.
4. Describe how to help a child learn to take good notes, make a good outline, and write a good summary.
5. Explain how to teach a child to use graphic aids in textbooks.

STUDY METHODS

SQ3R

Probably the best-known study method is Robinson's SQ3R Method—Survey, Question, Read, Recite, Review (Robinson, 1961).

Survey As you approach reading assignments you should notice chapter titles and main headings, read introductory and summary paragraphs, and inspect any visual aids such as maps, graphs, or illustrations. This initial survey provides a framework for organizing the facts you later derive from the reading.

Question Formulate a list of questions that you expect to be answered in the reading. The headings may give you some clues.

Read Read the selection in order to answer the questions you have formulated. Since this is purposeful reading, making brief notes may be helpful.

Recite Having read the selection, try to answer each of the questions that you formulated earlier without looking back at the material.

Review Reread to verify or correct your recited answers and to make sure that you have the main points of the selection in mind and that you understand the relationships between the various points.

Using a study method such as this one will help a student remember content material better than simply reading the material would. Consequently, it is worthwhile to take time in class to show pupils how to go through the various steps. The teacher should have group practice sessions on SQ3R, or any study method, before he or she expects the children to perform the steps independently.

Material chosen for SQ3R instruction should be content material on which the students should normally use the method. Ask all the students to survey the selection together, reading aloud the title and main headings and introductory and summary paragraphs, and discussing the visual aids, in the first practice session.

The step that needs most explanation from the teacher is the Question step. Show children how to take a heading, such as "Brazil's Exports," and turn it into a question: "What are Brazil's exports?" This question should be answered in the section, and trying to find the answer provides a good purpose for reading. A chapter heading, such as "The Westward Movement," may elicit a variety of possible questions: "What is the Westward Movement?" "When did it take place?" "Where did it take place?" "Why did it take place?" "Who was involved?" The teacher can encourage children to generate questions like these in a class discussion in initial practice sessions.

After they have formulated questions, the class reads to find the answers. The teacher might make brief notes on the chalkboard to model behavior the children can follow. Then he or she can have students practice the recite step by asking each child to respond orally to one of the purpose questions, with the book closed. During the review step the children reread to check all the answers they have just heard.

In further practice sessions, the teacher can merely alert the children to perform each step and have them all perform the step silently at the same time. It will probably take several practice sessions before the steps are thoroughly set in the students' memories.

Although SQ3R is probably the most well-known study method, it is not the only one. Spache and Spache (1977) recommend use of a similar method that does not include prereading questions but has the following steps: Preview, Read, Summarize, Test. Both methods are most often applied in the areas of social studies and science.

SQRQCQ

Another method that seems simple enough to utilize with good results at the elementary level is one developed especially for use with mathematics materials—SQRQCQ (Fay, 1965). SQRQCQ stands for Survey, Question, Read, Question, Compute, Question. This approach may be beneficial because youngsters frequently have great difficulty reading statement problems in mathematics textbooks.

Survey   You read through the problem quickly to gain an idea of its general nature.
Question   You ask, "What is being asked in the problem?"
Read   You read the problem carefully, paying attention to specific details and relationships.
Question   You make a decision about the mathematical operations to be carried out and in some cases the order in which they are to be performed.
Compute   You do the computations you decided upon in the preceding step.
Question   You decide whether or not the answer seems to be correct, asking, "Is this a reasonable answer? Have I accurately performed the computations?"

As is true with SQ3R, the teacher should have the whole class practice the SQRQCQ method before he or she expects students to use it independently. The teaching of the method takes little extra time, since it is a good way to manage mathematics instruction.

Other Techniques to Improve Retention

In addition to providing pupils with a good study method, a teacher can increase their ability to retain content material by following the suggestions provided below.

1. Conduct discussions about all assigned reading material. Talking about ideas that they have read helps to fix these ideas in students' memories.
2. Teach your pupils to read assignments critically. Have them constantly evaluate the material that they read, and avoid giving them the idea that something is true "because the book says so" by encouraging them to challenge any statement in the book if they can find evidence to the contrary. The active involvement with the material that is necessary in critical reading aids retention. (See Chapter 4 for a thorough discussion of critical reading.)
3. Encourage your pupils to apply the ideas they have read about. For example, after reading about parliamentary procedure, students could conduct a club meeting; after reading about a simple science experiment, they could actually conduct the experiment. Children learn those things that they have applied better than those about which they have only read.
4. Always be certain that the children have in mind a purpose for reading before beginning each reading assignment, since this increases their ability to retain material. You may supply them with purpose questions or encourage them to state their own purposes. Some examples of purpose questions are:
   a. What was the route Josey and her parents took on their bicycle trip? (sequence question)
   b. What caused Ian to forget about the promise he had made? (cause-and-effect question)
   (More information about purpose questions is found in Chapter 4.)
5. Use audiovisual aids to reinforce concepts presented in the reading material.
6. Read background material to the class to give students a frame of reference to which they can relate the ideas that they read.
7. Prepare study guides for content area assignments. Study guides, duplicated sheets prepared by the teacher, help children retain their content area concepts by setting purposes for reading and providing appropriate frameworks for organizing material. (Study guides receive extensive attention in Chapter 7.)
8. Teach the students to look for the author's organization. Have them outline the material.
9. Encourage the children to picture the ideas the author is describing. Visualizing information will help them remember it longer.

10. Teach note-taking procedures and encourage note-taking. Writing down information often helps children retain it.
11. After the children have read the material, have them summarize it in their own words in either written or oral form.
12. Have children use spaced practice (a number of short practice sessions extended over a period of time) rather than massed practice (one long practice session) for material you wish them to retain over a long period of time.
13. Encourage *overlearning* (continuing to practice a skill for a while after it has been initially mastered) of material that you wish pupils to retain for long periods of time.
14. When appropriate, teach some simple mnemonic devices—for example, "there is 'a rat' in the middle of 'separate'."
15. Offer positive reinforcement for correct responses to questions during discussion and review sessions.
16. Encourage students to look for words and ideas that are mentioned repeatedly, because they are likely to be important ones.

FLEXIBILITY OF READING HABITS

Flexible readers adjust their approaches and rates to fit the materials they are reading. Good readers continually adjust their reading approaches and rates without being consciously aware of it.

Adjustment of Approach

A flexible reader approaches printed material according to his or her purposes for reading and the type of material. For example, she may read poetry aloud so she can savor the beauty of the words, or she may read a novel for relaxation in a leisurely fashion, giving attention to descriptive passages that evoke visual imagery and taking time to think about the characters and their traits. If she is reading a novel simply to be able to converse with friends about its story line, she may read less carefully, only wishing to discover main ideas and basic plot.

Informational reading is approached with the idea of separating the important facts from the unimportant ones and paying careful attention in order to retain what is needed from the material. Rereading is often needed if materials contain a high density of facts or very difficult concepts and interrelationships. For such material, reading every word may be highly important, whereas it is not as important for materials that have few facts or less difficult concepts. Flexible readers approach materials for which they have little background with greater concentration than material for which they have extensive background.

Adjustment of Rate

Students will use study time more efficiently if they are taught to vary their rates to fit the reading purposes and materials. A student should read light fiction for enjoyment much faster than a mathematics problem that he hopes to solve. When reading to find isolated facts, such as names and dates, he will do better to scan a page rapidly for key words than to read every word of the material. When reading to determine main ideas or organization of a selection, he will find skimming more reasonable than reading each word of the selection.

Children often make the mistake of trying to read everything at the same rate. Some of them read short stories as slowly and carefully as they read science experiments, and will probably never enjoy recreational reading because they have to work so hard and it takes them so long to read a story. Other children read everything at a rapid rate, often failing to grasp essential details in content area reading assignments, although they complete the reading. Reading rate should not be considered separate from comprehension. The optimum rate for reading a particular piece is the fastest rate at which the child maintains an acceptable level of comprehension.

One way to help pupils fit their reading rates to reading materials is illustrated in the following activity.

● **MODEL ACTIVITY:** *Adjusting Reading Rates*

Ask pupils questions such as these:

1. What rate would be best for reading a science experiment?
   a. fast
   b. moderate
   c. slow
2. Which material could you read fastest and still meet your purpose?
   a. television schedule
   b. newspaper article
   c. science textbook

Follow up answers with the question "Why?" If students do not choose "slow" as the answer for the first question, analyze the reason they give and point out any problems, making clear to them that every step in a science experiment must be done accurately and in the proper sequence or the experiment will not work. In order to assure that he or she understands all details and follows the proper sequence, a person must read slowly enough not to overlook any detail, and may even have to reread to be absolutely accurate.

If children do not answer "a television schedule" for the second question, ask what purpose they would have in reading such a schedule. When they reply, "to find what is on at a particular time" or "to find out when a certain program is on," point out that it is possible to scan for this information and that scanning is the fastest type of reading. They might aim to locate specific facts in a newspaper or a science textbook, but the format of a television schedule facilitates scanning, and it would probably be faster to read one even if the purposes for reading each type of material were similar. ●

Another way to assist children in fitting appropriate rates to materials is to give them various types of materials and purposes, allow them to try different rates, and then encourage them to discuss the effectiveness of different rates for different purposes and materials. Emphasis on increasing reading speed is best left until children have a firm grasp of the basic word recognition and comprehension skills. By the time they reach the intermediate grades, some will be ready for help in increasing their reading rates. It is important to remember that speed without comprehension is useless, so be sure they maintain comprehension levels as work on increasing reading rate progresses. To help pupils increase their reading rates, teachers may use timed exercises or speed reading devices such as the tachistoscope, which presents printed material for brief periods of time; controlled reading machines that project material at varying speeds; and reading pacers with arms that move down a page of printed material from top to bottom at regulated speeds. Comprehension checks should accompany each lesson, and if the teacher plots rate on a graph to show children their improvement, he or she should also plot comprehension so the children will not forget the importance of understanding the material.

ReFlex Action

One method for developing flexible readers is known as ReFlex Action. It is designed to supplement the readiness portion of a guided reading activity. Its objective is to have children select the processing strategies that best fit a given reading context. The first step is analysis of context through questioning, whether teacher-directed, student-initiated, or reciprocal. Readers should question the purpose for reading; the difficulty, structure, and organization of the material; their background and interest in a particular area; the aids (such as teacher assistance, study guides, etc.) available for working with the selection; the social setting in which the reading will take place; and the time constraints, if any. The second step of the approach is strategy selection—determining whether skimming, scanning, reading to comprehend all of the ideas presented by the author, or a combination of strategies is needed. If the reader decides he or she should use a combination of strategies, he or she should determine the order in which to apply them in this step also. Obviously, teachers must provide varied contexts for reading—not a single unvarying approach with the same purpose, the same difficulty level, and so forth—in order to make this approach work (Hoffman, 1979).

Describe the SQ3R study method.

Explain the reasons that children should learn to read different materials at different rates.

(See Self-Improvement Opportunity 1.)

LOCATING INFORMATION

In order to engage in many study activities, pupils need to be able to locate the necessary reading material. A teacher can help by showing them the location aids in textbooks, reference books, and libraries.

Books

Most books offer pupils several special features that are helpful for locating needed information, including prefaces, tables of contents, indexes, appendices, glossaries, footnotes, and bibliographies. Teachers should not assume that children can adjust from the basal reader format to the format of content subject books without assistance. Basal readers have a great deal of narrative (story-type) material which is not packed with facts to be learned, as is the content material that students will encounter. Although most basals have a table of contents and a glossary, they contain fewer of the special features mentioned above than do content area textbooks. Therefore, teachers should present content textbooks carefully to the children.

Preface/Introduction

When a teacher presents a new textbook to pupils in the intermediate or upper grades, he or she can ask them to read the preface or introduction to get an idea of why the book was written and of the manner in which the author or authors plan to present the material. Children should be aware that the prefaces and introductions of books they plan to use for reference can give them valuable information.

Table of Contents

The table of contents of a new textbook can also be examined on the day the textbook is distributed. Even primary-level pupils can learn that the table of contents tells what topics the book discusses on which pages and makes it unnecessary for a person to look through the entire book to find the section that is of interest at the moment. Asking questions such as the following ones,

The dictionary can be a wonderful learning tool for children, but before they can use it proficiently, they must be familiar with certain fundamental skills, such as alphabetization and use of guide words. (© Ed Lettau/Photo Researchers)

the teacher can hold a brief drill with the new textbook that will emphasize these points.

> What topics are covered in this book?
> What is the first topic that is discussed?
> On what page does the discussion about _____ begin? (This question can be repeated several times with different topics inserted in the blank.)

Indexes

Pupils at the intermediate- and upper-grade levels should become familiar with indexes. They should understand that an index is an alphabetical list of items and names mentioned in a book and the pages upon which these items or names appear, and that some books contain one general index and some contain subject and author indexes as well as other specialized ones (for example, a first-line index in a music or poetry book). Most indexes contain both main headings and subheadings, and students should be given opportunities to practice using these headings to locate information within their

274

Teaching
Reading in
Today's
Elementary
Schools

books. The following lesson, which should follow a preliminary lesson about what an index is and how it can be used, provides practice in the use of an index.

● **MODEL ACTIVITY:** *Lesson Plan for Index Practice*

Use the children's own textbooks to teach index use. You can modify this lesson idea to fit an actual index in a content area textbook.

Sample Index
Addition
    checking, 50–54
    meaning of, 4
    on number line, 10–16, 25–26
    number sentences, 18–19
    regrouping in, 75–91, 103–104
Checking
    addition, 50–54
    subtraction, 120–25
Circle, 204–206
Counting, 2–4
Difference, 111–12
Dollar, 35
Dozen, 42
Graph, 300–306
    bar, 303–306
    picture, 300–303

Ask the children to use the sample index to answer the following questions:
1. On what pages would you look to find out how to check addition problems? Under what main topics and subheadings do you have to look to discover these page numbers?
2. On what page will you find "dollar" mentioned?
3. What pages contain information about circles?
4. On what pages would you look to find out how to add using a number line? What main heading did you look under to discover this? What subheading did you look under?
5. Where would you look to find information about picture graphs? Would you expect to find any information about picture graphs on page 305? Why or why not?
6. Is there information on regrouping in addition on pages 103 and 104? Is this information on any other pages?
Ask the following question if you are using an actual index.
7. Find the meaning of addition and read it to me. Did you look in the index to find the page number? Could you have found it more quickly by looking in the index? ●

Appendices

Students can also be shown that the appendices of books contain supplementary information that may be helpful to them—for example, bibliographies or tabular material. There are times when children need to use this material, but they will not be likely to use it if they do not know where to find it.

Glossaries

Primary children can be shown that glossaries, which are often included in their textbooks, are similar to dictionaries but include only the words presented in the book in which they are found. Textbooks often contain glossaries of technical terms which can greatly aid students in understanding the book's content. The skills necessary for proper use of a glossary are the same as those needed for using a dictionary. (See Chapter 3 for a detailed discussion of dictionary use.)

Footnotes and Bibliographies

These aids refer students to other sources with information about the subject being discussed in a book, and teachers should encourage students to turn to these sources for clarification of ideas, for additional information on a topic for a report, or simply for their own satisfaction.

The bibliography, which appears at the end of a chapter or at the end of the entire textbook, is generally a list of references that the author consulted when researching the subject or that contain additional information. In some cases, bibliographies list books by a particular author or appropriate selections for particular groups.

Reference Books

Elementary school children are often called upon to find information in such reference books as encyclopedias, dictionaries, almanacs, and atlases. Unfortunately, many students reach high school still unable to use such aids effectively. Though some skills related to the use of reference books can be taught in the primary grades (for example, use of picture dictionaries), the bulk of the responsibility for teaching use of reference books rests with the intermediate-grade teacher.

Important skills for effective use of reference books include:

1. knowledge of alphabetical order and that encyclopedias, dictionaries, and some atlases are arranged in alphabetical order.
2. ability to use guide words, knowledge of their location on a page, and understanding that they represent the first and last entry words on a dictionary or encyclopedia page.

276

Teaching
Reading in
Today's
Elementary
Schools

3. ability to use cross references (related primarily to use of encyclopedias).
4. ability to use pronunciation keys (related primarily to use of dictionaries).
5. ability to choose from several possible word meanings the one that most closely fits the context in which a word is found (related to use of dictionaries).
6. ability to interpret the legend of a map (related to use of atlases).
7. ability to interpret the scale of a map (related to use of atlases).
8. ability to locate directions on maps (related to use of atlases).
9. ability to determine which volume of a set of encyclopedias will contain the information needed.
10. ability to determine key words under which related information can be found.

Because of the fact that encyclopedias, almanacs, and atlases are often written on much higher readability levels than the basal materials used in the classroom, teachers must use caution in assigning work in these reference books. Children are not likely to profit from looking up material in books that are too hard for them to read; when children are asked to do so, they tend to copy the material word for word without trying to understand it.

Kristina MacCormick and Janet E. Pursel (1982) found that the overall readability levels of three encyclopedias often used in schools—the *Academic American Encyclopedia,* the *Encyclopaedia Britannica,* and the *World Book*—were all too high for elementary students, being sixteenth, sixteenth, and eleventh grade in difficulty respectively. None of the selections checked in the *Academic American* and the *Britannica* were below ninth-grade level; these books are clearly not good choices for the majority of elementary students, though some *parts* of their articles, in particular opening paragraphs, are written on lower levels and thus are not totally unusable. About 16 percent of the *World Book's* articles are written on fifth- through eighth-grade level, with the rest on higher levels. The common use of this encyclopedia in elementary schools makes knowledge of this fact very important to teachers, who should make assignments requiring use of encyclopedias with care and with specific students in mind.

Many skills related to the use of an atlas are included in the section of this chapter that is concerned with reading maps. Some aspects of dictionary use and use of encyclopedias are discussed below. (Other aspects of dictionary use are discussed in Chapters 3 and 4.)

Dictionaries

Before a child can use a dictionary for any of its major functions, he or she must be able to locate a designated word with some ease. Three important skills are necessary for this.

Alphabetical Order   Since the words in a dictionary are arranged in
alphabetical order, children must learn alphabetical order to gain access to the words they seek. Beginning with the first letter of the word, they gradually learn alphabetization by the first two or three letters, and learn that sometimes it is necessary to work through every letter in a word in the process.

Try these four ideas for developing and strengthening students' knowledge of alphabetical order.

● **MODEL ACTIVITY:** *Alphabetical Game*

Divide the class into two teams and line players up in alphabetical order by names. For the first round of the game have students take turns answering when you call a letter of the alphabet by responding with the next letter of the alphabet. Give the player's team a point if he or she answers correctly and deduct a point if the player answers incorrectly. After an incorrect answer, give the other team an opportunity to answer correctly on the same letter. In the second round the team member must answer with the preceding letter of the alphabet, and in the third round he or she must give the two letters that immediately precede and follow the letter you call. The same activity can be carried out in class without using teams.   ●

● **MODEL ACTIVITY:** *Alphabetical Order*

On the front side of each of 14 file cards write the words shown below. On the reverse side write the letters. Set the cards up at a learning center and have the children follow the directions shown below. (As you can see, this particular message is a seasonal one, but the activity can be redesigned for any number of cards with whatever message you choose.)

1. apple—M
2. bear—E
3. great—R
4. happy—R
5. heart—Y
6. height—C
7. learn—H
8. monster—R
9. noticeable—I
10. noticed—S
11. powerful—T
12. puppy—M
13. steak—A
14. streak—S

Directions: Place the words printed on the file cards in alphabetical order. When you have done so, take the cards and arrange them on your desk in left-to-right order with Card 1 containing the word that comes first in the alphabet. Place them as shown below.

Order for Cards
1 2 3 4 5
6 7 8 9 10 11 12 13 14

278

Teaching
Reading in
Today's
Elementary
Schools

Now turn the cards over. If you have alphabetized the cards correctly, they will spell out a message for you. If you do not find a message on the back of the cards, turn the cards over and study them carefully to see which ones are not in alphabetical order. Rearrange the cards correctly and look for the message again. The correct arrangement is in the answer key, if you find yourself unable to work this puzzle correctly. ●

● **MODEL ACTIVITY:** *Sections of the Dictionary*

Prepare four cardboard mailboxes labeled like the ones shown here. Then prepare index cards with a word printed on each one for students to place in the boxes. Set the mailboxes, the index cards, and a dictionary in a learning center, and have students follow the directions given below.

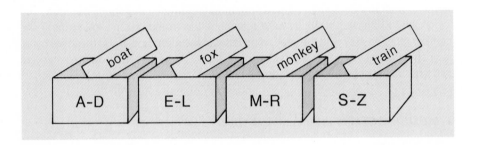

Directions: Pretend that the words on the word cards are ones you need to look up in the dictionary. The mailboxes are labeled with letters found in four sections of the dictionary (the first quarter of the dictionary, A–D; the second quarter, E–L; the third quarter, M–R; and the last quarter, S–Z). Place each card in the correct box. Time yourself to see how long it takes to place the cards. Check your work, using the answer key, when you are finished.

Follow-up: Mix up the cards again and time yourself once more to see if you can do the task more quickly this time. Be sure to check your work. For extra practice, actually look up the words in the dictionary and time yourself. Try again to see if you can improve your time. ●

● **MODEL ACTIVITY:** *Alphabetizing*

Write the following pairs of words on the board:

(1) baby   (2) window   (3) happen
    donkey   tractor   curve

(4) acorn	(5) teach	(6) scold
antler	bitter	sample
(7) advise	(8) straight	(9) church
add	stick	chief
(10) penthouse	(11) reaction	(12) planter
pentagon	reactor	plantation

Ask the children which word in each pair would appear first in the dictionary and why. The pairs are arranged so that each set of three is harder than the previous set. You can ask the slower pupils to respond to the easier pairs and the brighter pupils to respond to the more difficult ones. The last set of three pairs is quite difficult. ●

Guide Words Children need to learn that the guide words at the top of a dictionary page tell them the first and last words on that page. If they are proficient in use of alphabetical order, they should be able to decide whether or not a word will be found on a particular page by checking to see if the word alphabetically falls between the two guide words.

The following suggestions are for students' work with guide words in the dictionary.

ACTIVITIES

1. If the children each have copies of identical dictionaries, use dictionaries for this activity; otherwise, the glossary in the back of a textbook can be used. Tell the children to turn to a certain page and read the guide words. Then ask them to locate the first guide word on the page and tell where it is found. Follow the same procedure with the second guide word. Direct the students to repeat this activity with a number of different pages. Then ask them to explain what guide words tell dictionary users.
2. Write two guide words on the board. Have each child write as many words as possible that would be found on a dictionary page with those guide words. Set a time limit. The child with the largest number of correct words can be declared the winner, but this doesn't have to be a competitive activity.
3. Use worksheets such as those that follow.

● *WORKSHEET: Guide Words*

Directions: Pretend that the two words listed in all capital letters below are the guide words for a page of the dictionary. On the line beside each of the numbered words,

280

Teaching
Reading in
Today's
Elementary
Schools

write "yes" if the word would be found on that page and "no" if it would not. Be ready to explain your choices when the teacher checks this worksheet.

BRACE—BUBBLE

1. beaker _____
2. boil _____
3. break _____
4. braid _____
5. bud _____
6. buy _____
7. broke _____
8. bracelet _____
9. bunny _____
10. bribe _____

11. brave _____
12. border _____
13. bypass _____
14. brag _____
15. bring _____
16. brother _____
17. branch _____
18. bridge _____
19. brake _____
20. barber _____ ●

● **WORKSHEET:** *Guide Words*

Directions: Below are four guide words and the two dictionary pages on which they occur. Write the number of the page on which each of the numbered words would be found, unless it would be found on neither page; in that case, write "no" beside the word.

Page 300   RAINBOW—RAPID
Page 301   RAPPORT—RAVEN

1. rare _____
2. ramble _____
3. ranch _____
4. rabbit _____
5. rash _____
6. razor _____
7. rave _____

8. ratio _____
9. range _____
10. raw _____
11. rank _____
12. raincoat _____
13. race _____
14. raise _____ ●

Locating Variants and Derivatives   Variants and derivatives are sometimes entered alphabetically in a dictionary, but more often they are either not listed or are listed in conjunction with their root words. If they are not listed, the reader must find the pronunciation of the root word and combine the sounds of the added parts with that pronunciation. This procedure requires advanced skills in word analysis and blending.

Here are two ideas for exercises in locating variants and derivatives in the dictionary.

● **WORKSHEET:** *Determining the Correct Entry Word*

Directions: If you wanted to look up the following words in the dictionary, you might not be able to find them listed separately. These words have prefixes, suffixes, and inflectional endings added to root words, so you may need to locate their root words to find them. For each word, write the root word on the line.

1. happily _____
2. commonly _____
3. earliness _____
4. opposed _____
5. undeniable _____
6. gnarled _____
7. cultivating _____

8. customs _____
9. cuter _____
10. joyfully _____
11. computable _____
12. comradeship _____
13. concentrating _____
14. directness _____ ●

● **MODEL ACTIVITY:** *Locating Variants and Derivatives*

Write on the board a series of test words, all of which are variants or derivatives. See that each pupil has a dictionary. Then give a signal to the class members to begin to look up the words. The first one to locate each test word goes to the board and writes beside the word the entry under which he or she found the word.

Test Word　　*Student's Entry*
donating　　donate

Continue the process until all words have been located. It is a good idea to circulate and give assistance to children who are having difficulty. ●

Encyclopedia Use

Since different encyclopedias vary in content and arrangement, pupils should be exposed to several different sets. In addition to asking them to compare encyclopedias on an overall basis, noting such things as type of index used, number of volumes, and publication date, teachers should have them compare the entries on a specified list of topics. The following activities can be used to provide children with instruction and practice in use of the encyclopedia.

● **MODEL ACTIVITY:** *Encyclopedia Skills*

Have students find the correct volume for each of the following topics, without opening the volume:

George Washington
Declaration of Independence
Civil War
Turtles
Siamese Cats

Have them check their choices by actually looking up the terms. If they fail to find a term in the volume where they expected to find it, ask them to think of other places to

282

Teaching
Reading in
Today's
Elementary
Schools

look. Let them check these possibilities also. Continue the process until each term has been located. A possible interchange between teacher and pupil might be:

Teacher: In which volume of the encyclopedia would a discussion of George Washington be found?
Pupil: In Volume 23.
Teacher: Why did you choose Volume 23?
Pupil: Because *W* is in Volume 23.
Teacher: Why didn't you choose Volume 7 for the *G's*?
Pupil: Because people are listed under their last names.
Teacher: Look up the term and check to see if your decision was correct.
Pupil: It was. I found "George Washington" on page 58.
Teacher: Very good. Now tell me where you would find a description of Siamese cats.
Pupil: In Volume 19 under *Siamese*.
Teacher: Check your decision by looking it up.
Pupil: It is not here. It must be under *C*. I'll check Volume 3.
Teacher: Good idea.
Pupil: Here it is. It is under *Cats*. ●

● **WORKSHEET:** *Choosing the Right Volume*

Directions: Pretend you have an encyclopedia in which there is one volume for each letter of the alphabet. Look at the following names, decide which volume you should use to find each one, and write the letter of the volume in the space provided beside the name. When you finish, take the answer key and check your work. If you don't understand why you made your mistakes, ask the teacher or aide for help.

Abraham Lincoln _____
Clara Barton _____
Martin Luther King _____
Eleanor Roosevelt _____
Henry Wadsworth Longfellow _____
John Paul Jones _____
Martin Van Buren _____
Answer Key: L, B, K, R, L, J, V ●

● **WORKSHEET:** *Using the Encyclopedia*

Directions: Look up each of the following topics in the encyclopedia. Then write the letter of the volume in which you found the topic and the page numbers on which it is discussed on the line beside each topic.

1. Badminton _____
2. Constellations _____

3. U.S. Constitution _____

4. Lobster _____

5. Oleander _____

6. Sampan _____ ●

Other Reference Materials

Children are often asked to use materials other than books, such as newspapers, magazines, catalogues, transportation schedules, and pamphlets and brochures, as reference sources.

To help youngsters learn to locate information in newspapers, teachers can alert them to the function of headlines and teach them how to use the newspaper's index. Teachers also should devote some class time to explaining journalistic terms, which can help children better understand the material in the newspaper, and to explaining the functions of news stories, editorials, columns, and feature stories.

In helping children to use magazines, teachers can call attention to the table of contents and give the children practice in using it, just as they did with textbooks. Distinguishing between informational and fictional materials is important in magazines, as is analysis of advertisements to detect propaganda. Activities related to these critical reading skills are found in Chapter 4.

In order to use catalogues, children again need to be able to use an index. Activities suggested in this chapter for using indexes in newspapers and textbooks can be profitably used here also. Ability to read charts giving information about sizes and information about postage and handling charges may also be important in the use of catalogues.

A variety of transportation schedules, pamphlets, and brochures may be used as reference sources in social studies activities. Since their formats may vary greatly, teachers will need to plan practice in reading the specific materials that they intend to use in their classes.

The following activities can be aids in helping students to use newspapers and catalogues as reference materials.

ACTIVITIES

1. Use activities related to developing the concept of main idea (see Chapter 4) to sensitize youngsters to the function of headlines.
2. During class discussion explain the meanings of any of the following terms and abbreviations with which the children are not familiar: AP, byline, dateline, editorial, UPI.
3. Use activities found in Chapters 4 and 7 concerning types of stories, columns, features, and advertisements in the newspaper.
4. Develop worksheets similar to these for use of the newspaper's index and for practice with charts in catalogues.

284

Teaching
Reading in
Today's
Elementary
Schools

● **WORKSHEET:** *Use of a Newspaper's Index*

Directions: Below is an index from a newspaper. Study it and answer the questions that follow.

Index

Comics	B-11-12	Finance	A-4-7
Classified Ads	B-5-10	Horoscope	A-8
Crossword	B-11	Humor columns	A-8-9
Editorials	A-23	Obituaries	A-11
Entertainment	B-3-4		

1. Where in the newspaper would you find information concerning financial matters? _____
2. In what section would you look to find a movie that you would like to see or to find the television schedule? _____
3. On what page is the crossword puzzle found? _____
4. How many pages have comics on them? _____
5. Where would you look to find out which people had died recently? _____ ●

● **WORKSHEET:** *Reading Charts in Catalogues*

Directions: Study the chart below, which describes postage and handling charges assessed by one company. Answer the questions that follow it.

Postage and Handling Charges
If your order is:

up to $6.99	—	add 90¢
$7.00 to $10.99	—	add $1.30
$11.00 to $14.99	—	add $1.70
$15.00 to $18.99	—	add $2.10

1. Your order comes to $8.70. What are the postage and handling charges? _____ For what amount should you write your check? _____
2. Your order comes to $14.99. What are the postage and handling charges? _____
3. Your order is only 90¢. What are the postage and handling charges? _____ ●

Libraries

The teacher and the librarian should work together as a team to develop the skills that pupils need to use the library effectively. The librarian can help by showing students the location of books and journals, card catalogs, and reference materials (such as dictionaries, encyclopedias, atlases, and the *Reader's Guide to Periodical Literature*) in the library; by explaining the procedures for checking books in and out; and by describing the rules and regulations relating to behavior in the library. Demonstrations of the use of the card catalog and the *Reader's Guide* and explanations of the arrangement of books under the Dewey Decimal System, which is the system used most often in elementary school libraries, are also worthwhile. Prominently displayed posters can help remind children of check-out procedures and library rules.

By familiarizing children with reasons for using the library and by explaining to them why they may need to use such aids as the card catalog, the Dewey Decimal System, and the *Reader's Guide,* teachers can prepare students for a visit to the library. While they are still in the classroom, the children can learn that cards in the card catalog are arranged alphabetically and that the card catalog contains subject, author, and title cards. Sample cards of each type, similar to those shown in Example 6.1, can be drawn on posters and placed on the bulletin board. In addition, fifth and sixth graders will benefit from a lesson that explains the use of cross-reference cards (also shown in Example 6.1).

The teacher may want to construct a model of a card-catalog drawer and have the children practice using it. Children may enjoy constructing the three main types of cards for several books that they have read and then alphabetizing these cards to make a miniature card catalog.

Two other suggestions for practice with library skills follow.

1. The teacher can send the children on a scavenger hunt that requires use of the library by dividing the class into teams and giving the teams statements to complete or questions to answer (Example: The author of *The Secret Garden* is ―――――).
2. The teacher can give students questions and ask them to show on a map of the library where they would go to find the answers. (Muller and Savage, 1982).

✓ Self-Check: Objective 3

What are the special features of books that can help pupils locate desired information? Describe each feature briefly.

Name several types of reference books and enumerate special skills needed to use each one.

Describe three types of cards used in a card catalog.

(See Self-Improvement Opportunities 2, 3, and 4.)

ORGANIZATIONAL SKILLS

When engaging in such activities as writing reports, elementary school students need to organize the ideas they encounter in their reading. Too often teachers at the elementary level give little attention to organizational skills, such as note-taking, outlining, and summarizing, and too many youngsters enter secondary school without having mastered them.

286

Teaching
Reading in
Today's
Elementary
Schools

▶ **EXAMPLE 6.1:** Subject, Author, Title, and Cross-Reference Cards

Subject card

```
                        HORSES

            F

            Hen     Henry. Marguerite

                        Black gold; illus. by Wesley Dennis

                    Rand McNally. © 1957
```

Author card

```
            F

            Hen     Henry. Marguerite

                        Black gold; illus. by Wesley Dennis

                    Rand McNally. © 1957
```

Title card

```
                        Black gold

            F

            Hen     Henry. Marguerite

                        Black gold; illus. by Wesley Dennis

                    Rand McNally. © 1957
```

Cross-reference card

```
                        Zeus


                        see
                    Greek Mythology
```

Note-taking

Teachers may present note-taking skills in a functional setting when children are preparing written reports on materials they have read. Children should be taught

1. to include key words and phrases in their notes.
2. to include enough of the context to make the notes understandable after a period of time has elapsed.
3. to include bibliographical references (sources) with each note.
4. to copy direct quotations exactly.
5. to indicate carefully which notes are direct quotations and which are reworded.

Key words—the words that carry the important information in a sentence—are generally nouns and verbs, but they may include important modifiers. Example 6.2 shows a sample paragraph and a possible set of notes based upon this paragraph.

After reading the paragraph shown in Example 6.2, the note-taker first thinks, "What kind of information is given here?" The answer, "a problem for restaurant owners or managers—good help," is the first note. Then the note-taker searches for key words to describe the kind of help needed. For example, cooks who "are able to prepare the food offered by the restaurant" can be described as *good* cooks—ten words condensed into two that carry the idea. In the case of the nouns *dishwasher* and *waitresses* and *waiters,* descriptive words related to them are added; condensation of phrases is not necessary, although the *ands* between the adjectives may be left out, because the key words needed are found directly in the selection. The last part of the

▶ **EXAMPLE 6.2:** Sample Paragraph and Notes

A restaurant is not as easy a business to run as it may appear to be to some people, since the problem of obtaining good help is ever-present. Cooks, dishwashers, and waitresses or waiters are necessary personnel. Cooks must be able to prepare the food offered by the restaurant. Dishwashers need to be dependable and thorough. Waitresses and waiters need to be able to carry out their duties politely and efficiently. Poorly prepared food, inadequately cleaned dishes, and rude help can be the downfall of a restaurant, so restaurant owners and managers must hire with care.

Sample note card

> Problem for restaurant owner or manager—good help: good cooks; dependable, thorough dishwashers; polite, efficient waitresses and waiters. Hire with care.

288

Teaching
Reading in
Today's
Elementary
Schools

paragraph can be summed up in the warning "Hire with care." It is easy to see that key-word notes carry the message of the passage in a very condensed or abbreviated form.

A teacher can go through an example such as this one with the children, telling them what key words to choose and why, and then provide another example, letting the children decide as a group which key words to write down and having them give reasons for their choices. Finally, each child can do a selection individually. After completing the individual note-taking, the children can compare their notes and discuss reasons for choices.

Students can take notes in outline form, in sentences, or in paragraphs. Example 6.3 shows several sample note cards.

▶ **EXAMPLE 6.3:** Sample Note Cards

1st reference from source

> Berger, Melvin. "Folk Music." *The World Book Encyclopedia,* 1979, VII, p. 281.
>
> Folk songs are passed along from person to person and gradually change in form through the years.

Source previously used

> Berger, p. 281.
>
> "Most American and European folk songs have a stanza form, which consists of a verse alternating with a chorus. The verses tell the story, and so each verse is different. The words of the chorus remain the same in most folk songs."

Incomplete sentences

> Berger, p. 281.
>
> Kinds of folk music: ballads, work songs, union songs, prison songs, spirituals, dance songs, game songs, nonsense songs, American Indian "power" songs, call-response songs.

Outlining

Teachers can lead children to understand that outlining is writing down information from reading material in a way that shows the relationships between the main ideas and the supporting details, although, of course, children must already know how to recognize main ideas and details. Two types of outlines that are important for children to understand are the sentence outline, in which each point is a complete sentence, and the topic outline, which is composed of key words and phrases. Since choosing key words and phrases is in itself a difficult task for many youngsters, it is wise to present sentence outlines first.

The first step in forming an outline is to extract the main ideas from the material and to list these ideas beside Roman numerals in the order they occur. Supporting details are listed beside capital letters below the main idea they support and are slightly indented to indicate their subordination. Details that are subordinate to the main details designated by capital letters are indented still further and preceded by Arabic numerals. The next level of subordination is indicated by lowercase letters, though elementary pupils will rarely need to make an outline that goes beyond the level of Arabic numerals.

A blank outline form like the one shown in Example 6.4 may help students to understand how to write an outline in proper form.

▶ **EXAMPLE 6.4:** Sample Outline

Title
I. Main idea
   A. Detail supporting I
   B. Detail supporting I
      1. Detail supporting B
      2. Detail supporting B
         a. Detail supporting 2
         b. Detail supporting 2
      3. Detail supporting B
   C. Detail supporting I
II. Main idea
   A. Detail supporting II
   B. Detail supporting II
   C. Detail supporting II ◀

The teacher can supply pupils with partially completed outlines of chapters in their subject matter textbooks and ask them to fill in the missing parts, gradually leaving out more and more details until the pupils are doing the complete outline alone. In order to develop readiness for outlining as described above, use Model Activity: Readiness for Outlining.

290

Teaching
Reading in
Today's
Elementary
Schools

● *MODEL ACTIVITY: Readiness for Outlining*

1. Provide the children with a set of items to be categorized.
2. Ask them to place the items in categories. More than one arrangement may be possible; let them try several.
3. Provide the children with a blank outline form of this type:

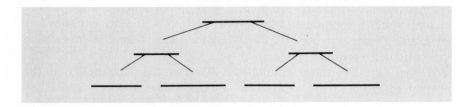

4. Have the children fill in the outline.
   Example:
   a. Provide plastic animals: horse, cow, chicken, pig, elephant, lion, sea gull, rooster, tiger.
   b. Give them time to categorize.
   c. Provide this outline.

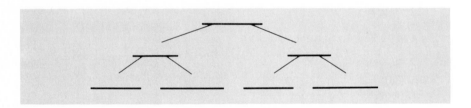

   d. Possible solution:

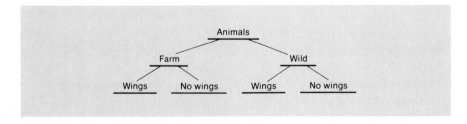

This activity can be used as a first step in teaching the concept of outlining to first and second graders. ●

The next step might be to have the students make free-form outlines, called arrays, for stories (Hansell, 1978). To make arrays, children use words, lines, and arrows to arrange key words and phrases from the story in a way that shows their relationships. Simple, very familiar stories allow children to concentrate on arranging the terms logically rather than on locating the details. Example 6.5 shows an array based upon the familiar story ''The Three Little Pigs.''

▶ **EXAMPLE 6.5:** Story Array

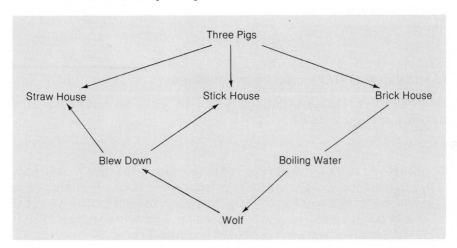

At first teachers will need to provide the key words and phrases. The children can then cooperatively develop arrays in small groups with help from teachers' probing questions about connecting lines, directions of arrows, and positions of phrases. The children may also ask the teacher questions about their decisions. As they develop proficiency with the task, the teacher can allow them to choose key words and phrases themselves, at first with his or her assistance and then independently. After mastering this step, the children can move on to forming arrays without assistance.

Summarizing

In a summary, a pupil is expected to restate what the author has said in a more concise form. Main ideas of a selection should be preserved, but illustrative material and statements that merely elaborate upon the main idea should not be included.

One possible activity for building experience with summarizing is to give children a long passage to read and three or four summaries of the passage. Let them choose the best summary and have them tell why they did not choose each of the other summaries. In addition, the following exercises may be helpful in teaching pupils to make summaries.

292

Teaching
Reading in
Today's
Elementary
Schools

● *MODEL ACTIVITY: Writing Headlines*

Give the children copies of news stories without headlines, like the one below, and let them provide headlines that contain the main ideas of the stories.

> Coopersville's pollution index has increased to a highly undesirable level this year. Chemists reveal that on a scale of 100, Coopersville's pollution is 95, compared to 75 for the average U.S. urban area. This report merely verifies what most residents of Coopersville have known for a long time—Coopersville exists under a cloud of smog. ●

● *MODEL ACTIVITY: Single-Sentence Summaries*

Have the children read a short passage, like the one below, and try to summarize its content in a single sentence.

> Sometimes your hair makes a noise when you comb it. The noise is really made by static electricity. Static electricity collects in one place. Then it jumps to another place. Rub your feet on a rug. Now touch something. What happens? Static electricity collects on your body, but it can jump from your finger to other places. Sometimes you can see a spark and hear a noise. ●

✔ **Self-Check: Objective 4**

Three types of organizational skills have been discussed in this section. Name and explain the function of each.

READING AIDS

Textbooks contain numerous aids to readers that children often disregard because they have had no training in how to use these aids. We have already discussed glossaries, footnotes, bibliographies, and appendices in this chapter, but we also need to consider other aids such as maps, graphs, tables, and illustrations.

Edward Fry (1981) believes that teachers should give more attention to the development of graphical literacy—the ability to read maps, graphs, pictures, and diagrams. As Harry Singer and Dan Donlan (1980) suggest, teachers can use reading comprehension questions (such as those discussed in Chapter 4) or a directed reading activity to teach how to understand these aids. Actually making graphic aids is also a good technique to help the students develop their communication abilities.

Maps

Many maps appear in social studies textbooks, and they are also sometimes found in science, mathematics, and literature books. As early as the first grade, children can begin developing skills in map reading, which they will use increasingly as they progress through school and maps appear with greater frequency in reading materials. Without comprehending the maps, children will find it more difficult to understand the concepts presented in narrative material.

A first step in map reading is to examine the title (for example, "Annual Rainfall in the United States") to determine what area is being represented and what type of information is being given about the area. The teacher should emphasize the importance of determining the information conveyed in the title before moving on to a more detailed study of the map. The next step is to teach the children how to determine directions. By helping students to locate direction indicators on maps and to use these indicators to identify the four cardinal directions, the teacher makes children aware that north is not always at the top nor south at the bottom of a map, although many maps are constructed in this manner.

Interpretation of the legend of the map is the next reading task. The legend contains an explanation of each of the symbols used on a map, and unless a reader can interpret it, he or she will be unable to understand the information conveyed by the map.

Learning to apply a map's scale is fairly difficult. Because it would be highly impractical to draw a map to the actual size of the area represented (for instance, the United States), maps show areas greatly reduced in size. The scale shows the relationship of a given distance on the map to the same distance on the earth.

Upper-elementary school pupils can be helped to understand about latitude and longitude, the Tropic of Cancer and the Tropic of Capricorn, the north and south poles, and the equator. Students should also become acquainted with map terms such as *hemisphere, peninsula, continent, isthmus, gulf, bay,* and many others.

Each time children look at a map of an area, encourage them to relate it to a map of a larger area—for example, to relate a map of Tennessee to a map of the United States. This points out the position of Tennessee within the entire United States.

Some suggestions for teaching map-reading skills are given below.

ACTIVITIES

1. In teaching children about directions on maps, give them pictures of direction indicators that are tilted in various ways, with north indicated on each one. Let the students fill in *S, E,* and *W* (for south, east, and west) on each indicator.

294

**Teaching
Reading in
Today's
Elementary
Schools**

Successful use of reading aids such as maps and graphs can greatly enhance students' understanding of content area textbooks. (© Bohdan Hrynewych/Southern Light)

2. To teach children to apply a map's scale, help them to construct a map of their classroom to a specified scale.
3. Have children practice using the map's legend by asking them questions such as the following:
   Where is there a railroad on this map?
   Where is the state capital located?
   Where do you see a symbol for a college?
   Are there any national monuments in this area? If so, where are they?
4. Let the children show that they understand terms such as *gulf* and *peninsula* by locating them on a map.
5. Give the children maps such as the one presented in Example 6.6 and have them answer questions about them.

▶ **EXAMPLE 6.6:** Sample Map and Questions

Questions
1. What is this map about?
   a. American Indian Tribes of the U.S.
   b. Number of American Indians in U.S. counties in 1970
   c. Number of American Indians in U.S. counties today

2. The example shows a main map and two inset maps. What is true about these three maps?
   a. They all are drawn to the same scale.
   b. Two of them are drawn to the same scale.
   c. They all are drawn to different scales.
3. What indicates the densest population?
   a. solid white
   b. gray and white stripes
   c. solid dark gray
4. What is the Indian population in most of Tennessee?
   a. under 100
   b. 100–2,499
   c. 2,500–9,999
5. The Indian population in Nevada varies from what to what?
   a. 100–2,499
   b. 2,500–10,000
   c. Under 100–10,000 and over
6. In what portion of the U.S. is there the largest concentration of Indians?
   a. Southwest
   b. Southeast
   c. Northeast

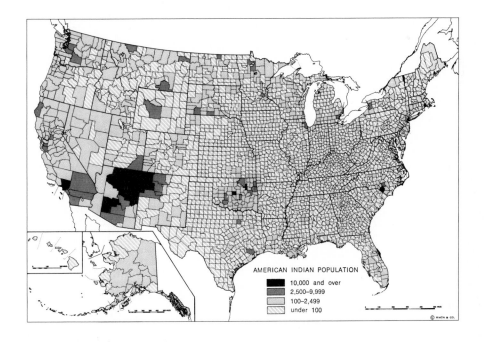

AMERICAN INDIAN POPULATION

- 10,000 and over
- 2,500–9,999
- 100–2,499
- under 100

© RMⁿ & CO.

Graphs

Graphs are diagrams that often appear in social studies, science, and mathematics books to clarify written explanations. There are four basic types of graphs. These are described below and illustrated in Example 6.7.

1. *Picture graphs* express quantities through pictures.
2. *Circle* or *pie graphs* show relationships of individual parts to the whole.
3. *Bar graphs* use vertical or horizontal bars to compare quantities. (Vertical bar graphs are easier to read than horizontal ones.)
4. *Line graphs* show changes in amounts.

Students can learn to discover from the graph's title what comparison is being made or information is being given (for example, time spent in various activities during the day or populations of various counties in a state), to

▶ **EXAMPLE 6.7:** Sample Picture, Pie, Bar, and Line Graphs

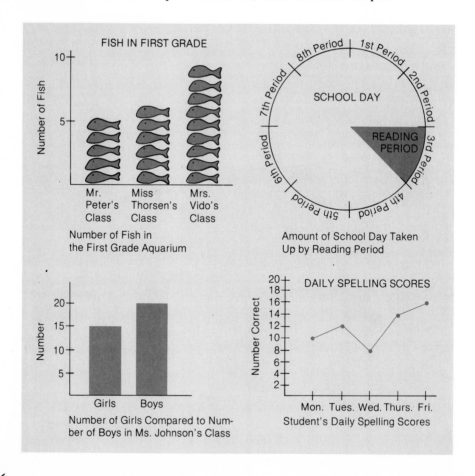

Number of Fish in the First Grade Aquarium

Amount of School Day Taken Up by Reading Period

Number of Girls Compared to Number of Boys in Ms. Johnson's Class

Student's Daily Spelling Scores

interpret the legend of a picture graph, and to derive needed information accurately from a graph.

One of the best ways to help children learn to read graphs is to have them construct meaningful graphs such as the ones below.

1. A picture graph showing the number of festival tickets sold by each class. One picture of a ticket could equal five tickets.
2. A circle graph showing the percentage of each day that a child spends in sleeping, eating, studying, and playing.
3. A bar graph showing the number of books read by the class members each week for six weeks.
4. A line graph showing the weekly arithmetic or spelling test scores of one child over a six-week period.

A teacher should also construct graphs like that shown in Example 6.8 and ask the children to answer the questions about them.

▶ **EXAMPLE 6.8** Sample Graph and Questions

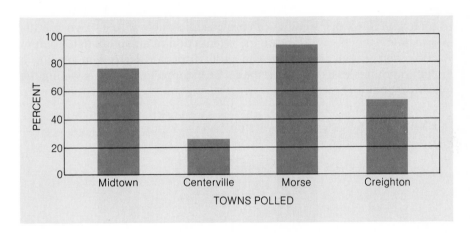

Questions
1. What percent of the voters from Midtown were for John Doe?
   a. 30
   b. 50
   c. 60
   d. 80
2. In which of the four towns shown was John Doe the least popular?
   a. Midtown
   b. Centerville
   c. Morse
   d. Creighton

298

Teaching
Reading in
Today's
Elementary
Schools

3. In which of the four towns shown did John Doe have the most support?
   a. Midtown
   b. Centerville
   c. Morse
   d. Creighton
4. In which town were 95 percent of the voters for John Doe?
   a. Midtown
   b. Centerville
   c. Morse
   d. Creighton ◀

Tables

Tables may appear in reading materials of all subject matters, and may present a problem because children have trouble extracting the particular facts needed from a large mass of available information. The great amount of information provided in the small amount of space on tables can confuse children unless the teacher provides a procedure for reading tables.

Just as the titles of maps and graphs contain information about their content, so do the titles of tables. In addition, since tables are arranged in columns and rows, the headings can provide information. To discover specific information, students must locate the intersection of an appropriate column with an appropriate row. They can profit from an exercise in reading a multiplication table, like the one shown in Example 6.9, and answering the following questions.

▶ **EXAMPLE 6.9:** Sample Table and Questions

	1	2	3	4	5	6	7	8	9
1	1	2	3	4	5	6	7	8	9
2	2	4	6	8	10	12	14	16	18
3	3	6	9	12	15	18	21	24	27
4	4	8	12	16	20	24	28	32	36
5	5	10	15	20	25	30	35	40	45
6	6	12	18	24	30	36	42	48	54
7	7	14	21	28	35	42	49	56	63
8	8	16	24	32	40	48	56	64	72
9	9	18	27	36	45	54	63	72	81

Questions
1. What is the product of 5 · 6?
2. What is the product of 9 · 3?
3. Is the product of 5 · 4 the same as the product of 4 · 5?
4. Which number is greater: the product of 3 · 8 or the product of 4 · 7?
5. When a number is multiplied by 1, what will the product always be?
6. Why is 24 where the 4 row and the 6 column meet?
7. How do the numbers in the 2 row compare with the numbers in the 4 row? ◀

Illustrations

Various types of illustrations are found in textbooks, ranging from photographs to schematic diagrams. All too often, children see illustrations merely as space fillers, reducing the amount of reading they will have to do on a page. As a result, they tend to pay little attention to illustrations even though illustrations are a very good source of information. For example, a picture of a jungle may add considerably to a child's understanding of that term, or a picture of an Arabian nomad may illuminate the term *Bedouin* in a history class. Diagrams of bones within the body can show a child things that he or she cannot readily observe first-hand.

✔ Self-Check: Objective 5

Name the four reading aids discussed in this section and briefly discuss the type of information each one offers.
(See Self-Improvement Opportunities 5, 6, and 7.)

Test Yourself

True or False

_____ 1. SQ3R stands for Stimulate, Question, Read, Reason, React.

_____ 2. SQ3R is a study method useful in reading social studies and science materials.

_____ 3. SQRQCQ is a study method designed for use with mathematical textbooks.

_____ 4. Students remember material better if they are given opportunities to discuss it.

_____ 5. Study guides are of little help to retention.

_____ 6. Writing information often helps children to fix it in their memories.

_____ 7. Massed practice is preferred over spaced practice for encouraging long-term retention.

_____ 8. Students should read all reading materials at the same speed.

_____ 9. Rereading is often needed for materials that contain a high density of facts.

_____ 10. Glossaries of technical terms are offered as reading aids in many content area textbooks.

_____ 11. Index practice is most effective when the children use their own textbooks rather than a worksheet index that has no obvious function.

_____ 12. Children need to be able to use subject, author, and title cards found in the card catalog.

_____ 13. Elementary school pupils have no need to learn how to take notes, since they are not asked to use this skill until secondary school.

_____ 14. Subordination in outlines is indicated by lettering, numbering, and indentation.

300

Teaching
Reading in
Today's
Elementary
Schools

_____ 15. The legend of a map tells the history of the area represented.

_____ 16. North is always located at the top of a map.

_____ 17. A good way to help children develop an understanding of graphs is to help them construct their own meaningful graphs.

_____ 18. Children may use newspapers, magazines, catalogues, and brochures as reference sources.

_____ 19. Teachers do not need to teach journalistic terms to elementary-level youngsters; this is a higher-level activity.

_____ 20. The ability to read charts is needed when using catalogues.

_____ 21. Key words are the words that carry the important information in a sentence.

_____ 22. Being able to recognize main ideas is a prerequisite skill for outlining.

_____ 23. Guide words indicate the first two words on a dictionary page.

_____ 24. ReFlex Action is an approach for developing flexible readers.

Vocabulary

Check your knowledge of these terms. Go back and reread parts of the chapter if necessary.

arrays	guide words	reading/study skills
bar graphs	legend	ReFlex Action
circle or pie graphs	line graphs	scale
	picture graphs	SQRQCQ
	reading rate	SQ3R

Self-Improvement Opportunities

1. Using materials of widely varying types, develop a procedure to help elementary students learn to be flexible in their rates of reading.
2. Take a content area textbook at the elementary level and plan procedures to familiarize children with the parts of the book and the reading aids the book offers.
3. Collect materials that youngsters can use as supplementary reference sources (newspapers, magazines, catalogues, brochures, etc.), and develop several short lessons to help the children read these materials more effectively.
4. Visit an elementary school library and listen to the librarian explaining the reference materials and library procedures to students. Evaluate the presentation and decide how you might change it if you were responsible for it.

5. After collecting a variety of types of maps, decide which features of each type will need most explanation for youngsters.
6. Make a variety of types of graphs into a display that you could use in a unit on reading graphs.
7. Collect pictures and diagrams that present information. Ask several children to study these pictures and extract as much information from them as possible. Then analyze the results.

Bibliography

Fay, Leo. "Reading Study Skills: Math and Science" in *Reading and Inquiry,* J. Allen Figurel, ed. Newark, Del.: International Reading Association, 1965, pp. 93–94.

Fry, Edward. "Graphical Literacy." *Journal of Reading* 24 (February 1981): 383–90.

Hansell, Stevenson F. "Stepping Up to Outlining." *Journal of Reading* 22 (December 1978): 248–52.

Hoffman, James V. "Developing Flexibility Through ReFlex Action." *The Reading Teacher* 33 (December 1979): 323–29.

MacCormick, Kristina, and Janet E. Pursel. "A Comparison of the Readability of the *Academic American Encyclopedia, The Encyclopaedia Britannica,* and *World Book.*" *Journal of Reading* 25 (January 1982): 322–25.

Muller, Dorothy H., and Liz Savage. "Mapping the Library." *The Reading Teacher* 35 (April 1982): 840–41.

Robinson, Francis P. *Effective Study.* Rev. ed. New York: Harper & Row, 1961, Chapter 2.

Singer, Harry, and Dan Donlan. *Reading and Learning from Text.* Boston: Little, Brown and Company, 1980, Chapter 12.

Spache, George D., and Evelyn B. Spache. *Reading in the Elementary School.* 4th ed. Boston: Allyn & Bacon, 1977, Chapters 11 and 12.

Suggested Readings

Burron, Arnold, and Amos L. Claybaugh. *Using Reading to Teach Subject Matter: Fundamentals for Content Teachers.* Columbus, Ohio: Charles E. Merrill, 1974.

Dallman, Martha, et al. *The Teaching of Reading.* 6th ed. New York: Holt, Rinehart and Winston, 1982, Chapters 7A and 7B.

Dechant, Emerald. *Improving the Teaching of Reading.* 2nd ed. Englewood Cliffs, N.J.: Prentice-Hall, 1970, Chapter 13.

Durkin, Dolores. *Teaching Them to Read.* 3rd ed. Boston: Allyn & Bacon, 1978, Chapters 14 and 15.

302

Teaching
Reading in
Today's
Elementary
Schools

Forgan, Harry W., and Charles T. Mangrum. *Teaching Content Area Reading Skills: A Modular Preservice and Inservice Program.* Columbus, Ohio: Charles E. Merrill, 1976, Chapter 7.

Heilman, Arthur W., et al. *Principles and Practices of Teaching Reading.* 5th ed. Columbus, Ohio: Charles E. Merrill, 1981, Chapter 9.

Karlin, Robert. *Teaching Elementary Reading: Principles and Strategies.* 3rd ed. New York: Harcourt Brace Jovanovich, 1980, Chapter 8.

Lapp, Dianne, and James Flood. *Teaching Reading to Every Child.* New York: Macmillan, 1978, Chapter 10.

Olson, Joanne P., and Martha H. Dillner. *Learning to Teach Reading in the Elementary School: Utilizing a Competency Based Instructional System.* 2nd ed. New York: Macmillan, 1982, Chapters 4 and 15.

Ransom, Grayce A. *Preparing to Teach Reading.* Boston: Little, Brown, 1978, Chapter 12.

Smith, Richard J., and Dale D. Johnson. *Teaching Children to Read.* 2nd ed. Reading, Mass.: Addison-Wesley, 1980, Chapter 15.

Tinker, Miles A., and Constance M. McCullough. *Teaching Elementary Reading.* 4th ed. Englewood Cliffs, N.J.: Prentice-Hall, 1975, Chapters 10 and 12.

Zintz, Miles V. *The Reading Process: The Teacher and the Learner.* 3rd ed. Dubuque, Iowa: William C. Brown, 1980, Chapter 11.

CHAPTER 7

Reading in the
Content Areas

Introduction

In order to read well in content area textbooks, children need good general reading skills, including word recognition, comprehension, and reading/study skills. If they cannot recognize the words they encounter, they will be unable to take in the information that the material is intended to convey. Without good literal, interpretive, critical, and creative reading comprehension skills, they will not understand the textbook's message. And if they lack good reading/study skills, they will be less likely to comprehend and retain the material. These skills may be initially acquired in reading class. However, because of the special reading problems presented by content area books, teachers should be aware that simply offering their students instruction in basal readers during reading class is not sufficient if the children are to read well in content area texts. Special help with content area reading, at the time when they are asked to do such reading, is important to children. They learn reading skills appropriate to specific subject areas and general techniques useful for expository or content reading best if the skills and techniques are taught when they are needed. In this chapter we discuss each content area (language arts, social studies, mathematics, and science and health) along with its reading difficulties and activities to promote readiness and good comprehension. In addition we present general content area reading strategies.

Setting Objectives

When you finish reading this chapter, you should be able to

1. Use a cloze test to determine the difficulty of written materials.
2. Name some readability formulas that you can use to determine the difficulty of written materials.
3. Describe several general techniques for helping students read content area materials.
4. Describe some procedures and materials helpful in presenting material in language arts, social studies, mathematics, science, and health books.

CONTENT TEXTS COMPARED TO BASAL READERS

Content textbooks, with the exception of many literature books, contrast dramatically with basal readers in their demands upon students. English, mathematics, social studies, science, and health books are in most cases more difficult to read and often are not as carefully graded for reading difficulty as are basal readers. In addition, teachers and students use many supplementary materials, some of which have been prepared not as textbooks but as trade books, in content areas. Whereas basal readers generally have carefully controlled vocabularies and planned repetition of key words to encourage their acquisition, content area texts present many new concepts and vocabulary terms rapidly and give little attention to planned repetition. All of the content areas have specialized vocabularies that students must acquire; generally, little technical vocabulary is presented in basal readers.

Large portions of basal readers are written in a narrative style that describes the actions of people in particular situations. They do not present the density of ideas typical of content textbooks, which are generally written in an expository style, with facts presented in concentrated form. Students must give attention to every sentence in the content books, for nearly every one will carry important information that they must acquire before they can understand later passages. This is rarely true of basal readers, for each selection is generally a discrete entity.

Basal reader selections usually have entertaining plots which children can read for enjoyment. Content selections rarely offer this enticement; therefore, few content books tend to be chosen by students for recreational reading.

Content textbooks contain large numbers of graphic aids to be interpreted by the students, whereas basal readers contain a much smaller percentage of these aids. The illustrations found in basal readers above first-grade level are primarily for interest value, but those in content books are designed to help clarify concepts and should be studied carefully.

Whereas typographical headings that signal the organization of the selection are abundant in content area textbooks, few such headings are used in basal readers, and the ones that are used are not as informative as those in the content books. Children using content books can be helped to see that in many cases the typographical headings outline the material for them, indicating main ideas and supporting details.

READABILITY

The first step in helping children read content material is for the teacher to be aware of the difficulty of the textbook that he or she assigns. Teachers must adjust their expectations accordingly for each pupil's use of the book, so that no child is assigned work in a book that is so difficult it will immediately be frustrating. Such a book, written on what is called the child's "frustration level," prevents students from being able to learn the content. If a child is forced to try to read it, he or she may develop very negative attitudes toward the subject, the teacher, and even school in general. A student will probably learn best from printed material that is written on his or her "independent level," that is, the level at which an individual reads with ease and comprehension. He or she can also learn from textbooks written on the "instructional level," the level at which a child reads with understanding when given sufficient help by the teacher. (See Chapter 9 for further discussion of independent, instructional, and frustration levels.)

306

Teaching
Reading in
Today's
Elementary
Schools

One way to estimate the suitability of a textbook for your pupils is to use a cloze test, which is constructed and administered in the following manner.

Cloze Tests

1. Select a passage of approximately 250 consecutive words from the textbook. This should be a passage that the pupils have not read, or tried to read, before.
2. Type the passage, leaving the first sentence intact and deleting every fifth word thereafter. In the place of deleted words, substitute blanks of uniform length.
3. Give the pupils the passage and tell them to fill in the blanks, allowing them all the time they need.
4. Score the test by counting as correct only the exact words that were in the original text. Determine each pupil's percentage of correct answers. If a pupil had less than 40 percent correct, the material is probably at that individual's frustration level and is too difficult. Thus, you should offer alternative ways of learning the material. If he or she had from 40 percent to 50 percent correct, the material is probably at the instructional level for that student, and he or she will be able to learn from the text if you provide careful guidance in the reading by developing readiness, helping with new concepts and unfamiliar vocabulary, and providing reading purposes to aid comprehension. If the child had more than 50 percent correct, the material is probably at his or her independent level, and he or she should be able to benefit from the material when reading it independently (Zintz, 1977).

If a teacher is using the percentages given above, he or she can count *only* exact words as correct, since the percentages were derived using only exact words. Synonyms must be counted as incorrect, along with obviously wrong answers and unfilled blanks.

Because all the material in a given textbook is unlikely to be written on the same level, teachers should choose several samples for a cloze test from several places in the book in order to make a decision about the suitability of the book for a particular child.

A cloze passage such as the one shown in this section, which contains 263 words, may be used to determine the difficulty of a science textbook. No words have been deleted from the first sentence in order to give the pupil an opportunity to develop an appropriate mental set for the material that follows. A score of less than 20 correct responses indicates that the material is too difficult; a score of 20 to 25 indicates that the child can manage the material if given assistance by the teacher; and a score of more than 25 indicates that the child can read the material independently.

Cloze tests are preferred to informal reading inventories, or IRIs, (see Chapter 9 for a discussion of IRIs) for matching textbooks to pupils by some authorities because they put the child in direct contact with the author's language without having the teacher in between (through the written questions). Frequently a child can understand the text but not the teacher's questions related to it, which can result in underestimation of the child's comprehension of the material. On the other hand, some children react with frustration to the cloze materials, and these children would fare better if tested with an IRI.

Children should have experience with cloze-type situations before teachers use this procedure to help match pupils with the appropriate levels of textbooks. If they have not had such experiences, they may not perform as well as they otherwise would.

● **WORKSHEET:** *Cloze Passage*

Directions: Read the following passage and fill in each blank with a word that makes sense in the sentence.

The electricity of an electron is called a *negative charge*. The amount of electrical ___(1)___ of one electron is ___(2)___. But when millions of ___(3)___ move together, their energy ___(4)___ great. Sometimes they jump ___(5)___ the air from one ___(6)___ to another. This heats ___(7)___ air. You see the ___(8)___ air as a spark. ___(9)___ may also hear a ___(10)___. Did you ever get ___(11)___ electric shock? If you ___(12)___, you felt electrons moving. ___(13)___ of your body was ___(14)___ path on which negative ___(15)___ of electricity traveled.

Static Electricity
Electrons ___(16)___ easy to take away ___(17)___ some atoms. Electrons can ___(18)___ rubbed away from wool ___(19)___ a balloon. They collect ___(20)___ the balloon. This gives ___(21)___ balloon a negative charge ___(22)___ electricity. Atoms of the ___(23)___ are missing some electrons. ___(24)___ have less negative electricity ___(25)___ they had. A material ___(26)___ is missing electrons has ___(27)___ positive charge. A material ___(28)___ has a positive charge ___(29)___ electricity can hold more ___(30)___.

The kind of electricity ___(31)___ by rubbing electrons from ___(32)___ material to another is ___(33)___ *static* (STAT ik) *electricity*. *Static* means "___(34)___ stay in one place." ___(35)___ materials may keep charges ___(36)___ static electricity for a ___(37)___ time.

When charges of ___(38)___ electricity jump through the ___(39)___, you see lightning. Sometimes ___(40)___ happens when electrons jump ___(41)___ one cloud to another. ___(42)___ the electrons may jump ___(43)___ the earth. Electrons always ___(44)___ to a place that ___(45)___ fewer electrons. The earth ___(46)___ things that touch it ___(47)___ always hold more electrons. ___(48)___ the electrons jump, they ___(49)___ no longer static electricity. ___(50)___ are *current* (KUHR-unt) *electricity*.

Answers: (1) energy (2) small (3) electrons (4) is (5) through (6) place (7) the (8) hot (9) You (10) sound (11) an (12) did (13) Part (14) a (15) charges (16) are (17) from (18) be (19) with (20) on (21) the (22) of (23) wool (24) They (25) than (26) that (27) a (28) that (29) of

308

Teaching
Reading in
Today's
Elementary
Schools

(30) electrons   (31) made   (32) one   (33) called   (34) to   (35) Some   (36) of
(37) long   (38) static   (39) air   (40) it   (41) from   (42) Or   (43) to
(44) jump   (45) has   (46) and   (47) can   (48) Once   (49) are   (50) They

After determining each student's ability to benefit from the class textbook, the teacher can form instructional groups. Group 1 (an independent-level group) will be able to read textbook assignments and prepare for class discussion independently, and its students will sometimes be able to set their own purpose questions to direct their reading. Group 2 (an instructional-level group) will need to have the teacher introduce material carefully, build concepts and vocabulary gradually, and assign purpose questions. Group 3 (a frustration-level group) will need to be introduced to the subject and, in order to understand the concepts and information involved, be given some simpler materials such as library books with a lower readability level than that of the text or selections written by the teacher on an appropriately low level.

All groups can participate together in discussing the material, and the teacher can record significant contributions on the board in the same way that he or she might do when recording a language experience story. (See Chapter 5 for a detailed discussion of the language experience approach.) When the teacher asks class members to read the contributions from the board at the end of the discussion period, even poor readers may be able to read fairly difficult contributions because they have heard the sentences being dictated and have seen them being written down. Before the next class, the teacher can duplicate the class summary for each student to use in reviewing for tests and he or she can help the youngsters in Group 3 to reread the notes, emphasizing the new words and concepts, during study periods.

Readability Formulas

Standardized tests are a good way to obtain information on the reading achievement levels of pupils. Teachers should remember, however, that a standardized test score is not necessarily a reliable measure of a child's reading ability in a content textbook, since these tests are not generally built on passages that are comparable in style and writing patterns. Informal tests based on actual content materials may be better indications of the material's difficulty. Having determined the pupils' reading levels, the teachers can determine whether a textbook is appropriate by testing it with a standard measure of readability. Among widely used readability formulas, the Spache Readability Formula is designed for primary-grade books (Spache, 1966); the Dale-Chall Readability Formula is designed for materials from fourth-grade through college level (Dale and Chall, 1948); and the Gunning Fog Index can be used on material at all levels (Gunning, 1968).

A quick way to estimate readability is shown in Example 7.1.

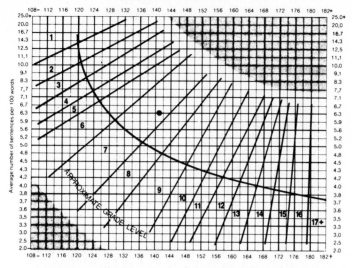

Expanded Directions for Working Readability Graph

1. Randomly select three (3) sample passages and count out exactly 100 words each, beginning with the beginning of a sentence. Do count proper nouns, initializations, and numerals.
2. Count the number of sentences in the hundred words, estimating length of the fraction of the last sentence to the nearest one-tenth.
3. Count the total number of syllables in the 100-word passage. If you don't have a hand counter available, an easy way is to simply put a mark above every syllable over one in each word, then when you get to the end of the passage, count the number of marks and add 100. Small calculators can also be used as counters by pushing numeral 1, then push the + sign for each word or syllable when counting.
4. Enter graph with *average* sentence length and *average* number of syllables; plot dot where the two lines intersect. Area where dot is plotted will give you the approximate grade level.
5. If a great deal of variability is found in syllable count or sentence count, putting more samples into the average is desirable.
6. A word is defined as a group of symbols with a space on either side; thus, *Joe, IRA, 1945,* and *&* are each one word.
7. A syllable is defined as a phonetic syllable. Generally, there are as many syllables as vowel sounds. For example, *stopped* is one syllable and *wanted* is two syllables. When counting syllables for numerals and initializations, count one syllable for each symbol. For example, *1945* is four syllables, *IRA* is three syllables, and *&* is one syllable.

Note: This "extended graph" does not outmode or render the earlier (1968) version inoperative or inaccurate; it is an extension. (REPRODUCTION PERMITTED—NO COPYRIGHT)

Source: Edward Fry, "Fry's Readability Graph: Clarifications, Validity, and Extension to Level 17" *Journal of Reading* 21 (December 1977): 249. Directions: Randomly select three 100-word passages from a book. Plot the average number of syllables and sentences per 100 words on the graph. Grade level scores that fall in the shaded area are invalid. Example: An average of 141 syllables and 6.3 sentences per 100 words indicates 7th grade readability.

310

Teaching
Reading in
Today's
Elementary
Schools

Microcomputer programs designed to test readability can ease the burden of making calculations by hand. Such programs are available for several formulas, including Dale-Chall, Flesch, and Gunning (Judd, 1981). Application of readability formulas is "the type of repetitive, high precision task for which computers were originally designed" (Keller, 1982).

It is worth noting that research has shown that many content area textbooks are written at much higher readability levels than are basal readers for the corresponding grades. Researchers have also discovered that subject-matter textbooks often vary in difficulty from chapter to chapter. If a teacher is aware of various levels of difficulty within a text, he or she can adjust teaching methods to help the students gain the most from each portion of the book, perhaps by teaching easier chapters earlier in the year and more difficult chapters later on. Of course, this technique is not advisable for teaching material in which the concepts in an early, difficult chapter are necessary for understanding a later, easier chapter.

✔ Self-Check: Objectives 1 and 2

Describe how to use a cloze test to estimate the suitability of a textbook for a child or group of children.
Name two widely used readability formulas.
(See Self-Improvement Opportunity 1.)

GENERAL TECHNIQUES FOR CONTENT AREA READING

Teachers can use a number of techniques to help children read in content areas more effectively. Several are discussed below.

Directed Reading-Thinking Activity (DRTA)

The DRTA is a general plan for directing children's reading of either basal reader stories or content area selections and for encouraging children to think as they read and to make predictions and check their accuracy. Russell Stauffer offers some background for understanding the DRTA.

Inquiry is native to the mind. Children are by nature curious and inquiring, and they will be so in school if they are permitted to inquire. It is possible to direct the reading-thinking process in such a way that children will be encouraged to think when reading—to speculate, to search, to evaluate, and to use. (1968, p. 348)

Stauffer (1969) further points out that teachers can motivate effort and concentration by a student by involving the student intellectually and encouraging him or her to formulate questions and hypotheses, to process information, and to evaluate tentative solutions. The DRTA is directed toward accomplishing these goals. It has two components—a process and a product.

Content area textbooks are very demanding upon students; they are generally written in an expository style, with a high density of facts and with frequent use of specialized and technical terms. (© Peter Vandermark/Stock, Boston)

The process consists of

1. identifying purposes,
2. guiding the reader's adjustment of rate to fit his or her purposes and material,
3. observing the reading in order to diagnose difficulties and offer help, and
4. developing comprehension.

The product component consists of skill-building activities.

Perhaps because the student is interacting with the material during reading, the DRTA is extremely useful for improving children's comprehension of selections.

The lesson plan in Example 7.2 illustrates the steps of a directed reading-thinking activity. It is designed for use with a selection entitled "Meeting the Need for Food" from Frederick M. King's *Social Studies and Our Country* (The Laidlaw Social Science Program; River Forest, Ill.: Laidlaw, 1972, pp. 56–60). It could also include activities for vocabulary or concept development. The teacher's manual (p. T34) suggests developing background for and understanding of the words *pemmican* and *caribou*. At the end of the selection under the heading "Think for Yourself," there is a thought-provoking question designed to help develop concepts about the effects of rainfall, soil, and temperature on the Indians' food supplies.

312

Teaching
Reading in
Today's
Elementary
Schools

▶ **EXAMPLE 7.2:** Social Studies Lesson Plan using the DRTA

Step 1: Making predictions from title clues.
Write the title of the chapter section to be studied on the chalkboard and have a child read it. Ask the children, "What do you think this part of the chapter will cover?" or "What do you think are the ways that the Indians met the need for food?" Give them time to consider the questions thoroughly and let each child have an opportunity to make predictions. All predictions should be accepted, regardless of how reasonable or unreasonable they may seem, but the teacher should not make any predictions during this discussion period.

Step 2: Making predictions from picture clues.
Have the students open their books to the beginning of the selection. Ask them to examine carefully the pictures shown in this section. Then, after they have examined the pictures, ask them to revise the predictions they made earlier.

Step 3: Reading the material.
Ask the children to read the selection to check the accuracy of their predictions. They may read this material in seven segments, corresponding to the seven subheadings, and check each segment to see if their predictions were accurate. On the other hand, since the entire selection is only five pages long, they may read it as a block.

Step 4: Assessing the accuracy of predictions, adjusting predictions.
When all the children have finished reading the material, lead a discussion by asking such questions as "Who was right about the ways the Indians met their food needs?" Ask the children who believe they were right to read orally to the class the parts of the selection that support their predictions. Children who were wrong can tell why they believe they were wrong. If the class has considered only the first segment, have the children adjust their predictions on the basis of what they have just read and the subheading of the second segment, "Hunting for caribou."

Step 5: Repeating the procedure until all parts of the lesson have been covered. ◀

Guided Reading Procedure

Manzo's guided reading procedure (GRP), designed to help readers improve organizational skills, comprehension, and recall, is appropriate for content area reading at any level. The steps in the procedure are as follows.

1. Set a purpose for reading a selection of about 500 words and tell the children to remember all they can. Tell them to close their books when they finish reading.
2. Have the students tell everything they remember from the material, and record this information on the board.

3. Ask students to look at the selection again to correct or add to the information that they have already offered.
4. Direct the children to organize the information in an outline (see Chapter 6), semantic web (see Chapter 4), or some other arrangement.
5. Ask synthesizing questions to help students integrate the new material with previously acquired information.
6. Give a test immediately to check on the children's short-term recall.
7. Give another form of the test later to check medium or long-term recall.

A study of the GRP by Paul Ankney and Pat McClurg (1981) showed that it was superior to more conventional methods (vocabulary presentation, purpose questions, and postreading discussion) for social studies but not for science, and that it seemed to have no differential effect on better and poorer readers, males and females, or higher achievers and lower achievers. The researchers concluded that the GRP offered an effective approach to reading in content areas and added variety to classes. Although it was time-consuming, it caused children to be eager to return to their books to verify information and search for additional facts.

The SAVOR Procedure

This procedure, developed by Ezra and Varda Stieglitz (1981), is based upon the semantic feature analysis technique, but its focus is reinforcement of essential content area vocabulary rather than merely increased awareness of likenesses and differences in words. It works well as a culminating activity for a lesson, since pupils must have some knowledge of the topic to use it.

To begin the procedure, the teacher introduces the topic and divides the class into groups of no more than five people each. The members of each group generate words related to the category involved, which one student lists in a column. Then the children identify features common to one or more of the examples. The student recorder writes these features across the top of the page. Group members then put pluses or minuses in the spaces where the category words and features intersect. If they disagree, the teacher should ask them to defend their choices, using any needed reference materials. The result of using SAVOR to discuss shapes might be as shown here:

	Straight lines	Curved lines	Four sides	Three sides	All sides must be equal in length
Triangle Rectangle Circle Square					

314

Teaching
Reading in
Today's
Elementary
Schools

After the matrix is finished, the children can discuss which features different shapes have in common and which are unique to one shape.

It is wise to introduce students to the SAVOR technique with a familiar topic not related to an area of study, such as "vehicles," so that the focus is on the technique. The teacher should write the list on the board as the children name category members, then list the features as the children name them, giving examples if they have trouble starting. One such completed matrix is illustrated below.

	Two-wheeled	Four-wheeled	motor-powered	pedal-powered
cars	−	+	+	−
bicycles	+	−	−	+
tricycles	−	−	−	+
motorcycles	+	−	+	−

When first using the procedure in content areas, the teacher might provide an incomplete matrix for the children to complete with pluses and minuses, under direct teacher supervision. Always discuss reasons for marks when there is disagreement. Then the pupils can work in small groups as the teacher circulates to assist and/or observe.

Oral Reading Strategy

Anthony Manzo (1980) has recommended using an oral reading strategy about once a week in a content class. The teacher reads aloud about two pages of the text while the children follow in their books. He or she stops at logical points and asks the children to summarize the information in their own words. This technique will reveal confusions, raise questions, and allow the teacher a chance to work on vocabulary and other points of concern.

Question-Only Strategy

With this strategy, the teacher first tells the students the topic for study and explains that they must learn all they can by asking questions about it. Then they will be given a test covering all the ideas the teacher believes are important, whether the questions have covered those ideas or not. The students then ask their questions, and the teacher answers them. Following the questions, a test is given. Later, the students discuss what questions they should have asked, but did not ask, during the questioning step. Finally they read their texts or use some other means of learning what they did not learn through their questions. A teacher may choose to give a follow-up test after the study (Manzo, 1980).

Directed Inquiry Activity (DIA)

Keith Thomas has developed this procedure based on the directed reading-thinking activity for study reading in content areas. Here the children preview a part of the reading assignment and predict responses to the questions who, what, when, where, how, and why, which are recorded on the chalkboard. After class discussion of the ideas takes place, students read to confirm or alter their predictions. The predictions provide purposes for reading and, along with discussion, provide the mental set needed for approaching reading (Manzo, 1980).

Study Guides

Study guides—duplicated sheets prepared by the teacher and distributed to the children—help guide reading in content fields and alleviate those difficulties that interfere with understanding. They can set purposes for reading as well as provide aids for interpretation of material through suggestions about how to apply reading skills, as shown in the example found in the social studies section of this chapter.

Pattern guides are study guides that stress the relationship among the organizational structure, the reading/thinking skills needed for comprehension, and the important concepts in the material. The first step in constructing such a guide is identifying the important concepts in the material. Then information about each concept must be located within the selection, and the author's organizational pattern must be identified. The teacher then integrates the identified concepts, the writing pattern, and the skills necessary for reading the material with understanding in a guide that offers as much direction as the particular students need—whether it be the section of text in which the information is located; the specific page number; or the page, paragraph, and line numbers.

A guide for a selection with a cause-and-effect writing pattern might be constructed in this manner.

1. Identify the reading/thinking process on the upper left portion of the guide and in the directions. Example:

   Cause/Effect
   As you read this material, look for the effects related to the causes listed below.

2. Offer page or page and paragraph numbers for each listed cause.
3. Consider offering some completed items to get the students started and model the correct responses (Olson and Longnion, 1982).

Teachers might want to turn the social studies activity on identifying contrasts and the science classification game found later in this chapter into pattern guides.

316

Teaching
Reading in
Today's
Elementary
Schools

Study guides should be carefully prepared and used with discrimination. Not all members of the class should be given the same study guide, since students should have questions geared to their level of development in reading skills. Remember that a study guide will not increase the likelihood that a student will understand a selection if the selection is too difficult for that student to read.

Several students may cooperate to find the answers to questions on a study guide, or they may work individually. In any case, be sure the class discusses the questions or items after reading the material.

Manipulative Materials

Teachers can use manipulative learning materials to teach both content objectives and the reading skills necessary to attain these objectives. After introducing and demonstrating these materials in whole class sessions, the teacher should place them in learning centers to be used independently by the students. The materials should have directions for easy reference, and there should be a way for the students to determine the accuracy of their answers or to receive reinforcement. If activities call for divergent thought, reinforcement is usually provided through a report or project. Among activities provided by the materials are matching technical vocabulary terms with illustrations of their meanings in a puzzle format, matching causes with effects, and following directions to produce an art product (Morrow, 1982).

Integrating Approaches

Because no single technique will make it possible for all students to deal with the many demands of content material, a teacher must know many approaches, must teach them directly, and must let the students know why they help. Children need to be able to pick out an appropriate approach for a particular assignment.

"The eight areas to be considered in planning a content lesson are objectives, vocabulary, background and motivation, survey and prediction, purposes for reading, guided reading, synthesis and reorganization, and application" (Gaskins, 1981, p. 324). The ultimate goal is to make students capable of studying effectively on their own.

To begin, the teacher should present to the class some content and process (reading/study skill) objectives for each lesson, then move on to vocabulary by presenting and teaching words through context clues or by relating the words to ones the children already know. Next comes a discussion designed to supply background information, motivate the students, and relate the material to things they already know. Then the teacher asks the students to survey the material and predict what it is going to tell. Purposes for reading are set, either through the predictions, or by other techniques. The teacher should guide the reading through use of a study guide; reading to verify hypotheses; reading to answer who, what, when, where, how, and why questions; or selective reading to discover important information. Then he or she should plan activities that guide students to synthesize and reorganize information—for example, use the guided reading procedure, construct main-idea statements, take notes, write a content-based language experience story on the material (first group, then individual), or make graphic representations of the content (graphs, charts, diagrams). Students need to be given an opportunity to apply the concepts they have read about in some way (Gaskins, 1981).

✔ Self-Check: Objective 3

Name seven general techniques for helping students read content area materials.
Describe two in detail.
(See Self-Improvement Opportunities 2 and 5.)

SPECIFIC CONTENT AREAS

Special reading difficulties are associated with each of the content areas. It is best to teach skills for handling these difficulties when students need them in order to read their assignments.

Language Arts

The content of the language arts block of the elementary school curriculum involves listening, speaking, reading, and writing instruction. It includes the subjects of reading, literature, and English. Since we have discussed basal readers that are used during reading class in other chapters in this textbook, they will not be considered here.

Literature

In literature classes children are asked to read and understand many literary forms, including short stories, novels, plays, poetry, biographies, and auto-biographies. (These forms are discussed in Chapter 8.) One characteristic of all these forms is the frequent occurrence of figurative or nonliteral language, which is sometimes a barrier to understanding. Children tend to interpret literally expressions that often have meanings different from the sums of the meanings of the individual words. For example, the expression "the teeth of the wind" does not mean that the wind actually has teeth, nor does "a

318

Teaching
Reading in
Today's
Elementary
Schools

blanket of fog" mean a conventional blanket. Context clues indicate the meanings of such phrases in the same ways that they cue word meanings.

Adults often assume that children have had exposure to an expression that is quite unfamiliar to them. Children need substantial help if they are to comprehend figurative language. Research has shown that even basal readers present many of these expressions. For instance, Hulda Groesbeck (1961) found many figurative expressions in third-grade basal readers, and she discovered that the frequency of such expressions increased as grade level increased. Some common kinds of figures of speech that cause trouble are

1. simile—a comparison using *like* or *as*
2. metaphor—a direct comparison without the words *like* or *as*
3. personification—giving the attributes of a person to an inanimate object or abstract idea
4. hyperbole—an extreme exaggeration
5. euphemism—substitution of a less offensive term for an unpleasant term or expression.

Teachers can use the following exercises to teach figurative language.

ACTIVITIES

1. Show students pictures of possible meanings for figurative expressions and ask them to accept or reject the accuracy of each picture. (For example, if you illustrate the sentence "She worked like a horse" with a woman pulling a plow, children should reject the picture's accuracy.)
2. Ask children to choose the best explanation of a figurative expression from a number of possible choices. Example:

   "The sun smiled down at the flowers" means:
   a. The sun was pleased with the flowers.
   b. The sun shone on the flowers.
   c. The sun smiled with its mouth.

3. Give each child a copy of a poem that is filled with figures of speech and have the class compete to see who can "dig up" all the figures of speech first. You may require students to label all figures of speech properly as to type or to explain them.
4. Have the children participate in an "idioms search," in which they look in all kinds of reading material and try to find as many examples of idioms as they can. Students must define each one in a way that corresponds with its usage.
5. Use a worksheet such as the one shown in Worksheet: Figures of Speech.

Directions: Look at this cartoon and caption and answer the questions that follow.

"Dennis the Menace" ® is © by Field Enterprises Inc.
Used with permission.

a. What does "been through the mill" really mean, as Dennis's mother used it?
b. What does Dennis *think* it means?
c. How is the woman likely to react to Dennis's question?
d. How does Dennis's mother probably feel about the question?
e. Can misunderstanding figurative language cause trouble at times? Why do you say so? ●

English

English textbooks cover the areas of listening, speaking, and writing and are generally comprised of a series of sections of instructional material followed by practice exercises. The technical vocabulary involved includes such terms as *determiner, noun, pronoun, manuscript, cursive,* and *parliamentary procedure.* The concepts presented in the informational sections are densely packed; each sentence is usually important for understanding, and examples are frequently given. Children need to be encouraged to study the examples because they help to clarify the information presented in the narrative portion of the textbook.

320

Teaching
Reading in
Today's
Elementary
Schools

Teachers are wise to plan oral activities in class to accompany the listening and speaking portions of the English textbook, since such practice allows immediate application of the concepts and facilitates retention of the material. Similarly, it is wise to ask pupils to apply the concepts encountered in the writing section as soon as possible in relevant situations to aid retention.

Social Studies

In social studies reading, youngsters encounter such technical terms as *democracy, communism, capitalism, tropics, hemisphere, decade,* and *century* as well as many words that have meanings different from their meanings in general conversation. When children first hear that a candidate is going to *run* for office, they may picture a foot race, an illusion that is furthered if they read that a candidate has decided to enter the *race* for governor. If the term *race* is applied to people in their texts, the children may become even more confused. Children who know that you *strike* a match or make a *strike* when bowling may not understand a labor union *strike.* Discussions about the *mouth* of a river could bring unusual pictures to the minds of youngsters.

Social studies materials also present children with maps, charts, and graphs to read. Ways of teaching the use of such reading aids have been suggested in Chapter 6. Social studies materials must be read critically. Students should be taught to check copyright dates to determine timeliness and to be alert for such problems as outdated geography materials that show incorrect boundaries or place names.

Fictionalized biographies and diaries used for social studies instruction are excellent for teaching children to evaluate the accuracy and authenticity of material, since authors have invented dialogue and thoughts for the characters to make the material seem more realistic. Teachers should lead children to see that these stories try to add life to facts but are not completely factual, perhaps by having them check in reference books for accuracy of dates, places, and names. Sometimes reading an author's foreword or postscript will offer clues to the fictional aspects of a story; for example, at times only the historical events mentioned are true. Students should also be aware that authors use first-person narrative accounts to make the action seem more personal, but that in reality the supposed speaker is not the one who did the writing. Also, any first-person account offers a limited perspective because the person speaking cannot know everything that all the characters in the story do or everything that is happening at one time. Alert students to look for the author's bias, and ask them to check to see how much the author depended on actual documents if a bibliography of sources is given (Storey, 1982).

Many other comprehension skills, such as the ability to recognize cause-and-effect relationships and to grasp chronological sequence, are necessary to understand social studies materials. (For more information on these comprehension skills, see Chapter 4.) These materials are generally written in a very precise and highly compact expository style in which many ideas are expressed in a few lines of print. Authors may discuss a hundred-year span in a single paragraph or on a single page or cover complex issues in a few paragraphs, even though whole books could be devoted to these issues. The sample content selection, "Problems Old and New," used for illustrating a study guide is an example of expository writing. (See Example 7.3.) Because children's reading should be purposeful, we recommend the use of student study guides for social studies material.

▶ **EXAMPLE 7.3:** Sample Selection and Study Guide

Problems Old and New (Page 192)

The West promised many wonderful things. But getting there to enjoy them was not an easy task. Wagon trains starting out on the Oregon or Santa Fe Trail faced long, difficult journeys. Sometimes supplies ran out, or no water and firewood could be found, or the wagons got stuck in prairie mud. All these were new problems for the people moving west.

But there were some familiar problems, too. They had to keep order on the wagon train, and see that rules were followed. They also had to make sure that important jobs were done, like fixing broken wagons, taking care of animals, cooking, caring for the sick, and hunting antelope and buffalo for meat. In other words, each group had to organize a small government for itself.

You have learned that different countries had different kinds of government. It was the same with the wagon trains. Some of them elected committees to make rules for the whole group. Some asked one man to be the leader. And other groups allowed anyone over sixteen to have a say in making rules.

(Page 193)

When the wagon trains finally reached the places where they were going, the problem of making a government came up again. The rules made for wagon trains would not work in the new settlements. The westerners usually kept some of the rules they had followed in the towns and villages in the East. But all the older rules could not be used in the wilderness. Some new rules were needed. But who would make the new rules? How would they be made? What kind of rules would they be? The national government did not make rules for the West until most of it had become states. There was a government for each of the new territories in the West. But the territories were so big that the territorial governments had trouble keeping in touch with every town, city, and settlement. So the new westerners had to make these important decisions about government all by themselves.

Source: William R. Fielder, ed. *Inquiring About American History: Studies in History and Political Science* (New York: Holt, Rinehart and Winston, 1972), pp. 192–93. Reprinted with permission of the publisher.

Study Guide

Overview Question: How did people govern themselves during and after journeys to the West?

322

Teaching
Reading in
Today's
Elementary
Schools

1. Read the first paragraph on page 192 to discover what new problems were faced by people moving west on wagon trains.

   What is a synonym for each of the following words: *task, journeys?*

2. Read the second paragraph to discover what familiar problems people moving west on wagon trains faced.

   What kinds of animals did they use for meat? Do these animals resemble animals commonly used for meat by today's Americans?

3. Read paragraph three to discover three different forms of wagon train governments.

   What is a committee? What are some advantages and some disadvantages of having decisions made by a committee?

   How is allowing sixteen-year-olds to vote similar to or different from the United States government today?

4. Study the picture at the top of the page [not reproduced here]. Describe the wagon in which the people traveled west.

5. Read the paragraph on page 193 to find out who made the important decisions about government after the people finally reached the places where they were going.

   What is a wilderness?

6. *Territory* is the root word from which *territories* and *territorial* are formed.

   What are the meanings of *territory, territories, and territorial?*

7. Why did territorial governments have trouble keeping in touch with the towns, cities, and settlements in the territories? ◄

Let us examine the way in which the study guide in Example 7.3 directs students' reading. First, the overview question offers an overall purpose for the reading, helping students read the material with the appropriate mental set. In Number 1 students are given a purpose for reading the first paragraph (in order to enhance comprehension and retention of important content). Following the purpose is a question focusing upon important vocabulary. Number 2 provides a purpose for reading the second paragraph and asks two questions, the first of which guides the children to information directly stated in the passage and the second of which encourages them to relate what they discover from reading the passage to their own lives. In addition to providing a purpose for reading the third paragraph, Number 3 asks three questions: the first focuses on important vocabulary; the second calls for critical thinking about a concept in the passage; and the third tries to relate the past time students are reading about to the present. In Number 4 the children are encouraged to study a picture to gain information to add to that gained from the printed word. In Number 5 they are given a purpose for reading the next paragraph and are asked about important vocabulary. Number 6 encourages students to apply their structural-analysis skills to determine the meanings of vocabulary terms, and Number 7 requires them to make an inference from the facts presented.

Social studies materials are organized in a variety of ways, including cause-and-effect relationships, chronological order, comparisons and/or contrasts, and topical order (for example, by regions, such as Asia and North America, or by concepts, such as transportation and communication). The content selection "Problems Old and New" is an example of the comparison/contrast arrangement. To help children deal with cause-and-effect and chronological order arrangements, use the ideas found in Chapter 4 for helping students determine such relationships and sequences. Drawing time lines is one good way to work with chronological order, and an idea for working with the comparison/contrast style is shown below.

● **MODEL ACTIVITY:** *Identifying Contrasts*

Ask the children to make a chart showing the contrasts (or comparisons) in a selection, using the following format. (The ideas are based on the selection "Problems Old and New.")

Familiar Problems	*New Problems*
Need for order	Supplies ran out
Fixing broken wagons	No water
Caring for animals	No firewood
Cooking	Wagons stuck in prairie mud
Caring for the sick	
Hunting animals for meat ●	

If the teacher points out the organizational pattern of the selection, children approach the reading with an appropriate mental set, which aids greatly in comprehension of the material.

Social studies materials frequently are written in a very impersonal style and may be concerned with unfamiliar people or events that are often remote in time or place. Also, students may already lack interest in the subject. For these reasons, teachers should use many interesting trade books to personalize the content and to expand on topics that are covered very briefly in the textbook. Among supplementary reading materials that are not too difficult are the following. (Approximate difficulty levels are given.)

The Childhood of Famous Americans Series. Indianapolis: Bobbs-Merrill. (Grade 4)

Follett Beginning Social Studies Series. Chicago: Follett. (Grades 1–6)

Frontiers of America Books: American History for Reluctant Readers, by Edith McCall et al. Chicago: Children's Press. (Grade 3)

324

Teaching
Reading in
Today's
Elementary
Schools

Indians of America Books. Chicago: Children's Press. (Grades 2–4)
The Piper Books. Boston: Houghton Mifflin. (Intermediate grades)
See and Read Beginning to Read Biographies. New York: G. P. Putnam. (Grade 2)

Using the Newspaper

The newspaper is a living textbook for social studies through which youngsters learn about tomorrow's history when it is happening. Different parts of the newspaper require different reading skills, as noted below.

1. news stories—identifying main ideas and supporting details (who, what, where, when, why, how), determining sequence, recognizing cause-and-effect relationships, making inferences, drawing conclusions
2. editorials—discriminating between fact and opinion, discovering the author's point of view, detecting author bias and propaganda techniques, making inferences, drawing conclusions
3. comics—interpreting figurative language and idiomatic expressions, recognizing sequence of events, making inferences, detecting cause-and-effect relationships, drawing conclusions, making predictions
4. advertisements—detecting propaganda, making inferences, drawing conclusions, distinguishing between fact and opinion
5. entertainment section—reading charts (TV schedule and the like), evaluating material presented
6. weather—reading maps

All of these skills have been discussed fully in either Chapter 4 or Chapter 6.

Student newspapers such as *Weekly Reader* (American Education Publications) and *Know Your World* (Columbus, Ohio: Xerox Education Publications) are often used in the elementary classroom. *Know Your World* is aimed at youngsters who are ten to sixteen years old but are reading on a second- to third-grade level, whereas *Weekly Reader* has a separate publication for each grade level.

Many regular newspapers are written on fourth- to eighth-grade levels. Most of these vary in difficulty from section to section. A check with a readability formula of available newspapers, especially local ones, will help teachers decide if the students in their classes can use the newspapers profitably.

Teachers can begin newspaper study by determining what the students already know with an inventory such as that shown in Example 7.4

After administering such an inventory, the teacher can decide where the students need to begin in newspaper study. Some will need initial orientation to the parts of the newspaper and the information found in each part; some will need help with location skills; and others will need help with newspaper terminology.

Directions: Answer the following questions about your use of the newspaper.

1. What newspaper(s) come to your home?
2. Do you read a newspaper regularly? How often?
3. What parts of the newspaper do you read? _____News _____Editorials _____ Comics _____Entertainment section _____ Features _____ Advertisements _____Columns _____ Other(Give names.) _____
_____
4. How do you locate the part of the newspaper that you want?
_____turn each page _____use the index
5. Where is the index in a newspaper?
6. What do the following terms mean?
   a. AP
   b. byline
   c. dateline
   d. editorial
   e. lead
   f. masthead
   g. UPI ◀

Following are several activities to help children read the newspapers more effectively.

ACTIVITIES

1. Have pupils locate the who, what, where, when, why, and how in news stories.
2. Using news stories with the headlines cut off, have pupils write their own headlines and compare these with the actual headlines.
3. Have children scan a page for a news story on a particular topic.
4. Give children copies of news stories about the same event from two different newspapers. Then ask them to compare likenesses and differences and discuss.
5. Using copies of conflicting editorials, have students underline facts in one color and opinions in another color and discuss the results. Also have them locate emotional language and propaganda techniques in each editorial.
6. Discuss the symbolism and the message conveyed by each of several editorial cartoons. Then ask students to draw their own editorial cartoons.
7. Have pupils compare an editorial and a news story on the same topic. Discuss differences in approach.
8. Tell youngsters to locate comics that are funny. Then ask them to tell why.
9. Cut out the words in a comic strip, have the children fill in words they think would fit, and compare with the original. Or show children comic strips with the last frame missing, ask them what they think will happen, and let them compare their ideas with the real ending.

326

Teaching
Reading in
Today's
Elementary
Schools

10. By studying the entertainment section, pupils can decide what movie or play would be most interesting to them or locate time slots for certain television programs.
11. Encourage the children to try to solve crossword puzzles.
12. To discover which type of writing is more objective, which has more descriptive terms, and so on, pupils should compare human interest features with straight news stories. Have them dramatize appropriate ones.
13. Ask pupils to search grocery advertisements from several stores for the best buy on a specified item or to study the classified advertisements to decide what job they would most like to have and why. Then ask them to write their own classified ads.
14. Have the youngsters study the display advertisements for examples of propaganda techniques.
15. Ask pupils to locate examples of the following types of columns: medical advice, love advice, household hints, humor, and how-to-do-it.
16. Ask students to use the index of the paper to tell what page to look on for the television schedule, weather report, and so on.
17. Ask the children to search through the newspaper for typographical errors, and then discuss the effect of these errors on the material in which they have appeared.
18. Have pupils search the sports page for synonyms for the terms *won* and *lost*. Ask them why these synonyms are used.

Mathematics

Reading in mathematics has its own difficulties. For one thing, there is again the problem of specialized vocabulary. Young children have to learn terms like *plus, minus, sum,* and *subtraction,* whereas older children encounter such terms as *perimeter* and *diameter.* Words with multiple meanings also appear frequently. Discussions about *planes, figures,* numbers in *base* two, or raising a number to the third *power* can confuse children who know other, more common meanings for these words. Nevertheless, many mathematics terms have root words, prefixes, or suffixes that children can use in determining their meanings. (For example, *triangle* means three angles).

To help build math vocabulary, teachers can assign a math word for each day, which students must identify and use in a sentence. One child may "own" the word, wearing a card on which the word is written and giving a presentation on it to the rest of the group, or students may have to identify or illustrate math terms written on cards before they can line up to leave the room. The teacher can ask questions about which terms being studied apply to a particular problem or ask the children to dramatize the problems or meanings of math terms (Kutzman and Krutchinsky, 1981).

Mathematical crossword puzzles are good to use to teach specialized vocabulary. An example is shown in Worksheet: Mathematical Crossword Puzzle.

● **WORKSHEET:** *Mathematical Crossword Puzzle*

```
¹P  L  U  ²S       ³E
 O        U         Q
⁴I  N     ⁵M  ⁶I  N  U  S
 N     ⁷O     N     A
⁸T  E  N     C     L
       E     H
```

Across

1. Two_____two equals four.
4. Abbreviation for inch
5. Ten_____one equals nine.
8. In the decimal system base_____ is used.

Down

1. A decimal_____shows place value.
2. Total
3. The same amount in all containers, or_____amounts
6. 1/12 of a foot
7. One × _____ = one. ●

Difficulties with words are not the only problems children have with math textbooks. They are also required to understand a different symbol system and to read numerals as well as words, which involves understanding place value. Children must be able to interpret such symbols as plus and minus signs, multiplication and division signs, symbols for union and intersection, equal signs and signs indicating inequalities, and many others, as well as abbreviations such as *ft., lb., in., qt., mm, cm,* and so on.

Symbols often are particularly troublesome to children, perhaps partly because some symbols mean other things in other contexts; for example, "–" means "minus" in math but is a hyphen in regular print.

Matching exercises such as the following one encourage youngsters to learn the meanings of symbols.

328

Teaching
Reading in
Today's
Elementary
Schools

● *WORKSHEET: Matching Exercise for Symbols*

Directions: Draw a line from each symbol in Column 1 to its meaning in Column 2.

Column 1	Column 2
=	is greater than
>	is less than
≠	equals
<	plus
−	is not equal to
+	minus
÷	divided by ●

To read numbers, pupils must understand place value. They must note, for example, that in the number 312.8 there are three places to the left of the decimal point (which they must discriminate from a period), which means that the leftmost numeral indicates a particular number of hundreds, the next numeral tells how many tens, and the next numeral tells how many ones (in this case, three hundreds, one ten, and two ones, or three hundred twelve). To determine the value to the right of the decimal, they must realize that the first place is tenths, the second place hundredths, and so forth. In our example, there are eight tenths; therefore, the entire number is three hundred twelve and eight tenths. This is obviously a complex procedure, involving not merely reading from left to right but reading back and forth.

Mathematical sentences also present reading problems. Children must recognize numbers and symbols and translate them into verbal sentences, reading $9 \div 3 = 3$, for example, as "nine divided by three equals three."

Students will need help in reading and analyzing word problems as well. Teachers should arrange such problems according to difficulty and avoid assigning too many at one time (Schell, 1982).

Story problems can present special comprehension difficulties. They require the basic comprehension skills (determining main ideas and details, seeing relationships between details, making inferences, drawing conclusions, and following directions). Emerald Dechant (1970) suggests that students follow a definite procedure in solving statement problems:

1. learn all word meanings
2. discover what is asked for in the problem
3. decide what facts are needed to solve the problem
4. decide what mathematical operations must be performed
5. decide upon the order in which the operations should be performed.

Calhoun C. Collier and Lois A. Redmond (1974) point out that mathematics material is very concise and abstract in nature and involves complex relationships. A high density of ideas per page appears in this kind of material, and understanding each word is very important, for one word may be the key to understanding an entire section. Yet elementary teachers too often approach a math lesson in terms of developing only computational skill, apparently not realizing that reading skills can be advanced during arithmetic lessons, or that arithmetic statement problems would be more comprehensible if attention were given to reading skills.

To understand mathematics materials, Collier and Redmond (1974) suggest students should

1. read the material rapidly or at a normal rate in order to get an overview and to see the main points.
2. read the material again, this time "more slowly, critically, and analytically" to determine details and relationships involved.
3. read some parts of the material a number of times, if necessary, varying the purpose each time.
4. look for relevant information.
5. decide what operations must be performed.
6. determine whether all needed information is given.
7. read the numbers and operation symbols needed to solve the problem.
8. adjust reading rate to the difficulty of the material.

Sometimes children find it useful to draw a picture of the situation involved in a problem or to manipulate actual objects, and teachers should encourage such approaches to problem solving when they are appropriate.

Graphs, maps, charts, and tables, which often occur in mathematics materials, were discussed in Chapter 6.

Science and Health

Extremely heavy use of technical vocabulary is typical in science and health textbooks, where students will encounter terms like *lever, extinct, rodent, pollen, stamen, bacteria, inoculation* and *electron*. Again, some of the words that have technical meanings also have more common meanings—for example, *shot, matter, solution,* and *pitch*. In these classes, as in all content area classes, the teacher has the responsibility of seeing that the pupils understand the concepts represented by the technical terms in their subjects. As an example, a science teacher might bring in a flower when explaining what the *stamen* are and where they are located. While diagrams are also useful, the more concrete an experience with a concept is, the more likely it is that the student will develop a complete understanding of the concept; a diagram is a step removed from the actual object.

Comprehension skills, such as recognizing main ideas and details, making inferences, drawing conclusions, recognizing cause-and-effect relationships, recognizing sequence, and following directions, are important in reading

330

Teaching
Reading in
Today's
Elementary
Schools

These students use many diverse reading and study skills in their science class, as they follow directions, interpret diagrams, and relate text exposition and description to scientific materials and models.   (© David Strickler/The Picture Cube)

science and health materials, as are critical reading skills. Because material can rapidly become outdated, awareness of copyright dates of these materials is important. The inquiring attitude of the scientist is the same as that of the critical reader. Ability to use such reading aids as maps, tables, charts, and graphs is also necessary.

Science and health materials, like social studies materials, are written in a highly compact, expository style that often involves classification, explanations, and cause-and-effect relationships. The suggestions in Chapter 6 for teaching outlining skills can be especially useful in working with classification, which involves arranging information under main headings and subheadings. A classification game, such as that shown in Worksheet: Classification Game, may also be helpful.

Explanations in science and health materials often describe processes, such as pasteurization of milk, which may be illustrated by pictures, charts, or diagrams designed to clarify the textual material. Material of this type needs to be read slowly and carefully and frequently requires rereading. Teachers might apply the material in Chapter 6 related to reading diagrams and illustrations, or the material in Chapter 4 on detecting sequence, since a process is generally explained in sequence. The oral reading strategy and the directed inquiry activity described earlier in this chapter would also be extremely useful in presenting material of this type. Similarly, the suggestions given in Chapter 4 for recognizing cause-and-effect relationships will help children handle this type of arrangement when it occurs in science textbooks.

Instructions for performing experiments are often found in science textbooks, and the reader must be able to comprehend the purpose of the experiment, read the list of materials to determine what he or she must assemble in order to perform the experiment, and determine the order of steps to be followed. The suggestions in Chapter 4 on locating main ideas, details, and sequential order and learning to follow directions should be useful when reading material of this nature. Before they perform an experiment, children should attempt to predict the outcome, based upon their prior knowledge. Afterward, they should compare their predicted results with the actual results, investigating the reasons for differences. Did they perform each step correctly? Can they check special references to find out what actually should have happened?

Because science textbooks are often written at higher difficulty levels than are the basal readers for the same grade level, some children will need

● **WORSHEET:** *Classification Game*

Directions: Place the terms at the bottom of the page under the correct headings.

Animal	Vegetable	Mineral

Terms: fox, fish, grass, rock, tree, iron, dog, flower, silver, gold. ●

332

Teaching
Reading in
Today's
Elementary
Schools

alternate materials to use for science instruction. Among these are:

Follett Beginning Science Books. Chicago: Follett.
Young Scott Science Books. New York: William Scott.
Science Picture Books. Herbert S. Zim. New York: William Morrow.

In addition, in some cases teachers can relate basal reader stories to science study by making science job cards to be used as follow-up activities to stories. An example of directions on one job card follows.

"What kind of weather do you believe was occurring in the story? Tell why you think this is true. Share your ideas with your reading group" (Whitfield and Hovey, 1981).

✔ Self-Check: Objective 4
Name some social studies and science and health reading problems that could occur.
Describe a procedure that you can follow in solving verbal mathematical problems.
(See Self-Improvement Opportunities 3, 5, 6, and 8.)

Test Yourself

True or False
_____ 1. Content area textbooks are carefully graded as to difficulty and are generally appropriate to the grade levels for which they are designed.
_____ 2. One difficulty encountered in all content areas is specialized vocabulary, especially regarding common words that have additional technical meanings.
_____ 3. The cloze technique can be used to help determine whether or not a textbook is suitable for use with a specific child.
_____ 4. All children in the fifth grade can benefit from the use of a single textbook designated for the fifth grade.
_____ 5. Readability formulas are too complicated for classroom teachers to use.
_____ 6. Students often must acquire early concepts and vocabulary in content textbooks before they can understand later content passages.
_____ 7. Offering youngsters instruction in basal readers is sufficient to teach reading skills needed in content area textbooks.
_____ 8. Children instinctively understand figures of speech; therefore, figurative language presents them with no special problems.
_____ 9. Story problems in mathematics are generally extremely easy to read.

_____ 10. Mathematics materials require a child to learn a new symbol system.

_____ 11. Concrete examples are helpful in building an understanding of new concepts.

_____ 12. Science materials need not be read critically since they are written by experts in the field.

_____ 13. An expository style of writing is very precise and highly compact.

_____ 14. The cause-and-effect pattern of organization is found in social studies and science and health materials.

_____ 15. Social studies materials frequently have a chronological organization.

_____ 16. All parts of the newspaper require identical reading skills.

_____ 17. The SAVOR procedure is designed to reinforce essential content area vocabulary.

_____ 18. In Manzo's oral reading strategy, children read aloud to each other.

_____ 19. The directed inquiry activity involves predictions made by the children.

_____ 20. Study guides may set purposes for reading.

_____ 21. The directed reading-thinking activity is a general plan for teaching either basal reader stories or content area selections.

Vocabulary

Check your knowledge of these terms. Reread parts of the chapter if necessary.

cloze procedure
content area textbook
directed inquiry
    activity
directed
    reading-thinking
    activity
euphemism
expository style

figurative language
frustration level
guided reading
    procedure
hyperbole
independent level
instructional level
language arts

language experience
    story
metaphor
oral reading strategy
question-only strategy
readability
SAVOR procedure
simile
study guides

Self-Improvement Opportunities

1. As a test of your ability to use the Fry Readability Graph, turn to the sample selection "Problems Old and New" in the section on social studies and determine its readability. Start counting your sample with "The

334

Teaching
Reading in
Today's
Elementary
Schools

West. . . ." If you get an incorrect answer, study the procedure again and determine where you made your error.

Answer
137 syllables
7.8 sentences
6th grade
(Did you count your sample right? Your last word should have been *taking*.)

2. Develop a directed reading-thinking activity (DRTA) for a content area lesson. Then try it out in an elementary school classroom or present it to a group of your peers in a reading or content methods course.
3. Develop a lesson for teaching students the multiple meanings of words encountered in science and health, social studies, mathematics, or literature. Try the lesson out in an elementary school classroom or present it to a group of your peers.
4. Collect examples of figurative language from a variety of sources and use them to develop a lesson on interpreting figurative language.
5. Select a passage from a social studies or science textbook. Prepare a study guide for children to use in reading/studying the passage.
6. Develop a bibliography of trade books that youngsters who are unable to read a particular content area textbook could use.
7. Demonstrate to your classmates the usefulness of newspaper reading in your particular content area.
8. Prepare a comparison/contrast chart as illustrated in the social studies section of this chapter for some topic in your content area.

Bibliography

Ankney, Paul, and Pat McClurg. "Testing Manzo's Guided Reading Procedure." *The Reading Teacher* 34 (March 1981): 681–85.

Collier, Calhoun C., and Lois A. Redmond. "Are You Teaching Kids to Read Mathematics?" *The Reading Teacher* 27 (May 1974): 804–808.

Dale, Edgar, and Jeanne S. Chall. "A Formula for Predicting Readability." *Educational Research Bulletin* 27 (January 21, 1948): 11–20 and 28, (February 18, 1948): 37–54.

Dechant, Emerald. *Improving the Teaching of Reading.* 2nd ed. Englewood Cliffs, N.J.: Prentice-Hall, 1970, Chapters 12 and 13.

Gaskins, Irene West. "Reading for Learning: Going Beyond the Basals in the Elementary Grades." *The Reading Teacher* 35 (December 1981): 323–28.

Groesbeck, Hulda Gwendolyn. "The Comprehension of Figurative Language by Elementary Children: A Study in Transfer." Ph.D. dissertation, University of Oklahoma, 1961.

Gunning, R. *The Technique of Clear Writing.* New York: McGraw-Hill, 1968.

Judd, Dorothy H. "Avoid Readability Formula Drudgery: Use Your School's Microcomputer." *The Reading Teacher* 35 (October 1981): 7–8.

Keller, Paul F. G. "Maryland Micro: A Prototype Readability Formula for Small Computers." *The Reading Teacher* 35 (April 1982): 778–82.

Kutzman, Sandra, and Rick Krutchinsky. "Improving Children's Math Vocabulary." *The Reading Teacher* 35 (December 1981): 347–48.

Manzo, Anthony V. "Three 'Universal' Strategies in Content Area Reading and Languaging." *Journal of Reading* 24 (November 1980): 147.

Morrow, Lesley Mandel. "Manipulative Learning Materials: Merging Reading Skills with Content Area Objectives." *Journal of Reading* 25 (February 1982): 448–53.

Olson, Mary W., and Bonnie Longnion. "Pattern Guides: A Workable Alternative for Content Teachers." *Journal of Reading* 25 (May 1982): 736–41.

Schell, Vicki J. "Learning Partners: Reading and Mathematics." *The Reading Teacher* 35 (February 1982): 544–48.

Spache, George D. *Good Reading for Poor Readers.* 6th ed. Champaign, Ill.: Garrard Press, 1966.

Stauffer, Russell G. "Reading as a Cognitive Process." *Elementary English* 44 (April 1968): 348.

Stauffer, Russell G. *Teaching Reading as a Thinking Process.* New York: Harper & Row, 1969.

Stieglitz, Ezra L., and Varda S. Stieglitz. "SAVOR the Word to Reinforce Vocabulary in the Content Areas." *Journal of Reading* 25 (October 1981): 46–51.

Storey, Dee C. "Reading in the Content Areas: Fictionalized Biographies and Diaries for Social Studies." *The Reading Teacher* 35 (April 1982): 796–98.

Tinker, Miles A., and Constance M. McCullough. *Teaching Elementary Reading.* 4th ed. Englewood Cliffs, N.J.: Prentice-Hall, 1975, Chapter 13.

Whitfield, Edie L., and Larry Hovey. "Integrating Reading and Science with Job Cards." *The Reading Teacher* 34 (May 1981): 944–45.

Zintz, Miles V. *Corrective Reading.* 4th ed. Dubuque, Iowa: William C. Brown, 1981.

Suggested Readings

Burmeister, Lou E. *Reading Strategies for Middle and Secondary School Teachers.* 2nd ed. Reading, Mass.: Addison-Wesley, 1978.

Burron, Arnold, and Amos L. Claybaugh. *Using Reading to Teach Subject Matter: Fundamentals for Content Teachers.* Columbus, Ohio: Charles E. Merrill, 1974.

Fay, Leo, and Ann Jared. *Reading in the Content Fields.* Rev. ed. Newark, Del.: International Reading Association, 1975 (annotated bibliography, listing periodicals, books, and research).

336

Teaching
Reading in
Today's
Elementary
Schools

Forgan, Harry W., and Charles T. Mangrum. *Teaching Content Area Reading Skills: A Modular Preservice and Inservice Program.* Columbus, Ohio: Charles E. Merrill, 1976.

Harris, Larry H., and Carl B. Smith. *Reading Instruction Through Diagnostic Teaching.* 2nd ed. New York: Holt, Rinehart and Winston, 1976, Chapter 14.

Herber, Harold L. *Teaching Reading in the Content Areas.* 2nd ed. Englewood Cliffs, N.J.: Prentice-Hall, 1978.

Hittleman, Daniel R. *Developmental Reading, K–8: Teaching From a Psycholinguistic Perspective.* 2nd ed. Boston: Houghton Mifflin, 1983, Chapter 10.

Karlin, Robert. *Teaching Elementary Reading: Principles and Strategies.* 3rd ed. New York: Harcourt Brace Jovanovich, 1980, Chapter 8.

Kennedy, Eddie C. *Methods in Teaching Developmental Reading.* 2nd ed. Itasca, Ill.: Peacock, 1981, Chapter 11.

Olson, Joanne P., and Martha H. Dillner. *Learning to Teach Reading in the Elementary School: Utilizing a Competency Based Instructional System.* 2nd ed. New York: Macmillan, 1982, Chapter 12.

Ransom, Grayce A. *Preparing to Teach Reading.* Boston: Little, Brown, 1978, Chapter 8.

Robinson, Richard D., *Introduction to the Cloze Procedure.* Newark, Del.: International Reading Association, 1972 (annotated bibliography listing periodicals, books, and research).

Seels, Barbara, and Edgar Dale, eds. *Readability and Reading.* Rev. ed. Newark, Del.: International Reading Association, 1971 (annotated bibliography, listing periodicals, books, and research).

Smith, Richard J., and Thomas C. Barrett. *Teaching Reading in the Middle Grades.* 2nd ed. Reading, Mass.: Addison-Wesley, 1979.

Smith, Richard J., and Dale D. Johnson. *Teaching Children to Read.* 2nd ed. Reading, Mass.: Addison-Wesley, 1980, Chapter 14.

Spache, George D., and Evelyn B. Spache. *Reading in the Elementary School.* 4th ed. Boston: Allyn & Bacon, 1977, Chapter 9.

Tinker, Miles A., and Constance M. McCullough. *Teaching Elementary Reading.* 4th ed. Englewood Cliffs, N.J.: Prentice-Hall, 1975, Chapter 13.

Willman, Betty. "Reading in the Content Areas: A 'New Math' Terminology List for the Primary Grades." *Elementary English* 48 (May 1971): 463–71.

Wright, Jane Perryman, and Nann L. Andreasen. "Practice in Using Location Skills in a Content Area." *The Reading Teacher* 34 (November 1980): 184–86.

CHAPTER 8

Literary Appreciation and Recreational Reading

Introduction

Elementary school teachers should make sure that there is a balance among developmental, functional, and recreational reading within the reading program. They should recognize that the recreational phase calls for planning just as the other phases do. In this chapter we consider the place of literature in the reading program, suggest ways for teaching literature skills, and give ideas for encouraging children to read for pleasure.

Without doubt, one of the most important long-range objectives for the elementary school reading program is the development of reading habits that will serve the individual throughout an entire lifetime. Evidence that a large percentage of adults are *able* to read but seldom *do* read either for information or enjoyment suggests that they were perhaps turned off by too much reading instruction and not enough experience in reading for informational and recreational reasons. Therefore, it is crucial that children be exposed to experiences with literature that are designed to promote reading enjoyment.

Setting Objectives

When you finish reading this chapter, you should be able to

1. Identify ways to use children's literature in different areas of the curriculum.
2. Know what literary elements children should learn and how to assess their understanding of these elements.
3. Teach several literary forms found in children's literature.
4. Locate sources for selecting and evaluating children's literature.
5. Recognize the different types of reading materials available for children.
6. Design a classroom environment conducive to recreational reading.
7. Discuss ways to motivate children to read for pleasure.
8. Understand when and how children should read orally.
9. Identify several ways in which children can respond to literature through drama.
10. Discuss a variety of ways to interpret literature creatively.

USING LITERATURE IN THE READING PROGRAM

The major purpose of using literature in the reading program is to promote children's development of reading tastes and a lifetime appreciation of fine reading materials. Literature also encourages children to learn about our literary heritage and develop skills of literary analysis and language, and it enriches the content of the curriculum and stimulates creative activities.

Developmental, functional, and recreational reading can easily be incorporated into the school day. During the instructional period, when students are probably reading from their basal readers, developmental reading occurs. Functional reading, however, takes place when students need to find information for a specific purpose or when they are studying in the content areas. Recreational reading and literary appreciation can indeed occur throughout the day as the teacher reads a story or a chapter from a book to the class, as the students read library books when they finish their work, or during a special period set aside for interpreting literature through such activities as choral reading, book sharing, or creative dramatics. Teachers might teach literary skills directly through a unit on poetry or a novel or integrate them with basal reader and language arts lessons, as shown in Table 8.1.

339
Literary
Appreciation
and
Recreational
Reading

In reviewing articles from the past twenty-five years of *The Reading Teacher* to determine the place of literature in reading programs over the years, Shirley Koeller (1976) found a rise in paperbacks and book clubs during the 1950s and a surge of new children's books in the 1960s. She also reported that reading specialists have consistently recommended combining reading instruction with children's free selection of books instead of using a single basal reader approach. Other themes that emerged were the importance of teachers' reading to students at every level, the accessibility of enough books to meet the interests of all pupils, the value of children's sharing books with

TABLE 8.1 Literary Skills and Recreational Reading During a Typical School Day

Time	Activity	Purpose
8:30–8:45	Teacher reads aloud to children.	Children develop an interest in reading for pleasure.
9:00–10:30	Children read from basal readers.	Children learn some literary skills as they read a selection from good literature.
11:00–11:20	Several children demonstrate and explain a science experiment to the rest of the class.	Children use informational books for a purpose.
12:45–1:30	Children read biographies and historical fiction.	Children investigate materials related to the social studies unit.
2:00–2:30	Teacher introduces a poem during language arts class.	Children listen to the poem and respond to its rhythm, visual images, and mood.

Whenever children have free time, they may read a library book.

340

Teaching
Reading in
Today's
Elementary
Schools

one another, and the importance of having them respond creatively to literature.

Whether or not teachers should use behavioral objectives (precise goals) for teaching literature and developing literary appreciation is an issue that has been debated by Gordon Peterson and Patrick Groff (1977). Peterson contends that such objectives are useful because they provide specific information about what a student should be able to do, suggest sequence and priorities for instruction, offer materials and techniques, and provide a means for student evaluation. Patrick Groff, on the other hand, opposes the use of behavioral objectives, believing that they may have a negative effect upon children's enjoyment, understanding, and appreciation of literature as well as a limiting influence on children's creative responses.

Teachers can use literature to enrich each subject in the curriculum; for example, children's literature readily extends into social studies, for which award-winning books can be found for nearly every period in history. Elizabeth Speare's *The Bronze Bow* is a novel about a boy who encounters Jesus in Rome; Marguerite De Angeli's *The Door in the Wall* treats the situation of a crippled boy in 14th century England; *The Courage of Sarah Noble* by Alice Dalgliesh describes a young girl who must face the difficulties of living in Connecticut in early pioneer days; Carol Brink's *Caddie Woodlawn* brings the reader into the excitement of living on the Wisconsin frontier during the last half of the 19th century; and Paula Fox's *The Slave Dancer* tells the story of a boy who becomes involved in the slave trade with Africa during pre-Civil War days. Biographies of famous people who lived during different historical periods also add spice to textbook accounts.

Teachers can use trade books to develop mathematical concepts as well (Huck, 1979; Radebaugh, 1981). Starting with simple counting books, such as the vividly illustrated *Brian Wildsmith's 1, 2, 3's,* teachers can use books to expand concepts dealing with shapes, with comparative size, and with ordinal numbers. An activity and craft book, *Right Angles: Paper-Folding Geometry,* by Jo Phillips, helps young children work out mathematical concepts, and Robert Froman's *Bigger and Smaller* shows relative sizes of objects.

Vocabulary lessons are lively and fun when the class uses trade books for word play and for learning interesting features of words (Blatt, 1978; Burke, 1978). In the Amelia Bedelia books, by Peggy Parish, Amelia takes everything literally, with disastrous results: her sponge cake is made of sponges! Fred Gwynne's *A Chocolate Moose for Dinner* illustrates figurative expressions and words with multiple meanings as a child might visualize them; William Steig's *CDB* uses letters of the alphabet to represent words for silly sayings; and Emily Hanlon uses homonyms to form nonsense verses in *How a Horse Grew Hoarse on the Site Where He Sighted a Bare Bear.*

Literature can also promote facility in the area of language arts, as demonstrated in the activities given on pages 368–69 for a folklore unit. Skills developed in a unit such as this are reading, reporting (orally and in written form), telling stories, literary appreciation, vocabulary, writing creatively, listening, and doing research.

341
Literary
Appreciation
and
Recreational
Reading

✔ **Self-Check: Objective 1**

Suggest some ways in which you can use trade books to enrich teaching in the content areas.
(See Self-Improvement Opportunity 1.)

TEACHING LITERATURE SKILLS

When teaching literature, teachers should plan diversity in children's exposure to literature rather than allow pupils to have random encounters with books (Stewig, 1980). Instruction may be organized by genres (forms), literary elements, or topics to vary pupils' experiences.

Teachers should also introduce students to the specialized vocabulary and skills they will need to develop an appreciation of literature. Children must understand words such as *characterization* and *theme* before they can fully participate in many lessons. Literature also presents them with very different meanings for words they use in their everyday language, such as *meter* and *plot*. In casual conversation children may discuss parking meters and plots of ground, but these meanings will be of little help in determining the meter of a poem or the plot of a short story.

Literary Elements

In order to understand literary passages, children should be able to recognize and analyze plots, themes, characterizations, and sequences. The *plot* is the overall plan for the story, and all the other elements contribute to it. The *theme* is the main idea that the writer wishes to convey to the reader, and *characterization* refers to the way in which the author makes the characteristics and motives of each person in the story evident to the reader. Of course, *sequence* refers to the order in which events occur.

To lead a child to examine a story closely, teachers should ask questions about plot, theme, characterization, and sequence. For example, the following questions are appropriate to a mystery that the children have just read:

1. Did the way the story was told hold you in suspense until the very end? (plot)
2. Did the story have a moral? If so, what was it? (theme)
3. Did you suspect John of being the thief? What things did he do and say that made you either suspect him or not suspect him? (characterization)
4. Did David act as a real person might have acted when he discovered the missing money? How did you feel toward David after you saw his reaction? (characterization)
5. Did David accuse John of the theft before or after John bought his new rifle? (sequence)

Two additional literary elements, setting and style, should be considered. An authentic *setting* will involve the past, present, or future, and an author

342

Teaching
Reading in
Today's
Elementary
Schools

Promoting reading enjoyment and fostering good lifetime reading habits are among the most important objectives of a school reading program.   (© Hugh Rogers/Monkmeyer)

may describe a specific locale or imply one through dialect and activities. The setting answers the questions of when and where and, in a well-written book, affects the actions, characters, and theme. Use questions of the following type to direct attention to the setting:

Where and when did the story take place?
Did the story capture the spirit and feeling of the place or the age?
How did the author reveal the setting?

Style—the author's mode of expressing thoughts in words—should be appropriate to plot, theme, and characters. Usually the writer strives for a variety of sentence patterns. Children prefer action and conversation; they do not like too much description or too many figurative and symbolic meanings. Style includes the author's point of view when telling the story: his or her own (first person), the main character's (first person), or the omniscient narrator's (third person). The latter can reveal the inner thoughts and emotions of all the characters. To direct attention to the author's style, ask:

343

Literary
Appreciation
and
Recreational
Reading

> What would you say about the way the author wrote?
> Did the author tell the story from a personal point of view?
> Was there an all-knowing narrator?

✔ Self-Check: Objective 2
Cite literary elements appropriate for study and provide several questions to help evaluate the child's understanding of each one. (See Self-Improvement Opportunity 2.)

Literary Forms

Children are asked to read and understand many literary forms, including short stories, novels, plays, poetry, essays, biographies, and autobiographies.

Short Stories

Short stories can cause reading difficulties because of their brevity. Because a large amount of information is packed into a small number of words, children must read every sentence carefully. They can be helped to understand short stories better if they are given some questions to guide their reading, such as

Setting
> Where did this story take place?
> When did the story take place?
> How did the setting of the story affect the action?

Characterization
> Which character in the story did you like best? Why?
> Which character in the story did you like least? Why?
> Which character in the story caused the most trouble? Did this person mean to cause trouble? What did the person do or say that caused you to answer as you did?

Sequence
> What was the first incident that caused problems for the characters?
> Name, in order, two other problems that developed.

Plot
> Did you expect the story to end as it did? Why or why not?

Theme
> Did the story have a moral or message? If so, what was it?

344

Teaching
Reading in
Today's
Elementary
Schools

Teachers can also enhance understanding of short stories by building background before reading—exposing students to information about the area and period in which the action takes place through discussion, films, filmstrips, and other audiovisual aids.

Novels

Novels can often be difficult for a poor or average reader to read because they have several intertwined plots that may be hard to follow, and long descriptive passages try the patience of reluctant readers, who tend to prefer action and dialogue. Teachers must read many novels to children to develop their expectations for "novel behavior" before they ask children to read one for study purposes. Many are available—*Mrs. Frisby and the Rats of NIMH, The Hobbit, Julie of the Wolves, Island of the Blue Dolphins, The Incredible Journey, A Wrinkle in Time, Rabbit Hill,* and the like.

Traditionally, teaching of novel-reading has been characterized by three basic weaknesses: overemphasizing the facts of the story; providing children with little opportunity to develop a positive self-concept; and offering infrequent opportunities to develop creative thinking. A number of recommended procedures for overcoming these weaknesses are listed below.

ACTIVITIES

1. After carefully selecting a novel that will best meet the needs and interests of the children, have the class read the novel in one of several ways:
   a. Provide time over several weeks to read the complete novel aloud during class time. Making sure each child receives ample time to read aloud, you could have the class read several chapters each day. First provide an opportunity for silent reading so that audience reading will be a pleasant experience.
   b. Set aside a portion of class time to supplement the pupil's independent reading of designated chapters, perhaps reading aloud the most crucial parts of the book to the class.
   c. The children can read the novel completely on their own. If you choose this procedure, be sure to provide time for private consultation and discussion of each child's progress.
2. After the novel has been completed, the class as a whole can discuss it in the following manner:
   a. Divide the class into groups of four or fewer and let each group discuss questions that you have provided on plot, setting, characters, theme, and style. (The questions can be typed beforehand on index cards.)
   b. Distribute questions to individual children so that each has a question of his or her own to answer. Perhaps two or three children could work together on the more difficult ones. Below are some sample questions for the novel *Where the Lilies Bloom,* by Vera and Bill Cleaver.

345
Literary
Appreciation
and
Recreational
Reading

Plot

At the beginning of the story, Mary Call feels that she must fight to keep her family together, but at the end we discover that she no longer feels she has to do this. What has happened in the story that causes Mary Call to change her mind?

Is one of the events in the story more important than all of the others? Why or why not?

Does the story keep your attention? How?

Why do you think the authors entitled their book *Where the Lilies Bloom*? What would you have called it?

Do you think this story could really happen?

Setting

Where did the story take place?

Do you think a family like the Luthers could be living in the 1980s, or would they have lived in the past?

Do you think the place where the story was set had anything to do with the type of person Mary Call was? Would the story change if it were set somewhere else outside of the mountains, such as in a city?

Characters

If you had to tell someone who had not read the story about Mary Call Luther, how would you describe her?

What makes Mary Call different from her brother and sisters?

Did any character (person in the story) change during the story? Explain.

Did the characters seem real to you? Do you think maybe the authors really knew a family like this when they wrote about the Luthers? Have you ever known or seen a family like the Luthers?

Theme

Mary Call has many problems in the story. Can you remember some of them?

After Roy Luther died, Mary Call became the leader of her family. What were some of her responsibilities as the head of her family?

All of the conflicts (problems) in the novel are very important, but the authors use them to try to tell us something else that is important—the "main idea" of the story. What do you think the authors are trying to tell us?

Style

Do you like the way Vera and Bill Cleaver write? Why or why not?

Were you always anxious to find out what was going to happen next?

Through whose eyes do the authors tell their story?

3. When the child, individually or as part of a group, has had ample time to think about the questions, direct discussion in one of the following ways:

   a. Set aside time each day to discuss the questions assigned to each group, calling upon members for discussion.

   b. Lead the class in a group dialogue, incorporating all the questions with which the class has been presented.

346

Teaching
Reading in
Today's
Elementary
Schools

4. Follow up with suitable class activities by letting children do the following:
   a. Sketch pictures of Trial Valley and either paint them with water colors or color them with crayons or colored chalk.
   b. Make a nature scrapbook. Have pupils collect some plants and flowers near their homes, place the specimens between the pages of a heavy book until pressed and dried, then tape each one on a different page of a scrapbook. Students should record the specimen's name, where it was found, and the like, so the scrapbook can be used as a class reference book.
   c. Talk to parents and grandparents about old home remedies, or check the *Farmer's Almanac* and old cookbooks. Report to the class and discuss.
   d. Discuss the foods students eat and compare them with the foods the Luther family ate.
   e. Compare *Where the Lilies Bloom* with the TV programs "The Waltons" and "Little House on the Prairie."
   f. Pantomime Mary Call trying to drive the car.
   g. Write a new ending to *Where the Lilies Bloom*.
   h. Write a paragraph on "Alone and On Our Own"; "Why My Family Grew Closer Together"; "I Wish I Were an Only Child"; "No Neighbor to Help."

Plays

Because plays are written in a different way from most narrative prose, they present problems. The characters in a play are generally listed at the beginning; then usually the setting is described; and finally, the dialogue is presented, with each part labeled to indicate the speaker. Aside from a few stage directions, much of the actual action is left to the imagination and is only implied by the dialogue. Children understand plays more easily if they act them out in the classroom.

Teachers can help youngsters understand plays by using some of the following activities:

ACTIVITIES

1. Develop background for the play before presenting it to the class. Emphasize the characteristics of the area and period in which the action occurs through verbal descriptions, films, filmstrips, pictures, or other audiovisual aids.
2. Explain to the children the importance of visualizing the action in the play as they read it. Help them to see how stage directions aid this process.
3. Ask the children to read the paragraph that describes the setting of the scene and encourage them to picture this scene mentally.
4. Call children's attention to the cast of characters. Show them how each character's words are indicated in the script, and encourage them to find out as much as they can about each character so that they will be better able to visualize each one.

5. Ask each pupil to read the entire play silently, picturing the characters, setting, and action.
6. Have each youngster pretend to be one of the characters, feeling the part and practicing reading the character's dialogue realistically. Assign parts and have the children read the play orally. Then discuss the effectiveness of the reading. Ask for positive comments as well as suggestions for improvement.
7. Assign parts to different children and have a second reading; record this attempt. Ask the performers to listen to the recording to evaluate themselves.
8. Ask questions such as those suggested for teaching a short story in order to determine youngsters' grasp of setting, characterization, sequence, plot, and theme.

347

Literary
Appreciation
and
Recreational
Reading

Poetry

Poetry uses rhythm, rhyme, repetition, and other techniques to develop moods and create visual and auditory impressions, and it is filled with difficult figurative expressions, such as similes and metaphors.

It is best not to overanalyze poetry at the elementary school level. Allow it to speak to the children and offer them visual and auditory sensations, without dissecting it line by line. Some analysis is acceptable, however, and in some cases it may be necessary— for example, meanings of figures of speech must be clarified if students do not understand them. Teachers can use questions such as the following, if they use them sparingly, when poetry is being read:

1. What words in the poem make you see, hear, feel, smell, and taste things? How does the poet make you feel the galloping motion of the horse?
2. How does the poet put you in a sad (happy) mood?
3. Which lines in each stanza of the poem rhyme?
4. Does this poem have a message? If so, what is it?
5. What do you think was the author's reason for writing this poem? Why do you think so?

Before letting students read a poem for themselves, the teacher should read it aloud fluently as a model. Then the children should read the poem silently, with teacher help with any unfamiliar words or phrases. After this preparation, students may read the poem orally, either to a group or privately (perhaps for a tape recorder), since poetry is intended for the ear and has its greatest effect when it is read aloud.

Essays

Essays are examples of nonfiction prose that are formal or informal, humorous or serious, and present the writer's personal viewpoint on a subject. Students need to be able to determine the purpose of the essayist.

348

Teaching
Reading in
Today's
Elementary
Schools

Ask students to read essays to decide whether they are designed to entertain, persuade, or inform. Also ask them to try to describe the characteristics of the writer. The teacher may wish to use comprehension questions such as:

Humorous essays—What parts of the essay did you think were funny? How did the author use words in an amusing way?

Persuasive essays—What did the author want to make you believe or do? How did the author try to encourage you to think or do as he or she wished? What emotional words were used? Did these words affect your feelings about what was said?

Informative essays—What was the author trying to explain? Was the explanation clear to you? Why or why not? What are the main points that you gained from this essay?

Biographies and Autobiographies

Biographies and autobiographies are stories about people's lives. The biographer has an opportunity to look at the life of another person more objectively than the autobiographer, who is writing about himself or herself. Unfortunately, this fact does not guarantee objectivity, and students must be encouraged to find out as much as they can about a biographer in order to help them determine whether or not he or she is likely to be biased. A staunch Republican writing a biography of a Democrat might look at things differently from the way a Democrat would view them. A biographer who writes about someone long after that person's death is, of course, at a disadvantage, since nothing can be discovered or observed first-hand. In contrast, the autobiographer has all the facts at hand but may not choose to present them all or may misrepresent some situations. A teacher can help youngsters to understand the difference between biography and autobiography by having them write their own life stories and the life stories of classmates. After comparing the biography and autobiography of each individual, the children can discuss differences and reasons for these differences.

The next step is to present the children with professionally written biographies and autobiographies of the same person and ask them to compare the accounts, discussing reasons for variations in class. The teacher might use questions such as the following to guide the discussion:

1. Who wrote the biography?
2. Did the author know the subject personally? If so, did the author like or dislike the subject? What differences might this make?
3. Did the biographer live about the same time as the subject? What difference might this make?
4. Did the biographer make the subject look less perfect than he or she seemed to be in the autobiography? What are some possible reasons for this?

🖝 **Self-Check: Objective 3**

349

Literary
Appreciation
and
Recreational
Reading

Name several literary forms. Discuss some ways of teaching each form.
(See Self-Improvement Opportunity 3.)

Story Reading and Storytelling

Reading aloud to children serves many purposes. Good oral reading by the teacher serves as a model and allows students to experience literature that they might not be able or inclined to read for themselves. It can also whet their appetites to read more on their own, since an exciting chapter or section of a book often stimulates children to read the entire book themselves. Besides providing exposure to specific books, reading to children can also introduce them to creative and colorful use of language in prose and poetry, present new vocabulary and concepts, and acquaint them with the variety of language patterns found in written communication.

Teachers should read in natural tones and with expression, providing time for sharing the illustrations, exploring key words and phrases, and evaluating reactions. The best stories to read aloud are those children cannot easily read for themselves, that the teacher personally likes and is thoroughly familiar with, and that possess the qualities assigned to the best literature.

Similarly, teacher storytelling acquaints children with literature and provides for good listening experiences. Folktales are especially good, for they were told and told and told again long before they were ever captured in print. Myths, stories from such authors as Andersen and Kipling, and even episodes from longer books may be adapted for telling.

Simply listening to stories is a valuable experience for children, but occasional follow-up discussions can bring out points that they might otherwise miss. The teacher should be prepared to lead discussions related to characters, theme, plot, or some other aspect of a story whenever the occasion warrants. A card file with questions to initiate a discussion about each book is useful. An example of a card for such a file is shown in Example 8.1.

To introduce children to books, teachers and librarians often use book talks about individual books or about several books that are related in some way. The teacher begins by telling a humorous or exciting part of the story and stops just short of the conclusion in order to make children want to read the ending for themselves.

Teachers can tape-record storybooks to build a library of recorded stories that children can listen to year after year. When the teacher has recorded several stories, he or she should place the tapes at a listening center along with the accompanying books. These teacher-recorded materials are better than commercially prepared tapes because they offer lower cost, wider choice of books, and pacing designed for the needs of special learners (Carbo, 1981).

350

Teaching
Reading in
Today's
Elementary
Schools

► **EXAMPLE 8.1:** Literature Discussion Card

Class Discussion

The Giving Tree, Shel Silverstein, Harper & Row, 1964.
A tree responds to the needs of a boy by giving of itself in many ways.
Discuss the following topics.

1. Do you think it was right for the boy to take so much from the tree?
2. Did the boy give anything back to the tree? What might he have done for the tree?
3. Suppose the tree had not given so much of itself. What would be the advantages for others?
4. Do you know a person who is like the Giving Tree?

ENCOURAGING RECREATIONAL READING

The test of a good recreational reading program is the quantity and quality of books that students read voluntarily. Teachers can encourage children to read for pleasure in a variety of ways.

Selecting Recreational Reading Materials

The kinds of literature that teachers make available to their students affect the success of their recreational reading programs. In order to satisfy their interests and accommodate their reading levels, students need a wide selection of materials. Achievement test scores may be used to establish a rough indication of reading levels. Teachers should make easier books available to encourage the slow reader and more difficult ones to challenge the gifted reader.

According to Huck (1979), children are interested in reading realistic fiction, biographies, stories about animals, tales of exploration and adventure, and stories of the past. They like suspense, action, humor, and make-believe. Increasingly, they are interested in seeking out information from nonfiction books on a wide range of subjects. Teachers can assess children's personal reading interests by simply asking them to list three things that interest them or by administering an interest inventory such as that on pages 240–41.

Many selection aids, or references that identify and evaluate publications, are available to help teachers and librarians select literature for specific purposes. Among the most comprehensive are the *Children's Catalog* (New York: H. W. Wilson, 1976) and *The Elementary School Library Collection* (Phyllis Van Orden and Lois Winkel, eds., Williamsport, PA: Bro-Dart Foundation,

1977). Both of these contain author, title, and subject indexes and provide annotations of the books listed.

Each year since the 1974–1975 school year, the International Reading Association–Children's Book Council Joint Committee has published an annotated list of "Children's Choices," which appears annually in the October issue of *The Reading Teacher*. Each list is compiled by approximately 10,000 children, working in teams, who read new books and vote for their favorites.

Another useful source in selecting children's books is a listing of Newbery and Caldecott award winners. The John Newbery Award is presented annually to the author whose book is selected by a special committee as the year's most distinguished contribution to American literature for children; excellence in illustration is the criterion used in awarding the annual Randolph Caldecott Medal.

Selecting appropriate poetry for children is especially difficult. Poorly chosen poems can prejudice children against poetry, whereas a suitable poem will amuse, inspire, emotionally move, or intellectually interest listeners. A poem should not only be understandable and enjoyable but should stimulate children to discover additional poems on their own. Among poetry collections that are popular with intermediate-level children, Shel Silverstein's *Where the Sidewalk Ends* and *The Light in the Attic* are favorites. They contain hilarious poems about children who think and behave much the same the world over, and the clever line drawings surrounded by open spaces help the reader visualize the scenes. The humor comes from alliteration, from plays on words, or from a highly exaggerated situation, such as in "Sarah Cynthia Sylvia Stout Who Would Not Take the Garbage Out" (*Where the Sidewalk Ends*).

Most of the books that children use in school have sturdy library bindings and have been carefully selected for content, but students sometimes prefer other forms of reading material. Most children enjoy reading paperback books because they are easy to carry around and inexpensive to own. Many teachers prefer paperbacks because multiple copies of one book cost the same as a single library edition, so teachers can order enough for small groups of children to read and use in follow-up activities and discussions.

Paperback books are often available at special reduced rates through book clubs, such as Scholastic Book Clubs (Englewood Cliffs, NJ 07632). For nearly two decades "Reading is FUNdamental," or "RIF" (600 Maryland Avenue S.W., Smithsonian Institution, Washington, D.C. 20560), has offered an inexpensive book distribution program in which each child receives three free books a year. Since paperbacks are so easily available, they are one way to make recreational reading appealing to children.

Easy-to-read books generally do not meet the criteria for good children's literature, but they are valuable in a beginning reading program. Written with a controlled vocabulary that a first grader can understand, these books are intended to be read *by* young children instead of *to* them. Youngsters who

352

Teaching
Reading in
Today's
Elementary
Schools

have just learned to read experience great delight in being able to read an entire book independently.

Many good children's magazines are available for different reading levels and different areas of interest. Classroom subscriptions to two or three favorites will enrich the reading program. Some popular choices are listed below.

Cricket (Open Court Publishing Co., Box 599, LaSalle, IL 61301). Excellent illustrations; high literary content; stories, poems, and articles by distinguished authors.

Ebony, Jr.! (Johnson Publishing Company, 820 S. Michigan Avenue, Chicago, IL 60605). Activities, poems, stories, and nonfiction articles about blacks who have made special contributions.

Humpty Dumpty's Magazine (Parent's Magazine Enterprises, 52 Vanderbilt Ave., New York, NY 10017). Games, puzzles, pictures, and stories for beginning readers.

National Geographic World (National Geographic Society, 17th and M Streets N. W., Washington, D.C. 20036). Feature stories on plant and animal life, and different cultures; color photographs; projects.

Ranger Rick's Nature Magazine (National Wildlife Federation, 1412 16th Street N.W., Washington, D.C. 20036). Stories and articles about science and conservation; suggested nature projects; color photographs.

Sesame Street Magazine (Children's Television Workshop, 1 Lincoln Plaza, New York, NY 10023). Parents' page with suggestions for adult reinforcement of activities; games, puzzles, posters, artwork, picture stories.

Stone Soup: A Journal of Children's Literature (Box 83, Santa Cruz, CA 95063). Letters, pictures, stories, and poems by children from five to thirteen years of age.

Your Big Backyard (National Wildlife Federation, 1412 16th Street N.W., Washington, D.C. 20036). Excellent illustrations and information about nature for young children.

During multimedia presentations children experience folk songs, storytelling with sound effects, and filmed versions of classics, through recordings, filmstrips, and films. Multimedia approaches can be springboards for getting children interested in reading good literature, since quite often a child who hears a story at a listening station later asks to read the book. Appendix B in Chapter 2 lists sources of multimedia materials.

The primary purpose of using comic books in the classroom is to motivate poor readers (Koenke, 1979; Wright, 1979). Though comics are not great literature and do not guarantee improvement in reading, they do offer a colorful, fast-paced alternative for the reluctant reader, and good teachers can find creative ways to use them. Those comics exhibiting the seal "Approved by the Comics Code Authority" on their front covers contain reasonably wholesome material for children aged nine to thirteen, their primary readers.

In readability, comics range from 1.8 (*Archie* and *Casper the Friendly Ghost*) to 6.9 (*Prince Valiant*) according to the Fry Readability Graph.

TV tie-ins are a relatively new form of reading material for young people, but they are remarkably popular, especially with slow and reluctant readers. TV tie-ins are paperback books based on the story lines and characters from popular television series. They are fast-moving, action-filled, and easy to read. Students are enthusiastic about reading them because they are already familiar with the characters and can anticipate the action. Jackie Busch (1978) found that 89 percent of 595 students in grades two through twelve had read a book as a result of watching a commercial television program.

✔ Self-Check: Objectives 4 and 5

Identify alternative sources for selecting children's literature. What are some types of literature that have special appeal for students? (See Self-Improvement Opportunities 5, 6, 7, 8, and 9.)

Creating an Environment for Recreational Reading

Teachers who want to encourage children to read for pleasure provide special areas for recreational reading and design bulletin boards and displays that attract attention to books. Imagination helps to create an interesting place for children to relax and read. Discarded refrigerator cartons with the backs removed can be transformed into grass shacks, log cabins, moon rockets, or witches' dens for children to visit in their free time; a raised platform covered with carpet scraps in a secluded corner is a special place to escape with a favorite book; old telephone cable spools make round library tables for young children; and old-fashioned bathtubs piled with cushions are appealing hideaways. Children also appreciate having their own private places for reading where they will not be disturbed, so teachers should provide carpet scraps, large pillows, pieces of plywood, and chains of beads for creating private nooks and crannies. Bookshelves filled with books within reach of all reading areas are a necessity, and the selection should be changed periodically.

Bulletin boards and dioramas can create interest in specific books or special topics. Small, portable bulletin boards are suitable for featuring books and authors, perhaps with displays of book jackets, which are colorful and easy to use. Three-dimensional dioramas take time to make, but the tiny figures intrigue children. To make a diorama, cut the top and one side off a small carton and set up a scene from a story inside the box. For example, to illustrate *Charlotte's Web*, weave the word TERRIFIC into a piece of fishnet, place a tiny pipe-cleaner spider in it, tack the net up over a corner of the box, and put a model of a pig with some straw on the bottom of the carton. Beside the scene place a copy of the book.

Working together, a teacher and a librarian can arrange attractive displays of new books, perhaps along with projects at interest centers in any curricular

354

Teaching
Reading in
Today's
Elementary
Schools

area. For instance, James Daugherty's *Daniel Boone* and Roberta Strauss Feuerlecht's *The Legends of Paul Bunyan* could be displayed in connection with a unit on the westward movement. Other ideas for book displays are suggested below.

Madeline, by Ludwig Bemelmans. Use a French flag, a model of the Eiffel Tower, and a poster of Paris from a travel agency.

White Snow, Bright Snow, by Alvin Tresselt. Include a display of student-made white paper snowflakes on a dark background and marshmallow snowmen standing in detergent snowflakes.

The Story of Johnny Appleseed, by Aliki. Display a map of Johnny Appleseed's travels, along with an apple, seeds from an apple, and apple blossoms (if in season).

A Gathering of Days: A New England Girl's Journal, 1830–32, by Joan Blos. Use a map of New England and a looseleaf notebook for students to record imaginary events that could have happened to them if they had been Catherine's friends.

Motivating Students to Read

With an abundant supply of books and a supportive reading environment, most children will be enthusiastic about recreational reading. But some will still need to be motivated, and even good readers occasionally appreciate added incentives for reading.

Book recording devices, which are ways of keeping track of the number and type of books that students read, provide good incentives (Whitehead, 1968). Bulletin-board charts, card files, and reading wheels and ladders are examples. The most familiar recording device is simply a large piece of poster board with each child's name listed at the left side. Beside each name is space for students to place tiny replicas of books that they have read, with the title and the author printed on them. Different colors of construction paper can represent different categories of books, such as yellow for science fiction, orange for biography, and red for realistic fiction.

Another familiar recording device is the bookworm, which consists of a series of connected circles. Whenever a child finishes a book, he or she adds a circle with the title and author. The bookworm is a joint endeavor that can run up and down the walls of the classroom. Again, different colors can represent different types of reading material.

Reading wheels and ladders are used individually to encourage children to diversify their reading. Each spoke of the wheel or each rung of the ladder represents a different type of book, and students color in or cover up a space for each book read. A sample bookworm and a reading ladder are shown in Example 8.2.

► **EXAMPLE 8.2:** Bookworm and Reading Ladder

355

Literary
Appreciation
and
Recreational
Reading

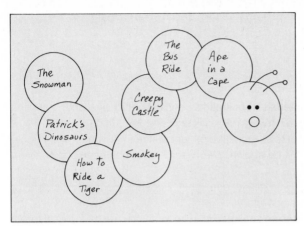

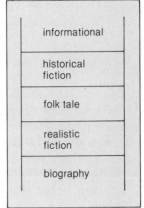

Students may keep personal card files or notebooks listing books they have read, or they may contribute to a class file. For their files, students should note brief comments on one side of the card and draw illustrations on the other.

Some schools use special programs to promote interest in reading. Media specialists organize book clubs to attract readers with similar interests who wish to share their knowledge. A Reading Olympics program awards gold, silver, and bronze certificates to each child who completes a specified number of books. On RIF distribution days some teachers hold special motivational programs, which are often seasonal: witches tell spooky stories at Halloween, the Easter bunny makes the spring distribution, or the Abominable Snowman pulls books from a sack during the winter season.

Sustained Silent Reading (SSR) is widely used as a means for stimulating interest in reading. The teacher sets aside a period of time, usually from fifteen to thirty minutes, each day for silent reading. SSR can be used by a single classroom or by the entire school—students and staff. Reading materials are freely chosen by the students, who now have the opportunity to use the skills that they have acquired for an uninterrupted period of reading for pleasure. As their teacher joins them, they realize that recreational reading has value even for adults. Of course, a wide selection of books, effective motivational strategies, and follow-up discussions of reading materials are important components of Sustained Silent Reading.

Book fairs are another way of acquainting children with new books, offering them books to own and creating enthusiasm for reading. Media specialists arrange with book distributors to deliver books on consignment for about a week, and then advertise the fair in advance so that children can look forward to buying new books. Special book-related events, such as puppet

356

Teaching
Reading in
Today's
Elementary
Schools

shows, visiting storytellers, dramatic presentations, and special displays, are often held in conjunction with the book fair.

Some other ideas for stimulating reader interest are given below.

ACTIVITIES

1. Use free promotional materials (bookmarks, posters, etc.) available from the Children's Book Council, 67 Irving Place, New York, NY 10003.
2. Using schedules from local television studios, announce in advance when book-related television shows will be shown. *The Wizard of Oz* has been shown every year for many years.
3. Set the mood for storytime with music, dim lights, a special room arrangement, or a feature related to a specific story.
4. Supply nonfiction and biographical books related to a current topic of great interest (a royal wedding or a space launch, for example).
5. Promote Book Week and Library Week and use related materials (also available from the Children's Book Council).
6. Ask your school librarian to show the children special features of the library (where new books are placed, what story filmstrips are available and how to use them, how to use the card catalog, where award-winning books are located, and so on).
7. Make a "Who's Who" of famous story characters, to which each student contributes one or more pages.
8. Invite a local author to speak to your class and discuss what it is like to write a book.
9. Use crossword puzzles, charades, and games based on stories.

Some things actually discourage young people from reading. For example, most children intensely dislike required reading lists and formal book reports. Students also find prolonged analysis of books tedious, and they lose interest in reading if the teacher shows no interest in reading for pleasure.

✔ Self-Check: Objectives 6 and 7

Cite several ways to create a stimulating environment for recreational reading and motivate children to read for pleasure. (See Self-Improvement Opportunity 10.)

Providing Opportunities for Responding to Literature

Reading a book is just the first step in developing appreciation for literature and interest in recreational reading. Children need opportunities to share what they have read and to respond creatively to good literature. On the next few pages we present some suggestions for reacting to stories and books.

357

Literary
Appreciation
and
Recreational
Reading

Creative Book Sharing

Even though children dislike formal book reports, they should be encouraged to respond to and share books on certain occasions. Teachers can devise dozens of ways for children to react to books, including the ones below.

ACTIVITIES

1. Set up mock interviews between the student and a character in the book, between two book characters, between the student and the author, or between a character and the author.
2. Arrange a panel discussion in which several students who have read different books by the same author talk about similarities and differences in the books, the writer's strengths and weaknesses, the writer's general philosophy, and how the author's style has changed over a period of time.
3. Once a month let students share in groups of four or five what they liked or did not like about a book they read, showing the book while they are telling about it.
4. Have students make book jackets. They can illustrate the cover and write a brief biographical sketch of the author and a "blurb" to make the book sound appealing.
5. When more than one student reads the same book, try the following suggestions: dramatize a scene from the story; set up a puppet show and tape-record the voices of the characters; compare views about character development, conflicts in the story, and the ending of the book.
6. For biographies, have students discuss the childhoods of famous people, what influences caused them to become famous, and what struggles they faced to accomplish their goals.
7. When students have read biographies of creative people, ask them to include examples of the subjects' famous works in their reviews: playing a recording by a well-known composer, showing an art print by a painter, or displaying a product of an inventor.
8. For books about travel, students might read several books about the same country and compare points of view, keep an imaginary travel diary of the country featured in the book, or give an illustrated lecture on the country by locating it on the map and by showing postcards and other travel materials.
9. For realistic fiction, encourage students to identify the problems of the characters and how they are solved, relate the situation in the book to the student's own environment, or propose alternate solutions for the characters' problems.
10. Encourage students to compare books with movie or television versions of the same title.

Interpreting Literature Orally

At times a child may ask to read a favorite story to the class or to a small group, and at other times the teacher should encourage children to share stories of general interest orally. Older children's reading of stories to younger ones can be highly beneficial to both groups.

Audience reading is an exercise in communication. Because the reader is trying to convey the author's message, he or she must pronounce all words correctly, enunciate distinctly, phrase appropriately, use proper intonation, and pace the reading appropriately. In order to accomplish these goals, the oral reader should have an opportunity to read silently first, during which preview he or she can become acquainted with the author's style of writing, determine the author's message, and check on the correct pronunciation of unfamiliar words. If the passage is particularly difficult, the reader may need to practice it, or portions of it, aloud in order to assure proper phrasing and intonation. A teacher should not ask a child to read before an audience without allowing time for preparation, and, of course some presentations will demand more preparation than others.

Some examples of purposes for audience reading are:

1. Confirming an answer to a question by reading the portion of the selection in which the answer is found.
2. Reading aloud the part of an assigned story that is funniest or saddest or that tells about a particular person, thing, or event.
3. Reading a news story in which the class should be interested or background information for a topic of discussion from a reference or trade book.
4. Reading instructions to a person or group so that they can carry them out.
5. Making announcements or issuing invitations.
6. Reading the part of a character in a play or the narration for a play or other dramatic presentation.
7. Reading news for a school radio broadcast.
8. Sharing a part of a story, a poem (poems are written to be read aloud), or an experience story that the reader has enjoyed.
9. Participating in choral reading or readers' theater.

Audience reading should have a true audience; that is, there should be one or more people with whom the reader is attempting to communicate through reading. Audience members should not have access to the book from which the performer is reading and should not be allowed to follow the reading with their eyes. Instead, they should listen to the reader in order to grasp the author's meaning, or, if the reader is reading to prove a point, to agree or disagree. The reader must attempt to hold the audience's attention through oral interpretation of the author's words. A stumbling performance will lead to a restless, impatient audience and a poor listening situation.

Oral reading skills require special attention. The teacher may demonstrate good and poor oral reading, let the children analyze these performances, and then help students draw up a list of standards or guidelines such as the one that follows.

359

Literary
Appreciation
and
Recreational
Reading

1. Be sure you can pronounce each word correctly before you read your selection to an audience. If you are not sure of a pronunciation, check the dictionary or ask for help.
2. Say each word clearly and distinctly. Don't run words together, and take care not to leave out word parts or to add parts to words.
3. Pause in the right places. Pay attention to punctuation clues.
4. Emphasize important words. Help the audience understand the meaning of the selection by the way you read it. Read slowly enough to allow for adequate expression and speak loudly enough to be easily heard.
5. Prepare carefully before you read to an audience.

Possible activities for developing good audience reading include the following.

1. Give the children opportunities to listen to good readers. Be a good model by preparing diligently before reading literature selections to the class. Good models are also available on tape recordings.
2. Let the children listen to tapes of their own oral reading efforts and analyze their own performances, using the class-developed guidelines.
3. Discuss the reading clues offered by punctuation marks and give the children practice in interpreting these marks in short selections or single sentences.
4. Discuss how voice inflection helps to convey meaning. Have the children say "She is going" in a way that indicates a fact, that denotes dislike of the idea, that emphasizes that the action will be taken, and that shows happiness about the information.
5. Give special attention to reading poetry in a way that avoids a singsong effect. Emphasize the value of punctuation marks for this purpose.

Several sources of material for helping children with specific oral reading skills are available; a sample page from one source is presented below.

▶ **EXAMPLE 8.3:** Sample Oral Reading Exercise

Using Your Voice in Oral Reading
Here are some sentences that have contrasts. Read one pair of sentences. See how the second sentence differs from the first. Make sure your voice changes to show the contrast.

1. The roaring wind banged the door shut.
   A gentle breeze drifted softly by.
2. The giant pounded his fist on the table.
   A wee fairy flitted to the rosebud.

360

Teaching
Reading in
Today's
Elementary
Schools

3. The bass drum boomed like thunder.
   The silver bells tinkled softly.

4. The Indian slipped silently through the trees.
   The speeding car crashed into the bridge.

5. The great clock boomed out the hours.
   The tiny watch ticked gently and steadily.

6. The girls tiptoed past the sickroom door.
   The shouting boys dived with a great splash.

7. The sneaky cat crept up on the birds.
   The elephant crashed through the brush.

Source: Mildred Dawson and Georgiana Newman, *Oral Reading and Linguistics*, Book 3, "Loud and Clear," p. 41. Westchester, Ill.: Benefic Press, 1969. ◀

✔ Self-Check: Objective 8

List the purposes for having children read aloud that seem most important to you.

(See Self-Improvement Opportunity 11.)

Responding through Drama

The dramatic process includes such activities as

1. pantomiming story situations.
2. characterizing objects or persons.
3. improvising situations and dramatizing stories.
4. reading and creating plays (and use of aids, such as puppets).
5. readers' theater.
6. reading/speaking choral verse.

Through the ages, communication has taken place through body actions. Movement stories or poems delight children and pantomiming is one way of dramatizing through movement. Beginning with simple activities such as being a toad under a mushroom, it can then progress to pantomimes involving the cooperation of several children. Since young children usually know some nursery rhymes when they enter school, these rhymes can be used for pantomime. It's fun to be Jack or Jill and run up the hill, to be Little Bo Peep looking for her sheep, or to be the scary spider chasing Miss Muffet away from her tuffet. Fables (such as Aesop's) are also good for a group to act out, as are folktales like *Little Red Riding Hood*.

Teachers can focus on characterization (being an animal or another person) by asking children to interpret the giant in *Jack and the Beanstalk*. How does he

361

Literary
Appreciation
and
Recreational
Reading

Drama activities—including reading and acting out plays—can be wonderful motivational experiences for children.　(© Donald C. Dietz/Stock, Boston)

walk? What kind of person is he? How old is he? What would his facial expressions be like? What is his relationship with the other characters in the story?

Acting without a script is called improvisation or creative dramatics. For example, children may use dialogue as they pretend to be (in order) the Three Billy Goats Gruff crossing the bridge.

One of the most advanced drama experiences for children is dramatizing parts of stories, books, or poems—in the primary years, works such as *The Three Bears,* and at the intermediate level, Washington Irving's *Rip Van Winkle.* The children must have the main points of the story in mind and understand the main characters and the setting of the story.

Puppets—either simple hand puppets that the children have made, in which the head is moved by the index finger and the arms by the third finger and thumb, or rod puppets, controlled by one or more rigid rods to which the puppet is attached—are very useful for presenting plays. Puppets may be constructed from a paper sack, Styrofoam, a rubber ball, papier-mâché, an old sock, fruits or vegetables, a stick, and so on. Tape-recording the script as the children read it (or act it out) and then playing it during the puppet performance may help some children concentrate on hand movements until they can coordinate both speaking and manipulating the puppets.

Reluctant readers are often motivated by the use of readers' theater in which the performers, with scripts in hand, read aloud in a dramatic style. It is

362

Teaching
Reading in
Today's
Elementary
Schools

quite simple to produce. Select a story, a poem, a scene from a play—one or a combination of several forms of literature with a theme or mood such as animals, holidays, heroes, sports—and make up the script, asking all participants to explore for suitable material. Groups read the choices and decide what will create a well-rounded program. Add a few clever hats for fun and simple musical instruments (cymbal, triangle, and so on) for dramatic effects. The readers become characters in the story, and as they change character, they change their hats and often their voices. No costumes or stage sets are needed, and the lines are read.

An important feature of readers' theater is that any number can participate, from as few as two or three to as many as twenty-five or thirty. If an entire class is involved, divide it into groups, each to present one segment of a story or a complete program.

Through readers' theater, reluctant readers make contact with literature in a rewarding way. Easy-to-read stories are often used and in many instances are preferable for dramatization, and rehearsal is reading practice with a purpose. In addition, children learn to interpret character and to pool ideas.

Another form of drama is choral reading/speaking. One of the simplest kinds is echoic verse. In this form of drama the reader says a line and the audience repeats it, word for word, intonation for intonation, and sometimes even action for action. Echoic activities have some advantages over other forms of choral reading since members of the audience do not need copies of the text. A couple of examples of poems that lend themselves well to echoic treatment are "The Mysterious Cat" by Vachel Lindsay and "The Night Will Never Stay" by Eleanor Farjeon.

Among the various types of choral reading/speaking arrangements are:

Line-a-child. Each child reads one or two lines individually. When the climax is reached, a few lines may be read in unison. "The Death of Cock Robin" is a good choice.

Refrain: One individual reads or speaks the narrative part and the whole group joins in on the refrain. Example:

> "Never, No Never"

Leader: Did you ever see an elephant
       Sitting in a tree?
Group: Never, no never, no never.
Leader: Did you ever see a rooster
       Swimming in the sea?
Group: Never, no never, no never.
Leader: Did you ever see a dog
       Carry doughnuts on his tail?
Group: Never, no never, no never.
Leader: Did you ever see a cat
       With green spots on his back?
Group: Never, no never, no never.

363

Literary
Appreciation
and
Recreational
Reading

Leader: Did you ever see a monkey
       Striped all pink and black?
Group: Never, no never, no never.
Leader: Did you ever see the mailman
       Bring milk instead of mail?
Group: Never, no never, no never.

Author Unknown

Two-part or *antiphonal:* Two groups of children are involved, such as boys and girls, light voices and deep voices, or questions and answers. Example:

"Cats"
Group 1: "Pussycat, pussycat, where have you been?"
Group 2: "I've been to London to look at the Queen."
Group 1: "Pussycat, pussycat, what did you there?"
Group 2: "I frightened a little mouse under a chair."

Author Unknown

✔ Self-Check: Objective 9

What are four types of choral reading? Consider ways that you might want to use choral reading in your classroom.

Reacting to Poetry

In addition to listening with appreciation and participating in choral reading, students can respond to poetry through music, art, and dramatization. Children may tape-record their own readings of poems or share poetry in small groups, or some students may wish to make their own illustrated poetry booklets or contribute to a class poetry notebook.

Another way to help children react to poetry is to encourage them to write their own poetry according to a pattern. Usually students listen to several examples of a particular type of poetry to become familiar with the pattern, then dictate one or two poems as a whole class for the teacher to write on the board. Some patterns are given below.

A *cinquain* is a simple five-lined poem that has the following structure (Burns and Broman, 1979):
Line 1: one word, giving title
Line 2: two words, describing title
Line 3: three words, expressing action
Line 4: four words, expressing a feeling in a phrase
Line 5: one word, repeating title or giving synonym for title.

Haiku is a short three-lined Japanese poem with seventeen syllables—five in the first line, seven in the second line, and five in the third line. It should capture a moment or an image in relation to nature or the seasons of the year.

364

Teaching
Reading in
Today's
Elementary
Schools

Limericks are five-lined poems with the following rhyme scheme:

_____	A
_____	A
_____ B	
_____ B	
_____	A

A *parody* is a contemporary version of a familiar poem, often from Mother Goose.

Responding Through Creative Writing or Art

As we have pointed out, children can respond creatively to literature in many ways, including through creative writing. Some ideas are given below.

ACTIVITIES

1. Let the students write a class newspaper on one of these themes: (a) news stories that are modern adaptations of fairy tales and Mother Goose rhymes, (b) a newspaper written at the same time and place as the setting of the book that the teacher is reading, or (c) a literary digest of news about books. Children may compose advertisements for favorite books to place in the newspaper.
2. Direct the students to write a class book, either a collection of short stories or a series of chapters about the adventures of an unusual character created by the class. Students may wish to check about getting the book bound at a local printing shop.
3. Ask the children to prepare an annotated list of their favorite books and then get together with other students, alphabetize the complete list, and compile a class bibliography for other students to use.
4. Ask students to collect as many Newbery Award books and Honor books (runners-up to Award books) as they can find, read several of them, and ask their friends to read others. After making up and filling out an evaluation checklist for each book, with criteria such as characterization, author's style, authenticity of setting, and plot development, they may add to the checklist comments about the merit of each book.
5. Encourage students to write a radio or television script based on a story. First they should read some plays to become familiar with directions for staging and appropriate writing style for dialogue.
6. Let the students write a different ending for a story or complete an unfinished story.

Stories can be interpreted through many art media: clay, paint, papier-mâché, scraps of felt and ribbon, or collage. Four specific ways of responding to literature through art are suggested here.

ACTIVITIES

365

Literary
Appreciation
and
Recreational
Reading

1. *Murals* are designed around a central theme: a scene from a story, a parade of characters, a series of episodes, or a synthesis of popular characters in an "animal fantasy" (Huck, 1979, pp. 649–50). For example, *A Tree is Nice,* by Janice Udry, would be a good basis for a mural that shows many kinds of trees. With the aid of the teacher, children plan how their mural will look; then each child sketches one part and attaches it to the appropriate place to get a general idea of the total effect. When they are satisfied with the plan, the children begin drawing with crayon, chalk, or tempera paint.

2. As with murals, *mobiles* begin with a theme and a plan for developing that theme. Tiny objects or two-dimensional cutouts of characters are attached to nylon thread, fishing line, or fine wire and are suspended from rods or some sort of frame. The balancing rods may be cut from metal coat hangers, or students can use a tree branch or umbrella frame for support. The mobile must be carefully balanced so that objects can move freely. Children might draw monsters from Maurice Sendak's *Where the Wild Things Are,* color them on both sides, cut them out, and fasten them to a mobile.

3. Students can make a *box movie,* or a series of drawings that represent scenes from a story, by drawing the scenes on a roll of shelf paper or on individual sheets of manila paper that are fastened together in sequence. The paper is attached at both ends to rods and rolled around one rod like a scroll. Then the roll is placed inside a box that has an opening the size of one frame. A student turns the rollers as the narrator tells the story. For instance, children could depict *Julie of the Wolves,* by Jean George, by showing Julie's developing relationship with the wolves, one scene at a time.

4. *Time lines* are drawn on long, narrow strips of paper to show time relationships within stories or of events. Each interval on the time line represents a specified span of time. Students can also make a *map* from the description of the setting of almost any story, such as one tracing the route of the slave ship in Paula Fox's *The Slave Dancer.*

✔ Self-Check: Objective 10

Recall some books that were your favorites when you were a child. What types of response to literature would be appropriate to use with these books?
(See Self-Improvement Opportunities 11 and 12.)

Responding at Learning Centers

Basically, a learning center is a collection of activities related to a central theme. Its physical arrangement should be attractive and practical but can vary according to the amount of space, the kinds of materials, and the locations available. Usually teachers place record-keeping forms at learning centers so that they can keep track of which children are completing certain

366

Teaching
Reading in
Today's
Elementary
Schools

activities. Ideally, learning centers should offer children choices so that they may select those activities that appeal to them most. Sometimes teachers must limit participation to a certain number of pupils at any one time, and it may be necessary to schedule times in advance. Not all children should be required to participate in every center, but they should be given the opportunity to work there if they wish.

It is a good idea to use one center in the classroom for literature all year long, with a permanent collection of cards for students to use independently. A sample card is shown in Example 8.4. Introduce special themes periodically to encourage students to react critically to certain types of literature. Such themes might include

a study of mythology.
a comparison of biographical books about a famous person.
an investigation of the history of children's books.
an analysis of authors' styles of writing.
a study of a particular author and his or her works.

▶ **EXAMPLE 8.4** Learning Center Card

CREATIVE WRITING   Independent Work

Many Moons, James Thurber, Harcourt Brace Jovanovich, 1943.

A young princess desires the moon, and the king sends for his wise men for help. It is the court jester, however, who solves the problem with the princess's help.

Choose one idea and write a story about it.

1. Imagine you are the Royal Magician. How would you keep Princess Lenore from seeing the moon?
2. Make a list of the things you would tell the king you had done for him if you were the Royal Magician.
3. Who was the cleverest of the king's assistants? Why do you think so?

Activities built around the theme of "Judy Blume and Her Books" are provided in Example 8.5 as a model for a literature center. We selected this theme because of Judy Blume's great popularity with intermediate-level readers. Her books contain humor, insight into the feelings of young adolescents, characters with whom readers can identify, and a straightforward treatment of contemporary issues. To use the center, students need multiple copies of several of Blume's books.

Directions: Read several Judy Blume books and think about them. Then read the activities at the literature center and choose two or more from each category. Keep your work in a file folder at the center. You may wish to work with other readers.

A. *About the Author*
  1. Write a letter to Judy Blume in care of the publisher and ask her
     a. Why did you become a writer?
     b. Are the characters real people?
     c. How do you know so much about how we feel?
     d. Whatever you would like to know.
  2. Name a theme that you would like Judy Blume to write about next.
     a. Write a paragraph suggesting a story line.
     b. Describe what you think the main character would be like.
  3. Find out all you can about Judy Blume. Consult magazine articles, books about authors, and information on book jackets. Then
     a. design a bulletin-board display using book jackets, a picture of Judy Blume, and interesting facts about her life.
     b. make an illustrated booklet containing reviews of her books and information about her background as a writer.
     c. prepare a presentation about her and her books to give to another class.
  4. Prepare a mock interview with Judy Blume for radio or television. After you have rehearsed it, present it to the class.
  5. Plan a panel discussion or debate with other Blume readers about whether or not authors should write on the kinds of themes that Judy Blume chooses.

B. *About the Books*
  1. Make a collage of magazine pictures related to the themes in Judy Blume's books.
  2. Choose favorite scenes from Blume's books. Find others who have read the same books and act out the scenes for your class.
  3. Write diary entries for five consecutive days in the life of one of the characters.
  4. Identify the theme for each book you read. Then relate these themes to yourself and people you know.
  5. Predict what the characters in the books you have read will be doing in five or ten years.
  6. Think about the characters and choose one to be your friend. Give reasons for your choice. Is there someone you would not like for a friend? If so, why?
  7. Should Judy Blume's books be translated into other languages for boys and girls in other countries to read? Why or why not?
  8. Create a television commercial to advertise one or more of Blume's books. You may want to include a musical jingle.
  9. Could one of Blume's books be made into a television series? Consider possible story lines and audience reactions.

368

Teaching
Reading in
Today's
Elementary
Schools

10. Make riddles of character descriptions for others to guess.
11. Make and play a game of Concentration using book titles and character names from Judy Blume's books.
12. Choose one book that several of you have read and talk about all the emotions or feelings that are discussed in the book. Make a list.

C. *About Specific Books*
  1. *Freckle Juice* (New York: Four Winds Press, 1971).
      a. Make up your own recipe for freckle juice.
      b. How would you like to change your appearance? What difference would it make? How important is appearance?
  2. *Then Again, Maybe I Won't* (Scarsdale, N.Y.: Bradbury Press, 1971).
      a. How would you feel if you suddenly became rich? poor?
      b. What problems was Tony facing in growing up?
  3. *Blubber* (Scarsdale, N.Y.: Bradbury Press, 1974).
      a. Write a page in Blubber's diary expressing her feelings about being fat.
      b. Suggest ways that Blubber could have defended herself.
  4. *Are You There God? It's Me, Margaret* (Scarsdale, N.Y.: Bradbury Press, 1970).
      a. What kind of relationship does Margaret have with God? How does her relationship compare with yours?
      b. What were some of the problems that Margaret had in moving to a new place? Make a list of the problems you might face if you moved. ◄

Participating in a Literature Unit

To help children appreciate a certain aspect of literature, a teacher can plan a unit around a story. The unit might actually replace basal reader instruction for a time, or it might be taught in addition to the basal reader, perhaps near the end of the school day. Such a unit might involve children in a number of related language arts skills, as in the following example. In it children read, report (orally and in written form), tell stories, write creatively, listen, learn new vocabulary words, and do research. At the same time they are learning to appreciate fables, folklore, fairy tales, legends, and myths.

ACTIVITIES FOR A UNIT ON FOLKLORE

1. Let children read and compare folktale variants, beginning with the Brothers Grimm tales and moving toward contemporary versions. (Reference source: *Household Stories*, New York: McGraw-Hill, 1966).
2. Encourage children to tell stories, repeating familiar favorites or creating new tales.
3. Read and/or tell classic folktales to the students.
4. Provide opportunities for discovering word origins and literary allusions, especially in myths (examples: echo, Pandora's box, Mercury, Atlas).

5. Let children dramatize folktales using puppets, pantomime, readers' theater, and creative dramatics.
6. Encourage children to write creatively. Have them
   a. study the characteristics of a fable (brevity, animal characters, a moral) and create new fables.
   b. write modern versions of fairy tales.
   c. make up a ballad based on folklore and set it to music.
   d. make up original *pourquoi* tales, such as "Why the Rabbit Has Long Ears."
   e. write new endings for fairy tales after changing a major event in the story, such as having the First Little Pig build his house out of stone and the Third Little Pig build his house out of spaghetti.
   f. select a newspaper story, find a moral for it (example: Theft doesn't pay), and write a fable about this moral.
7. Help students find out how folktales were originally communicated and how they came to be written.
8. Invite storytellers for children to listen to. Ask students to interview the storytellers about techniques and about the origins of the tales they tell.
9. Encourage students to compare similarities in characters and motifs of folktales from around the world (examples: the Jackal in India, the Weasel in Africa, and Brer Rabbit in the United States).

369

Literary
Appreciation
and
Recreational
Reading

Working With Support Personnel

Teachers and librarians should work together to use the library's resources both to reinforce subject matter and to encourage students to read for pleasure. By suggesting books and materials that will complement units of study and relate to the interests of their students, teachers work with librarians. By introducing new books, presenting stories to the class, and showing students how to use the library, librarians cooperate with teachers. In one program the teachers and the librarian work together to find books to use for individualized reading and classroom learning centers (Noyce, 1979).

In an all-school oral literature program coordinated by a media specialist, teachers select a theme around which four units are planned for the year (Boothroy and Donham, 1981). The media specialist helps teachers select books for reading aloud in keeping with the theme, and students make first, second, and third choices of unit topics. Each unit meets for two twenty-five-minute periods per week for nine weeks. At oral literature time groups of children visit the rooms of teachers to whom they have been assigned for the nine-week period. The teacher reads aloud from a book and leads a discussion about it during the session, asking children to respond creatively through art, drama, or writing projects.

Parents and the community should also be part of a school's literature program. If they realize the value of literature in their child's reading program, parents can encourage him or her to read for pleasure. Parent-teacher organizations can sponsor programs to review children's books and maga-

370

Teaching
Reading in
Today's
Elementary
Schools

zines that might be unfamiliar to parents and to suggest ways in which parents can provide a home atmosphere that promotes interest in reading. Parents or members of the community might also like to join children during an SSR or storytelling session; some nonschool personnel may be excellent storytellers or have books that they are willing to contribute. The school, the home, and the community can work together to encourage recreational reading.

Test Yourself

True or False

_____ 1. Children's literature can be a part of the entire curriculum.

_____ 2. The major purpose of teaching literature is to enable children to know the titles and authors of children's books.

_____ 3. A book's theme is the overall plan for the story.

_____ 4. Style is the author's mode of expressing thoughts in words.

_____ 5. A major purpose in teaching children how to read novels is to stress knowledge of facts.

_____ 6. Children should analyze poetry in depth at the elementary level.

_____ 7. When reading aloud, teachers should speak in natural tones and with expression.

_____ 8. Children who like to read usually enjoy reading realistic fiction and biographies.

_____ 9. Selection aids are people who advise librarians about which books to order.

_____ 10. The Newbery Award is for excellence in illustration.

_____ 11. Easy-to-read books are high-quality literature for children.

_____ 12. The RIF program is an inexpensive book-distribution program.

_____ 13. Many good children's magazines are being published.

_____ 14. TV tie-ins are copies of television scripts.

_____ 15. The classroom environment has little or no effect on recreational reading.

_____ 16. SSR is a Russian reading program.

_____ 17. Book fairs offer children opportunities to buy books and enjoy book-related activities.

_____ 18. Among good ways of motivating children to read books are required reading lists and formal book reports.

_____ 19. Since audience reading is an exercise in communication, it therefore demands a real audience.

_____ 20. In readers' theater the performers read aloud from their scripts in a dramatic style.

_____ 21. Choral reading is a useful activity for developing oral reading skills.

_____ 22. Children in the elementary school should not be expected to write any type of poetry.

_____ 23. Parents, librarians, and the community should all support the reading program.

Vocabulary

Check your knowledge of these terms. Reread parts of the chapter if necessary.

antiphonal choral reading	echoic verse	readers' theater
book-recording device	genre	recreational reading
Caldecott Medal	haiku	selection aids
characterization	improvisation	setting
choral reading/speaking	limerick	style
cinquain	Newbery Award	Sustained Silent Reading
creative dramatics	pantomime	theme
diorama	plot	trade books

Self-Improvement Opportunities

1. Think of some ways to use children's literature to enrich each area of the curriculum. Then choose one subject and find three books that you could use to supplement the textbook.
2. Become familiar with a children's book. Then do one of the following:
   a. Make a lesson plan for teaching its literary elements.
   b. Make a card to use in leading a class discussion.
   c. Make a card for students to use independently at a learning center.
3. Find an example of each literary form described in this chapter. Read one of them and make a list of questions to use in teaching it to children.
4. Select a read-aloud story for an age level of your choice. Then share it with a small group of children or your peers. Tape your reading and evaluate it.
5. After thinking about the best time of day for reading orally to a class, choose a grade level that you would like to teach and make a list of books that you would like to read aloud to your class.
6. Ask children to name their favorite books and see if some books are named by several children. If you have a chance, administer an interest inventory to these children to find out their reading interests.
7. Ask a child to evaluate a book by answering questions that you have prepared. Then see if your own evaluation agrees with the child's analysis.

372

Teaching
Reading in
Today's
Elementary
Schools

8. Find a selection aid and analyze its usefulness in helping you choose appropriate books for an elementary classroom.
9. Find copies of children's magazines and choose two or three that you would like for your classroom. Write a brief review of each.
10. List five techniques that you would like to use for motivating children to read for pleasure.
11. With some other students, make up a list of creative ways for children to report on books.
12. Find a group of children to work with you and make one of the four special art projects described in this chapter.

Bibliography

Blatt, Gloria T. "Playing with Language." *The Reading Teacher* 31 (February 1978): 487–93.

Boothroy, Bonnie, and Jean Donham. "Listening to Literature: An All-School Program." *The Reading Teacher* 34 (April 1981): 772–74.

Burke, Eileen M. "Using Trade Books to Intrigue Children with Words." *The Reading Teacher* 32 (November 1978): 144–48.

Burns, Paul C., and Betty L. Broman. *The Language Arts in Childhood Education.* 5th ed. Boston: Houghton-Mifflin, 1983, p. 210.

Busch, Jackie S. "Television's Effects on Reading: A Case Study." *Phi Delta Kappan* 59 (June 1978): 668–71.

Carbo, Marie. "Making Books Talk to Children." *The Reading Teacher* 35 (November 1981): 186–91.

Huck, Charlotte S. *Children's Literature in the Elementary School.* 3rd ed. updated. New York: Holt, Rinehart and Winston, 1979, pp. 549, 649–50.

Koeller, Shirley. "25 Years Advocating Children's Literature in the Reading Program." *The Reading Teacher* 34 (February 1981): 552–55.

Koenke, Karl. "ERIC/RCS: The Careful Use of Comic Books." *The Reading Teacher* 34 (February 1981): 592–95.

Noyce, Ruth M. "Team Up and Teach with Trade Books." *The Reading Teacher* 32 (January 1979): 442–48.

Peterson, Gordon, and Patrick Groff. "Behavioral Objectives for Children's Literature? Yes! No!" *The Reading Teacher* 30 (March 1977): 652–55.

Radebaugh, Muriel Rogie. "Using Children's Literature to Teach Mathematics." *The Reading Teacher* 34 (May 1981): 902–906.

Stewig, John Warren. *Children and Literature.* Chicago: Rand McNally, 1980.

Whitehead, Robert. *Children's Literature: Strategies of Teaching.* Englewood Cliffs, N.J.: Prentice-Hall, 1968, pp. 37–44.

Wright, Gary. "The Comic Book—A Forgotten Medium in the Classroom." *The Reading Teacher* 33 (November 1979): 158–61.

Butler, Francelia. *Sharing Literature with Children.* New York: David McKay, 1977.

Coody, Betty. *Using Literature with Young Children.* 2nd ed. Dubuque, Iowa: William C. Brown, 1979.

Coody, Betty, and David Nelson. *Teaching Elementary Language Arts: A Literature Approach.* Belmont, Calif.: Wadsworth, 1982.

Glazer, Joan I., and Gurney Williams III. *Introduction to Children's Literature.* New York: McGraw-Hill, 1979.

Lonsdale, Bernard J., and Helen K. Mackintosh. *Children Experience Literature.* New York: Random House, 1973.

Lukens, Rebecca J. *A Critical Handbook of Children's Literature.* Glenview, Ill.: Scott, Foresman, 1976.

Reasoner, Charles F. *Releasing Children to Literature.* Rev. ed. New York: Dell, 1976.

Rudman, Masha Kabakow. *Children's Literature: An Issues Approach.* Lexington, Mass.: D. C. Heath, 1976.

Sale, Roger. *Fairy Tales and After.* Cambridge, Mass.: Harvard University Press, 1979.

Sebesta, Sam Leaton, and William J. Iverson. *Literature for Thursday's Child.* Chicago: Science Research Associates, 1975.

Smith, James A., and Dorothy M. Park. *Word Music and Word Magic.* Boston: Allyn and Bacon, 1977.

Somers, Albert B., and Janet Evans Worthington. *Response Guides for Teaching Children's Books.* Urbana, Ill.: National Council of Teachers of English, 1979.

Sutherland, Zena, et al. *Children and Books.* 6th ed. Glenview, Ill.: Scott, Foresman, 1981.

Tiedt, Iris M. *Exploring Books with Children.* Boston: Houghton Mifflin, 1979.

CHAPTER APPENDIX: CHILDREN'S BOOKS CITED IN CHAPTER 8

Alcott, Louisa May. *Little Women.* Boston: Little, Brown, 1868.

Alexander, Martha. *Nobody Asked Me If I Wanted a Baby Sister.* New York: Dial, 1971.

Aliki. *The Story of Johnny Appleseed.* Englewood Cliffs, N.J.: Prentice-Hall, 1963.

Ashbjornsen, Peter Christian, and Jorgen E. Moe. *The Three Billy Goats Gruff.* New York: Harcourt, Brace and World, 1957.

Bemelmans, Ludwig. *Madeline.* New York: Viking, 1962.

374

Teaching
Reading in
Today's
Elementary
Schools

Blos, Joan. *A Gathering of Days: A New England Girl's Journal, 1830–32.* New York: Scribner's, 1979.

Blume, Judy. *It's Not the End of the World.* Scarsdale, N.Y.: Bradbury, 1972.

Brink, Carol. *Caddie Woodlawn.* New York: Macmillan, 1936.

Burnford, Sheila. *The Incredible Journey.* Boston: Little, Brown, 1961.

Byars, Betsy. *Summer of the Swans.* New York: Viking, 1970.

Cleaver, Vera, and Bill Cleaver. *Where the Lilies Bloom.* Philadelphia: Lippincott, 1973.

Collodi, Carlo. *Pinocchio.* New York: Franklin Watts, 1967.

Dalgliesh, Alice. *The Courage of Sarah Noble.* New York: Charles Scribner's Sons, 1954.

Daugherty, James. *Daniel Boone.* New York: Viking, 1932.

De Angeli, Marguerite. *The Door in the Wall.* New York: Doubleday, 1949.

Feuerlecht, Roberta Strauss. *The Legends of Paul Bunyan.* New York: Macmillan, 1966.

Fox, Paula. *The Slave Dancer.* Scarsdale, N.Y.: Bradbury, 1974.

Froman, Robert. *Bigger and Smaller.* New York: Crowell, 1971.

Galdone, Paul. *The Gingerbread Boy.* New York: Seabury, 1973.

George, Jean. *Julie of the Wolves.* New York: Harper & Row, 1973.

Gwynne, Fred. *A Chocolate Moose for Dinner.* New York: Dutton, 1973.

Hanlon, Emily. *How a Horse Grew Hoarse on the Site Where He Sighted a Bare Bear.* New York: Delacorte, 1976.

Irving, Washington. *Rip Van Winkle and the Legend of Sleepy Hollow.* New York: Macmillan (*The Sketch Book,* 1819).

Lawson, Robert. *Rabbit Hill.* New York: Viking, 1944.

L'Engle, Madeleine. *A Wrinkle in Time.* New York: Farrar, Strauss, 1962.

Lindgren, Astrid. *Pippi Longstocking.* New York: Viking, 1950.

O'Brien, Robert C. *Mrs. Frisby and the Rats of NIMH.* New York: Atheneum, 1971.

O'Dell, Scott. *Island of the Blue Dolphins.* Boston: Houghton Mifflin, 1960.

Parish, Peggy. *Amelia Bedelia.* New York: Harper & Row, 1963.

Phillips, Jo. *Right Angles: Paper-Folding Geometry.* New York: Crowell, 1972.

Sendak, Maurice. *In the Night Kitchen.* New York: Harper & Row, 1970.

Sendak, Maurice. *Where the Wild Things Are.* New York: Harper & Row, 1964.

Silverstein, Shel. *The Light in the Attic.* New York: Harper & Row, 1981.

Silverstein, Shel. *Where the Sidewalk Ends.* New York: Harper & Row, 1974.

Speare, Elizabeth. *The Bronze Bow.* Boston: Houghton Mifflin, 1961.

Steig, William. *CDB.* New York: Simon and Schuster, 1968.

Steptoe, John. *Stevie.* New York: Harper & Row, 1969.

Tolkien, J. R. R.   *The Hobbit*. Boston: Houghton Mifflin, 1938.

Tresselt, Alvin.   *White Snow, Bright Snow*. New York: Lothrop, 1947.

Twain, Mark.   *The Adventures of Huckleberry Finn*. New York: Harper & Row, 1884.

Udry, Janice.   *A Tree is Nice*. New York: Harper & Row, 1957.

White, E. B.   *Charlotte's Web*. New York: Harper & Row, 1952.

Wildsmith, Brian.   *Brian Wildsmith's 1, 2, 3's*. New York: Franklin Watts, 1965.

375

Literary
Appreciation
and
Recreational
Reading

CHAPTER 9

Assessment of
Pupil Progress

Introduction

Assessing children's mastery of what is being or has been taught is indispensable to good teaching and is frequently an integral part of instructional procedure. Such a statement as "Doing these exercises will give you an opportunity to see how well you can read and interpret tables" illustrates the close relationship between instruction and evaluation. Some evaluative procedures, however, are less easily identified with instruction. These consist of tests administered near or at the end of a unit of work and of standardized (and other) tests designed to measure pupil achievement at any particular time.

This chapter is divided into three major parts. The first is concerned with informal (nonstandardized) assessment procedures and devices; the second is concerned with norm-referenced (standardized) assessment instruments; and the third with criterion-referenced tests. Samples of different kinds of tests are provided throughout the chapter, and the purposes and uses of various assessment devices and instruments are discussed. By knowing what the child needs, the teacher will know what to teach. Therefore, as is further explained in Chapter 11, adjusting instruction in the light of appropriate information makes all the difference. Teachers must assess pupils frequently to detect the ongoing changes in their achievement. They must not consider assessment a once- or twice-a-year practice.

Among kinds of assessment procedures that a teacher will find useful are diagnosing specific reading skills on a day-by-day basis as reading instruction proceeds; determining the appropriate level of reading instruction for each individual in a class; judging each student's potential reading level; and assessing general reading achievement and areas of strengths and weaknesses in a class.

Setting Objectives

When you finish reading this chapter, you should be able to

1. Know how to assess the following reading skills informally: sight vocabulary, word attack, comprehension, study, and oral reading.
2. Evaluate the development of literary interests.
3. Explain how to use a graded word list to determine reading level.
4. Construct and interpret an Informal Reading Inventory (IRI) to find a child's reading level.
5. Name several ways to assess a child's ability to read content materials.
6. Recognize and analyze the significance of a reading miscue.
7. Describe tests for different aspects of reading readiness.
8. Use norm-referenced reading survey tests effectively.

378

Teaching
Reading in
Today's
Elementary
Schools

9. Describe the types and content of some norm-referenced tests.
10. Determine a reading expectancy level.
11. Identify some limitations of norm-referenced reading tests.
12. Differentiate between a norm-referenced and a criterion-referenced test.

INFORMAL (NONSTANDARDIZED) ASSESSMENT

In the day-to-day program, the classroom teacher will necessarily depend more upon informal assessment devices than formal assessment instruments. (Formal instruments are commercially available tests that have been standardized against a specific norm or objective.) In simple terms, this means that the effective teacher is observing and recording individual strengths and weaknesses during the educational process in order to adjust instruction to meet individual needs.

Assessment of Specific Skill Areas

Reading Readiness Skills

The importance of assessing a child's readiness for reading is discussed in Chapter 2. Here we suggest some types of informal assessment.

1. The teacher can create his or her own informal checklist of readiness skills and behaviors. He or she can make several copies of this checklist for each pupil, keeping them in individual file folders. By filling out the forms periodically, being sure to date each one, the teacher has a written record of each child's progress. In creating such a checklist a teacher might use criteria similar to those identified in the Clymer-Barrett Prereading Rating Scale shown in Example 9.8 on page 411.
2. It is possible to evaluate a child's readiness for any type of prereading skill through use of informal activities designed for that purpose. For example, naming the pictures on charts of people, animals, or things gives an indication of the extent of the student's vocabulary. Teachers can use sets of word pairs (such as *wall, fall,* and *cat, can*) to ask the child which rhyme and which do not, or alphabet cards (of capital letters and lower case letters) to assess progress toward alphabet reading.
3. Story retelling is useful for evaluating the language of students. After the teacher tells a short story to an individual student in a quiet setting, each child retells it into a tape recorder. This method also tests a child's ability to organize, comprehend, and express connected speech under controlled conditions (Pickert and Chase, 1978).

4. To assess children's prereading phonics abilities, use a prereading phonics inventory, such as the one designed by Durrell and Murphy (1978), which tests pupils' ability to recognize and write letters and their awareness of letter names. Children are asked to match spoken words with words in print.
5. Anecdotal records, or detailed running accounts of a child's activities, are useful in analyzing a child's social-emotional readiness, language development, interests, and attitudes. A teacher may focus attention on one child for a period of time and jot down exactly what the child is doing at each moment—sitting, walking, playing, talking, watching, listening, or looking at a book. These records may be kept in a file along with checklists and samples of the child's work.

Sight Vocabulary

In the case of a child who has had little reading experience, teachers may find file cards (3″ × 5″) useful. The cards should be numbered and arranged in the same order as the words on a test sheet, and the examiner should keep a copy of the test sheet with a record of words the child misses. If a teacher uses a test sheet in place of cards, the child should place a cardboard marker under each word as he or she proceeds down the page. Both the child and the examiner should have copies of the test sheet.

1. The child is told to say the words he or she knows. As the correct response is given, the examiner checks the word on his or her own test sheet, writing in a miscalled word or the types of errors a child makes while trying to pronounce each word.
2. The child should pronounce each word immediately, with no hesitation. If he or she miscalls the word but corrects it before going on, write "C" in front of the word that was corrected.
3. If the child makes no effort on the word, point to or present the next word.
4. If a child makes any of the following efforts, do not give credit for knowing the word:
   a. miscalls or omits the word and then a word or more later comes back and gives it correctly,
   b. miscalls the word and gives more than one mistaken word before getting the correct one,
   c. hestitates longer than a few seconds before giving the word.
5. The child's score is the number of words checked.

Word Recognition

As we note later in the listing of norm-referenced reading tests, several formal measures of this aspect of reading are available. Informal assessment of the

380

Teaching
Reading in
Today's
Elementary
Schools

various skills and techniques that relate to word recognition are discussed below.

Context The teacher can observe the child figuring out the meanings of words from sentences such as the following, which illustrate different types of contextual clues.

A *dulcimer* is a musical instrument with wires stretched over a soundboard. (definition)

Fran likes to participate in sports, but I prefer being a *spectator*. (contrast)

I saw the *astronauts* go walking on the moon. (familiar—the child is already acquainted with the word, in this case through TV)

Please *cooperate* with your partner and help finish the work. (experience—the child is already acquainted with the idea through experience)

Noting the reactions of a child trying to identify the italicized words in these sentences, the teacher can ask the following questions:

1. Does the pupil rely primarily on phonics, context, or something else?
2. Does she use the entire sentence to help her figure out a word, or does she just stop to get help before having used all the clues?
3. Does her attitude toward an unknown word reflect confidence or frustration?

Other informal assessment procedures include

1. a cloze procedure, used on a basal reader or content passage to see if the child can use context clues to supply missing words or synonyms. (See Chapter 7.)
2. word recognition exercises at appropriate levels. These may provide no clues to word recognition other than context (example: Rather than being *drowsy* after the long trip, Sonia was wide awake), or they may provide other clues as well (example: The g___s looks very green). (For other ideas, see Chapters 3 and 4.)[1]

Phonics While several norm-referenced word-analysis tests are available,[2] teachers may informally measure phonic analysis abilities by asking children to identify initial, medial, and final sounds in words.

---

[1] For more on preparing checkups on context clues, see Janis E. Timian and Richard Santeusanio, "Context Clues: An Informal Inventory." *Reading Teacher* 27 (April 1974): 706–709.

[2] These include Paul McKee, *Inventory of Phonetic Skills: Tests One, Two* and *Three* (Boston: Houghton Mifflin), for grades 1, 2, and 3, and Constance M. McCullough, *McCullough Word Analysis Tests* (Boston: Ginn and Company, 1963), for grades 4, 5, and 6.

What is the first sound you hear in *book, toy, forest, part, kitchen?* What are the first two letters in these words: *fright, snake, skate, scales, praise, dwelling?*
What is the middle sound you hear in *cabbage, balloon, reading?*
What is the vowel with which each word begins: *Indian, olives, elephant, umbrella, apple?*

Moreover, teachers can prepare exercises for each of the phonic elements introduced to a group of children.

Element: consonant digraphs
Assessment: Ask the child to tell you what two consonants go together to make a new sound in the words
*sh*e   tee*th*   bea*ch*   *wh*at

A more comprehensive informal inventory of phonics skills is presented in Example 9.1, which could be given to an entire class at one time as a pretest or posttest to help determine what skills students have or have not learned. Students should be given an answer form with categories and numbers on it to use in recording their responses.

▶ **EXAMPLE 9.1:** Informal Phonics Inventory

I. CONSONANT SOUNDS (initial)
Directions: Write the beginning letter of each word I say.

1. hit	6. work
2. just	7. town
3. goose	8. lamp
4. punt	9. never
5. zest	10. fox

II. CONSONANT SOUNDS (final)
Directions: Write the last letter of each word I say.

1. tub	6. chalk
2. head	7. rug
3. chief	8. pen
4. glass	9. dog
5. hoop	10. arm

III. CONSONANT BLENDS (initial)
Directions: Write the first two letters of each word I say.

1. step	6. skate
2. bright	7. glum
3. spout	8. black
4. claw	9. frown
5. draw	10. slap

382

Teaching
Reading in
Today's
Elementary
Schools

IV. CONSONANT DIGRAPHS (initial)

Directions: Write the first two letters of each word I say.

1. then   3. chief
2. shout   4. photo

V. CONSONANT DIGRAPHS (final)

Directions: Write the last two letters of each word I say.

1. sing   3. dish
2. sick   4. cloth

VI. LONG AND SHORT VOWELS

Directions: If the vowel is short as I say a word, write *short* and the vowel. If it is long, write *long* and the vowel.

1. hit   6. red
2. ate   7. hat
3. me   8. cut
4. go   9. hot
5. mule   10. ice

VII. VOWEL DIGRAPHS AND DIPHTHONGS

Directions: Write the two vowels that go together to form a unit—such as *oo, oi, oy,* and *ou*—in each word I say.

1. taught   5. toy
2. saw   6. cow
3. food   7. book
4. oil   8. foul ◄

The results from this type of inventory indicate what kinds of skills individual students need to learn. Using these results, the teacher can help children master those skills by working with them individually or in small groups. He or she may need to clear up misconceptions or review skills that children have studied previously; then students should practice applying the studied skill in new situations. If several students are deficient in the same skill, the teacher should create a temporary skill or needs group so that several students can learn the skill at the same time. As each child masters the skill, he or she may leave the group, until the group no longer exists.

Generally, a student is considered to have adequate knowledge of a skill if he or she gets 75 percent to 80 percent of the answers correct in a particular category. A teacher might administer the informal phonics inventory in Example 9.1 and find the following information: all of the children got 75 to 80 percent of the answers correct in I, Consonant Sounds (initial), and II, Consonant Sounds (final). One child made only 60 percent in III, Consonant Blends, and another child made just 50 percent in IV, Consonant Digraphs (initial). Four children scored below 75 percent on V, Consonant Digraphs (final); eight children made below 80 percent on VI, Long and Short Vowels;

and only three children made 75 percent or more on VII, Vowel Digraphs and
Diphthongs. Using these results, the teacher knows that the two children who
scored below 75 percent in skill categories III and IV should receive
individualized instruction and be required to complete skill sheets for
practice. The students who did not make 75 percent in categories V and VI
should meet with the teacher in special skill groups until they understand the
skill. In category VII, where nearly all of the students missed too many items,
the teacher needs to teach most of the class. The three students who have
already mastered this last skill should be allowed to work independently
during this instructional time.

Teachers should apply this same diagnostic-prescriptive principle to other
types of reading instruction as well, first making an assessment, next
analyzing the results to see which students are weak in certain areas, and then
planning specific activities to help students reach a certain level of competence in these areas.

Structural Analysis Again, an informal performance checkup through
observation is a reliable means of collecting data. The teacher can provide a
series of sentences such as those shown below and have the child complete
them by adding a correct beginning or ending to the word in parentheses.

An umbrella is _____ on a rainy day. (need)
A baby is _____ to drive a car. (able)

Teachers can prepare and administer an informal structural-analysis
inventory in the same way as a phonics inventory. Consisting of exercises
related to prefixes and suffixes, inflectional endings, contractions, compound
words, and syllabication and accent, the inventory might resemble the one in
Example 9.2.

▶ **EXAMPLE 9.2:** Structural Analysis Inventory

Directions: Write the following parts of the words listed below.

prefix: unable	_____
suffix: painful	_____
root word: funny	_____
contraction for: do not	_____
words used in the contraction: we've	_____ _____
words forming the compound: pancake	_____ _____
words forming the compound: bookcase	_____ _____
each syllable: window	_____ _____
each syllable: arithmetic	_____ _____ _____ _____
each syllable: handle	_____ _____ ◀

384

Teaching
Reading in
Today's
Elementary
Schools

Dictionary Usage To assess a specific objective or element of instruction related to working with dictionaries, a teacher can give the children a list of unfamiliar words and ask them to look the words up in the dictionary and then pronounce them by using information derived from the dictionary. Possible words are

anathematize
bludgeon
chimerical
dishabille
eustachian

The location skills and the pronunciation skills needed to use a dictionary (discussed in Chapters 3 and 6) are important elements to test in ongoing checkups. For example, can the child alphabetize words as to the first, first two, first three letters? Can he or she use guide words as clues to alphabetical position? Can the child use the symbols in the pronunciation key?

A more comprehensive informal inventory of dictionary skills is presented in Example 9.3.

▶ **EXAMPLE 9.3:** Informal Dictionary Inventory

1. Look up the word_____. What are the two guide words found on the page on which you found the word?
2. What does the word_____mean?
3. In the dictionary, on what page is the pronunciation and meaning of the word_____found?
4. What synonyms are provided for the term_____?
5. What is the derivation of the word_____?
6. What part of speech is the term_____?
7. What diacritical marks are used in the phonetic spelling of_____?
8. What is the dictionary entry for the word_____?
9. How many syllables does this word have:_____?
10. Which syllable of_____receives a secondary emphasis?
11. What vowel sounds are given for each accented syllable for the word_____?
12. Which syllable of the word_____contains a schwa sound? ◀

Comprehension

To measure meaning or comprehension abilities, teachers can ask questions about a passage that the child has read silently.

1. Literal level—Ask identification questions, such as *who, what, when, where, how many.*
2. Interpretive level—Ask explanatory questions, such as *how, why.*
3. Critical level—Ask judgment or evaluation questions.

For more specific assessment of comprehension skills (such as discovering main ideas and specific facts, following sequences of events, drawing conclusions, reacting to mood, and the like), prepare an informal comprehension inventory by providing the child with passages to read and questions to answer. Teachers might use appropriately leveled or sequenced sets of materials, such as Richard Boning's series (1976), which covers the following eight skills, providing passages and questions of varying difficulty:

1. locating the answer
2. drawing conclusions
3. following directions
4. getting the main idea
5. detecting the sequence
6. getting the facts
7. using the context
8. working with sounds.

In a day-to-day situation, accomplish informal assessment of comprehension through questions like the following:

1. What is the main idea of paragraph 3, page 150?
2. After reading pages 88 through 91, describe the events that lead to finding the lost dog.

Study Skills

Study skills, such as the ability to use tables of contents and indexes, to locate and use basic reference materials, and to read maps, globes, tables, charts, and graphs, may be assessed directly when students are using such materials. Examination of oral and written reports will reveal strengths and weaknesses in students' abilities to organize, summarize, outline, and take notes.

Informal exercises that require children to use actual reference sources are also informative (for examples, see Chapter 6). Teachers might use the following means to prepare sample test items.

1. Parts of textbook—Prepare questions that require children to make use of different aids in their textbooks, such as table of contents, glossaries, and appendices.
2. Interpretation of graphic aids—Prepare questions related to examples from the students' textbooks.
3. Reference materials—Develop questions designed to determine whether children know various reference sources and how to use them.
4. Outlining and note-taking—Using a passage from a content area textbook, ask children to read and then outline it, giving a certain number of main ideas and subtopics.

386

Teaching
Reading in
Today's
Elementary
Schools

5. Flexibility of rate—Use selections with different directions, such as "Read to remember the main ideas of the author," "Scan to find the answers to these three questions in the selection," and the like.

In assessing the ability to adjust reading rate during silent reading, teachers should observe and provide exercises to answer the following questions: What are the pupil's rates of speed in reading various materials for various purposes? Is the reading speed appropriate to reading purpose and material? Does the pupil vary rate according to the materials? Does the pupil insist on comprehending what he or she reads?

Oral Skills

Teachers often ask children to read orally in order to determine the extent of their sight vocabularies and their methods of deciphering unfamiliar words. When they use oral reading for this purpose, they should conduct the session on a one-to-one basis with the pupil, rather than publicly. This is the only situation for oral reading in which students should not do any prior silent reading, for the teacher needs to see the child's initial approach to words in order to gain useful information. A method for marking children's errors is offered later in this chapter in the section on informal reading inventories. Teachers can also use standardized oral reading tests, of which the two best known are probably the Gilmore Oral Reading Test and the Gray Oral Reading Test. Oral reading also provides the teacher with the opportunity to evaluate a child's oral reading expertise. For this purpose, however, oral reading should be preceded by silent reading.

Teachers working with beginning readers will want to use oral reading much more frequently than teachers of more mature readers will, since the processes by which beginning readers attack unfamiliar words should be monitored daily so that teachers can offer appropriate skills instruction. They will also need to hear beginners read aloud in order to help them develop the ability to read in thought units. In addition, oral reading is an ego-satisfying experience for beginning readers, who are eager to read aloud to prove their ability to perform adequately.

✓ Self-Check: Objective 1

Prepare one "check-up" exercise for each of these word recognition skills: context clues, phonic analysis, structural analysis, and using a dictionary. Do the same for a comprehension and a study skill. (See Self-Improvement Opportunity 1.)

Literary Interests

An observant teacher who takes time to be a sensitive and yet critical evaluator of each child's progress is probably the best judge of the quality of a child's reaction to literature. The following questions will help the teacher in the evaluating process. Are the children

1. growing in appreciation of good literature? How do you know?
2. making good use of time in the library and in free reading of books and periodicals?
3. enjoying storytelling, reading aloud, choral reading, and creative drama?
4. getting to know themselves better through literature?
5. increasing understanding of their own and other cultures through knowledge of the contributions of their own people and people of other lands?
6. becoming sensitive to sounds, rhythms, moods, and feelings as displayed in prose and poetry?
7. maturing in awareness of the structure and forms of literature?
8. enjoying dictating stories, reading aloud to each other, exchanging books with friends?

Teachers can gain answers to these questions through spontaneous remarks by the child (for example, "Do you know any other good books about space travel?"); through directed conversation with the class (for example, "What books would you like to add to our classroom library?"); and during individual conferences, when the children have an opportunity to describe books they like and dislike.

Within every school day countless opportunities are available for obtaining information: listening to conversations between children, observing their creative activities, studying their library circulation records, conferring with parents, and the like. Time spent looking through and discussing various books in the library with a child will provide the teacher with great insight into the child's reactions.

One excellent device for showing changes in literary taste over a period of time is a cumulative reading record, where children record each book they read, giving the author, title, kind of book, date of report, and a brief statement of how well they liked the book. Gradually, the children can tell more about what they liked and what they disliked about a particular book.

Another device is a *personal reading record,* maintained separately by (or for) each child. It classifies reading selections by topics such as poetry, fantasy, adventure or mystery, myths and folklore, animals (or more specifically, for example, horses and dogs), biography, other lands, sports, and the like. By focusing on the types of literature that the children read, teachers may encourage them to read about new topics and to expand their reading interests.

✔ Self-Check: Objective 2
Describe ways in which to assess development of literary interest. (See Self-Improvement Opportunity 9.)

Informal Assessment Procedures

Observation

It has long been recognized that observing a student's work is a good way to assess his or her achievement. The value of this way of obtaining information is evidenced by the fact that the competent teacher, after working with a class for several months, can select with remarkable accuracy the pupils who will make high scores on achievement tests.

Every day the teacher receives numerous clues related to reading performance levels. For example, as a child performs in an oral reading activity, the alert teacher can notice and jot down the child's ability to work with initial and final consonants, initial and final blends, vowel sounds, syllables, compound words, inflectional endings, prefixes and suffixes, possessives and contractions. If the pupil misses words like *there, what* and *were,* he or she may need more help with difficult sight words. If the child misses words like *car, hard,* and *burn,* perhaps he or she needs to do more work with the principle of the vowel sound when followed by *r.* The teacher can make mental note of how well the pupil handles picture clues, word-form clues, and various types of context clues, as well as of how well he or she selects meaning suitable to context. When the child reads orally the teacher has the opportunity to observe rate of reading, phrasing, and intonation. When he or she reads silently, the teacher can observe reading skill through asking oral questions and leading discussions. To check meaning vocabulary and level of concept development, seek answers to these questions:

1. Does the student grasp the main and supporting ideas of a selection? Does he know why the main ideas are important? Do his note-taking and outlining indicate a grasp of how the author organizes information?
2. Can the student follow precise directions given in print?
3. Can he relate ideas from various sources?

Content area instruction offers many occasions for observing the pupil at work, for detecting his grasp of special vocabularies, for checking his ability to use specialized references, and for noting his ability to adjust to different thought patterns. The teacher can ask herself:

1. How does the student attack reading tasks in social studies, mathematics, and science textbooks, and in trade books?
2. Does she know how to find information in resource materials?
3. Is she learning to read in different ways for different purposes?

To detect skill in creative and critical reading, the teacher can ask whether students

1. look below the surface, reading between the lines, thinking as they read.
2. react actively to the material.
3. read for implied meanings, using given facts to derive fresh meanings.

Informal observation of a student's work affords the teacher a valuable opportunity to assess learning and achievements.   (© Paul Fortin/Stock, Boston)

4. go beyond the stated facts.
5. sense hidden meanings.
6. call sensory imagery into play and read with sensitivity and appreciation of the situation.
7. detect the author's possible bias.
8. judge and compare materials critically, evaluating the logic of the selection and recognizing propaganda techniques.

   In terms of emotional response to reading, questions such as the following should be in the mind of the teacher.

1. Is the child eager to participate in reading activities and interested in finding information in books? Does she like to read orally and to listen to others, and does she enjoy choral reading of poetry or dramatization of a story? Does she use books in free-time periods?
2. What are the child's favorite books, magazines, and newspapers? What titles is she checking out from the school and public libraries?

   Of course, no student reveals all there is to know about his or her reading in any one or two samples of reading behavior, but when informal assessment procedures are continuous, patterns of strengths and weaknesses become more apparent. A teacher can learn something each time the child reads aloud, attempts to use worksheets independently, reads silently for a given purpose, or makes a trip to the library.

390

Teaching
Reading in
Today's
Elementary
Schools

The ability to learn a great deal from children's reading activities is an important facility, for which nothing can be adequately substituted, but teachers can increase the depth and accuracy of their observations by using structured reading checklists or lists of significant reading behaviors. Many basal reading series provide checklists for various reading activities, as do a number of professional reading textbooks. Comprehensive reading checklists are available from

Barbe, Walter B., and Jerry Abbott. *Personalized Reading Instruction.* Englewood Cliffs, N.J.: Prentice-Hall, 1975.

Guszak, Frank. *Diagnostic Reading Instruction in Elementary School.* 2nd ed. New York: Harper & Row, 1978, Chapter 11, "Reading Checklist."

Kennedy, Eddie C. *Methods in Teaching Developmental Reading.* 2nd ed. Itasca, Ill.: F. E. Peacock, 1981, Appendix, "Developmental Reading Skills."

Otto, Wayne, et al. *Focused Reading Instruction.* Reading, Mass.: Addison-Wesley, 1974, Chapters 7–10.

Even though it might not be easy to record the information gathered in day-by-day observation, a certain amount of record-keeping is highly desirable. To file information, some teachers keep a folder for each pupil and place material in it every two or three weeks, or each time they note something special. Samples of the student's work that include teacher's explanations or supplementary notes, special notes on the student's performance, and a general statement on a student's daily work during a report period are typical. Other valuable materials for the folder include samples that illustrate a student's skill on a particular reading task.

Self-Appraisal

Whenever possible, the teacher should encourage the child to discuss his or her own perception of personal strengths and weaknesses. An occasional interview, using such questions as the following, can provide much information.

1. Did you have a good reading period today? Did you read well? Did you get a lot done?
2. Did you read better today than yesterday?
3. Were you able to concentrate today on your silent reading?
4. Did the ideas in the book hold your attention? Did you have the feeling of moving right along with them?
5. Did you have the feeling of wanting to go ahead faster to find out what happened? Were you constantly moving ahead to get to the next good part?
6. Was it hard for you to keep your mind on what you were reading today?
7. Were you bothered by others or by outside noises?
8. Could you keep the ideas in your book straight in your head?

9. Did you get mixed up in any place? Did you have to go back and straighten yourself out?
10. Were there words you did not know? How did you figure them out?
11. What did you do when you got to the good parts? Did you read faster or slower?
12. Were you always counting to see how many pages you had to go? Were you wondering how long it would take you to finish?
13. Were you kind of hoping that the book would go on and on—that it would not really end?[3]

Use a self-check exercise with some pupils, incorporating questions like those suggested in Example 9.4.

▶ **EXAMPLE 9.4:** Self-Check Exercise

Directions: Read and answer the following questions.
1. What are some reading activities that you would like to know more about?
   a. how to learn new words
   b. how to understand what I read
   c. how to read aloud to a group
   d. how to use the library
   e. how to answer the questions in my science book
2. What reading skills do you think you need to work on most this month?
   a. how to use the dictionary to check word meanings
   b. how to get the main ideas from what I read
   c. how to do choral reading
   d. how to study better.
3. What reading activities do you feel satisfied about? Are there any that you feel need some improvement? ◀

Basal Reader Tests

Basal reader systems usually include tests to be used for determining how well pupils have learned the content of a specific unit of instruction. They are specific to each reader, and norms are ordinarily not supplied. Because basal reader tests help teachers determine if the children have actually learned the content of a specific unit, they can be valuable in the assessment program. They can help the teacher decide who needs corrective/remedial instruction, who can be advanced at the usual pace, and who might be somewhat accelerated.

Since these tests are generally given immediately following a unit of instruction and cover the basic objectives of that unit, they tend to be

[3]Lyman C. Hunt, "The Effect of Self-Selection, Interest, and Motivation Upon Independent, Instructional, and Frustrational Levels," *Reading Teacher* 24 (November 1970): 146–51, 158. Reprinted with permission of author and International Reading Association.

392

Teaching
Reading in
Today's
Elementary
Schools

somewhat easy. They do detect the problems of children who have not achieved well in a particular unit, but often provide inadequate assessments of the very high achievers.

In addition, many basal reader programs have tests built into their workbooks. While these tests are limited to specific skills, they can serve some diagnostic purposes. By analyzing a child's workbook, a teacher will find more insights into the types of problems the child has.

Graded Word Lists

The San Diego Quick Assessment is a graded word list that teachers can use to determine reading levels and identify errors in word analysis, applying the results to grouping pupils or to selecting appropriate reading material. To administer this instrument, they should follow the steps below.

1. Type out each list of ten words (see Table 9.1) on individual index cards.
2. Begin with a card on a level at least two years below the student's grade level.

TABLE 9.1:   "San Diego Quick Assessment" Graded Word List (Partial List)

Preprimer	Primer	Grade 1	Grade 2
see	you	road	our
play	come	live	please
me	not	thank	myself
at	with	when	town
run	jump	bigger	early
go	help	how	send
and	is	always	wide
look	work	night	believe
can	are	spring	quietly
here	this	today	carefully

Grade 3	Grade 4	Grade 5	Grade 6
city	decided	scanty	bridge
middle	served	certainly	commercial
moment	amazed	develop	abolish
frightened	silent	considered	trucker
exclaimed	wrecked	discussed	apparatus
several	improved	behaved	elementary
lonely	certainly	splendid	comment
drew	entered	acquainted	necessity
since	realized	escaped	gallery
straight	interrupted	grim	relatively

Source: M. LaPray and R. Ross, "The Graded Word List: A Quick Gauge of Reading Ability." *Journal of Reading* 12 (January 1969): 305–307. Reprinted with permission of the authors and the International Reading Association.

3. Ask the student to read the words aloud. If he or she misreads any words on the initial list, go back to easier lists until the child makes no errors.

4. Encourage the student to attempt to read unknown words aloud so that you can determine the techniques he or she is using for word identification.
5. Have the child read lists from increasingly higher levels until he or she misses at least three words.

If the reader misses no more than one out of ten words, he is at an independent reading level. If he makes two errors on a list, he is at the instructional level; and if he makes three or more errors, reading material at this level will be too difficult for him. Although these lists are available up to the eleventh-grade level, we present only the lists for the first six grades in Table 9.1.

To make your own graded word list inventory, compose a list of words from the glossaries of basal readers (choose about twenty words randomly from each level, preprimer through sixth reader). After you have placed the words on 3 × 5 cards, flash them at the rate of one card every two and a half seconds to the child. When the student becomes frustrated, present each word for about five seconds, stopping when the child misses 50 percent or more of the words from one grade level. By carefully recording the child's responses during the longer time presentation, you can get some idea of the child's word-attack skills. (Graded word lists do not produce as accurate an estimate of reading levels as teachers can obtain from the Informal Reading Inventory, as described in the next section.)

Teachers can develop an informal check for sight vocabulary (word recognition within five seconds), of course, from any basic sight word list.[4]

✔ Self-Check: Objective 3

Cite procedures for administering a graded word list to determine reading levels.

(See Self-Improvement Opportunity 3.)

Informal Reading Inventory

Once a teacher has determined the instructional level for word recognition, he or she may want to find out the child's ability to read words in context and to use comprehension skills. Here the purpose is to establish the child's

1. instructional level (that is, the reading level of the material the child will use with teacher guidance).
2. independent reading level (level to be read "on her own").

[4]Three basic sight word lists are the Dolch word list, found in Edward Dolch, *A Manual for Remedial Reading* (Champaign, Ill.: Garrard, 1945), p. 29; "Instant Words," found in Edward B. Fry, *Reading Instruction for Classroom and Clinic* (New York: McGraw-Hill, 1972), pp. 58–63; and "Kucera-Francis Corpus of 220 Service Words," found in Dale D. Johnson, "The Dolch List Reexamined." *The Reading Teacher* 24 (February, 1971): 449–57.

394

Teaching
Reading in
Today's
Elementary
Schools

3. frustration level (level that thwarts or baffles).
4. capacity level (potential reading level).

Four steps are involved in devising an inventory to establish a child's reading levels.

1. Selection of a standard basal series
   a. Use any series that goes from preprimer to the sixth level or above.
   b. Choose materials that the child has not previously used.
2. Selection of passages from the basal reading series
   a. Choose a selection that makes a complete story.
   b. Find selections of about these lengths:
      preprimer—book 1 (grade 1): approximately 75 words
      book 2: 100 words
      book 3: 125 words
      book 4: 150 words
      book 5: 175 words
      book 6 and above: 200 words
   c. Choose two selections at each level; plan to use one for oral reading and one for silent reading. Take the selections from the middle of the book.
3. Questioning
   a. Develop five to ten questions for each selection at each level.
   b. Include at least one of each type of question: main idea, detail, vocabulary, sequence, and inference.
4. Construction
   a. Cut out the selections and mount them on a hard backing.
   b. Put the questions on separate cards.
   c. Have a duplicate copy of the oral reading passage for marking purposes.

The oral reading sequence in an informal reading inventory should begin on the level at which the child achieved 100 percent in the word recognition flash presentation. During this part, the teacher should supply words when the child hesitates for more than five seconds. Many teachers have found it helpful to use a simple system like the following for marking the oral reading errors of pupils on reading inventories.

Error	*Marking*
(a) unknown word supplied by teacher	place *p* above unknown word
(b) word or word parts mispronounced	underline mispronunciation, indicate given pronunciation above word
(c) omitted words or word parts	circle omission
(d) insertion of new words	place caret ($\wedge$) and word where insertion was made

(e)   reversals of word order or word parts — use reversal mark ($\curlywedge$) as follows.

did⌐He⌐

(f)   repetitions — use wavy line, as the boy ran

(g)   self-correction — place © beside error that was self-corrected

Teachers may mark ignored punctuation marks and spontaneous corrections themselves, but some authorities suggest that these should not be scored as errors. Mispronounced proper names and differences due to dialect should also not be counted as errors. Some teachers have found it effective to tape a student's oral reading, replaying the tape to note the errors in performance.

After the oral reading, the teacher asks questions about the selection; then the child reads the silent reading part and is asked questions about that selection. When the child falls below 90 percent in word recognition, achieves less than 50 percent in comprehension (answers fewer than 50 percent of the questions correctly), or appears frustrated, he or she should not be asked to read at a higher level. Material read silently may be reread orally and scores compared with earlier oral reading. The teacher may also time the silent reading and get some indication of word-per-minute reading rate. After the child reaches *frustration* level material, the examiner should read aloud one selection of each level until the child is unable to answer 75 percent of the questions on the material.

Material is written at a child's independent reading level when he or she reads it without tension, correctly pronounces ninety-nine words in a hundred (99 percent correct), and correctly responds to at least 90 percent of the questions (for example, answers nine of ten questions). The material from which the child correctly pronounces 85 percent (in grades one and two) or 95 percent (in grades three and above) of the words and correctly answers at least 75 percent of the questions is roughly at the child's *instructional* level, the level at which the teaching may effectively take place.

If a student needs help on more than one word out of ten (90 percent) or responds correctly to fewer than 50 percent of the questions, the material is too advanced and at the frustration level. After the level of frustration has been reached, the teacher should read aloud higher levels of material to the child until he or she reaches the highest reading level for which the child can correctly answer 75 percent of the comprehension questions. The highest level achieved indicates the child's probable *capacity* (potential reading) level. (Note: Various writers in the field of reading suggest slightly differing percentages relative to independent, instructional, frustration, and capacity levels.) A reading capacity level is the highest level at which a child can understand the ideas and concepts in the material that is read to him or her. For example, if a child's instructional reading level is high second grade and his or her capacity, or *potential*, level is fourth grade, that child has the ability to read better than he or she is now doing.

396

Teaching
Reading in
Today's
Elementary
Schools

The percentages of correct answers do not always give clear-cut information. For instance, if the word recognition score of a fourth grader falls between 90 and 95 percent, the reading material might be at either the frustration or the instructional level. One way to decide which level reflects the student's actual ability is to observe the types of errors he or she makes. If errors seem to occur without loss of meaning, are the result of nervousness or carelessness, or are the result of dialect differences, the score may reflect the instructional level. On the other hand, if the errors interfere with the meaning and the miscalled words bear little or no resemblance to the actual words, the reading material is probably at the student's frustration level. Another type of confusion results when the pupil's scores indicate that the reading material is at the instructional level for word recognition but at the frustration level for comprehension. Since comprehension is the ultimate goal of reading, the comprehension score is more important. But in any case, the percentages are only an estimate of a reader's abilities, and decisions about placement should also be influenced by other factors such as the child's attitude toward reading, past performance, and determination. A good guideline to follow when a student's scores are borderline or contradictory is to give the pupil the lower-level material to ensure success.

The list below shows how to evaluate the scores of an informal reading inventory.[5]

Level	Word Recognition		Comprehension
Independent	99 percent or higher	and	90 percent or higher
Instructional	85 percent or higher (gr. 1–2) and 95 percent or higher (gr. 3–above)	and	75 percent or higher
Frustration	below 90 percent	or	below 50 percent
Capacity	_____		75 percent or higher

A form like that shown in Example 9.5 can be maintained for recording results of the informal reading inventory. Example 9.6 presents a teacher-made informal reading inventory based on a story from a fourth-grade basal reading series. It should give teachers some ideas about the items needed in an informal reading inventory.

---

[5]The set of criteria for the reading levels are basically those proposed by Johnson and Kress (Marjorie Sedden Johnson and Roy A. Kress, *Informal Reading Inventories*. Newark, Del.: International Reading Association, 1965), with an adjustment suggested by Powell (William R. Powell, "Reappraising the Criteria for Interpreting Informal Reading Inventories," in J. DeBoer, ed., *Reading Diagnosis and Evaluation*. Newark, Del.: International Reading Association, 1970) for word recognition for grades 1 and 2.

▶ **EXAMPLE 9.5:** Informal Analysis Sheet

Name _____ Age _____ Grade _____ Date _____

Sight Vocabulary Level	*Timed*	*Untimed*
Sight Word List	_____	_____
Recognition Inventory	_____	_____

Reading Levels
Independent _____
Instructional _____
Frustration _____
Capacity _____

Main Types of Word Recognition Errors
Unknown words _____
Mispronunciations _____
Omissions _____
Insertions _____
Reversals _____
Repetitions _____

Speed _____

Observations:
_____
_____

Word Recognition:
_____
_____

Comprehension:
_____
_____ ◀

An informal reading inventory (IRI) can provide valuable information about a child's sight vocabulary level, major types of word recognition errors, and reading levels. Many basal reader manuals contain individual reading inventories; other sources include

Burns, Paul C., and Betty D. Roe. *Informal Reading Assessment.* Chicago: Rand McNally, 1980.

Jacobs, H. Donald and L.W. Searfoss. *Diagnostic Reading Inventory.* 2nd ed. Dubuque, Iowa: Kendall/Hunt, 1979.

Johns, Jerry L. *Basic Reading Inventory—Preprimer to Grade Eight.* Dubuque, Iowa: Kendall/Hunt, 1980.

Silvaroli, Nicholas J. *Classroom Reading Inventory.* 4th ed. Dubuque, Iowa: William C. Brown, 1982.

Sucher, Floyd, and Ruel Allred. *Screening Students for Placement in Reading.* Oklahoma City: Economy, 1973.

Woods, Mary Lynn, and Alden J. Moe. *Analytical Reading Inventory.* Columbus, Ohio: Charles E. Merrill, 1977.

398

Teaching
Reading in
Today's
Elementary
Schools

▶ **EXAMPLE 9.6:** Graded Selection and Teacher-Made IRI

(172 words)

[Motivation Statement: Read to find out how Larry was cheered up.]

Larry stormed into the house. He slammed the door behind him. "I never get to do anything!" he shouted.

Larry's grandfather looked up from the book he was reading. "What happened?" he asked calmly.

"Alan won't even take me swimming with him," Larry said, frowning. "He says I can't go with him and his friends to swim in Lake Paz. He says the water is too deep for me."

"Well, I think your brother has a point," Grandfather said. "Alan has passed his lifesaving tests. You've only taken a few swimming lessons."

"But, Grandfather, it will be a long time before I can take my tests too. Do I have to wait until then?"

"I'm afraid so, if you want to swim in Lake Paz," said Grandfather. Then he smiled and his eyes twinkled. "But if you'd like to go to the City Pool, I'll drive you. It's not too deep, and there are good lifeguards at that pool."

Larry smiled too. "Thanks, Grandfather. You really know how to cheer me up."

Source: From *Scott, Foresman Basics in Reading, Flying Hoofs* by Ira E. Aaron, Dauris Jackson, Carole Riggs, et al. Copyright © 1978 by Scott, Foresman and Company. Reprinted by permission.

Vocabulary   *Types of Errors*

Number of words correct: _____   Mispronunciation _____

Accuracy   85%–146   Refusal to pronounce _____

         90%–155   Insertion _____

      100%–172   Omission _____

                                 Repetition _____

                                 Reversals _____

Questions:

(Main Idea)   1. What do you think would be a good title for this story? (Larry is left out)

(Sequence)   2. Larry stormed into the house. Name in order the next two things he did. (Slammed the door; shouted)

(Inference)   3. How did Larry feel at the start of the story? (Angry) Why do you think so? (Stormed into the house, slammed the door, shouted)

(Detail)   4. Who is one character in the story other than Larry? (Grandfather, Alan)

(Inference)   5. What did Larry want to do? (Go swimming with Alan)

(Inference)   6. Who is Alan? (Larry's brother)

(Detail)   7. Where did Grandfather say Larry could go swimming? (City Pool)

(Cause/Effect)   8. Why couldn't Larry go swimming at Lake Paz? (Water too deep; a beginning swimmer; hadn't passed lifesaving tests)

(Vocabulary)   9. What is the meaning of "calmly"? (Quietly, not excited)

(Vocabulary)   10. What is the meaning of "point" in "your brother has a point"? (Good reason)

Comprehension

Number of questions answered correctly: _____

Ten questions: 100%	*Types of Errors*
Nine questions: 90%	Main Idea _____
Eight questions: 80%	Detail _____
Seven questions: 70%	Sequence _____
Six questions: 60%	Cause/Effect _____
Five questions: 50%	Inference _____
	Vocabulary _____

Summary:

a. Major Word Recognition Errors: _____

_____

b. Major Comprehension Errors: _____

_____

_____ ◀

In a review of commercial informal reading inventories, Kathleen and Eugene Jongsma (1981) made several recommendations for selection and use. The teacher should choose an inventory that corresponds as closely as possible to the instructional materials she or he is using in the classroom, and she or he should agree with what the inventory considers to be an error. By noting the types of questions asked, the number of questions, and how scoring is handled, she or he examines the means of evaluating comprehension. The teacher should also give attention to the clarity of instructions for administering, scoring, and interpreting the inventory. Use of alternate forms for pre- and posttesting is questionable because forms may not actually be equivalent.

Example 9.7 shows a copy of a page from a published informal reading inventory. The Error Count letters and abbreviations stand for Omission,

400

Teaching
Reading in
Today's
Elementary
Schools

Insertions, Substitutions, Aided words, Repetitions, and Reversals. The parenthetical letters refer to types of questions: main idea, factual, terminology, cause-and-effect, and inferential. The scoring guide indicates the number of word recognition and comprehension errors for each level: independent, instructional, and frustration.

It is important to remember that the result of an informal reading inventory is an *estimate* of a reader's abilities. The percentages achieved by the child are

▶ **EXAMPLE 9.7:** Graded Selection from Informal Reading Inventory

Primer (50 words 8 sent.)
Examiner's Introduction
(Student Booklet page 21):

  Pat is thinking about fooling Mom. Have you ever thought about tricking your folks? Please read about Pat.

Pat sat by the tree.

"Mom wants me to work," Pat said.

"I do not want to help her work.

I will hide by this big tree.

She will not find me.

I will hide from her.

My mom will not find me.

I will hide by this big tree!"

Comprehension Questions and Possible Answers

(mi) 1. What would be a good title for this story?
("The Hiding Tree" or "No Work for Pat")

(f) 2. Where is Pat sitting?
(by the big tree)

(t) 3. What does the word work mean in this story?
(to do a chore)

(ce) 4. Why is Pat going to hide behind the big tree?
(so Pat's mom will not find Pat)

(f) 5. What does Pat's mom want Pat to do?
(help her work)

(inf) 6. What is said in the story which makes you think Pat really doesn't like his chores?
(Stated: I don't want to help her work so I'll hide from her.)

Error Count:
O___I___S___A___REP___REV___

Scoring Guide	
W R Errors	COMP Errors
IND 0–1	IND 0
INST 2–3	INST 1–2
FRUST 5+	FRUST 3+

Source: Mary Lynn Woods and Alden J. Moe. *Analytical Reading Inventory.* (Columbus, Ohio: Charles E. Merrill, 1977), p. 37. ◀

an important indication of levels of performance, but the teacher's observa-

tions of the child taking the test are equally important.[6]

✔ Self-Check: Objective 4

Prepare a chart or diagram showing the procedures for constructing and interpreting an IRI.

(See Self-Improvement Opportunities 4 and 5.)

Cloze Procedure

The cloze procedure may be used as an alternative to the graded silent reading passages of the informal reading inventory. It can help teachers determine reading levels for both basal (narrative) reading and content area reading. For instructions on the cloze procedure, see Chapter 7. Miles V. Zintz suggests using the distribution of correct responses in determining independent, instructional, and frustration levels, as cited in Chapter 7.

Content Area Procedures

To make a group reading inventory of content material, have children read a passage of 1,000 to 2,000 words from their textbooks and then ask them the following types of questions (Miller, 1978):

1. vocabulary (word meaning, word recognition, synonyms/antonyms, syllabication/accent, affixes)
2. open-ended questions (or questions that do not have a single correct response, as "Would you like to have had some other ending to the passage? If so, why?" or "What other titles could you think of for this selection?" or "For what reasons did you enjoy the passage?"
3. objective questions (or questions related to main idea, significant details, following directions, literal comprehension, interpretive comprehension, critical reading, and so on).

If children can comprehend 75 percent of what they read (answer six out of eight questions), the material can be classified as suitable for instructional purposes. These students' comprehension will increase if the teacher introduces specialized vocabulary words, helps with comprehension, teaches a study method, and provides specific purposes for reading. Of course students have many different reading levels depending upon their interests and the

[6]For a critical review of informal reading inventories, see John Pikulski, "A Critical Review: Informal Reading Inventories," *The Reading Teacher* 28 (November 1974): 141–51. Also see William R. Powell, "The Validity of the Instructional Reading Level," in *Diagnostic Viewpoints in Reading* (Newark, Del.: International Reading Association, 1971), pp. 121–33.

402

Teaching
Reading in
Today's
Elementary
Schools

background information that they may possess on any specific topic. Thus, teachers need to apply a group reading inventory for each specific content area.

The informal reading inventory described earlier can be modified to assess content reading skills by

1. choosing sight words that are specialized vocabulary terms from the content area (selected from glossary)
2. using oral and silent reading passages from a graded series of content textbooks.

Content books that children will study should be written on their instructional or independent level, and trade and supplementary books should be on their independent level. To account for the wide range of reading differences in a classroom, supplementary materials of many types, such as easy textbooks, readable trade books (nonfiction and fiction), and materials especially prepared for poorer readers, are required.[7]

✔ Self-Check: Objective 5

Explain two ways to inventory a child's ability to read content material.
(See Self-Improvement Opportunity 6.)

Miscue Analysis

Listening to a child read, a teacher must often evaluate the significance of different errors or miscues. A not very proficient reader might conceivably read "Have a good time" as "What a green toy," while a more proficient reader might read "He had a spot of dirt over his eye" as "He had a spot of dirt above his eye" (Goodman, 1970). Since different error types signify different things, educators often use the term "reading miscue analysis" to describe the interpretation of a child's oral reading performance.[8] The child who reads "The boys are playing" as "The boys is playing" may be a speaker of a nonstandard dialect and may be using his or her decoding ability to translate the printed text to meaning. While this miscue does not interfere with meaning, many miscues do reflect a problem.

Yetta M. Goodman and Carolyn L. Burke have suggested a series of questions that teachers can use to identify types of miscues. The possible

[7]See Chapter 11 for a list of such materials.

[8]This term is an outgrowth of considering reading a "psycholinguistic guessing game" in which the reader scans print line by line using graphic (visual) cues, phonological (sound) cues, syntactic (grammatical) cues, and semantic (meaning) cues. In short, readers guess and predict meaning from their knowledge of the language, testing and checking as they read. The mature reader decodes print directly into meaning, while the beginning reader probably moves from print to speech to meaning. See Kenneth S. Goodman, "Reading: A Psycholinguistic Guessing Game." *Journal of the Reading Specialist* 4 (May 1967): 126–35.

significance of each kind of miscue is indicated in the righthand column below.

Question	Possible Significance
1. Is a dialect variation involved in the miscue?	A "yes" answer may indicate that the child has gained enough proficiency in reading to use oral language competency.
2. Is a shift in intonation involved in the miscue?	A "yes" answer may suggest that the child has anticipated an unpredictable structure or is unfamiliar with the author's language structure.
3. How much does the miscue look like what was expected?	A high degree of similarity may indicate overuse of decoding in addition to lack of familiarity with the word in this context or material.
4. How much does the miscue sound like what was expected?	High similarity may indicate overuse of decoding and lack of familiarity with the word used.
5. Is the grammatical function of the miscue the same as the grammatical function of the word in the text (e.g., noun substituted for noun)?	A "yes" answer may indicate that the child probably is reading with comprehension and is aware of the grammatical function of the substitution.
6. Is the miscue corrected?	Self-correction probably indicates that the child comprehends the reading material but anticipated an alternate structure to that of the author.
7. Does the miscue occur in a structure which is grammatically acceptable?	A "yes" answer suggests that the child is sufficiently proficient in reading to use oral language communication competency.
8. Does the miscue occur in a structure which is semantically acceptable?	A "yes" answer suggests the same possibility as 7 and indicates that the child is predicting the author's intended meaning.
9. Does the miscue result in a change of meaning?	A "yes" answer may indicate that the child is trying to read ideas in the text that are unfamiliar.[9]

[9]Yetta M. Goodman and Carolyn L. Burke. *Reading Miscue Inventory, Manual, and Procedure for Diagnosis and Evaluation* (New York: Macmillan, 1972). Copyright © 1972 by Yetta M. Goodman and Carolyn L. Burke. Reprinted with permission.
Note: Also see Kenneth Goodman, ed., *Miscue Analysis* (Urbana, Ill.: National Council of Teachers of English, 1973).

404

Teaching
Reading in
Today's
Elementary
Schools

To conduct miscue analysis, a teacher has a student read orally while he or she marks any miscues on a copy of the selection. The marking system may be the same as recommended earlier in this chapter.

1. Choose a selection the child hasn't read, one somewhat ahead of the reader's current level.
2. Allow time for the child to do her best. Don't supply words, correct miscues, or answer requests for help. Just say, "Do the best you can."
3. Record miscues on the copy of the selection.
4. Use questions following the selection to check comprehension or ask the child to tell it in her own words.
5. In studying the child's reading record, remember that the number of miscues is less important than what they show about her reading.

In studying the miscues, check for particular items such as:

1. Is the miscue a result of the reader's dialect? If he says *foe* for *four*, he may be simply using a familiar pronunciation that does not affect meaning.
2. Does the miscue change the meaning? If he says *dismal* for *dismiss*, the meaning is likely changed and the substitution wouldn't make sense.
3. Does the reader self-correct? If he says a word that doesn't make sense but self-corrects, he is trying to make sense of reading.
4. Is he using syntactic cues? If he says *run* for *chase*, he still shows some use of syntactic cues, but if he says *boy* for *beautiful*, he is likely losing the syntactic pattern.
5. Is he using graphic cues? Comparing the sounds and spellings of miscues and expected words in substitutions will reveal how a reader is using graphic cues. Examples of such miscues include *house* for *horse*, *running* for *run*, *is* for *it*, and *dogs* for *dog*.

An easy way to check the quantity and quality of miscues is to do the following:

Total miscues   ____
Subtract dialect miscues   ____
            ____ Total nondialectal miscues
Subtract all corrected miscues   ____
            ____ Total uncorrected miscues
Subtract all miscues that don't
   change meaning   ____ Miscues that don't change meaning
            ____ Significant miscues

✔ Self-Check: Objective 6

What are nine statements you can make about the following situation?
Printed sentence: At the zoo, I had my first view of a zebra.
Child reads as: At the zoo, I heard my first view of a zebra.
(See Self-Improvement Opportunities 7 and 8.)

The use of informal assessment procedures is increasing in the field of special education, where such informal techniques as teacher-made tests and skill checklists are especially helpful when used in conjunction with formal measurement techniques. Teachers utilize these methods for documenting progress toward short-term objectives and annual goals, for developing and reviewing individual educational programs (IEPs), and for evaluating pre-placement. They use other types of informal procedures, such as observation and interviews with children and parents, for obtaining information necessary to make decisions about classification and eligibility.

The major advantage of informal assessment is its flexibility, which allows teachers to design it for a special purpose and construct it from materials that are being used for instruction. Information from these informal tests is therefore more instructionally relevant than data from formal tests, although it has the major disadvantage of lack of technical validity and reliability. Because of this technical inadequacy, informal tests must be constructed and interpreted with great care and used along with other types of assessment (Bennett, 1982).

NORM-REFERENCED TESTS

Norm-referenced tests provide objective data about reading performance, about intelligence, about content area achievement, and so on. Authors of these tests sample large populations of children to determine the appropriateness of test items. They seek to verify the *validity* and *reliability* of test results so that schools can be confident that the tests measure what they are intended to measure and that results will not vary significantly if students take the same test more than once.

Before saying more on norm-referenced testing instruments, we need to define a few terms:

1. An *achievement test* measures the extent to which a person has "achieved" something, acquired certain information, or mastered certain skills.
2. A *diagnostic test* analyzes and locates specific strengths and weaknesses and sometimes suggests causes.
3. An *intelligence test* measures general academic abilities or characteristics that indicate potential.
4. A *survey test* measures general achievement in a given area.

A norm-referenced achievement test is valid if it represents a balanced and adequate sampling of the instructional outcomes (knowledge, skills, and so on) that it is intended to cover. Validity is best judged by comparing the test content with the related courses of study, instructional materials, and educational goals. Evidence about validity is generally provided in a test's manual of directions. A careful inspection of the items on the test serves as a

406

Teaching
Reading in
Today's
Elementary
Schools

double-check of whether the test is designed to measure what it claims to measure. Predictive validity refers to the accuracy with which an aptitude or readiness test indicates future learning success in some area.

Reliability refers to the degree to which a test produces consistent results. It is usually checked by giving the same test twice to a large group of children. If each child makes approximately the same score in both situations, the test is considered to be reliable, while if many children make higher scores in one testing situation than in the other, the test has low reliability. When measuring the level of achievement of an individual child, teachers should use only a test of high reliability. A test of low reliability cannot be very valid; however, high reliability does not insure high validity.

A second method of measuring reliability is to take students' scores on the odd-numbered items and their scores on the even-numbered items and see if they are in the same rank order (or if they have a high correlation). Still another method is to compare one form of a test to a different but equivalent form.

The most common ways in which results of norm-referenced tests are expressed are grade equivalents (or grade scores), percentile ranks, and stanines. A grade equivalent indicates the grade level, in years and months, for which a given score was the average score in the standardization sample. For example, if a score of 25 has the grade equivalent of 4.6, then in the norm group, 25 was the average score of pupils in the sixth month of the fourth grade. After the test has been standardized, if another pupil in the sixth month of the fourth grade takes the same test and scores 25 correct, his or her performance is "at grade level" or average for this grade placement. If he or she gets 30 right, or a grade equivalent of 5.3, he or she has done as well as the typical fifth grader in the third month on *that* test. Similarly, a 3.3 grade equivalent for a fourth grader means that the performance is equal to that of the average student in the third month of the third grade on that test.

Concerned that grade equivalents were being misinterpreted and misused, the Delegates Assembly of the International Reading Association passed a resolution in April 1981 to abandon the use of these scores for reporting performance. They also resolved that test authors and publishers should eliminate grade-equivalent interpretations from their tests. This action was taken in part because delegates felt that misuse of grade equivalents was leading to a misunderstanding of a student's ability and that other information from norm-referenced tests was less likely to be misinterpreted.[10]

Percentile rank (PR) expresses a score in terms of its position within a set of 100 scores. The PR indicates the percent of scores in a reference group that is equal to or lower than the given score; therefore, a score ranked in the fiftieth percentile is equal to or better than the scores of 50 percent of the people in the reference group.

---

[10]See full statement of resolution in the January 1982 issue of *The Reading Teacher,* p. 464, or the November 1981 issue of the *Journal of Reading,* p. 112.

On a stanine scale the scores are divided into nine equal parts, with a score of five being the mean. The following interpretation for stanine scores gives information about a student's relationship to the rest of the group.

stanine 9: higher performance
stanines 7 and 8: above average
stanines 4, 5, and 6: average
stanines 2 and 3: below average
stanine 1: lower performance

Through the use of test norms—ways to express scores in relation to those of a standardization population—teachers can compare one child's score with the scores of other children of similar age and educational experience. It is also possible to determine how a child's performance on one test compares with his or her performance on other tests in a battery, and how it compares to his or her performance on the same test administered at another time. Scores from two different standardized reading tests cannot be easily compared, however, since the tests probably differ in purpose, length, and difficulty. Even the results of the same test administered on successive days may vary, depending on the reliability of the test.[11]

Formal Tests for Beginning Readers

Formal tests of vision, hearing, intelligence, language, and reading readiness can assess how ready to read young children are.

Vision

None of the commercial batteries of tests completely covers all important visual acuity skills, but two of the more inclusive are

Keystone Visual Survey Tests. Meadville, Penna.: Keystone View Co.
Orthorater. Rochester, N.Y.: Bausch and Lomb Optical Co.

These tests measure visual discrimination:

Harrison-Stroud Reading Readiness Profiles. Boston: Houghton Mifflin, 1957.
Murphy-Durrell Reading Readiness Analysis. New York: Harcourt Brace Jovanovich, 1965.

[11]For more on test norms, particularly on the strengths and weaknesses of grade equivalents, percentiles, and stanines, see Carolyn Massad, "Interpreting and Using Test Norms," *The Reading Teacher* 26 (December 1972) 286–92. See also James F. Baumann and Jennifer A. Stevenson, "Understanding Standardized Reading Achievement Test Scores," *The Reading Teacher* 35 (March 1982): 648–55.

Hearing

The audiometer, a device for testing auditory acuity, is available under trade names such as Ambco, Audiovoc, Beltone, Maico, and Zenith. Perhaps the most carefully designed test of articulation available to a classroom teacher is the *Goldman-Fristoe Test of Articulation* (Circle Pines, Minn.: American Guidance Service, 1972). This particular test assesses the child's ability to produce sounds in initial, medial, and final positions—an ability dependent upon adequate auditory discrimination. Some auditory discrimination tests include

Katz, Jack. *Kindergarten Auditory Screening Test.* Chicago: Follett, 1971.
Wepman, Joseph M. *Auditory Discrimination Test.* Rev. ed. Chicago: Language Research Associates, 1968. (Pairs of words are read to a child seated with his or her back to the teacher; the child tells whether the pair of words sounds the same or different.)

Auditory comprehension (ability to listen to, understand, and react to story material) may be evaluated with such tests as

Durrell Listening-Reading Series. New York: Harcourt Brace Jovanovich, 1969.
Spache Diagnostic Reading Scales. Monterey, Calif.: California Test Bureau, 1963.

Intelligence

As long as teachers can avoid prejudices about intelligence test scores and recognize the severe limitations in the predictive values of such tests, mental tests may be helpful. One of the best to use with young children is

Harris, Dale B. *Goodenough-Harris Drawing Test.* New York: Harcourt Brace Jovanovich, 1963. (This is a quick, nonverbal test of intellectual maturity, particularly effective with preschool children and with children who have hearing or language handicaps.)

Language

We cited tests for the encoding and decoding of phonemes of language in the preceding section on hearing (*Goldman-Fristoe Test of Articulation* and the *Wepman Auditory Discrimination Test*). Other features of language may be assessed by formal instruments:

Semantics: *Peabody Picture Vocabulary Test.* Circle Pines, Minn.: American Guidance Service, 1981.
Syntax: *Bilingual Syntax Measure (BSM),* New York: Harcourt Brace Jovanovich, Inc., 1975.

One rather complete language battery is *Tests of Language Development*, by P. L. Newcomer and D. D. Hammill, Austin, Texas: Empiric Press, 1977. (For children ages four to nine. Five subtests: picture vocabulary, oral vocabulary, grammatic understanding, sentence simulation, and grammatical completion. Two supplemental subtests: word discrimination and word articulation.)

Reading Readiness

Although reading readiness tests have certain limitations (such as the limited samplings of abilities tested, dependence upon measures of preschool learning, and possible inappropriateness of national norms to particular class being tested), the following commercial tests are available:

Clymer-Barrett Readiness Test. Rev. ed. Santa Barbara, CA: Chapman, Brook & Kent, 1983.
Gates-MacGinitie Tests: Readiness Skills. Boston: Houghton Mifflin, 1968.
Harrison-Stroud Reading Readiness Profiles. Boston: Houghton Mifflin, 1957.
Metropolitan Readiness Test. Rev. ed. New York: Harcourt Brace Jovanovich, 1976.
Murphy-Durrell Reading Readiness Analysis. New York: Harcourt Brace Jovanovich, 1965.

It is worthwhile to examine the content of reading readiness testing batteries to see which specific skills are assessed, since there is a lack of consensus among test authors as to which skills should be measured. Listening, letter recognition, visual-motor coordination, auditory discrimination, and visual discrimination are frequently measured, whereas a number of important factors, such as attention span or experiential background, are not.

The *Test of Basic Experience* (TOBE) (New York: McGraw-Hill, 1975) is designed to survey conceptual development of young children in mathematics, language, science, and social studies. It is useful in determining the school learning potential of children who show a language or cultural disadvantage on conventional readiness tests.

The *Stanford Early School Achievement Test* (SESAT) (New York: Harcourt Brace Jovanovich, 1969) also measures the learning that a child has gathered from home, neighborhood, peers, and general preschool activities. Level 1 (Grades K.1–1.1) provides the teacher with knowledge of what a child has already learned about environment (social and natural), mathematics, letters and sounds, and aural comprehension by the time he or she comes to school.

Many basal reading programs provide teachers with readiness tests designed to measure the skills with which their own programs deal. Such tests are criterion-referenced rather than norm-referenced—that is, they measure achievement but do not compare a child's score with the scores of other children, as standardized readiness tests do.

Since the results of a two-year study revealed that early diagnosis and consequent individualized instruction have a positive effect on later reading

410

Teaching
Reading in
Today's
Elementary
Schools

achievement, early testing is advisable. One testing device for prereaders is called *Prediction with Diagnostic Qualities* (PDQ) (Wilmette, Ill.: Eduscope, 1974). It contains items with diagnostic value, in that it has "direct implications for follow-up instruction to remove deficits" (Hillerich, 1978, p. 358). Test items are designed to evaluate a child's success with those receptive and expressive elements of language that are considered important for success in reading. PDQ is intended to be used by kindergarten teachers as a diagnostic tool.

According to Yetta Goodman's review (1981), Marie Clay's *Concepts about Print Test: Sand* (Exeter, N.H.: Heinemann Educational Books, 1972) and *Concepts about Print Test: Stones* (Exeter, N.H.: Educational Books, 1979) can provide insight into a child's knowledge of written language. The twenty-page booklets used for administering the tests are similar to children's picture storybooks. They enable the teacher to observe how a child responds to print as the teacher reads, to discover what should be taught as the child interacts with the printed page, and to find out what aspects of language the child is learning to control.

The Readiness Survey from the *Clymer-Barrett Readiness Test* identifies pupil characteristics that teachers should consider in determining children's readiness for reading. Example 9.8 presents this useful checklist.

Comprehensive

Some assessment batteries measure several aspects of the young child's development. Two such instruments are

Caldwell, Betty, *Cooperative Preschool Inventory*. Princeton, N.J.: Educational Testing Service, 1971.
CIRCUS: Comprehensive Program of Assessment Services for Preprimary Children. Princeton, N.J.: Educational Guidance Service, Inc., 1975.

SOMPA (The System of Multicultural Pluralistic Assessment; New York: Psychological Corporation, 1977) is a comprehensive instrument for assessing the level at which culturally different children function in cognitive, perceptual-motor, and adaptive behavior areas. It claims to provide a means of estimating learning potential masked by sociocultural and health factors. Norms are provided for black, Hispanic, and white children between five and eleven years of age. Parts of the SOMPA must be administered by especially qualified personnel.

✔ Self-Check: Objective 7

Describe one test for reading readiness in each of the following areas: vision, hearing, intelligence, and language.

Clymer-Barrett Readiness Survey

Directions: Put a check in the appropriate place for each of the characteristics below. The manual tells how to use and interpret this survey.

	Low	Average	High
1. Oral Language			
Takes part in classroom discussions			
Expresses needs effectively			
Relates a story clearly			
2. Vocabulary and Concepts			
Uses words and concepts related to people, places, things			
Knows nursery rhymes and old tales			
Describes personal experiences beyond the classroom			
3. Listening Skills			
Understands oral instruction			
Can memorize a short poem or story			
Listens attentively and responsively			
4. Thinking Abilities			
Interprets pictures			
Predicts outcome for a story			
Demonstrates flexibility in solving problems			

	Low	Average	High
5. Social Skills			
Is accepted by other children			
Plays cooperatively			
Waits patiently for a turn			
6. Emotional Development			
Seeks new tasks and activities			
Accepts changes in routine			
Is well adjusted in school setting			
7. Attitudes Toward Learning			
Asks questions about letters, words, numbers			
Enjoys stories and poems			
Learns enthusiastically			
8. Work Habits			
Completes assignments independently			
Is not easily distracted			
Takes pride in work			

	Low	Average	High
Overall Rating			

Source: *The Readiness Survey* from the Clymer-Barrett Readiness Test, Form A, p. 15. Copyright 1983, Institute for Reading Research, Inc. ◀

Norm-Referenced Reading Survey Tests

Reading survey tests can show in a general way how well children are performing in relation to others in the same grade. Through examination of the scores of all the class members, the teacher can obtain an indication of the range of reading achievement in the class.

The distribution in the list below shows the reading achievement scores for one fourth-grade class. Examination of this distribution shows that four

412

Teaching
Reading in
Today's
Elementary
Schools

children are performing below grade level, seventeen at grade level, and seven above grade level, which implies that the teacher must make provisions for individual differences. This information helps her to group children for instruction, placing children of comparable achievement together. Necessary group adjustments can be made as the teacher works with the students.

Grade Score	Number of Children
7.0–7.9	1
6.0–6.9	2
5.0–5.9	4
4.0–4.9	17
3.0–3.9	3
2.0–2.9	1
	(N = 28)

Teachers should be concerned not only with a student's total achievement score but with subtest scores, since two children may have the same total score but have different reading strengths and weaknesses, revealed in subtest scores.

	Child A	Child B
Word recognition	2.8	4.5
Word meaning	3.6	2.5
Comprehension	4.1	3.5
Reading achievement score	3.5	3.5

On first analysis, test scores indicate general areas in which students may need more help, but a more careful examination of individual test items and of children's responses to them can often supply a teacher with information about specific reading needs. Since children sometimes make even the correct responses for the wrong reasons, including random guessing, the teacher may wish to go over the test items to see if the children can explain how and why they made their responses. Teachers may be able to discern patterns of error by comparing similar test items and responses.[12]

When using norm-referenced tests for making decisions about instructional programs, teachers should also consider the student's academic potential as reported by an aptitude or intelligence test, test-taking ability or test anxiety, and current reading performance in the classroom. Intelligence test scores, despite their limitations, can be used to compare students' academic potential with their actual reading achievement. Observation of test-taking strategies may help teachers identify which students' test scores are invalid due to unusual stress or failure to attend to the task. Comparing achievement test scores with classroom performance enables teachers to decide whether a child

---

[12]These uses are based on Robert Karlin, *Teaching Elementary Reading*, 2nd ed. New York: Harcourt Brace Jovanovich, 1975, pp. 60–64.

Norm-referenced achievement tests are administered by many schools in the spring or fall of every year; if used properly, the results from these tests can aid the teacher in planning reading instruction.   (© David R. Frazier/Photo Researchers)

is doing as well as can be expected or should be challenged with more difficult work. By combining this information, teachers should be able to make reasonable instructional decisions about appropriate reading materials and programs for students (Baumann and Stevenson, 1982).

✔ **Self-Check: Objective 8**
**Suggest three uses of norm-referenced reading survey tests.
(See Self-Improvement Opportunities 10, 11, and 12.)**

Representative Reading Survey Tests

California Reading Test, Monterey, Calif.: California Test Bureau, 1970. Grades 1–2, 2.5–4.5, 4–6, 7–9, 9–14. Tests vocabulary and comprehension for all grades and word attack for grades 1–2, 2.5–4.5. (Group)

Gates-MacGinitie Reading Tests. Boston: Houghton Mifflin, 1978. Grades 1, 2, 3, 4–6, 7–9. Tests vocabulary and comprehension for grades 1, 2, 3; tests speed and accuracy for grades 2–3; tests speed, accuracy, vocabulary, comprehension for grades 4–6, 7–9. (Group)

Iowa Silent Reading Tests. New York: Harcourt Brace and Jovanovich, 1973. Grades 4–8, 9–14. Tests rate, comprehension, directed reading, word meaning, paragraph comprehension, sentence meaning, alphabetizing, using indexes. (Group)

414

Teaching
Reading in
Today's
Elementary
Schools

Metropolitan Achievement Tests: Reading. New York: Psychological Corporation, 1978. Grades K–1.4, 1.5–2.4, 2.5–3.4, 3.5–4.9, 5–6.9. Tests word knowledge, word analysis, comprehension; yields Instructional Reading Level. (Group)

Sequential Tests of Educational Progress: Reading. Princeton, N.J.: Cooperative Test Division, Educational Testing Service, 1972. Grades 4–6, 7–9, 10–12, 13–14. Tests comprehension. (Group)

S.R.A. Achievement Series. Chicago: Science Research Associates, 1978. Grades K–12. Tests vocabulary and comprehension. (Group)

A profile sheet from the *Gates-MacGinitie Reading Tests* is presented in Example 9.9 to give an indication of the content of the test and the recording of results.

Some norm-referenced reading survey tests, such as the *Metropolitan Achievement Tests: Reading,* provide valuable descriptions of the skill measured by each item in the tests. The Content Outlines for the Word Analysis sections of the Metropolitan Primary I Battery suggest item numbers for these topics:

1. often-confused sight words
2. reversals
3. initial consonants
4. final consonants
5. medial vowels
6. initial consonant digraphs and blends
7. *r*-controlled vowels
8. prefixes
9. suffixes
10. silent consonants
11. final blends and digraphs
12. silent letter *e*

Examining how a student responds to questions covering these topics can be useful. Schools can receive an item-analysis report on how well groups perform on every single item, as well as on the percent of the national sample of pupils who answered each item correctly.

Other Norm-Referenced Tests

Achievement Tests

Most schools administer achievement tests in the spring or fall every year as a way of assessing the gains in achievement of groups of children. Most of these tests are actually batteries, or collections of tests on different subjects, and should be given under carefully controlled conditions and over the course of several days. They may be sent to the publisher for machine scoring.

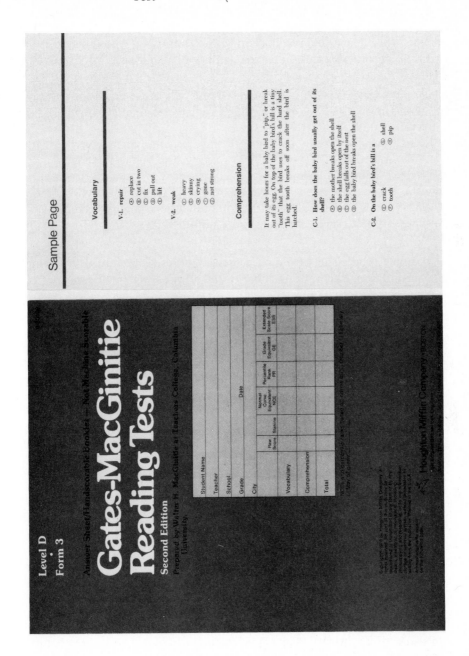

Source: *Gates-MacGinitie Reading Tests.* 2nd ed. Boston: Houghton Mifflin, 1978. ◀

416

Teaching
Reading in
Today's
Elementary
Schools

Many of these achievement tests contain subtests in reading and language, which provide useful information for identifying students' general strengths and weaknesses in reading. For instance, the *Iowa Tests of Basic Skills: Primary Battery* (New York: Riverside, 1978) contains subtests in listening, word analysis, vocabulary, and reading comprehension, along with other curricular areas. Some other norm-referenced achievement tests are listed below.

California Achievement Tests. Monterey, Calif.: CTB/McGraw-Hill, 1970 and
1978. Grades K–12.9. Tests reading, language, mathematics, spelling, and
reference skills.

S.R.A. Achievement Series. Chicago, Ill.: Science Research Associates, Inc.,
1978. Grades K–12. Tests skills in reading, mathematics, language arts,
reference materials, science, and social studies.

Stanford Achievement Test Series. New York, N.Y.: Psychological Corporation,
1982. Grades K–12. Tests reading comprehension, language skills, mathematics, science, social science, and auditory skills.

A sample profile sheet from an achievement test is presented in Example
9.10. It indicates the various subtests and the scoring procedure.

✔ Self-Check: Objective 9

Identify a norm-referenced test of each type: Reading Survey and
Achievement. What does each test specifically do?
(See Self-Improvement Opportunities 10, 11, and 12.)

Intelligence Tests and Reading Potential

Several group intelligence tests used in the elementary schools are listed
below.

California Short-Form Test of Mental Maturity. Monterey, Calif.: California Test
Bureau, 1963. Kindergarten through college levels. Gives language and
nonlanguage scores. Reports in percentiles, standard scores, stanines,
mental ages, and IQ.

Cognitive Abilities Test. Boston: Houghton-Mifflin, 1982. (Primary 1 and 2 for
Gr. K–3; Levels A–H for Gr. 3–12. Primary level is group nonreading,
using pictorial materials and oral instructions. Levels A–H provide separate
batteries: verbal, quantitative, and nonverbal.)

Otis-Lennon School Ability Test. Rev. ed. New York: Harcourt Brace Jovanovich,
1982. (Pri–K; Primary II–gr. 1); Elementary I (grades 1–3); Elementary II
(grades 4–6); Intermediate (grades 7–9). No reading required on Primary I,
II, or Elementary I. Samples fourteen different mental processes. Provides
percentile rank and stanine.

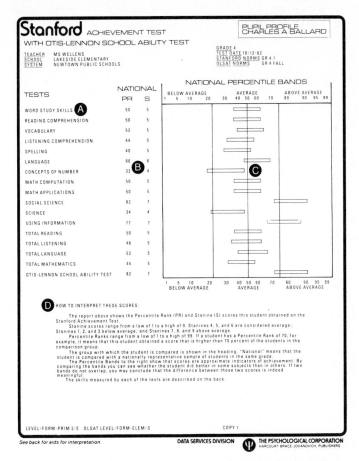

Source: *Stanford Achievement Test*, 7th Edition. Copyright © 1982 by Harcourt Brace Jovanovich, Inc. Reproduced by permission of the publisher. ◀

A frequently used test of scholastic aptitude is the *Peabody Picture Vocabulary Test* (PPVT) (Circle Pines, Minn.: American Guidance Service, 1981). The examiner using this test presents a page containing four pictures, provides a stimulus word, and asks the examinee to indicate the appropriate picture. The test takes approximately fifteen minutes and can be given by a teacher without special training in test administration. Raw scores can be converted into age equivalents and standard score equivalents. Another brief, individually administered test is the *Slosson Intelligence Test* (SIT) (East Aurora, N.Y.: Slosson Educational Publications, 1974).

Intelligence test scores are useful in identifying the underachiever. A child's score on a norm-referenced reading test only indicates relative performance

418

Teaching
Reading in
Today's
Elementary
Schools

and not the performance of which the child is capable; however, an intelligence test score can indicate his or her capability level, which can then be compared with the child's actual performance level. The teacher can then determine whether or not the child is performing up to capacity. One commonly used formula for finding the child's expected grade placement, or reading expectancy level, based on his or her intellectual capacity has been suggested by Guy L. Bond, Miles A. Tinker, and Barbara B. Wasson (1979).

$$\frac{IQ}{100} \text{ (years in school)} + 1.0 = \textit{Reading expectancy}$$

Thus, a mid-year fifth grader who scored 120 on an intelligence test would have a reading capacity or expectancy of 6.4 (mid-sixth-grade level).

$$(1.20 \times 4.5) + 1.0$$
$$= 5.4 + 1.0$$
$$= 6.4$$

In counting the years in school, begin with first grade and go through all of the following years, including any years that the student repeated a grade. Because of the differences in children's backgrounds and the limitations of norm-referenced tests, teachers should use formulas with caution, holding in mind the fact that most formulas for predicting reading potential are least accurate for extremely good and extremely poor readers.

A listening comprension test is another way of judging the reading potential of a child. One such test, the *Durrell Listening-Reading Series* (New York: Harcourt Brace and World, 1969), attempts to answer the following questions: Which children are limited because they lack understanding of the spoken language? How far above a child's reading level is his listening comprehension level? Among the candidates for corrective instruction, which have the highest learning potentials? The Durrell test has two levels: the Primary Level (grades 1–2) is divided into four sections—vocabulary listening, vocabulary reading, sentence listening, and sentence reading; and the Intermediate Level (grades 3–6) covers vocabulary listening, vocabulary reading, paragraph listening, and paragraph reading.

Other listening comprehension tests include

Sequential Tests of Education Progress, Listening. Princeton, N.J.: Educational Testing Service, Cooperative Test Division, 1957.
Cooperative Primary Test: Listening. Princeton, N.J.: Educational Testing Service, Cooperative Test Division, 1967.
Stanford Achievement Tests: Listening. New York: Harcourt Brace Jovanovich, 1973.

✔ Self-Check: Objective 10
Explain two ways to judge the reading potential of a child.
(See Self-Improvement Opportunity 13.)

Limitations of Norm-Referenced Reading Tests

If norm-referenced tests are properly understood and interpreted, they can assist teachers in planning reading instruction. But teachers need to understand the tests' limitations clearly, and they should begin by asking a series of questions about them.

Which test should I use? A test is inappropriate if the sample population used to standardize it is significantly different from the class to be tested. Test manuals should contain information about the selection and character of the sample population, pointing out, for example, from what geographical areas and socioeconomic groups the sample was drawn.

What about the content? How many different skills do the test items sample? Children who have participated in a comprehensive program will not be fairly tested by tests that are narrow in scope. Most tests require only a short period of time to complete and therefore cannot possibly sample many different skills or include more than a few items covering any one skill. Thus, many tests must be viewed as gross instruments at best.

How accurate are the scores? It is doubtful that teachers should accept the results of norm-referenced tests with great confidence. They should not assume that a grade score exactly indicates an actual performance level, since a single test score on a norm-referenced reading test frequently reflects the child's frustration level rather than his or her instructional or independent level. In other words, a child who achieves a fourth-grade score on a test may be unable to perform satisfactorily in a fourth-year reader or with fourth-grade content materials. This situation is particularly true for readers at the upper and lower ends of the class distribution.

The Metropolitan Achievement Tests: 1978 Edition (MAT) (New York, N.Y.: Psychological Corporation, 1978) may be an exception to this, however. In a recent study, researchers compared cloze tests, informal reading inventories, and placement tests with the MAT to determine its validity for estimating a student's instructional reading level. They found that the MAT correlated closely with other procedures and may therefore be a useful tool (Smith and Beck, 1980).

Even if a test's norms are based on populations closely approximating the class being tested, teachers must ask whether comparison with national achievement is a good way to describe class or student achievement. Consider, for example, a sixth-grade class in a residential district of a well-to-do community. In such a school, the ability of pupils, the interest of parents in education, the training and skill of the teachers, and other factors that encourage achievement would be far above the national average. What is really gained by comparing the reading achievement of this class with the performance of the national sample? Certainly the performance of children in these better schools is well above the norm, but that information is not very useful. Norm-referenced tests might be improved by being based on more homogeneous and more easily described populations rather than on the extremely varied national population.

420

Teaching
Reading in
Today's
Elementary
Schools

Is the test fair to minority groups and inner-city children? Test publishers have been giving increasing attention to the question of the fairness of their tests. They do not want to state questions in a way that will give certain children an unfair advantage or turn off some children so that they will not do their best. Many writers and editors from different backgrounds are involved in test-making, and questions are reviewed by members of several ethnic groups to correct unintentional, built-in biases.[13]

✔ Self-Check: Objective 11

List four cautions to keep in mind in using norm-referenced tests.

CRITERION-REFERENCED TESTS

A criterion-referenced (or objective-referenced) test is designed to yield scores interpretable in terms of specific performance standards—for example, to indicate that a student can identify the main idea of a paragraph 90 percent of the time. Such tests do not tell the teacher anything about how a child compares with other children, but are intended to be used as guides for developing instructional prescriptions. (For example, if a child cannot perform the task of identifying cause-and-effect relationships, the teacher should provide instruction in that area.) Such specific applications make these tests more useful than norm-referenced tests in day-to-day decisions about instruction.

Criterion-referenced tests are usually part of an objective-based reading program that uses pretests and posttests to measure a child's mastery of a skill (see Chapter 5). Such programs identify hundreds of discrete skills and arrange them in sequence. These skills become learning goals and are taught and tested. Each child must demonstrate adequate mastery of one skill before advancing to the next.

Educators have important questions, however, concerning criterion-referenced tests. How many correct answers are needed to show that the pupil has achieved an objective or performed up to standard? At what grade level should we expect a child to meet each objective? Should every pupil be expected to meet every objective? Other questions arise when a child does achieve an objective. Is it typical for a third grader to achieve this objective? Do most third graders know how to perform this task? These questions bring us back to comparing individuals—or to a norm-referenced interpretation of test scores.

Criterion-referenced testing is a comparatively new type of assessment and has both advantages and disadvantages. It is an effective way of diagnosing a child's knowledge of reading skills, and it helps in prescribing appropriate

[13]These limitations are based on Robert Karlin, *Teaching Elementary Reading:* 2nd ed. New York. Harcourt Brace Jovanovich, 1975, pp. 64–66.

instruction. Furthermore, students do not compete with other students but only try to achieve mastery of each criterion or objective. On the other hand, reading becomes nothing more than a series of skills to be taught and tested, and skills are learned in isolation rather than in combination. Knowledge gained in this way may be difficult for children to apply to actual reading situations.

An example of a criterion-referenced approach to reading is the *PRI Reading Systems*, which succeeds the *Prescriptive Reading Inventory*. Assessment and instructional materials provide data on each student's skill in reading to be used for placement, diagnosis and prescription, skill reinforcement, progress checks, and enrichment. Assessment materials measure the student's ability to achieve objectives that are usually identified for reading instruction in grades kindergarten through nine. Lesson plans and activities for helping students gain mastery of those skills they have not already learned are provided. An Individual Diagnostic Map from the *PRI Reading Systems* is shown in Example 9.11.

Below is a list of other commercially available criterion-referenced tests.

The Individual Pupil Monitoring Systems (IPMS). Available in two forms on six levels, grades 1–6, in reading. Is untimed and designed to assess the skills included in most standard reading programs. (Houghton Mifflin)

Skills Monitoring System in Reading (SMS). Designed to assess a pupil's understanding of and ability to perform specific reading tasks. Covers grades 3–5. (Harcourt Brace Jovanovich)

The Wisconsin Design. An extensive testing program that includes assessment of word attack, study skills, comprehension, and self-directed, interpretive and creative reading. Covers grades K–6. The Wisconsin Design is explained in detail in Chapter 5. (Wisconsin Design, NCS Educational Systems Division)

✔ Self-Check: Objective 12

Differentiate between a norm-referenced and a criterion-referenced test.
(See Self-Improvement Opportunity 14.)

REVIEW OF TESTS AVAILABLE TO THE CLASSROOM TEACHER

Given this myriad of tests, a teacher may well wonder what to use to assess students' knowledge and abilities. The following review may help to put assessment into a proper perspective.

Informal tests may be given at any time for a specific purpose to one or more children. These tests are usually designed to find out what a student knows about something and to determine if some students need more

422

Teaching
Reading in
Today's
Elementary
Schools

► **EXAMPLE 9.11:** Example of Criterion-Referenced Approach

PRI Reading Systems

Individual Diagnostic Map

Instructional Objectives Inventory
System 1, Level E

Name _____

Teacher _____

Grade _____ Date _____

DIRECTIONS

The items that test a specific instructional objective are listed by number in the ITEM NUMBERS column. To fill in the box under each item number, refer to the student's corrected answer sheet for the *PRI Reading Systems Instructional Objectives Inventory*. Record C for correct, X for incorrect, or O for item omitted. Add the number of correct items for each objective and enter that number on the line in the RAW SCORE column. Use the raw score to determine Mastery (+ = 3 or 4), Review (R = 2), or Nonmastery (− = 0 or 1). Enter +, R, or − for each objective in the box in the last column.

SKILL AREA	OBJECTIVE NUMBER AND NAME	ITEM NUMBERS (Enter C, X, or O)	RAW SCORE	+ = 3, 4; R = 2; − = 0, 1
Vocabulary	31 Antonyms	13 14 15 16		
	32 Synonyms	9 10 11 12		
	33 Word Definition	5 6 7 8		
	34 Multimeaning Words in Context	1 2 3 4		
Word Usage	36 Capitalization	21 22 23 24		
	37 Punctuation	25 26 27 28		
	38 Possessives	33 34 35 36		
	44 Context Clues	17 18 19 20		
	45 Verb Tense, Agreement	29 30 31 32		
	46 Modifier Placement	37 38 39 40		
	47 Complete Sentences	41 42 43 44		
Literal Comprehension	51 Event Sequence	47 49 53 54		
	52 Motivation	45 48 51 55		
	54 Paragraph Paraphrasing	46 50 52 56		

SKILL AREA	OBJECTIVE NUMBER AND NAME	ITEM NUMBERS (Enter C, X, or O)	RAW SCORE	+ = 3, 4; R = 2; − = 0, 1
Interpretive & Critical Comprehension	56 Passage Summary	61 74 83 88		
	57 Future Events	67 72 75 84		
	58 Character Analysis	60 63 79 81		
	59 Cause and Effect	59 68 71 82		
	60 Drawing Conclusions	57 66 78 87		
	61 Metaphors/Similes	62 70 76 85		
	62 Idiomatic Expressions	58 64 69 80		
	63 Tone/Mood	65 73 77 86		
Study Skills	64 Paragraph Structure	93 94 95 96		
	65 Outlines	97 98 99 100		
	69 Library Resources	89 90 91 92		
Content Area Reading	70 Directions (Social Studies)	113 114 123 124		
	71 Vocabulary (Social Studies)	117 118 119 120		
	72 Graphic Displays (Social Studies)	115 116 121 122		
	73 Directions (Science)	127 128 133 134		
	74 Vocabulary (Science)	129 130 135 136		
	75 Graphic Displays (Science)	125 126 131 132		
	76 Directions (Mathematics)	103 104 107 108		
	77 Vocabulary (Mathematics)	105 106 109 110		
	78 Graphic Displays (Mathematics)	101 102 111 112		

Published by CTB·McGraw-Hill, Del Monte Research Park, Monterey, California 93940. Copyright © 1980 by McGraw-Hill, Inc. All Rights Reserved. Printed in the U.S.A.

92104

Source: Reproduced by permission of the publisher, CTB/McGraw-Hill, Del Monte Research Park, Monterey, CA 93940. Copyright © 1980 by McGraw-Hill, Inc. All rights reserved. Printed in the U.S.A. ◄

instruction before moving on to another skill. Most of the time informal tests are constructed by the classroom teacher, but they may also be taken from commercially prepared inventories, word lists, or other specific skill checks.

Some types of informal tests used in reading are graded word lists (which give approximate reading levels based on word recognition only), informal reading inventories (which give reading levels based on both comprehension and word recognition), and the cloze procedure (which determines how well a student can read the textbook). Graded word lists and IRIs must be given individually, but the cloze procedure may be given to an entire class at once.

The teacher can construct criterion-referenced tests to determine how well a student understands a specific skill. More often these tests are part of an objective-based or systems management approach to reading and are used along with sets of skill-building materials. In addition, many basal reader series provide tests at the end of each unit to assess the student's knowledge of reading skills associated with the unit. Because these tests relate directly to the instructional materials, the teacher can tell from the results if he or she needs to reteach some skills to certain children.

The classroom teacher should also understand the purposes of various types of norm-referenced tests that may be part of the school program. A kindergarten or first-grade teacher may want to administer a reading readiness test to help determine whether a child is ready for reading instruction. Most schools require that achievement tests be given annually to find out how much progress students have made in overall academic achievement. Intelligence tests are usually given every few years to determine the academic aptitude of students, but results of these tests must be used with caution. Reading survey tests are used to obtain general information about a student's reading level, and diagnostic reading tests are given by special reading teachers to find specific skill deficiencies.

The teacher's most useful assessment tool is day-to-day observation. Informal tests may be used to reinforce or supplement such observation, whereas norm-referenced tests are usually given only as mandated by the school system.

Test Yourself

True or False

_____ 1. Study skills may be assessed most effectively in situations where they are being used.

_____ 2. A check sheet for recording the kinds of miscues children make in oral reading is not helpful to most teachers.

_____ 3. Results from the San Diego Quick Assessment are useful for grouping pupils or selecting appropriate reading materials.

_____ 4. The teacher must devise his or her own informal reading inventory, since none are commercially available.

_____ 5. Basal reader programs usually include tests specific to each unit or reader.

_____ 6. Material written on a child's independent reading level is less difficult than material written on her instructional level.

_____ 7. Selections of seventy-five words are used for each grade level in the IRI.

_____ 8. For first and second graders, an IRI presents material on the instructional level if the word recognition is 85 percent and comprehension is 75 percent.

424

Teaching
Reading in
Today's
Elementary
Schools

_____ 9. Teachers may use the cloze procedure as an alternative to the IRI in determining narrative or content material reading levels.

_____ 10. An IRI can be prepared for content reading material as well as for narrative (basal reader) passages.

_____ 11. Miscue analysis can help in understanding the nature of a child's reading errors.

_____ 12. Significant miscues are found in this manner: Total miscues − (dialectal miscues + corrected miscues + miscues that don't change meaning).

_____ 13. If a test has high reliability, high validity is assured.

_____ 14. Standardized reading survey tests can identify the range of performance differences within the class but cannot necessarily identify the precise achievement level of each class member.

_____ 15. Little is gained by examining responses to individual test items on a reading test.

_____ 16. A general survey reading test does not identify the specific reading strengths or weaknesses of the reader.

_____ 17. Reading readiness tests measure a child's attention span and experiential background.

_____ 18. Some formal tests measure a child's vision and hearing.

_____ 19. A child's grade placement score on a standardized reading test will reveal whether or not he is an underachiever.

_____ 20. One formula for determining reading expectancy is $\frac{IQ}{100}$ (years in school) + 1.0.

_____ 21. IQ scores can be used to identify the underachiever.

_____ 22. Teachers can utilize listening comprehension tests to judge the reading potential of a child.

_____ 23. Percentile rank (PR) refers to the percent of correct responses an examinee makes on a test.

_____ 24. A criterion-referenced assessment relates an individual's test performance to absolute standards rather than to the performance of others.

_____ 25. There are at present no criterion-referenced tests.

Vocabulary

Check your knowledge of these terms. Reread parts of the chapter if necessary.

achievement test	dialectal miscue	independent level
aptitude test	frustration level	informal assessment
cloze procedure	grade-equivalent scores	informal reading
criterion-referenced test	graded word list	inventory
diagnostic test	graphic cues	insertions

instructional level	reading checklist	survey test
miscue	reading readiness test	syntactic cues
norm-referenced test	reliability	underachiever
percentile rank	reversals	validity
potential reading level	stanine	

Self-Improvement Opportunities

1. Prepare a structured reading checklist for one of the following: word attack skills (including contextual analysis, phonics analysis, structural analysis, dictionary usage), study skills, or comprehension skills.
2. Study a set of basal reader tests to determine how you can use them.
3. Administer the San Diego Quick Assessment to a child. Then share your findings about reading level and word-analysis errors with peers.
4. Secure a published IRI and administer it to one or more elementary school pupils. Report the results to the class.
5. Prepare an IRI using basal reading materials, administer it to a child, record the results, and share your findings with the class.
6. Prepare a group inventory, using content reading materials. Administer your group inventory to a child, record the results, and share the findings with the class.
7. Utilize the procedures suggested for a miscue analysis. Check the quantity and quality of miscues.
8. Below are some errors made by a fourth-grade student in oral reading. What kind of help do these errors suggest that this student might need?

Correct Word	Incorrect Reading
and he hoped	hopped
they knew	know
on the map	mape
would come alive	aliv
of the few	fun
was a new	now
back home	here

9. Discuss with a teacher and a librarian some ways to assess development of children's literary interests.
10. Secure a copy (and manual) of a norm-referenced reading survey test. Study it and report on it to your peers, considering purpose, range, forms, testing time, reliability, validity, strengths, and weaknesses.
11. If feasible, observe the administration of a norm-referenced reading survey test to a child or group of children.

426

Teaching
Reading in
Today's
Elementary
Schools

12. If feasible, administer a norm-referenced reading survey test to a child and interpret the results.

13. Calculate the reading expectancy level, given these data for children who have not repeated a grade:
    a. IQ of 80; mid-year fifth grader
    b. IQ of 90; mid-year seventh grader
    c. IQ of 120; mid-year fourth grader

    Answers: 4.6

    6.9

    5.2

14. Examine several criterion-referenced tests.

15. From the following list, choose which type of test is appropriate for each of the following purposes. (More than one answer could be correct.)

    criterion-referenced   survey
    norm-referenced   achievement
    informal
    intelligence

    a. To find out if a child has mastered a specific skill
    b. To determine how much gain in general academic achievement the second grade class in a school made during the preceding year
    c. To find out how a child's reading achievement compares with that of the average child in the nation
    d. To find out what a child's potential for learning is
    e. To get a general idea of a student's reading ability
    f. To find out what a child knows about structural analysis

Bibliography

Bauman, James F., and Jennifer A. Stevenson. "Using Scores from Standardized Reading Achievement Tests." *The Reading Teacher* 35 (February 1982): 528–33.

Bennett, Rand Elliot. "Cautions for the Use of Informal Measures in the Educational Assessment of Exceptional Children." *Journal of Learning Disabilities* 15 (June/July 1982): 337–39.

Bond, Guy L., Miles A. Tinker, and Barbara B. Wasson. *Reading Difficulties: Their Diagnosis and Correction.* 4th ed. Englewood Cliffs, N.J.: Prentice-Hall, 1979, p. 62.

Boning, Richard A. *Specific Skills Series.* Rockville Center, N.Y.: Barnell Loft, 1976.

Durrell, Donald D., and Helen A. Murphy. "A Prereading Phonics Inventory." *The Reading Teacher* 31 (January 1978): 385–90.

Goodman, Yetta. "Test Review: Concepts about Print Test." *The Reading Teacher* 34 (January 1981): 445–48.

Goodman, Yetta. "Using Children's Reading Miscues for New Teaching Strategies." *The Reading Teacher* 23 (February 1970): 455–59.

Hillerich, Robert L. "A Diagnostic Approach to Early Identification of Language Skills." *The Reading Teacher* 31 (January 1978): 357–64.

Jongsma, Kathleen S., and Eugene A. Jongsma. "Test Review: Commercial Informal Reading Inventories." *The Reading Teacher* 34 (March 1981): 697–705.

Miller, Wilma. *Reading Diagnosis Kit.* West Nyack, N.Y.: Center for Applied Research in Education, 1978.

Pickert, Sarah M., and Martha L. Chase. "Story Retelling: An Informal Technique for Evaluating Children's Language." *The Reading Teacher* 31 (February 1978): 528–31.

Smith, Edwin H., et al. "Informal Reading Inventories for Content Areas: Science and Mathematics." *Elementary English* 49 (May 1972): 659–66.

Smith, William Earl, and Michael D. Beck. "Determining Instructional Reading Level with the 1978 Metropolitan Achievement Tests." *The Reading Teacher* 34 (December 1980): 313–19.

Suggested Readings

Baumann, James F., and Jennifer A. Stevenson. "Understanding Standardized Reading Achievement Test Scores." *The Reading Teacher* 35 (March 1982): 648–55.

Dallman, Martha, et al. *The Teaching of Reading.* 6th ed. New York: Holt, Rinehart and Winston, 1982, Chapter 12.

Dechant, Emerald. *Diagnosis and Remediation of Reading Disabilities.* Englewood Cliffs, N.J.: Prentice-Hall, 1981, Chapter 3.

Gillet, Jean Wallace, and Charles Temple. *Understanding Reading Problems: Assessment and Instruction.* Boston: Little, Brown, 1982, Chapters 4 and 8.

Guszak, Frank J. *Diagnostic Reading Instruction in the Elementary School.* 2nd ed. New York: Harper & Row, 1978.

Johns, Jerry L., et al., eds. *Assessing Reading Behavior: Informal Reading Inventories.* Newark, Del.: International Reading Association, 1977. (Annotated Bibliography Series).

Otto, Wayne, and Richard J. Smith. *Corrective and Remedial Teaching.* Boston: Houghton Mifflin, 1980, Chapter 4.

Rubin, Dorothy. *Diagnosis and Correction in Reading Instruction.* New York: Holt, Rinehart and Winston, 1982, Chapters 3 and 8.

Spache, George D. *Diagnosing and Correcting Reading Disabilities.* 2nd ed. Boston: Allyn and Bacon, 1981, Chapters 4 and 7.

Stauffer, Russell G., et al. *Diagnosis, Correction, and Prevention of Reading Disabilities.* New York: Harper & Row, 1978, Chapters 3, 4, and 5.

Wilson, Robert M. *Diagnostic and Remedial Reading for Classroom and Clinic.* 4th ed. Columbus: Charles E. Merrill, 1981, Chapter 4.

CHAPTER 10

Classroom Organization
and Management

Introduction

Classroom organization does not deal directly with the reading process, or with materials, methods, or approaches to teaching reading. Yet without good classroom organization and management, reading instruction may be totally ineffective. It is not enough for teachers to know what to teach; they must also know what organizational patterns and management techniques are conducive to learning.

In this chapter we deal with various types of organizational plans, offering practical suggestions for forming and managing different types of groups and discussing other plans, such as an individualized plan and an open curriculum. We also stress the significance of the role of the teacher in the student's learning environment, along with some factors that contribute to teacher effectiveness. After discussing the influence of parents on children's reading attitudes and achievement and considering ways of establishing good communication between parent and teacher, we point out the value of paraprofessionals in the school program.

Setting Objectives

When you finish reading this chapter, you should be able to

1. Name some general guidelines for organizing a classroom reading program.
2. Note some different ways that teachers might group students for reading-related purposes.
3. Explain how you might use interclass or cross-grade grouping.
4. Delineate the rationales behind several organizational plans used at the elementary school level.
5. Discuss how a teacher can be a facilitator and stimulator of learning within the reading program.
6. Name the ways in which teachers can communicate with parents.
7. Explain the roles paraprofessionals play within the reading program.

ORGANIZATIONAL PATTERNS

The fact that students vary a great deal in chronological age, maturity, cognitive abilities, interests, and personal experiences is no secret. In view of the obvious need to provide the most appropriate instruction for each learner, teachers must give careful consideration to plans that provide for individual differences. Students in a total reading program should participate in small-group, individualized, and whole-class activities. Many types of individualized activities are discussed in Chapter 5; other individualization plans

430

Teaching
Reading in
Today's
Elementary
Schools

and whole-class activities are treated later in this chapter. An extensive discussion of grouping immediately follows this section.

Some general guidelines for organization of the classroom are listed below.

1. No single classroom pattern or structuring is better than another; the local situation, the strengths of individual teachers, and the abilities of the children involved will help to dictate the best system for a particular school.
2. Teachers should consider many criteria in deciding upon a particular organizational plan, including results of informal and formal tests, children's interests, and specific goals of instruction.
3. Organizational patterns should be flexible, and should be altered as better ways are discovered.
4. No absolute criterion states the proper size for groups within a class. Corrective or remedial work usually requires small groups, but when children can assume considerable responsibility for independent work, the number involved may be much higher.
5. Children learn from each other, so opportunities to share within a group are basic to good instruction.
6. Organization is a technique or a system, not a "method of instruction." Organization can only facilitate, or hinder, effective instruction.

✔ Self-Check: Objective 1
Cite at least four guidelines for organizing a reading classroom. Can you suggest others not stated above?
(See Self-Improvement Opportunity 1.)

Grouping

Educators have made various attempts to create organizational plans for meeting the needs of all students in the most efficient way possible. These plans usually involve some form of grouping as a compromise between whole-class and totally individualized instruction.

Within each heterogeneous classroom, children generally have a wide range of reading levels, which increases with each succeeding grade. Using the findings from various studies, Dallman and others concluded that

At the first-grade level, the range of achievement in a class can be expected to be two or more years.

At the fourth-grade level, the range of achievement in a class may be four years or more.

At the sixth-grade level, the range of achievement in a class may be six years or more. (1982, p. 386)

While grouping by achievement may indeed reduce the spread of reading levels, teachers must not forget that many differences still exist among students. They can differ in their rates of progress, in their attitudes toward reading, in their backgrounds and experiences, and in their degree of motivation. Two students may have similar overall achievement scores; however, one may be weak in word recognition and strong in comprehension while the other may have the opposite problem.

Two major grouping plans have been used in heterogeneous classroom settings: intraclass (within the class) and interclass (between classes). A discussion of each major grouping plan follows.

Intraclass Group Plans

Types of Groups Dividing children into reading groups on the basis of reading level or ability (high, average, and low) is a popular practice in our schools. This is a kind of *achievement grouping,* a method of grouping children according to the level of reading material they are comfortable with. The teacher may divide the class into two, three, or four groups, usually using basal readers as the main fare, because the manuals and workbooks provide a careful and detailed skill-building program. Good teachers will note how difficult these materials are for each child in each group and will provide easier or harder related reading (supplementary reading, trade books, magazines, newspapers, and the like) as needed.

As children show specific skill deficiencies in their achievement groups, they need *special skills* or *needs grouping,* which groups together children who need work on the same skill. Several children from each of the groups may need help with word recognition (such as recognizing certain initial consonant sounds), comprehension (such as summarizing meaning of a paragraph), or a study skill (such as graph reading). Children with a common need can work together in one or perhaps more meetings. Such special needs groups will involve different children at different points in time.

Another type of grouping, *interest grouping* (on the basis of shared or common interest or concern), is recommended for certain reading activities. For example, if three or four children in a class like horse stories, the librarian, notified about this interest and the reading levels of the children, can find just the right books for them. After reading and talking, the children might prepare a discussion about the books for the entire class. Or they might make a poster advertising the books they read, write a story together, or make a scrapbook. From such temporary interest groupings, more formal and long-term groups often evolve (for example, library groups, choral groups, dramatic clubs, readers' theaters, and book fair groups).

A fourth type of grouping is based on *projects* or *research.* Such groups may grow out of a unit from another area of the curriculum, such as science or social studies. Pupils of varying ability levels work together to investigate a topic, choosing material written at appropriate levels for them and pooling their information. Their investigation usually results in a presentation to the class or the construction of something related to the topic, which might be

432

Teaching
Reading in
Today's
Elementary
Schools

space travel, types of mammals, community helpers, pioneer life, energy, environmental control, or something similar.

A popular form of grouping among students is *friendship grouping,* in which good friends work together for a specific purpose and within a specified time frame. Because friends understand each other, enjoy being together, and can usually cooperate well, this type of group can be particularly effective. There is a danger, however, that the primary activity may be social interaction rather than the accomplishment of the designated task. If this is the case, the teacher should disband the group until the students realize that they must *work* together, not just visit. Some purposes for friendship groups might be sharing favorite stories, responding to books through combined artwork (posters, dioramas, mobiles), and preparing a puppet show based on a story to present to the class.

Yet another type of grouping involves *pupil pairs* or *partners,* who may work cooperatively on such activities as

1. sight word practice with picture-word cards.
2. dictionary practice on location of words, location of definition that fits the context, and the like.
3. visual discrimination games—locating identical words or words that differ.
4. solving crossword puzzles based on new vocabulary words.

Partners may work better on skill tasks if they have about the same degree of reading ability and if they are congenial. The directions for a paired task must be clear, the task specific, and the time limited to that needed for the task.

Pupils may also work in pairs in *tutorial groups,* in which one student acts as a tutor and is assigned to help another student learn a specific skill. Tutors should be trained by the teacher in how to present the skill and should be encouraged to act in a helpful rather than superior manner. Tutorial pairing can benefit both the tutor and the tutee and can save the teacher's time, especially if the tutor occasionally works with more than one tutee at the same time.

An intraclass grouping plan that uses all these kinds of groupings offers certain advantages. The child has the opportunity to choose or be placed in a variety of group situations, and discovers that some things are best learned in groups and others on an individual basis. Most important, this kind of plan provides opportunities to correlate reading with other content areas and to use the interrelationships among the language arts, since the same teacher works with the same children in all subject areas throughout the school day.

Formation of Groups   Placing students in the appropriate ability group is not an easy task. Teachers must consider several factors and may want to wait from several days to a few weeks before making group assignments. Records from the previous year usually show which basal reader was last completed

Without good classroom organization and management, reading instruction may be totally ineffective. (© Sybil Shelton/Peter Arnold)

by each child, and teachers can place the child in the next book in the series. They can also use achievement test scores to help them place students. If a child has transferred into the school and no records are available, the teacher will want to make an informal assessment to determine his or her reading level and group placement. Remember: a good guideline to follow when in doubt is to place a student at a level where success is virtually assured, since it is much better for the child psychologically to move *up* than to move *back*.

Other factors enter into a teacher's decision on group placement. Some children may not have read a book all summer and will need to review before moving on, whereas others may have attended summer reading programs at the library or read extensively at home and be ready to continue immediately. A student's willingness to work, attitude toward reading, and rate of progress are also important considerations.

There is no optimal group size or number of groups for a classroom. Most teachers find that three ability groups work well in terms of classroom management and reduction of differences in reading levels, but some classes divide more logically into two or four groups. Since better readers are usually better independent workers, the high-achievement group may include a larger number of students than the low group, which should be small so that the teacher can give more attention to individual problems. During the year

434
Teaching
Reading in
Today's
Elementary
Schools

the number and composition of groups may change in response to the students' progress.

Ability groups generally last all year, but it is a good idea to move a student if that will facilitate learning. A teacher may have misjudged a student's placement, or a student may change his or her rate of learning to read. However, before moving a pupil the teacher should observe him or her closely and perhaps discuss the potential change with the student. A child who reads fluently, always finishes first, and knows all of the answers may be a candidate for a higher group or for an individualized approach. This student will probably be excited about advancing but must realize that the work will be more difficult; he or she might read with both the old and new groups for a period of time to avoid missing any skills and to ensure that the move is within his or her capability. Seatwork could be proportionately reduced for this period of time. On the other hand, a child who misses more than one word out of fifteen or twenty and has difficulty understanding the material should probably be moved to a lower group. This child may be disappointed initially, but will be relieved to find that the reading level is more comfortable and success is more likely to occur.

Students in the high group often finish the basal reader for their grade before the end of the school year, and when this happens the teacher should be ready to suggest other types of reading experiences. Individualized reading, a study of the newspaper, a unit on poetry or folklore, or a research activity is appropriate. One fifth-grade group who finished early evaluated Newbery books, first devising a checklist of criteria and then locating all of the available Newbery Award winners and runners-up. Each of the students read and evaluated several of the books, and the group then compiled the results of their evaluations.

Forming ability or achievement groups in first grade is a special problem because there are no records of any books that students might have read. A teacher at this level will probably wait longer to form groups and may experiment with temporary formations, using reading-readiness test scores, informal checklists, and observation to assign students to groups. Gradually the teacher will begin pulling together those children who seem to be ready for formal reading instruction in one group and placing those who are showing signs of interest in reading in a second group. The teacher will place children who will need many types of readiness experiences before they are ready for reading instruction in a third group.

Other than achievement groups, most groups are formed for a limited time and a specific purpose. For example, skills groups are formed on the basis of specific needs identified through criterion-referenced tests, informal assessments, or teacher observation. They are created when the teacher recognizes that several children have a similar weakness and are disbanded as the children learn the skill. Interest groups may be formed by using an informal interest inventory (see page 240) or by asking students to sign up for topics that they would like to investigate, and project or research groups may be formed by student preference or randomly by the teacher.

Psychological Impact of Grouping Even if a teacher tries to conceal the identities of the high and low groups, children are well aware of the level of each group. Many low-group students remain in the low group over the years and as a result form poor self-concepts. Teachers should try to minimize the stigma they feel due to their placement in the low group.

Members of the low reading group should be included in whole-class reading-related activities. Some of these students may be excellent artists who can contribute to a class mural; others may love acting and can interpret a story through creative dramatics. They can also mix with members of higher achievement groups through participation in interest, project, skills, or friendship groups. These children should be seated with other class members, not segregated by reading group.

Names of groups can be labels that reinforce a slow reader's negative feelings, so teachers should avoid identifying groups by numbers or letters (1 or A for the top group, 2 or B for the middle group, and 3 or C for the low group), or by names that connote quickness or slowness. Instead they might allow children to name their own group or call a group by the title of the book that is being used.

Perhaps the most important factor in building a slow reader's self-concept is the kind of group rapport that the teacher helps to create. Children are likely to feel good about themselves if the teacher encourages them, praises their efforts, cares about them, and makes the lessons interesting. A warm, intimate atmosphere within a group will help students to feel better about reading and about themselves.

Scheduling of Groups Reading achievement groups are generally held near the beginning of the day for about an hour and a half, and frequently this time period is used for instruction with the basal reader. A class with three ability groups might be scheduled as shown in Table 10.1.

The morning instructional period may be used for other approaches along with or instead of the basal reader. For instance, first graders might benefit from alternating basal reader instruction on Mondays, Wednesdays, and Fridays with language experience lessons on Tuesdays and Thursdays, while

TABLE 10.1 A General Plan for Grouping Within the Classroom

	Group A	*Group B*	*Group C*
10 min.	Total-class reading activities		
30 min.	Teacher-directed activity	Independent work	Library reading
30 min.	Independent work	Library reading	Teacher-directed activity
30 min.	Library reading	Teacher-directed activity	Independent work
10 min.	Total-class reading activities		

Note: The table suggests that all groups possess the same ability to work independently. In actual classroom situations, there may be a need for more teacher-directed activities for the slower learning reading group(s).

436

Teaching
Reading in
Today's
Elementary
Schools

older students might alternate basal reader lessons with skill-group instruction. A class of students who can work well independently might engage in individualized reading every morning.

The following is a variation of a group organizational plan designed for a one-hour reading session in the fifth grade where four groups are at work at the same time.

Group 1

(High-achievement group)

This group works independently, doing reading research on questions listed for the class unit. The teacher needs only to check with the group occasionally or to offer suggestions for new reading.

Group 2

(Low-achievement group)

The teacher starts the period with this group. Since this is the slow reading group, the children may read comfortably at about a second-grade level. The teacher helps them compose a story, from which they make a reading chart, which is then read by each member of the group. Using the chart, students work on word structure and some phonics before the teacher moves on to another group. The children are then given some easy books to read for pleasure. When the teacher has finished his work with Group 2, he checks on each of the other groups or helps individuals.

Group 3

This is a group of average readers who may have difficulty in discovering the main ideas in a story. They work with a worksheet designed by the teacher.

Group 4

Three or four capable children who are not working up to their capabilities get help from another student who is a good reader. The tutor has been coached by the teacher to help the children with words they do not know. They read a story silently and later read the story aloud to each other, working for expression.

Children should not read for instructional purposes only; teachers should offer opportunities for recreational and functional reading later in the day. For a half-hour to an hour in the afternoon students might participate in whole-class or special-purpose group activities such as those already suggested. This period should be relaxing and enjoyable so that students will realize that reading is more than skill building.

Management of Groups   No matter how good a lesson is, students will not learn much unless the teacher is able to control their behavior. Classroom management is a crucial factor in learning, especially when instruction is individualized or conducted in groups. Clear, sensible, consistent procedures can contribute to the maintenance of an orderly classroom.

The teacher must establish behavioral policies (perhaps with student input), which all students must understand. At the beginning of the year these policies might be listed on a chart as part of a language experience lesson. Generally it is advisable to permit children reasonable freedom of movement and to allow them to talk quietly about task-related topics, but low voices and quiet movement should be stressed at all times. A child who breaks her pencil point, for instance, should be permitted to sharpen it without waiting to ask permission, but a teacher may want to limit the number of children at a learning center or allow only one student at a time to go to the restroom.

Children must know exactly what they are to do if they are expected to work well independently. After writing assignments for each group on the chalkboard, the teacher should spend time going over these assignments and making sure the students understand what they are asked to do. A list of things to do when they finish should also be available for students who complete their work early.

Room arrangement affects classroom management. Children should know where to find materials that they will need to use, such as workbooks, paper, scissors, and crayons, and they should know where to put completed work. Space should be provided for independent small-group work, and children should be able to move quickly and quietly to and from those areas that they use frequently.

The teacher should select carefully the best place in the room to hold basal reader groups. She should sit in a corner facing a semicircle of children who are in the group. From this vantage point the teacher can also watch the rest of the class and be aware of any problems that may be developing. If possible, she should sit by the chalkboard in order to use it for instructional purposes during reading groups. When children are working in other types of groups, she will move quietly from one group to another, answering questions and offering suggestions.

A good policy for teachers to follow while working with groups is to prohibit other children from interrupting, because interruptions are distracting and usually unnecessary. Appointed monitors can help solve small problems, such as identifying a word or finding a pencil, but children may consult the teacher about bigger issues if necessary while others are moving into or out of groups.

In order to maintain class control, teachers should make organizational changes slowly and gradually. Only those students who can be trusted to work well independently should be included in the initial stages if new groups are being formed or individualized reading is beginning. As more children participate in the new plan, some may not be able to handle the unstructured situation; these children may need to return to their seats and continue with traditional assignments until they can behave responsibly.

Worthwhile and interesting activities should be available for students while teachers work with groups because they can be important learning experiences. These activities are also important for maintaining good discipline, because children who are interested in their work are not apt to cause problems. Most independent activities are related to basal reader lessons,

438

Teaching
Reading in
Today's
Elementary
Schools

either as skill development or enrichment, but teachers should also offer a variety of interesting choices that will motivate children. Ideas may be listed on the board, placed at centers, or written on slips of paper for students to pull from an activity box. They should be changed periodically so that the class does not get bored. Students might choose from such ideas as those listed below.

Design and put up a bulletin board about your basal reader story.

See how many two-, three-, four-, or more syllable words you can find in your story.

Dramatize a story with a few other students for the rest of the class.

Read books from the class library or the school library that the teacher has checked out in advance. (The selection should be changed periodically.)

Compose a poem or short story and illustrate it on a sheet of paper that will become part of a class book.

Write a different ending for a story; write what you liked or did not like about the main character; or write another type of reaction to the story.

Select an acetate-protected activity sheet from a file: a crossword puzzle, a seek-a-word puzzle, or some other type of activity.

Fold a strip of paper (maybe three inches by twelve inches) into four sections and make a comic strip.

Look through your story to find all of the descriptive words, action words, or naming words.

Make as many small words as you can from a large word that appears in your story, such as *Thanksgiving* or *spectacular*.

Write a story for the class newspaper.

Do research for a social studies or science project.

Work with a small group on a mural or diorama.

Write half a page about yourself for a class book and illustrate the rest of the page with a collage of things you like.

Arrange in sequence comic strips that have been cut into frames.

Write a story using the story starters in a commercial kit or that your teacher suggests. (Example: "I woke up in the middle of the night terrified by. . . .")

Solve riddles or puzzles and create some of your own.

First graders must learn to do some things independently before they are grouped, so the teacher will need to help these youngsters develop self-control, good work habits, and social-interaction skills. In planning independent work, he must keep in mind the children's immaturity and limited reading ability, gradually introducing activities such as the following.

Playing a commercial or teacher-prepared game such as Lotto, alone or with a partner

Illustrating stories

Painting pictures

Cutting out pictures in magazines or catalogues of things that begin with a certain sound or objects that belong together

Modeling clay

Putting puzzles together

Engaging in dramatic play

Looking at picture books

Listening to stories at a listening station

Working with reading readiness workbooks

Using felt figures or a flannel board to retell a story

Working with word-bank cards

✔ Self-Check: Objective 2

Describe some strategies that teachers might use for managing an entire class while they are working with one reading group. (See Self-Improvement Opportunities 2, 3, 4, and 5.)

Interclass Grouping

Interclass grouping involves parallel scheduling of reading lessons among several sections of a grade or grades. Groups go to different rooms (or spaces within an open classroom) and are divided according to general reading level. One teacher provides instruction for one ability group while another teacher works with another ability level, and so on. This kind of grouping is based on the assumption that the range of skills that needs attention will be limited by the needs of a particular group and will be reduced for each teacher. Evidence indicates, however, that the range of skills in such situations is not appreciably lessened.

For such grouping to be homogeneous, teachers must know about many criteria. They should discover each student's achievement levels, intelligence, interests, preferred learning modality, and academic motivation. Interclass grouping tends to ignore age and maturity differences, sometimes combining pupils from several grade levels, and often tends to separate reading activities from instruction in content areas.

✔ Self-Check: Objective 3

Describe several key characteristics of interclass groupings.

Other Organizational Plans

At times a teacher may find individualized or whole-class activities to be more appropriate than small groups. A discussion of these other arrangements is presented below. In addition, four alternative organizational plans—nongraded, departmentalization, team arrangement, and open curriculum—are discussed in this section.

Individualized

Two plans for individualizing instruction are given here: learning centers and reading contracts. (See also Chapter 5 for a discussion of individualization.)

Learning Center It is often necessary to supplement the reading program with additional skill development activities. After identifying skill needs of children and giving initial instruction, the teacher can prescribe activities for additional practice to be done in a learning center. These types of centers can also be used conveniently to provide resources and motivation for extensive reading for information and enjoyment.[1]

A successful learning center is one that contains these four components:

1. self-direction for the child
2. provision for different ability levels
3. stated objectives for each specific skill, with a sequence of tasks from easiest to most difficult
4. clearly defined means of evaluation.

A brief list of the types of reading stations applicable in the classroom includes

1. library corner for reading
2. center for creative drama or puppet shows
3. listen-and-read centers
4. oral reading with partners or on tape
5. language experience (writing) centers
6. reading game centers
7. centers for skill development with worksheets, tapes, activity cards or folders
8. project centers for research purposes
9. literature centers.

Among the techniques that have been found successful in handling pupil assignments to stations are

1. listing assignments on the chalkboard
2. listing assignments on a chart
3. listing assignments on duplicating paper
4. discussing assignments orally
5. giving tickets for the various stations
6. using a job sheet or contract.

[1]These learning-center ideas are based on *Reading Effectiveness Program in Elementary Schools.* Indiana Department of Education, 1975, pp. 75–80.

Some teachers have found a job-card box—a skill-based series of cards to coordinate the use of the material in the center—a handy tool. Designed to direct children to materials in the room and to independent activities of various sorts, the cards can be numbered and color-coded according to level, type of activity, and skill. They can be either chosen by the children or assigned by the teacher.

Teachers have found many ways of establishing learning centers. Screens, bookcases, corrugated cardboard boxes, portable chalkboards, and filing cabinets are but a few of the possibilities for dividers and center walls.

One way of recording a child's work at the center is presented in Example 10.1. Example 10.2 illustrates an idea for a learning center.

▶ **EXAMPLE 10.1:** Sample Learning Center Record

Name _____
I worked at the _____ center or station.
Time in _____ Time out _____
How did you like the work? _____ (good, fair, poor)

Activity:

I read _____
I worked on _____
I listened to _____
I read aloud with _____
I wrote _____
I played a reading game _____
I did a worksheet on _____
I also _____ ◀

Some teachers attempt to individualize to some degree by using reading laboratories, which are kits of materials that offer practice on reading skills at a variety of levels. They are generally designed to be scored by the students themselves, who are initially placed at an appropriate level by a test administered by the teacher and then expected to progress through materials of increasing difficulty at their own rates. These materials may be incorporated into learning centers.

Two excellent references about learning centers are

Dick, Norma, ed. *Ideas for Reading–Learning Centers.* California Reading Association, 1973.
Greff, Kasper N., and Eunice N. Askov. *Learning Centers: An Ideabook for Reading and Language Arts.* Dubuque, Iowa: Kendall/Hunt, 1974.

442

Teaching
Reading in
Today's
Elementary
Schools

▶ **EXAMPLE 10.2:** Mini Learning Center: "The *ow* Sound"

Place a learning package into a laminated file folder. In this case the learning package will focus on the *ow* sound, which can have the following variations:

ow sound as in *flower*
ow sound as in *arrow*
ow that can have either sound, depending on context, as in *bow*

Place word cards in envelopes attached to the folder. Directions should read "Look at each word card and decide in which envelope it should be placed (the one with the picture of the flower, the one with the picture of the arrow, or the one with no picture). Code the cards on the back so that the child can check the answers. Use a set of cards that includes the following words:

now	slow	row
towel	snow	sow
howl	tow	bow ◀
growl	show	
crown	throw	
power	blow	
powder	grow	
	flow	
	low	
	glow	

Student Contracts   Students may "contract" to complete certain sequences of instruction designed to help them with their individual needs. The agreement may be formalized through the use of a contract, signed by the teacher and the child, that simply states what the pupil is to do and when the task is to be completed. Once agreed upon, the contract should be completed as specified. Example 10.3 illustrates one such student contract.

A teacher can prepare and have available contracts calling for a variety of assignments and tasks, from which pupils can select those that most suit their needs, or the pupils can propose a contract and negotiate it with the teacher.

A possible modification of the contract plan is called the assignment or job sheet. The teacher first identifies a definite instructional goal—for example, the mastery of a specific skill or subskill—and then organizes available material (textbooks/workbooks, and so on) to guide the learner toward that goal. Each child can proceed as fast as mastery permits. At times, children can work in pairs or teams of three to complete the assignment, which may take from three to five class periods. Example 10.4 shows a sample assignment sheet. Again, a skill-based series of these sheets can be noted on cards in a box, as explained earlier.

► **EXAMPLE 10.3:** Sample Pupil Contract Form

443

Classroom
Organization
and
Management

1. After listening to the librarian read aloud *The Cay* by Theodore Taylor, read one of the following to learn more about the idea of survival.
   a. *Island of the Blue Dolphins* by Scott O'Dell
   b. *Stranded* by Matt Christopher
   c. *Three Without Fear* by Robert C. Dusoe
   d. *Landslide* by Veronique Day
   e. *The Summer I Was Lost* by Philip Viereck
2. Share your research in one of these ways:
   a. Illustrate one incident in the story.
   b. Write a play dramatizing one incident.
   c. Make a model of an object that may be useful for survival.
   d. Interview an authority on the subject of some sort of survival technique and write a report.
   e. Compare the character(s) of your story with Robinson Crusoe in terms of self-reliance.

Choose one book from Number 1 and one method from Number 2 for your contract.
I plan to do 1 _____ and 2 _____. I will have this contract completed by _____.
Student's signature _____
Teacher's signature _____ ◄

► **EXAMPLE 10.4:** Sample Job Sheet

How to Use an Encyclopedia #3 (_____ book)

Page	Directions
10	You and your partner take turns reading paragraphs to each other. Then read, answer, and check questions 1 and 2.
12	You and your partner take turns reading paragraphs to each other. Then do as directed on the lower half of page 12.
13	Read, answer, and check questions on lower half of page 13.
14	Do sections 3 and 5 as directed.
18	Read and discuss this section with your partner; answer questions at bottom of page 18.
22	Write, as directed, working alone. When finished, check your work with your partner.
25	Complete blanks in the bottom right corner. Check your answers in the Teacher's Edition.

Now go to the teacher for a review discussion and check test before picking up your next assignment sheet. ◄

Whole-Class Activities

Whole-class activities are appropriate when the teacher uses multisensory presentations, particularly oral or visual materials, since these can convey meaning to children of differing achievement levels. Another reason for whole-class activities is to build a spirit of class unity and to give each child a feeling of participation.

Among reading activities for the whole class are creative dramatics and choral reading, listening to stories read by the teacher or other students, taking part in sustained silent reading (see page 355), learning about reading study skills, going to the library, watching educational television, writing a class newspaper, creating a language experience story, watching and discussing a film or filmstrip of a story, sharing multiple copies of a student magazine or newspaper, playing word games, and sharing during a poetry hour.

Nongraded

A nongraded class incorporates students of a wider-than-usual age span with a wide range of academic performances. For example, if there are 90 children six, seven, and eight years old (traditionally first, second, and third graders), the principal might randomly select ten from each age level to form a class of thirty pupils, thus producing three nongraded classrooms instead of one first grade, one second grade, and one third grade. The children may continue with the same teacher for as long as three years. Sometimes this pattern is called a multiple-graded or -leveled or continuous progress pattern. Individual differences within a nongraded class may be no greater than those in a single grade situation, and it is again possible to group by specific skills and according to maturity and needs. Nongraded classes can provide for differing pupil rates of growth by directing the teacher's attention toward the need for individualization of instruction.

Departmentalization

This organization has seemed to be on the increase in the past few years, particularly in middle schools. Under a departmentalized plan of teaching, there is a separate teacher for each subject, such as one teacher for the reading (and possibly other language arts) program, one for the social studies program, one for the science program, etc. A teacher may teach the same subject for five to six classes a day with one period free or devoted to giving individual help. Some correlation between reading (or language arts) and other subjects is possible when a teacher works as part of a team with another teacher, such as the social studies teacher. In such a case, the two teachers can make use of a large block of time by teaching the two subjects back to back. Within the allotted time, many types of teaching and grouping can take place. The skills of one subject can be used to complement or develop the content of another subject. For example, since the children in social studies will need to know how to do research, the reading teacher can focus upon how to use reference materials. The major advantage of departmentalization is that the greater a teacher's understanding of a subject is, the greater the possibility for excellent instruction is, whereas the greatest disadvantage is probably that departmentalization tends to make the curriculum subject-centered rather than process- or child-centered.

Team Arrangement

This involves combining two or three classes in one large area with a staff of several teachers. Team teaching has developed from the belief that all teachers are not equally skilled or enthusiastic in all curriculum areas. While one teacher instructs the entire class or a group in an area of his particular competence, the other teachers work with other groups or individuals on other subjects. The team situation can offer a variety of activities in the best possible circumstances, making it possible to diagnose the word identification problems of a child, to group the child with other children who have the same problem, and to allow one teacher to give undivided attention to that group with no interference from the rest of the class. Meanwhile, another teacher can work with a group on a poetry unit, an activity she likes very much. Still another teacher can work with a group planning a book fair, while a fourth teacher can help some children with a particular content area reading difficulty. On other days, the teachers can work with the same children but on different problems or on the same problems with different children. Open physical arrangements in schools (three or four sections of children in a large undivided area) help to provide for this kind of teaching.

Open Curriculum

With this approach, modeled on the British infant and primary schools, classrooms are usually divided into separate areas, often called interest or learning centers (Robinson and Gold, 1974; Wiener, 1974). They are filled with learning materials related to science, art, or language arts, for example. The language arts center, for instance, might have word games and books designed for a variety of reading levels. Children actively engage in planning their activities and usually work independently or in small groups. A basic tenet of open classroom philosophy is that children learn reading skills in a "natural" way, as they learn about other subjects, and at their own pace, so skills are not programmed according to a predetermined sequence. The language experience approach is often used in an open curriculum during the primary years, and children's compositions are used as instructional reading material. Temporary groups are often formed around common interests, and individual and small-group conferences are part of the instructional plan. Dewey's concept of exploration (Dewey, 1938), Montessori's focus upon

446

Teaching
Reading in
Today's
Elementary
Schools

extensive use of objects and games as instructional materials (Hunt, 1964), Rousseau's faith in the child's natural curiosity and growth (Rousseau, 1964), and Piaget's idea that children learn in varying stages through direct experience (Piaget, 1955) are all roots of the program.

The following example illustrates one way of grouping in an open curriculum in terms of reading skill development.

A teacher gives diagnostic tests to check reading skills of all the children in her section of the classroom. Diagnostic testing is her particular job, while other teachers in the unit are taking the responsibility for different assignments. As part of her job, this teacher also groups the children according to skill difficulties and then divides these groups into subgroups according to general ability. When a group of children have difficulty selecting the main idea in a paragraph, the whole multi-aged group is provided with material geared to the ability of the poorest reader in the group, as the problem is common to easy and difficult reading material. As some reading tasks require subgrouping because of the nature and difficulty of the material, the teacher subdivides a group that has problems with summarizing what has been read. While older boys and girls may summarize well those reading materials written on a low reading level, they may have comprehension difficulties with material written at their own general achievement levels. Thus, the teacher sets up two (or more) groups divided as to reading level because the task is affected by the difficulty of the material being used.

As soon as the groupings have been determined, the teacher reports her plans to the other teachers in her unit, and a schedule is set up for meeting with various groups in quiet places to work on their specific problems. The schedule for special help is posted on a common announcement board or given to each person concerned on a dittoed schedule. Children plan their day's work and are responsible for being in the right place at the right time.

Too often, an open environment exists only in the physical arrangement of the classroom rather than in the operation of a flexible educational program.

✔ Self-Check: Objective 4

List several organizational patterns and provide a rationale for each. (See Self-Improvement Opportunity 6.)

ROLE OF THE TEACHER

A pure form of any organizational plan is rarely found in operation. Usually schools, sets of teachers, or teachers alone use a combination of plans, because there are strengths and weaknesses to each one. A teacher must develop an organizational system with which he or she is comfortable and which works effectively. Just as there is no one best way to teach reading for all children, so there is no one way to organize a class to suit the needs of every teacher or every group of children. We agree with others that while organizational plans have an indirect bearing on instruction, a competent teacher, not a particular structure, is what makes the major difference.

Thus it is safe to say that the most essential ingredient of a good reading program is a creative, organized, enthusiastic, knowledgeable teacher. Generally speaking, the excellent teacher (1) understands each learner's social, cultural, and linguistic backgrounds; (2) seeks to unify cognitive and affective learning processes; (3) utilizes the child's experiences and provides other experiences for development of ideas and feelings to be incorporated in the process of reading; and (4) sees himself or herself as a guide, listener, questioner, reactor, facilitator, and stimulator of learning rather than as a didactic instructor.

Ten desirable teacher behaviors (DTBs) were identified by the Institute of Development of Human Resources at the University of Florida at Gainesville for use by teachers in the classroom and by parents at home. They can be directly related to reading instruction and used by teachers as criteria for evaluating their instruction, according to Dixie Lee Spiegel (December, 1980, pp. 324–330). Most of them are based on teacher-child interactions.

DTB 1: Before starting an activity, explain what you are going to do. It is important to set purposes for reading and to explain each task clearly. Both DRA (see Chapter 5) and DRTA (see Chapter 7) provide opportunities for setting purposes during reading lessons.

DTB 2: Before starting an activity, give the learner time to familiarize him- or herself with the materials. Students should know something about the content of the reading material before they begin to read. This criterion is consistent with schema theory, which relates background knowledge to success in comprehension.

DTB 3: Ask questions that have more than one right answer. Literal questions with a single correct answer are easy to ask, but higher-order comprehension questions with many possible correct answers cause children to reflect and consider. Thinking questions require a child to become mentally involved with the reading material.

DTB 4: Ask questions which require multiple-word answers. These types of questions are also likely to be higher-order questions that call for divergent thinking. In addition, they provide opportunities for language development as children are required to express their ideas.

DTB 5: Encourage the learner to enlarge upon his or her answer. If students give incorrect or illogical answers, a teacher can help them to arrive at acceptable answers by questioning them about their reasoning. In a similar way, students who explain how they reached correct answers are modeling appropriate thought processes for their peers.

DTB 6: Get the learner to ask questions. Students should feel free to ask questions in order to clarify concepts and to explore the author's meaning.

448
Teaching
Reading in
Today's
Elementary
Schools

Manzo's ReQuest procedure (see page 208) helps children learn to form higher-order questions.

DTB 7: Give the learner time to think about the problem: don't be too quick to help. Too often teachers "rescue" students who seem to take too long to answer questions. Instead, they should allow time for students to use various decoding strategies and to consider answers to comprehension questions.

DTB 8: Get the learner to make judgments on the basis of evidence rather than by guessing. Readers should be encouraged to use information they already have in order to make inferences in reading. They should use evidence from both their own experiences and the text to support their answers.

DTB 9: Praise the learner when he or she does well or takes small steps in the right direction. Learning to read is a long-term, complex process, and teachers should celebrate any evidence of progress toward this goal. Progress, not perfection, should be rewarded.

DTB 10: Let the learner know when an answer or word is wrong, but do so in a positive or neutral manner. Whenever possible, the teacher should point out that part of a child's answer is correct or that his or her idea is reasonable. Then the teacher can lead the student to discover what is incorrect about the answer in order to develop skill in reading independently.

A study by Leinhardt, Zigmond, and Cooley was reported by John Guthrie (1982). This study used as its premise that learning occurs through engagement. "Children improve in reading in direct proportion to the amount of time they spend fruitfully engaged in reading activities at an appropriate level of difficulty" (p. 755). Leinhardt and others found that certain types of reading activities, or engagements, were more beneficial than others. For example, time spent in silent reading correlated positively with reading achievement, but no gains in achievement resulted from time spent in traditional oral reading or from indirect reading, including discussion and some types of workbook activities.

Three teacher behaviors seemed to be most effective in gaining student attention and engagement: (1) teacher instruction, including presentations, explanations, and feedback; (2) reinforcement of student learning, such as giving praise or recognition for student efforts; and (3) "cognitive press," expressed through the teacher's support and encouragement of the student's inclination toward academic material.

Jack Bagford (1981) described a staff development project in which teaching methodology was measured by outside, independent evaluators in the area of reading instruction. He used a Teacher Classroom Behavior Inventory for evaluation, which included the following behaviors:

1. Communicates with clarity.
2. Makes efficient use of instructional time.
3. Exhibits high rate of immediate corrective feedback.
4. Elicits high rate of active pupil response.

5. Asks questions of varying types and difficulty.
6. Establishes and maintains an environment which encourages reading.
7. Utilizes a variety of approaches to teaching reading.
8. Adjusts instruction for individual differences in reading ability.
9. Provides reading tasks that challenge pupils, but which also allow for a high rate of pupil success.
10. Exhibits a positive attitude toward pupils and their probable success in reading.
11. Selects and uses instructional materials of appropriate difficulty.
12. Communicates to pupils what is expected of them and how well they are meeting expectations.
13. Develops in pupils a positive attitude toward reading. (pp. 402–403)

At the end of three years, the evaluators found increases in ratings for reading teachers and gains in pupil achievement. By focusing on the priorities listed in the Inventory, teachers made desirable changes in instructional behaviors over the three-year period.

In a summary of findings from several research studies on the relationship between the teaching and learning of basic skills in the elementary grades, Jere Brophy (1979) reached several conclusions about teacher effectiveness. Some teachers are more successful in enabling students to learn than others, and success is related to differences in teacher behavior. Although no teaching skills have been identified as appropriate for all situations, several types of behavior are related to gains in reading achievement.

Effective teachers spend more time actually teaching than those teachers who are less effective, and they spend more time in productive activities and less time in disruptions and periods of confusion. Direct instruction is effective for helping students learn basic skills. It makes use of a structured curriculum, keeps students actively involved in academic work, and provides for student response with corrective feedback.

Effective teaching varies according to grade and student ability levels. In comparison with teaching in the upper elementary grades, effective teaching in the lower grades makes greater use of small-group instruction, teacher circulation among the students, praise, and drill and recitation. Lower-ability students need to move at a slower pace and have more repetition than higher-ability students.

H. Alan Robinson and Alvina T. Burrows (1974) have listed the attitudes and actions they consider essential to being a good teacher in the following general areas.

Reading

1. Considers reading an act of searching for the author's messages; recognizes that reading does not take place unless understanding takes place
2. In addition, considers reading a dialogue between the authors and the reader, in which the reader interacts with the authors, interprets what the authors say,

450

Teaching
Reading in
Today's
Elementary
Schools

evaluates the message, and uses, stores, or even discards the information and ideas obtained

3. Recognizes that each child brings a somewhat different cultural, social, emotional, intellectual, and language background to reading and uses that knowledge in the teaching-learning situation

4. Evaluates the strengths and weaknesses of pupils' language development and relates the knowledge gained to their reading progress

5. Evaluates individual needs in the skills of reading and continually plans suitable instruction

6. Helps pupils assess their own reading achievement

7. Uses oral reading as one evaluation technique without constant interference from the teacher and without an audience

8. Involves children in reading for a multitude of purposes in a variety of materials

9. Selects from many organization plans according to purpose(s) of instruction: flexible groupings, individual pupils, pupil teams, whole class

10. Has children read orally in purposeful audience situations, with material well prepared in advance, so as to enhance the experience of the listener

11. Permits children to read orally in their own dialects without correction unless the message is unclear to the listeners; works toward long-term development of reading orally in standard English

12. Often reads to pupils, involving and encouraging their responses and their interactions

13. Serves as an adult model by sharing some of his or her reading interests and experiences with children

14. Uses appropriate opportunities to stimulate wide reading, leading to lifetime reading habits

Literature

1. Selects literature to read to children and helps them select literature for themselves within their levels of conceptual maturity and language sophistication

2. Reads appropriate literature to children revealing his or her own satisfaction in the experiences without forcing agreement with adult tastes and interpretations

3. Exposes children to varied models of literary merit and discusses qualities of writing with them without extensive analysis; uses open-ended as well as specific questions to focus attention on style, characterization, plot, setting, point of view, theme

4. Provides much unstructured exploration of literature and exchange of responses based upon knowledge that this free experience leads to favorable reading attitudes and ability to read critically and creatively

5. Keeps rotating classroom library collection readily accessible to pupils; arranges for class and informal individual use of school library and visits to community library

6. Suggests books of both prose and verse to individuals and groups appropriate to their personal interests, as well as to topics in various curriculum areas

7. Arranges for deepening and intensifying literary experience through free conversation, discussions, dramatics, graphic arts, and written expression

Integration of Language Arts

451
Classroom
Organization
and
Management

1. Plans for interaction of reading, writing, listening, and speaking, and relates them to cognitive and affective learnings
2. Develops concepts through use of all the language arts, drawing upon firsthand experience and the media
3. Involves children in activities that show the relationship of simultaneous use of the language arts—viewing and listening (television), writing and listening (questions and notes after a speaker or interview), reading and dramatizing; demonstrates the unique contribution of each when used separately and together
4. Provides isolated practice in needed skills in each of the language arts, but makes sure that they are applied in meaningful, purposeful situations throughout the total school curriculum. (pp. 77–78, 80)

Obviously, many factors are involved in being an effective teacher. One important instructional activity that seems to have a strong impact upon pupil achievement is the questioning done by teachers in reading lessons (discussed in Chapter 4). Another, cited in the previous section, is making and using appraisals of pupil attitudes toward reading, and a third is discussed fully in Chapter 9, "Assessment of Pupil Progress." It is recommended that teachers begin the instructional program with a diagnosis of the specific reading needs of each child, design lessons to meet the identified needs, define in precise terms what is to be taught, and then evaluate the results of the instruction in terms of what the child has learned (Rutherford, 1971). Factors such as those mentioned in this section seem to characterize the first-rate, superior teacher of reading as distinguished from the less effective reading teacher.

✔ Self-Check: Objective 5

Give an explanation of at least three roles of the teacher related to (1) reading, (2) literature, and (3) language arts. (See Self-Improvement Opportunity 7.)

PARENTS AND PARAPROFESSIONALS

Parents can assist the teacher by providing educational opportunities for the child at home, and paraprofessionals can help in a variety of ways in the classroom. This section will include discussions of specific ways in which both parents and paraprofessionals can support teachers.

Parents

It is important to maintain communication between teachers and parents. Among the traditional methods of communication are newsletters (carefully written letters and bulletins to keep the parents informed about happenings at

452

Teaching
Reading in
Today's
Elementary
Schools

school), school booklets (including rules and regulations and helpful information that parents need to know before and after sending their child to school), Parent-Teacher Association meetings, written reports in the form of personal letters or checklists, telephone calls, social suppers, home visits (which give the parent and teacher a chance to discuss particular problems and acquaint the teacher with the home environment of the child), and Open House days (when the parents visit in the child's classroom—with or without the child—to familiarize themselves with the materials, schedules, and routines of the school day). For years schools have utilized these methods, in various combinations, to foster communication between school and home.

The major avenues open to the reading teacher who wishes to communicate with parents are

1. suggesting general and specific activities for the child to do at home.
2. conferring about reporting devices, tests, and homework.
3. sending letters or bulletins to keep parents informed.

Home Activities

Because language usage is initiated long before children have their first encounters with school, parents are important partners in the school's endeavors. Fortunate are those children whose homes provide an outward sense of love, a feeling of security, wholesome food, adequate rest—all of which contribute to a stable environment for learning. When a great deal of verbal interaction is encouraged, background experiences are broadened, and reading materials are made available, children are also being prepared for learning. Parents who talk with and listen to their children, who bring signs and labels to their attention, who share home experiences with them, and who read to them provide a natural background for beginning reading instruction. Since not all children experience the benefits of all these activities, some parents may need assistance and information about ways to provide a good home environment for their children's success in school.

Listening and speaking with children are of paramount importance. An attentive listener encourages further conversational efforts. Conversation with parents is an important way for children to learn to be willing to let others talk in turn and to interrupt less frequently. In talking with parents, children hear sentence patterns and rhyming words, have the opportunity to distinguish sounds of many types, and gain information and words. Casual conversations between parents and children may occur as children play house, build with blocks, or enjoy toys. Opportunities abound every day for talking and listening at home: weather, news, food, clothing, pictures, games, pets, furniture, and plants are all good topics for discussion between parents and children. Everyday opportunities for sharing experiences with younger children include visits to nearby parks, local shops, fire stations, and the like. Parents can easily answer children's questions and explain the meanings of

Parents are important partners in the school's endeavors—by stressing the value of reading and by actually reading to and with their children, they can help build positive attitudes toward books.   (© Elizabeth Crews)

new words while families are enjoying experiences together. More special trips might involve visits to a museum, zoo, bakery, dairy farm, or bottling company; longer trips provide even more talk about roads, rivers, mountains, or animals new to the children. A camping trip, for example, offers many opportunities for developing vocabulary in several areas:

Bedding: air mattresses, cots, mosquito netting, sleeping bags
Kitchen equipment: aluminum foil, charcoal, cooler, Dutch oven, grill, propane, spatula, tongs
Personal equipment and shelter: first-aid kit, ground canvas, tent, insect repellent, stakes, washbasin
Tools: ax, compass, lantern, pliers, radio, saw, screwdriver, shovel.

Parents' reading to children offers many benefits. Stories stimulate young imaginations and depict a wide variety of experiences; they increase children's listening and speaking vocabularies, provide information, and broaden concepts. As families converse about the poems and stories, children develop listening and oral language skills. As children ask questions, talk about pictures, and dramatize or retell stories, they establish a foundation for

454

Teaching
Reading in
Today's
Elementary
Schools

reading "on their own." The relationship between speech and print becomes evident to them. A part of children's reading experiences should certainly involve making use of the public library; children should have their own library cards and should be taken to the library often to check out books that are appropriate for them.[2]

Some topics for parent-teacher programs might include the following:

1. What we know about how children learn to read, emphasizing individual differences and levels of development
2. Techniques for reinforcing a child's learning behaviors (providing for success, using the child's interests, values of word games, and the like)
3. Making and using homemade educational products for the child
4. Classroom observation (how to observe)
5. Use of multimedia (library, comic books, television, and so on)
6. Parent-teacher conferences (importance of home-school partnership, for instance)

Reporting, Tests, and Homework

The report card is a report to parents and children about the child's performance in school. However, teachers want parents to know additional facts about their children and the school program that are not included on a report card.

To prepare an individual report on a child or to hold a parent-teacher conference about a child, the teacher needs a folder of samples of that child's work and a file of classroom charts of weekly test scores or other achievement records.

Many schools formally schedule three parent-teacher conferences per year—one around the last week of November, one the first week of February, and one the second week of May. Although teachers frequently use a standard form filled in with comments about the child's personal, social, and academic progress, an informal record is often maintained of main points discussed with parents, conclusions reached, and recommendations by teacher and parents.

The November conference is a good time to introduce parents to the reading materials used in the school and to describe the reading experiences and skills that are being emphasized in that particular year. A teacher may want to explain how the reading program is organized and the general approaches he or she uses. The teacher may also point out what (if anything) will be required of the child in terms of homework as well as what to do when the child requests help. In an early parent meeting, the teacher also might

[2]These and other ideas are explored in the article by Sammye J. Wynn, "The Ancillary Role of Parents in the Prevention and Correction of Reading Difficulties" in *Remedial Reading: Classroom and Clinic,* 2nd ed., by Leo M. Schell and Paul C. Burns, Boston: Allyn & Bacon, 1972, pp. 556–66.

suggest that the parents encourage supporting activities, such as reading games (homemade or commercially produced) and television logs (records of what the child watches).

In the February conference, the teacher can share children's work and test results with parents, reporting the results of norm-referenced reading tests and explaining the range of class scores, the median score of the class, and the individual student's score. These test results provide some tangible information to discuss, and this type of information is relatively free of teacher bias; therefore, it contributes toward easy discussion of problems. In parent-teacher conferences, just as in discussions with students, teachers should attempt to give a true picture of test results and of their implications, pointing out any particular difficulties of the child and discussing why these difficulties exist and how the teacher is attempting to help. Interested parents may request additional ideas to use with their children for reinforcing reading skills and attitudes.

The final conference is often more of an evaluation session. The child's progress since the last conference is again reported, along with possible ideas and suggestions for summer activities. Time should be afforded the parents to ask questions and to find ways they can be of help.

Parents are often interested in how homework is assigned. Most homework should be carefully planned and informal in nature, supplementing formal preparation in the classroom. It should only be assigned after children understand the concepts and ideas and are motivated sufficiently to do the homework unaided. Hopefully, most homework assignments will be personalized, suited to the individual, and there will be little or no regularly assigned drill-type homework for the entire class.

Letters/Bulletins

Teachers should recognize that the report card and the teacher-parent conference are only two of many ways to interpret a child's interaction with the school's language arts program. Another means is a simple progress report brought home by the children and written in their own handwriting. For example: "Everyone in the first grade can read the names of the numbers 1 to 10." A school- or district-wide pamphlet on "Our Reading Program" may also provide needed information and be more efficient than a teacher's individual efforts. Some teachers provide a letter with each individual report, such as the following sample.

During the past six weeks your child has been working on a folklore unit in reading class. He or she has studied the characteristics of tall tales and has attempted to write an original tall tale of his or her own after reading several examples and hearing other examples read by the teacher. Your child's story is attached to this report. You may wish to read it and discuss it with him or her. All of the children produced tall tales which indicated an understanding of this form of literature.

456

Teaching
Reading in
Today's
Elementary
Schools

Some topics suitable for bulletins or letters include the following:

1. Reading to your child
2. How to tell a story
3. Checklist for reading games
4. Listening to sounds
5. Use of rhymes
6. Using puppets
7. The importance of questioning
8. Games to make
9. Developing good book habits
10. Using the public library.

General Suggestions

Following are some general suggestions to offer parents.

1. Work from the beginning to keep in touch with your child's reading program.
2. Have your youngster explain her reading program to you. Play the role of the patient listener and curious questioner.
3. Encourage your child to complete assignments, read books, think independently, be curious, and read for ideas.
4. Help your child to study by providing her with the space, the time, and the tools she needs for lessons.
5. If your child has a natural talent for reading, be sure to capitalize on this potential. Encourage her to participate in book fairs or to complete optional projects for reading classes.
6. If your child is having difficulty with any part of the reading program, try to give her help at an early date.
7. To promote independent thinking, use good judgment in giving help with homework. Express interest when questions are asked and try to ask questions that will help your child find the answer for herself rather than answering the question directly.

✔ Self-Check: Objective 6
Name several ways in which parents work with the teacher for the benefit of the child.
(See Self-Improvment Opportunity 8.)

Paraprofessionals

A growing number of adults are working as paid or volunteer assistants or aides to the teacher, helping by working with an individual or small group while the teacher conducts a lesson for the others; tutoring after school hours; and performing clerical work, marking workbooks, making displays or other audiovisual materials, and doing many other tasks inherent in the operation of the classroom. Many teachers have reacted positively to this new source of assistance.

It is apparent that aides who are used to assist in the classroom need some professional training in how to relate to children positively, how to teach simple skills, and how to judge pupil progress. Under the best conditions, paraprofessionals in the reading classroom can be instructional aides as well as clerical aides. Basically, the classroom teacher is responsible for the activities the aide performs and for preparing the paraprofessional to carry out assigned activities. Teacher supervision of the aide is necessary. Some areas in which the paraprofessional may be of assistance in the classroom, assuming he or she is a capable and responsible person, are suggested below.

1. scoring teacher-made tests or work sheets
2. working with small groups or individuals on particular reading skills
3. reading to large or small groups
4. setting up and using audiovisual materials (such as transparencies, charts, posters, tape recorders, projectors, and so on)
5. preparing the instructional materials, such as word files, skills boxes, and the like
6. arranging for guests to speak with the class
7. assisting in planning and supervising field trips
8. working with small groups in instructional games
9. assisting children in the use of reference materials
10. setting up displays and bulletin boards
11. developing and setting up learning-center activities
12. assisting in maintaining records for evaluation of pupil progress

In addition to paraprofessionals, student tutoring systems (where older students help younger students) have been used during the past decade with varying degrees of success. Where most successful, there has been extensive preplanning. Special attention has been given to teaching attitude, approach, and record-keeping procedures, students have gone through an orientation to the program and materials, and there has been a clear-cut plan of organizational structure and supervision.

✔ Self-Check: Objective 7

Provide several examples of how parents and paraprofessionals may be of assistance in the reading program.

(See Self-Improvement Opportunity 9.)

Test Yourself

_____ 1. Once organizational patterns have been established, they should be consistently maintained.

_____ 2. Organization is synonymous with instructional procedures.

_____ 3. A wider range of reading levels within a single classroom is more common at lower elementary grade levels than at higher elementary grade levels.

_____ 4. Every classroom should contain three reading ability groups.

_____ 5. Achievement grouping is a method of grouping children according to the level of reading material they are comfortable with.

_____ 6. Other than achievement groups, most groups are formed for a limited time and a specific purpose.

_____ 7. Members of the low reading achievement group should be separated from the rest of the class during other activities as well.

_____ 8. Organizational changes should be made slowly and gradually.

_____ 9. If reading skills are adequately covered during the reading instructional period, there is no need for any other type of reading during the day.

_____ 10. Classroom management is an important factor in how well students learn.

_____ 11. Even within groups based on reading achievement, there will be a diversity of abilities.

_____ 12. Specific needs grouping puts together children who need to work on the same skill.

_____ 13. One major disadvantage of departmentalization is the tendency to focus upon reading as a subject rather than a process.

_____ 14. A predetermined sequence of reading objectives and skills is a characteristic of the open curriculum approach.

_____ 15. What is done within the organizational pattern has more to do with the learning that takes place than the structure itself does.

_____ 16. Effective teachers spend more time actually teaching than ineffective teachers do.

_____ 17. In reality, parents are their children's first teachers of reading.

_____ 18. In reading to their children, parents are providing a foundation for the school's reading program.

_____ 19. Sending bulletins or letters to parents is a valuable way for teachers to communicate about the school's reading program.

_____ 20. Teacher aides should only do clerical work in the classroom.

Vocabulary

achievement grouping	friendship grouping	homogeneous
departmentalization	heterogeneous	interest grouping

interclass grouping
intraclass grouping
learning center
nongraded

open curriculum
paraprofessional
pupil pairs/partners
research or project
   grouping

special skills (needs)
   grouping
student contract
team arrangement
tutorial grouping

Self-Improvement Opportunities

1. Talk to at least two teachers at different grade levels to determine how they organize their classes during formal reading instruction.
2. Plan a daily reading schedule that provides for group instruction, individualized instruction, and recreational reading for a group of your choice.
3. Using the information given below, divide a hypothetical third-grade class into reading achievement groups. In making your decisions, consider the guidelines about grouping in this chapter. Compare your grouping plan with the plans of other students in your class.

Number of Children	Reading Grade Level
1	1^2
3	2^1
4	2^2
8	3^1
7	3^2
1	4
2	5
1	6

4. Think of several types of recreational reading activities that you might want to include in your reading program.
5. What are some things you would do to help a child in the low reading group overcome feelings of inferiority?
6. In a small group, discuss the advantages and disadvantages of the various organizational plans.
7. Interview one teacher, asking him or her to react to Robinson and Burrows' list regarding knowledge of the field of reading.
8. Prepare a letter or bulletin to parents on one of the suggested topics.
9. Talk with a paraprofessional about his or her role in the reading program. Then share your findings with members of the class.

Bibliography

Bagford, Jack. "Evaluating Teachers on Reading Instruction." *The Reading Teacher* 34 (January 1981): 400–404.

Brophy, Jere E. "Advances in Teacher Effectiveness Research." Paper

460

Teaching
Reading in
Today's
Elementary
Schools

presented at the annual meeting of the American Association of Colleges for Teacher Education, Chicago, Illinois, 1979, 24 pp. [ED 170 281].

Dallman, Martha, et al. *The Teaching of Reading.* 6th ed. New York: Holt, Rinehart and Winston, 1982, p. 386.

Dewey, John. *Experience and Education.* New York: Macmillan, 1938.

Guthrie, John T. "Effective Teaching Practices." *The Reading Teacher* 35 (March 1982): 766–68.

Hunt, John McVey. *Revisiting Montessori: Introduction to the Montessori Method.* New York: Schocken, 1964.

Piaget, Jean. *The Language and Thought of the Child.* Cleveland, Ohio: World, 1955.

Robinson, H. Alan, and Alvina T. Burrows. *Teacher Effectiveness in Elementary Language Arts: A Progress Report.* Urbana, Ill.: ERIC Clearinghouse on Reading and Communication Skills, 1974, pp. 77–78, 80.

Rothstein, Evelyn B., and Barbara K. Gold. "Reading in an Open Classroom—Extending the Gift." *The Reading Teacher* 27 (February 1974): 443–45.

Rousseau, Jean-Jacques. *Emile, Julie, and Other Writings,* S. E. Frost, Jr., ed., and R. L. Archer, trans. Woodbury, N.Y.: Barron's Educational Series, 1964.

Rutherford, William L. "An Analysis of Teacher Effectiveness in Classroom Instruction in Reading." In *Reading Methods and Teacher Improvement,* Nila B. Smith, ed. Newark, Del.: International Reading Association, 1971, pp. 124–33.

Spiegel, Dixie Lee. "Desirable Teaching Behaviors for Effective Instruction in Reading." *The Reading Teacher* 34 (December 1980): 324–30.

Wiener, Roberta. "A Look at Reading Practices in the Open Classroom." *The Reading Teacher* 27 (February 1974): 438–42.

Wynn, Sammye J. "The Ancillary Role of Parents in the Prevention and Correction of Reading Difficulties." In *Remedial Reading: Classroom and Clinic.* 2nd ed., by Leo M. Schell and Paul C. Burns. Boston: Allyn and Bacon, 1972, pp. 556–66.

Suggested Readings

Durkin, Dolores. *Teaching Them to Read.* 3rd ed. Boston: Allyn and Bacon, 1978, Chapter 5.

Farr, Roger, and Nancy Roser. *Teaching a Child to Read.* New York: Harcourt Brace Jovanovich, 1979, Chapter 9.

Hall, Mary Anne, et al. *Reading and the Elementary School Child.* 2nd ed. New York: Van Nostrand, 1979.

Harris, Albert J., and Edward R. Sipay. *How to Increase Reading Ability.* 7th ed. New York: Longman, 1980, Chapter 5.

Harris, Larry H., and Carl B. Smith. *Reading Instruction through Diag-*

nostic Teaching. 2nd ed. New York: Holt, Rinehart and Winston, 1976, Chapters 16 and 17.

Mangrum, Charles T., II, and Harry W. Forgan. *Developing Competencies in Teaching Reading.* Columbus, Ohio: Charles E. Merrill, 1979, Modules 9 and 12.

Otto, Wayne, et al. *How to Teach Reading.* Reading, Mass.: Addison-Wesley, 1979, Chapter 13.

Rubin, Dorothy. *A Practical Approach to Teaching Reading.* New York: Holt, Rinehart and Winston, 1982, Chapter 13.

Smith, Richard J., and Dale D. Johnson. *Teaching Children to Read.* 2nd ed. Reading Mass.: Addison-Wesley, 1980, Chapter 9.

Spache, George D., and Evelyn B. Spache. *Reading in the Elementary School.* 4th ed. Boston: Allyn and Bacon, 1977, Chapters 10 and 14.

CHAPTER 11

Readers with Special Needs

Introduction

In this chapter we discuss youngsters who are somewhat different from the majority, for whom most instructional sequences are designed. We propose ways to deal with the child who has mild to moderate difficulties, but we do not attempt to cover children who are profoundly retarded, psychotic, autistic, aphasic, or severely impaired perceptually, since these children will probably need a special class, a special school, or a residential facility. We also deal in this chapter with the gifted child, who is often neglected in the regular classroom. Our suggestions focus upon what the classroom teacher, not the specialist, can do. We believe that the elementary school teacher who has had a general course in the field of special education for the exceptional learner will probably be better prepared to help these children.

Since many children who have been enrolled in special education classes are being integrated into regular classes, in the future teachers will no doubt be responsible for more exceptional children. The past trend of isolating these children has been reversed as educators recognize that association with nonhandicapped children may be beneficial for the exceptional child. In an effort to return these children to the educational mainstream, schools are making special provisions of various forms.

We begin this chapter with a presentation of Public Law 94-142 and its effects on the education of handicapped children, then move to a discussion of guidelines for working with students who have special needs. The chapter then focuses on the different types of exceptional learners covered under the law and on gifted learners. Other groups of special students—those with cultural and linguistic differences—are also discussed. Finally, we discuss corrective and remedial readers. In each case we suggest special teaching strategies.

Setting Objectives

When you finish reading this chapter, you should be able to

1. Explain mainstreaming and its effects in a regular classroom.
2. Identify learners who are classified as exceptional and suggest several guidelines for instructing them.
3. Understand what ''learning disabilities'' are.
4. Explain some strategies for helping slow learners.
5. Name some desirable instructional modifications for children who have impaired hearing or speech or who are visually handicapped.
6. Describe the types of problems a behaviorally disturbed or hyperactive child can cause in the classroom.
7. Understand how to adjust teaching strategies for gifted pupils.
8. Appreciate the effects of a child's culture and socioeconomic level on his or her reading achievement.

464

Teaching
Reading in
Today's
Elementary
Schools

9. Discuss several important features and promising approaches to consider in a reading program for children with dialectal differences.
10. Delineate some special needs of bilingual children and ways of meeting these needs.
11. Identify underachievers.
12. Name materials that are available for working with readers who have special needs.

HANDICAPPED CHILDREN IN THE CLASSROOM: PL 94–142

In 1975 Congress passed a law that altered the placement of handicapped students in the public schools; instead of being assigned to resource rooms, many of these children are now being mainstreamed into regular classrooms. A major reason for passage of the law was to enable handicapped students who were being neglected to receive special services. Also, under the law, these children spend time with nonhandicapped children, thus addressing the apparent ineffectiveness of teaching handicapped students in segregated classes.

PL 94-142, known as the Education for All Handicapped Children Act, states that the federal government will "assist States and localities to provide for the education of all handicapped children, and to assess and assure the effectiveness of efforts to educate handicapped children." According to this law, handicapped children are those who are mentally retarded, hard of hearing or deaf, speech impaired, seriously disturbed emotionally, visually handicapped, orthopedically impaired, or possessing specific learning disabilities. Students who are suspected of being handicapped are referred for appropriate testing to determine their status, and only those handicapped students who are expected to benefit from integration in a regular classroom are placed there.

PL 94-142 further requires that handicapped children receive the most appropriate education in the *least restrictive environment,* a concept that places children in a learning environment as close to the regular classroom as possible but in which they can still master skills and content. A series of placement levels ranging from the least to the most restrictive is as follows:

regular classroom with teacher consultant
itinerant teacher
resource room
self-contained special class
special school
residential institution

Ideally, children will advance from a more to a less restrictive environment (Kirk and Gallagher, 1983).

Severely handicapped children in a regular school may be placed in a self-contained special class, where the special teacher is responsible for most of their program. A less restrictive environment is the part-time special class, where handicapped children spend about half of the day under the direction of the special teacher. A resource room is generally a small classroom where mildly handicapped children spend a period of time on a regular basis with instruction provided by the resource room teacher. Itinerant teachers, such as speech pathologists and school psychologists, may travel from one school to another to work with children who need special help. Teacher consultants are highly trained, experienced teachers who offer help to regular teachers whose classes include exceptional children.

When the least restrictive environment for an exceptional child is the regular classroom, that child is said to be mainstreamed. These children have special needs that the classroom teacher should understand, so teacher-training institutions have in recent years added courses in special education at both the graduate and undergraduate levels to prepare teachers to work with mainstreamed children. In-service training is also required by PL 94-142 to inform teachers about the handicapped.

Because regular members of the classroom play an important role in terms of offering acceptance and support to the mainstreamed child, the teacher should prepare students to receive the new class member by frankly explaining the nature of the handicap and the student's special needs. In addition, he or she might read a story about a similarly handicapped individual to help the class realize that even though the new student has special needs, his or her feelings, interests, and goals are much like their own (Rubin, 1982). It is important that the mainstreamed child be fully accepted as an integral part of the class and not just occupy space in the classroom (Hoben, 1980). After the child begins attending class, students may become actively supportive by providing necessary services, by tutoring when special help is needed, and by including the child in activities.

Many mainstreamed children are reading at levels considerably below those of their classmates, which can cause feelings of inadequacy and frustration which may in turn lead to behavior problems. The teacher can do two things: enable the child to excel in some nonacademic area, and teach reading individually at the child's level (Kirk, Kliebhan, and Lerner, 1978). The special child may also have a skill or ability, such as mechanical aptitude, conscientiousness for carrying out a responsibility, dramatic talent, or athletic prowess, that he or she could develop. In teaching beginning reading to these children, teachers should follow the general guidelines and select appropriate instructional materials, such as those suggested later in this chapter.

A major provision of PL 94-142 is the development of an individualized education program (IEP) for each handicapped child who receives support

466

Teaching
Reading in
Today's
Elementary
Schools

through federal funding. The IEP states the child's present levels of educational performance, the projected starting date of the program, and the duration of the special services. It sets annual goals for the child's level of educational performance as well as short-term instructional objectives, which must be defined in measurable terms. The IEP also specifies educational services and special instructional media for the child.

The IEP is developed by a multidisciplinary team, sometimes called the M-team or core evaluation team, consisting of a representative of the local education agency (other than the child's teacher), the teacher, and one or both parents. The child and other professional personnel may be included when appropriate. The M-team for children with specific learning disabilities must also include a person qualified to give individual diagnostic exams and, when available, an appropriate learning disabilities specialist.

One format for an IEP follows:

I. Summary of assessment
   A. Areas of strengths
   B. Areas of weaknesses
   C. Approaches that have failed
   D. Learning style(s)
   E. Recommended placement, general program outline, and assignment of personnel responsibility
II. Classroom accommodations
   A. General teaching techniques
   B. Language arts modifications (and other subject matter modifications)
III. Instructional plans
   A. Long-range (yearly) objectives, along with materials, strategies, and evidence of mastery
   B. Specific (1–3 months) objectives
   C. Ancillary personnel and services

Working together to plan instructional activities for exceptional children whenever possible, the resource room teacher and the classroom teacher might want to cooperate by drawing up a contract—a written agreement about specific measurable objectives, one or more activities for meeting each objective, and the date for completion (Wilhoyte, 1977). A contract helps the student focus attention on developing specific reading skills, keeping careful records, and accepting responsibility. It is based on his or her strengths and moves the child very gradually to a higher level of performance.

Under a contract, the resource teacher explains the objectives and activities to the child and writes the information on a form attached to the child's work folder. The child then takes the folder to the regular classroom in order to work independently on the activities, under the supervision of the classroom teacher. At the end of the allotted time, the child returns to the resource room for an evaluation by the resource teacher. If he or she has achieved 100 percent success in an activity, some sort of recognition is in order. Example

11.1 illustrates one possible reading contract. (See Chapter 10 for more information about contracts.)

Even though mainstreaming has been in effect for a relatively short time, some strengths and weaknesses of the plan have already emerged (Dallman, 1982). Among the strengths of the program are:

1. The plan is an attempt to provide a free education for every child in the least restrictive environment.
2. Atypical students can join with their peers in learning experiences that they might not have otherwise.
3. Parents are included in the planning and implementation of the program.
4. An individual learning program is planned for each child.

Some weaknesses are:

1. Handicapped children may experience frustration in a room where others are working at higher levels.
2. Both the handicapped child and the nonhandicapped classmates may have problems of adjustment.
3. If the special student has behavioral problems, he or she may disrupt the class.
4. Attending to the special needs of one student may be too demanding a task for the classroom teacher who must also meet the needs of the rest of the class.

✔ Self-Check: Objective 1

Explain the impact of PL 94-142 on public schools.
What is an IEP? How is it developed and what does it include?

▶ **EXAMPLE 11.1:** Reading Contract

READING CONTRACT					
Larry H. Student			_Mrs. Morgan_ Teacher		
Objective	Activity	Date	Initials		Comments
			St.	Tch.	
To learn to read 3 new words.	Play word card game.	May 4	LH	EM	Good work!
To understand the events in a story.	Listen to a story at the listening station and tell someone about it.	May 6	LH	EM	You retold the story well.

General Guidelines

Most of the procedures and materials already recommended in this book can be effectively used with exceptional children when teachers make reasonable adjustments for particular difficulties. We recommend individualization of instruction and a de-emphasis upon arbitrary age/grade standards so as to focus upon each child's educational needs. The exceptional child's basic needs and goals are not so different from those of the "ordinary" child, but the means of achieving those goals and fulfilling those needs are different. The following general practices, which apply to all learners, are crucial in teaching handicapped children.

1. *The teacher's attitude toward a child is of paramount importance.* Special children require a great deal of encouragement and understanding. Show that you are interested in them; talk with them about their interests; note things they have done; be friendly and encouraging. The child's personal worth and mental health must be given primary consideration, and you should assist the child in every way possible to develop personally and socially as well as academically.
2. *Special children need to realize success in their undertakings.* Progress charts are one visible way of making growth apparent to a child. Compliment the child on gains made; indicate that she is competing with her own record rather than with others. Make every effort to build her self-confidence and avoid frustrating situations that may aggravate her learning problems.
3. *Provide materials the child is capable of using as well as ones that are of interest.* Carefully select what to use in initial instruction; usually concrete and firsthand experiences are safe beginning activities, and audiovisual materials can be very helpful. Do not use reading materials with which the child has previously failed. Become familiar with various instructional strategies and learn how to adapt them to the child's individual learning style(s), and don't overlook the power and usefulness of television commercials, games, comic books, and other contemporary materials.
4. *A well-planned readiness period is needed for each task.* For example, before a lesson on using beginning sounds and context to identify an unknown word, prepare the children by using spoken context alone as a clue to the identification of a missing word and by helping them discriminate between the initial sounds in words.
5. *One instructional item should be presented at a time.* Instead of teaching all or several comprehension skills at the same time, provide instruction on how to get the main idea, how to follow simple written directions, how to locate an important detail or fact in a short paragraph, and so on.
6. *For some exceptional children, instruction should probably be more direct and more systematic than for the average child.* Much instruction should be with small groups and with individuals.

One result of PL 94-142 is that exceptional children with special needs are often integrated, or "mainstreamed," into the regular classroom. (© David S. Strickler/ Monkmeyer)

7. *Continuous evaluation is needed.* Make provisions for checking on student progress frequently.
8. *Special equipment may be necessary to meet individual needs.* This includes special tables, desks, stimulus-reduced areas, "time out" spaces, and the like.
9. *Instruction may be largely individualized.* Provide what is appropriate for the individual in a given area at a given time. Fit teaching to the child's needs, strengths, and weaknesses. The reading instruction must be specific, not general. For example, if a child has a hearing disability, the teacher will need to alter reading methods to take this into account, and the teacher and child will have to depend more on the visual characteristics of words. This requires the teacher to understand what interferes with and what facilitates reading for the individual. Giving such consideration

470

Teaching
Reading in
Today's
Elementary
Schools

to the learning problems of each child will lead to specific teaching adjustments, such as providing appropriate seating arrangements for the visually handicapped.

10. *Sound teaching procedures should be utilized with all learners.* Skills should be emphasized through actual reading, not through artificial drills. Help the child see a reason for learning to read. Moreover, use a variety of instructional procedures, corrective techniques, and materials rather than searching for one magic elixir.

11. *Reading activities should be as highly motivational as possible.* Games, audiovisual materials, and high-interest/low-vocabulary materials may assist. Teachers should find ways for the handicapped pupil to meet with success and demonstrate progress. They should provide positive reinforcement for small improvements.

12. *Approaches should be geared to the needs of the different learner.* Three of the approaches discussed in Chapter 5 hold considerable promise for working with different learners within the classroom: the language experience approach, the individualized reading approach, and programmed instruction. The first of these is meaningful to children and uses all forms of language; the second offers self-selection, self-pacing, individual or small-group skills instruction and one-to-one pupil-teacher conferences; and the third is useful for presenting skills in small sequential steps, calling for responses, and providing immediate reinforcement.

✔ Self-Check: Objective 2

Name several guidelines for working with readers who have special needs.

(See Self-Improvement Opportunity 1.)

Students with Specific Learning Disabilities

Characteristics

The most widely accepted definition of specific learning disabilities is the one included in PL 94-142: "The term 'children with specific learning disabilities' means those children who have a disorder in one or more of the basic psychological processes involved in understanding or in using language, spoken or written, which disorder may manifest itself in imperfect ability to listen, think, speak, read, write, spell, or do mathematical calculations. Such disorders include such conditions as perceptual handicaps, brain injury, minimal brain dysfunction, dyslexia, and developmental aphasia. Such term does not include children who have learning problems which are primarily the result of visual, hearing, or motor handicaps, of mental retardation, or emotional disturbance, or environmental, cultural, or economic disadvantage."

The causes of a specific learning disability are attributed to an individual's constitution rather than environment, and low achievement is thought to be due to deficient psychological processes such as attention, perception, reasoning, and language (Harris, 1980). One fact basic to an understanding of specific learning disabilities is the existence of a significant discrepancy between the student's potential for learning and his or her actual achievement level. For instance, IQ scores may indicate that a student is capable of doing fifth-grade work, but he may only be working on a first-grade level. Gaps may also exist among different academic areas; in this case, a student may be quick to learn everything except how to read and write (Ludlow, 1982).

It is important to try to identify accurately those students who have specific learning disabilities. A conservative estimate by the Office of Education places the percentage of the school population with such disabilities at 1 to 3 percent. Four to six times as many boys as girls have been identified as learning-disabled. In determining which students have specific learning disabilities, a multidisciplinary team evaluates referrals by using various assessment procedures. Students are considered to be learning disabled if they have normal or above-normal intelligence and no major medical problems but have an achievement deficit of two or more years in some areas (Ludlow, 1982).

Weaknesses frequently observed among learning-disabled students include

1. visual perception problems, in which the student confuses letter shapes, makes reversals, and has difficulty in identifying a figure concealed in a picture.
2. auditory perception disorders, in which the student mispronounces and misspells similar-sounding words (*aminal* for *animal*) and is unable to blend the sounds of a word in order to pronounce it.
3. fine and gross motor function disorders, exhibited through poor physical coordination, illegible handwriting, and a poor sense of directionality (can't distinguish left from right).
4. attention disorders, manifested by a short attention span, high distractibility, hyperactivity, and impulsivity (writing answers or speaking without thinking).
5. language problems, in which students have difficulty with articulation, following oral and written directions, and expressing their thoughts accurately orally and in writing.
6. thinking disorders, involving inadequacies in memory, concept formation, judgment, and problem-solving.

Instructional Implications and Strategies

Many learning-disabled students have severe communication deficits which can be observed in their oral language and reading performance. They seem to have trouble using normal language structures to speak in an organized manner, and they also appear to have trouble comprehending continuous text. When comparing the learning disabled with normal children, researchers have found delays in language development and differences in the quality

472

Teaching
Reading in
Today's
Elementary
Schools

of language—especially in the comprehension of logical relations, in ways of using language on tests, and in the acquisition of rules related to patterns of word formation (Wallach and Goldsmith, 1977). In an effort to help these children learn a specific word formation skill, researchers provided special instruction in recognizing suffixes, including inflectional endings of verbs. They trained learning-disabled students to attend to the suffixes *-ed* and *-ing,* using paper-and-pencil exercises and oral drills. Students were praised for correct responses and given daily feedback, and errors and correct answers were recorded daily on a chart so that the children could see their progress. The researchers concluded that identifying individual errors was a good basis for instruction, a structured format for teaching a specific skill was effective, and oral reading performance improved significantly following the instruction (Henderson and Shores, 1982).

Reading improvement is the most widely recognized academic need of the learning-disabled child (Gaskins, 1982). The content and sequence of reading programs are much the same for all children, but the methods vary according to the nature of the student. Some strategies that may be helpful in teaching reading skills to the learning-disabled student are given below.

Respect the student. Acknowledge the child's feelings. Try to relieve his or her anxieties, and offer praise and encouragement whenever possible. Recognize special abilities and needs.

Create a structured environment. Develop a routine and provide security by having a time and a place for everything. Set clear and consistent rules with reasonable contingencies, and avoid events that distract and interfere with the instructional program.

Minimize and accept mistakes. When you make mistakes yourself, comment on them. (Example: "I tripped right over that box. Sometimes I feel so clumsy!") Admit that you can't remember something and look it up. Laugh at your own mistakes, help the student to laugh at his or her mistakes, and don't call attention to the student's awkward moments.

Help with language problems. When a child can't think of a word, supply it. Give directions clearly, briefly, and concisely. Make sure the child is looking directly at you. It may be advisable to have the child repeat the directions back to you.

Use varied instructional and assessment techniques. Present concepts by means of concrete objects, manipulative devices, and multimedia presentations (films, television, videotapes, recordings) to make use of the child's five senses. Provide various opportunities for practicing skills (learning center activities, projects, worksheets), various instructional techniques (science experiments, simulation activities, role-playing), and various types of assessment (creative projects, oral reports, written tests, and presentations).

Simplify learning tasks. Let the student concentrate on achieving one task at a time. Give small amounts of learning material to him or her at one time, and repeat and reinforce each step, providing systematic instruction (Ludlow, 1982; Smith, 1981).

Name some characteristics of learning-disabled children. What are
some ways to help these children learn?
(See Self-Improvement Opportunity 2.)

Slow Learners

Characteristics

The American Association on Mental Deficiency defined slow learners as
follows (Kirk, Kliebhan, and Lerner, 1978):

Borderline child	IQ between 85 and 68
Mildly retarded child	IQ between 67 and 52
Moderately retarded child	IQ between 51 and 36

The primary characteristic of slow-learning children is that they do not
learn as readily as others of the same chronological age. They are unable to
make complicated generalizations and are usually unable to learn material
incidentally without instruction, and they generally need systematically
presented instruction.

Reviews of the reading characteristics of slow learners reveal several points
that have implications for developing instructional programs (Buttery and
Mason, 1979).

1. No one approach is superior to any other.
2. The teacher is the most significant factor in determining a child's success
   with reading.
3. Slow learners make more progress when they are placed in regular
   classrooms than when they are in special classes.
4. Slow learners are inferior to most other children in comprehension skills
   and in oral reading.
5. Reading comprehension is the most difficult skill for them to learn.

Instructional Implications and Strategies

Whenever possible, slow learners should spend most of the school day in the
regular classroom with teachers who recognize and know how to deal with
their special needs and who are willing to try a variety of methods. Slow
learners need an extended reading readiness (prereading) program, one that
may last for as long as two years. Reading instruction *per se* should be
introduced later, progress more slowly, and develop more gradually than is
usually the case. Teachers should plan instruction with the understanding
that the slow learner will stay in each stage of reading development longer
than the average pupil. Slow learners will profit from using materials that do
not have demanding vocabularies and from repetition. They will need a great

474

Teaching
Reading in
Today's
Elementary
Schools

deal of help in developing adequate comprehension skills. Suitable techniques for teaching slow learners are presented below.

Characteristics of Slow Learners	*Recommendations for Teaching*
1. Short attention span	1. Activities should vary, move quickly, and be completed in a short amount of time. Set short-term goals that enable students to succeed at frequent intervals.
2. Need for close supervision	2. Give instruction individually or in small groups, providing frequent project checks, reinforcement, and encouragement.
3. Concrete rather than abstract learning	3. New words should be learned through association with concrete objects or pictures, and new concepts should be experienced directly or vicariously (field trips, films, simulation, and role-playing). Learning should be by rote.
4. Low self-concept	4. Provide opportunities for child to work as part of the whole class, giving recognition for small successes and using progress charts. The environment should be nonthreatening.
5. Poor language development	5. Provide opportunities for listening to stories and responding orally. Arrange time for sharing experiences and taking part in discussions.
6. High level of distractibility	6. Establish schedules and routines and minimize interruptions and distractions.
7. Short-term memory	7. Basic skills and new words should be overlearned through frequent practice. Repetition and review are necessary.

Many slow learners will be socially promoted and leave school before they can read beyond a second- or third-grade level, so teachers should provide these students with the basic functional reading skills they will need to use during their lives. (These skills are also useful for other types of disabled readers.) To teach functional or survival reading, use large assortments of product labels, old telephone books, catalogues, newspapers, magazines, order forms, movie and television schedules, cereal boxes, maps, transportation schedules, recipes, and manuals. If these resources are available, children can begin to apply the reading skills they have learned in a practical way, working with familiar materials and learning why reading is important.

Teachers can make a set of cards with imaginary situations for the children to use at a learning center where the resource materials are located. The teacher may need to pronounce some of the words on the cards and assist the children in locating appropriate materials. See suggested activities in Example 11.2.

Some other ideas for working with students on survival skills are suggested below.

1. Set up a post office. Children can write notes and address envelopes to their classmates.

▶ **EXAMPLE 11.2:** Imaginary Functional Situations

Your dog is sick. What number do you call for help? Where could you take your dog?

If the house is on fire, what number would you call? What are some other emergency phone numbers?

Look at several labels to find out what is dangerous about each product. Make a list of "danger" words.

You want to write a lost-and-found ad for the bicycle you lost. Write the ad and find the address of the newspaper.

Choose a magazine that you would like to order. Fill out the order form.

Follow a recipe and make something good to eat.

Your mother is coming home on the bus but you forget what time your father is supposed to meet her. Look it up in the schedule.

You want to order a game that is advertised on the back of a cereal box. Follow the directions for placing the order.

You want to watch a television special but you can't remember the time or channel. Find it in the newspaper.

Look at a menu and order a meal for yourself. Find out how much it costs.

Look through a catalogue and choose four items that you would like to have for less than $100 in all. Fill out the order blank.

You want to go to a football game in a nearby town. Find the stadium on the map and be able to give directions.

476

Teaching
Reading in
Today's
Elementary
Schools

2. Obtain multiple copies of last year's telephone directories and look up the number of each student; find emergency numbers; and look through the Yellow Pages to find restaurants, a skating rink, movie theaters, and other places that are familiar to the children. Let each student make a telephone directory of these numbers.

3. Give children forms to fill out about themselves, including their names, addresses, telephone numbers, Social Security numbers, etc.

4. Get copies of old and new drivers' manuals. Then have students match the old word signs with the new international symbols.

5. Make cards of words and phrases found in public places, such as *Wet Paint, No Trespassing, Danger, Ladies Room,* etc. Have the children see how many terms they can recognize.

6. Obtain city maps and let students locate landmarks. Simple map-reading skills involving their own school and neighborhood should precede work with a larger map.

7. Make a collection of grocery labels and product advertisements from magazines. Then let the children pretend to go food shopping by selecting some of the labels and advertisements. They should tell the teacher and other members of the group what they "bought." Have beginning readers match pictures and words from labels that have been cut apart.

8. Have students use newspapers for locating grocery-store and other advertisements, finding the classified section and looking for items that are for sale and jobs that are available, using the index to find the comics page, reading headlines, and looking at the sports pages to find out about local athletic events.

9. Keep a collection of simple recipes that are arranged alphabetically by category in a recipe box. Obtain basic ingredients and allow the children to make something.

10. Make a game of reading television schedules. Name a popular show and let the children compete with each other to see who can find the show first.

11. Collect coupons and distribute some to each child. Encourage the children to figure out who will save the most money by using the coupons. Be sure they check expiration dates and any other conditions (such as two for the price of one).

12. Use labels from different sizes and brands of the same product and help children find which one is the most economical by comparing prices and amounts.

✔ **Self-Check: Objective 4**

How can you identify the slow learner in a classroom? What are some reasonable expectations for a slow learner?
(See Self-Improvement Opportunities 3 and 9.)

Visually Handicapped Children

Characteristics

A *partially sighted* child is one whose visual acuity is better than 20/200 but not better than 20/70 in the better eye with the best correction available. Educationally, the partially sighted or *visually impaired* child has difficulty but is able to learn to read print, as opposed to the blind child, who must learn to read Braille.

Teachers have many opportunities to observe symptoms of visual difficulties when students are reading. Among these symptoms are

1. squinting.
2. scowling.
3. closing or covering one eye.
4. rubbing the eyes frequently.
5. holding the book too close or too far away.
6. frequently losing the place.
7. red or inflamed eyes.
8. frequent blinking.
9. moving head excessively.
10. frequent errors when copying board work.

Alert teachers should refer a child who has these symptoms to a visual specialist.

Instructional Implications and Strategies

In general, the language of visually handicapped children is not deficient, so their ability to listen and relate and remember must be developed as fully as possible. Several instructional ideas for the visually handicapped child are proposed below.

1. Since the child gains knowledge primarily through touch and hearing, he or she should be given many concrete objects to feel and manipulate. Accompanying these tactile experiences, verbal explanations describing shape, size, weight, hardness, texture, pliability, and temperature are very helpful. Teachers can provide homemade "boxes" in the classroom: cloth box (fabrics to develop concepts of soft, stiff, smooth, rough, silky, sticky, furry, thick, thin, hairy, bumpy), rock box, shell box, wood box, sandpaper box, and building materials box (brick, foam, plastic, sheet rock, rubber, metal pipes, wiring). They can also use tools of various types of work—carpentry, auto mechanics, gardening, architecture, baking, and the like. Conversations based on shape, size, texture, and

478

Teaching
Reading in
Today's
Elementary
Schools

usage will help expand basic concepts and vocabulary. A great deal of verbal information is desirable; tape recorders are good ways of presenting it.

2. The teacher must provide additional stimulation to expand the child's horizons, to develop imagery, and to orient him or her to a wide and varied environment. Mapping the classroom, the school, and, later, the community can help fulfill these needs. Trips and experiences concerning the school and the community are a natural base for writing activities. The child should be permitted to dictate many stories, either with the teacher or aide serving as transcriber or into a tape recorder.

3. Reading aloud to children is one of the most rewarding experiences that builds listening skills. This is especially true with the visually impaired child. Commercially prepared records in which well-known actors read aloud children's classics—Carol Channing reading the Madeline stories (Caedmon), Hans Conreid reading highlights from *Treasure Island* (Literary Records), Danny Kaye reading *Grimm's Fairy Tales* (Golden Records), and Sterling Holloway reading the *Winnie the Pooh* series (Disneyland Records)—are but a few available resources.

4. Utilize sets of cassette tapes on listening skills (such as the ones developed by Dorothy Bracken and available from Science Research Associates). Other records of sounds include *Authentic Sound Effects* (Electra Records), *Sound Effects* (Audio-Fidelity), and *Sounds of My City* (Folkways Records).

5. Children with impaired vision should be seated close to the chalkboard or wherever there is material to be studied. Many schools have large-type books (duplicated from original text or trade materials) for the visually impaired.

6. Encourage the child to use properly fitted glasses when reading.

7. Plan several short periods of close work (such as reading a book) rather than one extended period of continuous work.

8. Provide active assignments of some kind after close work.

9. Adjust shades so there is no glare on the chalkboard.

10. Minimize the use of machines that utilize a lighted screen.

Many schools have a T/O Vision Tester, a visual screening test to determine whether a child can see both near and far. However, this test only suggests visual deficiencies which should be checked more thoroughly by an eye specialist.

Hearing Impaired Children

Characteristics

The term *hard of hearing* or *hearing impaired* applies to those whose sense of hearing is defective but functional for ordinary purposes, with or without a hearing aid. The older a child is when his or her hearing becomes impaired, and the more advanced the child's speech is, the easier he or she will find learning to read. Of course, the extent of hearing impairment is also an important consideration.

As with visual difficulties, teachers are in an excellent position to observe telltale symptoms of auditory difficulties. Among these symptoms are

1. inattentiveness in class.
2. turning the head so that a particular ear always faces the speaker.
3. requests for repetition of directions and other verbal information.
4. frowning when trying to listen.
5. frequent rubbing of ears.
6. frequent earaches.
7. dizziness.

Children who exhibit these symptoms should be referred for auditory testing.

Instructional Implications and Strategies

Special arrangements within a classroom can often help hearing impaired youngsters. These children should be seated near the teacher so that they have adequate opportunities to hear explanations and directions and so they can see the teacher's face, thus having opportunities for lip-reading.

When she is presenting new words, the teacher should stand so that the hearing impaired child can easily see her lips when she pronounces a word. Light should fall on the teacher's face rather than come from behind, because this can cause a glare in the child's eyes and shadow the teacher's face. After the child has watched the teacher pronounce a word, he or she should be shown the printed form of the word on the chalkboard.

The child with impaired hearing may have particular trouble with phonics instruction. He or she will need to be shown how a sound "looks" on a person's mouth. A sight approach, accompanied by instruction on context and word structure, may prove to be more effective than phonics approaches.

A teacher who has children with auditory difficulties in her classroom should follow these directions:

1. Speak slowly, clearly, and with adequate volume.
2. Seat the child as far as possible from distracting sounds.
3. Emphasize silent reading.
4. Minimize the use of auditory channels in instruction.
5. Provide practice materials that have clearly written instructions.

Many schools have a Beltone Audiometer, a screening device to determine hearing loss and the sound frequency at which the loss occurs. This is a useful device for finding out the degree of a child's handicap.

480

Teaching
Reading in
Today's
Elementary
Schools

✔ **Self-Check: Objective 5**

Suggest some instructional ideas for teaching hearing impaired and visually handicapped children.
(See Self-Improvement Opportunity 2.)

Speech Impaired Children

Characteristics

Speech is considered abnormal "when it deviates so far from the speech of other people that it calls attention to itself, interferes with communication, or causes the speaker or his listener to be distressed" (Van Riper, 1978, p. 43). Such problems are considered by some authorities to be a part of the more extensive category sometimes called "communication disorders." Understanding the label, however, is significantly less important than understanding the types of speech difficulties that children might have and how they may affect the development of reading skills. In this chapter we shall highlight two of the most common speech disorders with which the classroom teacher must deal: articulation problems and stuttering problems.

1. *Articulation.* Articulatory disorders are by far the most common type of speech disorder among schoolchildren and the type with which a classroom teacher can accomplish the most. Such a disorder is indicated when a child persists in one or more of the following practices:

   substitutes one sound for another (for example, "wittle" for "little")
   omits a sound (for example, "pane" for "plane")
   distorts a sound (the sounds of *s, z,* and *r* are the most commonly distorted ones).

2. *Stuttering.* Stuttering is one of the most complicated and difficult of speech problems. Stuttering children may have silent periods during which they are unable to produce any sound, or they may repeat a sound, a word, or a phrase or prolong the initial sound of a word. They may also show signs of excessive muscular strain, such as blinking their eyes.

   It is normal for children between the ages of two and six years to repeat a sound, a word, or a phrase forty or fifty times in every hundred words spoken. If adults do not focus undue attention on speech during this period of nonfluency, maturation will usually enable the child to overcome repetition.

Instructional Implications and Strategies

Teachers of young children with impaired speech can make considerable use of rhymes, stories, and songs in groups. They can plan more formal lessons, organized around the speech sounds that are most likely to cause difficulties, where observation indicates a need. Some of the most common error patterns can be readily identified by teachers who have trained themselves to listen. Teachers should listen for substitution of *w* for *r* and *l* (as in *wed* and *wamp*), voiceless *th* for *s* (as in *thun*), voiced *th* for *z* (as in *thebra*), *f* for the voiceless *th* (as in *fumb*), *d* for the voiced *th* and *g* (as in *dis* and *det*), *b* for *v* (as in *balentine*), *s* or *ch* for *sh* (as in *soe* or *choe*), and *t* for *k* (as in *tandy*) (Byrne, 1965). Every experience in which language is used may become an opportunity for informal speech development and improvement. For many children, a social situation in which they are encouraged to talk freely can result in increased self-confidence and independence, reflected in rapidly increasing control of speech.

It is probably wise for the classroom teacher to face the problem of stuttering in a rather indirect way. Help from parents in eliminating sources of tension is important, as is the teacher's realization that there is no such thing as "perfect speech." Many nonfluencies are accepted as normal in adult speech.

The safest suggestion to the classroom teacher with regard to helping children who stutter is a general "don't." Do not ask them to stop and start over, to slow down, to speed up, to take a breath; this may only make them more concerned about the way they are talking and may cause them to stutter more. Do not deny them the right to read and recite in class as they choose—speaking should be made a rewarding experience for students as often as possible. In fact, students should be encouraged to talk and keep on talking even if they stutter. Help them to develop confidence in their speaking ability. So far as possible, treat children as if they had no stuttering problem. Accept and react to stuttering as you would to normal speech, and help the other members of the class develop this same attitude of acceptance.

Behaviorally Disturbed Children

Characteristics

Behaviorally disturbed children exhibit unexpected or uncontrollable behavior that often has no immediately identifiable cause or reason. This behavior is most often classified as either *conduct disorder,* including aggressive behavior—which we discuss in this section— or *personality problem,* which typically includes withdrawal (Quay, 1972, 1975). Usually children who exhibit these types of behavior either cannot or will not conform to school expectations (Bradley, 1978).

Samuel Kirk and James Gallagher define a child with a conduct disorder as "one who defies authority; is hostile toward authority figures (police officers, teachers, and so forth); is cruel, malicious, and assaultive, and has few guilt feelings. This category includes children who are described as hyperactive, restless, and hyperkinetic" (1983, p. 327). According to R.C. Bradley (1978),

482

Teaching
Reading in
Today's
Elementary
Schools

children who have serious conduct problems show intensive emotion, misbehave frequently, act compulsively, lose control of their emotions, and have poor interpersonal relationships.

Since nearly all children behave inappropriately at one time or another, the identification of children with behavioral disorders depends largely on the frequency, duration, and intensity of misbehavior. Authorities disagree about how much inappropriate behavior is required to classify a child as behaviorally disordered, so estimates of the prevalence of such children vary widely. It is generally agreed, however, that although only about 2 or 3 percent of the population needs intensive special education programs for behavior problems, at least one million school-aged children need help with these difficulties (Kirk and Gallagher, 1983).

One form of behavioral disorder is hyperactivity. According to William Cruickshank (1981), hyperactive children "present the most complex teaching problems of any in the entire spectrum of exceptional children." As with other types of behavioral disorders, hyperactivity is a matter of degree. Although most children will on occasion become excitable or distracted, hyperactivity can become so intense that it can interfere with a child's academic growth and social relationships.

Nine out of ten hyperactive children are boys. They may exhibit overactivity, impulsivity, distractibility, and excitability. More specifically, in the classroom hyperactive children are constantly on the move, can't focus on tasks because they are so easily distracted, don't think before they act, guess at words instead of trying to figure them out, and are easily frustrated. They may be irritable and destructive for no reason (Fairchild, 1975).

Instructional Implications and Strategies

What can teachers who have behaviorally disturbed or hyperactive children in their rooms do? Here are some ideas (Aukerman and Aukerman, 1981; Bradley, 1978; Fairchild, 1975).

1. *Reinforcement.* Reward good behavior even if it is just sitting still for five minutes. Use verbal reinforcers ("good work!"). If they don't work, use activity reinforcers ("When you finish you may go to the interest center"). If they don't work either, use tangible reinforcers (food, inexpensive toys). Try to ignore inappropriate behavior.
2. *Communication.* Speak clearly, precisely, slowly, and quietly. Ask students to paraphrase directions back to you. Let them know exactly what kinds of behavior are acceptable and unacceptable, and make sure that they understand the consequences for unacceptable behavior. Then be consistent in your reactions.
3. *Acceptance.* Accept the child as a person even though you cannot accept his or her behavior. Be realistic in your expectations. Show affection, make a

list of good qualities, and learn about the child's interests and family. Assign work at which the student can succeed.

4. *Environment.* Keep the room environment as simple as possible and help the child to keep clutter from collecting. Use an improvised study carrel to eliminate distractions and place the child's desk or carrel near your desk.
5. *Structure.* Adhere to schedules and routines and enforce class rules. Structure can make children feel secure. As they gain control over their behavior, such structure can be reduced.
6. *Teaching methods.* Eliminate failure as much as possible. Give step-by-step directions, individualize some instruction, and make reading sessions short. Warn the child in advance that you will call on him or her during the lesson, and use contracts and progress charts. (Remember that no single method works for all children.)
7. *Outside assistance.* Get help when you see problems developing. Try a team approach, using guidance counselors, school psychologists, consultants, or social workers.

✓ Self-Check: Objective 6

What are some characteristics of behaviorally disturbed children? What implications do these characteristics have for instructional procedures?
(See Self-Improvement Opportunity 5.)

GIFTED CHILDREN

Characteristics

Recognition of the importance of special educational opportunities for gifted students is growing: seventeen states have laws that require appropriate education for such children, and thirty-three have formulated guidelines for programs. Even so, federal expenditures are two hundred times greater for the handicapped than for the gifted (Lyon, 1981).

An early signal that a child is gifted or very bright may be precociously early reading. Extremely bright children frequently teach themselves to read without any formal instruction and are often able to read materials designed for beginning reading before they enter school. Studies show that approximately half the children who are gifted, as classified by intelligence tests, can read in kindergarten and that nearly all can read at the beginning of first grade.

Gifted children usually have advanced linguistic development, being above normal in their ability to use and understand vocabulary, in maturity of sentence structure, and in originality of expression. Although all normal

484

Teaching
Reading in
Today's
Elementary
Schools

young children learn the language of their environment without formal instruction, the bright child learns the language more rapidly.

Within the school setting, gifted children are likely to progress mentally at a rate of one and one fourth (or more) years within one calendar year, as compared to the average child, who has one year of mental growth for each year of his or her life. However, there are both "normal" achievers and underachievers among the gifted; they do not always live up to or demonstrate their potential. Physical defects, emotional instability, and poor study habits may interfere with the recognition of the abilities of the gifted. Too, some gifted children are nonconformists and tend to irritate a teacher, causing the teacher to consider them "brats" rather than "brains."

Although each mentally advanced child is, of course, different, some characteristics are common to most:

1. interest in books and reading
2. a large vocabulary, with an interest in words and their meanings
3. ability to express themselves verbally in a mature style
4. enjoyment of activities usually liked best by older children
5. curiosity to know more, shown by using the dictionary, encyclopedia, and other reference sources
6. long attention span combined with initiative and the ability to plan and set goals
7. a high level of abstract thinking
8. a creative talent with a wide range of interests.

Means for identifying the gifted vary. Typically, students in the top 5 percent of the school population are considered gifted (Lyon, 1981). A widely accepted definition introduced by the U.S. Office of Education (Marland, 1971) includes general intellectual ability, specific academic aptitude, talent in the visual and performing arts, leadership ability, and creative and productive thinking as criteria for giftedness. Students who are considered to be verbally gifted would score in the upper 3 percent among their peers in at least two of the following categories: verbal reasoning, foreign languages, reading, and creative writing (Fox and Durden, 1982).

Instructional Implications and Strategies

Renzulli recommends using a revolving-door model for working with gifted children (Renzulli and Smith, 1980; Reis, 1981; Reis and Renzulli, 1982), in which students are not arbitrarily assigned to a gifted class for a year but come and go according to their interest in pursuing special topics. As many as 25 to 30 percent of the entire student population may qualify for participation in the gifted program on this rotating basis. These students enter a resource room for involvement in a specialized or creative project that may require

from several weeks to a year or more for completion. They make up the work that they consequently miss in the classroom through curriculum compacting, which enables them to cover certain curricular material more rapidly than other children.

Renzulli's Enrichment Triad Model consists of three stages. Type I activities, designed to interest children in topics that are not a part of the regular curriculum, encourage exploration of these topics. In Type II activities students receive cognitive and affective training in such skills as problem-solving, critical thinking, investigating, and inquiry. Type III activities allow students to investigate a problem and develop a product. When a student finishes a project, he or she either revolves out of the resource room or chooses another topic for investigation.

Another strategy to use with gifted students is inquiry reading (Cassidy, 1981). In this approach good readers in grades three through six independently investigate subjects of special interest to them. During the first week they learn the procedure and each child selects one topic, identifying appropriate resources and developing contracts with deadlines for completing the task. Most of the time during the second and third weeks is spent working independently, often in the library, where students use references to take notes, or in interviews with resource people. Contracts are reviewed with the teacher and work on the culminating project is begun. In the fourth week students complete their projects and prepare and give presentations. Finally, inquiry reading projects are evaluated by the teacher and each student.

Within the classroom reading program teachers have many ways to attend to the special needs of gifted children. These ways include providing a wide supply of resource materials, offering opportunities for students to respond creatively to books, suggesting long-term enrichment or research projects (such as in-depth investigation of the newspaper), and developing a file of language puzzles and mindbenders for students to use (*Reader's Digest* is a good source).

Simply because the gifted are capable of completing their work more rapidly than other students, they should not be expected to do more of the same kind of work if they finish their assignments early. Instead, encourage them to choose challenging and creative activities from a resource file. A dozen stimulating ideas involving reading and language are given below (Click, 1981).

1. Complete the following: If I could be a vegetable, I would be _____ because _____.
2. If a raindrop could talk, what would it say to another raindrop if it fell on a flower petal, on a teacher's umbrella, etc.?
3. Invent a new holiday. Give a reason for its existence and suggest ways to celebrate it.

486

Teaching
Reading in
Today's
Elementary
Schools

4. What familiar expressions are represented by the following? When you know the answers, make up some similar puzzles of your own.[1]

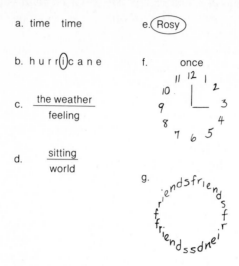

a. time   time

b. hurr(i)cane

c. the weather / feeling

d. sitting / world

e. (Rosy)

f. once

g.

5. Choose a political candidate to support. Write a slogan, design a campaign button, propose a budget, and develop campaign strategies.
6. Research the history of common objects, such as tin cans, buttons, or spoons.
7. Rewrite "The Twelve Days of Christmas" using more up-to-date gifts.
8. Investigate the meanings and language origins of such familiar names as Edward, Barbara, Arthur, Philip, Florence, George, Helen, Arnold, and Ethel. Decide if a name is suitable for someone you know who has that name. What name best describes you?
9. Pretend you are opening a new store to sell something unusual, such as spiders. Draw up a plan for advertising and marketing your product.
10. Put major events from your life on individual 3 × 5 cards and string them together in order with yarn. Illustrate the cards with photographs, drawings, or pictures from magazines. Do the same thing for the lives of famous people.
11. Write, illustrate, and bind a children's book.
12. Create your own animal by combining parts of different animals. Draw a picture of it, describe its habits and habitat, and write an adventure story about it.

✔ Self-Check: Objective 7

List several characteristics of gifted learners. What are some appropriate instructional procedures for them?
(See Self-Improvement Opportunities 3 and 10.)

[1]Answers: a. time after time; b. the eye of the hurricane; c. feeling under the weather; d. sitting on top of the world; e. Ring around a Rosy; f. once upon a time; g. circle of friends.

America has long been known as the "melting pot" because of its assimilation of people from all parts of the world. In recent years this idea has been modified by people who believe in the "salad bowl" concept, or the rights of different ethnic groups to retain their cultural diversity within American society.

Children from some families may differ in their values, their orientation toward school, and their speech patterns from those in the American mainstream. Many speak a dialect based on their socioeconomic or ethnic background or the region of the country in which they live. Others speak English as a second language or no English at all. Both their cultural and linguistic divergencies can make a difference in how these children learn and consequently in how they should be taught, and thus educational policies in our schools have been affected by their presence and needs.

Multiethnic education means developing an understanding and appreciation of various racial and ethnic minority groups in the United States. This awareness should permeate the curriculum (Garcia, 1981). Children should be taught with consideration for their cultural heritage, their language preferences, and their lifestyles. On the other hand, too much attention to the needs of special groups may weaken the educational program, so teachers must also concentrate on teaching the skills and content that are necessary for success in American society (Thomas, 1981).

Some general guidelines for working with children of diverse ethnic origins are listed below (ASCD Multicultural Education Commission, 1977; Barnes, 1977).

1. *Learn about their culture.* Find out about their language and what things are important to them. Make home visits to learn about children's living conditions.
2. *Participate in the community.* Become involved in recreational activities and community service projects. The children and their families will appreciate your efforts and you will get to know them in out-of-school settings.
3. *Value their contributions.* Take an interest in what children bring to share. Build activities around their holiday celebrations. Listen to what they say.
4. *Share ideas with other teachers.* Observe the techniques used by teachers whom children respect. During in-service and faculty meetings, share ideas that get results.
5. *Discuss universal concerns.* Show that all kinds of people have certain things in common, such as liking ice cream and caring about their families. Use these concerns in developing lessons and units.

While these ideas are useful in any instructional situation, the following list contains practical suggestions for teaching reading to children from multiethnic backgrounds (Foerster, 1976).

488

Teaching
Reading in
Today's
Elementary
Schools

1. *Choose materials carefully.* Some suitable materials include books written by the children themselves; trade books about differences in backgrounds, language, and interests; high-quality comic books; and paperback books, especially the high-interest/low-vocabulary variety.

2. *Make no assumptions.* Because of differences in background experiences, children vary in their readiness for understanding stories and concepts. Fill in gaps and clarify misunderstandings with direct or vicarious experiences.

3. *Use picture and context clues.* These clues are necessary for helping children to recognize words when their language differs from standard English in vocabulary, usage, and syntax.

4. *Let children read orally frequently.* In order to check children's pronunciation and intonation of standard English, listen to them read. You may want to use a tape recorder so that you can analyze the tapes and keep a record of linguistic changes.

5. *Plan for skill development.* Diagnose children's reading skill deficiencies and plan programs of instruction to meet individual needs.

The following discussions deal with how children's background and specific language characteristics may affect the way they learn, and consider strategies that teachers can use as they work with these children.

Culturally Different Students

Characteristics

Many children are from homes that differ economically, socially, and culturally from middle-class backgrounds. Although these children's cultural environments may be full and rich, they differ markedly from the school setting. Most teachers come from middle-class families and as a result have middle-class expectations regarding goals, behavior, and academic achievement. Instructional materials often deal with experiences unfamiliar to culturally different children, such as family vacations and visits to department stores. In school, children are expected to use standard English, but most culturally different children speak in nonstandard dialect. Therefore, a considerable gap exists between the environment of the culturally different children and the middle-class school situation. Because of this discrepancy, many of these children have difficulty learning in school.

Often the families of culturally different children have lived in poverty for generations. Educational levels are low, and some parents may be illiterate. Parents' jobs are usually poorly paid and on unskilled or semiskilled levels, if they exist at all. Their housing is often substandard and conditions are crowded; there are no books for children to read, and there is no place to do homework. Food and clothing are often inadequate, so that children are malnourished and uncomfortable. Most families see little hope for a better life and simply struggle to survive. In addition to being frequently absent, children who come from economically deprived homes such as these are likely to have low aspirations, poor self-concepts, suspicions about school and the teacher, and poor preparation for school tasks.

Culturally different children may be found in any part of the country and may represent any· ethnic heritage. Many of them are found in rural or mountainous areas, such as Appalachia, and many others are located in urban areas, such as inner-city ghettos. Migrant-worker families, found primarily in rural areas, have children with the lowest achievement rates, the highest dropout rates, and the most failures when compared with other children (Cardenas, 1976). Many of the problems of migrant children are due to lack of continuity in their school programs and to discriminatory treatment.

Many children who enter first grade from culturally different homes will not be ready for traditional reading readiness programs, since they will not know how to control their behavior and interact socially with other children, and their oral language will be inadequate for communication. They will be unfamiliar with pencils, scissors, paints, and books, and they may never have heard a story read to them.

Instructional Implications and Strategies

Teachers who work with culturally different children must first develop a positive relationship with them. Understanding their cultural heritage and learning more about it can serve as a basis for developing positive learning experiences.

During the prereadiness period, culturally different children must take part in oral language and listening activities that provide a foundation for reading and writing. Some things children can do are

1. name objects.
2. identify one object by name from several objects.
3. listen to the teacher read stories.
4. learn simple songs.
5. tell about something that happened.
6. carry on a brief conversation with another child or with the teacher.
7. point to a picture and tell what they see.
8. follow simple directions, such as "Clap your hands" and "Stamp your foot."
9. answer questions, such as "Who lives with you?" and "How did you get to school today?"
10. call other children in the class by name.

Among the several compensatory programs that have been developed to meet the needs of these children, the most familiar is Head Start, which was begun in order to give culturally different children a "head start" before

490

Teaching
Reading in
Today's
Elementary
Schools

entering school. Head Start was designed to enrich the background experiences of children from low-income families; although programs differ across the country, many of them focus on sensorimotor and language development.

In order to ease the adjustment between Head Start's preschool program and the traditional primary classroom, Project Follow Through was established. Also a compensatory program, Follow Through may take a variety of forms, including an academic intervention model referred to as DISTAR (see Example 11.3). This program features the direct teaching of language, reading, and math skills.

Several programs for helping migrant students are available through the ERIC Clearinghouse on Reading and Communication Skills (Reed, 1978). Most stress providing individualized instruction and helping children to become independent learners. They place curricular emphasis in the following four areas:

1. oral language programs for making the transition between language at home and at school
2. task-oriented activities for helping children solve problems
3. experience-based programs for relating home experiences to school and for expanding concepts beyond the immediate environment
4. affective programs for improving the child's self-concept.

A mastery-learning reading instructional program for improving reading achievement in inner-city schools has been introduced in Brooklyn (Levine, 1982). This program, the Chicago Mastery Learning Reading Program, consists of 194 units of instruction for teaching word attack, comprehension, and study skills for grades kindergarten through eight. Some of the advantages of this program are that it teaches children strategies for learning how to learn; provides specific, detailed instruction for teachers; meets the needs of low-achieving students; stresses comprehension skills; and allows children to be successful. Use of this plan is resulting in gains in reading achievement.

Basing his conclusions on extensive research, Jere Brophy (1982) recommends several teaching strategies that should be effective with inner-city children. He points first to the importance of teacher effectiveness in producing learning gains and stresses the teacher behaviors listed below.

1. *Good teachers take the responsibility for teaching.* Teachers do not accept the failures of their students but reteach, try other methods, and believe in the ability of their students to learn.
2. *Good teachers organize and manage their classes.* Most of the available time is spent in instruction; little time is spent in transitions between lessons and other nonproductive activities. Good teachers establish routines and schedules, minimize disruptions, and move instruction at a lively pace.

102

TASK 8 Some, All, None

You will need an extra piece of paper for
this exercise.
Look at the cows.
Tell me if I cover up some of the cows
or all of the cows or none of the cows.
 a. Cover three cows.
    Am I covering up some of the cows or all
    of the cows or none of the cows? Signal.
    Some of the cows.
 b. Cover six cows.
    Am I covering up some of the cows or all
    of the cows or none of the cows? Signal.
    All of the cows.
 c. Cover none of the cows.
    Am I covering up some of the cows or all
    of the cows or none of the cows? Signal.
    None of the cows.
 d. Cover two cows.
    What am I doing? Touch.
    Covering up some of the cows.
 e. Cover none of the cows.
    What am I doing? Touch.
    Covering up none of the cows.
 f. Cover six cows.
    What am I doing? Touch.
    Covering up all of the cows.
 g. Repeat a through f until all children's
    responses are firm. Praise the children.

Individual Test
Repeat a through f, calling on different
children for each step.

Source: From *Distar ® Language 1*, 2nd ed., by Siegfried Engelmann and Jean Osborn © 1976,
1972, 1969. Science Research Associates, Inc. Reprinted by permission. ◀

3. *The curriculum is geared for success.* Students should participate in a variety
   of meaningful activities, progressing in incremental steps and experiencing
   success at each level.
4. *Good teachers direct the learning process.* Teachers demonstrate skills, conduct
   activities, explain concepts, review materials, and actively direct students'
   learning experiences.
5. *Skills are taught to mastery level.* Following instruction, teachers let students
   practice and apply skills to the point of overlearning. Lower-level skills are
   learned thoroughly before higher-level skills are introduced.
6. *Teaching strategies differ at various grade levels.* In the early grades students
   need more individualized attention than in higher grades, but teachers
   must work closely with students and check their progress at all levels.
7. *Teachers need to be supportive.* Teachers offer instructional support to
   students by providing structured learning experiences, individualization,
   and continuous supervision. They also offer personal support through
   praise, encouragement, and appreciation of effort.

492

Teaching
Reading in
Today's
Elementary
Schools

✔ **Self-Check: Objective 8**

What are some of the problems that culturally different children encounter as they enter school? What are some ways that teachers can help them?
(See Self-Improvement Opportunities 6 and 9.)

Dialectal Differences

Characteristics

Children who exhibit cultural differences are also likely to have linguistic differences or variations, or "dialects." A dialect may be defined as a variation of a language that is sufficiently different from the original to be considered a separate entity but not different enough to be classed as a separate language. Dialectal variations are usually associated with socioeconomic level, geographic region, or national origin. In truth, we all speak a regional dialect of some sort, and differences exist even within a regional pattern. *Idiolect* is the term referring to an individual's unique language style.

The differences between dialects occur in phonology (pronunciation), vocabulary, and to a limited extent in grammatical construction (syntax). The term *dialect* carries no derogatory meaning; any dialect is as adequate and correct as another. An individual simply uses the forms he or she encounters in his or her environment.

Teachers of reading must be familiar with the principal systematic differences in pronunciation and syntactic rules in order to evaluate accurately the oral reading of the divergent speaker. Without this knowledge, teachers cannot distinguish between a child's oral misreading that results from a lack of decoding skills and oral misreading that results from dialectal differences.

Dialectal differences occur in both urban and rural areas. One example of each is discussed briefly below. According to Harber and Beatty, some of the characteristic speech patterns of black urban ghetto areas are as shown in Table 11.1.

William Stewart (1969) studied the speech patterns of Appalachian rural children and found various features, including

1. dropped endings of words: *goin'*, *comin'*, *seein'*
2. lack of distinction in the sound of different vowels before *r: far, fir, car, cur*
3. elimination of subjects in sentence patterns: *'m going down town*, *'e's doing his work*
4. incorrect use of the objective case of pronouns in compound subjects: *me and you, me and my sister*
5. addition of "n" to possessive pronouns: *his'n, her'n*
6. distortion of sounds: *cidy* for *city*, *tank* for *thank;* and mispronunciation of words: *duh* for *the*, *terry* for *very*.

Phonological Differences

Feature	Example (SE—BE)
Simplification of consonant clusters	test—tes, past—pas, went—win
th sounds	
voiceless *th* in initial position	think—tink or think
voiced *th* in initial position	the—de
voiceless *th* in medial position	nothing—nofin'
voiced *th* in medial position	brother—brovah
th in final position	tooth—toof
r and *l*	
in postvocalic position	sister—sistah, nickel—nickuh
in final position	Saul—saw
Devoicing of final *b, d,* and *g*	cab—cap, bud—but, pig—pik
Nasalization	
-ing suffix	doing—doin
i and *e* before a nasal	pen—pin
Stress—absence of the first syllable of a multisyllabic word when the first syllable is unstressed	about—'bout
Plural marker*	three birds—three bird or three birds the books—de book or de books
Possessive marker*	the boy's hat—de boy hat
Third person singular marker*	He works here—He work here
Past tense—simplification of final consonant clusters*	passed—pass, loaned—loan

*Some authorities include these under syntactical differences

Syntactical Differences

Feature	SE	BE
Linking verb	He is going.	He goin, or He is goin
Pronomial apposition	That teacher yells at the kids.	Dat teachah, she yell at de kid (kids).
Agreement of subject and third-person singular verb	She runs home. She has a bike.	She run home. She have a bike.
Irregular verb forms	They rode their bikes.	Dey rided der bike (bikes).
Future form	I will go home.	I'm a go home.
"If" construction	I asked if he did it.	I ask did he do it.
Indefinite article	I want an apple.	I want a apple.
Negation	I don't have any.	I don't got none.
Pronoun form	We have to do it.	Us got to do it.
Copula (verb "to be")	He is here all the time. No, he isn't.	He be here. No, he isn't, or No, he don't.

TABLE 11.1: *(continued)*

	Syntactical Differences	
Feature	*SE*	*BE*
Prepositions	Put the cat out of the house.	Put de cat out de house.
	The dress is made of wool.	De dress is made outta wool.

Note: The inventory of differences between SE and BE is far smaller than the inventory of similarities.
(Source: Jean Harber and Jane N. Beatty. *Reading and Black English Speaking Child.* International Reading Association, Newark, Delaware, 1978, pp. 46–47. Reprinted with permission of the author and the International Reading Association.)

Instructional Implications and Strategies

Dialectal variations have implications for the teacher of reading. Research has not established how strongly these variations influence learning to read standard English, but there have been a number of specific proposals, each of which represents a viewpoint about language and reading.

1. Teach the children standard English first; then teach them to read.
2. Use materials written in nonstandard dialect or in the child's own language.
3. Use conventional reading material but accept dialect transpositions.
4. Use materials written in standard English that are culturally relevant to the target group.
5. Use the language experience approach.

We feel that teachers should teach standard English along with beginning reading instruction. Certainly the teacher should speak standard English, serving as a model for speakers of divergent dialects, encouraging children to express themselves in whatever dialect they have, and leading them gently toward the more generally accepted classroom or school dialect. Introduction to reading instruction should not be delayed until the child has learned to speak standard English. In brief, reading activities and language usage may be developed concomitantly.

For those who plan to teach in regions where children have divergent dialects, these classroom practices may be useful:

1. Provide an unusually rich program of development in functional oral language.
2. Relate reading to personal experiences and oral language forms that are familiar to the child.
3. Provide reading materials about characters with whom the child can identify.

4. Know the possible points of interference between the dialect of the child and the standard dialect of the school.

5. Listen to the child's language carefully to determine the nature, regularity, and predictability of such dialectal differences.

6. Base instruction (particularly phonics) on a careful analysis of the child's language. Vowel phonemes are particularly likely to vary—as in words ending in -og, such as *dog, fog, frog, log*—as are the other morphological, syntactical, and vocabulary features previously mentioned.

7. Differentiate between oral reading errors and particular speech patterns related to different linguistic backgrounds. (See "Miscue Analysis" in Chapter 9.)

Speakers of black English should be able to use their own dialect in the classroom as well as become acquainted with standard English (Padek, 1981). Students who speak black English may

1. write their own stories and read them orally to the class.
2. read some poems from black literature.
3. discuss reasons for different dialects.
4. role-play situations that call for the use of both black and standard English.
5. observe television news commentators. Then pretend to give a national newscast, imitating the speech, style, and mannerisms of the commentators.
6. take a survey of television shows that use dialect.
7. practice standard English patterns by copying dictated passages.
8. compare black English and standard English by using examples of one dialect and then the other to express the same idea. (Alexander, 1980)

✔ Self-Check: Objective 9

Explain what dialect is.
Name some characteristics of black urban and rural Appalachian speech. Then suggest some appropriate teaching strategies for children whose dialect differs radically from standard English. (See Self-Improvement Opportunities 7, 8, and 9.)

Bilingual Children

Characteristics

The term *bilingualism* refers to the ability to speak or understand another language in addition to the individual's native tongue. In the classroom bilingual students include some children who speak very little English as well as others who speak English almost as well as they do their native language. Bilingualism is prevalent in the United States—in the large metropolitan areas, in the rural areas of the Midwest and South, in the five southwestern

496

Teaching
Reading in
Today's
Elementary
Schools

states, and in Hawaii. In some areas, such as the Puerto Rican districts in New York City; the Chicano sections in cities in the Southwest; and the Chinatown areas of New York City, San Francisco, and Los Angeles, nearly all of the school population is bilingual.

An estimated 7.5 million children in U.S. schools do not speak English as their first language, but only a half-million of them are in English-as-a-second-language (ESL) or bilingual programs. It is expected that another million youngsters will enter school each year for the next few years. Materials available for teachers who work with bilingual students are in short supply, and it is imperative for educators to work together to develop programs to serve the influx of non-English-speaking students (Ebel, 1980; Gonzales, 1981).

Each ethnic group has its own linguistic characteristics. Here we discuss two groups in terms of their speech patterns and implications for teaching.

Spanish The child from the home in which Spanish is spoken will probably come to school speaking a Spanish-American dialect. The Spanish-speaking child who has already learned the alphabet will pronouce the vowels *a, e, i, o, u* as: *ä* (as in *cot*), *ā* (as in *bait*), *ē* (as in *beet*), *ō* (as in *oak*), $\overline{oo}$ (as in *boot*) and not as: *ā, ē, ī, ō, ū*.

The Spanish language does not use the voiced *th*, the *z*, the *zh*, or the *j* sounds. The tendency of Spanish speakers is to substitute for these sounds the sounds in the Spanish language most like them. One of the most common sounds in English, the *schwa* (unstressed vowel, such as *a* in *about*), has no counterpart in Spanish. The blend of *s* with other consonant sounds (*t, p, k, f, m, n,* and *l*) may present a problem, since no Spanish words begin with these combinations. A vowel always precedes the *s* in Spanish, and the second consonant becomes the beginning of the second syllable (as *estar* for *star*). The child may have difficulty in pronouncing two consonants together at the end of a word (as *wasp, disk, last*), and will often pronounce words ending in *r* plus *d, t, l, p,* and *s* without the final consonant (as *car* for *card*). The Spanish letter *h* elicits silence (*hotel* becomes *otel*). There are only two contractions in Spanish; stress and intonation in Spanish are different; and Spanish adjectives follow rather than precede nouns (*The dress blue is pretty*).

Some other points of difficulty might be the negative (*Jim is no here*); plurals (*The two boys are bigs*); omission of he (*Is fireman?*); comparisons (*Is more small*); omission of article (*He is policeman*); subject-verb agreement (*The girls runs* or *The girl run*); possessive (*the book of the boy*); and past tense (*He need help yesterday*).

Navajo The specific problems that Navajo children may have with English are considered here because the Navajos are the largest tribe in the United States; the features mentioned below cannot be generalized to include all Indian languages. Navajo speakers do not distinguish between the English /*p*/

Bilingual children who are learning to read English often pose a challenge for teachers, since approaches and materials will have to be varied according to the children's special needs.   (© Elizabeth Crews)

and /b/ and usually substitute their own slightly different /b/ for both. This sound never occurs at the end of a syllable in Navajo, however, so they often substitute either a glottal stop or the Navajo /d/ for a final /p/ or /b/. This /d/, which sounds like the /t/ in *stop*, is also typically substituted for the English /t/ and /d/ when they occur at the beginning of words. In Navajo, there are no correspondents to /f/, /v/, /th/, and /ng/. Vowel length and nasalization are differentiated to distinguish meaning, and the vowel sounds /ae/ (*a*) and /e/ (*u*)

498

Teaching
Reading in
Today's
Elementary
Schools

do not occur and are thus the hardest for Navajo pupils to learn. Navajo speakers must learn to distinguish among English /o/ (*o* as in *joke*), /u/ (*oo* as in *book*), and /uw/ (*oo* as in *loot*).

Groups of adjacent consonants present a major problem for Navajo speakers, who often substitute similar clusters of their own. Although tonal pitch is the only distinctive feature with which to differentiate meaning between such Navajo words as *nili* (*you are*) and *nili* (*he is*), Navajo uses particles to convey meanings expressed by intonation in English—for example, -iš and -ša, added to Navajo words, signal questions.

Navajo speakers find many features of English syntax difficult to understand. Articles and adjectives are troublesome because, with a few exceptions, they do not exist in Navajo. Few Navajo nouns are changed to make the plural (*four dog*), and the possessive /'s/ is a problem since the Navajo pattern for *the boy's book* would be *the boy his book.* Furthermore, the Navajo *bi* translates as any of the third-person pronouns: *he, she, it, they, them, him, her, his, its, their.* To add to the problem, the Navajo child is faced with a semantic system that categorizes experiences in a very different way (Saville, 1970).

Instructional Implications and Strategies

Bilingual children learn English as a second language by moving their bodies, by working with concrete objects, and through experiences. Songs, games, and choral readings with motions reinforce a child's understanding of words, as does acting out a sentence ("Tina sits down") or dramatizing a simple story. Dramatic play helps children relate English words to meaningful situations. To teach prepositions such as *on, under,* and *beside,* encourage appropriate body movements. Naming, labeling, and talking about concrete objects are also good ways to increase vocabulary. Audiovisual media—especially films and filmstrips, puppets, and pictures—enable children to associate words with experiences, as do field trips.

It is important to note that the best reading materials to use with bilingual children are those that relate to their culture. Whenever possible, the teacher should find books about the culture to read to the children and for them to read themselves. Since the supply of such books is probably limited, the teacher may let children create their own reading material by using the language experience approach (see Chapter 5). At first have the children dictate stories using only key words, such as nouns and verbs ("Boy run"), and gradually encourage them to expand such sentences to conform more closely to standard English. Children can also write and illustrate booklets about themselves, which then become the basis for building sight word vocabularies.

In teaching bilingual children to read basal readers, teachers must consider the relationship between the linguistic features of the text and the child's language proficiency (Gonzales, 1981), providing instruction on linguistic structures and forms if necessary. The teacher may discuss pictures by using simple sentences, avoiding the use of phrases, clauses, or other structures that the child does not understand. She may rewrite part of the text by reducing compound and complex sentences to series of simple sentences (for instance, changing the sentence "Tim ran and played" to "Tim ran" and "Tim played"). Aukerman and Aukerman (1981) recommend, however, that teachers should speak in the natural grammatical sequences of standard English as a model for the children to follow. They also suggest teaching those phonics elements that are common to both the child's native tongue and standard English first. Errors or miscues that reflect the structure of the child's first language should not be corrected until after the child becomes a fairly proficient reader.

In suggesting appropriate teaching strategies for bilingual Mexican-American children, Carol Dixon (1976) took into consideration their cultural values. Her suggestions are as follows:

1. Use activities that stress improving the skills of the entire group rather than of single individuals.
2. Use activities that require cooperation instead of competition.
3. Provide interaction between the student and the teacher or other students.
4. Allow children to assume authority roles in the classroom. Dixon feels that the cultural characteristics of these children justify the use of peer tutoring (one student teaching another) in the classroom. She also recommends use of the language experience approach, having students dictate stories in English, in Spanish, or in a combination of both languages.

According to Audrey Simpson-Tyson (1978), native American children's major handicap in learning to read may be their inability to use standard English well. Thus these children should have more time with language experiences before formal reading instruction begins. Appropriate experiences with language include the following:

1. Children should *listen* to language in many different situations: listening to stories, watching films, and listening to visitors.
2. Children must *use* language for communicating with each other and for expressing ideas. Language is stimulated by exploring, manipulating, constructing, moving, and singing. Native American culture should be central to these activities.
3. Children should *produce* language that can be read. They may dictate words for captions, labels, and charts.
4. Children may *read* what other children have written. The written words are familiar and meaningful.

500

Teaching
Reading in
Today's
Elementary
Schools

✔ **Self-Check: Objective 10**

What are some factors to consider in working with bilingual children?
(See Self-Improvement Opportunities 7, 8, and 9.)

CORRECTIVE AND REMEDIAL READERS:

UNDERACHIEVEMENT

It is a common misconception that every child who is reading below grade level is a poor reader. From the preceding discussion of exceptionalities, it is easy to see that not all children have the same abilities, linguistic facility, or experiences. Therefore, it is unreasonable to expect all children to read at grade level, and teachers should instead be concerned that children read up to their individual potential.

A child's reading potential is difficult to determine. Most measures of potential are based on *reading expectancy* (RE) formulas that use IQ scores or mental age, but IQ scores can be misleading. They are criticized for being culturally biased and for failing to measure all aspects of intelligence. Group intelligence tests are usually dependent on the individual's ability to read; therefore, a poor reader may receive a low score because his or her reading ability is inadequate rather than because he or she cannot answer the questions. IQ scores can also be affected by personal reasons, such as the individual's failure to understand directions or lack of effort.

Regardless of these weaknesses, a reading expectancy formula based on IQ score or mental age is one way of roughly assessing a child's reading potential. One such formula is the Harris 1 formula, which is simple to use: RE (Reading Expectancy) = MA (mental age) − 5.0. Mental age can be computed from IQ scores in the following way:

$$\text{MA (Mental Age)} = \text{CA (Chronological Age)} \times \frac{\text{IQ}}{100}$$

Thus, a child whose mental age is 11.2 would be expected to read at beginning sixth-grade level (11.2 − 5.0 = 6.2). Another RE formula, the Bond and Tinker formula, is given in Chapter 9.

Once a teacher has estimated a student's potential, he or she should compare it with the child's reading achievement level. A few children who are determined to learn may be working above their measured potential. Others may be working at their potential, even if they are not reading at grade level. For instance, a ten-year-old in fifth grade with an IQ score of 80 has a mental age of eight and an RE level of grade three. This child should not be expected to read at fifth-grade level because of his limited mental ability. On the other hand, a ten-year-old fifth grader with an IQ score of 120 has a mental age of twelve. By applying the Harris 1 formula, the teacher finds that this student is potentially capable of reading at the seventh-grade level. If this student reads only at fifth-grade level, he or she is an underachiever.

Two terms that designate reading instruction for underachieving readers are *corrective* and *remedial*. A *corrective reader* is generally one who reads about six to eighteen months below potential; this child should receive help in skill development in the classroom from the teacher before the disparity between potential and achievement increases. A student is usually considered to be a *remedial reader* if there is a gap of approximately two or more years between expectancy and achievement levels; this student needs special help in a reading resource room from a reading specialist. Whereas reading instruction for average readers is *developmental* and proceeds normally according to a prescribed sequence, gifted readers may take part in *accelerated* reading programs. Slow learners need instruction that is *adapted* to a slower pace.

Underachievement in reading is affected by considerably different factors for each type of exceptionality. Inability to read is a common characteristic of learning-disabled children who appear to have adequate mental ability for learning to read. By any RE formula, most of these children are underachievers. Because of the specific nature of learning disabilities, such children will probably need to go to a resource room for additional help with reading. On the other hand, many slow learners are actually reading up to their potential even if they are not reading at grade level. Since the IQ scores of children who are slow learners are lower than those of most other children, they should receive instruction that is adapted to a slower pace and uses easier material. Many gifted children are underachieving in terms of their potential even though they are reading at, or even slightly above, grade level. Teachers should challenge these children to read more difficult materials, encouraging them to participate in accelerated programs. Visually handicapped children may be reading below their potential because they have trouble seeing clearly, but when provisions are made for accommodating reading materials to their needs, they often reach their potential through corrective or remedial instruction. Similarly, hearing and speech impaired students are often underachievers because they cannot hear or reproduce sounds accurately and thus are generally unable to profit from phonics instruction. Teachers should use alternate methods in teaching word recognition to help these children reach their potential. Because children who are behaviorally disturbed or hyperactive cannot keep their attention on the lesson, they often fail to work up to their ability. Teachers must find ways to help these children calm down before providing corrective or remedial instruction.

Children who are culturally and linguistically different also frequently underachieve in reading. As we have mentioned, these children come from environments that do not provide them with the experiences and language skills necessary for coping with a middle-class curriculum and standard

502

Teaching
Reading in
Today's
Elementary
Schools

English. Therefore, even though they have the ability to succeed in school, the gap between their background and the school is so great that they do not learn all that they should. In order to help these children reach their potential, teachers should use instructional strategies and materials that help them make the transition from home to school.

Children who are not handicapped and who come from middle-class homes where standard English is spoken also may be underachievers. The causes for their underachievement are varied, and there is generally no easy solution. In some homes parents are either disinterested or so concerned that they create emotional problems for their children; in others children are bothered by problems such as a new sibling, an impending divorce, or child abuse. When children come to school hungry, they cannot concentrate. Perpetual colds or headaches interfere with learning. Children who are frequently absent miss so many lessons that they do not ever learn essential skills. Their foundation in reading is so weak that it collapses at higher levels. Some children have developed negative attitudes toward reading as a result of frustrations and failure and may have such low self-concepts that they have stopped trying.

Teachers who understand the causes for underachievement are sometimes able to alleviate the situation, but at other times they can only offer understanding. In the case of vision and hearing impairments, a teacher can recommend that the parents or guardian see that the child gets professional attention. When children come to school hungry, a teacher can arrange for the cafeteria to provide them with food before school starts. If children are abused or neglected, a teacher can contact the proper authorities. Solving any one of these problems, however, seldom changes a child's reading level appreciably.

When trying to help underachievers reach their potential, classroom teachers have two major types of responsibilities. First, they should help corrective readers in the classroom by identifying specific deficiencies (see Chapter 9 on assessment) and developing plans to help these readers improve. Second, after remedial readers have been identified, classroom teachers must cooperate with the resource teacher and/or reading specialist to help plan reading instruction, arranging a time to coordinate reading programs for these children.

A teacher needs to concentrate on both developing positive attitudes and building reading skills when working with underachieving readers. Teacher behaviors and instructional procedures that are effective with these children may be found in the general guidelines near the beginning of this chapter.

✔ Self-Check: Objective 11

Explain how teachers can identify underachievers and how they can help them to reach their potential.
(See Self-Improvement Opportunity 11.)

It was not too long before they saw the river. As Johnny ran ahead, he turned and called, "Come on! I want to see Big Red and Ranger Finley."

"Well, Johnny, you will not have to wait much longer," called Dan. "Look ahead where the river turns. Do you see those two men fishing?"

104

Source: *Dan Frontier Goes Exploring*, by William Hurley. Chicago: Benefic Press, 1971, p. 104. ◀

MATERIALS FOR READERS WITH SPECIAL NEEDS

Guideline 3 near the beginning of this chapter emphasizes selecting materials that exceptional children are capable of using as well as those that are of interest to them. High-interest/low-vocabulary books meet both of these requirements. These books contain especially interesting and appealing

504

Teaching
Reading in
Today's
Elementary
Schools

▶ **EXAMPLE 11.5:** Sample Rebus Material

Source: R.W. Woodcock, *Rebus Reader Two* (Circle Pines, Minn: American Guidance Service, 1969), p. 16. ◀

stories for slow learners, culturally different students, and poor readers; they are written at a low readability level so that these students can read them easily. (Example 11.4 presents a page from a high-interest/low-vocabulary book.) A sampling of these and other materials that are especially suited to the needs of special students is found in Table 11.2; the listed materials are only a few of the many varied publications and programs that are available.

Test Yourself

True or False

_____ 1. The exceptional child's basic needs and goals are quite different from those of the average child.

_____ 2. The handicapped child often needs more direct, systematic instruction than the average child usually needs.

TABLE 11.2: Materials for the Exceptional Child

Program/Publisher	Levels	Audience	Components	Remarks
Peabody Rebus Program.[1] American Guidance Service, Circle Pines, MN	Readiness and beginning reading; Head Start	Remedial; bilingual/ESL[2]	Programmed workbooks	Pictured words (rebuses) as a transition to spelled words
Tales for Transfer Skill Series.	Intermediate	Slow reader[3]	Reusable books	High-interest adventure series, complete program
The Sly Spy. Ann Arbor Publishers, Naples, FL 33940	2nd, 3rd reading level	Slow reader	Reusable books	Phonic rules in high-interest format
Multiple Skills Series, Spanish and English.	K–6	Spanish speakers	Booklets, tests, spirit masters	Skill development lessons, 4 booklets at each level
Basic Word Sets, Spanish and English. Barnell Loft, Baldwin, NY 11510	1–9	ESL, LD,[4] hearing impaired	Booklets, spirit masters	Quick mastery of 720 key words
Ranger Don.	1–6	Spanish	Multimedia	English and Spanish editions
Cowboy Sam.	Preprimer–6	Slow reader	Multimedia	High-interest/low-vocabulary series
Cowboys of Many Places. Benefic Press, Chicago, IL 60639	Preprimer–6	Multiracial	Multimedia	

[1]See Example 11.5 for sample material.
[2]ESL stands for English as a second language.
[3]The term *slow reader* as used in this table refers to any child who is reading below grade level.
[4]LD stands for learning-disabled.

TABLE 11.2: Materials for the Exceptional Child *(continued)*

Program/Publisher	Levels	Audience	Components	Remarks
Monster Books in Spanish. Bowmar/Noble, Los Angeles, CA 90039	K–4	Spanish speakers	Books, filmstrips	Lovable monster to teach beginning reading
Reading for Comprehension. Continental Press, Elizabethton, PA 17022	2 and up	Spanish speakers	2 books, spirit masters	High-interest stories, comprehension questions
Life Skills Reading Books. Creative Publications, Palo Alto, CA 94303	3–8	Slow, reluctant readers	Books with foldouts, reproducible pages	Real-life, high-interest situations
Context Phonetic Clues. Curriculum Associates, North Billerica, ME 01862	3–6	Readers with poor word recognition skills	300 cards, manual	High-interest phonics, multimodality activities for word analysis
Using Functional Word Signs. Developmental Learning Materials, Allen, TX 75002	(not given)	Slow reader	Cards, spirit masters, class profile, manual	Familiar word signs for training students to recognize important signs
Variety of programs. Disseminators of Knowledge, Buffalo, NY 14214	K–12	Gifted, talented	Kits, puzzles, activity cards and books, games	Wide selection of materials for challenging the gifted

TABLE 11.2: Materials for the Exceptional Child (*continued*)

Program/Publisher	Levels	Audience	Components	Remarks
Teaching Essential Language Skills. Communicaid. Ebsco Curriculum Materials, Birmingham, AL 35202	Primary	ESL, sensory Special education	Word cards, booklets Study manual	Conversational standard English Five-language publication
Edmark Rdng. Program. Functional Reading. Edmark Associates, Bellevue, WA 98009	Any (not given)	Nonreader Slow reader	Tests, lessons. Cards, picture/phrase, filmstrip, guides	Sight-word approach Learning by doing
Safe Life Reading Series	2.5 reading level	ESL, LD, slow readers	Filmstrips, readers, dittos	High-interest/low-vocabulary, functional
I Hate to Read Series. Educational Activities, Freeport, NY 11520	1–2 reading level, 4–up interest.	Slow readers	Filmstrip, books, and cassettes	High-interest/low-vocabulary, humorous
Recipe for Reading. Multi-Sensory Approach to Language Arts. Educational Pub. Service, Cambridge, MA 02238	Early primary 1–3 and up	Remedial Language disabled	Charts, books Books, charts, word lists	Structured approach Multisensory, phonetically structured
Storybooks for Beginners. Jamestown Publishers, Providence, RI	1 reading level, K–3 interest	Spanish, bilingual	Storybooks	Easy-to-read stories for Spanish or English, controlled vocabulary
Power Reading Series. Stepping into English. London Bridge, Baltimore, MD 21208	3–6 (not given)	Multi-ethnic, ESL	Comic books Filmstrips, books	Motivational program Fables with activities for fun and skills

TABLE 11.2: Materials for the Exceptional Child (*continued*)

Program/Publisher	Levels	Audience	Components	Remarks
Real Life Reading. Phonetic Reading Chain. Mafex Associates, Johnstown, PA 15907	Elementary 8–adult	Slow readers	Workbooks, flash cards	Application of basic skills to real situations; structured multisensory program
Building Life Skills. Modern Curriculum Press, Cleveland, OH 44136	Intermediate	Slow reader, any reader	Workbooks	Practical, everyday problems
Indian Reading Series.	Elementary	Native American	Activities, books	Sequenced reading, legends
Multi-Cultural Reading Comprehension. Opportunities for Learning, Chatsworth, CA 91311	2–6	Multiethnic reader	Five books, spirit masters	Multiethnic stories for reading skills
Varied programs. Resources for the Gifted, Phoenix, AZ 85018	K–12	Gifted	Puzzles, kits, activity books, cards, games	Critical and creative activities for the gifted
Distar. Science Research Associates, Chicago, IL	Preschool–2	Culturally and dialectally different children, ESL	Series of programmed reading instructional materials	Careful programming and sequencing, immediate reinforcement
Ear-Eye-Hand Phonics. Special Educational Materials, Yonkers, NY	K–2; slow learners, 2–4	Slow learner, remedial	Albums, activity books, manual	Stories for each sound

_____ 3. The language experience approach and individualized reading are generally good approaches to use with the different learner.

_____ 4. Many children who have been enrolled in special education classes are being integrated into regular classrooms.

_____ 5. The purpose of PL 94-142 is to place every exceptional child in a regular classroom.

_____ 6. The least restrictive environment enables a child to do whatever he or she pleases in the classroom.

_____ 7. Children who are being mainstreamed may have difficulty adjusting to a regular classroom.

_____ 8. IEP stands for Instant Environmental Plan.

_____ 9. A learning-disabled student is one who has a low level of functioning in all areas.

_____ 10. Many learning-disabled students have severe communication deficits.

_____ 11. Reading improvement is the most widely recognized academic need of the learning-disabled child.

_____ 12. Slow learners are those children whose IQ scores range between 85 and 100.

_____ 13. Slow learners should be given difficult material to read so they will be challenged.

_____ 14. Functional or survival skills include correct use of the telephone as well as the ability to interpret maps and schedules.

_____ 15. Observant teachers can usually detect a child who has a visual or hearing problem.

_____ 16. Visually handicapped children need to be taught to listen and remember well.

_____ 17. Hearing impaired children should be taught to read primarily with a phonics approach.

_____ 18. Two of the most common speech disorders with which the classroom teacher deals are articulation and stuttering.

_____ 19. In order to help the hyperactive or behaviorally disordered child, the teacher should keep the room environment simple and free of clutter.

_____ 20. The revolving-door policy for the gifted refers to allowing children to attend school every other day.

_____ 21. Children from homes of a low socioeconomic level have no problems adapting to a middle-class school.

_____ 22. Compensatory programs are designed for gifted students.

_____ 23. Children who have cultural differences are also likely to have linguistic differences.

_____ 24. Understanding the backgrounds of multiethnic children is a good way to begin relating to them.

_____ 25. It is impossible for a gifted child to be an underachiever.

_____ 26. A corrective reader is one whose problems have been corrected.

Vocabulary

behavioral disorder
bilingualism
compensatory program
corrective reader
dialect
ESL
exceptional
gifted
handicapped
hearing impaired

hyperactivity
IEP
itinerant teacher
least restrictive
   environment
mainstreaming
multidisciplinary team
multiethnic
PL 94-142
reading expectancy

remedial reader
resource room
self-contained special
   class
slow learner
specific learning
   disabilities
speech impaired
underachiever
visually impaired

Self-Improvement Opportunities

1. List the twelve general guidelines given for instructing exceptional children in order of importance (in your opinion). Be prepared to justify your reasoning.
2. Go to a school office and find out how the needs of learning-disabled children are met. Ask to visit a classroom where a student with a physical or sensory handicap is being mainstreamed, and observe how this child participates in class activities and how he or she is accepted by classmates.
3. Plan six activities for using the newspaper with the slow reader and six for using it with the gifted student.
4. Talk with a speech correction teacher about the role of the regular classroom teacher in helping speech impaired children.
5. Visit a classroom to see if any child appears to be hyperactive. If there is such a child, observe how the teacher works with him or her.
6. Visit a compensatory program, such as Head Start, in your community and observe how the program tries to prepare children for school.
7. Study the characteristics of the people who live in your area. How do their language patterns compare with standard English? What cultural and ethnic variations do you find? What implications do these findings have for teaching?
8. Determine which linguistically different children are in evidence in a classroom. Then compare your judgments with those of the teacher.
9. Get permission from a classroom teacher to work with a culturally or linguistically different child on a one-to-one basis for one week, and ask the teacher to help you plan an instructional program for this child.
10. Find a book you think would appeal to one type of exceptional child and plan how you would present it.
11. Visit a school and find out what provisions are made for different types of

learners. Are resource rooms being used? Is there a program for the
gifted? What special personnel are available to provide services?

12. If feasible, become familiar with one or more of the special materials cited near the end of this chapter. Report to the class on possible uses.

Bibliography

Alexander, Clara Franklin. "Black English Dialect and the Classroom Teacher." *The Reading Teacher* 33 (February 1980): 571–77.

The ASCD Multicultural Education Commission. "Encouraging Multicultural Education." *Educational Leadership* 34 (January 1977): 288–91.

Aukerman, Robert C., and Louise R. Aukerman. *How Do I Teach Reading?* New York: John Wiley & Sons, 1981.

Barnes, Willie J. "How to Improve Teacher Behavior in Multiethnic Classrooms." *Educational Leadership* 34 (April 1977): 511–15.

Bradley, R. C. *The Education of Exceptional Children,* 3rd ed. Wolfe City, Texas: University Press, 1978.

Brophy, Jere. "Successful Teaching Strategies for the Inner-City Child." *Phi Delta Kappan* 63 (April 1982): 527–30.

Buttery, Thomas J., and George E. Mason. "Reading Improvement for Mainstreamed Children Who Are Mildly Mentally Handicapped." *Reading Improvement* 16 (Winter 1979): 334–37.

Byrne, Margaret C. *The Child Speaks: A Speech Improvement Program for Kindergarten and First Grade.* New York: Harper & Row, 1965.

Cardenas, Jose A. "Education and the Children of Migrant Farmworkers: An Overview." (October 1976). [ED 134 367]

Cassidy, Jack. "Inquiry Reading for the Gifted." *The Reading Teacher* 35 (October 1981): 17–21.

Click, Aliene. "Activities for Gifted Children in Elementary School." Unpublished paper, Tennessee Technological University, 1981. 114 pp.

Cruickshank, William M. *Concepts in Learning Disabilities: Selected Writings.* Vol. 2. Syracuse, N.Y.: Syracuse University Press, 1981.

Dallman, Martha, et al. *The Teaching of Reading.* 6th ed. New York: Holt, Rinehart and Winston, 1982.

Dixon, Carol N. "Teaching Strategies for the Mexican American Child." *The Reading Teacher* 30 (November 1976): 141–43.

Ebel, Carolyn Williams. "An Update: Teaching Reading to Students of English as a Second Language." *The Reading Teacher* 33 (January 1980): 403–407.

Fairchild, Thomas N. *Managing the Hyperactive Child in the Classroom.* Austin, Texas: Learning Concepts, 1975.

Flygare, Thomas. *The Legal Rights of Students.* Bloomington, Ind.: Phi Delta Kappa Educational Foundation, 1975.

512

Teaching
Reading in
Today's
Elementary
Schools

Foerster, Leona M. "Teaching Reading in Our Pluralistic Classrooms." *The Reading Teacher* 30 (November 1976): 146–50.

Fox, Lynn H., and William G. Durden. *Educating Verbally Gifted Youth.* Bloomington, Ind.: Phi Delta Kappa Educational Foundation, 1982.

Garcia, Ricardo L. *Education for Cultural Pluralism: Global Roots Stew.* Bloomington, Ind.: Phi Delta Kappa Educational Foundation, 1981.

Gaskins, Irene W. "Let's End the Reading Disabilities/Learning Disabilities Debate." *Journal of Learning Disabilities* 15 (February 1982): 81–83.

Harris, Albert J. "An Overview of Reading Disabilities and Learning Disabilities in the U.S." *The Reading Teacher* 33 (January 1980): 420–25.

Harris, Albert J., and Edward R. Sipay. *How to Increase Reading Ability.* 7th ed. New York: Longman, 1980.

Henderson, Anne J., and Richard E. Shores. "How Learning Disabled Students' Failure to Attend to Suffixes Affects Their Oral Reading Performance." *Journal of Learning Disabilities* 15 (March 1982): 178–82.

Hoben, Mollie. "Toward Integration in the Mainstream." *Exceptional Children* 47 (October 1980): 100–105.

Kirk, Samuel A., and James J. Gallagher. *Educating Exceptional Children.* Boston: Houghton Mifflin, 1983.

Kirk, Samuel A., Joanne Marie Kliebhan, and Janet W. Lerner. *Teaching Reading to Slow and Disabled Learners.* Boston: Houghton Mifflin, 1978.

Levine, Daniel U. "Successful Approaches to Improving Academic Achievement in Inner-City Elementary Schools." *Phi Delta Kappan* 63 (April 1982): 523–26.

Ludlow, Barbara L. *Teaching the Learning Disabled.* Bloomington, Ind.: Phi Delta Kappa Educational Foundation, 1982.

Lyon, Harry C., Jr. "Our Most Neglected Natural Resource." *Today's Education* 70 (February–March 1981): 18 E.

Marland, Sidney. *Education of the Gifted and Talented: Report to Congress of the United States by the U.S. Commissioner of Education.* (Washington, D.C.: U.S. Office of Education, 1971).

Padek, Nancy D. "The Language and Educational Needs of Children Who Speak Black English." *The Reading Teacher* 35 (November 1981): 144–51.

Quay, H.C. "Classification in the Treatment of Delinquency and Antisocial Behavior." In *Issues of the Classification of Children,* N. Hobbs, ed., Vol. 1. San Francisco: Jossey-Bass, 1975.

Quay, H.C. "Patterns of Aggression, Withdrawal and Immaturity." In *Psychopathological Disorders of Childhood,* H.C. Quay and J. S. Werry, eds. New York: Wiley, 1972.

Reed, Linda. "ERIC/RCS The Migrant Child in the Elementary Classroom." *The Reading Teacher* 31 (March 1978): 730–33.

Reis, Sally M. "TAG Serves the Gifted and Talented." *Today's Education* 70 (February–March 1981): 22 E–25 E.

Reis, Sally M., and Joseph S. Renzulli. "A Case for a Broadened Conception of Giftedness." *Phi Delta Kappan* 63 (May 1982): 619–20.

Renzulli, Joseph S., and Linda H. Smith. "Revolving Door: A Truer Turn for the Gifted." *Learning* 9 (October 1980): 91–93.

Rubin, Dorothy. *A Practical Approach to Teaching Reading.* New York: Holt, Rinehart and Winston, 1982.

Saville, Muriel R. "Providing for Mobile Populations in Bilingual and Migrant Education Programs." In *Reading for the Disadvantaged: Problems of Linguistically Different Learners,* Thomas D. Horn, ed. Newark, Del.: International Reading Association, 1970, pp. 115–34.

Simpson-Tyson, Audrey K. "Are Native American First Graders Ready to Read?" *The Reading Teacher* 31 (April 1978): 798–801.

Smith, Sally L. "Plain Talk About Children with Learning Disabilities." *Today's Education* 70 (February–March 1981): 46 E–52 E.

Stewart, William A. *Appalachian Advance* 4 (September 1969): 12.

Thomas, M. Donald. *Pluralism Gone Mad.* Bloomington, Ind.: Phi Delta Kappa Educational Foundation, 1981.

Van Riper, C. *Speech Correction: Principles and Methods.* 6th ed. Englewood Cliffs, N.J.: Prentice-Hall, 1978.

Wallach, G. P., and S. C. Goldsmith. "Language-based Learning Disabilities: Reading Is Language Too!" *Journal of Learning Disabilities* 10 (March 1977): 178–83.

Wilhoyte, Cheryl H. "Contracting: A Bridge between the Classroom and Resource Room." *The Reading Teacher* 30 (January 1977): 376–78.

Suggested Readings

Banks, James A. *Multiethnic Education: Theory and Practice.* Boston: Allyn and Bacon, 1981.

Fairchild, Thomas N., and Ferris O. Henson, II. *Mainstreaming Exceptional Children.* Austin, Texas: Learning Concepts, 1976.

Gottlieb, Jay, ed. *Educating Mentally Retarded Persons in the Mainstream.* Baltimore: University Park Press, 1980.

Heilman, Arthur W., et al. *Principles and Practices of Teaching Reading.* 5th ed. Columbus: Charles E. Merrill, 1981, Chapter 11.

Henson, Ferris O., II. *Mainstreaming the Gifted.* Austin, Texas: Learning Concepts, 1976.

Hittleman, Daniel R. *Developmental Reading, K–8: Teaching from a Psycholinguistic Perspective.* 2nd ed. Boston: Houghton Mifflin, 1983.

Horn, Thomas D. *Reading for the Disadvantaged: Problems of Linguistically Different Learners.* New York: Harcourt Brace Jovanovich, 1970.

Myers, Patricia I., and Donald D. Hammill. *Methods for Learning Disorders.* 2nd ed. New York: John Wiley, 1976.

514
Teaching
Reading in
Today's
Elementary
Schools

Newcomer, Phyllis L. *Understanding and Teaching Emotionally Disturbed Children.* Boston: Allyn and Bacon, 1980.

Pelow, Randall A., and Sally A. Chant. *The How-To Book of Survival Reading.* Dansville, N.Y.: Instructor Publications, 1980.

Savage, John F., and Jean F. Mooney. *Teaching Reading to Children with Special Needs.* Boston: Allyn & Bacon, 1978.

Smith, Richard J., and Dale D. Johnson. *Teaching Children to Read.* 2nd ed. Reading, Mass.: Addison-Wesley, 1980, Chapters 10, 11, and 12.

Appendix: Answers to "Test Yourself"

Chapter 1 True-False

1. F	8. T	14. T	20. F
2. T	9. T	15. T	21. T
3. T	10. F	16. F	22. F
4. F	11. F	17. F	23. F
5. F	12. T	18. T	24. T
6. F	13. F	19. F	25. T
7. T			

Chapter 2 True-False

1. F	9. T	15. F	21. F
2. F	10. F	16. T	22. T
3. T	11. F	17. F	23. T
4. F	12. F	18. T	24. T
5. T	13. F	19. F	25. F
6. T	14. F	20. T	26. T
7. T			
8. T			

Chapter 3 True-False

1. F	10. T	19. T	28. T
2. F	11. T	20. F	29. T
3. T	12. F	21. F	30. F
4. F	13. T	22. T	31. T
5. T	14. T	23. T	32. T
6. T	15. T	24. T	33. T
7. F	16. T	25. T	34. T
8. T	17. T	26. F	35. T
9. F	18. F	27. F	36. F

Chapter 3   Multiple-Choice

1. a	6. a	9. b	12. c
2. c	7. c	10. b	13. b
3. a	8. b	11. a	14. a
4. b			
5. c			

Chapter 4   True-False

1. F	11. T	21. F	31. T
2. T	12. F	22. T	32. T
3. F	13. T	23. T	33. T
4. F	14. F	24. F	34. F
5. T	15. T	25. F	35. T
6. T	16. F	26. T	36. T
7. F	17. T	27. F	37. F
8. T	18. F	28. T	38. F
9. T	19. T	29. T	39. T
10. T	20. T	30. F	40. T

Chapter 5   True-False

1. T	7. T	12. T	17. F
2. F	8. T	13. T	18. F
3. F	9. F	14. T	19. F
4. T	10. T	15. T	20. T
5. T	11. T	16. F	21. F
6. F			

Chapter 6   True-False

1. F	7. T	13. F	19. F
2. T	8. F	14. T	20. T
3. T	9. T	15. F	21. T
4. T	10. T	16. F	22. T
5. F	11. T	17. T	23. F
6. T	12. T	18. T	24. T

Chapter 7 True-False

1. F	7. F	12. F	17. T
2. T	8. F	13. T	18. F
3. T	9. F	14. T	19. T
4. F	10. T	15. T	20. T
5. F	11. T	16. F	21. T
6. T			

Chapter 8 True-False

1. T	9. F	14. F	19. T
2. F	10. F	15. F	20. T
3. F	11. F	16. F	21. T
4. T	12. T	17. T	22. F
5. F	13. T	18. F	23. T
6. F			
7. T			
8. T			

Chapter 9 True-False

1. T	8. T	14. T	20. T
2. F	9. T	15. F	21. T
3. T	10. T	16. T	22. T
4. F	11. T	17. F	23. F
5. T	12. T	18. T	24. T
6. T	13. F	19. F	25. F
7. F			

Chapter 10 True-False

1. F	6. T	11. T	16. T
2. F	7. F	12. T	17. T
3. F	8. T	13. T	18. T
4. F	9. F	14. F	19. T
5. T	10. T	15. T	20. F

1. F	10. T	16. T	22. F
2. T	11. T	17. F	23. T
3. T	12. F	18. T	24. T
4. T	13. F	19. T	25. F
5. F	14. T	20. F	26. F
6. F	15. T	21. F	
7. T			
8. F			
9. F			

Index

Concrete experiences, 62–63; activities to develop skills, 63, 85

Concrete-operational period, 61, 62, 65, 114

Conservation of substance, 62, 64, 65; activities to develop skills, 64, 86

Consonant blends, 91, 109, 134; activities to develop skills, 122, 124; assessing skills, 381; teaching, 111–112, 118, 120

Consonant diagraphs, 91, 110, 115, 134; activities to develop skills, 122, 124; assessing skills, 381–382; teaching, 111–112, 118, 120

Consonants, 109–110; activities to develop skills, 118–119, 122–124; assessing skills, 381–382; key words, 120–121; syllabication, 134; teaching, 110–115, 118, 120–121, 236. *See also* Phonics

Consonant substitution, 120–121

Content area reading, 22–23, 339; assessing, 377, 388; compared to basal readers, 272, 304–305, 331–332; determining readability, 305–310; determining reading level, 401–402; and direct inquiry activity, 315; and DRTA, 310–312; and guided reading procedure, 312–313; integrating approaches to, 316–317; language arts, 317–320; and manipulative materials, 316; mathematics, 326–329; and oral reading strategy, 314; and question-only strategy, 314; and Savor procedure, 313–314; science and health, 329–332; social studies, 320–326; and study guides, 315–316. *See also* Textbooks

Context clues, 91, 124, 136, 139, 140; assessing use of, 380, 388; as comprehension aids, 148, 153–154; pictures clues,

102–103; syntactic and semantic clues, 102–105; teaching, 104–108; in vocabulary building, 95, 157, 160, 316, 318

Continuous progress pattern, 444

Contractions, 125, 131–132; activities for, 132, 228; assessing skills, 383

Coody, Betty, 41

Cooper, Charles R., 17, 18

Cordts, Anna D., 120

Corrective readers, 463, 501–502

Cox, Mary B., 65

Cramer, Ronald, 200

Creative reading, 149, 177, 304; assessing, 388–389; discussed, 198–201; and objective-based approach, 245–246

Creative response questions, 43, 203, 205, 207

Criscuolo, Nicholas P., 164

Crist, Barbara, 164

Criterion-referenced tests, 250, 255, 377–378, 409, 434; discussed, 420–421; and objective-based approach, 245, 246, 423

Critical reading, 42, 149, 177, 190, 198; assessing, 384, 388–389; and author, 191, 193–194; in content areas, 268, 287, 304, 320, 330; evaluating material, 191–192, 194–197

Cross references, 276, 285–286

Crowell, Doris C., 205

Cruickshank, William M., 482

Cultural variations, 463, 470, 501; books for, 508; discussed, 487–492

Cunningham, Pat, 176, 232

Cuyler, Richard, 94

Dale, Edgar, 308

Dale-Chall Readability Formula, 308, 310

Dallman, Martha, 430, 467

Dash, 168

Davis, Hazel Grubbs, 72

Decentralization, 64

Dechant, Emerald, 328

Departmentalization, 439, 444–445

Derivatives, 130, 135; locating in dictionary, 280–281. *See also* Prefixes; Suffixes

Desirable teacher behaviors (DTBs), 447–448

Detail questions, 202, 203, 207, 208

Details, recognizing, 150, 182, 289, 305; activities for, 178–179; discussed, 177

Dewey, John, 445

Diacritical marks, 116, 136

Diagnostic/prescriptive program, *see* Objective-based program

Diagnostic tests, 21, 392, 405–410, 423

Dialect, 395, 396, 402–404, 496

Dialectical variations, 463, 464, 501; books for, 508; discussed, 487–488, 492–495

Dictionaries: activities for developing skills, 136–138, 158, 276–281; alphabetical order, 277–279; assessing use of, 384; guide words, 279–280; introducing use, 138; locating variants and derivatives, 280–281; phonetic respellings and accent marks, 136–138; picture, 98, 135, 138, 237, 265, 275; and pronunciation, 135–137; 140, 159; as references, 237, 265, 275, 276–281, 284; in word definition, 140, 149, 157–159; and word recognition, 91, 113, 135–138, 139, 140

Dictionary method, 153

Di Lorenzo, L. S., 72

Directed inquiry activity (DIA), 315, 331

Directed reading activity (DRA), 150, 218, 219, 232, 292, 447; discussed, 223–231

Directed reading-thinking activity (DRTA), 150, 200, 232, 315, 447; discussed, 310–312

Directionality, 59, 69, 234, 235, 471; activities for, 61, 85; discussed, 61

Student Response Form

Many of the changes made in this edition of *Teaching Reading in Today's Elementary Schools* were based on feedback and evaluations of the earlier editions. Please help us respond to the interests and needs of future readers by completing the questionnaire below and returning it to: College Marketing, Houghton Mifflin Company, One Beacon Street, Boston, MA 02108.

1. Please tell us your overall impressions of the text.

	Excellent	Good	Adequate	Poor
a. Was it written in a clear and understandable style?	___	___	___	___
b. Were difficult concepts well explained?	___	___	___	___
c. How would you rate the frequent use of illustrative Examples?	___	___	___	___
d. How comprehensive was the coverage of major issues and topics?	___	___	___	___
e. How does this book compare to other texts you have used?	___	___	___	___
f. How would you rate the activities?	___	___	___	___
g. How would you rate the study aids at the beginning and end of each chapter?	___	___	___	___

2. Please comment on or cite examples that illustrate any of your above ratings.

_____

_____

_____

3. Were there any topics that should have been included or covered more fully?

_____

_____

_____

532

Teaching
Reading in
Today's
Elementary
Schools

4. Which chapters or features did you particularly like? _____

_____

_____

5. Which chapters or features did you dislike? _____

_____

_____

6. Which chapters taught you the most? _____

_____

_____

7. What changes would you like to see in the next edition of this book?

_____

_____

8. Is this a book you would like to keep for your classroom teaching experience?

_____ Why or why not? _____

_____

_____

9. Please tell us something about your background. Are you studying to be an elementary school classroom teacher or a reading specialist? Are you inservice or preservice? Are you an undergraduate or graduate student? _____

_____